WESTERN HEMISPHERE

GEOGRAPHY
HISTORY
CULTURE

PRENTICE HALL
Needham, Massachusetts
Upper Saddle River, New Jersey

Program Authors

Heidi Hayes Jacobs

Heidi Hayes Jacobs has served as an educational consultant to more than 500 schools across the nation. Dr. Jacobs is an adjunct professor in the Department of Curriculum on Teaching at Teachers College, Columbia University. She completed her undergraduate studies at the University of Utah in her hometown of Salt Lake City. She received an M.A. from the University of Massachusetts, Amherst, and completed her doctoral work at Columbia University's Teachers College in 1981.

The backbone of Dr. Jacobs's experience comes from her years as a teacher of high school, middle school, and elementary school students. As an educational consultant, she works with K–12 schools and districts on curriculum reform and strategic planning.

Brenda Randolph

Brenda Randolph is the former Director of the Outreach Resource Center at the African Studies Program at Howard University, Washington, D.C. She is the Founder and Director of Africa Access, a bibliographic service on Africa for schools. She received her B.A. in history with high honors from North Carolina Central University, Durham, and her M.A. in African studies with honors from Howard University. She completed further graduate studies at the University of Maryland, College Park, where she was awarded a Graduate Fellowship.

Brenda Randolph has published numerous articles in professional journals and bulletins. She currently serves as library media specialist in Montgomery County Public Schools, Maryland.

Michal L. LeVasseur

Michal LeVasseur is an educational consultant in the field of geography. She is an adjunct professor of geography at the University of Alabama, Birmingham, and serves with the Alabama Geographic Alliance. Her undergraduate and graduate work is in the fields of anthropology (B.A.), geography (M.A.), and science education (Ph.D.).

Dr. LeVasseur's specialization has moved increasingly into the area of geography education. In 1996, she served as Director of the National Geographic Society's Summer Geography Workshop. As an educational consultant, she has worked with the National Geographic Society as well as with schools to develop programs and curricula for geography.

Special Program Consultant

Yvonne S. Gentzler, Ph.D.
School of Education
University of Idaho
Moscow, Idaho

PRENTICE HALL
Upper Saddle River, New Jersey
Needham, Massachusetts

ISBN 0-13-434123-6

3 4 5 6 7 8 9 10   01 00 99

Content Consultants for the World Explorer Program

TABLE OF CONTENTS

GEOGRAPHY TOOLS AND CONCEPTS

1

LATIN AMERICA 270

OF SPECIAL INTEREST

A hands-on, active approach to practicing and applying key social studies skills

Engaging, step-by-step activities for exploring important topics in the Western Hemisphere

LITERATURE High-interest selections written by authors from the Western Hemisphere

CITIZEN HEROES

EXPLORING TECHNOLOGY

STUDENT ART

MAPS

MAPS

CHARTS, GRAPHS, AND TABLES

READ ACTIVELY

How can I get the most out of my social studies book?

How does my reading relate to my world? Answering questions like these means that you are an active reader, an involved reader. As an active reader, you are in charge of the reading situation!

The following strategies tell how to think and read as an active reader. You don't need to use all of these strategies all the time. Feel free to choose the ones that work best in each reading situation. You might use several at a time, or you might go back and forth among them. They can be used in any order.

BEFORE YOU READ

Give yourself a purpose

The sections in this book begin with a list called "Questions to Explore." These questions focus on key ideas presented in the section. They give you a purpose for reading. You can create your own purpose by asking questions like these: How does the topic relate to my life? How might I use what I learn at school or at home?

Preview

To preview a reading selection, first read its title. Then look at the pictures and read the captions. Also read any headings in the selection. Then ask yourself: What is the reading selection about? What do the pictures and headings tell about the selection?

Reach into your background

What do you already know about the topic of the selection? How can you use what you know to help you understand what you are going to read?

Ask questions

Suppose you are reading about the continent of South America. Some questions you might ask are: Where is South America? What countries are found there? Why are some of the countries large and others small? Asking questions like these can help you gather evidence and gain knowledge.

Predict

As you read, make a prediction about what will happen and why. Or predict how one fact might affect another fact. Suppose you are reading about South America's climate. You might make a prediction about how the climate affects where people live. You can change your mind as you gain new information.

Connect

Connect your reading to your own life. Are the people discussed in the selection like you or someone you know? What would you do in similar situations? Connect your reading to something you have already read. Suppose you have already read about the ancient Greeks. Now you are reading about the ancient Romans. How are they alike? How are they different?

Visualize

What would places, people, and events look like in a movie or a picture? As you read about India, you could visualize the country's heavy rains. What do they look like? How do they sound? As you read about geography, you could visualize a volcanic eruption.

Respond

Talk about what you have read. What did you think? Share your ideas with your classmates.

Assess yourself

What did you find out? Were your predictions on target? Did you find answers to your questions?

Follow up

Show what you know. Use what you have learned to do a project. When you do projects, you continue to learn.

GEOGRAPHY
TOOLS AND CONCEPTS

Are you curious about our Earth? Do you want to know why some places in the world are cold and some are hot? Have you wondered why more people live in cities and fewer people live in other places? Would you like to find mountaintops or valleys to explore? If you answered yes to any of these questions, you want to know more about geography. Farmers grow corn, traders cross the ocean, and you walk or take a bus to school. Geography explains all of these activities— and many more.

Guiding Questions

The readings and activities in this book will help you discover answers to these Guiding Questions.

☛ What is the Earth's geography like?

☛ Where do the world's people live?

☛ What is a culture?

☛ How do people use the world's resources?

Project Preview

You can also discover answers to the Guiding Questions by working on projects. Preview the following projects and choose one that you might like to do. For more details, see page 126.

The Geography Game Create a team game the whole class can play. Write clues about the unique physical features, climate, population, culture, and natural resources of a country.

World News Today Prepare a short speech about a country's economy and natural resources. Use a collection of newspaper articles.

Focus on Part of the Whole Set up a classroom map and picture display based on your research of the geography, climate, and population of a country.

Desktop Countries Make a desktop display. Include food samples, a flag, souvenirs, and other items typical of a country from which your ancestors came.

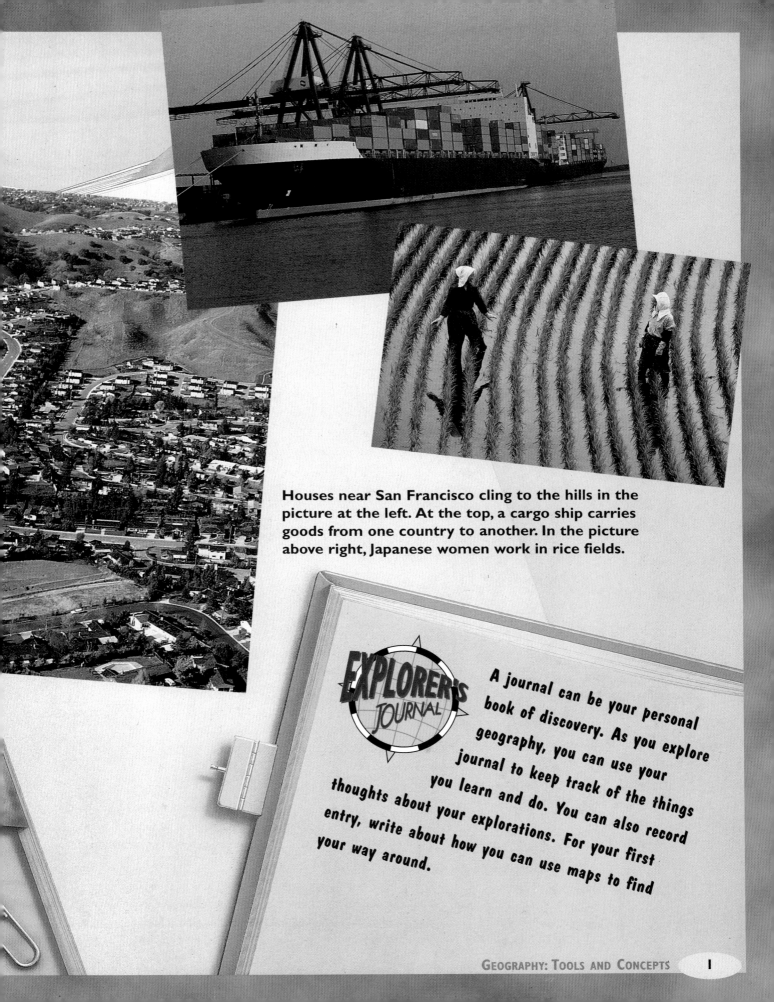

Houses near San Francisco cling to the hills in the picture at the left. At the top, a cargo ship carries goods from one country to another. In the picture above right, Japanese women work in rice fields.

EXPLORER'S JOURNAL

A journal can be your personal book of discovery. As you explore geography, you can use your journal to keep track of the things you learn and do. You can also record thoughts about your explorations. For your first entry, write about how you can use maps to find your way around.

ACTIVITY ATLAS

Geography

Learning about geography tools and concepts means being an explorer, and no explorer would start out without first checking some facts. Use the activities on the following pages to begin exploring the world of geography. They will help you learn what geography is and how it can help you.

▲ Why do people in this place wear this type of clothing?

▼ Why do relatively few people live in this area?

World: Physical

PLACE

1. Explore the Meaning of Geography Think about the word *geography*. The word part *geo* comes from a Greek word meaning "earth." *Graphy* means "science of," from an earlier word that meant "to write." How would you define *geography*?

People who are interested in geography are very curious about our world. They often ask questions such as "Where are things?" and "Why are they where they are?"

Look at the pictures on these two pages. The question that accompanies each picture is the type of question that geographers ask. For each picture, write another question a geographer might ask.

▲ Why did ancient people in this area become expert sailors?

▶ Why do visitors to this area become short of breath easily?

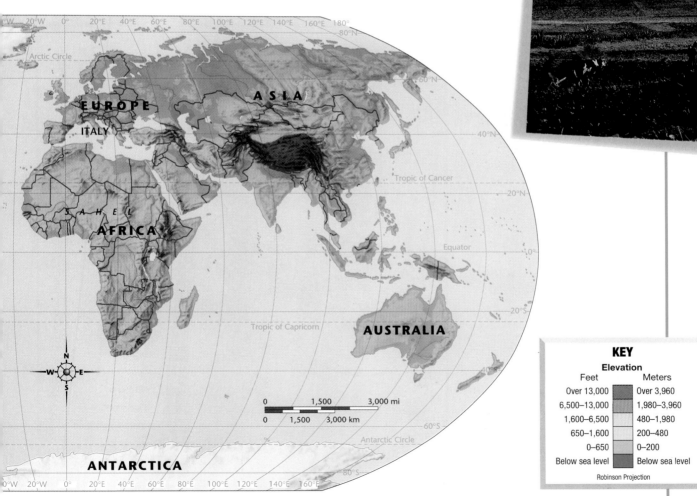

KEY

Elevation

Feet		Meters
Over 13,000		Over 3,960
6,500–13,000		1,980–3,960
1,600–6,500		480–1,980
650–1,600		200–480
0–650		0–200
Below sea level		Below sea level

Robinson Projection

LOCATION

2. What Kinds of Maps Does Geo Leo Need?

Geographers do more than ask questions about the Earth. They also gather, organize, and analyze geographic information. Geographers use many different types of maps to do this work.

Examine the map below and the maps on the next page. Be sure to read the title of each map so you know what the map is about. Then help Geo Leo plan a trip to South Asia, an area that includes the countries of Afghanistan, India, Pakistan, and Bangladesh.

A. *"If I wanted to find out how many people live in the city of Mumbai, India, which map would I use?"*

B. *"On my trip to South Asia, I want to search for gigantic insects that live in tropical rain forests. Which map do I use to find the tropical rain forests?"*

C. *"South Asia is a region that has many different types of climate. Which map will help me bring the right gear for Pakistan's arid climate?"*

GEO LEO

BONUS

Which type of vegetation grows in only one South Asian country?

South Asia: Vegetation Regions

AFGHANISTAN

PAKISTAN

Delhi

BHUTAN

NEPAL

Karachi

BANGLADESH

Tropic of Cancer

INDIA

Calcutta

Mumbai
(Bombay)

Bay of Bengal

Arabian Sea

SRI LANKA

INDIAN OCEAN

KEY

- Tropical rain forest
- Deciduous forest
- Mixed forest
- Tropical savanna
- Temperate grassland
- Desert scrub
- Highlands (vegetation varies with elevation)

Lambert Azimuthal Equal-Area Projection

South Asia: Climate Regions

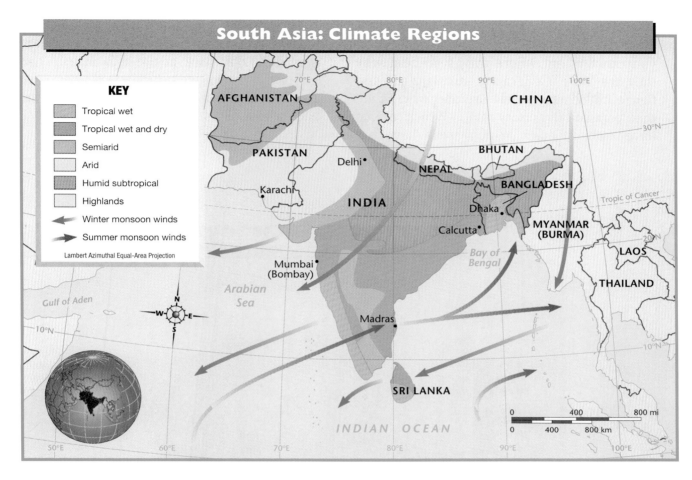

KEY

- Tropical wet
- Tropical wet and dry
- Semiarid
- Arid
- Humid subtropical
- Highlands
- → Winter monsoon winds
- → Summer monsoon winds

Lambert Azimuthal Equal-Area Projection

AFGHANISTAN
PAKISTAN
Delhi
Karachi
INDIA
CHINA
BHUTAN
NEPAL
BANGLADESH
Dhaka
Calcutta
MYANMAR (BURMA)
LAOS
THAILAND
Tropic of Cancer
Mumbai (Bombay)
Arabian Sea
Gulf of Aden
Madras
Bay of Bengal
SRI LANKA
INDIAN OCEAN

0   400   800 mi
0   400   800 km

South Asia: Population Density

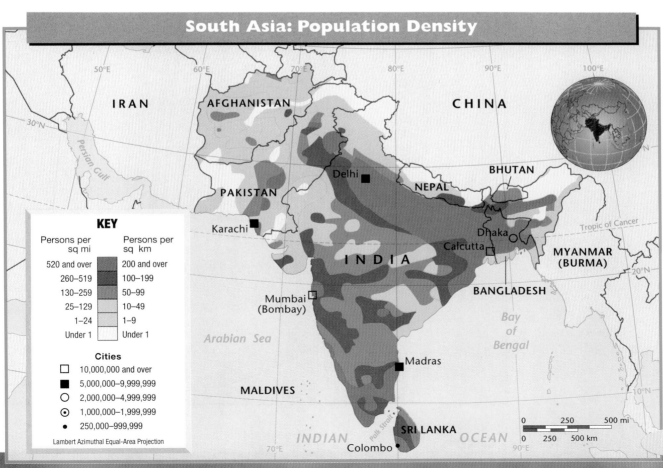

IRAN
AFGHANISTAN
CHINA
PAKISTAN
Karachi
Delhi
NEPAL
BHUTAN
Dhaka
Calcutta
MYANMAR (BURMA)
BANGLADESH
INDIA
Persian Gulf
Mumbai (Bombay)
Arabian Sea
Bay of Bengal
Madras
MALDIVES
SRI LANKA
Colombo
Polk Strait
INDIAN OCEAN
Tropic of Cancer

KEY

Persons per sq mi	Persons per sq km
520 and over	200 and over
260–519	100–199
130–259	50–99
25–129	10–49
1–24	1–9
Under 1	Under 1

Cities

- □ 10,000,000 and over
- ■ 5,000,000–9,999,999
- ○ 2,000,000–4,999,999
- ◉ 1,000,000–1,999,999
- • 250,000–999,999

Lambert Azimuthal Equal-Area Projection

0   250   500 mi
0   250   500 km

5

3. Analyze Density As you explore geography, you can find out where things are and why they are there. Geography can also help you figure out where people are and why. Study this population density map. Which places have many people? Which areas have the fewest? Why do you think people live where they do? Look back at the first map in this Activity Atlas for some clues. Try to draw conclusions about how physical features influence where cities are located.

World: Population Density

KEY

Persons per sq mi	Persons per sq km
520 and over	200 and over
260–519	100–199
130–259	50–99
25–129	10–49
1–24	1–9
Under 1	Under 1

Robinson Projection

MOVEMENT

4. Create a "Mental Map" Mental maps exist in people's minds, not on paper. Each of us has a file of mental maps, which show the routes to and around places such as school, home, or the mall. To put a mental map on paper, simply choose somewhere you like to go, and draw a map of how you get there. Include as many details as you can—landmarks, streets, buildings, and other details. Then, test the map by giving it to another person to follow. Is it clear? If not, make corrections. Finally, compare it with the maps on the previous pages. What is different? What is the same?

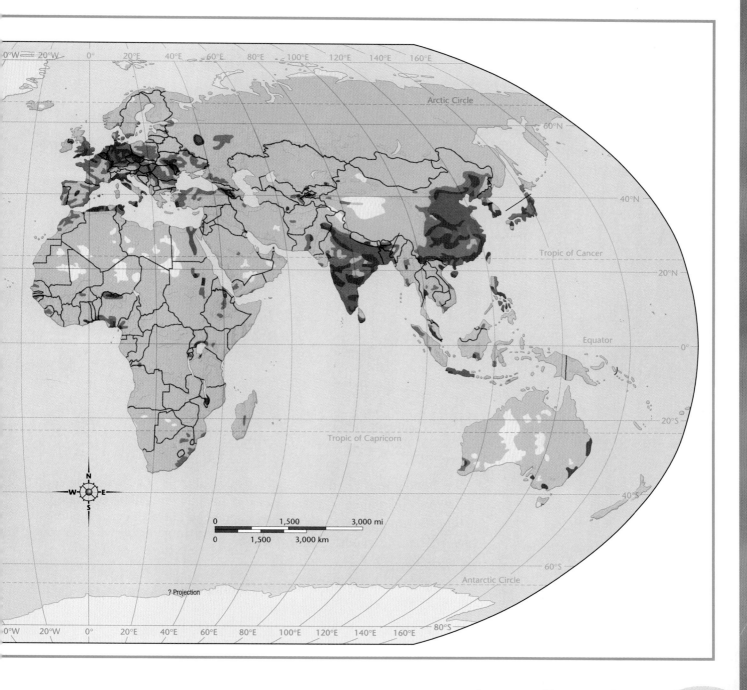

CHAPTER 1

The World of Geography

PICTURE ACTIVITIES

This photograph of San Francisco, California, was taken from the air. Pictures like this tell something about the world of geography. The following activities will help you understand how.

Study the picture
Find several natural features such as forests, hills, or oceans. Notice things that people have made such as roads, towns, and industries. If someone in a plane took a photograph of your region, what do you think the picture would show?

Make a prediction
In this picture, dense fog all but covers San Francisco's Golden Gate Bridge. How do you think the fog might affect traffic across the bridge and ships in the water?

The Five Themes of Geography

BEFORE YOU READ

Reach Into Your Background

If you were going to tell someone how to get to your school from where you live, what would you say? You might say something like "Go six blocks north and one block east." Or you might say your school is next to a local park or shopping center. These directions are examples of geography at work in your everyday life.

Questions to Explore

1. What is geography?

2. How can the five themes of geography help you understand the world?

Key Terms

geography
latitude
parallel
degree
Equator
longitude
meridian
Prime Meridian
plain

What would it be like to look at the Earth from a spaceship? Michael Collins, an astronaut who went to the moon, did just that. In his book *Carrying the Fire,* Collins described what he saw in July 1969 from his space capsule, 200 miles above the Earth. Even that far away, Collins could see natural features of the planet and evidence of the Earth's people.

▼ From hundreds of miles in space, huge clouds drifting over the Indian Ocean look like haze. What features can you see on the land?

"The Indian Ocean flashes incredible colors of emerald jade and opal in the shallow water surrounding the Maldive Islands; then on to the Burma [Myanmar] coast and nondescript green jungle, followed by mountains, coastline, and Hanoi. We can see fires burning off to the southeast, and we scramble for our one remaining still camera to record them. Now the sun glints in unusual fashion off the ocean near Formosa [Taiwan]. There are intersecting surface ripples just south of the island, patterns which are clearly visible and which, I think, must be useful to fishermen who need to know about these currents. The island itself is verdant—glistening green the color and shape of a shiny, well-fertilized gardenia leaf."

The Study of the Earth

From his high perch, Michael Collins described the colors of the ocean and the plant life on the land. He wrote about how land and water looked. He saw fires set by human beings. Collins was looking at the world as a geographer does.

Geography is the study of the Earth, our home. Geographers analyze the Earth from many points of view. They may discuss how far one place is from another. You do this when you tell someone directions. But they also study such things as oceans, plant life, landforms, and people. Geographers study how the Earth and its people affect each other.

The Themes of Geography: Five Ways to Look at the Earth

In their work, geographers are guided by two basic questions: (1) Where are things located? and (2) Why are they there? To find the answers, geographers use five themes to organize information. These themes are location, place, human-environment interaction, movement, and regions.

Location Geographers begin to study a place by finding where it is, or its location. There are two ways to talk about location—absolute location and relative location. Absolute location describes a place's exact position on the Earth. You might call absolute location a geographic address. Geographers identify the absolute location by

Predict What do you think each of the five geographic themes means?

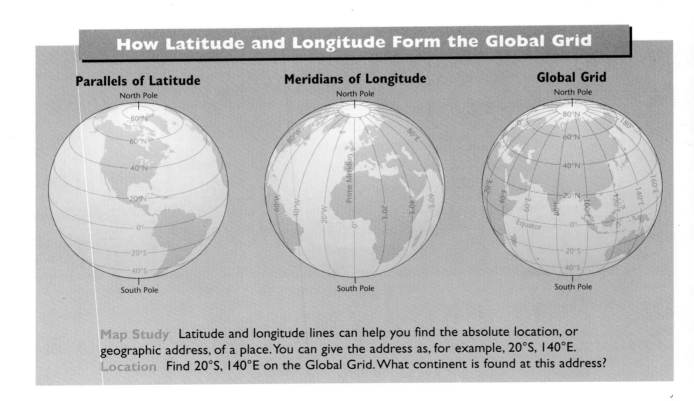

How Latitude and Longitude Form the Global Grid

Parallels of Latitude

North Pole
80°N
60°N
40°N
20°N
0°
20°S
40°S
South Pole

Meridians of Longitude

North Pole
80°W
80°E
60°W
40°W
Prime Meridian
20°W
20°E
40°E
60°E
0°
South Pole

Global Grid

North Pole
0°
180°
80°N
60°N
40°N
20°E
40°E
60°E
20°N
160°E
140°E
120°E
Equator
0°
20°S
40°S
South Pole

Map Study Latitude and longitude lines can help you find the absolute location, or geographic address, of a place. You can give the address as, for example, 20°S, 140°E.
Location Find 20°S, 140°E on the Global Grid. What continent is found at this address?

The Hemispheres

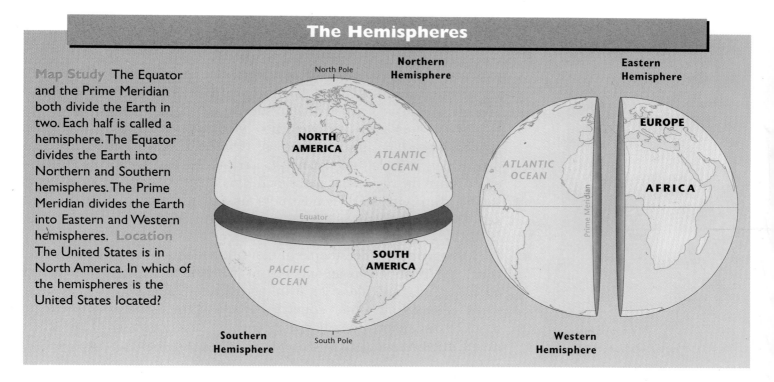

Map Study The Equator and the Prime Meridian both divide the Earth in two. Each half is called a hemisphere. The Equator divides the Earth into Northern and Southern hemispheres. The Prime Meridian divides the Earth into Eastern and Western hemispheres. **Location** The United States is in North America. In which of the hemispheres is the United States located?

using two kinds of imaginary lines around the Earth: latitude and longitude. With these lines, they can pinpoint any spot on the Earth.

Lines of **latitude** are east-west circles around the globe. They are also called **parallels,** because they are parallel to one another. They never meet. These circles divide the globe into units called **degrees.** In the middle of the globe is the parallel called the **Equator,** which is 0 degrees latitude. Geographers measure locations either north or south of the Equator. The farthest latitude north of the Equator is 90° north, the location of the North Pole. The farthest latitude south of the Equator is 90° south, the location of the South Pole.

Geographers also must pinpoint a place from east to west. For this they use lines of **longitude.** These lines, also called **meridians,** circle the globe from north to south. All meridians run through the North and South poles. The **Prime Meridian,** which runs through Greenwich, England, is 0 degrees longitude. Geographers describe locations as east or west of the Prime Meridian. The maximum longitude is 180°, which is halfway around the world from the Prime Meridian.

Geographers also discuss relative location. This explains where a place is by describing places near it. Suppose you live in Newburg, Indiana. You might give Newburg's relative location by saying: "I live in Newburg, Indiana. It's about 180 miles southwest of Indianapolis."

Place Geographers also study place. This includes a location's physical and human features. To describe physical features, you might say the climate is hot or cold. Or you might say that the land is hilly. To emphasize human features, you might talk about how many people live in a place and the kinds of work they do.

Using Latitude
Latitude can be used to measure distance north or south. One degree of latitude is equal to about 69 miles. For example, Fort Wayne, Indiana, is located 6 degrees north of Chattanooga, Tennessee. Therefore, we can determine that Fort Wayne is located about 414 miles north of Chattanooga (6 × 69 = 414).

Predict What two things about the environment of a place do you think the theme of interaction stresses?

Human-Environment Interaction The theme of interaction stresses how people affect their environment, the physical characteristics of their natural surroundings, and how their environment affects them. Perhaps they deliberately cut trails into the mountainside. Perhaps they have learned how to survive with little water.

Geographers also use interaction to discuss the consequences of people's actions. For instance, because farms in Turkey receive little rain, people have built dams and canals to irrigate the land. On the good side, everyone in the region has more food. On the bad side, irrigation makes salt build up in the soil. Then farmers must treat the soil to get rid of the salt. As a result, food could become more expensive.

Movement The theme of movement helps geographers understand the relationship among places. Movement helps explain how people, goods, and ideas get from one place to another. For example, when people from other countries came to the United States, they brought traditional foods that enriched the American way of life. The theme of movement helps you understand such cultural changes.

Regions Geographers use the theme of regions to make comparisons. A region has a unifying characteristic such as climate, land, population, or history. For instance, the Nile Valley region is a snake-shaped region on either side of the Nile River. The region runs through several countries. Life in the valley is much different from life in the regions alongside the valley. There the landscape is mostly desert.

The Rift Valley—Lake Naivasha

Edwin Rioba
Age 16
Kenya
The Great Rift Valley of East Africa was formed over millions of years by earthquakes and volcanic eruptions. Running from Syria in Asia to Mozambique in Africa, it stretches some 4,500 miles (7,200 km). **Place** Based on this picture, what landforms do you think are commonly found in the Great Rift Valley?

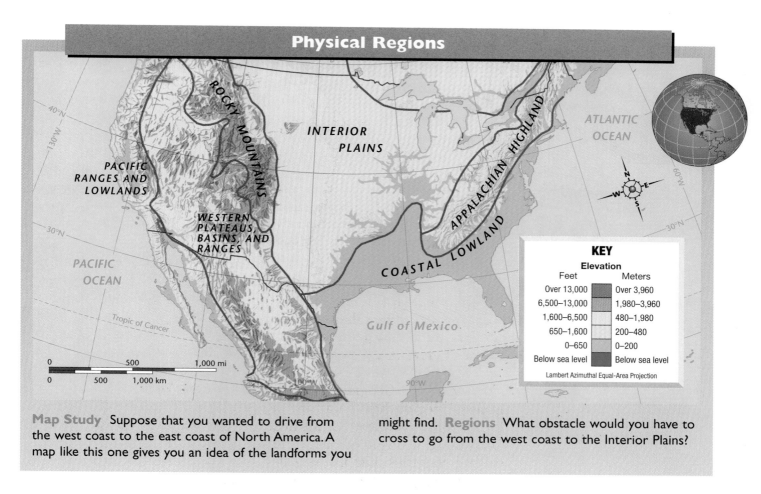

Physical Regions

ROCKY MOUNTAINS

INTERIOR PLAINS

PACIFIC RANGES AND LOWLANDS

WESTERN PLATEAUS, BASINS, AND RANGES

APPALACHIAN HIGHLAND

COASTAL LOWLAND

PACIFIC OCEAN

ATLANTIC OCEAN

Gulf of Mexico

Tropic of Cancer

40°N
30°N
30°N

130°W
60°W

100°W
90°W

0   500   1,000 mi
0   500   1,000 km

KEY

Elevation

Feet		Meters
Over 13,000		Over 3,960
6,500–13,000		1,980–3,960
1,600–6,500		480–1,980
650–1,600		200–480
0–650		0–200
Below sea level		Below sea level

Lambert Azimuthal Equal-Area Projection

Map Study Suppose that you wanted to drive from the west coast to the east coast of North America. A map like this one gives you an idea of the landforms you might find. **Regions** What obstacle would you have to cross to go from the west coast to the Interior Plains?

On maps, geographers use color and shape or special symbols to show regions. One map may show a **plain,** a region of flat land. The map above shows different regions of elevation, to show the height of land above sea level. A place can be part of several regions at the same time. For example, Houston, Texas, is in both a plains region and an oil-producing region.

SECTION 1 REVIEW

1. **Define** (a) geography, (b) latitude, (c) parallel, (d) degree, (e) Equator, (f) longitude, (g) meridian, (h) Prime Meridian, (i) plain.

2. What are two questions geographers ask when they study the Earth?

3. List the five themes of geography.

4. Give an example of how each theme can be used.

Critical Thinking

5. **Identifying Central Issues** You decide to start a geography club. When you invite a friend to join, she tells you she thinks geography is boring. She would rather learn about people, not just places. What could you say to change her mind?

Activity

6. **Writing to Learn** Make a chart listing the five geography themes. Find the location of your town or city on a map. Write down a relative location that tells where your city or town is. Then, take a walk around your neighborhood and think about the other four themes. Complete the chart by adding descriptions of your neighborhood that relate to each theme.

The Geographer's Tools

BEFORE YOU READ

Reach Into Your Background

Skulls-and-crossbones. Ships with black sails. Cannons. Swords. Treasure maps. That's right, MAPS. These things are all tools in great pirate tales. Maps are also one of the most important tools geographers use. Geographers and movie pirates aren't the only ones who use them. You do too!

Questions to Explore

1. What are some of the different ways of showing the Earth's surface and why do geographers use them?
2. What are the advantages and disadvantages of different kinds of maps and globes?

Key Terms
globe
scale
distortion
projection
compass rose
cardinal direction
key

Key People
Gerhardus Mercator
Arthur Robinson

▼ The Marshall Islanders made wood maps of the southwest Pacific Ocean. Curved palm sticks show ocean currents and shells show islands.

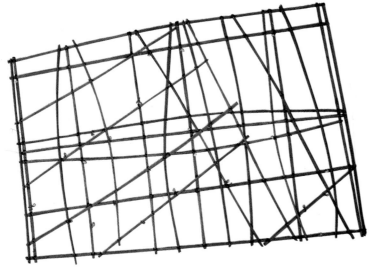

You might expect a map to be printed on a piece of paper. But hundreds of years ago, people made maps out of whatever was available. The Inuit (IN oo it) people carved detailed, accurate maps on pieces of wood. The Inuits were once called Eskimos. These Native Americans have lived in northern regions of the world for centuries. They needed maps that were portable, durable, and waterproof. Carved maps remind us that making maps is not just an exercise in school. People rely on maps, sometimes for their very survival.

Globes and Maps

Hundreds of years ago, people knew very little about the land and water beyond their own homes. Their maps showed only the areas they traveled. Other places either were left out or were only an empty space on their maps. Sometimes they filled the empty spaces with drawings of lands, creatures, and people from myths and stories.

As people explored the Earth, they collected information about the shapes and sizes of islands, continents, and bodies of water. Mapmakers wanted to present this information accurately. The best way was to put it on a **globe,** a round ball like the Earth itself. By using the same shape, mapmakers could show the continents and oceans of the Earth much as they really are. The only difference would be the **scale,** or size.

But there is a problem with globes. Try putting a globe in your pocket every morning. Try making a globe large enough to show the details of your state or community. A globe just cannot be complete enough to be useful and at the same time be small enough to be convenient. People, therefore, invented flat maps.

Flat maps, however, present another problem. The Earth is round. A map is flat. Can you flatten an orange peel without tearing it? There will be wrinkled and folded sections. The same thing happens when mapmakers create flat maps. It is impossible to show the Earth on a flat surface without some **distortion,** or change in the accuracy of its shapes and distances. Something is going to look larger or smaller than it is.

READ ACTIVELY

Predict Why do you think it would be hard to make an accurate map of the world on a flat sheet of paper?

An Orange Peel Map

Chart Study It is almost impossible to flatten an orange peel. The peel tears, wrinkles, and stretches. Mapmakers can make a flat map of an orange—or of the Earth—by using mathematics. But even a map laid out to look like this flattened orange peel is not accurate. **Critical Thinking** Look carefully at the photographs. As the orange peel is flattened, what distortions do you think might occur?

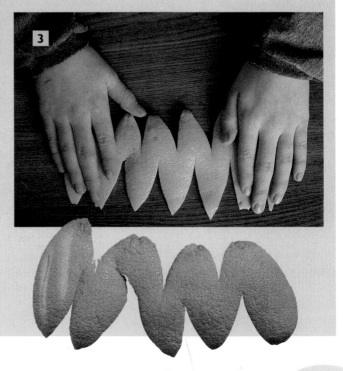

Getting It All on the Map

In 1569, a geographer named Gerhardus Mercator (juh RAHR duhs muhr KAYT uhr) created a flat map to help sailors navigate long journeys around the globe. To make his map flat, Mercator expanded the area between the longitudes near the poles. Mercator's map was very useful to sailors. They made careful notes about the distortions they found on their journeys. More than 400 years after he made it, those notes and the Mercator **projection,** or method of putting a map of the Earth onto a flat piece of paper, is used by nearly all deep-sea navigators.

When Mercator made his map, he had to make some decisions. He made sure that the shape of the landmasses and ocean areas was similar to the shapes on a globe. But he had to stretch the spaces between the longitudes. This distorted the sizes of some of the land on his map. Land near the Equator was about right, but land near the poles became much larger than it should be. For example, on Mercator's map Greenland looks bigger than South America. Greenland is actually only one eighth as large as South America.

Ask Questions What would you like to ask Gerhardus Mercator about the map he made in 1569?

Geographers call a Mercator projection a conformal map. It shows correct shapes but not true distances or sizes. Other mapmakers used other techniques to try to draw an accurate map. For instance, an equal area map shows the correct size of landmasses but their shapes are altered. The Peters projection on the next page is an equal area map.

Mapmakers have tried other techniques. The interrupted projection (see next page) is like the ripped peel of an orange. By creating gaps in the picture of the world, mapmakers showed the size and shape of land accurately. The gaps make it impossible to figure distances correctly. You could not use this projection to chart a course across an ocean.

Today, many geographers believe Arthur Robinson's projection is the best world map available. This projection shows the size and shape of most of the land quite accurately. Sizes of the oceans and distances are also fairly accurate. However, even a Robinson projection has distortions, especially in areas around the edges of the map.

There are many other types of projections. Each has advantages and draw-backs. It all depends on how you want to use each one. The illustrations on this page and the next page show several projections.

The World: A Mercator Projection

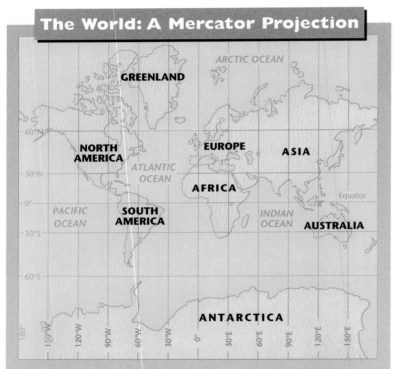

Map Study Mercator maps make areas near the poles look bigger than they are. This is because on a globe, the lines of longitude meet at the poles, but on a flat Mercator map, they are parallel. However, Mercator maps are useful to navigators because the longitude and latitude lines appear straight. Navigators can use these lines and a compass to plot a ship's route. **Place** Here Greenland looks bigger than it really is. It actually is about the size of Mexico. What other areas do you think might look larger than they should? Why?

The World: Interrupted, Equal Area, and Peters Projections

Interrupted Projection

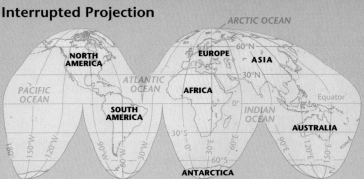

Map Study There are many ways to show a globe on a flat map. The interrupted projection map, on the left, shows the real sizes and shapes of continents. The equal area map, below left, shows size accurately. The Peters projection, below, shows land and ocean areas and correct directions accurately. **Location** Compare each projection with the more accurate Robinson projection below. What do each of these three projections distort?

Equal-Area Projection

Peters Projection

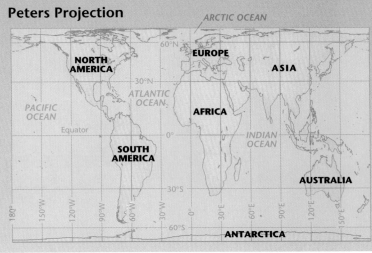

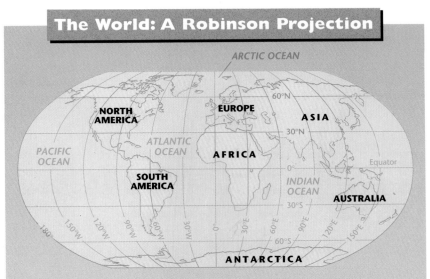

The World: A Robinson Projection

Map Study In 1988, the National Geographic Society adopted the Robinson projection as its official projection for world maps. While the Robinson projection does distort the globe a little, it shows the sizes and shapes of countries most accurately. **Movement** Do you think the Robinson projection would be as useful to a navigator as the Mercator projection? Why or why not?

The Parts of a Map

Look at the two maps below. One is an imaginary pirate map. The other is a map of the Grand Bahama Island, in the Caribbean Sea. Believe it or not, the pirate map has some features that you will find on any map. Of course, regular maps don't have the X that tells where the treasure is, but you will find a mark of some sort that shows your destination.

A Pirate Map and a Road Map

Map Study Almost all maps have some things in common. A compass rose shows direction. A key explains special symbols. A grid often shows longitude and latitude. The road map below has a grid of numbers and letters to help locate places.

Location What airport is located at B-1?

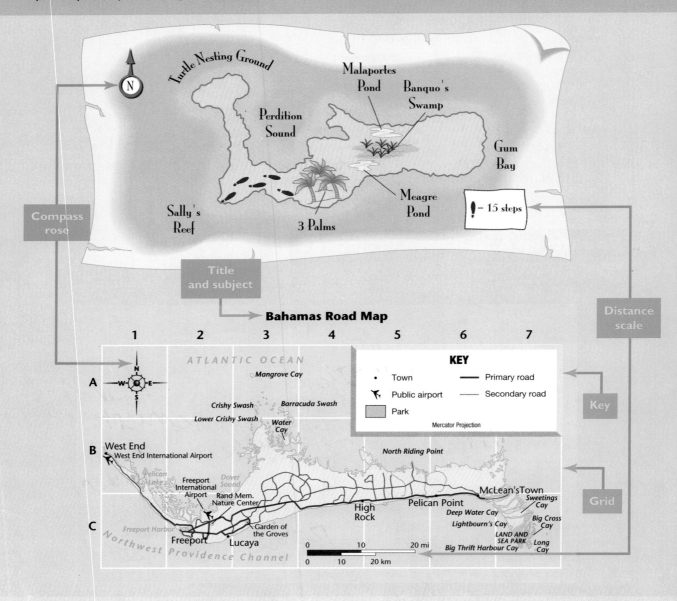

The pirate map has an arrow pointing north. On the regular map, you will find what geographers call a **compass rose,** which is a model of a compass. It tells the **cardinal directions,** which are north, south, east, and west.

On a pirate map, marks will tell you how many paces to walk to find the treasure. On a conventional map, an indicator for scale tells you how far to go to get to your destination. The scale tells you that one inch on the map represents a particular distance on the land. Scales vary, depending on the map. On one map, an inch may equal one mile. On another map, an inch may equal 100 miles.

On the pirate map, special symbols indicate landmarks such as trails, an oddly shaped rock, a tree with a broken branch, a small stream, or a cave. Regular maps also have symbols. They are explained in the section of the map called the **key,** or legend. It may include symbols for features such as national and state parks, various types of roads, sizes of towns and cities, or important landmarks.

A regular map includes some things that the pirate map doesn't. For instance, the pirate map doesn't have a map title. On a regular map, a title tells you the subject of the map.

A treasure map does not have a grid, either. Some maps use a grid of parallels and meridians. Remember that parallels show latitude, or distance north and south of the Equator. Meridians show longitude, or distance east and west of the Prime Meridian. On some maps, the area is too small for longitude and latitude to be helpful. These maps usually have a grid of letters and numbers to help people find things.

Every part of a map has a very simple purpose. That is to make sure that people who use maps have accurate information they need. The more you know about maps, the easier it will be for you to use them well—even if you're hunting for buried treasure!

READ ACTIVELY

Connect What parts of a map do you think are most helpful to you?

SECTION 2 REVIEW

1. **Define** (a) globe, (b) scale, (c) distortion, (d) projection, (e) compass rose, (f) cardinal direction, (g) key.

2. **Identify** (a) Gerhardus Mercator, (b) Arthur Robinson.

3. What are some advantages and disadvantages of using a globe to show the Earth's surface?

4. Why are there so many different types of map projections?

5. How can knowing the parts of a map help you?

Critical Thinking

6. **Making Comparisons** You are planning a hiking trip with your family to a nearby state park. Your family uses two maps: a road map and a map of the park. What advantages does each map have?

Activity

7. **Writing to Learn** Think of a place that you like to visit. How would you tell a friend to get there? Make some notes about directions and landmarks you could include in a map. Then make a map that shows your friend how to get there.

SKILLS
ACTIVITY

Expressing Problems Clearly

Geographers know that geography is not just about maps and where places are. Geography is about change. After all, the Earth is always being changed by natural forces. You and the nearly six billion other people on the planet also change it. Geographers use geography to view and understand these changes.

"Geography," as one of the world's leading geographers put it, "turns out to be much more, and much more significant, than many of us realized."

Are you still having a problem understanding what geography is? You can help yourself by expressing that problem clearly.

Get Ready

One way geographers help organize their study of the Earth is to use the five themes of geography. Look for them in Chapter 1. Understanding the five themes will help you express the meaning of geography.

▲ What can a geography walk teach you about your surroundings?

Try It Out

A. Identify the problem. You may think that geography is only about maps and the names of countries. You need to know what geography really is.

B. Think about exactly what the problem is. You know that the five geography themes should help you figure out what geography is. But maybe you have trouble understanding the five themes.

C. Put the problem into words. Write a sentence that tells the problem. There are many sentences that will work. Perhaps you will think of one something like this.

> What are the five geography themes, and how are they connected to what I know about the world?

Apply the Skill

Practice understanding the five themes of geography by going for a geography walk. Find out how the themes are reflected in the world around you. You don't have to walk near mountains or rivers. You can walk near your home or school.

1 Take a notebook and a pencil. You will need to take notes on your walk. Put into the notebook a list of the five geography themes and their definitions.

2 Take someone with you. Walk with a family member or a friend. Be sure to walk in a safe place.

3 Look for geography. As you walk, look for examples of the five themes. Does a delivery truck drive by? That is an example of movement. Is it carrying bread? Wheat for the bread was grown on a farm. That's human-environment interaction.

4 Record the geography around you. Find as many examples of each theme as you can. Record each one in your notebook.

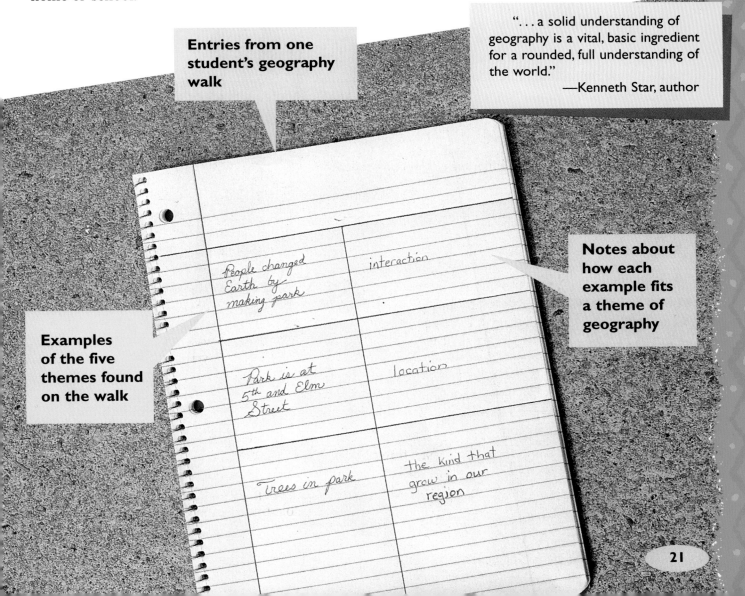

Entries from one student's geography walk

"...a solid understanding of geography is a vital, basic ingredient for a rounded, full understanding of the world."
—Kenneth Star, author

Notes about how each example fits a theme of geography

Examples of the five themes found on the walk

People changed Earth by making park — interaction

Park is at 5th and Elm Street — location

Trees in park — the kind that grow in our region

CHAPTER 1

Review and Activities

Reviewing Main Ideas

1. (a) What two questions do geographers always ask about a place? (b) What do geographers use to help answer the questions?

2. Explain how geographers locate any spot on the Earth.

3. You read in the newspaper that geographers are part of a team of people planning a new highway in your area. List and describe three geography themes that the team might use.

4. If you had to make a map, how would you show the Earth so that the size and shape of its features and the distances between them were accurate?

5. An ocean navigator uses one particular map to determine the best route from New Hampshire to Florida. An official who must solve an argument about which country owns a certain piece of land uses a different kind of map. Why do these two people use different maps?

Reviewing Key Terms

Use each key term below in a sentence that shows the meaning of the term.

1. geography
2. latitude
3. parallel
4. degree
5. Equator
6. longitude
7. meridian
8. Prime Meridian
9. plain
10. globe
11. scale
12. distortion
13. projection
14. compass rose
15. cardinal direction
16. key

Critical Thinking

1. **Recognizing Cause and Effect** Explain why today's maps are more accurate than maps drawn hundreds of years ago.

2. **Expressing Problems Clearly** Explain why there are so many different types of map projections.

Graphic Organizer

Choose a place that interests you. It might be a place you know very well or a place you have never seen. Fill in the web chart on the right. Write the name of the place in the center oval. If you know the place well, list facts or information under each theme. If you don't know the place, list questions that would fit each theme.

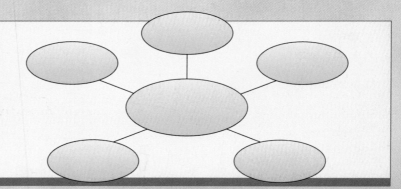

Map Activity

The Globe

For each place listed below, write the letter from the map that shows its location.

1. Prime Meridian

2. Equator

3. North Pole

4. South Pole

5. Europe

6. Africa

7. South America

8. North America

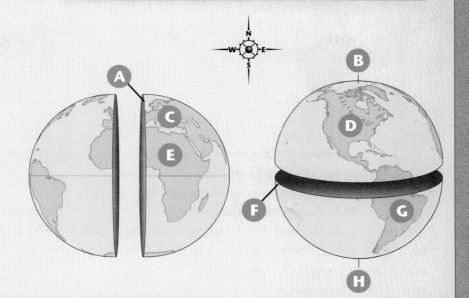

Writing Activity

Writing a Paragraph

Write a paragraph describing ways that you have seen people use maps. You may include such things as road maps, maps for seats in a sports arena or areas in a museum, or even hand-drawn maps to a friend's house.

Internet Activity

Use a search engine to find the **National Geographic Society** site. Click on the passport, then click on **Map Machine**. Choose **Political Maps** or **Physical Maps**. Click on the different regions to see the maps. With a partner, make a physical or a political map of the region of your choice.

Skills Review

Turn to the Skills Activity.

Review the steps for expressing problems clearly. Then complete the following: (a) Name one strategy you can use to help you express problems clearly. (b) How can expressing problems clearly help you to solve problems?

How Am I Doing?

Answer these questions to help you check your progress.

1. Can I list the five themes of geography and describe how they are used?

2. Do I understand the advantages and disadvantages of different ways of showing the Earth's surface?

3. What information from this chapter can I use in my book project?

INTERDISCIPLINARY ACTIVITY SHOP

A Five-Theme Tour

As discussed in Chapter 1, geographers use five themes to organize their study of the world and its people: location, place, human-environment interaction, movement, and regions. As you use this book, you will also be a geographer. You will gather, organize, and analyze geographic information. The five themes can help you. Before you use them, however, it helps to thoroughly know what they mean. A good way to explore the themes is through real-life examples.

Purpose

In this activity, you will plan a world tour. Your destination is either the world's mountains or the world's rivers. As you plan your tour, you will also explore the five geography themes.

Decide Where You Will Go

First, select the mountain tour or the river tour. Then, use a physical map of the world to choose five places you will visit along the way. Research each place so you can describe its relative location. That is, you will be able to write down descriptions such as "The Nile River in northeast Africa flows through Sudan and Egypt." This is an example of the theme of location, which answers the question "Where is this place?"

◄ ▲ Tourists enjoy the Nile River and the sights of Egypt.

Describe the Places on Your Tour

Use the theme of place to write an exciting description of each place on your tour. The theme of place answers the question "What is this place like?" Include both physical and human characteristics. Physical characteristics are the natural features of the Earth. Things related to people are human characteristics. Your research will help you focus on what makes your places unique.

Next, focus on the theme of human-environment interaction. This theme answers the questions: "How do people use this place? How and why have people changed this place?" For each place on your tour, gather information that answers these two questions. Add the information to your descriptions.

Plan a Travel Route

The theme of movement answers the question "How has this place been affected by the movement of people, goods, and ideas?" To explore this theme, choose just one place. Do research to plan a travel route from your community to that place.

Call or visit a travel agent to find the number of miles for each section of the journey. Add the distances together to find the total number of miles for the trip.

Learn About the Language

The theme of regions answers the question "How is this place similar to and different from other regions?" To help you learn about this theme, focus on the same one special place. Do research to find out what languages people speak there. Then find other places in the world where people speak the same languages. This activity will show you one type of region—a

language region. Your place belongs to a group of places that share something similar: the same language.

Do additional research to make a chart of some common words in the languages spoken in your place. For instance, you might find the words for "hello," "good-bye," "thank you," and "please." These are words a visitor will need to know.

Create a Travel Brochure

Now, use the information you have gathered to create a brochure about the places you will visit on your tour. The brochure will tell everyone about your plans. Include the descriptions you wrote for each place on the tour. Also include your travel route and language chart. Decorate the brochure with drawings or magazine pictures.

ANALYSIS AND CONCLUSION

Write a summary that tells which type of tour you planned—mountains or rivers. Be sure to answer the following questions in your summary.

1. How did the process of planning your tour help you learn about the five themes?

2. Which of the five themes do you think are most important in your tour?

CHAPTER 2

Earth's Physical Geography

PICTURE ACTIVITIES

Before we had satellites in space, people could only imagine how the Earth truly looked. Now, satellites let people see the Earth's land and water beneath a swirling mix of clouds. The following activities will help you get to know your planet.

Be a global weather forecaster

Weather forecasters use satellite pictures like the one above to see weather patterns. The white areas in the picture are clouds. What land areas do you recognize? How do you recognize them? On the day this picture was taken, what areas seem cloudier? Swirling patterns may indicate storms. Do you see any storm patterns?

Become an Earth expert

Watch especially for one of these topics as you read this chapter: Beneath the Earth's Surface, On the Earth's Surface, and Beyond the Earth's Atmosphere. Which one would you like to be an expert on?

Our Planet, the Earth

BEFORE YOU READ

Reach Into Your Background

What is spring like where you live? What is winter like? How long do these seasons last where you live? If you can answer these questions, consider yourself an amateur geographer. You have noticed the changes in your region at different times of the year.

Questions to Explore

1. How does the Earth move in space?
2. Why do seasons change?

Key Terms
orbit
revolution
axis
rotation

low latitudes
high latitudes
middle latitudes

Key Places
Tropic of Cancer
Tropic of Capricorn
Arctic Circle
Antarctic Circle

"The Sky Father opened his hand. Within every crease there lay innumerable grains of shining maize [corn]. In his thumb and forefinger he took some of the shining grains and placed them in the sky as brilliant stars to be a guide to humans when the bright sun was hidden."

This is part of an ancient myth of the Pueblos, who lived in what today is the southwestern United States. They used the story to explain the appearance of the night sky.

The Earth and the Sun

The Earth, the sun, the planets, and the twinkling stars in the sky are all part of a galaxy, or family of stars. We call our galaxy the Milky Way because the lights from its billions of stars look like a trail of spilled milk across the night sky. Our sun is one of those stars. Although the sun is just a tiny speck in the Milky Way, it is the center of everything for the Earth.

▼ Thousands of years ago, Native Americans laid this wheel out in Wyoming's Bighorn Mountains. They may have used it to track the movements of the stars.

Predict What causes day to change into night?

Understanding Days and Nights   The sun may be about 93 million miles (150 million km) away, but it still provides the Earth with heat and light. The Earth travels around the sun in an oval-shaped path called an **orbit.** It takes 365¼ days, or one year, for the Earth to complete one **revolution,** or circular journey, around the sun.

As the Earth revolves around the sun, it is also spinning in space. The Earth turns around its **axis**—an imaginary line running through it between the North and South poles. Each complete turn, which takes about 24 hours, is called a **rotation.** As the Earth rotates, it is daytime on the side facing the sun. It is night on the side away from the sun.

Understanding Seasons   At certain times of the year, days are longer than nights, and at other times, nights are longer than days. This happens, in part, because the Earth's axis is at an angle. At some points in the Earth's orbit, the tilt causes a region to face toward the sun for more hours than it faces away from the sun. Days are longer. At other times, the region faces away from the sun for more hours than it faces toward the sun. Days are shorter.

The Earth's tilt and orbit also cause changes in temperatures during the seasons. The warmth you feel at any time of year depends on how directly the sunlight falls upon you. Some regions receive a great deal of fairly direct sunlight, while other regions receive no direct sunlight. Special latitude lines divide up these regions of the world. You can see them on the map on the next page.

How Night Changes Into Day

Chart Study This diagram shows how places on the Earth move from night into day. Today, it takes almost 24 hours for the Earth to make one complete rotation. But when the Earth first formed millions of years ago, it spun 10 times faster. A full cycle of day and night on the Earth lasted just over two hours. **Critical Thinking** As time passes, the Earth spins more and more slowly. What will eventually happen to the length of a day? Find North America on the globe. Which coast gets daylight first?

North Pole

Night

Earth's rotation

Day

Rays of sun

South Pole

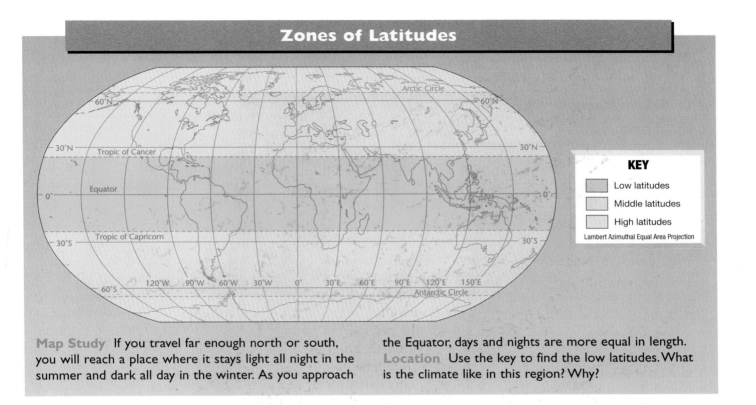

Map Study If you travel far enough north or south, you will reach a place where it stays light all night in the summer and dark all day in the winter. As you approach the Equator, days and nights are more equal in length. **Location** Use the key to find the low latitudes. What is the climate like in this region? Why?

Looking at Latitudes

Look at the diagram on the next page. In some places on the Earth, the sun is directly overhead at particular days during the year. One place is the Equator, an imaginary latitude line that circles the Earth at 0°, exactly halfway between the North Pole (90°N) and the South Pole (90°S). On about March 21 and September 23, the sun is directly over the Equator. On those days, all over the Earth, days are almost exactly as long as nights. People call these days the spring and fall equinoxes.

Two other imaginary latitude lines lie $23\frac{1}{2}°$ north and $23\frac{1}{2}°$ south of the Equator. At $23\frac{1}{2}°$N is the Tropic of Cancer. Here, the sun shines directly above on June 20 or 21. This is the first day of summer, or the summer solstice (SOHL stiss), in the Northern Hemisphere. At $23\frac{1}{2}°$S is the Tropic of Capricorn. Here, the sun shines directly above on December 21 or 22. This is the first day of winter, or the winter solstice, in the Northern Hemisphere. The seasons are reversed in the Southern Hemisphere. When would the summer solstice occur there?

The area between the Tropic of Cancer and the Tropic of Capricorn is called the **low latitudes,** or the tropics. Any location in the low latitudes receives direct sunlight at some time during the year. In this region, it is almost always hot.

Two other latitude lines set off distinct regions. To the north of the Equator, at $66\frac{1}{2}°$N, is the Arctic Circle. To the south of the Equator, at $66\frac{1}{2}°$S, is the Antarctic Circle. The regions between these circles and the poles are the **high latitudes,** or the polar zones. The high latitudes receive no direct sunlight. It is very cool to bitterly cold.

Midnight Sun Earth's axis is at an angle, which makes the Earth seem to lean. When the North Pole leans toward the sun, the sun never sets. At the same time, the South Pole leans away from the sun, so at the South Pole, the sun never rises. This lasts for six months. When the South Pole leans toward the sun, this pole has six months of continuous sunlight. Sunlight at the poles falls at an angle, so the poles receive very little heat.

Summer On June 21 or 22, the sun's direct rays are over the Tropic of Cancer. The Northern Hemisphere receives the greatest number of sunlight hours. It is the beginning of summer there.

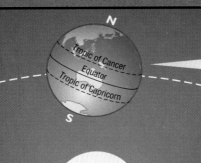

Spring On March 20 or 21, the sun's rays shine strongest near the Equator. The Northern and Southern Hemispheres each receive almost equal hours of sunlight and darkness. It is the beginning of spring in the Northern Hemisphere.

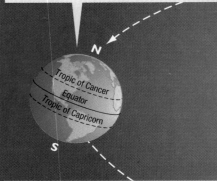

Sun

Autumn On September 22 or 23, the sun's rays shine strongest near the Equator. Again, the Northern and Southern Hemispheres each receive almost equal hours of sunlight and darkness. It is the beginning of fall in the Northern Hemisphere.

Winter Around December 21, the sun is over the Tropic of Capricorn in the Southern Hemisphere. The Northern Hemisphere is tilted away from the sun and it is the beginning of winter there.

Chart Study As the Earth moves around the Sun, summer changes to fall and fall changes to winter. But the warmest and coldest weather does not start as soon as summer and winter begin. Why? Oceans and lakes also affect the weather, and they warm up and cool off slowly. **Critical Thinking** Australia lies in the Southern Hemisphere. What is the season in Australia when it is winter in the United States?

Two areas remain: the **middle latitudes,** or the temperate zones. At some times of the year, these areas receive fairly direct sunlight. At other times, they receive fairly indirect sunlight. So, the middle latitudes have seasons: spring, summer, winter, and fall. Each lasts about three months and has distinct patterns of daylight, temperature, and weather.

SECTION 1 REVIEW

1. **Define** (a) orbit, (b) revolution, (c) axis, (d) rotation, (e) low latitudes, (f) high latitudes, (g) middle latitudes.

2. **Identify** (a) Tropic of Cancer, (b) Tropic of Capricorn, (c) Arctic Circle, (d) Antarctic Circle.

3. The Earth revolves and the Earth rotates. Explain the difference between the two.

4. Why are seasons different in the Northern and Southern hemispheres?

5. What causes the Earth to have seasons?

6. Describe conditions in the high, middle, and low latitudes.

Critical Thinking
7. **Drawing Conclusions** What would happen to plant and animal life if the Earth did not tilt on its axis? Why?

Activity
8. **Writing to Learn** Write a storybook for a young child explaining the relationship between the Earth and the sun.

Land, Air, and Water

BEFORE YOU READ

Reach Into Your Background
Think of one of your favorite outdoor activities, such as skiing, cycling, or hiking. Tell how the shape of the land helps you enjoy it.

Questions to Explore
1. What forces shape the land?
2. What are the Earth's major landforms?

Key Terms
landform
mountain
hill
plateau
plain
plate tectonics
plate
weathering
erosion
atmosphere

Key Places
Ring of Fire
Pangaea

L isten to the words of Megumi Fujiwara, a Japanese medical student who lived through the Great Hanshin Earthquake in 1995.

> "E arly that morning, I had awakened hearing explosions and feeling my body rising. I knew immediately that it was an earthquake and expected the shaking to last only a moment. It didn't, and after landing back on my futon [bed], I lay frozen, listening to windows rattling and breaking [and] seeing objects flying above. Then everything blacked out. I awoke some time later, inhaling dust and unable to see anything. [I] found myself outside at ground level, rather than in my second-story apartment. Open sky had replaced my ceiling."

Fujiwara was lucky. The Great Hanshin Earthquake killed 5,500 people when it struck Kobe (KOH bay), Japan, on January 17, 1995.

Forces Inside the Earth

Japan knows about earthquakes because it is part of what geographers call the "Ring of Fire." About 90 percent of the world's earthquakes and many of the world's active volcanoes occur on the Ring, which circles the Pacific Ocean. Earthquakes and volcanoes are two forces that shape and reshape the Earth. They provide clues about the Earth's structure, and they are one reason why the Earth's surface constantly changes.

What Is the Earth Made Of?   To understand events like volcanoes and earthquakes, you must study the Earth's structure. Pictures of the Earth show a great deal of water and some land. The water covers about 75 percent of the Earth's surface in lakes, rivers, seas, and oceans. Only 25 percent of the Earth's surface is land.

In part, continents are unique because of their **landforms,** or shapes and types of land. **Mountains** are landforms that rise usually more than 2,000 feet (610 m) above sea level. They are wide at the bottom and rise steeply to a narrow peak or ridge. **Hills** are lower and less steep than mountains, with rounded tops. A **plateau** is a large, mostly flat area that rises above the surrounding land. At least one side of a plateau has a steep slope. **Plains** are large areas of flat or gently rolling land. Many are along coasts. Others are in the interiors of some continents.

Pangaea: The Supercontinent   For hundreds of years, as geographers studied the Earth's landforms, they asked "where" and "why" questions. When they looked at the globe, they thought they saw a relationship between landforms that were very far apart.

Predict Why do scientists think the Earth once had only one, large landmass?

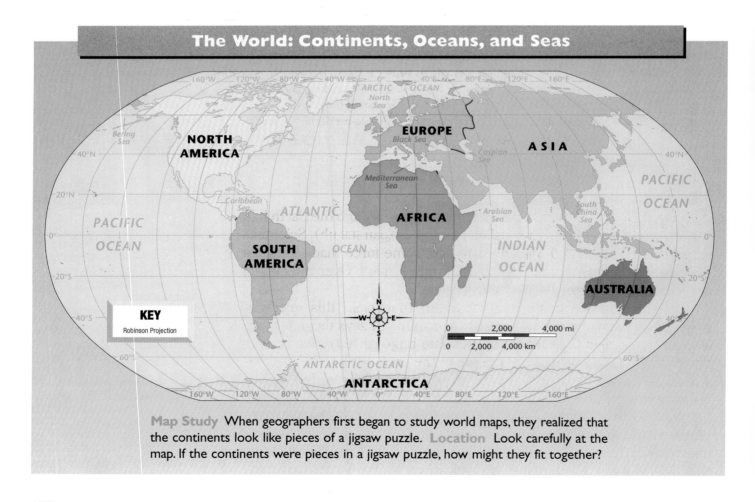

The World: Continents, Oceans, and Seas

Map Study When geographers first began to study world maps, they realized that the continents look like pieces of a jigsaw puzzle. **Location** Look carefully at the map. If the continents were pieces in a jigsaw puzzle, how might they fit together?

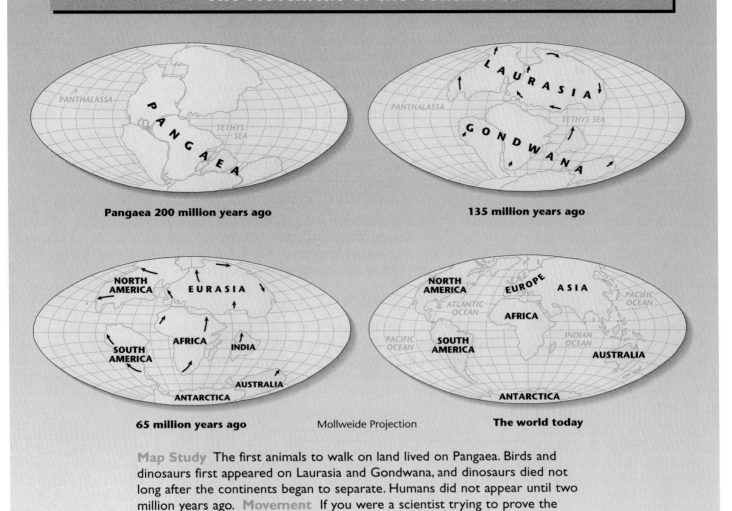

Pangaea 200 million years ago

135 million years ago

65 million years ago

Mollweide Projection

The world today

Map Study The first animals to walk on land lived on Pangaea. Birds and dinosaurs first appeared on Laurasia and Gondwana, and dinosaurs died not long after the continents began to separate. Humans did not appear until two million years ago. **Movement** If you were a scientist trying to prove the theory of plate tectonics, what clues would you look for?

Today, geographers theorize that millions of years ago the Earth had only one huge landmass. They called it Pangaea (pan JEE uh). Scientists reasoned that about 200 million years ago, some force made Pangaea split into several pieces, and it began to move apart. Over millions of years, the pieces formed separate continents.

But why did the continents separate? To explain this question, geographers use a theory called **plate tectonics.** It says the outer skin of the Earth, called the crust, is broken into huge pieces called **plates.** The continents and oceans are the top of the crust. Below the plates is a layer of rock called magma, which is hot enough to be fairly soft. The plates float on the magma, altering the shape of the Earth's surface. Continents are part of plates, and plates shift over time. We cannot see them move because it is very slow and takes a long time. When geographers say a plate moves quickly, they mean it may shift two inches (five cm) a year.

The World: Plate Boundaries

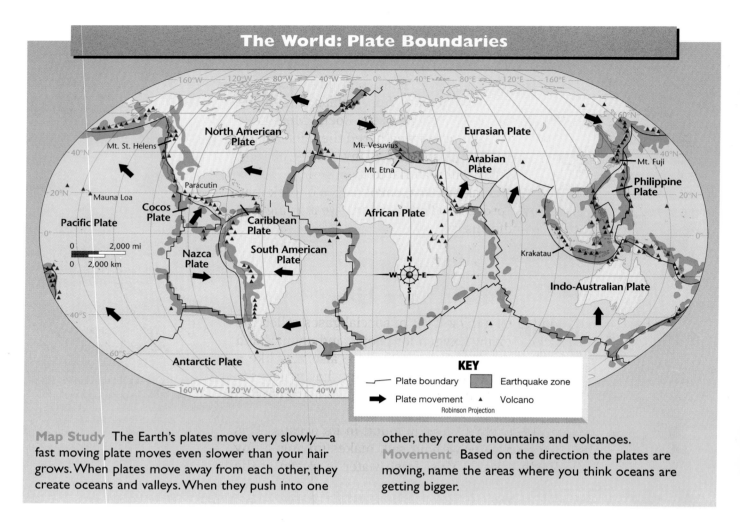

KEY
- —— Plate boundary
- ➡ Plate movement
- ▲ Volcano
- ▓ Earthquake zone

Robinson Projection

Map Study The Earth's plates move very slowly—a fast moving plate moves even slower than your hair grows. When plates move away from each other, they create oceans and valleys. When they push into one other, they create mountains and volcanoes.

Movement Based on the direction the plates are moving, name the areas where you think oceans are getting bigger.

A New Island For thousands of years, magma from underwater volcanoes built up until it rose above sea level to create the Hawaiian islands. Today, a new island, named Loihi (low EE hee), is forming. Already two miles (3.2 km) high, it has 3,000 feet (914 m) to go before it breaks the ocean's surface. Loihi erupts almost all the time. It causes earthquakes and tidal waves that threaten the other islands.

Volcanoes, Earthquakes, and Shifting Plates Look at the map of plate boundaries on this page. It shows that plates move in different directions. In some places, plates move apart, and magma leaks out through cracks in the crust. In the oceans, over time, the cooling rock builds up to form lines of underwater mountains called ridges. On either side of the line, the plates move away from each other.

In other places, the plates push against one another, forcing one plate under the other. Tremendous pressure and heat builds up. Molten rock races upward, exploding onto the surface and producing a volcano.

Along plate boundaries, there are many weak places in the Earth's crust. When plates push against one another, the crust cracks and splinters from the pressure. The cracks are called faults. When the crust moves along faults, it releases great amounts of energy in the form of earthquakes. These movements can cause dramatic changes.

Forces on the Earth's Surface

Forces like volcanoes slowly build up the Earth; other forces slowly break it down. Often, the forces that break the Earth down are not as dramatic as volcanoes, but the results can last just as long.

Weathering is a process that breaks rocks down into tiny pieces. Three things cause weathering: wind, rain, and ice. Slowly but surely, they wear away the Earth's landforms. Hills and low, rounded mountains show what weathering can do. The Appalachian Mountains in the eastern United States once were as high as the Rocky Mountains of the western United States. Wind and rain weathered them into much lower peaks. Weathering helps create soil, too. Tiny pieces of rock combine with decayed animal and plant material to form soil.

Once this breaking down has taken place, small pieces of rock may be carried to new places by a process called **erosion.** Weathering and erosion slowly create new landforms.

Predict What two things do people, other animals, and plants need to survive?

Air and Water:
Two Ingredients for Life

The Earth is surrounded by a thick layer of special gases called the **atmosphere.** It provides life-giving oxygen for people and animals and life-giving carbon dioxide for plants. The atmosphere also acts like a blanket. It holds in the amount of heat from the sun that makes life possible. Winds, as you can see in the map below, help to distribute this heat around the globe.

About 97 percent of the Earth's water is found in its oceans. This water is salty. Fresh water, or water without salt, makes up only a tiny percentage of all the Earth's water. Most fresh water is frozen at the

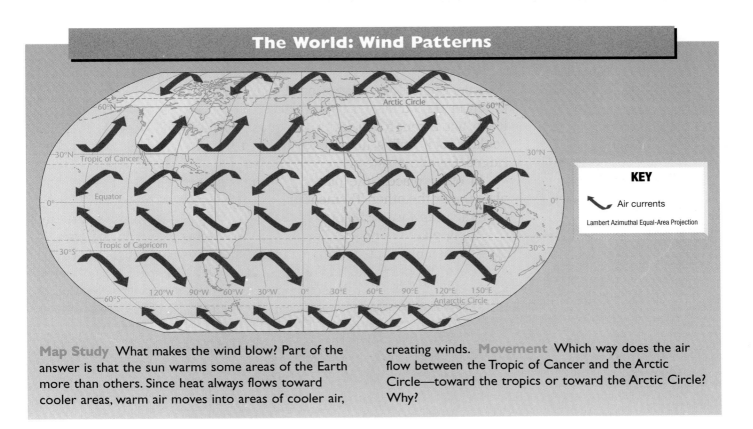

The World: Wind Patterns

KEY

Air currents

Lambert Azimuthal Equal-Area Projection

Map Study What makes the wind blow? Part of the answer is that the sun warms some areas of the Earth more than others. Since heat always flows toward cooler areas, warm air moves into areas of cooler air, creating winds. **Movement** Which way does the air flow between the Tropic of Cancer and the Arctic Circle—toward the tropics or toward the Arctic Circle? Why?

The Water Cycle

Chart Study Ocean water is too salty to drink or to irrigate crops. However, the oceans are a source of fresh water. How does this happen? When water evaporates from the ocean's surface, salt is left behind. The water vapor rises and forms clouds. The rain that falls to the Earth is fresh. **Critical Thinking** Once rain has fallen, how does water return to the ocean?

Clouds

Precipitation

Condensation

Rain, snow, sleet, hail

Transpiration (moisture from plants)

Surface runoff

Evaporation from lakes and streams

Evaporation from ocean

Groundwater

Subsurface runoff

North and South poles. People need fresh water for many things. This fresh water comes from lakes, rivers, and rain. Also, much fresh water, called groundwater, is stored in the soil itself. The diagram above shows the movement of all the water on the Earth's surface, in the ground, and in the air. The Earth does have enough water for people. However, some places have too much water and other places have too little.

SECTION 2 REVIEW

1. **Define** (a) landform, (b) mountain, (c) hill, (d) plateau, (e) plain, (f) plate tectonics, (g) plate, (h) weathering, (i) erosion, (j) atmosphere.

2. **Identify** (a) Ring of Fire, (b) Pangaea.

3. Why are there earthquakes and volcanoes?

4. What forces on the Earth's surface break down rocks?

5. Why is the atmosphere important?

Critical Thinking

6. **Distinguishing Fact From Opinion** What facts support the theory of plate tectonics?

Activity

7. **Writing to Learn** Suppose you were able to see the region you live in 10,000 years from now. Describe how the landforms might look. Explain what might have caused those changes.

Climate and What Influences It

Reach Into Your Background
Thunderstorms can knock down power lines and trees. Hurricanes can destroy whole communities. What is the worst weather you have experienced? How did you feel? How did you stay safe?

Questions to Explore
1. What is climate?
2. How do landforms and bodies of water affect climate?

Key Terms
weather
temperature
precipitation
climate

Key Names and Places
Gulf Stream
Peru Current
California Current
St. Louis
San Francisco

In late May 1996, a tornado's furious winds tore down the movie screen of a drive-in theater in St. Catherine's, Ontario, Canada. Ironically, the week's feature movie was *Twister,* a film about tornadoes.

Richard and Daphne Thompson spend their time tracking tornadoes in Oklahoma. Daphne Thompson recalls one particular storm: "The car was hit by 50- to 70-mile-per-hour gusts," she says. "Tumbleweeds were blowing so hard one left a dent in the car."

Weather or Climate?

These two stories show that weather like tornadoes can be dangerous. Or is it "climate" like tornadoes? What is the difference between weather and climate?

Every morning, most people check the temperature outside before they get dressed. But in some parts of India, people have very serious reasons for watching the **weather,** or the day-to-day changes in the air. In this region, it rains only during one period of the year. No one living there wants the rainy days to end too soon. That rain must fill the wells with enough fresh water to last through the coming dry spell.

▼ Tornadoes can easily flatten buildings. Tornado winds are the most powerful and violent winds on the Earth.

Map Study Many factors, including nearness to the Equator and to bodies of water, affect climate.

Regions What are the two major climate regions of South America? What is the major climate region of North Africa?

KEY

Tropical
- Tropical wet
- Tropical wet and dry

Dry
- Semiarid
- Arid

Mild
- Mediterranean
- Humid subtropical
- Marine west coast

Continental
- Humid continental
- Subarctic

Polar
- Tundra
- Ice cap
- Highlands
- Ice pack

Robinson Projection

ATLANTIC OCEAN

PACIFIC OCEAN

80°N   120°W

60°N

40°N

Tropic of Cancer

20°N

Equator

Tropic of Capricorn

60°S

Antarctic Circle

160°W   120°W   80°W   40°W

Predict What do you think influences the climate of an area?

Weather is measured primarily by temperature and precipitation. **Temperature** is how hot or cold the air feels. **Precipitation** is water that falls to the ground as rain, sleet, hail, or snow.

Climate is not the same as weather. The **climate** of a place is the average weather over many years. Weather is what people see from day to day. A day is rainy or it is dry. Climate is what people know from experience happens from year to year.

Latitude, Landforms, and Climate   The Earth has many climate regions. Some climates are hot enough that people rarely need to wear a sweater. In some cold climates, snow stays on the ground most of the year. And there are places on the Earth where between 30 and 40 feet (9 and 12 meters) of rain fall in a single year. Geographers know climates are different in the low, middle, and high latitudes, because latitude affects temperature. Major landforms such as mountains also affect climates in neighboring areas. Wind and water also play a role.

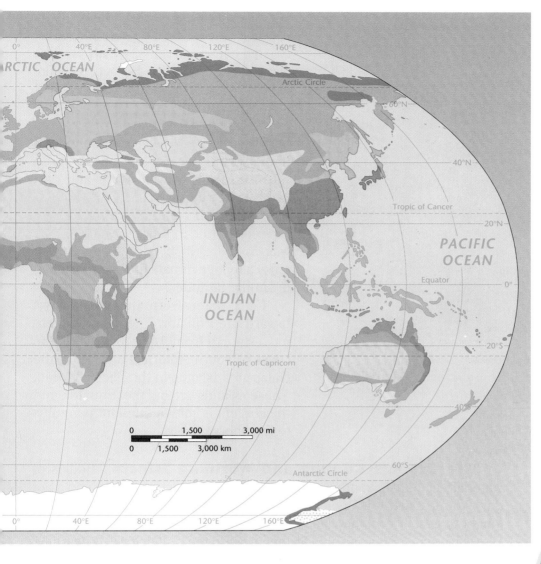

0	1,500	3,000 mi
0	1,500	3,000 km

Wind and Water

Without wind and water, the Earth would overheat. If you sit in the sun for a while on a hot day, you will feel warmer and warmer. The same thing could happen to the tropical regions of the Earth if wind and water did not help spread the sun's heat.

The Blowing Winds   In part, the Earth's rotation creates our winds. Because of it, air moves in an east-west direction, as the map at the end of the last section shows. Two other factors make air move in a north-south direction: (1) Hot air rises and circulates toward regions where the air is not as hot. (2) Cold air sinks and moves toward regions where the air is warmer. As a result, hot, moist air from the Equator rises in the atmosphere, then moves toward the North Pole or the South Pole. Cold, dry air from the poles moves toward the Equator. This movement helps keep the Earth from overheating.

Smog Normally, air is cooler at higher altitudes. During a temperature inversion, however, a layer of warm air sits on top of the cooler air. The warm air traps pollution near the ground. This mixture of dangerous smoke and fog is called smog. The brown air seen in cities such as Los Angeles and Denver is smog caused by car exhaust.

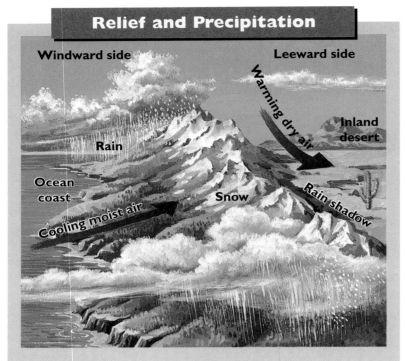

Relief and Precipitation

Windward side

Leeward side

Warming dry air

Inland desert

Rain

Ocean coast

Cooling moist air

Snow

Rain shadow

Chart Study As moist air blowing from the ocean rises up a mountain, it cools and drops its moisture. **Critical Thinking** Describe the climate on a mountain's leeward side—or side away from the wind.

Ocean Currents: Hot and Cold The Earth's rotation also creates ocean currents, which are like fast-moving rivers in the oceans. Like winds, ocean currents travel great distances. As you can see on the map on the next page, warm water from near the Equator moves north or south. In the Atlantic Ocean, the Gulf Stream, a warm current, travels north and east from the tropics. The Gulf Stream merges with the North Atlantic Current to to carry warm water all the way to the British Isles. People there enjoy a milder climate than people living in similar latitudes.

Cold water from the poles flows toward the Equator. The Peru Current moves north from Antarctica, along the coast of South America, and on to the Galapagos Islands in the Pacific Ocean. These islands sit on the Equator, but the current is cold enough for penguins to live there.

The Ocean's Cooling and Warming Effects Bodies of water affect climate in other ways, too. Have you gone to a beach on a hot day? You learned it is cooler by the water. That is because water takes longer to heat or cool than land. So in summer, a place near the ocean or a lake will be cooler than an area farther away. In the winter, it will be warmer.

For example, consider two places in the United States—San Francisco, California, and St. Louis, Missouri. Both cities have an average annual temperature of about 55°F (13°C). Their climates, however, are quite different. San Francisco borders the Pacific Ocean. The California Current passes by the city, carrying cool water from the waters off Alaska. In winter, the ocean current is warmer than the air, so the current gives off warmth and the air temperature rises. A San Franciscan traveling to St. Louis in December would find it much colder there than at home. In summer, the current is colder than the air, so the current absorbs heat, making the air temperature fall. A San Franciscan probably would find the summer months in St. Louis uncomfortably warm.

Raging Storms Wind and water can make climates milder, but they also can create storms. Some storms cause great destruction. Hurricane Andrew, for example, struck south Florida in the early morning hours of August 24, 1992, and left 160,000 people homeless. Julius Keaton recalls what happened:

READ ACTIVELY

Ask Questions What would you like to know about the raging storms that are part of the Earth's climate?

"I heard one window break, so I jumped up and put a mattress against it. But I guess that storm really wanted to get in, 'cause it blew out another window and beat down the front door.**"**

Hurricanes are wind and rain storms that form over the tropics in the Atlantic Ocean. The whirling winds at the center of a hurricane travel over 73 miles (122 km) per hour and can reach speeds of more than 100 miles (160 km) an hour. Hurricanes produce huge waves called storm surges, which flood over shorelines and can destroy homes and towns. Typhoons are similar storms that take place in the Pacific Ocean.

Hurricanes and typhoons affect large areas. One single hurricane can threaten islands in the Caribbean Sea, the east coast of Mexico, and the southern coast of the United States. Other storms are just as dangerous, but they affect smaller areas. Tornadoes, for example, are swirling funnels of wind that can reach 200 miles (320 km) per hour. The winds and the vacuum they create in their centers can wreck almost

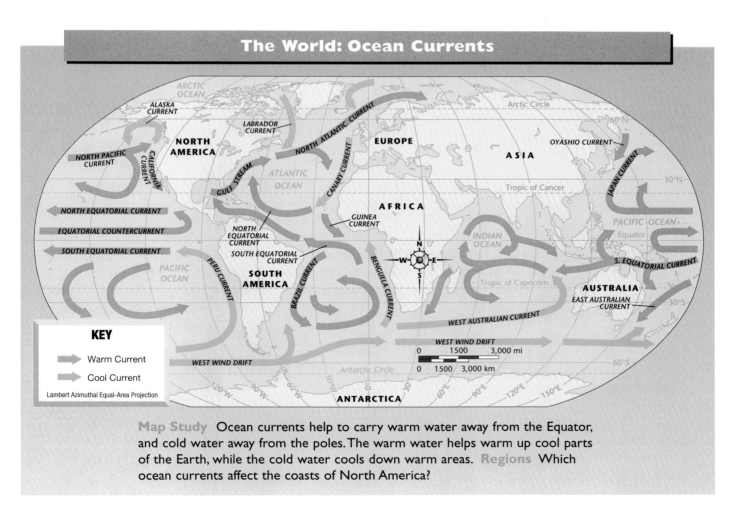

Map Study Ocean currents help to carry warm water away from the Equator, and cold water away from the poles. The warm water helps warm up cool parts of the Earth, while the cold water cools down warm areas. **Regions** Which ocean currents affect the coasts of North America?

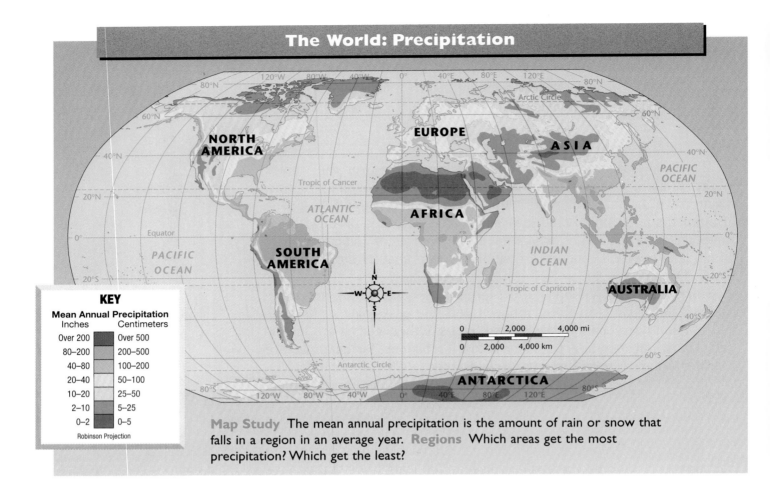

KEY

Mean Annual Precipitation

Inches		Centimeters
Over 200		Over 500
80–200		200–500
40–80		100–200
20–40		50–100
10–20		25–50
2–10		5–25
0–2		0–5

Robinson Projection

Map Study The mean annual precipitation is the amount of rain or snow that falls in a region in an average year. **Regions** Which areas get the most precipitation? Which get the least?

everything in their path. However, tornadoes only average about one-half mile in diameter. Therefore, they affect a more limited area than hurricanes.

Some storms are less severe. In winter, blizzards dump huge amounts of snow on parts of North America. And severe rainstorms and thunderstorms strike the continent most often in spring and summer.

SECTION 3 REVIEW

1. **Define** (a) weather, (b) temperature, (c) precipitation, (d) climate.

2. **Identify** (a) Gulf Stream, (b) Peru Current, (c) California Current, (d) St. Louis, (e) San Francisco.

3. Explain the difference between weather and climate.

4. How does latitude affect climate?

5. How do mountains affect neighboring climates?

Critical Thinking

6. **Recognizing Cause and Effect** Explain how currents from the tropics affect climates far away.

Activity

7. **Writing to Learn** Check a newspaper's local weather forecasts for the last several weeks. Make a chart. Then write a paragraph about your climate. Use what you know about your region's climate to describe the weather as normal or abnormal for this time of year.

How Climate Affects Vegetation

Reach Into Your Background
Make a list of some plants and trees native to your area. How much rain and sunlight do they seem to need? How do they react to unusual weather?

Questions to Explore
1. Where are the Earth's major climate regions?
2. What kinds of vegetation grow in each climate region?

Key Terms
vegetation
canopy
tundra
vertical climate

Key Place
Great Plains
Arctic Circle

Suppose you live in Arizona. You may walk past cactus plants on the way to school. In Minnesota, you may see leafy trees that change color in the fall. In Georgia, you may see Spanish moss draped along bald cypress trees. All these differences are related to climate.

Climate and Vegetation

A climate must provide plants with water, sunlight, and certain nutrients, or elements, plants use as food. Also, plants have features, called *adaptations,* that enable them to live in their particular climate. That means that over a very long time, small, accidental changes in a few individual plants made them better able to survive in a particular place.

How do geographers use such information? They can predict the kinds of plants they will find in a climate. Geographers discuss five broad types of climates: tropical, dry, moderate, continental, and polar. Each has its unique **vegetation,** or plants that grow there naturally.

Tropical Climates   In the low latitudes, you will find two types of tropical climates. Both are hot and wet. A tropical wet climate has two seasons—one with a great deal of rain and one with a little less rain. A tropical wet and dry climate also has two seasons: one with much rain and one with very little rain. The vegetation associated with these climates is tropical rain forest.

▼ Cacti have waxy skins that hold water in. Prickly spines protect a cactus from being eaten by animals that want its water.

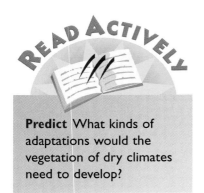

Predict What kinds of adaptations would the vegetation of dry climates need to develop?

Because growing conditions are so perfect—there is so much light, heat, and rain—thousands of kinds of plants grow in a rain forest. Some trees rise 130 feet (40 meters) into the air. Their uppermost branches create a **canopy.** Little sunlight can break through this dense covering of leafy branches. Other types of trees, which are adapted to the shade, grow to lower heights. Thousands of kinds of vines and ferns thrive in the rain forest.

Dry Climates Arid and semiarid climates are very hot but receive very little rain. Since there is so little moisture, vegetation in dry regions is sparse. Plants grow far apart in sandy, gravelly soil. Their shallow roots are adapted to absorb scarce water before it evaporates in the heat. Some plants have small leaves, which lose little moisture into the air through evaporation. Other plants flower only when it rains so that as many seeds survive as possible.

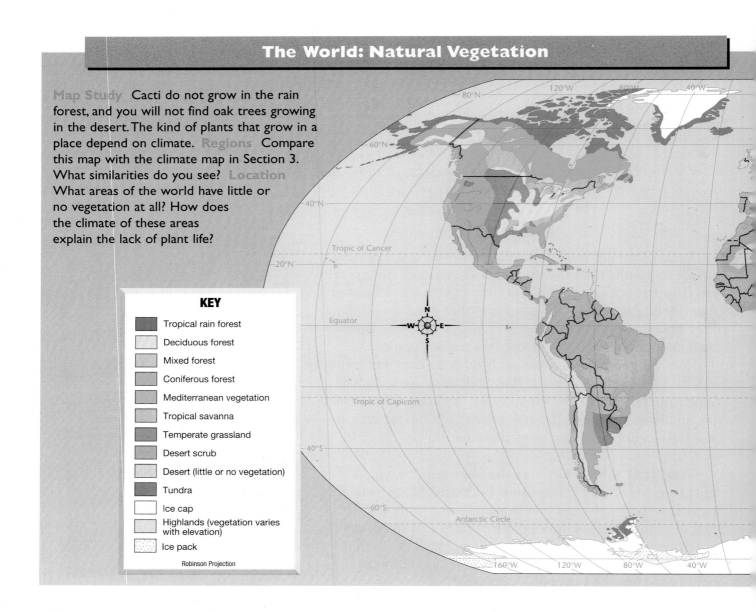

The World: Natural Vegetation

Map Study Cacti do not grow in the rain forest, and you will not find oak trees growing in the desert. The kind of plants that grow in a place depend on climate. **Regions** Compare this map with the climate map in Section 3. What similarities do you see? **Location** What areas of the world have little or no vegetation at all? How does the climate of these areas explain the lack of plant life?

KEY

- Tropical rain forest
- Deciduous forest
- Mixed forest
- Coniferous forest
- Mediterranean vegetation
- Tropical savanna
- Temperate grassland
- Desert scrub
- Desert (little or no vegetation)
- Tundra
- Ice cap
- Highlands (vegetation varies with elevation)
- Ice pack

Robinson Projection

Moderate Climates Moderate climates are found in the middle latitudes. There are three types: Mediterranean, marine west coast, and humid subtropical. In all three climate types, rain is moderate. There are seasonal changes, but temperatures hardly ever fall below freezing.

Moderate climates have a wide variety of vegetation. Forests of deciduous trees, which lose their leaves in the fall, grow here. So do tall shrubs, low bushes—or scrub—wildflowers, and a variety of grasses. The Mediterranean climate receives most of its rain in winter and summers are hot and dry. In this climate, plants have leathery leaves, which hold in moisture during the dry summers. Of the three moderate climates, the humid subtropical climate has the most precipitation, heat, and humidity. It supports many types of vegetation. Most marine west coast climates are mountainous and are cooled by ocean currents. Therefore, they support more forests than grasses.

CITIZEN HEROES

To Be a Leader
In the 1970s, Michael Stewartt was a charter airplane pilot in Alaska. Every day he flew over its vast forests, where he could see the damage to national forests from clear-cut logging. Lawmakers should see this for themselves, he thought. So, Stewartt founded Lighthawk, an environmental plane service that took people on educational "tours" in the air. Lighthawk continues today. It also creates plans for change.

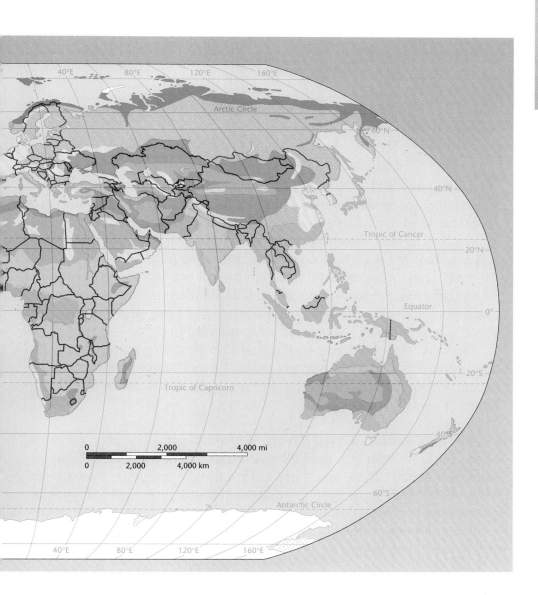

Antarctica (right) is an "icy desert"—a world of permanent ice and snow. In contrast, Oregon (below) is a world of constant green, teeming with life. **Critical Thinking** How do you think humans could adapt to living in each of these environments?

Continental Climates

In a humid continental climate, summer temperatures are moderate to hot, but winters can be very cold. This kind of climate supports grasslands and forests. Grasses tend to be tall. The first European settlers on the Great Plains of the United States noted that the grass there was high enough to hide a horse and its rider! Certain areas in this climate region support large deciduous forests. In areas where winters are colder, coniferous forests are found. Coniferous trees have needles, not leaves, and have cones to produce seeds. These adaptations provide protection through the winter.

Regions with subarctic continental climates are much drier, with cool summers and cold winters. Grasses are much shorter. Some subarctic continental areas have huge coniferous forests. Others, however, have few trees.

Polar Climates and Their Vegetation

The polar climates of the high latitudes are cold all year around. The **tundra,** which lies along the Arctic Circle, has short, cold summers and long, even colder winters. No trees grow here. Low shrubs bloom during brief summers. Mosses and strange plants called lichens (LY kuhns) grow on the surfaces of rocks. In the northern regions of the tundra, it is even colder and precipitation is very scarce. Only low grasses, mosses, lichens, and a few flowering plants grow.

LINKS ACROSS TIME

Plant Fossils In ancient rocks in Wyoming, scientists have found fossils of palm trees. Centuries ago, sediments such as sand or ash buried the plants quickly. Over thousands of years, the buildup continued. Slowly, the plants turned to rock. Scientists study fossils to learn about ancient climate and vegetation. Scientists also learn how climate and vegetation have changed over time.

A Vertical Climate

The climate at the top of Mount Everest, in Nepal in Southeast Asia, is like Antarctica's. But Mount Everest is near the Tropic of Cancer, far from the South Pole. Why is it so cold at the top of the mountain? A mountain is an example of **vertical climate,** where the climate changes according to the mountain's height.

Picture yourself on a hike up a mountain in a moderate climate. Grasslands surround the base of the mountain, and temperatures are warm. You begin to climb and soon enter a region with less precipitation than below. There are short grasses, like those in a continental climate. As you climb higher, you move through deciduous forests. It is cooler and drier here. Slowly the forests change to coniferous trees.

As you continue to climb, you find only scattered, short trees. Finally, there are only low shrubs and short grasses. Soon it is too cold and dry even for them. Mainly you see only the mosses and lichens of a tundra. And at the mountain top, you find an icecap climate, where no vegetation grows.

Vertical Climate Zones

Vertical climate zones determine land use. At an elevation of 6,762 feet (2,061 m), this Swiss village can grow hay and graze cattle. **Critical Thinking** What activities do you think happen at the higher elevations seen in this photograph?

SECTION 4 REVIEW

1. **Define** (a) vegetation, (b) canopy, (c) tundra, (d) vertical climate.

2. **Identify** (a) Great Plains, (b) Arctic Circle.

3. Why do polar climates have sparse vegetation?

4. What climate region has the most varied vegetation? Why?

5. How are continental climates different from moderate climates?

Critical Thinking

6. **Drawing Conclusions** Choose a climate region. Explain why certain kinds of plants do *not* grow there.

Activity

7. **Writing to Learn** Research three different cities. Find out what climate and vegetation regions they are in. Write an essay explaining how climate and vegetation affects everyday life in these cities.

Using Special Geography Graphs

"Everybody talks about the weather," Mark Twain is supposed to have said, "but nobody does anything about it." The great humorist was both right and wrong. People have always talked about the weather. Where we live and what we do are all affected by weather and climate.

Because weather is such a big part of life, people have tried to do something about it. For example, hundreds of years ago people in Europe tried to get rid of thunderstorms by ringing church bells. Today, people "seed" clouds with chemicals to try to cause rainfall.

Trying to "do something" about the weather is not very successful. Geographers have managed to do one thing very well, however. That is to gather information about weather and climate. One of the ways geographers do this is by making a climate graph. It usually shows average precipitation and average temperature.

Get Ready

A climate graph is really two graphs in one. Look at the climate graph on this page, for the city of São Paulo, Brazil.

The graph has two parts: a line graph and a bar graph. The line graph shows temperature. The scale for temperature is along the graph's left side. The bar graph shows precipitation. The scale for average precipitation in inches is along the right side of the graph. Finally, along the bottom of the graph are the labels for months of the year.

A good way to learn more about climate graphs is to make one of your own. You will need:

- a sheet of graph paper
- a lead pencil
- two different colored pencils

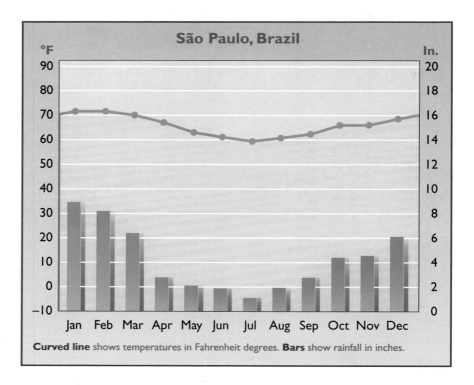

São Paulo, Brazil

Curved line shows temperatures in Fahrenheit degrees. **Bars** show rainfall in inches.

▶ During which months do you think most thunderstorms occur in South Carolina?

Try It Out

A. Draw a grid. Use the graph paper and the lead pencil to draw a large square. Divide the square into 10 horizontal rows and 12 vertical rows.

B. Label the grid. At the top of the graph, write Charleston, the name of the city you will graph. Using the lead pencil, copy the labels on the climate graph as shown on the previous page. Put labels for temperature on the left side of the graph. Put labels for precipitation on the right side. Finally, put labels for the months of the year along the bottom of the graph.

C. Make a line graph. The data on this page is for Charleston, South Carolina. Use the temperature data to plot a line graph. Use the climate graph on the opposite page as a model. Plot your line graph with one of the colored pencils.

D. Make a bar graph. Now use the data for precipitation to make a bar graph. Use the climate graph on the opposite page as a model. Plot your bar graph with the other colored pencil.

Apply the Skill

Use the steps below to practice reading your climate graph.

❶ **Compare differences in temperature.** (a) Which month has the highest temperature in Charleston? (b) Which month has the lowest?

❷ **Compare differences in precipitation.** (a) Which months have the highest precipitation? (b) Which month has the lowest?

❸ **Describe the climate.** Temperature and precipitation are two major factors that determine a climate. Using the information presented in the climate graph, how would you describe Charleston's climate?

Charleston, South Carolina		
	Temperature (Fahrenheit)	Precipitation (inches)
January	48	3.5
February	51	3.5
March	58	4.5
April	65	3.0
May	73	4.0
June	78	6.5
July	82	7.0
August	81	7.0
September	76	5.0
October	67	3.0
November	58	2.5
December	51	3.0

CHAPTER 2 Review and Activities

Reviewing Main Ideas

1. What causes day and night?
2. Why are the seasons at higher latitudes different from seasons at latitudes near the Equator?
3. How do plate tectonics shape the Earth?
4. What is the difference between weathering and erosion?

5. Why can two places have the same average temperatures but still have different climates?
6. How are climates closer to the poles similar to the tops of vertical climates?

7. (a) List five major climate regions in the world. (b) Then choose one of them and describe plants that live there.

Reviewing Key Terms

Use each key term below in a sentence that shows the meaning of the term.

1. orbit
2. revolution
3. axis
4. rotation
5. plate tectonics
6. weathering
7. erosion
8. atmosphere
9. weather
10. temperature
11. precipitation
12. climate
13. vegetation
14. tundra
15. vertical climate

Critical Thinking

1. **Identifying Central Issues** How does water affect a region's landforms and climate?
2. **Recognizing Cause and Effect** Why is the Earth continually changing form?

Graphic Organizer

Copy the chart on a separate sheet of paper. Select three climates from tropical, dry, moderate, continental, or polar. Write one term in each box of column 1. In column 2, write temperature, precipitation, plus other important information.

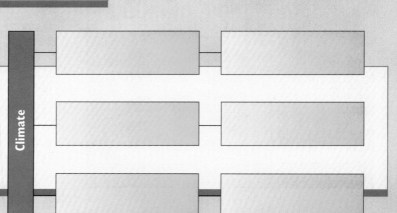

Map Activity

North America

For each place listed below, write the letter on the map that shows its location. Use the Atlas at the back of the book to complete the exercise.

1. Tropic of Cancer

2. Appalachian Mountains

3. Rocky Mountains

4. Arctic Circle

5. Great Plains

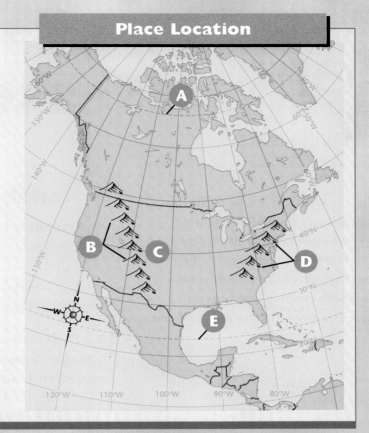

Place Location

Writing Activity

Writing a News Report

Choose a well-known natural disaster such as Hurricane Andrew or the eruption of Mount St. Helens. Find out where it happened, why it happened, and what were the immediate and long-term effects. Then, write a news report that explains the natural disaster in geographic terms.

Internet Activity

Use a search engine to find the **Weather Map** site. Look at the satellite map and click on your state or town to determine today's weather. Make a chart showing the temperature, humidity, wind, pressure, and weather throughout the day. What does the chart tell you about today's weather patterns?

Skills Review

Turn to the Skills Activity.

Review the steps for understanding special geography graphs. Then complete the following: (a) What two kinds of information are included in a climate graph? (b) How does a line graph help geographers describe a climate?

How Am I Doing?

Answer these questions to help you check your progress.

1. Do I know how the Earth's movements through space create day, night, and seasons?

2. Do I understand the forces that shape the Earth?

3. Can I explain the influences on the Earth's weather and climate?

4. Do I know why the Earth's climates support a variety of vegetation?

5. What information from this chapter can I use in my book project?

LAB ACTIVITY SHOP

The Earth's Seasons

We take seasons for granted. Summer always follows spring, and winter follows fall. Anywhere in the United States, you can usually tell when the seasons begin to change. Two factors cause seasons. One is the way the Earth revolves, or travels around the sun. The other is the angle of the Earth's axis.

Purpose

In this activity, you will make a model that shows how the revolution of the Earth around the sun causes the seasons.

Materials

- masking tape
- marker
- lamp
- globe

Procedure

STEP ONE

Make a model of the Earth's path around the sun. Use masking tape to mark a spot on the floor for the "sun." Following the diagram, use the tape to mark the Earth's orbit around the sun. Next, label the tape where each season begins. Now, tape the globe firmly to its frame. Because the Earth's rotation does not

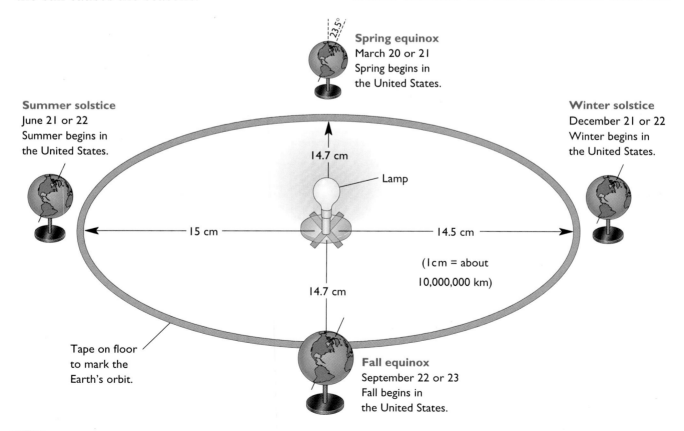

23.5°

Spring equinox
March 20 or 21
Spring begins in
the United States.

Summer solstice
June 21 or 22
Summer begins in
the United States.

Winter solstice
December 21 or 22
Winter begins in
the United States.

14.7 cm

Lamp

15 cm — 14.5 cm

(1cm = about
10,000,000 km)

14.7 cm

Fall equinox
September 22 or 23
Fall begins in
the United States.

Tape on floor
to mark the
Earth's orbit.

affect the seasons, the globe can remain in place. Put a lamp on the mark for the sun. Remove the shade and turn on the lamp.

STEP TWO

Show winter in the United States. Move the globe to the spot in the orbit where the season is winter in the United States. Be sure that the Earth's axis matches the position in the diagram. Notice that at other times of the year the Earth will be farther from the sun. Something besides distance must cause the season to be winter.

Let the globe sit for five minutes. Study how the sun's light hits the globe. Then, feel it by placing one hand on the Northern Hemisphere and the other on the Southern Hemisphere. Because of the tilt of the Earth's axis, the Northern Hemisphere gets less direct sunlight from the sun than the Southern Hemisphere. That means that the Northern Hemisphere receives less energy from the sun. So temperatures are cooler in the United States than in the Southern Hemisphere.

STEP THREE

Show spring in the United States. Place the globe on the floor at the spot where it is spring in the United States. Line up the Earth's axis correctly. Let the globe sit for five minutes. Place one hand on the Northern Hemisphere and the other on the Southern Hemisphere. Both hemispheres should feel about the same. Notice how the sun's light strikes the Earth. All parts of the Earth get about the same amount of energy.

STEP FOUR

Show summer in the United States. Place the globe at the spot where the season is summer in the United States. Notice that the Earth is farther from the sun than it was in winter. Line up the axis correctly. Let the globe sit for five minutes. Study the effect of the sun on both the Northern and Southern hemispheres. This time, because of the tilt of the axis, the Northern Hemisphere gets more direct sunlight from the sun, and therefore energy, than the Southern Hemisphere. Now, it is summer in the United States.

STEP FIVE

Show fall in the United States. Place the globe on the floor at the spot where it is fall in the United States. Line up the axis correctly. Let the globe sit for five minutes. Study both the Northern and the Southern hemispheres. Again, both hemispheres should feel about the same because all parts of the Earth get about the same amount of energy.

Observation

1. Which affects the seasons more—the angle at which the sun's rays hit the Earth or its distance from the sun? Explain your answer.

2. Which season does the Southern Hemisphere have when it is winter in the Northern Hemisphere?

3. When will you have about the same amount of daylight as night—January 8, July 20, or September 22? Explain your answer.

ANALYSIS AND CONCLUSION

1. If the Earth was not tilted on its axis, how do you think the seasons would be affected? Explain your answer.

2. In a science fiction story, the Earth's orbit is disturbed. The planet travels in a straight line, not around the sun. How would this affect the seasons?

CHAPTER 3

Earth's Human Geography

PICTURE ACTIVITIES

Many people live in New York City, Los Angeles, and other large American cities. To learn more about these people, carry out the following activities.

Study the picture
Look at this crowd of people hurrying along a busy New York City street. Many have come from other countries. List some places you think people in New York City might be from.

Rename the city
With a population of over seven million, New York City has more people than many small countries. The city has enough business and industry to be a country. What would you name the crowded "country" of New York City? Why?

Where Do People Live?

SECTION 1

Reach Into Your Background
Would you like to live in a city or in the country? List some interesting things you could do if you lived far from a city. List the things you would enjoy most about city life.

Questions to Explore
1. Where do most of the world's people live?
2. How is the world's population changing?

Key Terms
population
population distribution
demographer
population density

Key Places
Nile River valley

Imagine that you go to school in Tokyo, the capital of Japan. Every day you ride the Tokyo "bullet train" to school. What is it like? You probably must stand up for your two-hour ride. Every day more and more people jam the train. Often the car is so crowded that special station guards push people inside so the doors can close behind them.

This is not an exaggeration. The country of Japan is smaller than California. But it is home for 125 million people. Over 26.5 million of them live in Tokyo and its suburbs. Public transportation, roads, and living space are extremely crowded.

What Is Population Distribution?

The world's population, or total number of people, is spread unevenly over the Earth's surface. Some places have large numbers of people. In other places, the population is very small. Population distribution describes the way the population is spread out over the Earth.

▲ At rush hour in Tokyo, white-gloved guards jam two more passengers onto an already full train.

The reasons population is distributed as it is may seem unclear. Scientists called demographers try to figure it out. **Demographers** study the populations of the world. They examine such things as rates of birth, marriage, and death. And they look at the reasons why people choose to live in certain areas.

Why Is Population Distribution Uneven? To answer this question, demographers start with the idea that people are choosy. Recall an important fact about the Earth's surface. Many of the Earth's landforms are rugged mountains, hot deserts, and dry land with little vegetation. Few people can live in these places.

Many factors make a location a good place for people to live. Most major civilizations of world history began along bodies of water. Rivers and lakes form natural "roads" for trade and travel. Also, rivers and lakes supply fresh water for drinking and farming. People also prefer areas of flat, fertile soil. There they can grow food and build easily. Therefore, plains and valleys are easy to settle. Flat coastal areas make it easy for people to trade by ship with other countries. Look at the maps on this page and the opposite page to see how landforms affect where people live.

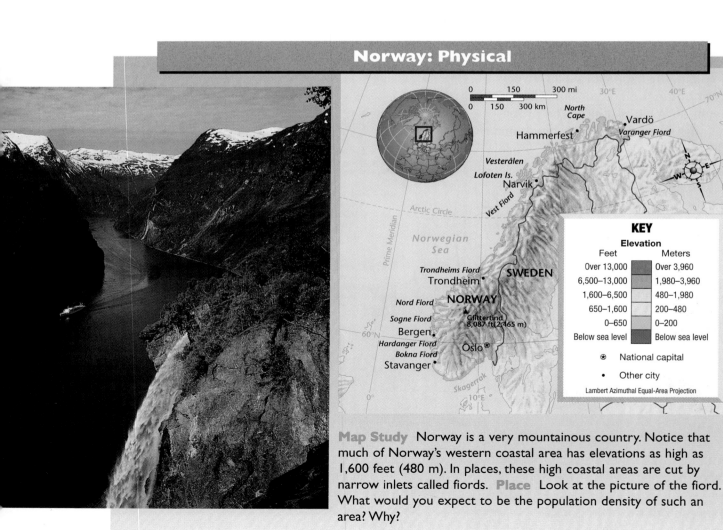

Norway: Physical

Map Study Norway is a very mountainous country. Notice that much of Norway's western coastal area has elevations as high as 1,600 feet (480 m). In places, these high coastal areas are cut by narrow inlets called fiords. **Place** Look at the picture of the fiord. What would you expect to be the population density of such an area? Why?

Other factors affect where people live. People prefer areas where the climate is not too hot or too cold, and where there is adequate rainfall. These places make it easier to raise food crops and animals. People also prefer places with natural resources to build houses and make products. For instance, few trees grew on the America's Great Plains. Few people settled there at first. They went on to other regions.

Continents Populous and Not Populous These reasons explain why more than 81 percent of the Earth's people—about 4.5 billion—live in Asia, Europe, and North America. These continents total only about 35 percent of the world's land. However, they have fertile soil, plains, valleys, and other favorable landforms. They also have fresh water, rich natural resources, and good climates.

Other continents have smaller populations partly because it is harder to live there. For example, Australia is about three million square miles, about as large as the continental United States. Only about 18 million people live in Australia, however. About the same number of people live in just the state of New York. Australia's environment is mostly desert or dry grassland. There are few rivers and little rainfall. As a result, most people live along the coasts, where conditions are better.

In Africa, too, landforms and climates limit population. Africa has about 15 percent of the world's land. But it has only 12 percent of the world's population. Africa has two of the world's largest deserts, one in the

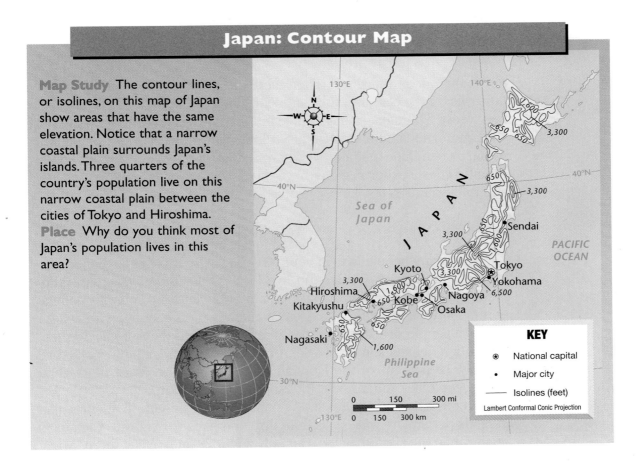

Japan: Contour Map

Map Study The contour lines, or isolines, on this map of Japan show areas that have the same elevation. Notice that a narrow coastal plain surrounds Japan's islands. Three quarters of the country's population live on this narrow coastal plain between the cities of Tokyo and Hiroshima. **Place** Why do you think most of Japan's population lives in this area?

KEY
⊗ National capital
• Major city
— Isolines (feet)
Lambert Conformal Conic Projection

In many countries, people can choose to live in very different places. For example, these photographs show apartments in Boston's Back Bay (above), houses in a Texas suburb (above right), and farms dotting the rich land near Lancaster, Pennsylvania (right). **Critical Thinking** What factors might cause people to choose homes in the city, the suburbs, or the country?

north and one in the south. Then there are broad bands of land that get little rain. In the center of the continent, along the Equator, there is a vast rain forest. Therefore, many people in Africa live along its narrow coasts.

Landforms and climates also limit South America's population. About 309 million people live there. Most live along the continent's Atlantic coast. Other regions have soaring mountains, vast dry plains, and thick rain forests. Fewer people live in these areas.

What Is Population Density?

How many people live on your street or in your neighborhood? The average number of people who live in a square mile (or square kilometer) is called **population density.** In every city and country, population density varies from one area to another. In a country with a high density, people are crowded together. Japan has one of the highest population densities in the world. Almost all of its 125 million people live on only 16 percent of the land. In Tokyo alone, there are more than 1,000 people per square mile (5,380 people per sq km).

In contrast, Canada has a low population density. It is about seven persons per square mile (less than three persons per sq km). Canada is bigger than the United States. But only about 28 million live there. Many factors affect Canada's population. For instance, its cool climate has a short growing season. This limits farming.

Studying Population Density How do demographers measure population density? They divide the number of people living in a place by the number of square miles (or sq km) of that place. For example, California's population is 31,430,697 people. Its land area is 155,973 square miles (403,970 sq km). Therefore, California's average population density is 201.5 persons per square mile (77.8 persons per sq km).

Remember that population density is an *average*. People are not evenly distributed over the land. New York City has a very dense population. However, New York state has many fewer people per square mile. Even in the city, some areas are more densely populated than others.

On a world population density map, different colors show how world population is distributed. Darker colors show areas with heavy population. Find this map in the Activity Atlas. Find the most densely populated areas of each continent. Now, find these places on the world physical map in the Activity Atlas. Compare the landforms to the population density. Notice that people tend to live on level areas near bodies of water.

Find the Nile River valley in Egypt. This region is very densely populated. In some areas the population density is about 5,000 people per square mile (1,930 per sq km). This is one of the highest population densities in the world. Why do so many people live here? If you think it is because the Nile is a great source of water and the land around it is flat and fertile, you are right. The land beyond the river is desert. Life there is difficult.

Some people do live in areas most of us would find uncomfortable. The Inuit and the Sami people live in frozen Arctic regions. Herders in desert regions of Africa and Asia survive in places that would challenge most people. Over many generations, these people have developed ways of life suited to their environments.

Connect Would you rather live in a place where the population density was high or low? Explain why.

SECTION 1 REVIEW

1. Define (a) population, (b) population distribution, (c) demographer, (d) population density.

2. Identify Nile River valley.

3. How do the physical characteristics of a country tend to affect its population distribution?

4. Why is it important to understand that population density is an average?

Critical Thinking

5. Making Comparisons A large percentage of the world's population lives on a small percentage of the world's land. How do the population distributions in Japan and Canada reflect this fact?

Activity

6. Writing to Learn You are a demographer studying your community. Make a list of questions to ask and possible sources for answers. Include in your list some population issues that are important to your community.

A Growing Population

BEFORE YOU READ

Reach Into Your Background

If you called a hospital in your community, you could find out how many babies were born last week. Multiply that number by all the hospitals in the world. Then, add the number of babies who were not born in hospitals. Subtract from this figure the number of people who died both in and out of hospitals. That's one way to find out how much the world's population increased in seven days.

Questions to Explore

1. How fast is the world's population growing?
2. What challenges are created by the world's growing population?

Key Terms

birthrate
death rate
life expectancy
Green Revolution

Imagine that all the years from A.D. 1 to the year A.D. 2000 took place in just 24 hours. Now you have an imaginary clock to measure how fast the world's population is growing. The list below shows that the Earth's population doubled several times in those 24 hours.

12:00 AM	200 million people in the world
7:48 PM	Population doubles to 400 million
10:12 PM	Population doubles to 800 million
11:00 PM	Population doubles to 1.6 billion
11:36 PM	Population doubles to 3.2 billion
11:59 PM	Population will double to 6.4 billion

How large was the world population at 12:00 AM (A.D. 1)? At 10:12 PM? During the 24 hours, how many times has the world's population doubled? How long did it take for the world population to double the first time? The last time?

Population Growth Is Worldwide

The example above makes it easy to see that world population has grown rapidly. Even more important, the rate of growth has increased greatly in modern times. For example, in 1960 the world population was 3 billion. By 2000—only 40 years later—it will climb to 6.4 billion people.

Population Birthrate and Death Rate During different historical periods, populations grew at different rates. Demographers want to understand why. They know that population growth depends on the birthrate and the death rate. The **birthrate** is the number of live births each year per 1,000 people. The **death rate** is the number of deaths each year per 1,000 people. By comparing birthrates and death rates, demographers can figure out population growth.

For centuries, the world population grew slowly. In those years, farmers worked without modern machinery. Food supplies often were scarce. Many thousands died of diseases. As a result, although the birthrate was high, so was the death rate. The **life expectancy,** or the average number of years that people live, was short. A hundred years ago in the United States, men and women usually lived less than 50 years.

Better Health Care for the Young

A mother and baby await medical help at the Kenyatta National Hospital in the East African country of Kenya. **Critical Thinking** How has modern medical care helped to increase the world's population growth?

Reasons for Population Growth Today Today, things have changed. The birthrate has increased dramatically. The death rate has slowed. As a result, populations in most countries have grown very fast. In some countries, the population doubles in less than 20 years. People live longer than ever. In the United States, for example, the average life expectancy for women is about 80 years and for men about 73 years.

Two scientific developments have made this possible. First, new farming methods have greatly increased the world's food supply. Starting in the 1950s, scientists developed new varieties of important food crops and new ways to protect crops against insects. Scientists developed new fertilizers to enrich the soil so farmers can grow more crops. Scientists also discovered ways to raise crops with less water. These changes in agriculture are called the **Green Revolution.**

The second set of scientific advancements came in medicine and health. Today, new medicines and types of surgery treat health problems that used to kill people, such as heart disease and serious injuries. Researchers also have created vaccines to fight diseases such as smallpox, polio, and measles, and antibiotics to fight infections. As a result, many more babies are born and stay healthy, and people live many more years.

LINKS TO SCIENCE

Hydroponics How can you grow a plant without soil? People called hydroponics farmers grow plants in water and necessary nutrients. The techniques are used where there is no soil, such as on ships. Today some groceries sell hydroponic vegetables. Some scientists say hydroponics may help feed the world's rapidly growing population.

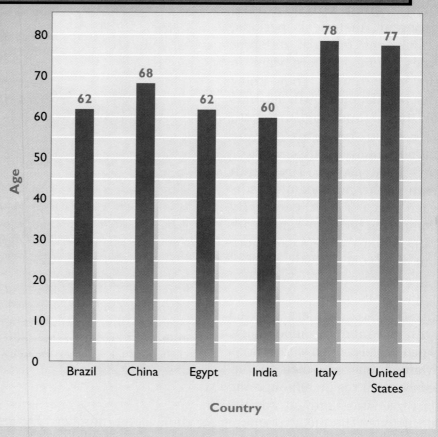

Life Expectancy in Selected Countries, 1995

Graph Study Life expectancy, or the number of years a newborn baby can expect to live, has soared in many countries since 1900. In some countries, however, life expectancy remains low. Which countries on this chart have the highest life expectancies? Which have the lowest? **Critical Thinking** What has contributed to the rise in life expectancy over the last few years?

Ask Questions What would you like to learn about the problems of population growth?

The Challenges of Population Growth

Today, food supplies have increased and people live longer. Even so, the people in many countries still face very serious problems. Growing populations use resources much faster than stable populations. Some nations, like those in Southwest Asia, face shortages of fresh water and energy. In Asia and Africa, food supplies cannot keep up with the growing population. Often, these countries do not have enough money to purchase imported food.

Population growth puts pressure on all aspects of life. The population of many countries is increasing so fast that many people cannot find jobs. There are not enough schools to educate the growing number of children. Decent housing is scarce and expensive. Public services like transportation and sanitation are inadequate.

A recent study by the World Bank describes the situation.

> "Today, South Asia is home to a quarter of the world's population, but it accounts for 39 percent of the world's poor [people] . . . . Out of every 12 children born, at least one is expected to die before reaching the age of one."

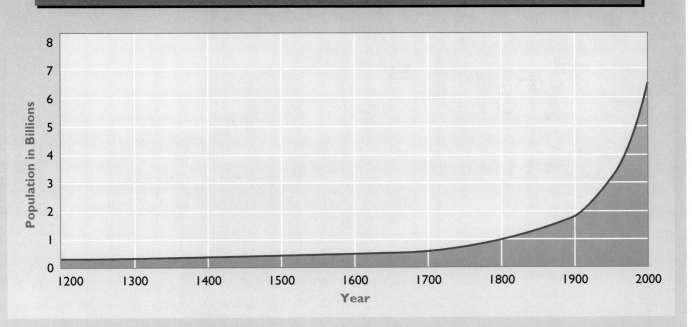

World Population Growth, A.D. 1200–2000

Graph Study For hundreds of years, the world's population rose very slowly. Recently, however, the rate of growth has skyrocketed.

Critical Thinking How does the graph show the change in the growth of the world's population?

Rapid population growth also affects the environment. For instance, forests in areas of India and Pakistan are disappearing. People cut the trees to use the wood for building and for fuel. Cutting forests affects the supply of clean air. Before, tree roots held soil in place. Now heavy rainfall may wash away the soil.

Look at the population changes indicated in the graph on this page. It shows how rapidly change has occurred in the last 300 years. The Earth's resources must now be shared by six times as many people than in earlier times. All the Earth's people must work to meet this challenge.

SECTION 2 REVIEW

1. **Define** (a) birthrate, (b) death rate, (c) life expectancy, (d) Green Revolution.

2. Why has the world's population increased so dramatically in the last four or five decades?

3. How have science and technology contributed to the growing population?

Critical Thinking

4. **Drawing Conclusions** The world's population has been growing at a fast rate. What are some of the dangers of a rapidly increasing population?

Activity

5. **Writing to Learn** World hunger is one of the major concerns caused by the rapid population growth. Write one or two suggestions to help solve this problem.

SECTION 3

Why People Migrate

BEFORE YOU READ

Reach Into Your Background

There may have been a time in your life when you or your family moved to a new home. Or perhaps a close friend moved away from your neighborhood. You probably felt a little sad and uncertain then. Imagine how you would feel if you moved to another country!

Questions to Explore

1. Why do people migrate?
2. What are some important population issues?

Key Terms
migration
immigrant
"push-pull" theory
urbanization
rural area
urban area

Key Places
Cuba
Vietnam
Jakarta

Roberto Goizueta heads Coca-Cola, one of the largest companies in the world. Yet when he came to the United States from Cuba in 1960, he had nothing. This is how he describes his escape from Cuba:

▼ On July 4, 1996—Independence Day—hundreds of people celebrate receiving their citizenship in El Paso, Texas.

"When my family and I came to this country [the United States], we had to leave everything behind . . . our photographs hung on the wall, our wedding gifts sat on the shelves."

Like millions of others who came to the United States, Roberto Goizueta has helped the nation become a land of prosperity.

Migration: The Movement of People

For centuries people have moved from one place to another. This is called migration. Immigrants are people who leave one country and move to another. From 1881 to 1920, almost 23.5 million Europeans moved to the United States. Since the late 1970s, more than 773,700 people migrated here from the country of

Vietnam. Over 818,000 came from El Salvador and other Central American countries, and over 3.5 million came from Mexico. More than 919,000 immigrants came from the Dominican Republic, Haiti, Jamaica, and Trinidad and Tobago.

Demographers use the **"push-pull" theory** to explain immigration. It says people migrate because certain things in their lives "push" them to leave. Often, the reasons are economic. Perhaps people cannot buy land or find work. Or changes in a government may force people to leave.

For instance, in 1959 there was a revolution in Cuba. Some Cubans lost land and businesses. Many fled to America to find safety and a better life. In the 1800s, many Scandinavians moved to Minnesota and Wisconsin. They wanted their own land, which was scarce in Scandinavia. Some also left to escape religious persecution.

What about the "pull" part of the theory? The hope for better living conditions "pulls" people to a country. Cubans settled in Florida because it was near their former home. It already had a Spanish-speaking population. Also, Florida's climate and vegetation are similar to Cuba's. Scandinavians were "pulled" by the United States government's offer of free land for immigrants willing to set up farms. They also moved to a familiar place. The long, cold winters in Minnesota and Wisconsin were similar to those in northwestern Europe.

Connect Did you or any members of your family or your ancestors immigrate to the United States? Why?

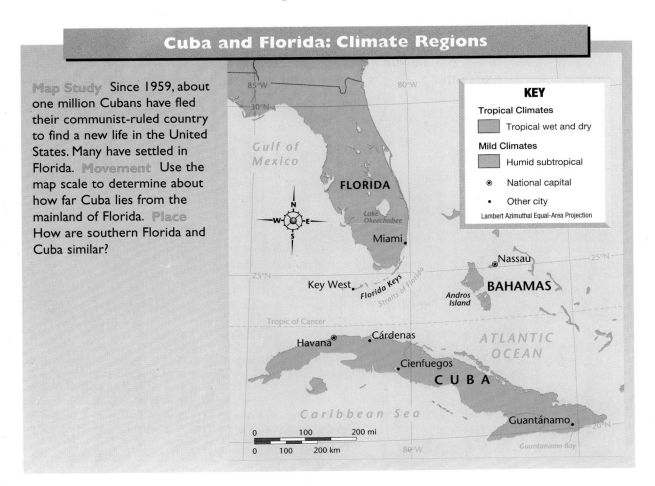

Cuba and Florida: Climate Regions

Map Study Since 1959, about one million Cubans have fled their communist-ruled country to find a new life in the United States. Many have settled in Florida. **Movement** Use the map scale to determine about how far Cuba lies from the mainland of Florida. **Place** How are southern Florida and Cuba similar?

KEY

Tropical Climates
Tropical wet and dry

Mild Climates
Humid subtropical

⊛ National capital

• Other city

Lambert Azimuthal Equal-Area Projection

Settlement of Polynesia
Not all people end up in a location by choice. Thousands of years ago people settled in Polynesia, a group of islands in the Pacific Ocean. Scholars theorize that these people left eastern Asia in search of new land. Then violent storms blew them off course. Ocean currents carried these people to the islands they now call home.

Irish Immigrants in the United States   Demographers use the push-pull theory to explain the great Irish immigration in the 1840s and 1850s. In those years, 1.5 million people left Ireland for the United States. Why did so many Irish people come to America? Ireland was a farming nation. In the 1840s, disease destroyed its main crop—potatoes. Hunger and starvation pushed people to migrate. Also, England ruled Ireland very harshly. There were very few ways for Irish people to improve their lives. These things also pushed people to move. Job opportunities pulled Irish families to the United States.

Vietnamese Come to the United States   The push-pull theory also explains Vietnamese immigration. These people came from southeastern Asia to the United States. After many years of war between North and South Vietnam, peace came in 1975. North Vietnam had won. Soon, it extended its communist form of government to South Vietnam. This was a serious change for many South Vietnamese. Thousands left the country. They were not welcome in nearby Asian countries. But the United States and the South Vietnamese had been allies during the war. The United States accepted the immigrants. That pulled the Vietnamese here.

An Irish-American President

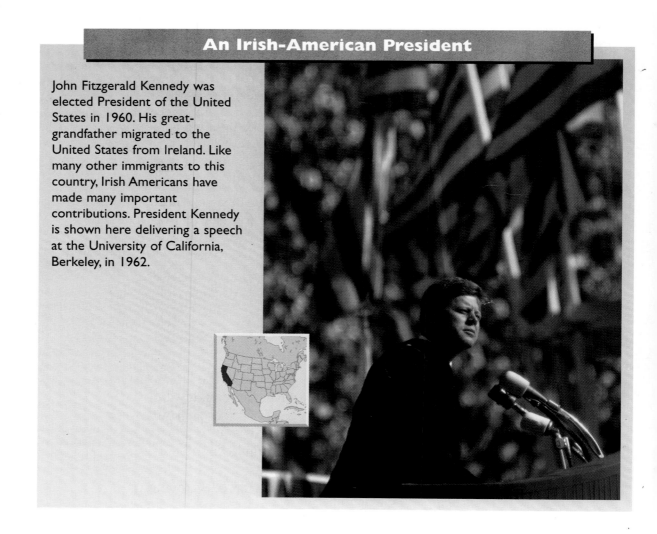

John Fitzgerald Kennedy was elected President of the United States in 1960. His great-grandfather migrated to the United States from Ireland. Like many other immigrants to this country, Irish Americans have made many important contributions. President Kennedy is shown here delivering a speech at the University of California, Berkeley, in 1962.

▲ Sometimes war forces people to migrate. In 1995, thousands of refugees fled a brutal civil war in the Central African country of Rwanda. They moved to the neighboring country of Zaire.

Other Kinds of Immigration Sometimes, people are forced to migrate. Australia was colonized by the English. Some were convicts serving their sentences in Australia. When their sentences were done, they stayed. War also forces people to migrate. In the mid-1990s, war broke out among three ethnic groups in the former Yugoslavia, in Eastern Europe. Many refugees fled to escape the warfare. Also, victorious soldiers of one group often forced entire communities of other groups to leave. Millions of immigrants flooded into countries in Eastern and Western Europe.

Other people leave their countries for a few years to help their families. Young men from Morocco and Turkey often go to Europe to find work. They leave their families behind. For a few years they work hard and save their money. Then they return home.

The World Becomes More Urban

Migration also occurs within a country. This happens in the United States. Americans migrate more than citizens of any other country, but most move from one state to another. Recently, the population has shifted from the northeastern states to the southern and southwestern states. People may be searching for better job opportunities or a better climate. This growth in urban areas of southern states has put great stress on services. Southwestern cities, for example, are developing new ways to ensure an adequate supply of fresh water.

Ask Questions What questions would you like to ask someone who plans to migrate to a city from a rural area?

One of the biggest challenges to today's nations is people migrating to cities from farms and small villages. In recent years, the population of major cities has grown tremendously. The movement of people to cities and the growth of cities is called **urbanization.** What pushes people from rural areas? What pulls people to cities?

Growing Cities, Growing Challenges   Cities in Indonesia are an example. In the past, most Indonesians were farmers, fishers, and hunters. They lived in **rural areas,** or villages in the countryside. Recently, more and more Indonesians have moved to **urban areas,** or cities and nearby towns. Its urban population is increasing rapidly. For example, in 1978, about 4.5 million people lived in the capital of Jakarta. By 1994, its population was about 11 million. That is an increase of 138 percent. And demographers estimate that by 2015 the population will have risen to about 21 million.

Jakarta is not unique. In South America, too, large numbers of people are moving from rural to urban areas. São Paulo, Brazil, is now the largest city in South America. The city has hundreds of tall office buildings, stores, banks, businesses, and small factories. In 1991, its population was 15.4 million. By 2015, it is expected to be 21 million.

The problem in cities like São Paulo is that too many people are coming too fast. Cities cannot keep up. They cannot provide housing,

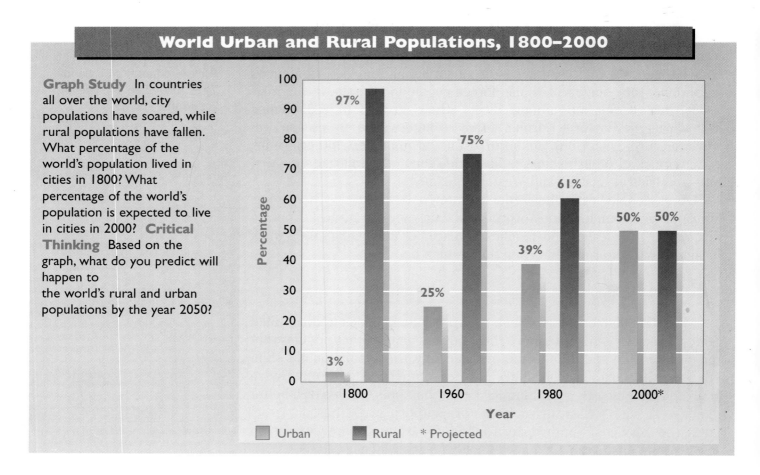

World Urban and Rural Populations, 1800–2000

Graph Study In countries all over the world, city populations have soared, while rural populations have fallen. What percentage of the world's population lived in cities in 1800? What percentage of the world's population is expected to live in cities in 2000? **Critical Thinking** Based on the graph, what do you predict will happen to the world's rural and urban populations by the year 2050?

Crowded Conditions in Cairo, Egypt

Across the world, growing cities face special challenges. Sometimes, there is not enough housing for newcomers to the cities. Sometimes, newcomers cannot afford the housing that is available. Until they find better housing, many newcomers build whatever shelters they can. These shelters are in Cairo, Egypt's capital.

jobs, schools, hospitals, and other services that people need. The country as a whole also suffers. With fewer farms, there is less food.

If you visited São Paulo, you would see why some migrants have a hard life. Schoolrooms are crowded. The city's four million cars and buses pollute the air. Traffic noise echoes day and night. Traffic jams and crowds often make it a struggle to get around.

With so many daily problems, why do immigrants flock to São Paulo and other big cities? Most are seeking a better life for their families. They are looking for jobs, decent houses, and good schools. Above all, most want more opportunities for their children.

READ ACTIVELY

Visualize Visualize what it would be like to move to a city like São Paulo, Brazil.

SECTION 3 REVIEW

1. **Define** (a) migration, (b) immigrant, (c) "push-pull" theory, (d) urbanization, (e) rural area, (f) urban area.

2. **Identify** (a) Cuba, (b) Vietnam, (c) Jakarta.

3. What are some of the reasons why people migrate from place to place?

4. Why have some immigrants left their homelands to live in the United States?

Critical Thinking

5. **Making Comparisons** What is the difference between migration within a country and migration from one country to another?

Activity

6. **Writing to Learn** When too many people migrate from rural to urban areas, it can mean hardships. List suggestions and ideas to help people decide whether to migrate to the city.

GEOGRAPHY: TOOLS AND CONCEPTS   **69**

Using Distribution Maps

magine yourself in a spaceship, floating high above the Earth. Although there is no day or night in space, you can see day and night on the planet beneath you. Half the Earth is lit by the sun, and half of it is in darkness. As you begin to glide over the night side, the Earth comes between you and the sun. Looking out of the spacecraft, you see that in many places there are small smudges of light spaced across the dark land. Some huge areas are brightly lit.

You are seeing the lights of human settlement. They include firelight, street lights, floodlights in parking lots, and the combined effect of millions of lights in homes. Where there are people, there is light. The distribution of the light reflects the distribution of people on the planet. The term geographers use to refer to where people live on the planet is population distribution. Floating over the Earth, you are looking at a living population distribution map of the Earth.

Get Ready

Why do geographers study population distribution? People live all over the world, yet population is concentrated in certain places. Consider this. Nearly six billion people live in the world. Yet all of us, standing close to each other, could easily fit into the state of Connecticut! Why do

we live where we do? Figuring out this answer and the reasons behind it are basic to understanding human life on the Earth. The first step is to find out where we do live. A population distribution map shows this best.

To see how population distribution maps are made and used, make and use one of your own. You will need paper, a pen, and a ruler.

Try It Out

A. **Draw a map of your school.** Use a large sheet of paper. Use the ruler to draw straight lines. Show and label classrooms, hallways, and so on.

B. **Make a key for your map.** Use stick figures as symbols. Each figure will represent five people. See the example on the next page.

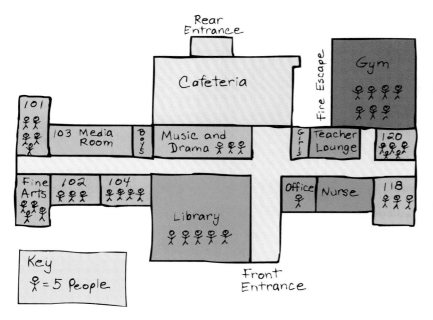

Key
🧍 = 5 People

C. **Add stick-figure symbols to your map.** Remember to put the symbols where the people are. Put the right number of symbols to show how many people are in each room. If there are 24 students and 1 teacher in your classroom, for example, you would draw 5 stick-figure symbols on the part of the map that shows your classroom.

D. **Give your map an appropriate title.** You have just made a population distribution map. It answers the same two questions that any such map does: Where are the people? How many people are in each place? Your map also provides clues about another question. Why is the population distributed in the way it is? See if you can answer this question about your school map.

Apply the Skill

Now that you see how population distribution maps are made and what questions they answer, you can learn a great deal from one of Mexico. Use the map here to answer these questions.

① **Read the map key.** Look at the key to get a sense of what the map is about. How is population represented on the map? How many people does each symbol stand for?

② **Answer the "where" and "how many" questions that population distribution maps can answer.** Where do most of the people of Mexico live?

③ **Answer the "why" question that population distribution maps can address.** Why do you think the population of Mexico is distributed the way it is? Think about physical factors such as climate and landforms as well as historical factors.

④ **Think about distribution maps generally.** This map shows population distribution. Other maps show the distribution of such things as natural resources, technology, and wealth. Find another type of distribution map and share it with the class.

Mexico: Population Distribution

KEY
• One dot represents 200,000 people

Lambert Azimuthal Equal-Area Projection

Review and Activities

Reviewing Main Ideas

1. How does geography affect where people settle?

2. (a) List the three continents with the most population and the four continents with the least population. (b) Choose one continent in each group and describe its landforms. Explain how those landforms affect population.

3. What kind of region is most attractive to new settlers? Which is least attractive?

4. Why does the Nile River valley of Egypt have such a high population density?

5. What factors have caused a rapid increase in human population?

6. Explain why people in many parts of the world are moving from rural areas to cities. Name two of these cities.

7. What are some conditions that push people to leave their country and pull them to migrate to another country?

Reviewing Key Terms

Use each key term below in a sentence that shows the meaning of the term.

1. population
2. population distribution
3. population density
4. urbanization
5. rural
6. urban
7. Green Revolution
8. life expectancy
9. birthrate
10. death rate
11. migration
12. immigrants
13. demographer
14. "push-pull" theory

Critical Thinking

1. **Recognizing Cause and Effect** How have Africa's landforms and climate limited its population?

2. **Identifying Central Issues** Explain the meaning of this statement: "Today, many countries of the world are becoming more urban." What does this statement tell about the movement of people in those countries?

Graphic Organizer

Copy the chart below onto a sheet of paper. Then fill the empty ovals with other effects that are the result of population growth.

more schools

Population Growth

more workers

Map Activity

Continents

For each place listed below, write the letter from the map that shows its location.

1. Asia
2. Antarctica
3. Africa
4. South America
5. North America
6. Europe
7. Australia

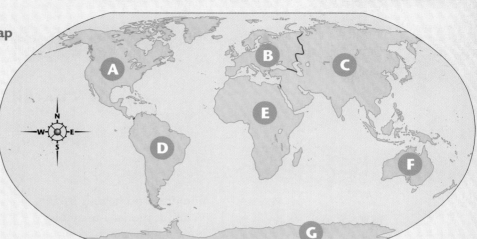

Place Location

Writing Activity

Writing to Learn

Find out how the population of your state has changed in the last 50 years. Write a paragraph that explains the main reasons why people migrated to or from your state.

Internet Activity

Use a search engine to find the **U.S. Census Bureau.** Click on **Just for Fun,** then click on **data map.** Click on your state. Find out the population of your state for 1990. Choose **Subject A-Z** and explore other data such as frequently occurring first names and birthrate. With the data you have explored, make a graph of census data for your state.

Skills Review

Turn to the Skills Activity.

Review the steps for using distribution maps. Then complete the following: (a) What can you learn from a population distribution map? (b) Would you learn more if you compared a population distribution map with a landform map or a climate map? Explain your answer.

How Am I Doing?

Answer these questions to help you check your progress.

1. Do I understand why the world's population is distributed unevenly?
2. Can I identify the continents with the highest population density? The continents where fewer people live?
3. Can I describe how the Earth's landforms and climates affect where people live?
4. Do I understand why many people move from rural to urban areas?
5. What information from this chapter can I use in my book project?

My Side of the Mountain

BY JEAN CRAIGHEAD GEORGE

Reach Into Your Background

Has your electricity ever gone out during a storm or a power failure? Suppose you had no electricity at all, or your home had no heating system. Without modern technology, how would you cope with the natural world around you?

Most people would have a hard time. But Sam Gribley, the fictional hero of the novel *My Side of the Mountain,* decided to live close to nature. He went to the Catskill Mountains in New York state and built a treehouse in a tall hemlock tree. His only companion was his falcon, Frightful. This excerpt tells how Sam managed during his first winter in the mountains.

Questions to Explore

1. What did Sam learn about nature as he lived alone in a forest in winter?
2. What skills did Sam need to survive alone in the wilderness?

hemlock (HEM lahk) *n.* pine trees with drooping branches and short needles
copse (kahps) *n.* a thicket of small trees or shrubs

Connect What would you do to pass the time if you did not have television, radio, or other electronic gadgets?

I lived close to the weather. It is surprising how you watch it when you live in it. Not a cloud passed unnoticed, not a wind blew untested. I knew the moods of the storms, where they came from, their shapes and colors. When the sun shone, I took Frightful to the meadow and we slid down the mountain on my snapping-turtle-shell sled. She really didn't care much for this.

When the winds changed and the air smelled like snow, I would stay in my tree, because I had gotten lost in a blizzard one afternoon and had to hole up in a rock ledge until I could see where I was going. That day the winds were so strong I could not push against them, so I crawled under the ledge; for hours I wondered if I would be able to dig out when the storm blew on. Fortunately I only had to push through about a foot of snow. However, that taught me to stay home when the air said "snow." Not that I was afraid of being caught far from home in a storm, for I could find food and shelter and make a fire anywhere, but I had become as attached to my hemlock house as a brooding bird to her nest. Caught out in the storms and weather, I had an urgent desire to return to my tree, even as The Baron Weasel returned to his den, and the deer, to their copse.

◀ Sunrise over Mongaup Pond in the Catskill Mountains, New York

We all had our little "patch" in the wilderness. We all fought to return there.

I usually came home at night with the nuthatch that roosted in a nearby sapling. I knew I was late if I tapped the tree and he came out. Sometimes when the weather was icy and miserable, I would hear him high in the trees near the edge of the meadow, yanking and yanking and flicking his tail, and then I would see him wing to bed early. I considered him a pretty good barometer, and if he went to his tree early, I went to mine early too. When you don't have a newspaper or radio to give you weather bulletins, watch the birds and animals. They can tell when a storm is coming. I called the nuthatch "Barometer," and when he holed up, I holed up, lit my light, and sat by my fire whittling or learning new tunes on my reed whistle. I was now really into the teeth of winter, and quite fascinated by its activity. There is no such thing as a "still winter night." Not only are many animals running around in the breaking cold, but the trees cry out and limbs snap and fall, and the wind gets caught in a ravine and screams until it dies.

yank (yangk) *v.* the sound made by a nuthatch
barometer (bah RAH muh tur) *n.* an instrument for forecasting changes in the weather; anything that indicates a change
whittle (witl) *v.* to cut or pare thin shavings from wood with a knife
teeth of winter the coldest, harshest time of winter

EXPLORING YOUR READING

Look Back
1. How has Sam's relationship with the weather changed?

Think It Over
2. Sam's relationship with his environment is different from most people's. In places, he talks about wind and trees as if they were alive. Think about your relationship with nature. How is it like Sam's? How is it different?

Go Beyond
3. What things does Sam do without that you take for granted?

Ideas for Writing: Essay
4. How might you decide what to wear to school in the morning without hearing a weather forecast? Write an essay that explains to your classmates how to watch for weather signs.

GEOGRAPHY: TOOLS AND CONCEPTS **75**

CHAPTER 4

Cultures of the World

PICTURE ACTIVITIES

Have you ever jumped for joy? The Inuits of Alaska toss one another for joy. People gather in a circle, grab the sides of an animal skin blanket, and use it to toss one another sky-high. The people here are celebrating a whaling festival. The Inuits also toss one another to celebrate the arrival of spring or a religious holiday or a successful hunt.

Look for clues
What can you find out about where the people in this picture live? List the clues you find. Explain what they tell you about the place shown.

Write a letter
Write a letter to someone in this photograph. Describe your thoughts about the tossing ceremony. Tell them about an activity you enjoy. Explain how these two activities are similar and different.

What Is Culture?

Reach Into Your Background

You and the people you know have certain ways of doing things. You have a way of celebrating birthdays. You have a way of greeting your friends. You have a way of eating a meal. You have a way of speaking. You have ways of gesturing. Many of the ways you do things are unique to you alone. Others you share with people around you.

Questions to Explore

1. What is culture?
2. How do cultures develop?

Key Terms

culture
cultural trait
technology
cultural landscape
agriculture

"**A**ll right, students," your teacher says, "time to clean the room. Kaitlyn—I'd like you to sweep today. Guy and Keisha, please use these feather dusters to clean our shelves and windowsills. Eric and Bobby, you can do the lunch dishes today. Serena and Zack, please empty the wastebaskets and take out the trash."

Would you be surprised if this happened in your classroom? Would you pitch in—or complain? In Japan, students would pitch in to help keep their classrooms clean. Hard work and neatness are important lessons. Although Japanese schools are similar to American ones, there are differences. Japanese students generally spend more time studying than many American students. In Japan, most children go to school five days a week and often on Saturdays for half a day. Many students do many hours of homework every afternoon and evening and over vacations.

Japanese students, like many American students, also enjoy sports, music, drama, and science. They join teams and clubs. They paint and take photographs. They play baseball, soccer, and tennis. They do karate and judo. They play musical instruments.

▼ These students in Japan are listening closely as their classmate speaks. How is your own classroom like this one? How does it differ?

Culture: A Total Way of Life

READ ACTIVELY

Predict What do you think the word *culture* means?

What if you met students from Japan? You would probably ask many questions. "How do you feel about cleaning your classroom?" you might ask. When you heard about how much homework they do, you might also ask "How do you find time to have fun?" Later, you might wonder about other things. What do Japanese students eat for lunch? What kinds of music do they like? What makes them laugh?

Answers to these questions will tell you something about the culture of Japan. **Culture** is the way of life of a group of people who share similar beliefs and customs. The language Japanese students speak and the way they dress are both a part of their culture. So are the subjects Japanese students study and what they do after school.

Elements of Culture   Culture includes the work people do, their behaviors, their beliefs, and their ways of doing things. Parents pass these things on to their children, generation after generation. A particular group's individual skills, customs, and ways of doing things are called **cultural traits.** Over time, cultural traits may change, but cultures change very slowly.

Some elements of a culture are easy to see. They include material things, such as houses and other structures, television sets, food, or clothing. Sports, entertainment, and literature are also visible elements of culture. The things you cannot see or touch are also part of culture. They include spiritual beliefs, ideals, government, and ideas about right and wrong. Language is also a very important part of culture.

▼ How people live is part of their culture. Different cultures sometimes interact with their environment in similar ways. In mountainous Japan, farmers build terraces on the hillsides to increase the amount of land available for farming. Terrace farming is also used in other cultures, including those in South America and South Asia.

Some aspects of culture, like the clothes people wear, may not seem important. When you visit another country, however, these differences can make you feel like an outsider. This photograph shows children who are watching an international track meet held in Los Angeles. The children are from the Los Angeles area. To make athletes from other countries feel welcome, they dressed in many different national costumes.

People and Their Land Geographers study culture, especially activities that relate to the environment. These things are part of the theme of human-environment interaction. Geographers want to know how landforms, climate, vegetation, and resources affect culture. For example, fish and seaweed are popular foods in Japan, a nation of islands. These islands are mountainous, with little farmland. Therefore, the Japanese get food from the sea.

Geographers are also interested in the effect people have on their environment. Often the effect is tied to a culture's **technology,** or tools and the skills people need to use them. People use technology to take advantage of natural resources and change the environment. Technology can mean tools like computers and the Internet. But technology also means stone tools and the ability to make them. Geographers use levels of technology to see how advanced a culture is.

A group's **cultural landscape** includes any changes to its environment. It also includes the technology used to make the changes. They vary from culture to culture. For example, Bali, in Indonesia, has many mountains. Therefore, people carved terraces in them to create flat farmland. Other regions, such as central India, have much level land. Farmers there would not develop a technology to create terraces.

Think about your culture. What do people eat? What are the houses like? What kind of work do people do? Can you identify some beliefs and values of your culture? In your mind, describe your culture. You may find it is harder to look at your own culture than at someone else's.

HEROES

Working Together
Sometimes the old ways are best. Two Bolivians, Bonifacia Quispe and Oswaldo Rivera, discovered the ancient Aymara Indians cut terraces into the sides of mountains to create flat farmland. Terraces are easier to irrigate and fertilize than slopes. In 1986, Quispe and Rivera taught the method to today's Aymara farmers. These farmers then grew 28 times more food.

The Development of Culture

Cultures develop over a long time. Geographers say early cultures went through four stages: the invention of tools, the discovery of fire, the growth of **agriculture**, or farming, and the use of writing.

Technology and Weather Forecasting

Technology is a very important part of culture because it changes the way we do things. For thousands of years, people have looked up at the sky to try to forecast the weather. Today, meteorologists—scientists who study the weather—still look up at the sky. However, they use very advanced technology, including various kinds of satellites, to do their job. Our ancestors could do little more than guess about the weather. Modern meteorologists, however, can make highly accurate forecasts about the weather several days into the future. Below is a diagram of a weather tracking satellite system.

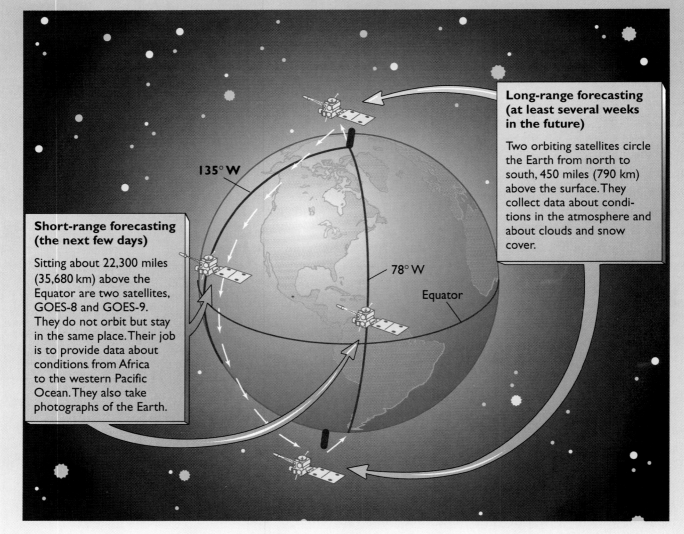

Long-range forecasting (at least several weeks in the future)

Two orbiting satellites circle the Earth from north to south, 450 miles (790 km) above the surface. They collect data about conditions in the atmosphere and about clouds and snow cover.

Short-range forecasting (the next few days)

Sitting about 22,300 miles (35,680 km) above the Equator are two satellites, GOES-8 and GOES-9. They do not orbit but stay in the same place. Their job is to provide data about conditions from Africa to the western Pacific Ocean. They also take photographs of the Earth.

135° W

78° W

Equator

Early Technology For most of human history, people were hunters and gatherers. Traveling from place to place, they collected wild plants, hunted game, and fished. Wood and stone tools and weapons helped them hunt, prepare food, and do other work. Later they learned to make and use fire, so some people began living in colder climates.

The Start of Agriculture Then, people discovered how to grow crops and tame wild animals to use as food or to help them with work. Now people no longer had to spend all their time following herds or moving from campsite to campsite in search of wild plants. Over time, societies relied on farming for most of their food. Historians call this great change the Agricultural Revolution.

By 3,000 years ago, the Agricultural Revolution had changed much of the world. Agriculture provided a steady food supply. Birthrates rose; death rates fell; population increased. Agriculture also led to the creation of cities and complex societies. Some people produced food, and others developed special skills. For example, people became potters, tailors, or metal workers. People began to develop laws and government. To record information, they developed writing. Now, people could store knowledge and pass it on to others. When a culture creates a writing system, it is called a civilization.

Early civilizations also created unique forms of art and music. They organized their beliefs into religions, with priests, temples, and ceremonies. Their roads and canals became features of the landscape. People learned to control and change their environment. Because of technological inventions such as irrigation and terracing, people could grow more and better crops in more areas. People spread over more and more regions. As they moved, they made changes to the Earth's landscape.

ACROSS TIME

The Domestication of Grain Early people gathered the seeds of the wild grains for food. However, about 10,000 years ago, people in Southwest Asia decided to try to plant wild wheat to tide them over. The first crop was poor. But farmers saved seeds from the best plants and tried again the next year. Over time, this led to today's domesticated wheat.

SECTION 1 REVIEW

1. **Define** (a) culture, (b) cultural trait, (c) technology, (d) cultural landscape, (e) agriculture.

2. If someone asked you to describe your culture, what would you tell them?

3. Describe four important developments in human culture. Tell why they are important.

Critical Thinking

4. **Recognizing Cause and Effect** Agriculture encouraged people to settle in one area and provided a steady food supply. How did agriculture lead to civilization?

Activity

5. **Writing to Learn** Find a photograph of a familiar scene in your town or city. List at least ten features of your culture shown in the photograph.

SECTION

Social Groups, Language, and Religion

BEFORE YOU READ

Reach Into Your Background

Even if you can't speak a word of Chinese, Italian, French, or Spanish, you can probably get Chinese, Italian, French, or Spanish food. Here is a list of four restaurants: Hoy Hing, Bella Vista, Café de Paris, Casa Mexico. Where would you go for enchiladas? For egg rolls? You know where to go because you connect food and language. Both are parts of culture. What else is part of culture?

Questions to Explore

1. Why is social organization important to cultures?
2. What elements make cultures distinct from one another?

Key Terms

social structure
nuclear family
extended family
ethics

▼ The end of Ramadan means a joyous celebration for these Egyptian Muslims.

It is still dark when the muezzin (moo EZ in) calls the people of Cairo to prayer. Roosters crow. As you wake, you remember that today is the first day of Ramadan (ram uh DAHN). During this religious season, Muslims, followers of the religion of Islam, eat and drink nothing from sunrise to sunset. This year, Ramadan will be special. Young children do not fast during Ramadan, but now you are 12. Now you are old enough to join the fast.

You are excited and a little nervous. You want to fast. It is a way to praise Allah, and it shows you are an adult. Still, you wonder if you can go all day without eating or drinking. You join your family for the *suhoor* (soo HOOR), the meal eaten before daybreak. Your parents and grandparents smile at you proudly. In the evening, you will join them for the *Iftar* (if TAHR), or the meal eaten after dark. That meal will taste especially good. And a month from now, when you celebrate the end of Ramadan, you will be prouder than ever. Every year you receive gifts, but this year they will be very special. You will give the prayers of thanksgiving, knowing you have joined with Muslims all over the world to celebrate Ramadan.

How Society Is Organized

Although the children of Cairo join with Muslims all over the world to celebrate Ramadan, they do so within their own households. Every culture has a **social structure.** This is a way of organizing people into

In the United States, a mother, father, and their two sons enjoy a day in the park (top left). In Malaysia, children join their parents, aunts, uncles, and grandparents to make music (top right). In the mountains of Tibet, a mother leads her child on a yak (bottom). As these pictures show, a family can be as small as two people or as large as a roomful of people.

READ ACTIVELY

Ask Questions What questions would you like to ask about different kinds of families?

smaller groups. Each smaller group has particular tasks. Some groups work together to get food. Others protect the community. Still others raise children. Social structure helps people work together to meet the basic needs of individuals, families, and communities.

The family is the basic, most important social unit of any culture. Families teach the customs and traditions of the culture. Through their families, children learn how to dress, to be polite, to eat, and to play.

Kinds of Families   All cultures do not define family in the same way. In some cultures, the basic unit is a **nuclear family,** or a mother, father, and their children. This pattern is common in industrial nations such as the United States, Great Britain, and Germany. Adults often work outside the home. They usually have money to buy what they need. They depend on the work of machines like vacuum cleaners and automobiles.

Other cultures have extended families. An **extended family** includes several generations. Along with parents and their children, there may be grandparents, aunts, uncles, cousins, and other relatives who live with them or close by. In extended families, older people are very respected. They pass on traditions. Extended families are less common than they used to be. As rural people move to cities, nuclear families are becoming more common.

Cultures also differ when deciding who is in charge in families. Many cultures have patriarchal (PAY tree ar kal) families. That means men make most family decisions. But some African and Native American cultures have matriarchal (MAY tree ar kal) families. In these, women have more authority than in patriarchies. Today, family organization is changing. Men and women have started to share family power and responsibility.

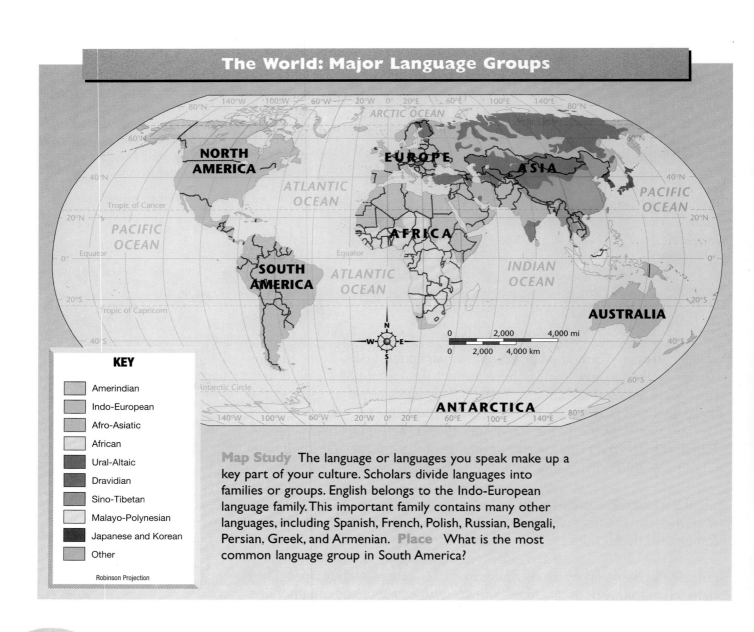

The World: Major Language Groups

KEY

- Amerindian
- Indo-European
- Afro-Asiatic
- African
- Ural-Altaic
- Dravidian
- Sino-Tibetan
- Malayo-Polynesian
- Japanese and Korean
- Other

Robinson Projection

Map Study The language or languages you speak make up a key part of your culture. Scholars divide languages into families or groups. English belongs to the Indo-European language family. This important family contains many other languages, including Spanish, French, Polish, Russian, Bengali, Persian, Greek, and Armenian. **Place** What is the most common language group in South America?

Social Classes   Cultures also have another kind of social organization—social classes. These rank people in a culture. A person's status or position may come from such things as wealth, land, ancestors, or education. In some cultures in the past, it was often hard—or impossible—for people to move from one social class to another. Today, people in many societies can improve their status. They can get a good education, make more money, or even marry someone of a higher class.

Language

Culture is a total way of life. Whoever you are, wherever you live, you are part of the culture of your society. You learn your culture from your family or from others. You also learn a great deal through language. Think of how hard it would be if you had no way to say, "Meet me by the gate after school," or "I'll have a tuna sandwich." How could you learn if you could not ask questions?

All cultures have language. In fact, every culture is based on language. It lets people communicate everything they need to share in their culture. Without language, people could not pass on what they know or believe to their children.

A culture's language reflects the things that its people think are important. For example, English has the word *snow* and several adjectives for the white stuff that falls in some places in winter. But the Inuits of North America have over 13 words for snow. Why? Where the Inuits live, snow covers the ground for a good part of the year. Snow is a more important part of their environment than it is to people of other cultures. The Inuits, therefore, have created words to meet their needs. All cultures have their own unique terms.

In some countries, people speak different languages. For example, the official language of Egypt is Arabic. It is spoken by most Egyptians. But some Egyptians speak Italian, Greek, or Armenian. Canada has two official languages, French and English, and Native Americans there speak a number of languages. People who speak these languages are culturally different in some ways from other people in their country. They may celebrate different festivals, wear different clothes, or have different customs for such things as dating or education.

Ways of Believing

Language is basic to cultures. Other basics are values and religion. At the beginning of this section, you read about Ramadan, a religious celebration of Muslims, followers of the religion of Islam. Ramadan is a very important part of Islam. And Islam is a major part of Egyptian culture. Other religions are important in other cultures.

Religion helps people understand the world. Religion can provide comfort and hope for people facing difficult times. And religion helps answer questions about the meaning and purpose of life. It helps define the values that people believe are important. Religions guide people in **ethics,** or standards of accepted behavior.

Ancient Alphabets The Phoenicians were ancient traders along the Mediterranean Sea. Their alphabet had 22 letters, and they wrote from right to left. The Greeks saw this writing system and based their own alphabet on it—with one difference. The Greeks, like us, wrote from left to right. We owe our alphabet, in part, to these two ancient cultures.

Predict Why are religions an important part of cultures?

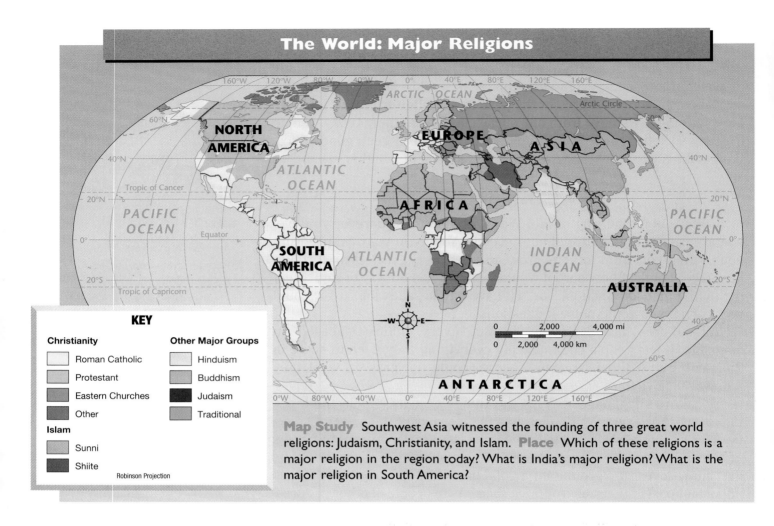

The World: Major Religions

NORTH AMERICA

EUROPE

ASIA

AFRICA

SOUTH AMERICA

AUSTRALIA

ANTARCTICA

KEY

Christianity
- Roman Catholic
- Protestant
- Eastern Churches
- Other

Islam
- Sunni
- Shiite

Other Major Groups
- Hinduism
- Buddhism
- Judaism
- Traditional

Robinson Projection

Map Study Southwest Asia witnessed the founding of three great world religions: Judaism, Christianity, and Islam. **Place** Which of these religions is a major religion in the region today? What is India's major religion? What is the major religion in South America?

Religious beliefs vary. Some religions such as Islam, Judaism, and Christianity believe in one god. Other religions worship more than one god. But all religions have prayers and rituals. Every religion celebrates important places and times. Most religions expect people to treat one another well and behave properly.

SECTION 2 REVIEW

1. Define (a) social structure, (b) nuclear family, (c) extended family, (d) ethics.

2. What is the basic unit of a culture's social structure?

3. What are three important features of a culture?

4. Explain the difference between a matriarchy and a patriarchy.

5. What is the role of religion in a culture?

Critical Thinking

6. Recognizing Bias How do you know that one language is not better than another?

Activity

7. Writing to Learn Make notes about your own culture. Draw three circles labeled "social structure," "language," and "religion." In each circle, make notes about your own culture's social structure, language, and religion. Include information about others in your family or neighborhood whose culture influences you.

Economic and Political Systems

BEFORE YOU READ

Reach Into Your Background

Many schools are polling places where people vote. You may have seen adults going into the gym or another part of your school to use a voting machine or mark a ballot.

Signs nearby often urge people to vote for a candidate or a certain way on an issue. Perhaps your student body holds elections, too. They are part of the political process in many places in the United States.

Questions to Explore

1. What is an economic system?

2. How do governments differ in their structure?

Key Terms

economy
producer
goods
services
consumer
capitalism
socialism
communism

government
direct
 democracy
monarchy
constitution
representative
 democracy
dictator

Muhammad Yunnus is a professor of economics in the country of Bangladesh. Bangladesh (bahng gluh DESH) is a very poor nation in South Asia. Yunnus wanted to understand how the people in his country really lived. His goal was to help them. He knew Bangladeshis ate only one or two meals a day. Though many had not gone to school, they were intelligent. Yunnus knew they were hard-working and could be trusted.

In the early 1970s, Yunnus met Sufiya Khatun. She made bamboo stools. But she earned only two cents a day because she had so few stools to sell. If she had more money for supplies, she could make more. But Sufiya had no way to borrow money to buy supplies. At first, Yunnus thought he would simply give her the small sum she needed. Then he wondered if others in the village were also like Sufiya. He found 42 people that needed to borrow about $26 each for their businesses.

Yunnus was shocked. So little money meant the difference between success and failure. But banks would

▼ Most of Muhammad Yunnus's customers are women seeking to open small businesses. This woman used her loan to start a weaving shop.

not bother with such small loans. In 1976, Yunnus decided to do something about this situation. He started up a bank to loan small amounts of money only to poor people. Every borrower must join a group of five people. Every group member is responsible for the loans of every other member, so members must all trust and help each other. To build trust, they meet once a week to talk over their problems.

Yunnus's bank is called the Grameen Bank, which means "village bank." Today, the Grameen Bank has more than 1,000 offices and has loaned money to 2 million customers. Its interest rates are fairly high, but 98 percent of its loans are paid back. People in other countries are starting banks like Grameen. There are even some in the United States.

READ ACTIVELY

Connect Think about each member of your family and what he or she does. Is each a consumer, a producer, or both? Explain why.

Economic Systems

Banks like the Grameen help people become productive members of their nation's economy. An **economy** is a system for producing, distributing, and consuming goods and services. Owners and workers are **producers.** They make products, such as bamboo baskets or automobiles. Those products are called **goods.** Some products are really **services** that producers perform for other people. They may style hair, provide hotel rooms, or heal diseases. **Consumers** are people who buy and use the goods and services.

There are two categories of businesses. Basic businesses are essential for a nation to function. They include things like transportation, communication, and electricity. Non-basic industries are "nice but not necessary." They may make products such as compact disks or sports equipment. Services can also be basic or non-basic businesses. Hospitals are basic businesses. Singing telegram companies are non-basic businesses.

◀▼ Neighbors in the New York town of Ithaca have a very interesting system of exchange. Instead of paying dollars, they trade "Ithaca Hours" for goods like fresh bread, as well as for services like babysitting. Each hour is worth $10—the average hourly wage in Ithaca. "Prices" depend on the amount of labor involved in producing the good or service.

Capitalism Replaces Communism

This photograph was taken in Berlin shortly after Communist East Germany united with capitalist West Germany. These East German children had never seen so many different school supplies before. The supplies came from the West, where the free market forces businesses to compete for customers.

Cultures choose the way they want to organize their economies. Today, most cultures choose from three basic systems: *capitalism, socialism,* and *communism.*

In **capitalism,** most basic and non-basic businesses are privately owned. Workers produce the goods or services. When a company sells its products, it earns profits, or money. The owners decide how much to pay workers and how to use profits.

The consumer is important in capitalism. Companies make products, but consumers might refuse to buy them. Successful companies supply goods or services that consumers need, want, and can afford. Capitalist countries include the United States, South Africa, and Japan. Capitalism is also called a free-market economy.

In **socialism,** the government owns most basic industries. It runs them for the good of society, not for profit. The government decides how much to pay workers and how much to charge for goods. It uses profits to pay for services such as health and education. Non-basic industries and services follow the capitalist model. They are privately owned, and consumers decide which products to buy. A few countries follow socialism or have socialistic programs. These countries include Spain, Portugal, and Italy.

READ ACTIVELY

Predict What do you think the three basic types of economic systems are?

In **communism,** the government owns all basic and non-basic industries. It provides all goods and services that people need. It also decides what is produced, how much workers will be paid, and how much everything will cost. Today, only a few of the world's nations practice communism. They include Cuba, China, and North Korea.

Hardly any nation has a "pure" economic system. For example, the United States has a capitalistic economy. However, state, local, and federal governments provide educational services, build and repair roads, and regulate product safety. In communist countries, you will find some private businesses such as small farms and special stores.

Political Systems

Small groups of people can work together to solve problems that affect them all. But that is impossible in complex cultures. Still, they also have to resolve conflicts between individuals and social groups. People also need protection from other countries and cultural groups. Communities need laws, leaders, and organizations that make decisions. **Government** is the system that sets up and enforces a society's laws and institutions. Some governments are controlled by a few people. Others are controlled by many.

ACROSS THE WORLD

Quebec In Quebec, a province in Canada, many people are descendants of French settlers. So, they speak both French and English. Some residents want Quebec to become a separate nation. This has led to much political debate. Canada is a democracy, so residents of Quebec could vote on the issue. For now, Quebec has decided to remain part of Canada, but the argument continues.

Ask Questions What would you like to find out about different kinds of government?

Lacquer Painting

Olga Loceva
Age 14
Russia
Under communism, traditional Russian arts and crafts, such as lacquer painting of boxes and vases as shown here, were discouraged. Since the collapse of the Soviet Union, many Russians have begun to practice these arts once again. What traditions do you value? How would you feel if the government banned those traditions?

Direct Democracy The earliest governments were probably simple. People lived in small groups and practiced **direct democracy.** That means everyone participated in running the day-to-day affairs of the group. Chiefs or elders decided what was right or what to do. Decisions were based upon the culture's customs and beliefs. Today, government plays much the same role for complex cultures.

Monarchy Until about 100 years ago, one of the most common forms of government was a **monarchy.** In this system, a king or queen rules the government. The ruler inherits the throne by birth. Monarchies still exist today. Sweden, Denmark, Great Britain, Spain, and Swaziland are examples. But the rulers of these countries do not have the power their ancestors did. Instead, they are constitutional monarchs. Their countries have **constitutions,** or sets of laws that define and often limit the government's power. In a constitutional monarchy, the king or queen is often only a symbol of the country.

▲ In Great Britain's constitutional monarchy, the monarch has little authority. The real power is wielded by Parliament, an elected body like our Congress.

Representative Democracy A constitutional monarchy usually is a **representative democracy.** That means citizens elect representatives to run the country's affairs. Democracy comes from the Greek word *demos,* which means "common people." In a representative democracy, the people indirectly hold power to govern and rule. They elect representatives, who create laws. If the people do not like what a representative does, they can refuse to re-elect that person. They can also work to change laws they do not like. This system ensures that power is shared. The United States, Canada, and Israel are examples of representative democracies.

Dictatorship "If I ruled the world. . . . " Have you ever said or heard those words? It's fun to think about. You could give away free ice cream. You could give 12-year-olds the right to vote. Maybe you could end war and poverty.

◀ Josef Stalin was one of the world's cruelest dictators. He ruled the former Soviet Union from 1929 until 1953. He controlled every aspect of Soviet life and jailed or executed anybody who opposed him.

Of course, no one person rules the world. There are some countries, though, where one person rules. A government leader who has almost total power over an entire country is called a **dictator.**

Dictators decide what happens in their countries. They make the laws. They decide if there will be elections. When dictators take over, they often make promises that sound good. They may promise to end crime or to make a country strong. Sometimes they keep their promises. More often, they do not. Either way, people lose the right to make their own decisions.

SECTION 3 REVIEW

1. **Define** (a) economy, (b) producer, (c) goods, (d) services, (e) consumer, (f) capitalism, (g) socialism, (h) communism, (i) government, (j) direct democracy, (k) monarchy, (l) constitution, (m) representative democracy, (n) dictator.

2. Describe the three main types of economic systems.

3. Which form of government gives power to make decisions to the greatest number of people—a monarchy, a democracy, or a dictatorship?

Critical Thinking
4. **Drawing Conclusions** You hear on the news an announcement from the newly elected leader of a foreign country. The announcement states that the country's representatives will not meet. It also says that no elections will be held until further notice. What kind of a government does this country have? How do you know?

Activity
5. **Writing to Learn** You are working on a project to increase voting in your community. A statewide election is approaching. On behalf of your project, write a letter to a newspaper. In it, describe two reasons why people who are eligible to vote should do so.

Cultural Change

SECTION
4

BEFORE YOU READ

Reach Into Your Background

If you like to listen to rap, rock, folk, or jazz music, you like music from many different cultures. The rhythms you like might have come from Ireland, Jamaica, or Peru. You probably like some artists from different countries, too. Name some music you like that you think is a cultural blend.

Questions to Explore

1. What causes cultures to change?

2. Why has the rate of cultural change been increasing?

Key Terms

cultural diffusion
acculturation

Most people think that blue jeans are typical American clothes. But many cultures contributed to them. Blue jeans were created in the United States in the 1800s, by Levi Strauss, a German salesman who went to California. He made the jeans with cloth from France, called *serge de Nîmes*. The name was shortened to denim. Strauss dyed the denim with indigo, a plant from India and China. The indigo colored the denim dark blue.

In the 1980s, the Japanese and the French developed stonewashing. It made brand-new denim jeans look worn. Then, an Italian company created acid-washed jeans. Today, jeans are still popular in America. They are also very popular in Britain, the former Soviet Union, India, and parts of Africa. And the name *jeans*? It's French, for Italian sailors who wore sturdy cotton pants. What is more American than jeans?

Always Something New

Just as jeans have changed over time, so, too, has American culture. Cultures change all the time. Because culture is a total way of life, a change in one part changes other parts. Changes in the natural environment, technology, and new ideas affect culture.

▼ Blue jeans are a popular form of casual wear across the world. These blue-jeans clad dancers are from Barcelona, Spain.

◄ Explorers brought crops native to the Americas, such as corn, squash, potatoes, and tomatoes back to Europe. This greatly changed the diet—and life—of Europeans.

Predict What are some changes that technology has made in our culture in modern times?

A Change in the Environment   If the weather changes long enough, the climate will change. That affects the kinds of food people can grow. It affects the kinds of clothes they wear. Changes in climate affect ways of making a living. But other changes can affect a culture, too.

A New Idea   New ideas also change a culture. People used to take nature for granted. They thought anyone could use resources without damaging the overall supply. Since the 1950s, people in the United States and all over the world have become concerned about the environment. They recycle and work to protect endangered species and preserve forests. People also realized that we can use up or pollute many natural resources. The desire to save nature is a cultural change.

Technology Equals Change   Cultural change has been going on for a long time. New technological discoveries and inventions may have had the most effect on cultures. The discovery of fire helped early people to survive colder climates. When people invented wood and stone tools and weapons, ways of living also changed. Hunters could kill animals such as the mammoth and the giant bear. These animals had been too large to hunt without weapons.

Think of how technology has changed the culture of the United States. Radio and television brought entertainment and news into homes. Such things as TV dinners and instant information are now part of our culture. Computers change how and where people work. Computers even help people live longer. Doctors use computers to treat patients. Radio, television, and computers add new words to our language. *Broadcast, channel surfing,* and *hacker* are three. What other new words can you think of?

Sharing Ideas   People are on the move all over the world. People come to the United States from other countries. Americans travel to other countries. In the process, they all bring new things such as clothing and tools with them. They also bring ideas about such things as ways to prepare food, teach children, or worship and govern. Sometimes a culture adopts these new ideas. The movement of customs and ideas is **cultural diffusion.**

The blue jeans story is a good example of cultural diffusion. Jeans were invented in the United States but now are popular around the world. People in other countries made changes to jeans. People in the United States adopted the changes. The process of accepting, borrowing, and exchanging ideas is called **acculturation.**

You can see cultural diffusion and acculturation if you study the history of baseball. It began as an American sport, but today it is played all over the world. That is an example of cultural diffusion. The Japanese love baseball. However, they changed the game to fit their culture. This change is an example of acculturation. Americans value competition. They focus on winning. But in Japan, a game can end in a tie. The

LINKS TO MUSIC

Tuning In to Cyberspace
Many record companies are now on the Internet. They talk about things like a band's latest musical release and upcoming tours. Some let people hear a band's music before buying it. Some bands have even tried live concerts over the Internet. This could be a big cultural change—listening to live performances at home instead of at a concert!

Working in a Canning Factory, 1912

Immigrants to the United States, like these young workers in a New York canning factory, came from many different ethnic backgrounds. The mixing of their various cultures produced a new, American culture.

Ask Questions Imagine you meet someone on the Internet from another culture. What questions would you ask to learn more about his or her culture?

Japanese do not mind a tie game for several reasons. For instance, in Japan, how well you play is more important than winning. Also, people try hard not to embarrass someone.

Technology and the Speed of Change

What's the fastest way to get from your house to Japan? A jet plane? A phone call? A television broadcast? The Internet? A fax? All these answers can be right. It depends on whether you want to transport your body, your voice, a picture, an interactive game, or a sheet of paper.

For thousands of years, cultures changed slowly. People moved by foot or wagon or sailing ship, so ideas and technology also moved slowly. Recently, technology has increased the speed of change. People no longer have to wait for a newcomer to bring changes. Faxes and computers transport information almost instantly. Magazines and television shows bring ideas and information from all over the world to every home. This rapid exchange of ideas speeds up cultural change.

A Global Village A village is a small place where people all know each other. It doesn't take long to get from one place to another. Today, many people call the Earth a "global village." That is because modern transportation and communications tell everyone about faraway people, businesses, and governments almost instantly.

Technology has brought many benefits. Computers let scientists share information about how to clean up oil spills. Telephones let us instantly talk to relatives thousands of miles away. In the Australian Outback, students your age use closed-circuit television and two-way radios to go to school in their own homes.

International Travel

Chart Study More and more people visit foreign countries each year. In 1995, 47 million Americans traveled to other nations. That's nearly as many people as live in California and Texas combined. **Movement** How have today's forms of transportation, such as jet planes, affected international travel? **Critical Thinking** How do you think the increase in international travel has affected the "global village"?

Year	U.S. Travelers to Foreign Countries	Foreign Visitors to the United States
1980	22 million	22 million
1985	35 million	25 million
1990	45 million	40 million
1995	47 million	43 million

In recent years, people across the world have made greater efforts to preserve their traditions. In this picture, for example, young people from 20 Native American nations perform a dance at a gathering near Lake Casitas, California. **Critical Thinking** Why do you think it has become more important in recent years for people to preserve their traditions?

Information Overload? Change can help, but it can also hurt. If things change too fast, people can become confused, and culture is threatened. Valuable traditions can disappear. Once important sources of knowledge are lost, they can never be regained. In many parts of the world, people are working to save their own cultures before it is too late. They do not want to lose what is good in their culture. They understand it is important to remember where they came from if they are to understand where they are going.

SECTION 4 REVIEW

1. **Define** (a) cultural diffusion, (b) acculturation.
2. List three things that can cause a culture to change.
3. Explain the meaning of the term "global village."

Critical Thinking

4. **Distinguishing Fact From Opinion** A friend who has a computer tells you she has an e-mail pal in Singapore. "You learn more by having a pen pal on the Internet than by having one through regular mail," she says. You point out that you get drawings and photos in the mail from your pen pal in Turkey. Which of you has stated a fact? Which has stated an opinion? How do you know?

Activity

5. **Writing to Learn** Interview an older person about what changes she or he has seen in the culture over the years. Write two paragraphs summarizing what they say.

Locating Information

Rhonda was puzzled. "Did you hear that?" she whispered to Denise. "He just told me to shrink the panic! What does he mean?" Rhonda and Denise were staying in the home of a family in Argentina, a country in South America. They had traveled there as exchange students. The family had a mother, a father, a young girl, and a teenage boy. Rhonda had just told the teenage boy that she felt nervous about finding her way around.

That's when he turned to her and said, "Achicar el panico! I'll help you." Rhonda knew "achicar el panico" translated as "shrink the panic" in English. But what did it mean? The boy smiled at her puzzled look. "In Argentina, that's how we say 'chill out!'" he said. Rhonda smiled back.

"I get it," she said. "I guess I also need help learning the slang you use here!"

You know that people in different cultures live lives that are very different from yours. But do you know just how different? Even little things like slang can have completely different meanings. Before you travel to another country, it helps to learn as much about its culture as possible. The trick, believe it or not, is to build a pyramid!

Get Ready

This pyramid is not a real pyramid, of course, but a "pyramid of knowledge." There

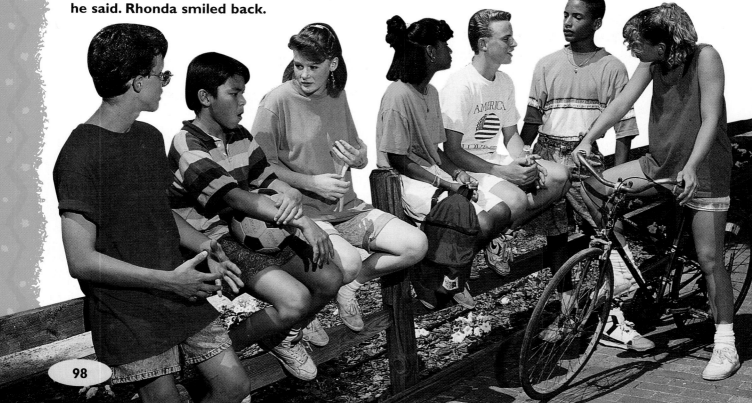

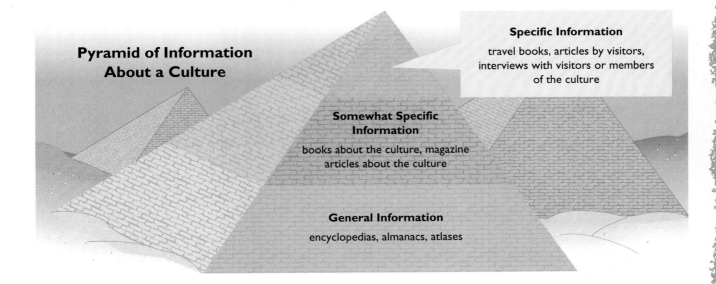

Pyramid of Information About a Culture

Specific Information
travel books, articles by visitors, interviews with visitors or members of the culture

Somewhat Specific Information
books about the culture, magazine articles about the culture

General Information
encyclopedias, almanacs, atlases

are thousands of sources of information about the peoples and cultures of the world. By organizing your search into the form of a pyramid, you can easily learn what you need to know. You will build your pyramid in a library.

Try It Out

Follow the steps below to build a pyramid of knowledge. As you work, refer to the diagram.

A. Choose a culture to learn about. You might choose a culture in a country in Europe, Latin America, Africa, or Asia.

B. Build a base of general information. Pyramids are built from the bottom up. The base of your pyramid of knowledge about a culture is general information. This includes such things as the correct name of a cultural group, its geographic location, the language the people speak, the population, and so on. Find this information by consulting the sources listed in the diagram of the pyramid.

C. Build the middle of the pyramid with more detailed information. The middle of the pyramid is made up of more detailed information about how people live in the culture. What are schools like? What customs are important? What are some common foods? What types of jobs do people have?

D. Build the top with specific information. Complete the pyramid by building the very top. It is made up of specific information about how individuals in the culture interact. Find out, for example, what proper greetings are and what certain gestures mean. Learn how to say basic phrases such as "How do you do?" and "Good-bye" in the language of the culture. Add specific information about anything else that interests you.

You can see you have learned a great deal about the culture in a short time. It takes a lifetime to develop a deep understanding of any culture. But by building a pyramid and continually adding to it, you can add to what you know.

Apply the Skill

Building a "pyramid of knowledge" is as simple as 1-2-3:

1. **Build the base.**
2. **Build the middle.**
3. **Build the top.**

As the pyramid grows, so does your knowledge. Practice applying this skill the next time you have any assignment requiring research. Find general information first, then more detailed information, and then very specific information. Work your way from the bottom to the top.

Review and Activities

Reviewing Main Ideas

1. What is the relationship between the environment people live in and their culture?

2. Describe three developments that have affected human culture.

3. Explain how the technology used in a culture reveals things about the culture's daily life, work, and values.

4. Why was the Agricultural Revolution so important in human history? What changes did it bring about?

5. Explain three important ways in which cultures can differ from one another.

6. Compare the three economic systems described in this chapter: capitalism, socialism, and communism.

7. Explain why people formed governments.

8. Why has culture changed more rapidly in modern times than in the past?

Reviewing Key Terms

Use each key term below in a sentence that shows the meaning of the term.

1. culture
2. technology
3. cultural landscape
4. social structure
5. nuclear family
6. extended family
7. economy
8. producer
9. goods
10. services
11. capitalism
12. socialism
13. government
14. constitution
15. representative democracy
16. dictator
17. cultural diffusion
18. acculturation

Critical Thinking

1. **Identifying Central Issues** Why is no culture exactly like any other culture?

2. **Expressing Problems Clearly** Why do you think people in one culture sometimes do not understand people in another?

Graphic Organizer

Think about how having less fresh water would affect society. Copy this cause-effect organizer. Then consider these topics: social organization, language, economic system, or government. Fill in the boxes, explaining how a water shortage might affect each topic.

Less Fresh Water

Vocabulary Activity

Many terms in this chapter compare and contrast similar ideas or activities. For instance, in capitalism, businesses are run by private individuals, but in communism, businesses are run by government. On a separate sheet of paper, explain how these terms compare and contrast similar ideas or activities.

1. goods and services

2. direct democracy and representative democracy

3. nuclear family and extended family

Writing Activity

Writing a Public Service Message

Your town or city is going to have a culture fair. The fair will introduce people to new cultures. It will also introduce people to different cultures within the United States. Write a public service message for a local radio station. A public service message includes the time, place, and purpose of a cultural event. Your notice should tell people why and how they should get involved with the culture fair.

Internet Activity

Use a search engine to find the Human-Languages Page. Click on Languages and Literature. Use the dictionaries and common phrases sections to learn how to say and write a greeting in five languages. Write your greetings, and an English translation, on a sheet of construction paper. Hang your greetings on a class "World Greetings" bulletin board.

Skills Review

Turn to the Skills Activity.

Review the steps for locating information. Then complete the following: (a) How can building a pyramid of knowledge help you to locate information? (b) Explain the difference between general information and specific information.

How Am I Doing?

Answer these questions to help you check your progress.

1. Do I understand how environment affects culture and how culture affects environment?

2. Can I list the major elements of culture and the forms that they take?

3. Can I describe the ways that cultures change?

4. What information from this chapter can I use in my book project?

LITERATURE

Rough Country

BY DANA GIOIA

BEFORE YOU READ

Reach Into Your Background

Think about the area where you live. It has many characteristics that make it unique. Perhaps there is a flood plain, hills, flat land, or an earthquake fault. Perhaps there are special stores or restaurants in your neighborhood. Perhaps the people who live there speak several languages. Or, perhaps, when you first think about it, you cannot see anything about your neighborhood that is different from anywhere else.

Most people are so used to their surroundings that they do not pay any attention to them. But Dana Gioia goes into great detail to explain why "Rough Country" is a very special place. As you read the poem, notice how Gioia emphasizes the unique nature of "Rough Country."

Questions to Explore

1. What characteristics make the country described in the poem "rough"?
2. What is so special about this spot in the country?

Rough Country

Give me a landscape made of obstacles,
of steep hills and jutting glacial rock,
where the low-running streams are quick to flood
the grassy fields and bottomlands.
                              A place
no engineers can master—where the roads
must twist like tendrils up the mountainside
on narrow cliffs where boulders block the way.

Where tall black trunks of lightning-scalded pine
push through the tangled woods to make a roost
for hawks and swarming crows.
                              And sharp inclines
where twisting through the thorn-thick underbrush,
scratched and exhausted, one turns suddenly
to find an unexpected waterfall,

glacial (GLAY shul) *adj.* from a glacier; here, rocks left behind by a glacier
bottomlands *n.* low land through which a river flows; flood plain
tendril (TEN drihl) *n.* thread-like part of a climbing plant that supports the plant

not half a mile from the nearest road,
a spot so hard to reach that no one comes—

a hiding place, a shrine for dragonflies
and nesting jays, a sign that there is still
one piece of property that won't be owned.

READ ACTIVELY

Visualize What does this place look like in your mind's eye?

◀▼ Where do you call home? Some people live in the Canadian Rockies, and others live in Washington farmlands. What unique features might you find if you lived in those places?

▲ What might you find if you lived in Chicago, Illinois?

EXPLORING YOUR READING

Look Back
1. What human activities would be difficult or impossible in this place?

Think It Over
2. In the fourth stanza of "Rough Country," the poet describes a hike that suddenly opens onto a waterfall. What makes the waterfall seem especially beautiful to the poet?

Go Beyond
3. In "Rough Country," the poet describes "one piece of property that won't be owned." Antarctica is another place that no one "owns." No country can claim any part of it. Why might people think a place was so important that no one should own it?

Ideas for Writing: Poem
4. Think about the place where you live. Make a list of its characteristics, and draw a picture of it. Then, write a poem about your place. Finally, compare your poem with "Rough Country."

CHAPTER 5

Earth's Natural Resources

PICTURE ACTIVITIES

Think of the power of a waterfall as it tumbles from high places to low ones. Today, dams like this one on the Brazil-Paraguay border create waterfalls. In the process, they harness river power to create electricity for homes and businesses. This helps economies grow. A dam across a river also has a huge effect on the environment. The dam holds back the water of the river. It floods acres of land and creates a lake. Sometimes such lakes flood forests, farmland, and even towns and villages.

Examine both sides of an issue

Think about how this dam changes the natural landscape and how it helps people. Make a list of the advantages and disadvantages of such a project.

Study the picture

Each country has natural resources. From this picture, what resources do you think Brazil has? As you read this chapter, think about how a country's wealth relates to its land and climates.

What Are Natural Resources?

SECTION 1

BEFORE YOU READ

Reach Into Your Background

How much do you throw away each day? How much do you recycle? What do you own that is made of recycled material? Jot down your answers.

Questions to Explore

1. What are natural resources?
2. What is the difference between renewable and nonrenewable natural resources?

Key Terms

natural resource
raw material
recyclable resource
renewable resource
nonrenewable resource
fossil fuel

What can we do with the garbage we create? People are searching for answers. Some are unique. In 1995, architect Kate Warner built a house in Martha's Vineyard, Massachusetts. She used materials most people call trash. The builders mixed concrete with ash left over from furnaces that burn trash. Then they used the mixture to make the foundation of the house. To make the frame of the house, they used wood left over from old buildings, not fresh lumber. Warner wanted glass tiles in the bathroom. So she had glassmakers create them out of old car windshields. "We ask people to recycle, but then we don't know what to do with the stuff," Warner says. "By making use of waste materials, the manufacturers of these new building materials are creating exciting new markets and completing a loop." In this loop, materials are used over and over again. Garbage becomes a natural resource.

▼ Factories make new steel for bicycles and buildings by combining iron and other natural resources with recycled or "scrap" steel.

Natural Resources

Kate Warner is one of many people who want to use the Earth's natural resources wisely. These people believe this is the only way for humans to survive. A **natural resource** is any useful material found in the environment. Usually when people talk about natural resources, they mean such things as soil, water, minerals, and vegetation. A natural resource, then, is anything from the Earth that helps meet people's needs for food, clothing, and shelter.

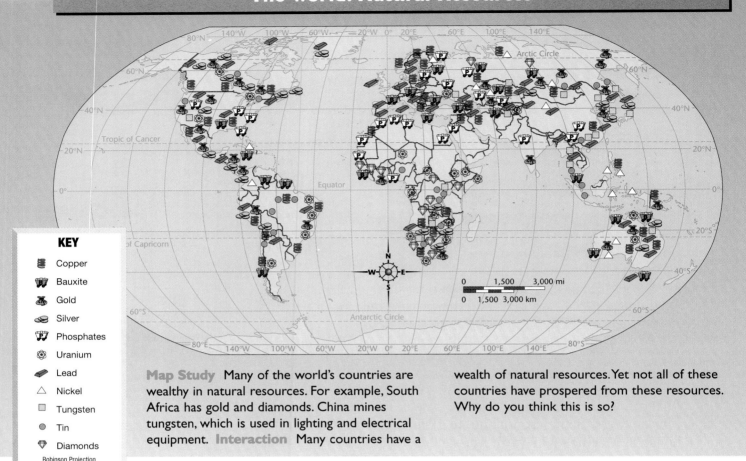

The World: Natural Resources

KEY

🗇 Copper
🗇 Bauxite
🗇 Gold
🗇 Silver
🗇 Phosphates
◉ Uranium
▬ Lead
△ Nickel
▢ Tungsten
● Tin
◇ Diamonds

Robinson Projection

Map Study Many of the world's countries are wealthy in natural resources. For example, South Africa has gold and diamonds. China mines tungsten, which is used in lighting and electrical equipment. **Interaction** Many countries have a wealth of natural resources. Yet not all of these countries have prospered from these resources. Why do you think this is so?

All people need food, clothing, and shelter to survive. People drink water. People eat the food that the soil produces. So do the animals that provide eggs, cheese, and meat. People get such things as fish and salt from the ocean. Homes are made from wood, clay, and steel. Every day you benefit from the natural resources in the environment.

People can use some resources just the way they come from nature. Fresh water is one. But most resources must be changed before people use them. For example, people cannot just go out and cut down a tree to make a house. Even if they want to build a log cabin, they must cut the tree into pieces first. For a modern home, the wood must have the bark shaved away. Then the wood is cut into boards of various sizes. Resources that must be altered, or changed, before they can be used are called **raw materials.** Trees are the raw material for paper and wood.

Three Kinds of Resources The environment is full of natural resources. But not all resources are alike. Geographers divide them into three groups. The first group of resources cycle naturally through the environment. They do so because of the way the Earth works. In the water cycle, water evaporates into the air and falls as rain, snow, hail, or sleet. This happens over and over again. Therefore, the Earth has the same amount of water, although there may be too much of it in some places and not enough in others. For this reason, geographers call water a **recyclable resource.** Some other materials that cycle through natural processes as recyclable resources are nitrogen and carbon.

A second group of resources includes trees and other living things on the Earth. These things are different from recyclable resources. It is possible for people to gather plants or hunt animals until they no longer exist. But it does not have to happen. For example, a timber company may cut down all the trees in an area. But the company may then plant new trees to replace the ones they cut. Every day the people of the world eat many chickens and ears of corn. But farmers and chicken ranchers make sure there are always more corn plants and chickens to replace the ones people eat. If a resource can be replaced, it is called a **renewable resource.** If people are careful, they can have a steady supply of renewable resources.

The third group of resources is called **nonrenewable resources.** When they are used up, they cannot be replaced. Most nonliving things, such as minerals, coal, natural gas, and petroleum—or oil—are nonrenewable resources. So are metals. City recycling programs are often eager to recycle aluminum cans and plastic bottles. That is because these cans and bottles are made of nonrenewable resources.

Ancient Energy: Fossil Fuel Often people take some things for granted. Lights turn on when a switch is flicked. The house is warm in winter or cool in summer. The car runs. All of these things require

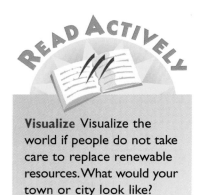

Visualize Visualize the world if people do not take care to replace renewable resources. What would your town or city look like?

Rain Forests: A Fragile Resource

Rain forests once covered millions of acres in Asia. Today, the rain forests of Asia are rapidly disappearing. Using heavy equipment to harvest the most valuable woods, loggers often damage huge areas of forest. In this photograph of the Malaysian rain forest, notice the sawmills that process the valuable tropical lumber and the roads that carry the wood out of the area. Once this rain forest is cut down, it will be very difficult to replace.

fossil fuels, which include coal, natural gas, and petroleum. Fossil fuels were created over millions of years from the remains of prehistoric plants and animals. These fuels are no longer being created. As a result, fossil fuels are nonrenewable resources. If people continue using coal, natural gas, and petroleum at today's rate, the Earth will run out of fossil fuels in 100 to 200 years.

A Special Resource: Energy

Imagine that you are in your room, reading your geography book. What items around you require energy? Some are obvious. A clock, a radio, or a lamp all use energy directly, in a form called electricity. Others are not so obvious because they use energy indirectly. Consider a water glass on a dresser or athletic shoes on the floor. These things were manufactured in a factory, and that process uses energy.

What about things made of plastic—a toy, a comb, or a pen? If you have a rug, it may be made of a synthetic material that looks like wool but is really a kind of plastic. These things are manufactured, so they use energy indirectly. But they also use energy directly. The reason is that plastics are made from petroleum, and petroleum is an energy source.

Getting everything to your room required energy, too. Your family bought them at a store, so you used energy to travel back and forth. The store bought them from a manufacturer, which required more energy. It takes a great deal of energy to put a small plastic glass in your room. So it is easy to see why people value energy sources so highly.

Energy "Have's" and "Have Not's" Everyone in the world needs energy. But energy resources are not evenly spread around the world. Certain areas are rich in some energy resources. Others have very few.

World Petroleum Consumption

Country	Percentage
United States	25%
Canada	2.7%
Mexico	1.8%
China	8.5%
Japan	5.3%
India	2.5%
Russia	10.6%
Germany	4.6%
Ukraine	2.8%
France	2.8%
United Kingdom	2.8%
Italy	2.1%

Percentage of World Petroleum Consumption

Chart Study Products made from petroleum are used to provide heat for buildings and power for automobiles, airplanes, and factories. People use so much petroleum that experts think that world supplies will be almost exhausted in 100 to 200 years. **Critical Thinking** What countries consume the most petroleum? Think of some ways that these countries could reduce their consumption of petroleum.

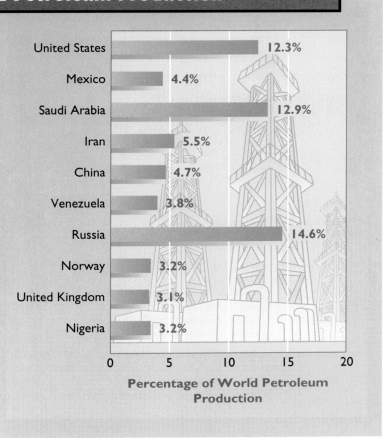

Chart Study Petroleum is a nonrenewable resource, one that cannot be replaced once it is used. As a result, it is very valuable. Countries that have deposits can sell petroleum for a profit. **Critical Thinking** Compare this chart with the one on the previous page. Notice that the United States uses about twice as much petroleum as it produces. How does Russia's production compare with its consumption?

United States 12.3%
Mexico 4.4%
Saudi Arabia 12.9%
Iran 5.5%
China 4.7%
Venezuela 3.8%
Russia 14.6%
Norway 3.2%
United Kingdom 3.1%
Nigeria 3.2%

0   5   10   15   20

Percentage of World Petroleum Production

Countries like Saudi Arabia and Mexico have huge amounts of oil. Others, like the United States and China, have coal and natural gas. Countries with many rivers, such as the countries of Northwestern Europe, can use water energy to create electricity. Others, such as Japan, have very few energy sources. These countries must buy their energy from other countries.

Growing Needs and the Search for New Supplies In 1973, members of the Organization of Petroleum Exporting Countries (OPEC) decided to sell less of their oil. In the United States, this caused a shortage of gasoline, which is made from oil. When there is a shortage of something, it is more expensive. The price of gas more than doubled. Drivers sat in long lines at gas stations. Companies that used fuel oil to make electricity sent notices to families and businesses. The notices asked people to use as little electricity as possible. How could OPEC members have such an effect on the United States?

The answer is that just because a country uses large amounts of energy does not mean that country has its own large energy resources. The biggest users of energy are industrial countries like the United States and the nations of Western Europe. Japan, which has few petroleum resources of its own, uses over twice as much energy as all of

Connect What things can you and your family do to use fewer fossils fuels in your everyday life?

Oil From Under the Ocean

In the chilly waters of the North Sea, European companies drill deep wells to tap the area's large oil deposits. Increased production of North Sea oil may reduce the world's demand for oil from Southwest Asia. **Critical Thinking** How might technological improvements such as more modern drilling rigs cut the cost of oil?

Africa. If a country does not have enough energy resources of its own, it must buy them from other countries. In the 1970s, the United States used so much energy that it had to buy oil from OPEC members. When they limited the supply of oil, they could charge much more for their product. The United States had to pay whatever the producing country asked. The oil shortages of the 1970s made people see they needed to find more sources of energy, including petroleum.

SECTION 1 REVIEW

1. **Define** (a) natural resource, (b) raw material, (c) recyclable resource, (d) renewable resource, (e) nonrenewable resource, (f) fossil fuel.

2. (a) Name two renewable resources. (b) What are two nonrenewable resources?

3. Name some ways that people use fossil fuels.

4. What is the difference between indirect energy use and direct energy use?

Critical Thinking

5. **Expressing Problems Clearly** Explain why people must be careful about how they use nonrenewable resources.

Activity

6. **Writing to Learn** Early pioneers in North America used forests and grasslands as they pleased. Write a paragraph explaining why it might have been less important then to replace those resources.

How People Use the Land

Reach Into Your Background

How many manufactured, or factory-made, items do you use in a day? What natural resources were used to make them? Make a list of these resources.

Questions to Explore

1. What are the stages of economic development?

2. How do different cultures use land?

Key Terms

manufacturing
developed nation
developing nation
commercial farming
subsistence farming
plantation
foreign aid

"**A**ll this water started flowing, but we were told it was restricted for use only by the oil company and we were not allowed to use it," said Li Lixing, a Chinese farmer. "We had to go at night and secretly take some for our crops." Li Lixing lives in a village by the banks of the Huang He. People have farmed here for hundreds of years. In Li's region, the government wants to help the economy by supporting businesses like the oil company. Farmers, therefore, face problems.

Many countries face problems of limited resources, increasing population, and growing demand. Studying how countries use their natural resources shows three basic patterns of economic activity.

Stages of Resource Development

Water from the Huang He is essential for Chinese farmers like Li. But industry needs resources, too. Which group is more important? In some cultures, industry comes first. In others, farmers do. Geographers study how people in different cultures use land and develop their resources. This tells geographers much about a culture. Geographers also compare land use and resource development all over the world.

First-Level Activities Geographers study three stages of economic activity. In the first, people use land and resources directly to make products. They may hunt, cut wood, mine, and fish. They also may herd animals and farm. This is the first stage of activities. People are beginning to develop their land. About half the world's population works in first-level activities. In countries like the United States, however, fewer people do this kind of work every year.

Harvesting Corn

Farmers in the midwest United States are part of the first level of economic activity. Before you eat this corn, it may be frozen, canned, or processed. It may be made into corn meal, cornflakes, corn tortillas, grits, or even corn muffins. Then it must be delivered to a store where you can buy it.

Connect Think about members of your family and friends who work. Do they do first-, second-, or third-level activities?

Second-Level Activities Suppose a farmer takes his corn crop to a mill and has the miller grind the corn into corn meal. This is an example of the second step in developing a resource. People turn raw materials into things they use. When a product is processed, it is changed from a raw material into a finished product. That process is called **manufacturing.** The farmer can pay the miller for his service and take the corn meal back home. Or the miller can sell the corn meal to someone else for further processing. Manufacturing may turn the farmer's corn crop into cornflakes for your breakfast.

Third-Level Activities In the third stage, a person delivers boxes of corn flakes to a local grocery store so you can buy one. In this stage, products are distributed to people who want them. People who distribute products do not make them. They produce a service by making sure products are delivered to people who want and need them.

Industrial nations require service industries. Transportation systems carry products from manufacturer to consumer. Communication for people and businesses comes from telephones, computers, and satellites. Other services—doctors' offices, shopping malls, and fast-food stores—are part of everyday living.

Economic Patterns: Developed and Developing Countries

Today, most manufacturing takes place in factories. Two hundred years ago, that was not so. People produced goods in their homes or small shops. Then came a great change. People invented machines to make goods. They built factories to house the machines. They found new sources of power to run the machines. This change in the way people made goods was called the Industrial Revolution.

The Industrial Revolution created a new pattern of economic activity. It separated countries into two groups—those with many industries and those with few. Countries that have many industries are called developed nations. Countries with few industries are called developing nations. People live differently in developed and developing nations.

Industrial Societies: Providing Goods and Services

Only about one quarter of the people in the world live in developed nations. These nations include the United States, Canada, Japan, Singapore, Australia, and most European countries. People in these nations use goods made in factories. Their industries consume great amounts of raw materials. They also use power-driven machinery. Businesses spend money on technology, transportation, and communications. Factories produce goods for the country's citizens and extra goods to sell to other countries.

▼ In a Detroit factory, a worker carefully assembles the same part on each automobile that comes down the power-driven assembly line.

160°W 120°W 80°W 40°W 0° 40°E 80°E 120°E 160°E

Arctic Circle

NORTH
AMERICA

EUROPE

ASIA

60°N

40°N   40°N

Tropic of Cancer

20°N   20°N

AFRICA

Equator 0°   0°

SOUTH
AMERICA

Tropic of Capricorn

AUSTRALIA

20°S   20°S

40°S

N
W E
S

0   2,000   4,000 mi

0   2,000   4,000 km

60°S

Antarctic Circle

ANTARCTICA

160°W 120°W 80°W 40°W 0° 40°E 80°E 120°E 80°S

KEY

- Nomadic herding
- Hunting and gathering
- Forestry
- Livestock raising
- Commercial farming
- Subsistence farming
- Manufacturing and trade
- Commercial fishing
- Little or no activity

Robinson Projection

Map Study This map uses a color-coded key to show the most common economic activities that take place across the world. Use the key to make comparisons among the continents. **Interaction** Read the paragraphs on developed and developing countries. Then look at the map and identify the continents where you think the most developed countries might be located. Explain your answer.

Predict What are the problems of developed nations?

In developed countries, most people live in towns and cities. They work in business and industry. Machines do most of the work. Most people have enough food and water. Most citizens can get a good education and adequate health care.

Developed nations rely on **commercial farming** to produce enough food for their people. Commercial farms are very large. Companies run most of them, not single families. These farms rely on modern technology, so they often need far fewer workers than small traditional farms. Commercial farms are very successful. In the United States, a few million farmers raise enough food to feed more than 250 million people. There is plenty left over to sell to other countries.

People in developed nations depend on each other. Farmers rely on industries for goods and services. City people depend on farmers for food. Anything, like wars and natural disasters, that stops the movement of goods and services can make life hard for everyone.

Developed nations can have some serious problems. Unemployment is a challenge. Not everyone can find a job. Manufacturing can also threaten the environment with air, land, and water pollution. Heavy production uses up natural resources, so shortages develop. Developed nations are working to solve these problems.

Developing Nations   It is important to remember that every culture is not like that of the United States. Most of the people of the world live in developing countries. Many of these countries are in Africa, Asia, and Latin America.

Developing countries often do not have great wealth. Many people work at **subsistence farming.** That means farmers raise enough food and animals to feed their own families. The farms require much labor, but they do not yield many crops. Often, the only commercial farms are **plantations.** These farms employ many workers but are owned by only a few people. Plantations usually raise a single crop for export, such as bananas, coffee, sugar cane, or tea.

In some developing countries, certain groups herd animals that provide families with milk, meat, cheese, and skins. In the deserts of Africa and Asia, vegetation and water are scarce. Herders in these regions are nomads. They travel from place to place to find food and water for their animals. In some developing nations, some people live as hunter-gatherers. Such groups are found in the Kalahari Desert in Africa and the Amazon region of South America.

Challenges in Developing Nations   Developing countries often face great challenges. These include disease, food shortages, unsafe water, poor education and health services, and changing governments. Farmers often rely on one or two crops. That puts farmers at risk if the crops fail. Thousands move to cities, but jobs there are often scarce.

Some challenges are connected to rapid population growth. It strains resources. For example, in the late 1990s, the supply of fresh water was becoming a problem. As populations grow, they need more water. Larger populations also need more food. This means that farms need more water. Industries also require large amounts of fresh water.

Developing countries are working to improve their people's lives. One way is to use their natural resources or sell them to other countries. Some countries have grown richer by selling natural resources, such as oil and other minerals, to others.

ACROSS THE WORLD

A Nation of Herders The Tuareg of the Sahara in northern Africa herd camels, goats, sheep, and cattle. They travel along the edge of the great desert. Here there are seasonal rains so there is pasture for the herds. Men and women are equals in Tuareg culture. Both can own their own herds of animals and other property.

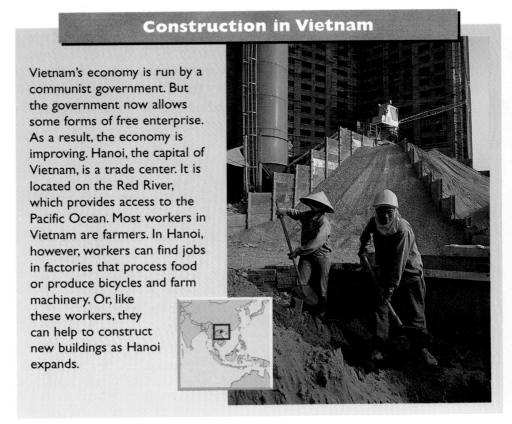

Construction in Vietnam

Vietnam's economy is run by a communist government. But the government now allows some forms of free enterprise. As a result, the economy is improving. Hanoi, the capital of Vietnam, is a trade center. It is located on the Red River, which provides access to the Pacific Ocean. Most workers in Vietnam are farmers. In Hanoi, however, workers can find jobs in factories that process food or produce bicycles and farm machinery. Or, like these workers, they can help to construct new buildings as Hanoi expands.

▶ This woman works in the city of Bangalore, India. In recent years, many Indian businesses have improved their services by using computers.

Developing countries sometimes receive help from developed nations. The help could be in the form of **foreign aid,** or gifts and loans from one government to another or from the United Nations. This aid is often used for special projects, such as building roads to move food and other goods from one area to another. Sometimes conflicts arise when the two governments do not agree on the best way to use foreign aid funds.

Sometimes help comes from businesses in developed countries. They may build factories in developing nations. This provides jobs and money for people. Sometimes building communication systems helps spread new ideas for farming and industries.

SECTION 2 REVIEW

1. **Define** (a) manufacturing, (b) developed nation, (c) developing nation, (d) commercial farming, (e) subsistence farming, (f) plantation, (g) foreign aid.

2. What are the characteristics of a developed nation? Of a developing nation?

3. How is subsistence farming different from commercial farming?

4. How can countries use their natural resources?

5. What challenges face developed nations? Developing nations?

Critical Thinking

6. **Identifying Central Issues** How are developing nations working to improve their people's lives?

Activity

7. **Writing to Learn** People who work at your school have jobs in a service industry. Interview a teacher, a server in the cafeteria, or a receptionist in the office. Find out what that person's duties are and what that person likes about his or her job. Write a brief profile for your school newspaper.

People's Effect on the Environment

BEFORE YOU READ

Reach Into Your Background

Many of the environmental problems we face are the result of actions people took in the past. Now people pay more attention to environmental issues. Make a list of things you and your community are doing to improve the environment.

Questions to Explore

1. How do people's actions affect the environment?

2. What are people doing to improve the environment?

Key Terms

ecosystem
deforestation
habitat
acid rain
ozone layer
global warming
recycle

ry to picture the United States as one huge desert. Africa's Sahara is even bigger than that. What's more, the Sahara is spreading. Wangari Maathai of Kenya, in East Africa, works to stop it. She heads Africa's Green Belt Movement. It urges people in a dozen African countries to plant trees. Tree roots hold valuable topsoil in place, stopping the spread of the desert. When their leaves fall to the ground, trees add nutrients to the soil. This will make rich soil good for other plants. Since 1977, this organization has planted more than 10 million trees.

▼ Coral reefs, like this one, take millions of years to construct. They can be completely destroyed in a matter of decades by such things as water pollution.

Danger to Land, Water, and Air

Wangari Maathai is saving forests in Africa. Other people around the world are also working to preserve the environment. If we learn to identify environmental problems, we too can protect our world.

The Sahara is a desert. The Amazon River valley is a rain forest. The Great Plains is an area of grasslands. Each of these regions is an **ecosystem,** a place where living elements depend on one another—and on nonliving elements—for their survival. Living elements are plants and animals. Nonliving elements are water, soil, rocks, and air. Desert birds cannot live in a rain forest. Grassland plants cannot survive in a desert. Living things are tied to their ecosystems.

Death of a Sea The border between Kazakstan and Uzbekistan in western Asia runs through the Aral Sea. Until about 1960, this shallow sea was the fourth largest inland lake or sea in the world. Two rivers fed into the Aral. Then people started diverting the water for irrigation projects. By 1987, the Aral Sea had less than half as much water as before. Its fish were dead. Fishing villages now sat far from the water's edge. Some experts believe it may take 30 years to repair the damage done to the Aral Sea.

If one part of an ecosystem changes, other parts are also affected. For example, ecosystems that have standing water like puddles have mosquitoes. They lay their eggs on the surface of water. A rainy summer produces more standing water. This means that more mosquito eggs will hatch. A dry summer means less water and fewer mosquitoes.

Some changes can destroy an ecosystem. Probably the greatest loss of ecosystems is happening in South America. Rain forests cover more than one third of the continent. They are home for more species, or kinds, of plants and animals than anywhere else in the world. But South Americans need land for farms, so they are cutting down the forests. This process is called **deforestation.** When the forests are gone, many plant and animal species become extinct, or die out.

Protecting Endangered Species   How can we prevent species of animals and plants from dying out? One way is through laws. In 1973, Congress passed the Endangered Species Act. It gave the government power to protect not only species that might become extinct but also the places that they live, or their **habitats.** Today, the act protects almost 1,000 kinds of living things in the United States that are threatened, or endangered.

Extinction has many causes. People may build houses or businesses on land that is the habitat of particular animals or plants. The air, soil, or water may be too polluted for a species of plant or animal to survive. Sometimes, a species is hunted until it disappears. Usually, more than one thing threatens a species. The goal of the Endangered Species Act is to stop extinction. But people disagree about the law. Some think humans should be allowed to use natural resources as they need them. Others think people should stop doing things that hurt other species.

Factories and Acid Rain
Often, endangered animal species are just one sign of an ecosystem with problems. Visitors to the New York's Adirondack Mountains see an ecosystem in trouble. Its vast forests are centuries old. But today, the needles of the spruce trees are brown, and birch trees have no leaves at all. There are few fish in the rivers. Frogs, certain kinds of birds, and many insects are hard to find. What happened?

According to scientists, **acid rain** is to blame. Acid rain is rain that carries

Saving the Gray Whale

Temporarily trapped in Alaska's ice, this gray whale may survive to make its yearly journey down the Pacific Coast to Mexico. Whaling nearly destroyed the world's population of gray whales. Protection as an endangered species, however, brought their numbers back up.

The Greenhouse Effect

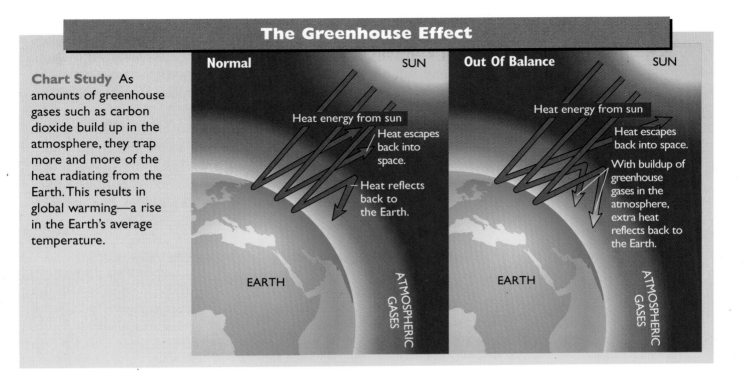

Chart Study As amounts of greenhouse gases such as carbon dioxide build up in the atmosphere, they trap more and more of the heat radiating from the Earth. This results in global warming—a rise in the Earth's average temperature.

Normal

SUN

Heat energy from sun

Heat escapes back into space.

Heat reflects back to the Earth.

EARTH

ATMOSPHERIC GASES

Out Of Balance

SUN

Heat energy from sun

Heat escapes back into space.

With buildup of greenhouse gases in the atmosphere, extra heat reflects back to the Earth.

EARTH

ATMOSPHERIC GASES

dangerous chemicals. The fossil fuels used by industries and automobiles release chemicals into the air. The chemicals combine with water vapor in the air, making the rain as acid as vinegar.

Canada and the United States now have laws to reduce acid rain. Coal-burning electricity plants must cut pollution in half by the year 2000. Factories are installing new devices called filters and scrubbers to clean up the fumes they release. Car makers have added devices to reduce the dangerous chemicals in car exhaust.

Rivers and Sewage Pollution   People have always dumped waste products into rivers, lakes, and oceans. These wastes can harm or destroy living things in the water. They also endanger people. Water creatures take in substances from the water. Little fish eat the creatures, big fish eat the little fish, and animals and people eat the fish. The substances pass from one living thing to another. Some of these substances are poisons.

Fertilizers and pesticides from farms also pollute water. (Pesticides are chemicals that kill insects.) Rainwater washes the substances into lakes and rivers. There, the fertilizers cause water plants to grow too fast, and they use up oxygen needed by fish and other water life.

The Ozone Layer and Ultraviolet Rays   In the 1970s, scientists realized that chemicals called chlorofluorocarbons (CFCs) were destroying the atmosphere's ozone layer. This is a layer of gas in the upper part of our atmosphere. The ozone layer blocks most of the harmful ultraviolet rays from the sun. These rays cause skin cancer in humans. They also damage other forms of life.

READ ACTIVELY

Connect What are some things you and your friends could do to protect the environment?

Until recently, aerosol spray cans, refrigerators, and air conditioners used CFCs. In 1985, a United Nations conference discussed the ozone layer. Many nations agreed to get rid of ozone-destroying chemicals by 2000. And scientists are searching for safe chemicals to replace CFCs.

Global Warming   The summer of 1995 in New England was unusually hot and dry. Temperatures stayed above 90 degrees for weeks. Heat and drought caused water shortages and killed crops. Some scientists feared this was the start of **global warming,** a slow increase in the Earth's temperature. Global warming may be caused by

A Sun-Powered House

If you have spent a few hours outside on a hot summer day, then you are well aware of the heating power of the sun. Scientists knew all about it, too. They also knew that if they could find a way to store that power, they would have a cheap, abundant source of energy. The diagram below shows how they solved the problem of storing the heat of the sun.

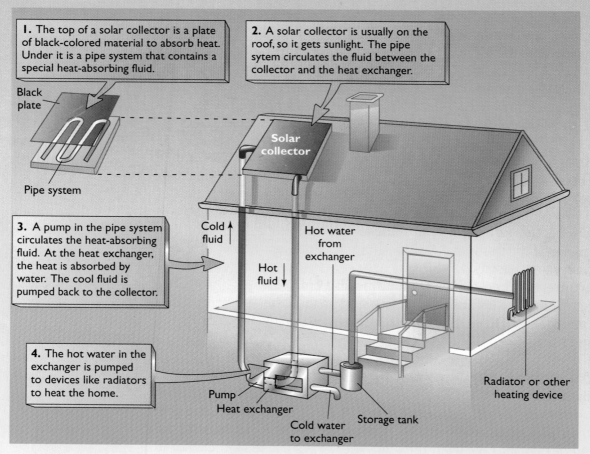

1. The top of a solar collector is a plate of black-colored material to absorb heat. Under it is a pipe system that contains a special heat-absorbing fluid.

2. A solar collector is usually on the roof, so it gets sunlight. The pipe sytem circulates the fluid between the collector and the heat exchanger.

3. A pump in the pipe system circulates the heat-absorbing fluid. At the heat exchanger, the heat is absorbed by water. The cool fluid is pumped back to the collector.

4. The hot water in the exchanger is pumped to devices like radiators to heat the home.

Black plate

Pipe system

Solar collector

Cold fluid

Hot fluid

Hot water from exchanger

Pump

Heat exchanger

Cold water to exchanger

Storage tank

Radiator or other heating device

gases like carbon dioxide that are released into the air. They are called greenhouse gases. Industrial countries produce about 75 percent of these gases. They are released when fossil fuels burn. These fuels produce most of the world's electricity. They also run the world's 550 million cars, buses, and trucks. Developing countries produce these gases when they burn forests to clear land and use wood for heating and cooking.

Normally, heat on the Earth escapes back into space. Some scientists theorize that greenhouse gases trap the heat and reflect it back to Earth. The result is a rise in the Earth's average temperature.

The Challenge of Energy

Because pollution is often tied to using fossil fuels, scientists are exploring other ways to get inexpensive energy. Their research concentrates on nuclear power, water, wind, and the sun. Individuals can protect the environment, too. For example, the United States produces more waste than any other nation in the world. To change that, people now **recycle**, or re-use old materials to make new products. Today, most American cities have recycling programs.

◀ It looks as if a fire burned these trees near the peak of Mount Mitchell in North Carolina. In fact, acid rain killed them.

SECTION 3 REVIEW

1. **Define** (a) ecosystem, (b) deforestation, (c) habitat, (d) acid rain, (e) ozone layer, (f) global warming, (g) recycle.

2. How do fossil fuels create pollution?

3. Why is global warming a problem?

4. What alternatives to fossil fuels are scientists researching?

Critical Thinking

5. **Expressing Problems Clearly** Explain why some species are endangered. Why do people disagree about reserving land for them?

Activity

6. **Writing to Learn** Write a persuasive paragraph explaining why fresh water should be protected. Include facts to support your reasons.

SKILLS ACTIVITY

Writing for a Purpose

"SAVE THE EARTH NOT JUST FOR US BUT FOR FUTURE GENERATIONS" ™

Have you ever testified before Congress about pollution? Or stopped a company from pumping poison into a river? Or organized a demonstration to make people more aware of the environment? You may think kids your age do not do such things. But the kids of KAP do.

KAP stands for Kids Against Pollution. These young people work to stop pollution. Nineteen students in Closter, New Jersey, formed KAP in 1987. Today, there are more than 13,000 KAP chapters across the United States and in other countries. KAP's motto is "Save the Earth Not Just For Us But For Future Generations."

One of KAP's main weapons is writing. It can be very powerful. KAP members use the power of persuasive writing, or writing that tries to show other people how their point of view can help solve a problem.

Get Ready

Writing to persuade means taking a stand and trying to convince others to agree with your opinion. There are four basic steps:

1. **Decide what your opinion is.** Your opinion is the position you plan to take. For example, suppose your opinion is "Our city should make a law to require people to recycle newspapers."

2. **Choose your audience.** Your audience is the people to whom you will be writing. You might write to a senator or a mayor. You might write to the general public in a magazine article or letter to the editor of a newspaper.

3. **Find support for your opinion.** Your writing must give reasons for your opinion and the facts to support each reason. For example, the statement "Recycling would prevent burying six tons of paper trash in our town's landfill every month" is a fact that supports an opinion. Find as many facts as you can to support your opinion. They will help make your message stronger.

4 **Write persuasively.** Finally, write a letter or an essay. Present one idea at a time, and defend it with facts. Although persuasive writing emphasizes facts, it often includes an appeal to emotions. Add a sentence or two that does this. KAP's motto, for instance, is an emotional appeal. The combination of facts and emotion can make persuasive writing work.

Try It Out

Suppose you are concerned about the growing amount of litter in a local park. Follow these four steps to write a persuasive letter.

A. What is your opinion? Decide upon a plan to solve the park's problem. Should there be stronger anti-litter laws? Should people be urged to litter less, or should they be required to participate in a community cleanup? Choose one of these opinions or develop your own solution.

B. Who is your audience? If you want a local law passed, write to a member of your local government. To address your fellow citizens, write to the editor of a local newspaper.

C. Why do you hold this opinion? Identify at least two reasons for your opinion. Then support each reason with facts.

D. How will you persuade your audience to agree with your opinion? Before you write your letter, make an outline. Start your letter with a catchy opening. Then present your reasons in logical order. In the conclusion, sum up your arguments and appeal to people's emotions.

Apply the Skill

Now, apply the skill to the real world. Choose a topic, and write a persuasive letter about it to the editor of your local newspaper. Try to persuade your fellow citizens to agree with your opinion.

To the Editor:
The time has come to do something about the litter ruining Peace Park. First of all, the Parks Department has released a study that shows littering has increased 10 percent in two years.

Review and Activities

Reviewing Main Ideas

1. (a) Name two natural resources. (b) Describe how they are used.
2. What is the difference between renewable resources and nonrenewable resources?
3. (a) What kind of nation has mainly agricultural activities? (b) What kind of nation has mainly industrial activities?
4. Why is commercial farming part of a developed nation instead of a developing nation?
5. How can foreign aid help a developing nation?
6. Why might one simple change in an ecosystem have many effects in the system?
7. Acid rain hurts forests and lakes. How could acid rain endanger people?
8. What can governments do to protect endangered species?
9. Why is recycling a good use of natural resources?
10. How can people work to prevent global warming?

Reviewing Key Terms

Use each key term below in a sentence that shows the meaning of the term.

1. natural resource
2. raw material
3. recyclable resource
4. renewable resource
5. nonrenewable resource
6. fossil fuel
7. manufacturing
8. developed nation
9. developing nation
10. commercial farming
11. subsistence farming
12. plantation
13. foreign aid
14. ecosystem
15. deforestation
16. habitat
17. acid rain
18. ozone layer
19. global warming
20. recycle

Critical Thinking

1. **Identifying Central Issues** Do you think people should do more to protect the environment? Use facts from the chapter to support your answer.
2. **Recognizing Cause and Effect** Think about the problems that arose during the oil shortage of 1973. It affected the supply of gasoline and heating fuel. Write a paragraph about how a gasoline shortage today would affect the lives of people in your family.

Graphic Organizer

Copy and fill in the table to show how pollution damages the environment and suggest some solutions.

Sources	Damage to Environment	Possible Solutions
Water Pollution		
Land Pollution		
Air Pollution		

Writing Activity

Writing a Letter

Become part of the global community by contacting an organization that works to protect the environment. Two groups are listed here. Describe what you have learned about threats to the environment. Explain how you use natural resources responsibly. Find out if the organization has suggestions for other actions.

Addresses:

Greenpeace
1436 U Street NW
Washington, D.C. 20009

World Wildlife Fund
1250 24th Street, NW
Washington, D.C. 20037

Skills Review

Turn to the Skills Activity.

Review the steps for writing for a purpose. Then complete the following: (a) Why do you think that it is important to know your audience when you are writing to persuade? (b) Do you think that you need to do research in order to write to persuade? Why or why not?

Internet Activity

Use a search engine to find the **U.S. Geological Survey.** Click on **Fact Sheets.** Scroll down and click on **State** to find a USGS program in your area. Click on your state and then choose a program. Write a paragraph that explains the goal of the program and the actions taken to reach the goal.

How Am I Doing?

Answer these questions to help you check your progress.

1. Can I describe natural resources and how different countries use them?

2. Do I understand how the stages of economic development are related to a nation's wealth?

3. Can I identify some threats to the environment?

4. What information from this chapter can I use in my book project?

GEOGRAPHY
TOOLS AND CONCEPTS
PROJECT POSSIBILITIES

*The chapters in this book have some answers
to these important questions.*

☛ **What is the Earth's geography like?**

☛ **Where do the world's people live?**

☛ **What is a culture?**

☛ **How do people use the world's resources?**

Doing a project shows what you know about geography! The knowledge and skills you have gained will help you do a great job.

GEO LEO

Project Menu

Now it's time for you to find your own answers by doing projects on your own or with a group. Here are some ways to make your own discoveries about geography.

The Geography Game
Every place in the world has unique characteristics. Use them to create a geography game with your classmates. Choose a country. Find one fact each about its (1) physical features, (2) climate, (3) population, (4) cultures, and (5) natural resources. These facts will be clues in the game. Practice writing them out until they are short and clear. Clues should not be too easy or too hard. They must provide enough information so that someone can figure out the answer. Now make five playing cards. On one side of each card, write a clue. On the other side, write the name of your country.

Divide into three teams. Each team needs the Atlas in the back of this book. Mix up the cards. Have your teacher or a volunteer pick a card and read the clue to team one. Members have 30 seconds to agree on an answer. If it is correct, the team earns one point. If not, the next team has a chance. Play until the cards are gone. The team with the most points wins.

From Questions to Careers

JOBS IN THE EARTH SCIENCES

People who want to preserve the Earth often have jobs in the sciences. Environmental engineers may figure out how to clean up oil spills or make better use of natural resources. Soil scientists find ways to increase the crops a farmer can grow on a piece of land, or they may work on soil conservation. Ethnobotanists study how certain cultures use plants, especially as medicines. These jobs require a college degree.

Some jobs that help preserve the Earth require less education. People who assist scientists are called technicians. Usually they need only an associate's degree, which takes two years. Technicians may work in agriculture, chemistry, energy, or weather research. All these jobs are vital to helping preserve the environment.

▼ A scientist and technician are shown collecting water quality samples from a stream.

World News Today

Collect newspaper and magazine articles about natural resources, economies, and businesses in countries around the world. Display the clippings on a poster. Choose one country, and study the relationship between its economy and its natural resources. Prepare a five-minute speech to tell your class what you found.

Focus on Part of the Whole

The world and its population are extremely varied. Choose a particular region or country. If you are working with a group, have each person choose a different country on a continent. Learn everything you can about the land's physical geography, the population, and the lifestyles of the people there. Use encyclopedias, almanacs, or other books.

Set up a display based on your research. Prepare a large map that includes important physical features of the land. Add captions that explain how the land's physical geography affects people's lives.

Desktop Countries

What countries did your ancestors come from? Select one and do some research on it. Interview someone, perhaps a relative from there, or read about it. Find a recipe you can prepare to share with the class. Then make a desktop display about your country. Write the name of the country on a card and put it on your desk. Add a drawing of the country's flag or map, or display a souvenir. On place cards, write several sentences about each object. Take turns visiting everyone's "desktop countries."

THE UNITED STATES AND CANADA

Spreading "from sea to shining sea," the United States and Canada take up nearly seven-eighths of North America. From the groups who migrated to these areas before the dawn of history to later settlers from around the world, a wide variety of people have flocked to North America. Out of the region's natural riches and varied cultures have grown successful nations. In this book, you'll see how the United States and Canada are working to create a good life for every citizen.

Guiding Questions

The readings and activities in this book will help you discover answers to these Guiding Questions.

- ☛ How has physical geography affected the cultures of the United States and Canada?

- ☛ How have historical events affected the cultures of the United States and Canada?

- ☛ How has the variety of peoples in the United States and Canada benefited and challenged the two nations?

- ☛ How has modern technology benefited and challenged the United States and Canada?

- ☛ How did the United States and Canada become two of the wealthiest nations in the world?

Project Preview

You can also discover answers to the Guiding Questions by working on projects. Preview the following projects and choose one that you might like to do.

Write a Children's Book Write a short book for young students about a topic in the United States and Canada.

Make a Time Line of Local History Make an illustrated time line of the history of your community.

Set Up a Weather Station Keep a log of local weather conditions. Compare your weather to other parts of the country.

Create a Diorama Sculpt the physical features of a geographic region in the United States and Canada with clay or dough. Add details to the landscape.

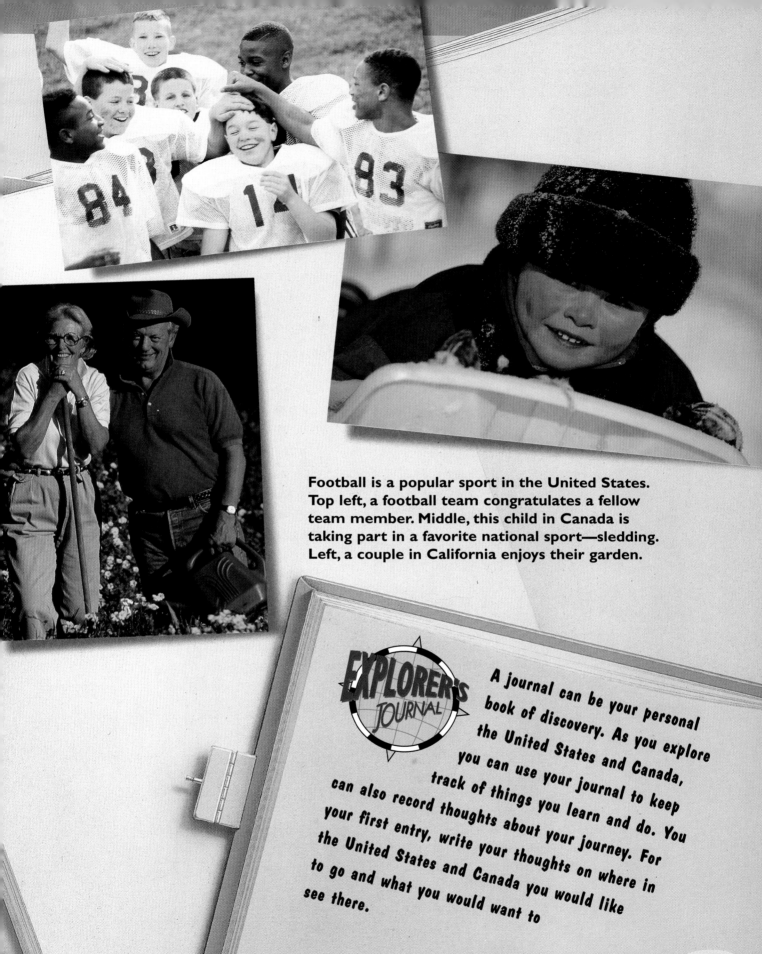

Football is a popular sport in the United States. Top left, a football team congratulates a fellow team member. Middle, this child in Canada is taking part in a favorite national sport—sledding. Left, a couple in California enjoys their garden.

EXPLORER'S JOURNAL

A journal can be your personal book of discovery. As you explore the United States and Canada, you can use your journal to keep track of things you learn and do. You can also record thoughts about your journey. For your first entry, write your thoughts on where in the United States and Canada you would like to go and what you would want to see there.

The United States and Canada

Learning about Canada and the United States means being an explorer and a geographer. No explorer would start out without first checking some facts. Begin by exploring the maps of the United States and Canada on the following pages.

Relative Location

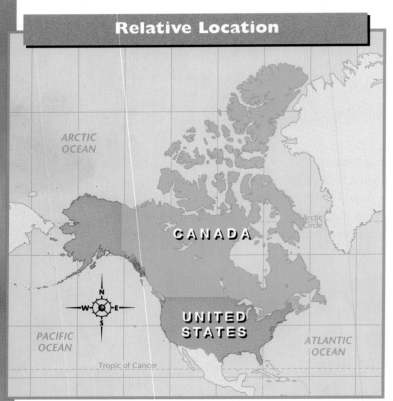

LOCATION

1. **Explore the Location of the United States and Canada** Look at the map at left. In this book you will read about the United States, which is colored orange on the map, and Canada, which is green. Which country extends farther north? If you were on the east coast of the United States, which direction would you travel to get to the Pacific Ocean? Why do Canadians think of the United States as their neighbor to the south?

Relative Size

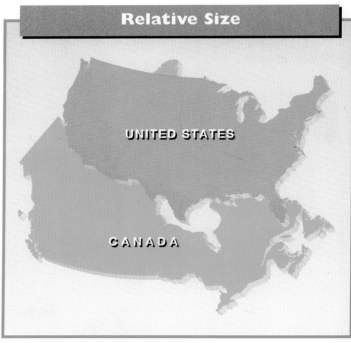

REGIONS

2. **Compare the Sizes of the United States and Canada** Look at the map to the right. Compare it to the map above. Notice that not all of the United States is shown on the map at right. Which country do you think is bigger, the United States mainland or Canada? Check your estimate by looking up both of the countries in the World View at the back of this book.

PLACE

3. Explore the United States and Canada
The United States and Canada together take up most of the continent of North America. Look at the map. What other country is on the same continent? What country borders Canada? What countries border the United States? Name the cities that are the national capitals of the United States and Canada. Which 2 of the 50 United States do not share a border with any other state? Which of the Canadian cities on the map is the farthest south? North?

PLACE

4. Locate Bodies of Water Important to the United States and Canada What three oceans surround the United States and Canada? Find the Great Lakes on the map. How many are there? Which one lies entirely within the United States? What river connects the Great Lakes to the Atlantic Ocean? The largest bay in the world is located in Canada. What is its name? Would you enter the bay from the Pacific Ocean or from the Atlantic Ocean?

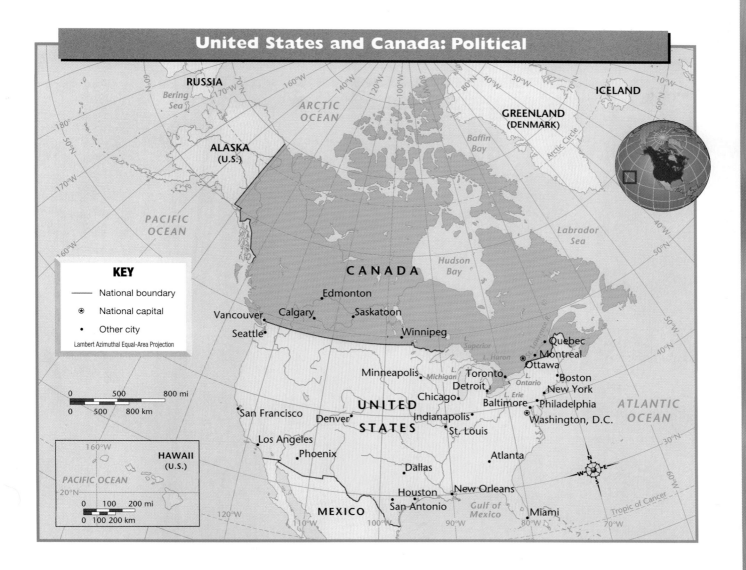

United States and Canada: Political

KEY
— National boundary
⊛ National capital
• Other city
Lambert Azimuthal Equal-Area Projection

PLACE

5. Find Geo Cleo Geo Cleo is traveling through the United States and Canada. Use her clues and the map below to answer her questions about where she has been on her tour of the United States and Canada.

A. *Whew! I've been hiking through the Rocky Mountains! Right now I'm heading south. I just crossed the Colorado River. What country am I in?*

B. *Today, I crossed the border of the United States, and I'm flying to Victoria Island in Canada. Which direction am I going?*

C. *Now I'm on a ship. We're heading from the Gulf of St. Lawrence to the Great Lakes. What river will we travel on?*

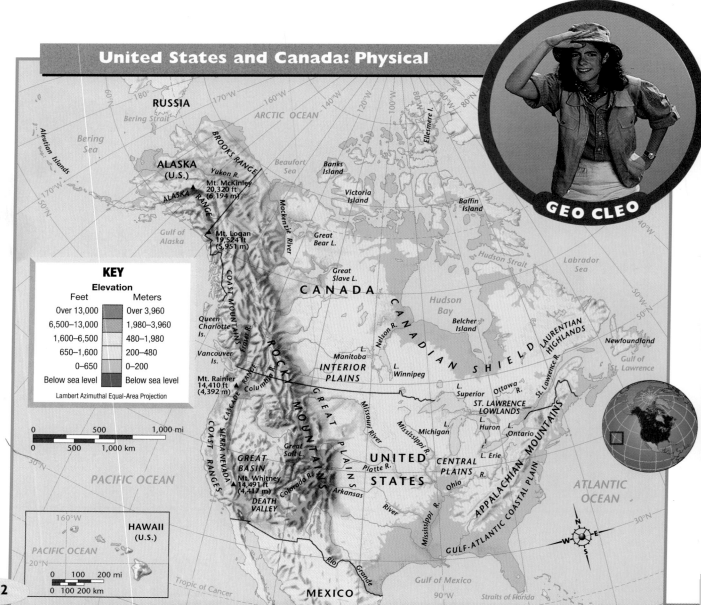

GEO CLEO

United States and Canada: Physical

RUSSIA

Bering Strait

ARCTIC OCEAN

Aleutian Islands

Bering Sea

ALASKA (U.S.)

Yukon R.

Mt. McKinley 20,320 ft (6,194 m)

ALASKA RANGE

BROOKS RANGE

Beaufort Sea

Banks Island

Victoria Island

Ellesmere I.

Baffin Island

Gulf of Alaska

Mt. Logan 19,524 ft (5,951 m)

Mackenzie River

Great Bear L.

Great Slave L.

CANADA

Hudson Strait

Labrador Sea

Hudson Bay

Belcher Island

CANADIAN SHIELD

LAURENTIAN HIGHLANDS

Newfoundland

KEY

Elevation

Feet		Meters
Over 13,000		Over 3,960
6,500–13,000		1,980–3,960
1,600–6,500		480–1,980
650–1,600		200–480
0–650		0–200
Below sea level		Below sea level

Lambert Azimuthal Equal-Area Projection

Queen Charlotte Is.

COAST MOUNTAINS

Vancouver Is.

Fraser R.

ROCKY MOUNTAINS

Nelson R.

L. Manitoba

INTERIOR PLAINS

L. Winnipeg

L. Superior

Ottawa R.

St. Lawrence R.

ST. LAWRENCE LOWLANDS

Gulf of St. Lawrence

Mt. Rainier 14,410 ft (4,392 m)

Columbia R.

CASCADE RANGE

GREAT PLAINS

Missouri River

Mississippi R.

L. Michigan

L. Huron

L. Ontario

L. Erie

APPALACHIAN MOUNTAINS

0   500   1,000 mi

0   500   1,000 km

COAST RANGES

SIERRA NEVADA

GREAT BASIN

Great Salt L.

Mt. Whitney 14,491 ft (4,417 m)

DEATH VALLEY

Colorado R.

UNITED STATES

Platte R.

Arkansas River

CENTRAL PLAINS

Ohio R.

GULF-ATLANTIC COASTAL PLAIN

ATLANTIC OCEAN

PACIFIC OCEAN

HAWAII (U.S.)

PACIFIC OCEAN

0   100   200 mi

0   100 200 km

Tropic of Cancer

Rio Grande

MEXICO

Mississippi R.

Gulf of Mexico

Straits of Florida

N E S W

INTERACTION

6. Investigate Land Use in the United States and Canada The use of land is one of the main features of a place. How many different types of land use are identified on the map? Which is the most common use of the land in Canada? In the United States? Compare the use of land in the eastern half of the United States to that in the western half. What are the main differences?

INTERACTION

7. Compare Land Use to Physical Features Look at the physical map on the opposite page. Compare it to the land use map on this page. What relationship do you see between physical features and the way people use the land? How do people use the land in mountainous regions? What type of land seems to be good for farming? Look at the manufacturing areas. What physical feature is close to most of them?

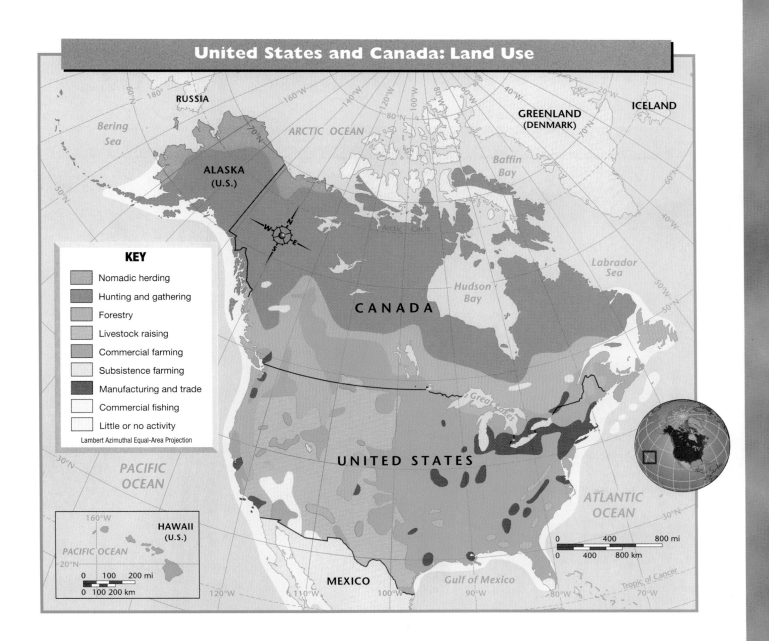

United States and Canada: Land Use

KEY
- Nomadic herding
- Hunting and gathering
- Forestry
- Livestock raising
- Commercial farming
- Subsistence farming
- Manufacturing and trade
- Commercial fishing
- Little or no activity

Lambert Azimuthal Equal-Area Projection

RUSSIA

Bering Sea

ARCTIC OCEAN

GREENLAND (DENMARK)

ICELAND

ALASKA (U.S.)

Baffin Bay

Arctic Circle

Labrador Sea

Hudson Bay

CANADA

Great Lakes

UNITED STATES

PACIFIC OCEAN

ATLANTIC OCEAN

0   400   800 mi
0   400   800 km

HAWAII (U.S.)

PACIFIC OCEAN

0   100   200 mi
0   100 200 km

MEXICO

Gulf of Mexico

Tropic of Cancer

8. Investigate the Climates of the United States and Canada You already know that climate affects the way people live. For example, you don't find snowplows on the beach or skis in the desert! Look at the map below. How many different types of climate regions are there in the United States and Canada? Do the climates seem to change more from east to west or from north to south? Which of the two countries has a region of humid subtropical climate? Which has the biggest area of subarctic climate?

9. Investigate How Climate Affects the Way People Live Look at the climate map below. What city fits each of these descriptions?

• In this area of marine west coast climate, winds blowing from the ocean help keep the climate very damp. People in this Canadian city are used to a climate with lots of rain.

• People who live here are in a tropical wet and dry climate. They do not own winter coats or boots, and many have never seen snow.

• The humid continental climate region includes some major cities of both countries. People here usually need clothes for all four seasons. Their houses must have good heating systems. Many are also air conditioned in the summer. This city is on Lake Michigan.

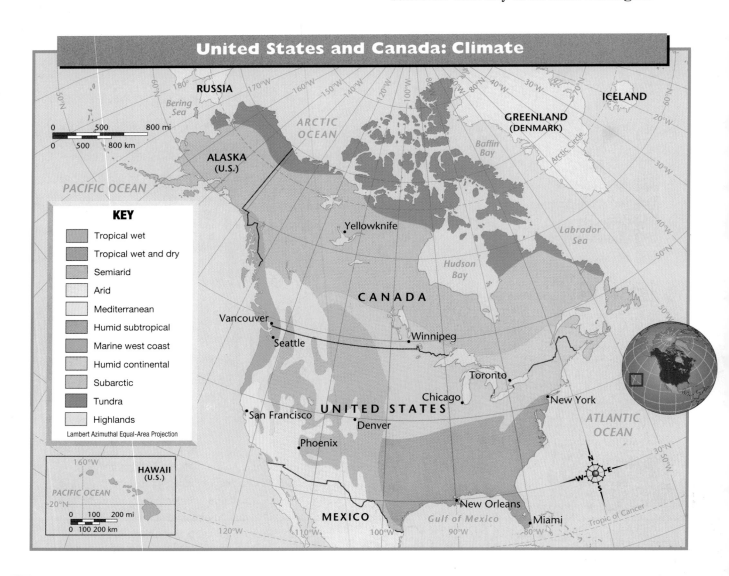

United States and Canada: Climate

KEY

- Tropical wet
- Tropical wet and dry
- Semiarid
- Arid
- Mediterranean
- Humid subtropical
- Marine west coast
- Humid continental
- Subarctic
- Tundra
- Highlands

Lambert Azimuthal Equal-Area Projection

10. **Analyze the Populations of the United States and Canada** The United States and Canada are often referred to as "countries of immigrants." Through the years, people have moved to both of these countries from other places around the world. The chart below lists the percentages of the populations of the United States and Canada whose ancestors came from some other places.

(Only the places of ancestry for the highest percentages of people are listed in the table.) Which are the three most common places of ancestry for people in the United States? How does this compare to the most common places of ancestry for people in Canada? Both Canada and the United States belonged to England in the early part of their histories. What effect has this had on the populations of Canada and the United States?

Most Common Sources of Ancestry		
Source	Percent of United States Population	Percent of Canadian Population
Africa	9.6 percent	0.8 percent
China	0.6 percent	2.2 percent
England	13.1 percent	14.6 percent
France	4.1 percent	22.7 percent
Germany	23.3 percent	3.4 percent
Ireland	15.6 percent	2.6 percent
Italy	5.9 percent	2.7 percent
Mexico	4.7 percent	less than 1 percent
The Netherlands	2.5 percent	1.3 percent
North America	3.5 percent	1.4 percent
Poland	3.8 percent	1.0 percent
Scotland	2.2 percent	3.3 percent
Ukraine	less than 1 percent	1.5 percent

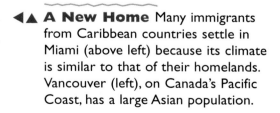

◀▲ **A New Home** Many immigrants from Caribbean countries settle in Miami (above left) because its climate is similar to that of their homelands. Vancouver (left), on Canada's Pacific Coast, has a large Asian population.

THE UNITED STATES AND CANADA

Physical Geography

PICTURE ACTIVITIES

These scenic peaks are part of a huge mountain system called the Rocky Mountains. They stretch across parts of the United States and Canada. To get to know this mountain system, do the following activities.

Study the picture
What do you think the weather is like in the Rocky Mountains? Based on what you see in the photograph, what kind of vegetation probably grows here?

Tour the Rockies
Why do you think tourists visit national parks in the Rocky Mountains? What sports or other activities might they enjoy in the parks? What effect do you think tourism has on the economies of the Rocky Mountain states and provinces?

Land and Water

BEFORE YOU READ

Reach Into Your Background

Have you ever climbed a hill or mountain—or been to the top of a skyscraper? What could you see from such a high place that you could not see from the ground? You probably saw the landscape and how places related to each other. Keep that idea in mind as you read this section.

Questions to Explore

1. What are the main physical features of the United States and Canada?

2. How do the physical environments of the United States and Canada affect the way people live?

Key Terms

glacier
tributary
Continental Divide

Key Places

Rocky Mountains
Appalachian Mountains
Death Valley
Great Lakes
St. Lawrence River
Mississippi River

Alaska's Mount McKinley is the highest mountain in North America and attracts thousands of visitors every year. In 1992, Ruth Kocour joined a team of climbers to scale the 20,320-foot (6,194-m) peak. After the team had set up camp at 9,500 feet (2,896 m), the first storm arrived. The team quickly built walls of packed snow to shield their tents from the wind. They dug a snow cave to house their kitchen and waited for the storm to blow itself out. Kocour recalls, "Someone on another team went outside for a few minutes, came back, and had a hot drink. His teeth cracked."

Maybe camping in the cold mountains is not for you. Perhaps you would prefer the sunny beaches of Florida or the giant forests of the Northwest. Maybe you would like to see the Arizona desert or the vast plains of central Canada. The landscape of the United States and Canada varies greatly.

▼ Dressed for warmth and carrying heavy backpacks, hikers stride across Mount McKinley's Kahiltna Glacier.

Where in the World Are We?

The United States and Canada are located in North America. To the east is the Atlantic Ocean, to the west, the Pacific. To the north, Canada borders the Arctic Ocean, while to the south, the United States borders Mexico and the Gulf of Mexico. The United States also includes Alaska and Hawaii.

Which is bigger, the United States or Canada? Canada has more land—it is the second-largest country in the world. The United States is the fourth largest. But the United States has more people—almost 10 times more people—than Canada. The United States has the third-largest population in the world, after China and India.

Landforms of the United States and Canada

From outer space, the United States and Canada appear as one landmass, with mountain ranges and vast plains running from north to south. Locate these mountains and plains on the physical map in the Activity Atlas at the front of your textbook.

Extending about 3,000 miles (4,830 km) along the western section of the continent, the Rocky Mountains are the largest mountain system in North America. In the east, the Appalachian (ap uh LAY chun) Mountains are the second largest. They stretch about 1,600 miles (2,570 km). In Canada, the Appalachians become the Laurentian (loh REN shun) Highlands. Tourists visit these mountain ranges year round.

Predict What are the major landforms of the United States and Canada?

▼ White-water rafters splash their way down a mountain stream in the Appalachians in West Virginia.

Visitors to Volcanoes National Park in Hawaii can marvel at the natural fireworks provided by one of the state's active volcanoes, Kilauea. The 122 islands that make up Hawaii, like many other islands in the Pacific Ocean, were created by volcanoes long ago. **Critical Thinking** How do you think volcanic eruptions affect the people who live in Hawaii?

Between the Rockies and the Appalachians lies a huge plains area. In Canada, these lowlands are called the Interior Plains. In the United States, they are called the Great Plains and the Central Plains. Much of this region has rich soil. In the wetter eastern area, farmers grow crops like corn and soybeans. In the drier western area, farmers grow wheat, and ranchers raise livestock.

Special Features of the United States The United States has several unique features. A plains area runs along its eastern and southern coasts. In the Northeast, this plain is narrow; it broadens as it spreads south and west. Flat, fertile land and access to the sea attracted many settlers to this area. Large cities developed here.

West of the Rockies lies a region of plateaus and basins. Perhaps the most notable feature of this area is the Great Basin. In the northeast section of this bowl-shaped valley is the Great Salt Lake. Death Valley is in the southwest section. Much of Death Valley lies below sea level. It is also the hottest place in North America. Summer temperatures here regularly climb to 120°F (50°C).

To the west of this region of plateaus and basins lie two more mountain ranges. These are the Sierra Nevada in California and the Cascades in Washington and Oregon. The Cascades were formed by volcanoes. One of these volcanoes—Mount St. Helens—erupted in 1980. People over 1,000 miles (1,609 km) away, in Denver, had to scrape volcanic ash from the eruption off of their cars.

LINKS TO SCIENCE

The Next Hawaiian Island Loihi, off the southern tip of Hawaii, is the world's most active volcano. But no one has seen it erupt. Its peak is 3,000 feet (914 m) below the ocean's surface. Years of continuous eruption have produced layer after layer of molten lava. Scientists predict that in 100,000 years Loihi will rise above the surface of the ocean and become the next Hawaiian Island.

Far to the north, snow and ice cover Alaska's many mountains. **Glaciers,** huge, slow-moving sheets of ice, fill many of the valleys between these mountains. Most of Alaska's people live along the warmer southern coast.

Special Features of Canada Canada, too, has a number of unique features. East of Alaska lies the Yukon (YOO kahn) Territory of Canada. Mount Logan, Canada's highest peak, is here. It is part of the Coast Mountains, which stretch south along the Pacific almost to the United States border.

Further east, beyond the Interior Plains, lies the Canadian Shield. This huge region of ancient rock covers about half of Canada. The land on the shield is rugged. As a result, few people live here.

Southeast of the shield are the St. Lawrence Lowlands. Located along the St. Lawrence River, these lowlands are Canada's smallest land region. However, they are home to more than half of the country's population. The region is also Canada's manufacturing center. And because the lowlands have fertile soil, farmers in this region produce about one third of the country's crops.

Major Bodies of Water

Both the United States and Canada have important lakes and rivers. People use these bodies of water for transportation, recreation, and industry. Many American and Canadian cities developed near these bodies of water. As you read, find these water bodies on the physical map in the Activity Atlas.

Explosion of Life Burgess Shale is a layer of rock in the Rocky Mountains in British Columbia. About 515 million years ago, mudslides swept up tiny forms of animal life. They were instantly buried. Over centuries, the mud hardened to rock. In 1909, geologist Charles D. Walcott discovered more than 60,000 different kinds of fossils in the shale. Scientists think these fossils come from the time of the greatest explosion of life ever on the Earth.

▶ French Canadians own this farmland in Canada's fertile St. Lawrence Lowlands. Unlike English Canadian farmers, who favor square fields, French Canadians prefer farming long strips of land.

A Ship on the St. Lawrence Seaway

This picture shows a ship passing through the Welland Canal on the St. Lawrence Seaway. The canal, which connects lakes Erie and Ontario, is 27.6 miles (44.4 km) long. **Critical Thinking** Why do you think that people sometimes call the St. Lawrence Seaway "Canada's highway to the sea"?

The Great Lakes Lakes Superior, Michigan, Huron, Erie, and Ontario make up the Great Lakes, the world's largest group of freshwater lakes. Of the five, only Lake Michigan lies entirely in the United States. The other four lakes are part of the border between the United States and Canada.

During an ice age long ago, glaciers formed the Great Lakes. As the glaciers moved, they dug deep trenches in the land. Water from the melting glaciers filled these trenches to produce the Great Lakes and many other lakes. Today, the Great Lakes are important waterways in both the United States and Canada. Shipping on the Great Lakes helped industry to develop in the two countries.

Mighty Rivers Canada has two major rivers. The Mackenzie River, the country's longest, forms in the Rockies and flows north into the Arctic Ocean. The St. Lawrence River connects the Great Lakes to the Atlantic Ocean. A system of locks and canals enables large ships to navigate the river. As a result, the St. Lawrence is one of North America's most important transportation routes.

In Canada, the St. Lawrence is called the "Mother of Canada." In the United States, America's largest river has an equally grand title.

READ ACTIVELY

Visualize Picture the Great Lakes region during the Ice Age. How is the scene different today?

The Mississippi Delta

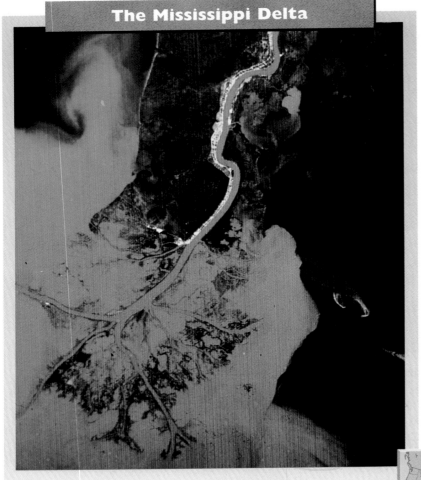

As the Mississippi River flows into the Gulf of Mexico, it dumps silt, forming a huge triangular plain called a delta. This satellite image shows the shape of the delta. The waters of the Mississippi are shown as light blue, the land is shown in shades of black.

Native Americans call the Mississippi River the "Father of Waters." It has its headwaters, or starting point, in Minnesota. From here, the river flows through the Central Plains to the Gulf of Mexico. Two other major rivers, the Ohio and the Missouri, are tributaries of the Mississippi. A **tributary** (TRIB yoo ter ee) is a stream that flows into a larger river.

Look again at the physical map in the Activity Atlas and find the Rocky Mountains. Notice that the Fraser, Columbia, and Colorado rivers form in the Rockies and flow west. Now find the Platte and Missouri rivers. They flow east from the Rockies. This is because the Rockies form the **Continental Divide,** the boundary that separates rivers flowing toward opposite sides of the continent.

SECTION 1 REVIEW

1. **Define** (a) glacier, (b) tributary, (c) Continental Divide.

2. **Identify** (a) Rocky Mountains, (b) Appalachian Mountains, (c) Death Valley, (d) Great Lakes, (e) St. Lawrence River, (f) Mississippi River.

3. (a) Which lakes lie on the border between the United States and Canada? (b) Why are these bodies of water important?

4. Give two examples of ways in which physical features have affected life in the United States and Canada.

Critical Thinking

5. **Drawing Conclusions** Hundreds of years ago, many people coming to the United States and Canada settled along coastal plains and rivers. Why do you think these areas attracted settlers?

Activity

6. **Writing to Learn** Suppose that you are planning a vacation. If you had your choice, what physical features of the United States and Canada would you like to see? Write a paragraph describing the places you would like to visit and why.

Climate and Vegetation

Reach Into Your Background

Would you like to go snow skiing in summer? Or how about taking a dip in an open-air pool at the height of winter? The climates of the United States and Canada are so varied that you can do these things!

Questions to Explore

1. What kinds of climates and vegetation do the United States and Canada have?

2. How do climate and vegetation affect where and how the people of the United States and Canada live?

Key Terms

rain shadow
tropics
tundra
permafrost
prairie
province

Key Places

Vancouver
Winnipeg

On a hot and sunny February morning, a reporter left his home in Miami Beach, Florida, and headed for the airport. Wearing lightweight trousers and a short-sleeved shirt, he boarded a plane to snowy Toronto. Was he forgetting something? Surely he knew that the temperature would be below freezing in Toronto.

He did, indeed, know all about the bitter cold that would greet him when he got off the plane. But he was going to research an article on Toronto's tunnels and underground malls. He wanted to find out whether people could really visit hotels, restaurants, and shops without having to go outside and brave the harsh Canadian winter.

Climate Zones

As the reporter well knew, Toronto and Miami Beach have very different climates. Climate zones in the United States and Canada range from the polar climate of the northern reaches of Canada to the desert climate of the southwestern United States. What accounts for this great variety in climates? The size of the region, first of all. Also, such factors as latitude, mountains, and oceans affect the kinds of climates found in the region.

▼ Whatever the weather outside, it is always pleasant in climate-controlled Eaton Center, a shopping mall in Toronto, Ontario.

Predict How do you think the ocean affects Canada's climate?

▼ In Canada's humid continental climate zone, moist air and hot summer temperatures can combine to produce heavy rainstorms. People in Winnipeg (below) shelter under the first thing to hand—garbage bags. In winter, temperatures can be so cold that rivers and canals freeze. People in Ottawa, Ontario (below right), skate on a frozen canal.

Canada's Climates—Braving the Cold Generally, the farther a location is from the Equator, the colder its climate. Look at the climate regions map in the Activity Atlas at the front of your textbook. Notice that much of Canada lies well to the north of the 40° line of latitude, a long way from the Equator. Therefore, much of Canada is very cold!

The ocean affects Canada's climates, too. Water heats up and cools down more slowly than land. Winds blowing across water tend to warm the land in winter and cool the land in summer. Therefore, areas that are near an ocean generally have fairly mild climates year round. Also, winds blowing across the ocean pick up moisture. When these winds blow over land, they drop the moisture in the form of rain or snow.

The climate regions map shows how oceans influence climate. Notice that much of the northwestern coast of Canada has a marine west coast climate. The waters of the Pacific Ocean help make the climate mild all year. And moisture-carrying winds blowing from the Pacific make the northwestern coast rainy, especially during winter. If you are planning a vacation in the west coast city of Vancouver, take an umbrella and a raincoat. It rains year round.

Being a great distance from the ocean also affects climate. Inland areas often have climate extremes. Find Winnipeg, in Canada's Interior Plains, on the map. Winter temperatures here are very cold, averaging around 0°F (–18°C). Yet summer temperatures run between 70°F and 90°F (20°C and 32°C).

One final factor—mountains—influences climate, especially rainfall. Winds blowing from the Pacific Ocean rise as they meet the various mountain ranges in the west. As they rise, they cool and drop their moisture. The air is dry by the time it reaches the other side of the

mountains. The area on the side of the mountains away from the wind is in a rain shadow. A **rain shadow** is an area on the dry, sheltered side of a mountain that receives little rainfall.

Climates of the United States   Latitude also influences climate in the United States. On the climate map in the Activity Atlas, you will see that Alaska lies north of the 60°N line of latitude. Far from the Equator, Alaska is cold for a good part of the year. Now find the southern tip of Florida and Hawaii. They lie near or within the **tropics,** the area between the $23\frac{1}{2}$°N and $23\frac{1}{2}$°S lines of latitude. Here, it is almost always hot.

The Pacific Ocean and mountains affect climate in the western United States. Wet winds from the ocean drop their moisture before they cross the mountains. As a result, the eastern sections of California, Nevada, and Arizona are semiarid or desert. Death Valley, which is located here, has the lowest average rainfall in the country—about 2 inches (5 cm) a year.

East of the Great Plains, the country has continental climates. In the north, summers are warm and winters are cold and snowy. In the south, summers tend to be long and hot, while winters are mild. The coastal regions of these areas sometimes experience violent weather. In

Predict How do you think the mountains affect climate in the western United States?

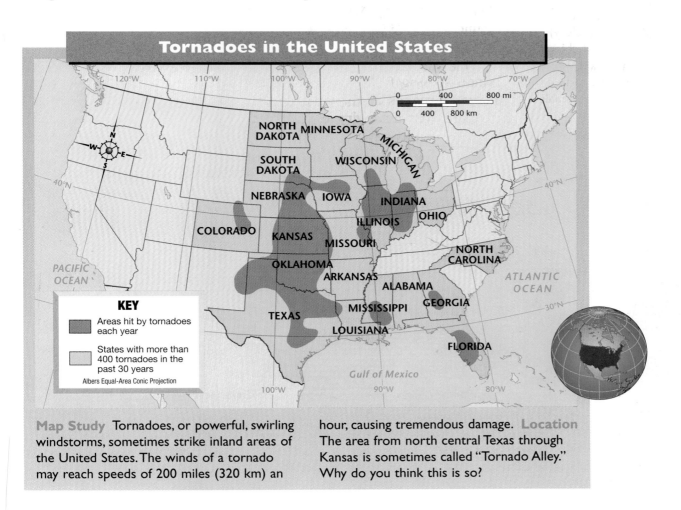

Tornadoes in the United States

KEY

Areas hit by tornadoes each year

States with more than 400 tornadoes in the past 30 years

Albers Equal-Area Conic Projection

Map Study Tornadoes, or powerful, swirling windstorms, sometimes strike inland areas of the United States. The winds of a tornado may reach speeds of 200 miles (320 km) an hour, causing tremendous damage. **Location** The area from north central Texas through Kansas is sometimes called "Tornado Alley." Why do you think this is so?

summer and fall, hurricanes and tropical storms develop in the Atlantic Ocean. These storms sometimes hit the coasts of the southeastern and eastern United States. Bringing winds of more than 75 miles (121 km) per hour, the storms can do incredible damage.

Natural Vegetation Zones

Climate in the United States and Canada helps produce four major kinds of natural vegetation or plant life. As you can see on the map below, these are tundra, grassland, desert scrub, and forest.

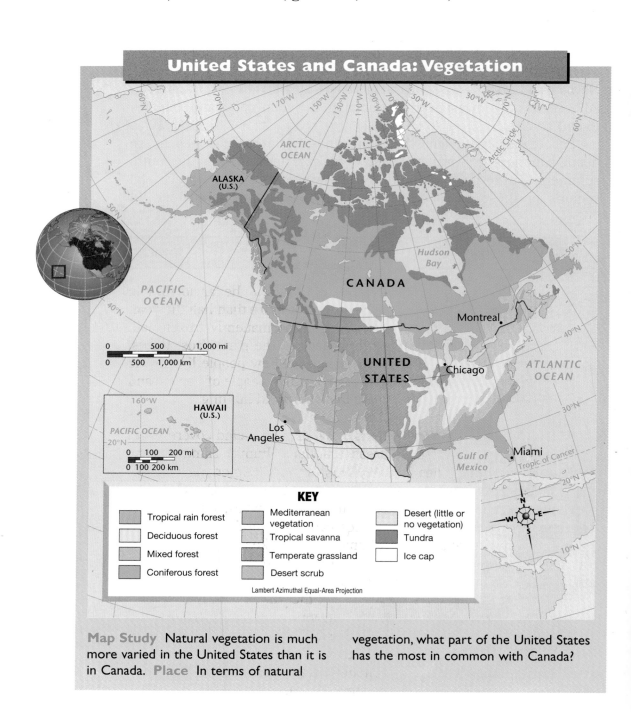

United States and Canada: Vegetation

KEY

- Tropical rain forest
- Deciduous forest
- Mixed forest
- Coniferous forest
- Mediterranean vegetation
- Tropical savanna
- Temperate grassland
- Desert scrub
- Desert (little or no vegetation)
- Tundra
- Ice cap

Lambert Azimuthal Equal-Area Projection

Map Study Natural vegetation is much more varied in the United States than it is in Canada. **Place** In terms of natural vegetation, what part of the United States has the most in common with Canada?

Cattle Raising in the West

Many people in the plains and other lowland areas of western North America make a living by raising cattle. These cowhands in California are rounding up cattle and bringing them into a fenced area. **Critical Thinking** Why do you think that areas of flat or rolling land are better for raising cattle than mountainous areas?

Northern Tundras The **tundra** is found in the far north. It is a cold, dry region that is covered with snow for more than half the year. The Arctic tundra contains **permafrost,** or permanently frozen soil. During the short, cool summer, the surface of the permafrost thaws. Mosses, grasses, and bright wildflowers grow. Few people live in the tundra. However, some Inuits (IN oo wits), a native people of Canada and Alaska, live here. They make a living by fishing and hunting.

Prairies Prairies are regions of flat or rolling land covered with grasses. They are located in areas that have humid climates. The world's largest prairie lies in the plains of North America. It covers much of the American central states and stretches into the Canadian provinces of Alberta, Saskatchewan (suh SKACH uh wun), and Manitoba. These three provinces are sometimes called the Prairie Provinces. A **province** is a political division of Canada, much like our states. Look at the physical map in the Activity Atlas to locate the prairies, or plains areas, of the United States and Canada.

When pioneers first saw the prairies of the Midwest, they described the land as "a sea of grass." Today, farmers grow fields of corn and soybeans here. Further west, the Great Plains receive less rainfall. Therefore, only short grasses will grow. These grasses are ideal for grazing cattle. And the land is suitable for growing wheat. The Prairie Provinces, too, have many wheat farms and cattle ranches.

LINKS
ACROSS TIME

Hundreds of Years of Storms Between 1493 and 1870, 400 hurricanes struck the Gulf of Mexico and Florida. Residents suffered because they did not know that the storms were coming. Things improved when sailing became more common and radios were invented. Sailors, therefore, could warn that storms were coming. Today, high-tech weather satellites provide the warning people on land require.

► The forests of the United States and Canada are ideal places for many kinds of outdoor activities. These people are bird watching in the forests of Quebec (kwih BEK) province, Canada.

Desert Scrub   With little rainfall, desert and semiarid regions have few plants. The Great Basin is a large, very dry region between the Rocky Mountains and the Sierras in the United States. The land cannot support large numbers of people, but many sheep graze on the area's short grasses and shrubs.

Forests   Forests cover nearly one third of the United States and almost one half of Canada. The mild climate of the northern Pacific Coast encourages great forests of coniferous (koh NIF ur us) trees, such as fir and spruce. Coniferous trees have cones that carry and protect their seeds. The Rockies and the Appalachians, too, are blanketed with coniferous forests. From the Great Lakes across southeastern Canada and New England and down to the southeastern United States, you will find forests of coniferous trees mixed with deciduous (dee SIJ oo us) trees. The latter shed their leaves in the fall.

SECTION 2 REVIEW

1. **Define**   (a) rain shadow, (b) tropics, (c) tundra, (d) permafrost, (e) prairie, (f) province.

2. **Identify**   (a) Vancouver, (b) Winnipeg.

3. (a) Describe the climate and vegetation of the American prairie. (b) What are the climate and vegetation of Canada's Pacific Coast?

4. What geographic features might lead someone to settle in Vancouver, rather than in Winnipeg?

Critical Thinking

5. **Making Comparisons** Contrast the climate and vegetation of the tundra with the climate and vegetation of the area around the Great Lakes.

Activity

6. **Writing to Learn**   You are taking a journey from northwestern Canada to the southeastern United States. Describe some of the climate zones you pass through.

Natural Resources

BEFORE YOU READ

Reach Into Your Background

Jot down four or five activities that you do in a typical day— take a shower, eat lunch, ride the bus to school, and so on. As you read this section, think about how natural resources play a part in these activities.

Questions to Explore

1. What are the major resources of the United States and Canada?
2. How do these resources affect the economies of these countries?

Key Terms
alluvial
agribusiness
hydroelectricity

Key Places
Imperial Valley
Grand Coulee Dam
St. Lawrence Lowlands

Surrounded by redwood forests, Carlotta, California, has little more than a gas station and a general store. Yet on one day in September 1996, police arrested more than 1,000 people here. Was Carlotta filled with outlaws like some old Wild West town? No, but it was the scene of a showdown. A logging company wanted to cut down some of the oldest redwood trees in the world. Protesters wanted to preserve the forest and the animals that live there. Both sides believed in the importance of natural resources. But they disagreed strongly about how to use them.

As in Carlotta, people all over North America use their natural resources for recreation, industry, and energy. In this section, you will read about the natural resources of the United States and Canada. You will also learn how people use them.

Natural Resources of the United States

Native Americans, pioneers, and explorers in North America knew it was a land of plenty. Fertile soil, water, forests, and minerals were abundant. These resources helped to build two of the leading economies in the world.

▼ These redwood trees are part of Muir Woods, a national park just northwest of San Francisco, California.

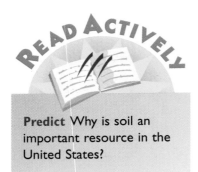

Predict Why is soil an important resource in the United States?

Soil The United States has vast expanses of fertile soil. Two soil types are especially important. The Midwest and the South have rich, dark soils. Along the Mississippi and other river valleys are **alluvial** (uh LOO vee ul) soils. These are deposited by water; they are the fertile topsoil left by rivers after a flood. Areas that have good soil are suitable for farming. Until the 1900s, most American farms were owned by families. Since then, large companies have bought more and more family farms across the country. For example, southern California's Imperial Valley has vast vegetable fields operated by **agribusinesses.** These are large companies that run huge farms.

Water Water is a vital resource all over the United States. People need water to drink. And they need it to grow crops. Factories rely on water for many industrial processes, including cooling moving parts. And both industry and farmers transport goods on rivers. Canada's St. Lawrence and Mackenzie rivers serve as shipping routes. The same is true of the Mississippi, Ohio, and Missouri rivers in the United States.

A Modern Irrigation System

Where rainfall averages less than 10 inches (25 cm) a year, as in the southwestern United States, irrigation supplies the water that crops need to thrive. However, the Southwest's limited supply of river water must be carefully rationed. This photograph shows a high-technology irrigation system watering several fields on a California farm. **Critical Thinking** Look back at the photograph of French-Canadian farmland in Section 1. How do the shapes of fields in that photograph compare with the shapes of fields here?

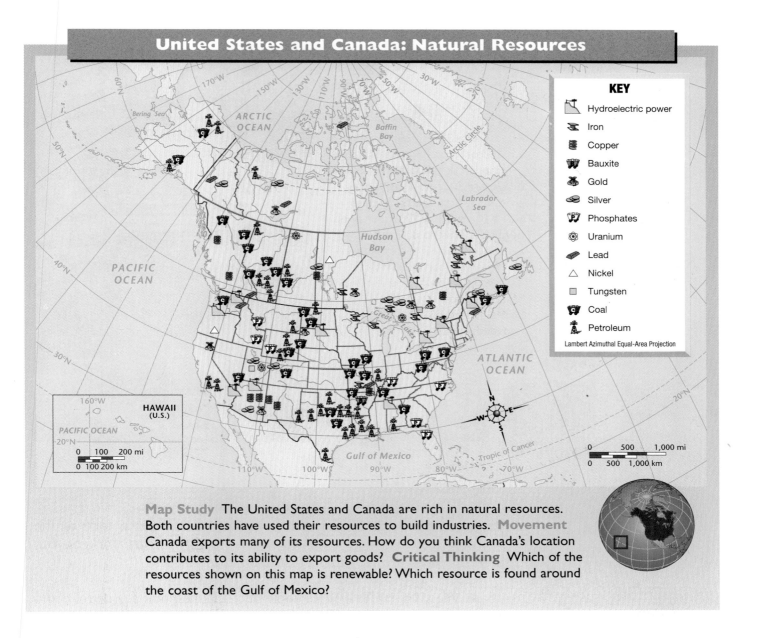

KEY

- Hydroelectric power
- Iron
- Copper
- Bauxite
- Gold
- Silver
- Phosphates
- Uranium
- Lead
- Nickel
- Tungsten
- Coal
- Petroleum

Lambert Azimuthal Equal-Area Projection

Map Study The United States and Canada are rich in natural resources. Both countries have used their resources to build industries. **Movement** Canada exports many of its resources. How do you think Canada's location contributes to its ability to export goods? **Critical Thinking** Which of the resources shown on this map is renewable? Which resource is found around the coast of the Gulf of Mexico?

Water is used for other purposes, too. Dams along many rivers generate **hydroelectricity** (hy dro ee lek TRIS ih tee), or power generated by moving water. The Grand Coulee (KOO lee) Dam on the Columbia River in the state of Washington produces more hydroelectricity than any other dam in the United States.

Abundant Energy and Mineral Resources The United States is the second-largest producer of coal, petroleum, and natural gas in the world. North America's biggest oil reserves are along the northern coast of Alaska. A pipeline carries crude oil south from the wells to the port of Valdez. From here, giant tankers carry the oil to the south to be refined. Abundant energy resources have fueled industrial expansion. They have also helped to provide Americans with one of the world's highest standards of living.

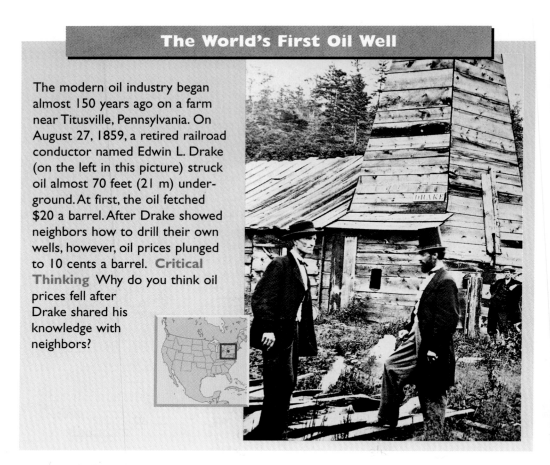

The modern oil industry began almost 150 years ago on a farm near Titusville, Pennsylvania. On August 27, 1859, a retired railroad conductor named Edwin L. Drake (on the left in this picture) struck oil almost 70 feet (21 m) underground. At first, the oil fetched $20 a barrel. After Drake showed neighbors how to drill their own wells, however, oil prices plunged to 10 cents a barrel. **Critical Thinking** Why do you think oil prices fell after Drake shared his knowledge with neighbors?

Predict What resources do the United States and Canada share?

The United States also has valuable deposits of copper, gold, granite, iron ore, and lead. Mining accounts for a small percentage of the country's economy and employs about 1 percent of its workers. But these minerals are very important to other industries.

A Wealth of Trees People once claimed that a squirrel could leap from one tree to another all the way from the Atlantic Coast to the Mississippi River. That is no longer true, but America's forests are still an important resource. In the Pacific Northwest, the South, the Appalachians, and areas around the Great Lakes, forests produce lumber, wood pulp for paper, and fine hardwoods for furniture.

Natural Resources of Canada

Canada's first European settlers earned their living as fur trappers, loggers, fishers, and farmers. Today, the economic picture has changed. Less than 5 percent of Canada's workers earn their living in these ways.

Farmland About 12 percent of Canada's land is suitable for farming. Most is located in the Prairie Provinces. This region produces most of Canada's wheat and beef. The St. Lawrence Lowlands are another major agricultural region. This area produces grains, milk, vegetables, and fruits.

◄ Powerful tugboats tow huge booms of logs harvested from Canada's forests.

Minerals and Energy Resources   The Canadian Shield contains much of Canada's mineral wealth. About 85 percent of the nation's iron ore comes from mines near the Quebec-Newfoundland border. The region also has large deposits of gold, silver, zinc, copper, and uranium. The Prairie Provinces, particularly Alberta, have large oil and natural gas deposits.

Canada harnesses the rivers of Quebec Province to make hydro-electricity. These rivers generate enough hydroelectric power that some can be exported to the northeastern United States.

Forests   With almost half its land covered in forests, Canada is a leading producer of timber products. These products include lumber, paper, plywood, and wood pulp. The major timber-producing provinces include British Columbia, Quebec, and Ontario.

SECTION 3 REVIEW

1. **Define**   (a) alluvial, (b) agribusiness, (c) hydroelectricity.

2. **Identify**   (a) Imperial Valley, (b) Grand Coulee Dam, (c) St. Lawrence Lowlands.

3. Describe the major natural resources in the United States and Canada.

4. Why is water an important resource? Give two examples of how it is used in the United States and Canada.

Critical Thinking

5. **Making Comparisons**   Based on what you know about the physical geography of the two countries, why do you think their resources are similar?

Activity

6. **Writing to Learn**   What do you think is the most important resource in the United States and Canada? Write a paragraph explaining your choice.

Using Distribution Maps

Your weekend adventure includes hiking alone in a deep, dark forest. You carry everything you need—tent, sleeping bag, stove, food, and water—in a backpack. Tree branches creak in the wind, and a hawk calls in the distance. You hear the rustle of a small animal scurrying through the leaves.

You soon realize there are sounds you do not hear—the sounds of people. You do not hear traffic, or the hum of a washing machine, or anyone talking.

Where can you go to have such a wonderful experience? There are many wilderness areas in the United States and Canada. Some are forested, others are desert areas, and still others are in mountain regions. What they all have in common, however, is that few people live there.

You can find these places by looking at a special kind of map called a population distribution map. Such a map will also show you a lot more about people and where they live.

Get Ready

A population distribution map is a map that shows the areas in which people live as well as the areas in which people do not live.

You can use a population distribution map to better understand a country or region you are learning about. But a population distribution map also provides clues to why people live where they do. This information is basic to understanding human life on the Earth.

Try It Out

Knowing how population distribution maps are made will help you understand how to use one. Make a population distribution map of your school. A model of such a map is shown below.

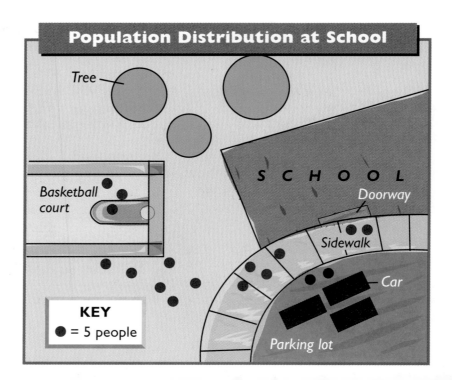

Population Distribution at School

Tree

Basketball court

SCHOOL

Doorway

Sidewalk

Car

KEY
● = 5 people

Parking lot

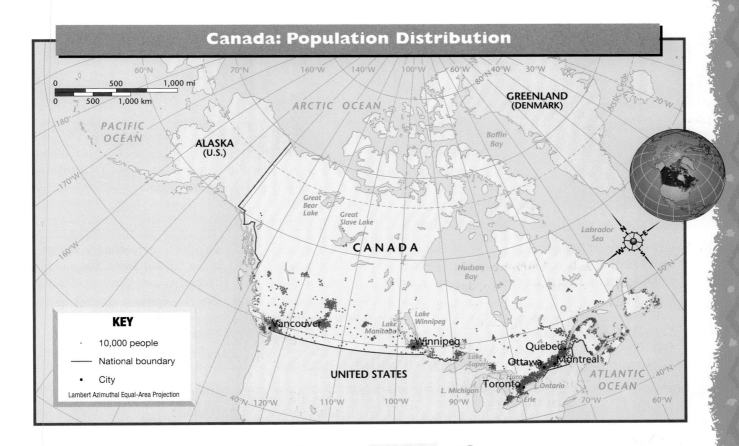

Canada: Population Distribution

KEY
- · 10,000 people
- — National boundary
- • City

Lambert Azimuthal Equal-Area Projection

A. Draw a map of your schoolyard or playground. It does not have to be perfect, but it should show the area around the school, the entrances to the school and the sidewalks leading to the school's doorways, and the school parking lot.

B. Make a key for your map. Have each dot represent five people.

C. Add dots to your map to represent how the population of your school is distributed. Choose a specific time of day, such as 11:00 A.M. Place the dots in the places where people are at 11:00 A.M. on an average day. Remember to draw the right number of dots to show how many people are in the area around the school.

D. Give your map a title. Now study your population distribution map. Your map answers the same two questions that any population distribution map answers: Where are the people? How many people are in each place? Your map also provides clues about another question: Why is the population distributed in the way that it is?

Apply the Skill

Now you know how population distribution maps are made and what questions they answer. Try looking at one that shows a whole country. Use the map to follow the steps below.

① **Familiarize yourself with the map.** Look it over to get a sense of what it is about. What country is shown? How is population represented? How many people does each dot stand for?

② **Answer the "where" and "how many" questions that population distribution maps address.**
- Where do the people of Canada live?
- Where do *most* of the people live?

③ **Answer the "why" question that this population distribution map addresses.** Write a paragraph to answer this question.
- Why do you think the population of Canada is distributed the way it is? Consider geographic reasons such as climate and landforms.

Review and Activities

Reviewing Main Ideas

1. List two major geographic features of the United States and Canada and describe their importance.

2. Why do relatively few people live in the deserts of the United States or in the Canadian Shield region in Canada?

3. How does the climate in the Great Basin affect the area's vegetation?

4. (a) What is Canada's smallest land region? (b) Why do most Canadians live there?

5. Of which three energy sources is the United States the world's second-largest producer?

6. Which natural resources help support the economy of Canada's Prairie Provinces?

Reviewing Key Terms

Match the definitions in Column I with the key terms in Column II.

Column I

1. an area on the dry, sheltered side of a mountain that receives little rainfall
2. a region of flat or hilly land covered with tall grasses
3. a large mass of ice that flows slowly over land
4. relating to soil deposited by a river or stream
5. a river that flows into a larger river
6. a cold, dry region that is covered with snow for more than half the year

Column II

a. tributary

b. glacier

c. rain shadow

d. tundra

e. prairie

f. alluvial

Critical Thinking

1. **Drawing Conclusions** If you were going to build a new city in the United States or Canada, where would you locate it? What geographic features would influence your decision?

2. **Recognizing Cause and Effect** How does climate affect the growth of vegetation in the United States and Canada? Give two examples.

Graphic Organizer

Copy this web on a sheet of paper and complete it. You may choose any region in the United States or Canada.

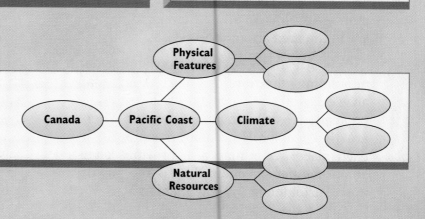

Map Activity

United States and Canada

For each place listed below, write the letter from the map that shows its location. Use the maps in the Activity Atlas to help you.

1. Canadian Shield
2. Great Basin
3. Great Plains
4. Rocky Mountains
5. Appalachian Mountains
6. Pacific Ocean
7. Atlantic Ocean
8. Great Lakes

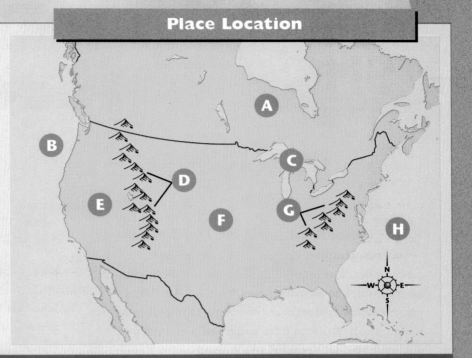

Place Location

Writing Activity

Write a Poem

Write a poem describing some aspect of the geography of the region where you live. Choose from landforms, bodies of water, climate, vegetation, or other natural resources.

Internet Activity

Use a search engine to find **Natural Resources Research Information Pages.** Click on **Canada.** Choose **Natural Resources Canada** and then click on **For Kids Only.** Create your own natural resources interactive map. Click on **United States** then choose **State Level.** Research a natural resources program in your state.

Skills Review

Turn to the Skills Activity.

Review the parts of a population distribution map. Then list the three questions a distribution map answers.

How Am I Doing?

Answer these questions to help you check your progress.

1. Can I describe the main physical features of the United States and Canada?

2. Do I understand how geography and climate affect the way people live in the United States and Canada?

3. Can I identify some of the natural resources of the United States and Canada?

4. What information from this chapter can I use in my book project?

Making a Model River

Charles Kuralt, a famous traveler and journalist, knows how important rivers are. "I started out thinking of America as highways and state lines," he wrote. "As I got to know it better, I began to think of it as rivers. . . . It wouldn't be much of a country without the rivers, and the people who have figured out a way to make a living beside them. . . . America is a great story, and there is a river on every page of it."

People of both the United States and Canada have long depended on their rivers. Native Americans and immigrants alike built their villages and towns on the banks of rivers, where they could fish and hunt and water their crops. These natural highways have carried boats through rugged land from the earliest times. Recently, they have become sources of hydroelectric power. Even today, most major cities stand on riverbanks.

Purpose

Rivers have an important place in both the geography and history of the United States and Canada. This activity will help you understand the growth and behavior of rivers.

Materials

- a plastic or flexible 12-by-9-inch aluminum tray with sides at least 4 inches high
- sand
- scissors
- a bucket or pan
- a pitcher of water
- a ruler
- duct tape
- a plastic or rubber hose about 3 feet long
- a brick or square object
- a funnel small enough to fit inside the hose

◄ The Chenoga River meanders through eastern New York state.

Procedure

STEP ONE

Predict how your river will flow. You will make the model river in a box of sand. What do you think it will look like? Will it flow in a straight line, or will it wind back and forth? Will the channel of the river be shallow or deep? Will the channel be the same along the whole length of the river, or will it change? Draw a sketch of how you think your river will look.

STEP TWO

Construct a river box. First, fill the tray with sand, leaving 1 inch at the top of the tray. Then use the scissors to cut a 1-inch V-shaped notch into the center of one end of the tray. This notch will allow the "river" water to drain away. Arrange the tray so that the water will drain into a pan or a bucket.

STEP THREE

Create a landscape for the river's flow. With a pitcher of water, wet the sand evenly until it is damp and packed, but not soupy. With the scissors, poke a small hole below the notch to drain excess water from the sand. Drag the ruler across the sand to make it level. Use duct tape to secure the hose at the end of the tray opposite the notch. Prop the tray up on the brick so that the landscape slopes toward the notch.

STEP FOUR

Let the river run! Put the funnel into the end of the hose. Use the pitcher to slowly pour a stream of water into the funnel. The water will start to make a river in the landscape. Then watch. You'll see a river form before your very eyes!

Observations

1. How did the shape and size of your river compare with the way you predicted it would look in Step One?

2. What happened to the sand in the river's channel?

3. Sediment is material picked up, carried, and deposited by a river. Describe the shape made in the sand as your river deposited its sediment near the drainage notch.

ANALYSIS AND CONCLUSION

1. What factors influenced the form your river took?

2. Increase the flow of water in your river. How does this affect the size and shape of your river?

3. Explain why knowledge of how rivers behave is important to each of the following groups of people: city planners, farmers, people who live near rivers, and boaters.

THE UNITED STATES AND CANADA
Shaped by History

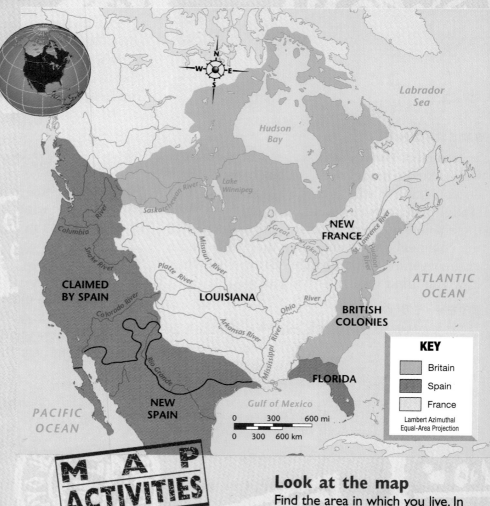

Labrador Sea

Hudson Bay

Lake Winnipeg

Saskatchewan River

Columbia River

Snake River

Great Lakes

NEW FRANCE

St. Lawrence River

Hudson River

ATLANTIC OCEAN

Platte River

Missouri River

CLAIMED BY SPAIN

LOUISIANA

Ohio River

BRITISH COLONIES

Colorado River

Arkansas River

Mississippi River

FLORIDA

Rio Grande

PACIFIC OCEAN

NEW SPAIN

Gulf of Mexico

0   300   600 mi
0   300   600 km

KEY
Britain
Spain
France
Lambert Azimuthal Equal-Area Projection

MAP ACTIVITIES

As you can see, three different European countries influenced North America in the 1700s. To help you identify which country influenced which areas, do the following activities.

Look at the map
Find the area in which you live. In 1753, what country controlled that area?

Compare and contrast
Which European country held the largest territory? Which European country had the territory farthest north?

The First Americans and the Arrival of the Europeans

BEFORE YOU READ

Reach Into Your Background

Suppose you go on a world trip. You land on an isolated island and meet the inhabitants. How do you react? Are you suspicious and frightened because the inhabitants' culture and yours are so different? Or are you excited and eager to learn from them and teach them about your culture?

Questions to Explore

1. Who were the first Americans?
2. What effect did the arrival of Europeans have on Native Americans?
3. How did the United States win its independence from Great Britain?

Key Terms

indigenous
missionary
indentured servant
plantation
boycott
Revolutionary War

Key People and Places

Christopher Columbus
William Penn
Thomas Jefferson
George Washington
Jamestown
Pennsylvania Colony

Perhaps as early as 30,000 years ago, small family groups of hunters and food gatherers reached North America from Asia. This migration took place during the last ice age. At that time, so much water froze into thick ice sheets that the sea level dropped. As a result, a land bridge was exposed between Siberia and Alaska. Hunters followed herds of bison and mammoths across this land bridge. Other migrating people may have paddled small boats and fished along the coasts.

Over time, the first Americans spread throughout North and South America. They developed different ways of life to suit the environment of the places where they settled.

▼ These bone tools were found near the area where scientists think a land bridge once connected Asia and North America.

A Southwestern Pueblo

Some Native American groups in the Southwest—the modern-day states of New Mexico, Arizona, Utah, and Colorado—used very distinctive building styles. Around A.D. 700, they began building their villages into the sides of steep cliffs or on top of flat-topped hills called mesas. These villages, or pueblos, were a lot like our high-rise apartment buildings. As many as 1,200 people might live in one village. Below is a diagram of a room in a pueblo.

The thick (4–6 in, or 10–15 cm) walls were made of adobe, a clay mixture. It was poured into special molds to make bricks, which dried in the sun. After a wall was built, it was coated with a layer of adobe similar to paint.

Pueblos were also designed for defense. In case of an attack, someone could pull away the ladder from the rooftop "door." This made it hard for intruders to enter the house.

In one corner of the room were the *metates*, specially shaped stones for grinding corn for cooking.

Who Were the First Americans?

Louise Erdrich is an American writer. She is also part Native American. In her novel *The Crown of Columbus,* she describes the variety of Native American cultures before the Europeans arrived:

> "[T]hey] had hundreds of societies, millions of people, whose experience had told them that the world was a pretty diverse place. Walk for a day in any direction and what do you find: A tribe with a whole new set of gods, a language as distinct from your own as Tibetan is from Dutch—very little, in fact, that's even slightly familiar."

The Europeans Arrive

Some scientists think that Native Americans migrated from Asia. But many Native Americans disagree. They believe they are **indigenous** (in DIJ uh nus) people. That means they originated in this place. One thing is clear, however. Native Americans' ways of life began to change after 1492. That year, Christopher Columbus, a sea captain sailing from Spain, explored islands in the Caribbean Sea. Later, Europeans changed North America forever.

Spanish and French Claims to the Americas Spanish settlers spread out across the Americas. Some went to today's southwestern United States and Mexico. Others went to Florida and the Caribbean islands. Still others went to South America. These colonists often enslaved Native Americans. The colonists forced Native Americans to work in mines or on farms. Working conditions were so harsh that thousands died. Spanish missionaries tried to make Native Americans more like Europeans, often by force. **Missionaries** are religious people who want to convert others to their religion.

Spain gained great wealth from her American colonies. Seeing this, other countries soon also wanted colonies in the Americas. French explorers claimed land along the St. Lawrence and Mississippi rivers. Unlike the Spanish, the French were more interested in furs than gold. French traders and missionaries often lived among the Native Americans and learned their ways. The French did not take over Native American land.

The English Colonists Grow Powerful
English settlers established 13 colonies along the Atlantic Coast. These settlers came to start a new life. Some wanted to be free from debt. Others wanted to own land. Still others wanted to practice their religions in their own ways. Some came as **indentured servants,** or people who had to work for a period of years to gain freedom.

LINKS TO SCIENCE

Migrating Plants When Columbus returned from the Americas to Spain, he brought gold. But he carried something else that may have been even more valuable—corn. In the next hundred years, European travelers brought back beans, squash, potatoes, peppers, and tomatoes. These foods changed European diets forever.

▼ Explorers used compasses like this one, which dates from 1580, to help them find their way to the Americas.

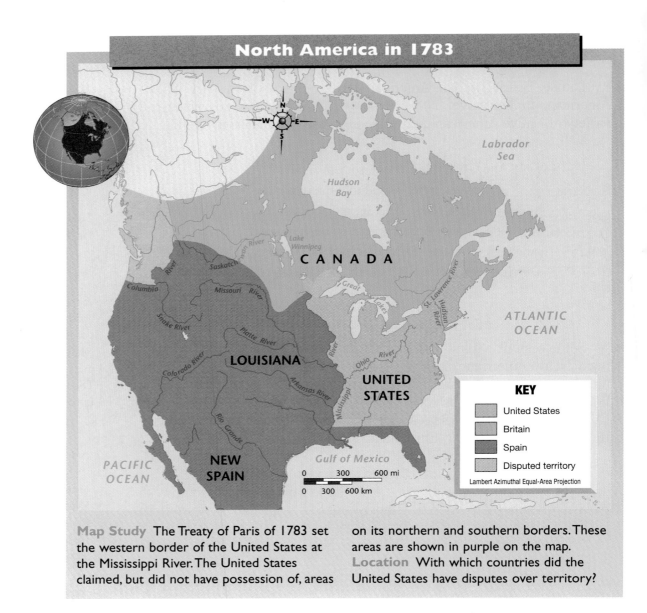

North America in 1783

Labrador Sea

Hudson Bay

Lake Winnipeg

CANADA

Saskatchewan River

Columbia River

Missouri River

Snake River

Platte River

Great Lakes

St. Lawrence River

Hudson River

ATLANTIC OCEAN

LOUISIANA

Colorado River

Arkansas River

Ohio River

Mississippi

UNITED STATES

Rio Grande

PACIFIC OCEAN

NEW SPAIN

Gulf of Mexico

KEY

United States

Britain

Spain

Disputed territory

Lambert Azimuthal Equal-Area Projection

0   300   600 mi
0   300   600 km

Map Study The Treaty of Paris of 1783 set the western border of the United States at the Mississippi River. The United States claimed, but did not have possession of, areas on its northern and southern borders. These areas are shown in purple on the map. **Location** With which countries did the United States have disputes over territory?

The first permanent English settlement was Jamestown, Virginia, founded in 1607. By 1619, it had the beginnings of self-government. In the same year, the first Africans arrived here as indentured servants. Later, about 1640, Africans were brought as slaves. Many were forced to work on the **plantations.** These were large farms in the South.

In 1620, the Pilgrims arrived in Massachusetts from England. They wanted to worship God in their own way and to govern themselves. They named their settlement Plymouth. About 60 years later, William Penn founded the Pennsylvania Colony. He wanted a place where all people, regardless of race or religion, were treated fairly. Penn was unusual because he paid Native Americans for their land. Before Penn—and after—most settlers took land, then fought Native Americans to control it.

In 1754, Britain and France went to war over land in North America. Americans call this war the French and Indian War. (At this time, Native

READ ACTIVELY

Visualize Visualize a meeting between William Penn and Native American groups. What issues do you think were discussed?

Americans were called "Indians," because early European explorers thought that they had found India.) With the colonists' help, the British were victorious.

The Break With Britain

The war with France had been very expensive. And, despite the victory over France, the British felt they needed an army in North America to protect the colonists. The British thought the colonists should help pay for the war and for their defense. Therefore, the British put taxes on many goods the colonists bought from Britain. No one represented the colonists in the British Parliament. The colonists demanded, "no taxation without representation." They also boycotted, or refused to buy, British goods.

Patriots such as Samuel Adams, Thomas Paine, and Patrick Henry encouraged colonists to rebel against British rule. The Revolutionary War began in 1775. In July 1776, representatives from each colony voted for independence. Thomas Jefferson wrote the official Declaration of Independence. His powerful words *liberty, equality,* and *justice* inspired many colonists to fight. George Washington led the American forces to victory in 1781. The Treaty of Paris, signed in 1783, made American independence official.

After the war, the 13 new states agreed to work together. But they had no strong central government. To form one, leaders from each state except Rhode Island met in Philadelphia in 1787 and wrote the Constitution. It set up the framework of our federal government. The Constitution was approved in 1789. It is still the highest law of the United States.

▲ Great Britain imposed several different kinds of taxes on the colonies. Many colonists especially hated the tax which required them to buy stamps, like this one, for legal documents and almost every other type of printed matter.

SECTION 1 REVIEW

1. **Define** (a) indigenous, (b) missionary, (c) indentured servant, (d) plantation, (e) boycott, (f) Revolutionary War.

2. **Identify** (a) Christopher Columbus, (b) William Penn, (c) Thomas Jefferson, (d) George Washington, (e) Jamestown, (f) Pennsylvania Colony.

3. Where do many scholars think the first Americans came from?

4. What was a major conflict between Native Americans and the European colonists?

Critical Thinking

5. **Recognizing Cause and Effect** Why did the colonists object to the taxes placed on them by the British?

Activity

6. **Writing to Learn** How were Native Americans involved with the people who arrived from Europe? Do some research about one Native American group. Write a report telling what happened as its people met the Europeans.

Growth, Settlement, and Civil War in the United States

BEFORE YOU READ

Reach Into Your Background

Have you ever gone camping? As you lay in your sleeping bag surrounded by trees and stars, what thoughts did you have about the wilderness? Did you think of keeping it just the way it was, or did you picture it as it might look if people lived there?

Questions to Explore

1. What were the effects of westward movement in the United States?
2. What were the causes and effects of the United States Civil War?

Key Terms

Louisiana Purchase
Manifest Destiny
immigrant
Industrial Revolution
abolitionist
Civil War
Reconstruction
segregate

Key People

Meriwether Lewis
William Clark
Thomas Jefferson
Andrew Jackson
Harriet Beecher Stowe
Abraham Lincoln
Andrew Johnson

▼ It took Meriwether Lewis (left) and William Clark (right) three years to complete their exploration of the lands west of the Mississippi River.

In 1803, President Thomas Jefferson sent Meriwether Lewis and William Clark to explore land west of the Mississippi River. They traveled all the way to the Pacific Coast. As they journeyed up the Missouri River, Lewis and Clark found plants and animals completely new to them. They also created accurate, highly valuable maps of the region. Much of the information was new. Lewis and Clark also met Native American groups along the way. During these meetings, the two men tried to learn about the region and set up trading alliances. Few of those Native Americans had any idea how the visit would change their way of life.

A Growing Nation

In 1803, President Jefferson had a great piece of luck. France offered to sell to the United States all the land between the Mississippi River and the eastern slopes of the Rocky Mountains—for only $15 million. This sale of land, called the **Louisiana Purchase**, doubled the size of the United States.

Before this new land could be settled, the United States faced another challenge from Great Britain. The War of 1812 lasted two years. Again, the United States was victorious.

The Nation Prospers

Peace and prosperity followed the War of 1812. As the country grew, so did the meaning of democracy. In the 13 original states, only white males who owned property could vote. New states passed laws giving the vote to all white men 21 years old or older, whether they owned property or not. Soon, all states gave every adult white male the right to vote. Women and African Americans, however, could not vote.

In 1828, voters elected Andrew Jackson as President. He looked after the interests of poor farmers, laborers, and settlers who wanted Native American lands in the Southeast. In 1830, President Jackson persuaded Congress to pass the Indian Removal Act. It required the

▲ In the 1820s, a Cherokee leader named Sequoyah developed a system of writing that enabled his people to read and write in their own language.

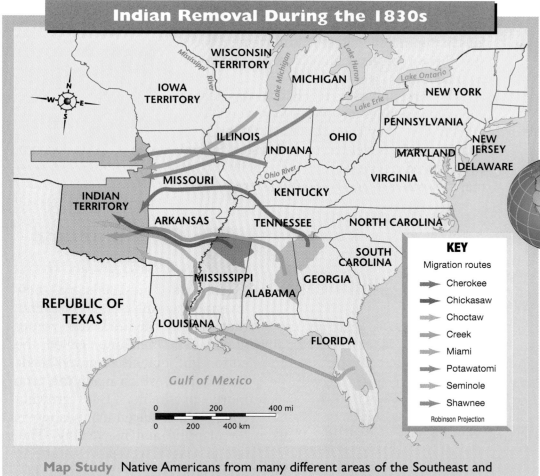

Indian Removal During the 1830s

KEY
Migration routes
→ Cherokee
→ Chickasaw
→ Choctaw
→ Creek
→ Miami
→ Potawatomi
→ Seminole
→ Shawnee
Robinson Projection

Map Study Native Americans from many different areas of the Southeast and Midwest were forced to leave their lands. **Movement** Which Native Americans crossed the Gulf of Mexico on their journey west?

Cherokee and other Native Americans in the area to leave their homelands. They were sent to live on new land in Oklahoma. So many Cherokee died on the journey that the route they followed is known as the Trail of Tears.

More Room to Grow The United States continued to gain land. In 1836, American settlers in the Mexican territory of Texas rebelled against Mexican rule. The Texans then set up the Lone Star Republic. In 1845, Texas became part of the United States. Only a year later, the United States went to war with Mexico. The U.S. won the war and gained from Mexico much of what is now the Southwest region.

Many Americans believed that it was the United States' Manifest Destiny to "own" all the land from the Atlantic to the Pacific. By this they meant the United States had a right to it. They also meant that it was America's fate to rule it. In the 1840s, American wagon trains began to cross the continent heading for the West.

The Industrial Revolution At the same time, thousands of people were pouring into cities in the Northeast. Some had left farms to work in factories. Others were immigrants, or people who move from one country to another. These people came from Europe in search of jobs in the United States. This movement was spurred by the Industrial Revolution, or the change from making goods by hand to making them by machine.

The first industry to change was clothmaking, or textiles. New spinning machines and power looms enabled people to make cloth more quickly than they could by hand. Other inventions, such as the steam engine, made travel easier and faster. Steamboats and steam locomotives moved people and goods rapidly. By 1860, railroads linked most major Northeastern and Southeastern cities.

READ ACTIVELY

Predict How did the cotton gin and new lands affect slavery in the United States?

▼ Settlers heading west moved their belongings in covered wagons like this one. Some people called the wagon a *prairie schooner* because, from a distance, its white canvas cover looked like a ship's sail.

The Civil War and Reconstruction

In the mid-1800s, a new invention set off a chain of events that deeply divided the young nation. The machine, called the cotton gin, quickly removed seeds from cotton, which made the crop more profitable. But growing cotton still required many laborers for planting and harvesting. This is one reason why slaves were an important part of plantation life. Cotton wore out the soil, though. Plantation owners wanted to expand into new western lands. But that meant that slavery would spread into the new territories. Some people did not want this. The debate began. Should the states or the federal government decide about slavery in the new territories?

Causes of Conflict   Until 1850, there were equal numbers of slave and free states in the United States. Then California asked to be admitted to the union as a free state. After a heated debate, Congress granted the request. The Southern states were not pleased. To gain their support, Congress also passed the Fugitive Slave Act. It said people anywhere in the country must return runaway slaves to their owners. This action only increased the argument over slavery. In 1852, Harriet Beecher Stowe published *Uncle Tom's Cabin,* a novel about the evils of slavery.

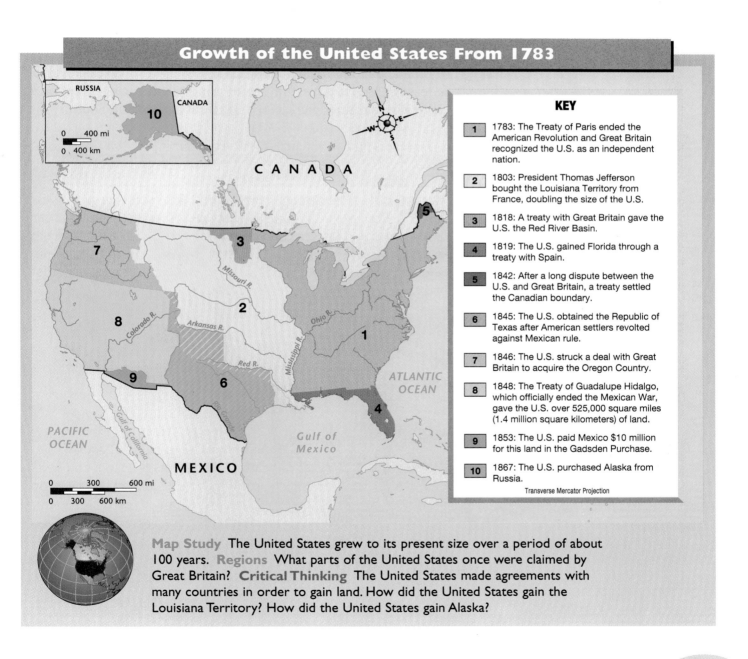

Growth of the United States From 1783

KEY

1 1783: The Treaty of Paris ended the American Revolution and Great Britain recognized the U.S. as an independent nation.

2 1803: President Thomas Jefferson bought the Louisiana Territory from France, doubling the size of the U.S.

3 1818: A treaty with Great Britain gave the U.S. the Red River Basin.

4 1819: The U.S. gained Florida through a treaty with Spain.

5 1842: After a long dispute between the U.S. and Great Britain, a treaty settled the Canadian boundary.

6 1845: The U.S. obtained the Republic of Texas after American settlers revolted against Mexican rule.

7 1846: The U.S. struck a deal with Great Britain to acquire the Oregon Country.

8 1848: The Treaty of Guadalupe Hidalgo, which officially ended the Mexican War, gave the U.S. over 525,000 square miles (1.4 million square kilometers) of land.

9 1853: The U.S. paid Mexico $10 million for this land in the Gadsden Purchase.

10 1867: The U.S. purchased Alaska from Russia.

Transverse Mercator Projection

Map Study The United States grew to its present size over a period of about 100 years. **Regions** What parts of the United States once were claimed by Great Britain? **Critical Thinking** The United States made agreements with many countries in order to gain land. How did the United States gain the Louisiana Territory? How did the United States gain Alaska?

After reading this book, thousands of Northerners became **abolitionists** (ab uh LISH un ists). These people wanted to end slavery. Many helped slaves escape to Canada. There, slavery was illegal. Most Southerners, however, felt that abolitionists were robbing them of their property.

The debate over slavery raged. When Abraham Lincoln, a Northerner, was elected President in 1860, many Southerners feared they would have little say in the government. As a result, some Southern states seceded, or withdrew, from the United States. They founded a new country—the Confederate States of America, or the Confederacy.

Conflict Erupts Into War   In 1861, the **Civil War** between the Northern states and the Confederacy erupted. It lasted four years. The North, known as the Union, had more industry, wealth, and soldiers. The Confederacy had experienced military officers. They also had cotton. Many foreign countries bought southern cotton. Southerners hoped that they would help supply the Confederacy.

Despite the North's advantages, the war dragged on. In 1863, Lincoln issued the Emancipation Proclamation. This freed slaves in areas loyal to the Confederacy. And it gave the North a new battle cry—freedom! Thousands of African Americans joined the fight against the South.

Overcoming Obstacles
When the Civil War began, Clara Barton wanted to help. She set up an organization to deliver supplies to men wounded in battle. She also worked as a nurse in hospitals located near battlefields. Because of her gentle and helpful ways, Barton earned the name "Angel of the Battlefield."

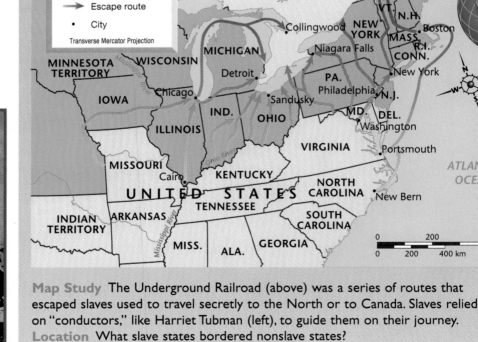

The Underground Railroad

KEY
Slave states
Non-slave states
Escape route
City
Transverse Mercator Projection

Map Study The Underground Railroad (above) was a series of routes that escaped slaves used to travel secretly to the North or to Canada. Slaves relied on "conductors," like Harriet Tubman (left), to guide them on their journey.
Location What slave states bordered nonslave states?

The picture to the left shows African American soldiers outside their barracks at Fort Lincoln, Washington, D.C., in early 1865. Twenty-one African Americans received the Congressional Medal of Honor (below), the country's highest award for bravery. **Critical Thinking** Why do you think African Americans were willing to fight for the Union?

The Civil War ended in 1865. Lincoln wanted the Southern states to return willingly to the Union. This was the first step in his plan for the **Reconstruction,** or rebuilding, of the nation.

Reconstructing the Union   Less than a week after the end of the war, Lincoln was killed. Vice President Andrew Johnson tried to carry out Lincoln's plan. But Congress resisted his efforts. Finally, Congress took complete control of Reconstruction. The Union Army governed the South until new state officials were elected.

That happened in 1877. But as soon as the Union Army withdrew, Southern lawmakers voted to **segregate,** or separate, blacks from whites. Segregation affected all aspects of life. The difficult struggle to preserve the United States had succeeded. But the long struggle to guarantee equality to all Americans still lay ahead.

SECTION 2 REVIEW

1. **Define**   (a) Louisiana Purchase, (b) Manifest Destiny, (c) immigrant, (d) Industrial Revolution, (e) abolitionist, (f) Civil War, (g) Reconstruction, (h) segregate.

2. **Identify**   (a) Meriwether Lewis, (b) William Clark, (c) Thomas Jefferson, (d) Andrew Jackson, (e) Harriet Beecher Stowe, (f) Abraham Lincoln, (g) Andrew Johnson.

3. (a) What was the Indian Removal Act? (b) How did it affect Native Americans?

4. How did the Industrial Revolution affect the United States?

5. Why did the Southern states withdraw from the Union?

Critical Thinking

6. **Expressing Problems Clearly**   How did the issue of slavery become a cause of the Civil War?

Activity

7. **Writing to Learn**   Write an entry that Lincoln might have made in his diary on his plan for Reconstruction.

The United States Becomes a World Power

BEFORE YOU READ

Reach Into Your Background

Have you ever wondered about the contrast between rich and poor neighborhoods in a city? Such contrasts have always been part of city life, where rich, middle-class, and poor people live near each other but live very different lives.

Questions to Explore

1. How did the United States become a world power?
2. How did the citizens of the United States gain more equality from the 1950s to the present?

Key Terms

labor force
settlement house
Homestead Act
communism
Cold War
civil rights movement

Key People

Jacob Riis
Jane Addams
Woodrow Wilson
Franklin D. Roosevelt
Harry S. Truman
Martin Luther King, Jr.

▼ Jacob Riis argued that tenements like these in New York City, which crowded as many as 10 people to a room, bred misery, disease, and crime.

Jacob Riis was an angry man. In his book *How the Other Half Lives,* he took his readers on tours of slum life in the late 1800s. He wanted other people to be angry, too—angry enough to change things.

"Come over here. Step carefully over this baby—it is a baby, in spite of its rags and dirt—under these iron bridges called fire escapes, but loaded down . . . with broken household goods, with washtubs and barrels, over which no man could climb from a fire . . . That baby's parents live in the rear tenement [slum] here. . . . There are plenty of houses with half a hundred such in."

The United States From 1865 to 1914

The Industrial Revolution made life easier for the rich and the middle class. By the late 1800s, a handful of people had made millions of dollars in industry. But life did not improve for the poor. City slums were crowded with poor immigrants. Many could not speak English. These newcomers were a huge **labor force,** or supply of workers. Employers paid them very little. Even small children had to work so that families could make ends meet.

Reformers like Jacob Riis began to protest such poverty. In Chicago, Jane Addams set up a **settlement house,** or community center, for poor immigrants. Mary Harris Jones helped miners organize for better wages. Because of her work to end child labor, people called her "Mother Jones."

One way for people to leave poverty behind was to move to the open plains and prairies of the Midwest. To attract settlers to this region, the United States government passed the **Homestead Act** in 1862. It gave 160 acres (65 hectares) of land to any adult willing to farm it and live on it for five years. Life on the plains was not easy. Trees and water were in short supply. And settlers faced swarms of insects, wild prairie fires, and temperatures that were very hot in summer and cold in winter. Still, most homesteaders held on for the five years. Railroads helped connect the East Coast with the West, which speeded up settlement.

READ ACTIVELY

Visualize Visualize life on a homestead farm on the prairie.

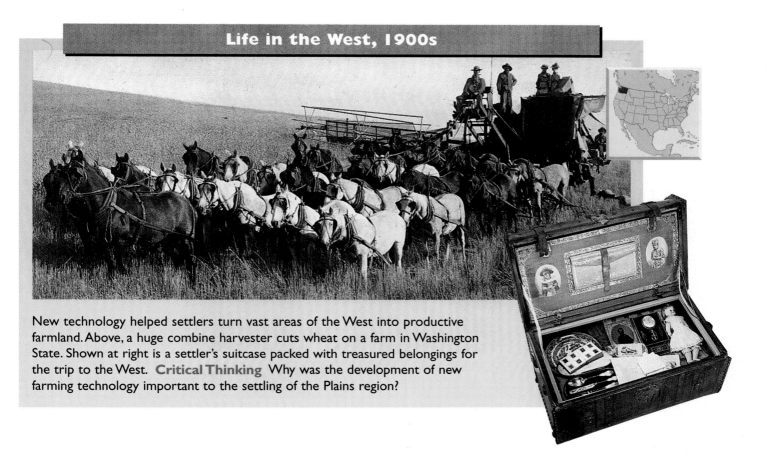

Life in the West, 1900s

New technology helped settlers turn vast areas of the West into productive farmland. Above, a huge combine harvester cuts wheat on a farm in Washington State. Shown at right is a settler's suitcase packed with treasured belongings for the trip to the West. **Critical Thinking** Why was the development of new farming technology important to the settling of the Plains region?

The United States Expands Beyond Its Shores The United States also expanded beyond its continental borders. Russia owned the territory of Alaska. In 1867, Secretary of State William Seward arranged for the United States to buy it. In 1898, the United States took control of Hawaii, another territory. The same year, the United States fought and won the Spanish-American War. The victory gave the United States control of the Spanish lands of Cuba, Puerto Rico, Guam, and the Philippines. America had a strong economy, military might, and overseas territory.

The World at War

Now the United States was a player in world affairs. As a result, the country was drawn into international conflicts. In 1914, World War I broke out in Europe. President Woodrow Wilson did not want America to take part. But when Germany began sinking American ships, Wilson had no choice. He declared war. The United States joined the Allied Powers of Great Britain and France. They fought against the Central Powers, which included Germany, Austria-Hungary, and Turkey. In 1917, thousands of American soldiers sailed to Europe. With this added strength, the Allies won the war in 1918. The terms of peace in the Treaty of Versailles punished Germany severely. Its harshness led to another worldwide conflict 20 years later.

▲ During World War I, the United States government paid for the war effort by selling bonds. These were certificates that included a promise to pay back the face amount plus interest. Posters like this urged Americans to buy bonds to win the war.

Fighting World War I

American troops in World War I and World War II served with great bravery. Here, a United States Army soldier in World War I rests during a pause in the shooting. More than 4 million Americans served in World War I. About 15 million Americans served in World War II.

Charles Lindbergh, a 25-year-old stunt flier and airmail pilot from Minnesota, made the world's first nonstop flight between the Americas and Europe in 1927. Lindbergh and his plane, *Spirit of St. Louis,* became a symbol of a daring, adventuresome spirit.

In the United States, during the 10 years after World War I, the economy boomed. Women enjoyed new freedoms and the hard-won right to vote. More and more people bought cars, refrigerators, radios, and other modern marvels.

In 1929, however, the world was grabbed by an economic disaster called the Great Depression. In America, factories closed, people lost their jobs, and farmers lost their farms. Many banks closed, and people lost their life's savings. By 1933, people were losing hope. But that year, President Franklin D. Roosevelt took office. He created a plan called the New Deal. This was a series of government programs to help people get jobs and to restore the economy. Some of these programs, like Social Security, are still in place today. Social Security provides income to people who are retired or disabled.

The Great Depression was very hard on Germany. Its people also lost hope. In 1933, they responded by turning to Adolf Hitler. Soon he had become dictator of Germany. Hitler convinced Germans that their nation would become wealthy and powerful by taking over other countries. Also, he claimed that Germans were a superior ethnic group—and should lead Europe. In 1939, Hitler's armies invaded Poland. This started World War II.

By the end of the war in 1945, Europe was in ruins. People around the world learned that Hitler had forced countless Jews, Gypsies, Slavs, and others into brutal prison camps. Millions of people, including some six million Jews, were murdered in these camps. This horrible mass murder is called the Holocaust (HAHL uh kawst).

READ ACTIVELY

Connect Why is it important that women, as well as men, can vote?

A New Home During the Cold War, the United States built underground "silos" for missiles. As new missiles were built, the Air Force removed the old ones and sold the silos. Some were used to store crops and other materials. One Kansas county turned a silo into a school. In 1984, a family bought a silo and built a home inside. The family paid $40,000 for the silo. Originally, it had cost the American people $4 million to build.

▼ Which of the wars shown on this time line did not involve open warfare?

As with World War I, the United States tried to stay out of the conflict. But in 1941, Japan attacked the United States naval base at Pearl Harbor, Hawaii. The Japanese were allied with the Germans, so the United States declared war on both nations. The United States sent armed forces to fight in Europe and in the Pacific. President Roosevelt, who led the nation in war, did not live to see peace. He died in April 1945. Vice President Harry S. Truman became President.

In May, the Allies defeated the Germans. During the summer, President Truman decided to drop two atomic bombs on Japan. That convinced Japan to give up. Finally, World War II was over.

Postwar Responsibilities

After World War II, the United States took on new international responsibilities. During World War I, the Soviet Union had been created. It adopted a form of government called **communism.** Under this system, the state owns all industries. In theory, the people share work and its rewards equally. After World War II, the communist Soviet Union took control of many Eastern European countries. The United States feared that the Soviets were trying to spread communism throughout the world. As a result, the United States and the Soviet Union entered the **Cold War.** This was a period of great tension, although the two countries never faced each other in an actual war. Two wars grew out of this tension. One was the Korean War, and the other was the Vietnam War. The Cold War lasted more than 40 years.

The economy of the United States boomed after World War II. But not all citizens shared in the benefits. In the South, segregation was a way of life. Many people began the **civil rights movement** to fight this injustice. People like Martin Luther King, Jr., led the movement to end segregation and win rights for African Americans. This success inspired others who felt they were treated unequally. Mexican American farmworkers, women, and disabled people also made gains in civil rights.

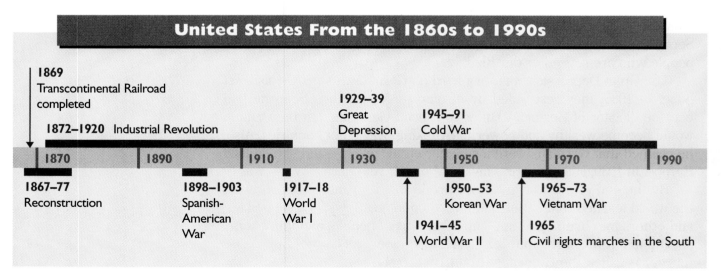

United States From the 1860s to 1990s

1869 Transcontinental Railroad completed

1872–1920 Industrial Revolution

1929–39 Great Depression

1945–91 Cold War

1870   1890   1910   1930   1950   1970   1990

1867–77 Reconstruction

1898–1903 Spanish-American War

1917–18 World War I

1950–53 Korean War

1965–73 Vietnam War

1941–45 World War II

1965 Civil rights marches in the South

A Birthday Celebration

On July 4, 1976, the United States celebrated its bicentennial, or two hundredth birthday. One of the most spectacular events of the celebration was a review of a huge fleet of tall sailing ships sent from the United States and foreign countries. Here, one of the ships sails into New York Harbor. **Critical Thinking** What events do you think would be appropriate for a country's two hundredth birthday? Why?

Many challenges remain, however. There are problems of homelessness and hunger, of low wages and pollution. But Americans have faced such problems before. Once, children worked in factories and mines for 12 hours a day, 6 days a week. During the Great Depression, hundreds of thousands of people were out of work. Droughts destroyed farms all through the Plains states. Again, Americans found ways to solve these problems. They did it by harnessing their energy, creativity, and willingness to work hard in the face of any challenge.

SECTION 3 REVIEW

1. **Define** (a) labor force, (b) settlement house, (c) Homestead Act, (d) communism, (e) Cold War, (f) civil rights movement.

2. **Identify** (a) Jacob Riis, (b) Jane Addams, (c) Woodrow Wilson, (d) Franklin D. Roosevelt, (e) Harry S. Truman, (f) Martin Luther King, Jr.

3. List three events that helped make the United States a world power.

4. What gain in equality did African Americans make after World War II?

Critical Thinking

5. **Recognizing Cause and Effect** How did the Homestead Act help settle the Plains of the Midwest?

Activity

6. **Writing to Learn** People who stay home during a war also find ways to help the country. Do research in the library about such things as rationing, volunteer work, and the employment of women during World War II. You can also interview friends or family members about that period. Then write a report about what life was like at home during the war.

Growth, Settlement, and Independence in Canada

BEFORE YOU READ

Reach Into Your Background

Have you ever seen a commercial for a product—or talked to a friend about some item—then rushed out immediately to buy it? Fads like this can make a company rich. The same thing happened back in the 1600s and 1700s. French businessmen got rich by selling American beaver skins. Many Europeans wanted hats made from the beaver's thick, glossy fur.

Questions to Explore

1. Why were France and Britain rivals in Canada?
2. How did Canada become an independent nation?
3. How did Canada become a world power?

Key Terms
dominion
bilingual

Key People and Places
Louis Papineau
William Mackenzie
Earl of Durham
Ontario
Quebec
Yukon

▼ The trade in beaver furs was so profitable during the 1700s and 1800s because beaver hats like this were the height of fashion in Europe.

The Haida people of British Columbia tell this tale. As in many Native American tales, nature plays an important role.

❝**W**hile he was crying and singing his dirge [sad song], a figure emerged from the lake. It was a strange animal, in its mouth a stick that it was gnawing. On each side of the animal were two smaller ones also gnawing sticks. Then the largest figure . . . spoke, 'Don't be so sad! It is I, your wife, and your two children. We have returned to our home in the water. . . . Call me the Beaver woman.❞

To the Haida and other native peoples in Canada, beavers were especially important. Imagine how they felt when European trappers killed almost all of the beavers to make fur hats.

The Battle of Quebec, 1759

The Battle of Quebec was a turning point in the Seven Years' War. This painting illustrates how British troops found a path through the cliffs that protected Quebec. **Critical Thinking** Do you think that Quebec would have fallen to the British if troops had not found a path in? Why or why not?

The French and the British in Canada

The profitable fur trade in Canada brought two European powers— France and Great Britain—into conflict there. Actually, the two rivals fought wars all over the world. In 1713, they signed a peace treaty. The treaty gave Great Britain the Hudson Bay region and the southeastern corner of Canada, called Acadia.

The peace was uneasy. Against their will, French Catholics in Acadia came under the rule of British Protestants. The French controlled the lowlands south of Hudson Bay and around the St. Lawrence River. Both countries wanted to control the Ohio River Valley, farther to the south. The French wanted its beavers for furs. The British wanted its land for settlement.

The contest for this region was so intense that in 1754, it erupted into the Seven Years' War. In the United States, this conflict is called the French and Indian War. The British won the decisive Battle of Quebec in 1759. The Treaty of Paris, signed four years later, gave Great Britain complete control over Canada. Some French settlers returned to France. Those who stayed resisted English culture. The first two British governors of Canada were sympathetic. They gained passage of the Quebec Act. It gave the French people in Quebec the right to speak their own language, practice their own religion, and follow their own customs.

LINKS ACROSS THE WORLD

Acadia Until 1763, France and Britain claimed land that today is Nova Scotia, New Brunswick, and part of Maine. The French called this region Acadia. When the British took over, Acadians who refused to pledge loyalty to Great Britain were driven from their homes. Some formed a colony in Louisiana. The name *Acadian* came to sound like "cajun." Now the Cajun culture is an important part of life in Louisiana.

British Loyalists in Canada

Some British Loyalists remained in the United States after the American Revolution. Many, however, moved to Canada. In Canada, the British government gave the Loyalists land to make up for the homes they had left behind. This painting shows Loyalists drawing lots for land.

During the American Revolution, some Americans did not want independence. They were called British Loyalists. After the war, many Loyalists moved to Canada. But most did not want to live in a French culture. To avoid problems, Great Britain divided the land into two colonies, Upper and Lower Canada. Most Loyalists moved into Upper Canada. It is now called Ontario. French Canadians remained in Lower Canada. It is now Quebec.

During the War of 1812, the French and British groups worked together. This was crucial when the United States tried to invade Canada. The United States had troops on the border between the two countries. The French, British, and native peoples forced the Americans back.

Canada Seeks Self-Rule

Once the war ended, however, Canadians again could not cooperate. Both French Canadians and British Canadians hated British rule. Many felt Britain was too far away to understand their needs. But the two groups did not join in rebellion. In 1837, a French Canadian named Louis Papineau (pah pee NOH) organized a revolt in Lower Canada. His goal was to establish the region as a separate country. The British easily defeated the rebels. The same thing happened in Upper Canada. William Mackenzie led the people against British rule. Again, the British easily defeated the rebels.

READ ACTIVELY

Ask Questions What do you want to know about how Canada became independent from Britain without going to war?

Still, British leaders were afraid more trouble was coming. They sent the Earl of Durham to learn what was wrong. When Durham returned, he had many suggestions. First, he suggested that the Canadians be given more control of their government. He also thought all the Canadian provinces should be united. But the British government united only Upper and Lower Canada to form the Province of Canada. Nova Scotia, Newfoundland, Prince Edward Island, and New Brunswick were not included in this union. If Canada were completely united, the British feared, the Canadians might make a successful rebellion.

But Canadians felt that all provinces should be represented in their government. Otherwise it could not be effective. In 1864, leaders from every province met. Together they worked out a plan to form a union. On July 1, 1867, the British Parliament accepted the plan. It passed the British North American Act. This made Canada "one Dominion under the name of Canada." A **dominion** is a self-governing area. Canada was still subject to Great Britain. But now a central government would run the country. Canadians would solve their own problems. Without a war, Canadians had won the right to control their own government.

After its "peaceful revolution," Canada saw years of growth and change. Skilled European farmers settled Canada's western plains. The region filled with productive farms. Gold and other valuable minerals were discovered in the Yukon in the 1890s. That brought miners to the far northwest. Canada was becoming rich and important.

CITIZEN HEROES

A Voice of Protest In 1869, the Canadian government wanted to finish the cross-country railroad across the flat plains region. Louis Riel, leader of the *métis* (may TEE)—mixed European and Native American people—objected to the plan. The *métis* said the railroad would bring new settlers, who would take away their land. The government refused to stop, so Riel led an armed revolt. It failed, and Riel was executed for treason, but the government did set aside land for the *métis*. Today, French Canadians consider Riel a hero.

▼ On November 7, 1885, Canada's far-flung provinces were tied together as the last spike was driven in, completing the Canadian Pacific Railway.

Canada Takes Its Place in the World   When Britain entered World War I, Canadians were still British subjects. Canada, therefore, entered the war, too. Canada willingly sent soldiers and resources overseas. Canada contributed so much to the Allied victory that the young country became a world power. Great Britain recognized Canada's new strength and granted it more independence. During the Great Depression, Canada focused on solving problems at home. But when World War II began in 1939, Canada took part. Once again, Canadian efforts helped win the war.

Canada: Postwar to the Present

During the war, Canadians built factories. They made war supplies and goods like clothes and shoes. Because of the war, people could not get such products from Europe. After the war, Canadian goods found a ready market in Europe.

Also during the postwar years, immigrants poured into Canada. They came from Asia, Europe, Africa, and the Caribbean. The newcomers filled jobs in new factories and other businesses. Soon, Canada became the world's fourth-largest industrial nation.

Toronto and the CN Tower

Rebecca Bond
age 10
Ajax, Ontario, Canada

The CN Tower is a communications and observation tower in downtown Toronto. "I painted the CN Tower," the artist said, "because it's my favorite place in Toronto. You can see the whole city from the top." **Critical Thinking** If you were asked to paint a picture of one of your area's landmarks, which one would you choose? Why?

Industrialization brought back old arguments. British Canadians built new factories in Quebec. That alarmed French Canadians. By 1976, some French Canadians were tired of being part of Canada. Quebec, they argued, should be independent. Instead, in 1982, the Canadians wrote a new constitution. Special sections spelled out ways to respect French Canadian culture and concerns. New laws made Canada a **bilingual** country. That is, Canada had two official languages— English and French. In addition Canadians could now change their constitution without Great Britain's permission. Canada was completely independent.

Fort York, Toronto

During the War of 1812, United States forces crossed Lake Ontario and occupied York, then Canada's capital, for four days. American soldiers burned government buildings and looted private houses. Today York is called Toronto. Here, in the shadow of Toronto's modern skyline, militia dressed in British uniforms of the period parade at historic Fort York.

Canada's government is modeled on the British parliamentary system. It is called a constitutional monarchy. It is also called a parliamentary democracy because the group of representatives that makes its laws is modeled on the English parliament. Another thing ties Canada to Great Britain. Canada belongs to the Commonwealth of Nations. All member countries were once British colonies. Great Britain gives members financial aid, advice, and military support.

SECTION 4 REVIEW

1. **Define** (a) dominion, (b) bilingual.

2. **Identify** (a) Louis Papineau, (b) William Mackenzie, (c) Earl of Durham, (d) Ontario, (e) Quebec, (f) Yukon.

3. (a) Why was the Ohio River Valley important to the French? (b) Why was it important to the English?

4. How did Canada become an industrial power after World War II?

Critical Thinking

5. **Making Comparisons** Compare the ways in which Canada and the United States became independent nations.

Activity

6. **Writing to Learn** Write a few reasons that a French Canadian might give for separating from British Canada.

Partners and Friends

THE UNITED STATES AND CANADA TODAY

BEFORE YOU READ

Reach Into Your Background

Think about the land on which your community is built. What do you think it looked like 300 years ago? What natural resources did it have? How have people changed it? Which changes are improvements and which are not? If you had the job of protecting the environment of your community, what would you do?

Questions to Explore

1. What environmental concerns do the United States and Canada share today?

2. What economic ties do the United States and Canada have to each other and to the world?

Key Terms

fossil fuel
acid rain
clear-cut
interdependent
tariff
free trade
NAFTA

Key Places

Cuyahoga River
Lake Erie
Niagara Falls
St. Lawrence Seaway

▼ The United States and Canada worked together to construct several buildings astride the border between the two countries at Derby Line, Vermont.

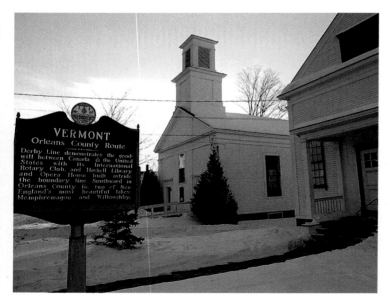

A minke whale swam northward in the Atlantic Ocean. She was very large—weighing four tons and about as long as a classroom—but still she swam gracefully. Every few minutes she dived for fish and came back up for air. The sight was breathtaking.

But there were people on the ocean that day. They wanted to do more than watch the whale. They were whale hunters from Norway, where whale meat is still part of people's diets.

A hundred years ago, Canadians, Americans, and others from all over the world also hunted whales. These animals were valued for their meat, oil, and bones. Then people began to realize that whales were disappearing. Today, the United States and Canada are members of the International Whaling Commission. Members work together to protect whales. This is just one of the ways the United States and Canada have become cooperative neighbors.

Environmental Issues

Protecting whales is one of many environmental issues that concern both the United States and Canada. Both countries share many geographic features—the coasts of the Atlantic and Pacific oceans, the Great Lakes, and the Rocky Mountains, for example. Both countries use natural resources in similar ways. And both have used technology to meet their needs. But technology has left its mark on their water, air, forests, and futures.

Solving Water Problems   Can you picture a river on fire? Impossible, you say? In 1969, a fire started on the Cuyahoga (KY uh hoh guh) River. That river flows past Cleveland, Ohio, and then empties into Lake Erie. Along the way, Cleveland's factories had poured waste, garbage, and oil into the river. The layer of pollutants was so thick that it burned without being put out by the water beneath it.

The Cuyahoga was typical of the rivers that empty into Lake Erie. So much pollution had been dumped into the lake that most of the fish had died. Swimming in the river was unthinkable. But the fire on the Cuyahoga was a wake-up call. The United States and Canada signed a treaty promising to cooperate in cleaning up the lake. Such treaties as this have greatly reduced freshwater pollution in the United States. Today, people again enjoy fishing and boating on the Cuyahoga.

The Cuyahoga River, Yesterday and Today

On August 22, 1969, a fireboat hosed down a burning pier that had been set on fire by flames from the Cuyahoga River (above right). Today, after a huge cleanup campaign, the view is different. Waterfront attractions such as restaurants and cruise boats (above left) offer visitors and residents a chance to enjoy the river views.

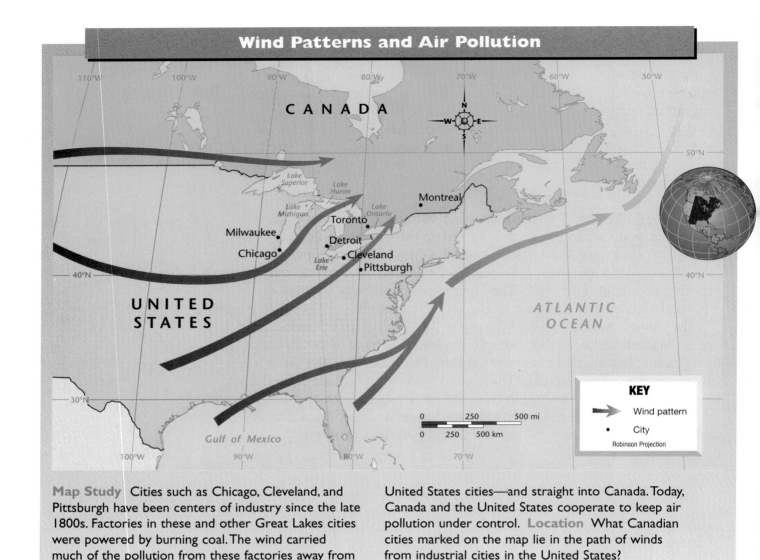

Wind Patterns and Air Pollution

CANADA

Lake Superior
Lake Huron
Lake Michigan
Lake Ontario
Lake Erie

Montreal
Toronto
Milwaukee
Detroit
Chicago
Cleveland
Pittsburgh

UNITED STATES

ATLANTIC OCEAN

Gulf of Mexico

KEY
Wind pattern
City
Robinson Projection

0 250 500 mi
0 250 500 km

Map Study Cities such as Chicago, Cleveland, and Pittsburgh have been centers of industry since the late 1800s. Factories in these and other Great Lakes cities were powered by burning coal. The wind carried much of the pollution from these factories away from United States cities—and straight into Canada. Today, Canada and the United States cooperate to keep air pollution under control. **Location** What Canadian cities marked on the map lie in the path of winds from industrial cities in the United States?

READ ACTIVELY

Predict What happens to the air pollution created in the Northeast or in Great Lakes areas of the United States?

Improving Air Quality On many days, you can look around most big cities and see that the air is filled with a brown haze. This pollution is caused by cars and factories burning **fossil fuels,** such as gasoline and coal. Not only is this air unhealthy for people to breathe, but it can also create other serious problems hundreds of miles away. Wind picks up pollutants in the air, where they combine with moisture to form an acid. When the moisture turns into rain, it is **acid rain.** Acid rain kills plants and trees. When enough acid rain falls on lakes, it kills fish and water plants. Coal-burning power plants in the Northeast and in Great Lakes areas have created this situation.

But polluted winds do not stop at international borders. Acid rain caused by United States power plants has affected forests and lakes in Canada, from Ontario to Newfoundland. When the Canadian government protested the situation in the 1980s, the two countries signed agreements to control air quality.

Renewing Forests "I'm like a tree—you'll have to cut me down," cried Kim McElroy in 1993. The other demonstrators with her agreed. They were blocking the path of logging trucks trying to enter the forest of Clayoquot Sound on Vancouver Island, British Columbia. The protesters believed that cutting down the trees would damage the environment. In similar forests throughout the United States and Canada, logging companies practiced **clear-cutting,** or cutting down all the trees in an area. Without trees, soil washes away, other plants die, and animals lose their homes.

On the other hand, people need lumber for houses. Paper companies need wood pulp to make their products. People who work for logging companies need their jobs.

The Canadian and American governments want to maintain both the forests and the timber industry. They are working to develop ideas that will do that. For example, British Columbia passed a law that sets aside parts of the Clayoquot Sound's forests for logging. The law also imposes new rules on loggers to prevent damage in the areas where cutting is allowed.

"Economics Has Made Us Partners"

Not all next-door neighbors get along as well as the United States and Canada. President John F. Kennedy once described the relationship this way: "Geography has made us neighbors. History made us friends. And economics has made us partners." With 3,000 miles (4,827 km) of border between the two countries, economic cooperation has benefited both. Part of this cooperation has been in transportation between the countries, particularly around the Great Lakes.

▼ Clear-cutting in Oregon's Mount Hood National Forest scars the land with large bare patches.

Ask Questions What would you like to know about the economic relationship between the United States and Canada?

The St. Lawrence Seaway   Have you ever heard of someone going over Niagara Falls in a barrel? The barrel would drop about 190 feet (58 m)—a pretty crazy stunt! But suppose you had a cargo of manufactured goods in Cleveland to send to Montreal. You decide to ship by water, because it is the cheapest and most direct means of transportation. Now what do you do? Niagara Falls lies between lakes Erie and Ontario. After that, your cargo would have to travel down a total drop of another 250 feet (76 m) in the St. Lawrence River before it reached Montreal. And once your cargo was unloaded, how would you get the ship back to Cleveland?

To solve this problem, the United States and Canada built the St. Lawrence Seaway. Completed in 1959, it is a system of locks, canals, and dams that allows ships to move from one water level to another. Now, ships can travel from Duluth, Minnesota, on Lake Superior, all the way to the Atlantic Ocean. The St. Lawrence Seaway makes it much easier for the United States and Canada to trade with each other and with Europe.

Trade   What country is the biggest trading partner of the United States? It is Canada. And the United States is Canada's largest trading partner, too. About three fourths of all of Canada's foreign trade—both exports and imports—is with the United States. Our economies are **interdependent.** That means that in order to be successful, each country needs to do business with the other.

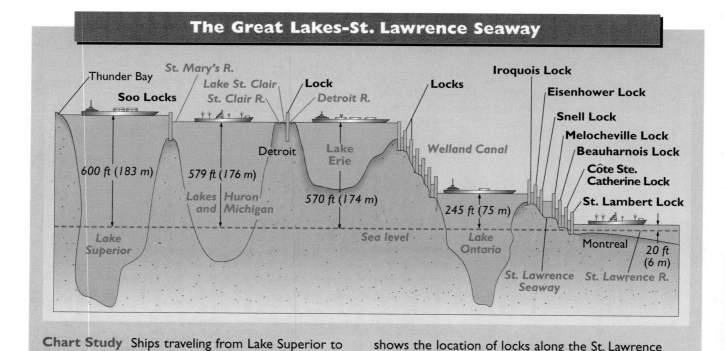

The Great Lakes-St. Lawrence Seaway

Chart Study Ships traveling from Lake Superior to the Atlantic Ocean must go through a series of locks. A lock is an enclosed part of a canal with a watertight gate at each end. Letting water into the lock raises ships. Letting water out lowers them. This diagram shows the location of locks along the St. Lawrence Seaway. **Critical Thinking** How do you think building the St. Lawrence Seaway affected the economies of the United States and Canada?

The Grain Industry in Alberta

This train is taking on a load of wheat from the nearby grain elevator. A grain elevator is a tall building where grain is stored. The train takes the wheat west to the Pacific Coast or east to the Great Lakes. The wheat then is loaded on ships for export. Wheat is one of Canada's most important exports. In fact, Canada is the world's second leading grain exporter. The United States leads the world in grain exports.

Before 1989, both countries charged fees called **tariffs** on many things they imported from each other. Tariffs raise the cost of goods, so they can limit the amount of trade. In 1989, Canada and the United States agreed to eliminate tariffs and have **free trade.** Since then, trade between them has increased. And in 1994, Mexico joined the United States and Canada to sign the North American Free Trade Agreement, or **NAFTA.** The goal of this agreement is to encourage trade and economic growth in all three countries.

SECTION 5 REVIEW

1. **Define** (a) fossil fuel, (b) acid rain, (c) clear-cut, (d) interdependent, (e) tariff, (f) free trade, (g) NAFTA.

2. **Identify** (a) Cuyahoga River, (b) Lake Erie, (c) Niagara Falls, (d) St. Lawrence Seaway.

3. Why is there disagreement about logging in some forests?

4. Why is acid rain from the United States a problem in Canada?

5. How has geography contributed to the trade partnership between Canada and the United States?

Critical Thinking

6. **Expressing Problems Clearly** Explain briefly why the United States and Canada cooperated to build the St. Lawrence Seaway.

Activity

7. **Writing to Learn** Write a paragraph that explains the main reasons why Canada and the United States are important to each other.

SKILLS ACTIVITY

Interpreting Diagrams

Suppose that your pen pal in Canada wants to know what your school looks like. Which would you rather do, write her a letter describing your school, or send her a photograph?

Many people would probably choose to send the photograph. A photograph would show her in an instant what your school looks like. But writing a letter also has its benefits. You can describe details a photograph might not show.

Which should you do—send a letter or send a photograph? The best solution would be to send both. The photograph would show your pen pal what your school looks like, and the letter would tell her about it. In a way, you would be playing a long-distance game of show-and-tell with your pen pal!

Get Ready

You can also have show-and-tell with a diagram. As you know, a diagram is a picture that shows how something works or is made. It usually includes labels that tell about certain parts of the picture. It is like a combination of the letter and the photograph you would send to your pen pal. A diagram can both show things through a picture and tell about them through labels.

A diagram is like a game of "show-and-tell"—the picture *shows,* and the labels *tell.*

Try It Out

To understand how diagrams are made—and how to learn more from them—make one yourself. Complete these steps:

A. Find a photograph of a bicycle. You can cut one out of an old catalog or a magazine. Look for a photograph that is about the same size as the diagram on the next page.

B. Write a description of the bicycle. Describe in words the bicycle for someone who has never seen one before. Be sure to describe what it looks like, what its different parts are, and how the parts work.

C. Draw a diagram of the bicycle. Using the picture and your paragraph as a reference, draw a diagram of the bicycle. Be sure to label each part and explain how it works.

D. Compare the picture, the paragraph, and the diagram. Which of the three does the best job of showing and explaining what a bicycle is, what its parts are, and how it works?

As you can see, both pictures and words are useful. But nothing works as well as the combination of pictures and words you find in a diagram.

Apply the Skill

Now that you see how a simple diagram can "show and tell," you are ready to see how a more complicated diagram does the same thing. Use the diagram to complete the steps that follow.

① **Read and look at the diagram below.** Look it over to get a sense of what it is about. What does this diagram illustrate? What do the labels tell?

② **Study the picture.** What does the picture tell you about how a locomotive works?

③ **Study the words.** What path does the steam take through the engine?

④ **Think about diagrams.** Write a few sentences that explain how this diagram helps you understand locomotives.

How a Locomotive Works

Steam is superheated and goes to the steam chest.

Burning coal turns water in the boiler to steam.

superheater pipes

boiler

steam pipe

steam chest

firebox

drive rods

The pistons move the drive rods, which turn the wheels.

pistons   cylinder

Steam moves into the cylinders, where it pushes the pistons back and forth.

Steam locomotives drove trains for about a century beginning in 1830.

Review and Activities

Reviewing Main Ideas

1. Some scholars say that the first people in North America were not indigenous. According to this theory, how did the first people get here?

2. How did Europeans change Native American ways of life?

3. Name two reasons why early colonists wanted to break away from Great Britain.

4. How did westward expansion affect voting laws?

5. How did the United States become a world power?

6. Besides African Americans, which groups campaigned for civil rights after the 1950s?

7. Why did Canada become more independent from Britain after World War I?

8. After World War II, Canada's influence on the rest of the world increased. Why?

9. How is acid rain produced?

10. What is the value of the St. Lawrence Seaway?

Reviewing Key Terms

Use each key term in a sentence that shows the meaning of the term.

1. indigenous
2. Manifest Destiny
3. immigrant
4. Industrial Revolution
5. abolitionist
6. Reconstruction
7. Cold War
8. civil rights movement
9. dominion
10. bilingual
11. fossil fuel
12. acid rain
13. interdependent
14. tariff
15. free trade

Critical Thinking

1. **Identifying Central Issues** Explain why Southern colonists believed that they needed slaves.

2. **Making Comparisons** Compare the ways in which the United States and Canada gained their independence from Great Britain.

Graphic Organizer

On a sheet of paper, copy this chart and fill in the empty ovals with forces that made the United States a world power.

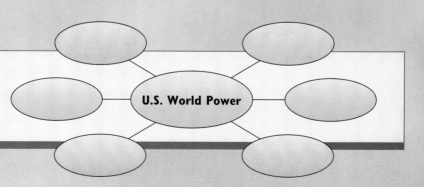

U.S. World Power

Map Activity

Place Location

Canada

For each place listed below, write the letter from the map that shows its location.

1. Ontario

2. Quebec

3. Yukon

4. Lake Erie

5. St. Lawrence Seaway

Writing Activity

Writing Activity

Think about ways in which the United States and Canada are similar. How are they different? Write a summary comparing the two countries.

Internet Activity

Use a search engine to find and browse **Selected Civil War Photographs.** Use a search engine to find **Civil War Slang.** Print out the sheet then use the search engine again to find **Civil War Letters of Galutia York.** Use the slang sheet to help you read the letters. Give a presentation on the daily life of a Civil War soldier.

Skills Review

Turn to the Skills Activity.

Review the four steps for reading a diagram. Then write a few sentences explaining why a diagram is more effective than a paragraph or a picture in providing information.

How Am I Doing?

Answer these questions to help you check your progress.

1. Do I understand how differences between the North and South led to the Civil War?

2. Can I describe how the United States became a world power?

3. Can I recognize the differences between the ways in which the United States and Canada gained their independence?

4. What information from this chapter can I use in my book project?

Transportation

By foot and in flight, in horse-drawn wagons and in locomotives, the people of Canada and the United States have always been on the move.

Transportation has played an important role in the histories of both countries. Early Native Americans spread across the continent on foot, on horseback, and in canoes. European colonists arrived in sailing ships, and settlers traveled west in covered wagons. History has always been affected by the ways in which people have traveled.

Purpose

In this activity, you will conduct an investigation of the ways in which people have crossed the rugged land and vast distances of the United States and Canada.

Find the Routes

Some of the roads in Canada and the United States have existed since Native Americans followed animal trails through the wilderness. Others have only existed since town or city planners decided to build them. Many roads change over time. Footpaths became cement sidewalks or paved highways. Look for different roads and paths in your community. Make a note of even the largest highway or the smallest path across the corner of someone's lawn. How old do you think the different routes are? Make a map of all the routes you take on your way to school.

◀▼ From trails to highways, transportation routes come in many forms.

194

Do a Sailboat Study

Ships with great sails brought the first Europeans to this continent. Read about sailboats and sailing ships to see how they work. Then make a model sailboat. Draw a plan for your sailboat and choose your materials very carefully. Test your sailboat by floating it in water and blowing on it to create wind. Make any changes you need to improve the boat.

Calculate Travel Times

As the United States and Canada have grown older, travel times have become shorter and shorter. The chart below shows how long it has taken to travel from New York to St. Louis, the "Gateway to the West," in various years between 1800 and today. The distance between New York and St. Louis is 870 miles (1400 km).

New York to St. Louis

Year	Method	Approximate Travel Time
1800	stagecoach and horseback	5 weeks
1860	passenger train	3 days
1930	passenger train	1 day
1950	automobile	24 hours
Today	passenger jet	3 hours

Use the chart to see how much travel speeds have improved. First, calculate the average speed in miles per hour of each method of transportation shown in the chart (distance in miles ÷ time in hours = speed in miles per hour). Then, draw a line graph of your results.

Links to Other Subjects

Finding routes .... **Geography**

Doing a sailboat study...................... **Science**

Calculating travel times .... **Math**

Singing transportation songs................ **Music**

Telling a travel tale .... **Language Arts**

Sing Some Transportation Songs

"I've been workin' on the railroad, all the livelong day. . . ." Sound familiar? People have written many folk songs about trains, cars, boats, and other ways of getting around. What other transportation songs can you think of? Find the words and music to a few, and perform them with your classmates.

Tell a Travel Tale

You may not be a world traveler yet, but you have traveled. You've walked, ridden in cars and buses, and perhaps you've even ridden a train, boat, or plane. Write the story of your most exciting journey. Explain how you traveled, and what made the voyage exciting.

ANALYSIS AND CONCLUSION

Write a summary of your investigation. Describe the steps you followed and consider the following questions in your summary.

1. Why is transportation so important?

2. How has transportation affected the histories of the United States and Canada?

3. People are continually trying to make transportation faster and more efficient. Why do you think this is so?

CHAPTER 8

Cultures of the United States and Canada

PICTURE ACTIVITIES

In addition to official U.S. holidays, like the Fourth of July, Americans celebrate many ethnic holidays. These people in New York City are enjoying the Puerto Rican Day Parade, which is held every June. To help you think about the mixture of people in the United States, do the following activities.

Take a poll
Ask students in your class where their great-grandparents are from. Many will be from the United States, of course. What other countries are represented?

Study restaurant listings
Use a telephone book to list the kinds of food served in restaurants in your community. How many countries are represented?

The United States

A NATION OF IMMIGRANTS

BEFORE YOU READ

Reach Into Your Background

"So what'll it be tonight? Italian, Mexican, Chinese?" Does someone ask this question when your family is trying to decide on a restaurant or where to get take-out food? A wide variety, or diversity, of food is just one advantage of living in a society made up of different cultures. What else do you like about cultural diversity?

Questions to Explore

1. What influences have made the United States a culturally diverse nation?

2. How does this diversity affect life in the United States?

Key Terms
cultural diversity
cultural exchange
ethnic group

This view of **cultural diversity,** or a wide variety of cultures, comes from Tito, a teenager from Mexico. What do you think of it?

"My parents say, 'You have to learn the American culture.' I listen to them, but then I think about an ideal society where there's a little bit of every culture and it goes together just right. Say there's a part of the United States that's very hot. The problem to solve: What can we do to keep these people from overheating? The people who came here from the tropics have certain secrets of surviving in hot climates. Well, they come along and would say, 'When I lived in the tropics . . . we made our buildings with thick walls and a lot of windows. The buildings were white to reflect away the sun.' And the others would say, 'Hey, what a great idea. It works!' Different ideas would come together and make everything a whole lot better."

▼ A family enjoys dinner at a Mexican restaurant in San Antonio, Texas.

Diverse Cultures in the United States

The United States has always been culturally diverse. The country is geographically diverse, too—that is, it has a variety of landforms, climates, and vegetation. The cultures of the first Americans reflected their environments. Native Americans near the ocean ate a great deal of fish and told stories about the sea. Native Americans in forests learned how to trap and hunt forest animals. Native American groups also traded with each other. When groups trade, they get more than just goods. They also get involved in **cultural exchange.** In this process, different cultures share ideas and ways of doing things.

Cultural Exchange When Europeans came to North America, they changed Native American life. Some changes came from things that Europeans brought with them. For example, there were no horses in the New World when the Spanish explorers came. Once horses arrived, they changed the way that many Native Americans lived and became an important part of Native American culture.

Predict What kinds of things do you think the Europeans learned from Native Americans?

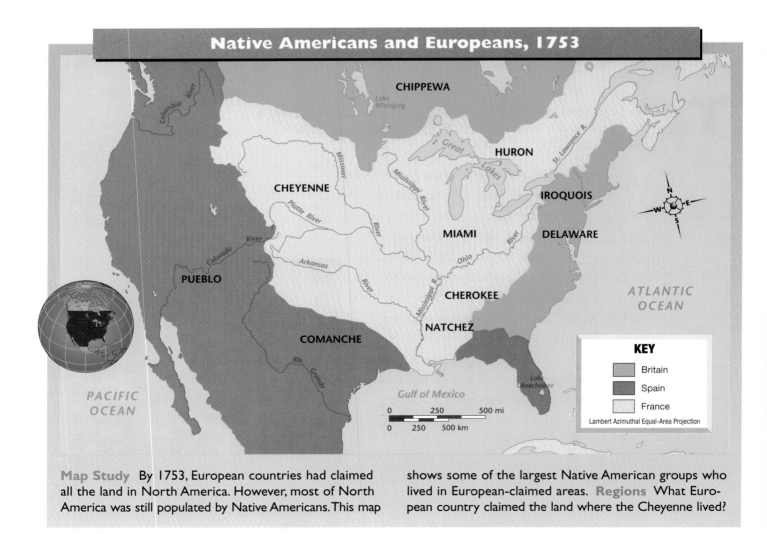

Native Americans and Europeans, 1753

CHIPPEWA

Lake Winnipeg

Columbia River

Great Lakes

HURON

St. Lawrence R.

Missouri

Mississippi River

CHEYENNE

IROQUOIS

Platte River

River

MIAMI

DELAWARE

Colorado River

River

Ohio

Arkansas

PUEBLO

River

Mississippi R.

CHEROKEE

ATLANTIC OCEAN

NATCHEZ

COMANCHE

Rio Grande

Lake Okeechobee

Gulf of Mexico

PACIFIC OCEAN

0   250   500 mi
0   250   500 km

KEY
- Britain
- Spain
- France

Lambert Azimuthal Equal-Area Projection

Map Study By 1753, European countries had claimed all the land in North America. However, most of North America was still populated by Native Americans. This map shows some of the largest Native American groups who lived in European-claimed areas. **Regions** What European country claimed the land where the Cheyenne lived?

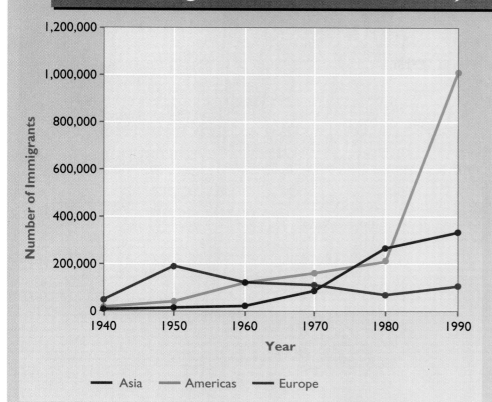

Immigration to the United States, 1940–1990

Number of Immigrants (y-axis): 0, 200,000, 400,000, 600,000, 800,000, 1,000,000, 1,200,000

Year (x-axis): 1940, 1950, 1960, 1970, 1980, 1990

— Asia   — Americas   — Europe

Chart Study This chart shows how many immigrants came to the United States from Asia, the Americas, and Europe between 1940 and 1990. **Critical Thinking** In 1940, roughly equal numbers of immigrants moved to the United States from each region. By 1950, most immigrants to the United States were European. How had things changed by 1990?

Cultural exchange occurred in two ways. Native Americans contributed many things to European culture. The French learned how to trap and to survive in the forest. English families learned to grow local foods such as corn and pumpkins. Cultural exchange also took place between enslaved Africans and their owners. The Africans learned English and used European tools. African music and foods entered the daily lives of slave owners.

This give-and-take happens every time immigrants come to a country. When Russian settlers came to the Midwest, they brought a kind of hardy wheat from their home country. Farmers soon learned that this tough wheat grew well in the Midwestern climate. These immigrants helped the Midwest become the leading wheat-growing area in the country today. In fact, so much wheat is grown here that it is called "America's breadbasket." Members of other ethnic groups have made important contributions to American culture, too. An **ethnic group** is a group of people who share a language, history, and culture.

What to Keep and What to Change? When immigrants move from one country to another, they must make difficult decisions. For instance, what things in their original culture should they keep, and what should they change? They must learn the language, laws, and manners of the people in their new home. For some, this is difficult. Others, however, want to forget the life they lived before.

Using Your Fingers and Toes Native Americans created the first number systems north of the Mexican border. The San Gabrielino in California used "all my hand finished" to mean 10. "All my hand finished and one my foot" was 15. The Chukchee used their fingers to count. Their word for "five" is *hand,* for "ten" *both hands,* and for "twenty" *man*—meaning both hands and both feet.

▶ Chinese American boy scouts in San Francisco proudly show off a dragon, which symbolizes Chinese New Year. Do you have to be Chinese to observe this holiday? Of course not—Americans of all ethnic backgrounds join in the joyous celebration.

For instance, Florence Benjamin, a third-generation American, asked her grandfather to teach her Russian. He replied, "From the time I came to this country, America has been my home and English my language. It is the only country that has been good to me and to the Jews. It is the one that is best for you. You don't need Russian." This man was grateful because American laws protected him. To him, being an American meant having the freedom *not* to use his native language.

On the other hand, some newcomers have difficulty adjusting to new ways. The United States is so different from their home country. Adults are sometimes afraid that the differences will come between them and their children. Anna, a teenager from Greece, describes the tensions that can grow among family members:

    "Once I understood English, once I started to see a whole American world out there that I never knew existed, a world that you don't see in Greece, I felt a little distant from [my parents]. The distance grew. They would be proud of me, but they also began to feel threatened. My new knowledge had no meaning for them. This has been hard and sad for all of us."

Almost all immigrants cling to things that remind them of their former homes. Think about your family or your friends' families. Does someone play an instrument special to your heritage? Do they use special phrases from the language they learned from their parents or grandparents? These customs give people a sense of identity. They also enrich American life.

United States Culture

Have you ever listened to music at a Caribbean carnival or watched a dragon parade amid bursting firecrackers at Chinese New Year? Although these traditions came from other countries, they are now a part of the diverse culture of the United States.

Regions of the United States also have cultural differences. Some things make all places seem alike, such as television and radio. But regional differences remain, in foods, accents, and pastimes. Consider musical styles. There is Cajun zydeco from Louisiana and bluegrass music from the Southeast. These styles "belong" to particular regions. However, people everywhere in the country enjoy them. Exchanging such things helps us appreciate the diversity of American life.

American culture also includes ordinary, everyday items. They often appear in the work of American artists. Composer Aaron Copland used cowboy songs in his ballet *Billy the Kid*. Andrew Wyeth painted haunting pictures of ordinary people in humble country surroundings. In

Connect What traditions do you think reflect your ethnic heritage?

▼ In small towns—like Elm Grove, Wisconsin—and large cities, people celebrate the Fourth of July with big parades.

Joseph Andereasen
age 11
United States

Sports are very much a part of a nation's culture. Baseball has been called the national pastime of the United States. Perhaps as many as 50 million people attend major league baseball games each season. **Critical Thinking** Who do you think the artist feels is the most important player? Why?

John Steinbeck's novel, *The Grapes of Wrath,* a poor farm family escapes dust storms of the 1930s. The African American poet Langston Hughes described life in Harlem, New York City in the early 1900s.

Cultures around the world also influence America's art. Musicians borrow sounds and ideas from Asia, South America, Africa, and Eastern Europe. Painters use techniques and images from Europe, Africa, and Asia. Writers use themes from the world's folk tales. Like Tito, the boy from Mexico, American artists all believe in different ideas coming together to "make everything a whole lot better."

SECTION 1 REVIEW

1. **Define** (a) cultural diversity, (b) cultural exchange, (c) ethnic group.

2. How has the arrival of immigrants affected the culture of the United States?

3. Why are the cultures in different environments so different from each other?

4. Describe the cultural exchange that occurred between Native Americans and Europeans.

Critical Thinking

5. **Recognizing Cause and Effect** Why do you think Anna's parents felt threatened when she began to feel like a part of American society?

Activity

6. **Writing to Learn** Write a brief poem about a custom that is important to your family or the family of a friend.

Canada

A Mosaic

BEFORE YOU READ

Reach Into Your Background

Have you ever made a mosaic, or a picture from tiles, beads, or other small bits of material? If you have, you know how satisfying it is to create a single pattern from many different shapes and colors. Canadians are proud of their "mosaic" society. It is the product of different cultures that keep their own identities while contributing to the culture of the whole nation.

Questions to Explore

1. Why do Canadians consider their society a mosaic?

2. How have the indigenous peoples of Canada worked to preserve their cultures?

Key Term

reserve

Key People and Places

Gordon Lightfoot
Nunavut

Channel-surf Canadian radio or television, and you may be surprised at the different languages you hear. Journalist Andrew H. Malcolm describes the variety of languages in Canada this way:

> "**O**ne Toronto radio station broadcasts in thirty languages, including announcements of arrival delays for flights from 'back home.' In many Vancouver neighborhoods the street signs are in . . . English and Chinese. One Toronto television station survived simply by broadcasting programs in many languages aimed at many different ethnic communities, including [Pakistani] movies in Urdu with English subtitles. Toronto's city government routinely prepares its annual property tax notices in six languages: English, French, Chinese, Italian, Greek, and Portuguese."

▼ For people across the world, the Royal Canadian Mounted Police, or Mounties, symbolize Canada.

Canada: Ethnic Groups

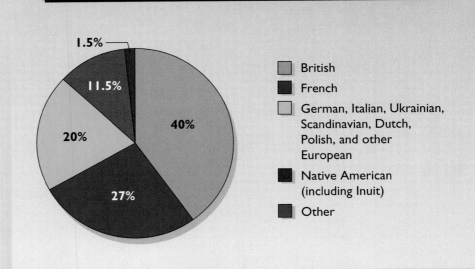

British

French

German, Italian, Ukrainian, Scandinavian, Dutch, Polish, and other European

Native American (including Inuit)

Other

40%

27%

20%

11.5%

1.5%

Chart Study Like the United States, Canada is very ethnically diverse.
Critical Thinking Hundreds of years ago, Native Americans were the largest ethnic group in Canada. What group is largest today? What percentage of Canada's people are of European descent?

Forming an Identity
Until the 1830s, no French-Canadian poets or novelists had any of their work published in Canada. The Quebec Movement of 1860 was the first attempt to preserve French culture. In the 1960s, Quebec poets worked to create a French-Canadian identity. One example is Paul Chamberland. In his book called *Terre Québec,* which means "the land of Quebec," he uses language to encourage pride in the province's French roots.

▼ Some French-Canadian drivers have license plates that refer to Quebec as *la belle province,* or "the beautiful province."

The People of Canada

The people who speak these languages came to Canada in search of better lives. Since Canada is the second-largest country in the world, it was attractive to newcomers in search of land and new opportunities. From the beginning, Canada's leaders made immigration easy. At first, they preferred European settlers. Laws set limits on immigrants who were Jews, Asians, or Africans. But that has changed. Today, people of all ethnic groups may move to Canada as long as they can support themselves.

Sometimes the ties among Canadians are not as strong as those among Americans. People in the United States may disagree with one another. But they rarely talk about forming independent states or countries. Some Canadian groups do.

For instance, the French Canadians of Quebec are very concerned about preserving their heritage. They are glad that Canada is a bilingual country. It has two official languages—English and French. In Quebec, special laws promote French culture and language. For instance, all street and advertising signs are written in French. An English translation of the sign appears below the French. But many French Canadians want more. They want Quebec to become a separate country. To show their determination, they have license plates that read *Je me souviens,* or "I remember." This refers to remembering their French heritage.

Canada's indigenous peoples also want to preserve their culture. Most, however, do not want to be independent. Instead, they are trying to fix problems from the past. In Canada, as in the United States, early European settlers took over the indigenous peoples' lands. Many indigenous peoples were sent to **reserves.** These were areas that the government set aside for them. Others were denied equal rights and facilities. In Canada, new laws allow the indigenous peoples to use their own languages in their schools. Now, people want their own languages on the street signs in their communities.

The Chippewa have a special problem. During World War II, the Canadian army took over Chippewa land for a military base. The Chippewa were sent to a reserve. The government said it would return the land after the war. Although the war ended in 1945, the land was not returned until 1994. The Chippewa sued the government for breaking its promise. They will use the money awarded to them for many projects. One big project is cleaning up dangerous waste that the military left behind. Chippewa chief Thomas M. Bressette feels his people deserved better treatment from the government:

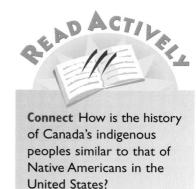

READ ACTIVELY

Connect How is the history of Canada's indigenous peoples similar to that of Native Americans in the United States?

Remembering Canada's History

The community of Chemainus, British Columbia, is famous for its collection of 32 historical murals. The murals are huge, and the people depicted in them are larger than life. This mural honors the role that the country's indigenous peoples have played in Canada's history.

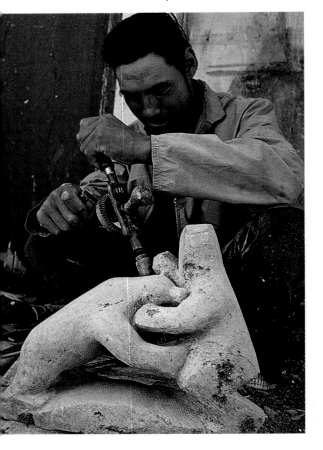
▼ An Inuit artist uses a drill to put the finishing touches on a soapstone carving. Creating such traditional artwork is one way the Inuits retain their identity.

READ ACTIVELY

Ask Questions What do you want to know about the ways in which Canadians have encouraged artists to express Canadian ideals?

"While our people were giving their lives [in the war] in Europe, the Government here in Canada was taking their land away from them and putting us on postage-stamp [size] reserves. We're asking for a share in the resources. We don't want to appear as beggars dependent on the government handouts, but we are now being denied the resources that we so willingly gave up to support this nation."

Canada's Inuits are also trying to improve their lives. For centuries, these nomadic hunters lived in the Arctic. They had great survival skills and were fine craftworkers and artists. They made everything they needed. Modern technology, however, allows them to buy the clothes, tools, and weapons they once used to make. Many Inuits have lost their traditional skills. As a result, some feel they are losing their identity as Inuits. In the early 1990s, the Inuits convinced the Canadian government to grant them a huge section of land. It is located in the Northwest Territory. At the turn of the century, they will move into their new homeland. They call it *Nunavut,* or "Our Land."

Canadian Culture—The Mosaic

Canada has made a special effort "to recognize all Canadians as full and equal participants in Canadian society." This means that people can be Canadian and express their ethnic heritage at the same time. There is one cultural issue that unites most Canadians. They feel that the United States has too much influence on their culture. This worry is not new. As early as 1939, Canada established the National Film Board. Its job is to support movies with Canadian national themes and concerns.

Canadians still search for ways to express their unique culture. Painters have played a role. In the 1920s and 1930s, several painters formed the "Group of Seven." These artists developed bold new techniques for their paintings of Canada's landscape. The group inspired other Canadian artists to experiment. Many are still doing this today. Some ethnic artists follow other paths. For instance, Inuit printmakers and sculptors give new life to the images and ideas of their ancestors.

Many Canadian writers and musicians are famous for their work. American writer Mark Twain highly praised Lucy Maud Montgomery's *Anne of Green Gables.* The heroine, Anne, was "the dearest and most moving and delightful child since Alice in Wonderland," Twain said. Today, writers such as Margaret Atwood and Alice Munro are praised for their work. "The Wreck of the Edmund FitzGerald" is a well-known

A Canadian Export

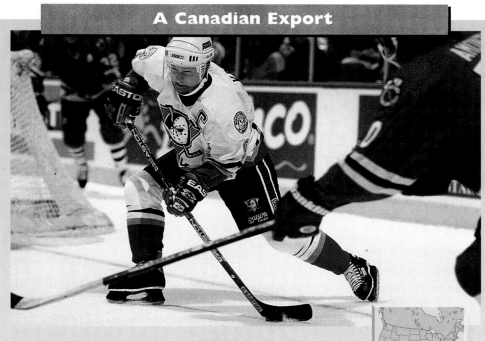

Hockey began in Canada, probably in the mid-1800s. Since that time, the Canadians have exported their national game to the United States. Twenty of the 26 teams in the National Hockey League are located in U.S. cities. Also, some 60 percent of players in the NHL are Canadians. Above, Canadian Paul Kariya of the Anaheim Mighty Ducks prepares to move forward with the puck.

folk song about a ship that sank in a storm on Lake Superior. Most people think the song is old. Actually, it was written in the 1970s by Canadian folksinger Gordon Lightfoot.

In sports, Canada has turned the tables. It has influenced the United States. Ice hockey and lacrosse are two of Canada's athletic exports. Every year, hockey teams from the United States and Canada compete for the Stanley Cup, a Canadian prize.

CITIZEN HEROES

Overcoming Obstacles Terry Fox never earned millions a year or had an athletic shoe named after him. But he was one of the greatest Canadian athletes. In 1980, for 143 days in a row, he ran a daily marathon, which is 26 miles (42 km) long! Through snow, hail, and intense heat, he ran 3,339 miles (5,374 km). But why? When Terry was 19, his right leg was amputated because of bone cancer. He ran to raise money to help others with the disease. When his "Marathon of Hope" was over, he had raised $25 million for cancer research.

SECTION 2 REVIEW

1. **Define** reserve.

2. **Identify** (a) Gordon Lightfoot, (b) Nunavut.

3. How does Canadian society seem like a mosaic?

4. How have Canada and Quebec tried to protect French culture?

5. What have the Inuits done to protect their culture?

Critical Thinking
6. **Making Predictions** Think about the Inuits moving into a new homeland. What do you think might happen to their culture? Why?

Activity
7. **Writing to Learn** Write a brief paragraph explaining why you think ice hockey developed in Canada.

SKILLS ACTIVITY

Organizing Information

What tools do you use to help you study? You certainly use your books, and you probably use a pencil and paper. Perhaps you use a dictionary or note cards. What about maps? You can make a map of the material you want to learn, and not just for your geography class.

When you think of a map, you might picture a map of a country or a continent from your textbook. Perhaps you think of a globe or of a street map. There are dozens—maybe even hundreds—of different kinds of maps. But there is an entirely different kind of map that you may not know of. It does not show the land or the water or even the sky.

This kind of map is called a concept map. As you read about a new topic, you can draw a concept map of the information. When you take notes, a concept map can help you organize information in a way that can be easier to understand and remember.

Get Ready

A concept map shows how concepts, or ideas, are related to one another. You can make a concept map about almost anything. Look at the concept map below.

The *subject* of this concept map, "lamps," is in the middle. Two important *features* of this subject are identified in the circles. Lines connect the features to the subject to show that they are related.

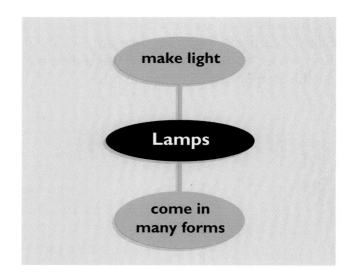

Now look below at how this concept map can grow. Can you see where *details* have been added to each of the features of lamps? Lines connect the details to each feature to show that they are related.

The subject of the concept map is in the middle. The features of the subject are identified at the next level. The final level identifies details of the features. As you get farther away from the middle of a concept map, it becomes more specific.

This type of concept map is sometimes called a "web." Can you see how its shape is similar to that of a spider web?

How do the concept maps show a great deal of information in a simple way? Notice that they show how all the ideas are related to each other. That is what makes concept maps so useful.

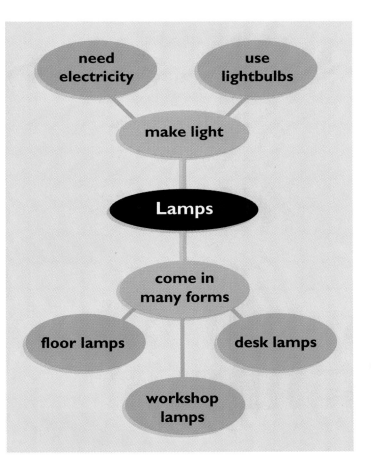

Try It Out

Try drawing your own concept maps. Draw a web for each of the subjects below.
- cars
- school
- music

Start with the subject in the center of the web. Then add features in circles connected to the subject with lines. Next add details of each feature. Some information you could include in a web about cars is shown in the chart.

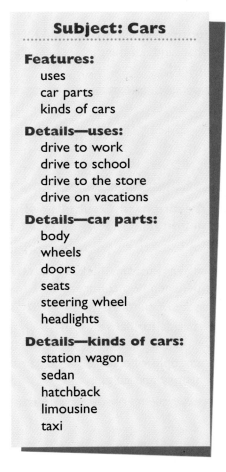

Subject: Cars

Features:
uses
car parts
kinds of cars

Details—uses:
drive to work
drive to school
drive to the store
drive on vacations

Details—car parts:
body
wheels
doors
seats
steering wheel
headlights

Details—kinds of cars:
station wagon
sedan
hatchback
limousine
taxi

Apply the Skill

Concept maps can be especially useful when you use them in your schoolwork. Reread Chapter 3 and create a web for each of the subjects below.
- Nunavut
- immigration
- traditions

Review and Activities

Reviewing Main Ideas

1. What contributions have Native Americans made to American culture?

2. If you went to an ethnic street festival, what kinds of things might you find?

3. What challenges face immigrants who move to the United States?

4. Why did the Chippewa sue the Canadian government?

5. How is Canadian culture similar to a mosaic?

Reviewing Key Terms

Match the definitions in Column I with the key terms in Column II.

Column I

1. the exchange of customs, ideas, or things between two cultures

2. a wide variety of cultures

3. an area set aside for native peoples

4. a group of people who share a language, history, and culture

Column II

a. **cultural diversity**

b. **cultural exchange**

c. **ethnic group**

d. **reserve**

Critical Thinking

1. **Drawing Conclusions** What do you think will be the effect on Canada if Quebec eventually becomes a separate country?

2. **Expressing Problems Clearly** Why do some French Canadians want Quebec to be a separate country?

Graphic Organizer

Immigrants have contributed much to the cultures of the United States and Canada. Copy the chart onto a sheet of paper. Then fill in the empty boxes with examples of regions from which immigrants to the United States and Canada came.

	United States	Canada
Regions from which immigrants came		

Map Activity

Native American Groups

For each Native American group listed below, write the letter from the map that shows its location.

1. Miami
2. Chippewa
3. Cherokee
4. Iroquois
5. Pueblo
6. Cheyenne
7. Comanche
8. Huron

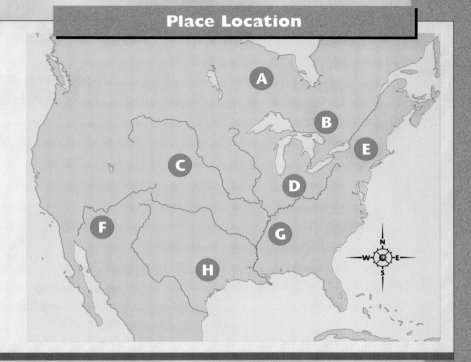

Place Location

Writing Activity

Writing a Letter

Suppose that Anna and Tito are pen pals. Write a letter from Tito to Anna, suggesting ways she might get her parents more involved in American culture. Remember, Tito believes problems can be solved when different ideas come together. Perhaps he might suggest that her parents contribute ideas to a community project. What kind of project could they participate in? How could participation make Anna's parents feel like they are part of their new society?

Internet Activity

Use a search engine to find the **Canadian Heritage** page. Choose English or French and explore the various links. Make a travel brochure for Canada including national historic sites, official languages, and cultures. Include text, photos, and illustrations in your brochure.

Skills Review

Turn to the Skills Activity.

Review how concept maps are used to organize information. Then answer the following questions: (a) What three levels of information are shown on a concept map? (b) What is another name for a concept map?

How Am I Doing?

Answer the following questions to check your progress.

1. Can I identify the important contributions immigrants have made to the United States?

2. Do I understand why Canadian culture is described as a mosaic?

3. Can I describe some challenges faced by immigrants to a country such as the United States or Canada?

4. What information from this chapter can I use in my book project?

Western Wagons

BY STEPHEN VINCENT BENÉT

prairie-schooner a covered wagon used by American pioneers to travel across the country

Ask Questions What questions would you like to ask someone who went West in the wagons?

They went with axe and rifle, when the trail was still to blaze,
They went with wife and children, in the prairie-schooner days,
With banjo and with frying pan—Susanna, don't you cry!
For I'm off to California to get rich out there or die!

We've broken land and cleared it, but we're tired of where we are.
They say that wild Nebraska is a better place by far.
There's gold in far Wyoming, there's black earth in Ioway,
So pack up the kids and blankets, for we're moving out today!

The cowards never started and the weak died on the road,
And all across the continent the endless campfires glowed.
We'd taken land and settled—but a traveler passed by—
And we're going West tomorrow—Lordy, never ask us why!

◄ This photograph was taken in 1866. The colors were hand painted on the photograph. It shows a wagon train on its way through the Strawberry Valley in the Sierra Nevada, a mountain range in California.

We're going West tomorrow, where the promises can't fail.
O'er the hills in legions, boys, and crowd the dusty trail!
We shall starve and freeze and suffer. We shall die, and tame the lands.
But we're going West tomorrow, with our fortune in our hands.

EXPLORING YOUR READING

Look Back

1. In "Western Wagons," what hopes do the people have for their future?

Think It Over

2. What is the mood of the travelers in "Western Wagons"?

Go Beyond

3. This poem mentions men and boys but barely refers to women or girls. Why do you think that is so? How could the poem be changed to include the women and girls who were part of these beginnings?

Ideas for Writing: Poem

4. Think of some important or unusual element of your family, community, or some other group to which you belong. It could be a special custom or a more general way of living. Write a poem that explains how this began, using historical facts or inventing a story.

Exploring the United States

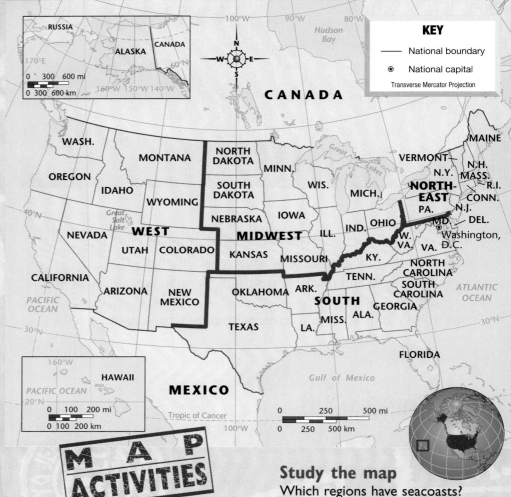

MAP ACTIVITIES

The United States can be divided into distinct regions. These are the Northeast, the South, the Midwest, and the West. To learn more about these regions, do the following activities.

Study the map
Which regions have seacoasts? Which region has the largest states, and which has the smallest?

Look for clues
Think about what it would be like to live in each region. What has attracted people to different parts of the United States? What kinds of work do you think people in different regions do?

The Northeast

LAND OF BIG CITIES

BEFORE YOU READ

Reach Into Your Background

Draw a quick sketch of your neighborhood. Do the houses have big yards, or are they close together? Do you live in an apartment with other families next door, or is your nearest neighbor some distance away? How do you think closeness to other people affects the ways people live?

Questions to Explore

1. How do the large cities of the Northeast contribute to the economy of the United States?

2. Why is the Northeast a region of many cultures?

Key Terms

commute
megalopolis
population density

Key Places

New York City
Philadelphia
Boston

For at least a century, life in New York City has been described in one way: crowded. One hundred years ago, horse-drawn carriages caused traffic jams. Now, 5 million riders squeeze into New York's subway cars every day. Others travel the 1,745 miles (2,807 km) of bus lines or catch one of the city's 12,000 taxis. And many people drive their own cars through the city's busy streets. The ferryboat is another way to travel in New York.

New York is not unique. Washington, D.C., Philadelphia, and Boston are also crowded. In these big cities, millions of people **commute,** or travel to work, each day. Many drive to work from suburbs that are far from the city's center. Even people who live in the city must travel from one area to another to work.

A Region of Cities

Did you ever hear of Bowash? That is what some people call the chain of cities from Boston to New York to Washington, D.C. This coastal region of the Northeast is a **megalopolis** (meg uh LAHP uh lis). In this type of region, cities and suburbs have

▼ During rush hour, New York City's streets fill with cars. If you are in a hurry, try walking or grabbing a subway train instead of driving.

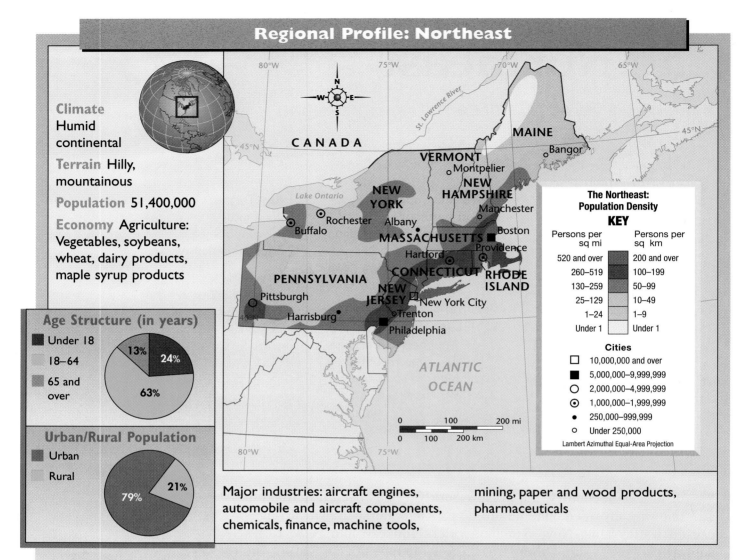

Climate Humid continental

Terrain Hilly, mountainous

Population 51,400,000

Economy Agriculture: Vegetables, soybeans, wheat, dairy products, maple syrup products

Age Structure (in years)

- Under 18
- 18–64
- 65 and over

13%
24%
63%

Urban/Rural Population

- Urban
- Rural

79%
21%

The Northeast: Population Density

KEY

Persons per sq mi	Persons per sq km
520 and over	200 and over
260–519	100–199
130–259	50–99
25–129	10–49
1–24	1–9
Under 1	Under 1

Cities

☐	10,000,000 and over
■	5,000,000–9,999,999
○	2,000,000–4,999,999
◉	1,000,000–1,999,999
•	250,000–999,999
○	Under 250,000

Lambert Azimuthal Equal-Area Projection

Major industries: aircraft engines, automobile and aircraft components, chemicals, finance, machine tools, mining, paper and wood products, pharmaceuticals

Map and Chart Study This map shows the population density of the Northeast. Note that city population figures in the key are for the metropolitan area, or the city and its surrounding suburbs. **Regions** Where are the most densely populated parts of the Northeast? Where are the least densely populated areas? **Critical Thinking** Compare the urban/rural population chart with the map. In which part of the region do you think most northeasterners live?

grown so close together that they form one big urban area. Look at the map on the next page to see how large this area is.

The Northeast is the most densely populated region of the United States. A region's **population density** is the average number of people per square mile (or square kilometer). The population is denser in parts of New Jersey than in crowded countries like India or Japan!

The Northeast's economy is based on cities. Many were founded in colonial times, along rivers or near the Atlantic Ocean. These cities began as transportation and trade centers. Today, manufacturing, finance, communications, and government employ millions of urban Northeasterners.

Philadelphia and Boston Philadelphia and Boston were important in our nation's early history. In Philadelphia, America's founders adopted the Declaration of Independence and the Constitution. Some early struggles against the British took place in Boston. In Philadelphia and Boston, you can visit buildings that date from before the American Revolution. Yet you will find that they are very modern cities, too.

Today, Philadelphia is an industrial powerhouse. It is located near the mouth of the Delaware River. Important land and water transportation routes pass through here. Ships, trucks, and trains bring in raw materials from other parts of Pennsylvania and from all over the world. Thousands of factories process food, refine petroleum, and manufacture chemicals. Hundreds of products are then shipped out for sale.

The Boston area is famous for its more than 20 colleges and universities. Cambridge (KAYM brij) is the home of Harvard, which is America's oldest university. The city is also famous for its science and technology centers. Boston's universities and scientific companies often work together to design new products and to carry out medical research.

LINKS TO LANGUAGE ARTS

Good-bye City Life In 1845, Henry Thoreau moved to Walden Pond in Massachusetts. His life there was an experiment in living alone and with only the essentials. He cut down trees and built a one-room house. He planted a vegetable garden and gathered wild fruit. And he wrote *Walden*, a classic of American literature.

An Urban Megalopolis

KEY

Metropolitan area

Freeway

Tollway

National capital

Other city

Lambert Azimuthal Equal-Area Projection

Map Study You can drive from Washington, D.C., to Boston, Massachusetts, without leaving the urban areas. **Place** Compare this map with the one in the Regional Profile. What similarities are there between the two maps?

The Brooklyn Bridge is a suspension bridge in New York City. A suspension bridge hangs from cables that are anchored at either end and supported by several towers along the bridge's length. Completed in 1883, the bridge crosses the East River, connecting two boroughs, or sections, of the city— Manhattan and Brooklyn. At the time of its completion, the Brooklyn Bridge was the longest suspension bridge in the world. There are six lanes for traffic. A wide walkway for pedestrians runs along the center of the bridge.

Each tower is 275 feet (84 m) tall. The two towers are seated firmly in underwater piers buried deep in the riverbed.

The suspender cables connect the cables and the roadbed.

The anchorages at either end of the bridge are huge blocks of concrete, set deep in the ground.

The roadbed, or deck, has special braces, called *trusses*, that prevent the bridge from swinging during high winds.

The main cable runs from one anchorage, across two towers, to a second anchorage. This cable is nearly 16 inches (41 cm) thick and is made of steel.

New York City One word describes New York City—huge. In terms of population, it is the largest city in the United States and one of the 10 largest in the world. More than 7 million people live in New York City. Most states do not have populations that large. The city covers an area of about 320 square miles (830 sq km) on islands and the mainland around the mouth of the Hudson River. The various parts of the city are connected by tunnels and bridges. One of the oldest and most interesting bridges is the Brooklyn Bridge. The diagram on the opposite page shows how the Brooklyn Bridge was built.

New York City is our nation's "money capital." The word *millionaire* was invented here. About 500,000 New Yorkers work for banks and other financial institutions. The headquarters of many of the country's wealthiest corporations are in New York. The famous New York Stock Exchange is on Wall Street.

New York is also a center of fashion, publishing, advertising, television, radio, and the arts. New York's Broadway is famous for its plays. About eight million people see plays in New York every year.

◀ New York City's financial district is a maze of skyscrapers. One of the streets hidden among these towers is Wall Street, the heart of New York's banking and financial industries.

A Gateway for Immigrants

On January 1, 1892, 15-year-old Annie Moore made her way down the gangplank of a steamship onto American soil. Annie and her two younger brothers had sailed from Ireland. Annie stepped into the registry room of the Ellis Island Immigrant Station. Here she received a $10 gold piece for being the first immigrant to arrive at the new station.

From 1892 to 1943, the first stop for millions of immigrants to the United States was Ellis Island. From here, immigrants could see the Statue of Liberty, half a mile away in New York Harbor. Today, Ellis Island and the Statue of Liberty are national monuments.

New York and other port cities of the Northeast have been important gateways for immigrants. In the 1800s, many Irish and Germans immigrated to New York. Later, immigrants poured in from southern and Eastern Europe. During the 1900s, people also have come from the Caribbean, Asia, and Africa. In one recent year, New York City welcomed immigrants from more than 100 different countries.

After entering through the port cities, many immigrants stayed in those cities and built a new life. Today, New York is rich in ethnic diversity. You can visit Little Italy, Little India, and Chinatown. To get a real sense of the ethnic diversity of the United States, just look at a list of restaurants in a big city like New York.

▶ The Statue of Liberty symbolizes the United States' tradition of providing a home to immigrants. The statue stands on Liberty Island in New York Harbor.

SECTION 1 REVIEW

1. **Define** (a) commute, (b) megalopolis, (c) population density.

2. **Identify** (a) New York City, (b) Philadelphia, (c) Boston.

3. (a) How does the population density in the Northeast compare with densities in other regions of the country?
(b) How does population density affect the ways people live and work?

4. If you were looking for work in the Northeast, what kinds of jobs might you find?

5. How have immigrants affected the culture of the Northeast?

Critical Thinking

6. **Making Comparisons** Think about the histories of, and major industries in, Philadelphia and Boston. How are the two cities similar? How have they developed differently?

Activity

7. **Writing to Learn** Which city described in this section are you most interested in learning more about? Make a list of things you would like to learn about this city. Then write a brief paragraph explaining why you want to learn these things.

The South

A CHANGING LANDSCAPE

Reach Into Your Background

Think about a time in your life when you experienced a big change. Perhaps you moved to another community or started at a new school. How did you adapt to the change? Did you find yourself thinking and behaving in new ways?

Questions to Explore

1. How is the South's land and water important to its economy?
2. How has the growth of industry changed the South?

Key Terms

petrochemical
industrialization
Sun Belt

Key Places

Atlanta
Washington, D.C.

From July 19 to August 4, 1996, the city of Atlanta, Georgia, was the center of the world. More than two million people from 172 countries visited the city during that time. They came to see a very special event. It was the 1996 Summer Olympic Games.

The people who watched the 1996 Olympics saw more than great athletes. They also saw a world-class city. Atlanta today is a center of trade, transportation, and communication. Atlanta is also in one of the fastest-growing regions of the United States: the South. With strong urban areas like Atlanta, plus rich agriculture, the South is helping to lead the United States into the future.

The Varied Land of the South

People in the South today can make a living in many different ways. The South's geography makes many of these jobs possible. The South is warmer than regions of the United States that are farther north. Most parts of the region also receive plenty of rain. The wide coastal plains along the Atlantic

▼ Famous boxer Muhammad Ali lights the Olympic torch at the 1996 Summer Olympic Games in Atlanta, Georgia.

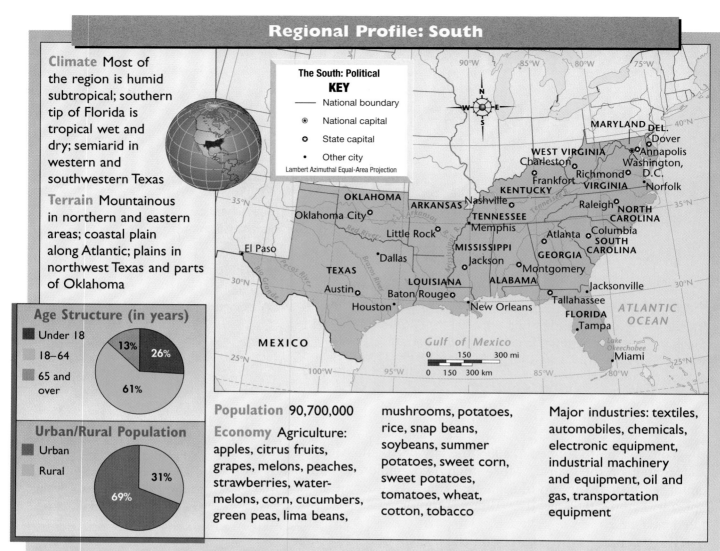

Climate Most of the region is humid subtropical; southern tip of Florida is tropical wet and dry; semiarid in western and southwestern Texas

Terrain Mountainous in northern and eastern areas; coastal plain along Atlantic; plains in northwest Texas and parts of Oklahoma

The South: Political
KEY
— National boundary
⊛ National capital
✪ State capital
• Other city
Lambert Azimuthal Equal-Area Projection

Age Structure (in years)
- ■ Under 18
- ■ 18–64
- ■ 65 and over

13% 26% 61%

Urban/Rural Population
- ■ Urban
- ■ Rural

31% 69%

Population 90,700,000

Economy Agriculture: apples, citrus fruits, grapes, melons, peaches, strawberries, water-melons, corn, cucumbers, green peas, lima beans, mushrooms, potatoes, rice, snap beans, soybeans, summer potatoes, sweet corn, sweet potatoes, tomatoes, wheat, cotton, tobacco

Major industries: textiles, automobiles, chemicals, electronic equipment, industrial machinery and equipment, oil and gas, transportation equipment

Map and Chart Study This map shows the borders and major cities of the southern states of the United States. **Interaction** Notice that most southern cities are located near waterways, such as rivers and the ocean. How do you think southern cities benefit from this location? **Critical Thinking** Look at the urban/rural population chart. Earlier in the 1900s, the South was a mostly rural region. Today, however, more southerners live in urban areas than live in rural areas. Based on your reading of this section, what change in the South's economy might have contributed to this population change?

Ocean and the Gulf of Mexico have rich soil. Together, these features make much of the South a great place for growing crops. Some places in the region are also good for raising animals for food. People in the South can take advantage of many different natural resources.

Farming in the South Farming has always been one of the most important parts of the South's economy. For years, the South's most important crop was cotton. Southern farmers once depended on cotton as their only source of income. Today, cotton still brings a lot of money to the South, especially to Alabama, Mississippi, and Texas. But

"King Cotton" no longer rules this region. In the 1890s, the boll weevil (bowl WEE vuhl)—a kind of beetle—began to attack cotton plants in the South. Over the next 30 years, it destroyed fields across the area. Without money from cotton, many farmers went bankrupt. Most southern farmers now try to raise more than one crop. Together they produce a wide variety of crops and farm animals.

Some of these crops need very special growing conditions. Citrus fruits require year-round warmth and sunshine. Florida has plenty of both. More oranges, tangerines, grapefruits, and limes are grown here than in any other state. Rice needs warm, moist growing conditions. Farmers in Arkansas, Louisiana, and Mississippi can supply this. They grow rice along the coast of the Gulf of Mexico and in the Mississippi River valley.

Some areas of the South have become famous for their agricultural products. Georgia has taken one of its products as its nickname. It is the Peach State. Georgia is also known for its peanuts and pecans. Texas raises more cattle than any other state. Arkansas raises the most chickens and turkeys. All of these items are just a sample of what southern agriculture produces. You can read about more of the South's farm products in the Regional Profile.

Drilling and Mining in the South In some parts of the South, what is under the soil is as important as what grows in it. In Louisiana, Oklahoma, and Texas, companies drill for oil and natural gas. These can be used as fuel. They are also made into **petrochemicals.** These are substances, like plastics, paint, and asphalt, that come from petroleum. In Alabama, Kentucky, West Virginia, and Tennessee, miners dig for coal. Southern states are also leading producers of salt, sulfur, lead, zinc, and bauxite—a mineral used to make aluminum.

READ ACTIVELY

Predict Think about what happened when oil and natural gas were discovered In Louisiana, Oklahoma, and Texas. How do you think that discovery affected the economies of those states?

◀ Cotton is no longer the South's major crop, but it still plays an important part in the region's economy.

Southern Fish and Forests   People in the South can also make a living in fishing and forestry. The Chesapeake Bay area near Maryland and Virginia is famous for its shellfish. However, the South's fishing industry is strongest in Louisiana and Texas. The timber industry works in every southern state except for Delaware. Softwood trees like southern pine are used for building or for paper. People use hardwood trees to make furniture. North Carolina has the nation's largest hardwood furniture industry.

Southern Cities and Industries

Until recently, people often thought of the South as a slow-moving, mostly rural region. But over the past 50 years, this region has gone through lots of changes. Though the South's rural areas are still important, most people in the South today live in cities. Some work in factories or in high-technology firms. Others work in tourism or in one of the other industries in this region's growing economy. This change from an agriculture-based economy to an industry-based economy is called **industrialization.**

Textiles and Technology   One of the most important industries in the South is the textile industry. Textile mills make cloth. They were first built in this region to use the South's cotton. Today, many mills still make cotton cloth. Many others now make cloth from synthetic, or human-made, materials. The textile industry is strongest in Georgia, the Carolinas, and Virginia.

READ ACTIVELY

Visualize Visualize how a rural area might change to an urban area. What do you think might be built? What features might disappear?

▼ One of the largest cities in the United States, Dallas, Texas, is a center of banking, industry, and trade.

The tourists on this steamboat are getting a taste of what it was like to travel on the Mississippi River more than 100 years ago. They are taking a trip on the *Natchez*, which sails out of New Orleans, Louisiana. In the 1800s and early 1900s, steamboats were an important form of transportation on rivers in the United States. **Critical Thinking** What part of a steamboat is used to push the ship through the water?

The textile industry was an early arrival in the South. The first mills in the region were built in the 1800s. Now, more than 100 years later, new industries are growing all across the South. One is the high-technology industry. Workers in this industry try to improve computers and figure out better ways to use them. Some centers of high technology are Raleigh, North Carolina, and Austin, Texas. Another forward-looking industry is the aerospace business. In Cape Canaveral, Florida; Houston, Texas; and Huntsville, Alabama, people work for the National Aeronautics and Space Administration (NASA). Some train as astronauts and run the space shuttle program. Atlanta, Georgia, is now a center for the cable television industry. If you watch the news on cable television, you are probably watching a program from Atlanta.

Transportation and Tourism A big part of the South's economy depends on moving goods and people into and out of the region. Most of the South's largest cities play big roles in this transportation industry. Miami, Florida, and New Orleans, Louisiana, are major ports. Miami is a center for goods and people going to and from Central and South America. New Orleans is a gateway between the Gulf of Mexico and the Mississippi River system. It is also an important port for oil tankers.

Some of the people the transportation industry brings to the South come to stay. Thousands come to work in the South's new industries. Thousands more choose to move to the South because of its climate. The South is part of the **Sun Belt.** This broad area of the United States

Jazz Jazz music is arguably the South's greatest contribution to the arts in America. Most people consider New Orleans to be the birthplace of jazz. Mainly African in origin, jazz grew out of many different kinds of music. African American work songs, hymns, and spirituals are all part of its roots. Today, musicians in New Orleans play many forms of jazz. One of the most popular is called Dixieland or New Orleans jazz.

stretches from the southern Atlantic Coast to the coast of California. It is known for its warm weather. The population of the Sun Belt has been rising for the past few decades. Some arrivals are older adults who want to retire to places without cold winters. Others come to take advantage of both the weather and the work that the Sun Belt offers.

Warm weather also brings people to the South who only plan to visit. These people fuel the region's tourist industry. In winter, tourists come to enjoy the sunny beaches of Florida and the Gulf Coast. In the summer, they can hike in the mountains of the Appalachians and Ozarks. They can visit historic cities like Charleston, South Carolina, or New Orleans, Louisiana, at any time of the year. In states throughout the South, there are always fun and exciting things to see and to do.

Our Nation's Capital The city of Washington is not in any state. Instead, it is in the District of Columbia, which lies between the states of Maryland and Virginia. This area of land was chosen as the site for the nation's capital in 1790. Located on the shore of the Potomac River, Washington, D.C., was the first planned city in the nation. It has wide avenues, public buildings, and dramatic monuments. Many people consider Washington to be one of the most beautiful cities in the world. As the nation's capital, it is home to the nation's leaders and to hundreds of foreign diplomats.

U.S. Space Camp

Every year, people from ages 10 to 92 come to Huntsville, Alabama, to go to U.S. Space Camp. Here, a student experiences "weightlessness."

SECTION 2 REVIEW

1. **Define** (a) petrochemical, (b) industrialization, (c) Sun Belt.

2. **Identify** (a) Atlanta, (b) Washington, D.C.

3. How have the geography and climate of the South shaped its economy?

4. How has the South changed in the 1900s?

Critical Thinking

5. **Recognizing Cause and Effect** In this section, you have learned that the population of the South is growing. How have the South's geography and economy affected this growth?

Activity

6. **Writing to Learn** You work in an advertising firm in Atlanta, Georgia; Houston, Texas; or Miami, Florida. Create an advertisement to persuade people to move to your city or state. The advertisement can be designed for a newspaper or a magazine. It can also be for radio, television, or the Internet.

The Midwest

MOVING FROM THE FARM

BEFORE YOU READ

Reach Into Your Background

Have you ever introduced a new food or activity to your family? Can you think of a time when you pursued a new interest on your own? In the Midwest, many people are building ways of life very different from the ways their parents lived.

Questions to Explore

1. How is technology changing agriculture in the Midwest?
2. How is the change in agriculture affecting the growth of cities?

Key Terms
mixed-crop farm
recession
corporate farm

Key Places
Chicago
Detroit
St. Louis
Minneapolis-St. Paul

Camille LeFevre grew up in Black River Falls, Wisconsin. Her family included many generations of farmers. Camille spent her childhood on her parents' sheep farm.

> "As a skinny, pigtailed youngster, I spent a lot of time naming lambs, . . . falling off horses named Ginger and Lucky, building hay forts, riding tractors, stuffing freshly sheared wool into gunny sacks and perching on fence gates staring dreamily into space."

Camille remembers her childhood with deep affection. Yet, like thousands of farm children who grew up in the 1980s and 1990s, she did not follow in her parents' footsteps. Farming in the Midwest changed, and Camille chose a different path.

Technology Brings Changes to the Midwest

The Midwest is often called "the heartland" because it is the agricultural center of our nation. The soil is rich, and the climate is suitable for producing corn, soybeans, and livestock. Technology helped make farms productive. Inventions like the

▼ On most farms, sheep-shearing takes place once a year. The wool from this breed of sheep—the Suffolk—is used to make industrial and upholstery fabrics.

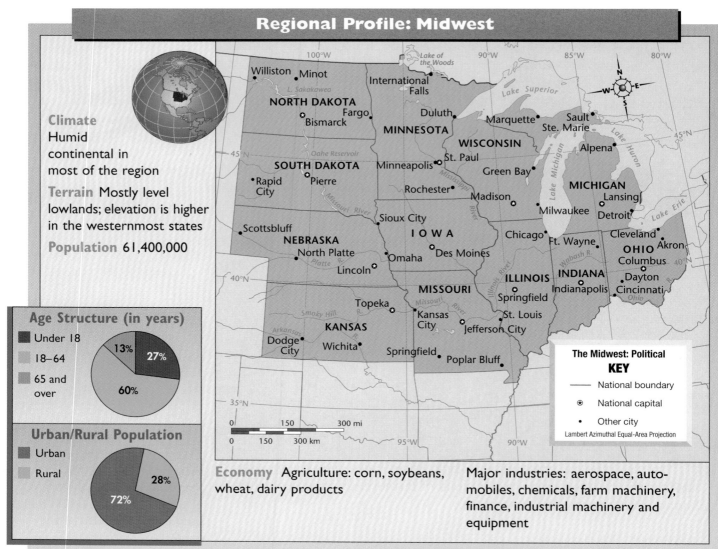

Climate Humid continental in most of the region

Terrain Mostly level lowlands; elevation is higher in the westernmost states

Population 61,400,000

Age Structure (in years)
- Under 18
- 18–64
- 65 and over

13%
27%
60%

Urban/Rural Population
- Urban
- Rural

28%
72%

The Midwest: Political
KEY
— National boundary
⊛ National capital
• Other city
Lambert Azimuthal Equal-Area Projection

Economy Agriculture: corn, soybeans, wheat, dairy products

Major industries: aerospace, automobiles, chemicals, farm machinery, finance, industrial machinery and equipment

Map and Chart Study This map shows the borders and major cities of states in the Midwest United States. **Location** The Great Lakes are part of a major shipping route. What Midwest states border the Great Lakes?

Critical Thinking Read the information about the Midwest's economy. Then look at the urban/rural population chart. How do you think most people in the Midwest make a living—in farming or in industry and services? Why?

steel plow, the windmill, and barbed wire helped settlers carve out farms on the plains. Today, technology continues to change the way people farm the land.

Family Farms Dwindle Until the 1980s, small family farms operated in this region. Many of these farms were **mixed-crop farms.** That is, they grew several different kinds of crops. This was a sensible way for farmers to work. If one crop failed, the farm had others. Camille's family, for example, sometimes raised cattle as well as sheep.

In the 1960s and 1970s, family farms prospered. The world population was rising, and demand for American farm products was high. Farmers felt that they could increase their business if they enlarged their farms. To build bigger farms, farmers bought more land and equipment. But all of this cost money. Many farmers borrowed from local banks.

In the early 1980s, there was a country-wide **recession** (rih SESH un), or a downturn in business activity. The demand for farm products dropped. At the same time, interest rates on loans increased. As a result, many farmers were not able to make enough money to pay their loans. Some families sold or left their farms. Over one million American farmers have left their land since 1980.

Corporate Farms Expand　What happened to the farms that were sold? Many of them were bought by agricultural companies. Small farms were combined to form large ones called **corporate farms.** These large farms could be run more efficiently. Large agricultural companies could afford to buy the expensive land and equipment that modern farming requires. And they could still make a profit.

Corporate farmers rely on machines and computers to do much of the work. This means that corporate farms employ fewer workers. Kansas offers a good example of corporate farming—having fewer

Dwindling Farms in Minnesota In Minnesota, the number of farms has fallen quickly. In 1959, Minnesota had 146,000 farms. In 1992, 88,000 farms were left. Further, about 38 percent of Minnesota's population was rural in 1960. In 1990, only 30 percent of the population lived in rural areas.

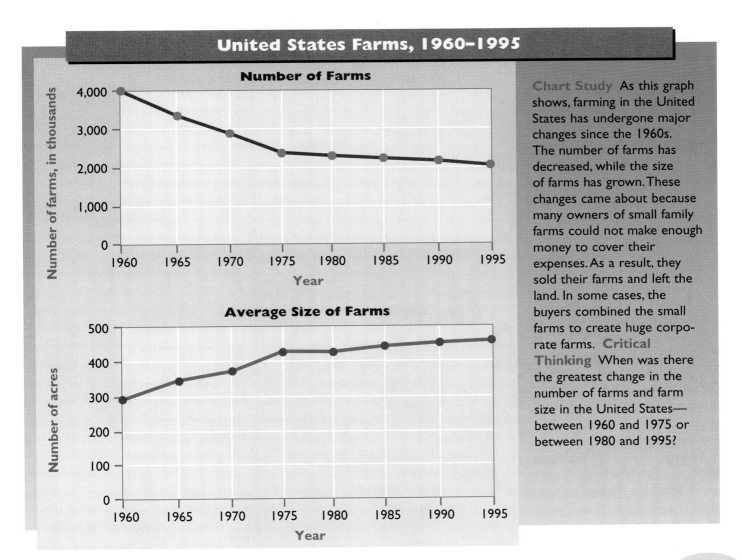

United States Farms, 1960–1995

Number of Farms

Average Size of Farms

Chart Study As this graph shows, farming in the United States has undergone major changes since the 1960s. The number of farms has decreased, while the size of farms has grown. These changes came about because many owners of small family farms could not make enough money to cover their expenses. As a result, they sold their farms and left the land. In some cases, the buyers combined the small farms to create huge corporate farms. Critical Thinking When was there the greatest change in the number of farms and farm size in the United States— between 1960 and 1975 or between 1980 and 1995?

workers and larger farms. In Kansas, 90 percent of the land is farmland, but only 10 percent of the people are farmers.

Not every farm in the Midwest is a corporate farm. But most small farms do not earn enough money to support a family. Family farmers usually have another job as well. Camille LeFevre's father, for example, advises other farmers on the best foods for their livestock.

Camille's parents did not lose their farm, but they did sell all their livestock to send Camille to college. When she graduated, she did not go back to the land. Farming these days is a very difficult way to make a living, she explains. She felt that she would have more opportunities in the city.

The Midwest Grows Cities

Camille is not alone. Most people in the Midwest today live in towns and cities. Yet many of these cities got their start as places to process and ship farm products.

Chicago: At the Center of Things   Chicago, Illinois, is a good example. Located on Lake Michigan, it was surrounded by prairies and farms in the mid-1800s. Farmers sent their corn, wheat, cattle, and hogs to Chicago. Mills and meat-packing plants turned these products into foods and shipped them east on the Great Lakes. When railroads were built, Chicago really boomed. By the late 1800s, it had become a steel-making and manufacturing center. What was one of the most important manufactured products made in Chicago? You probably guessed it: farm equipment.

Ask Questions What questions would you like to ask a person who grew up on a farm and later moved to a city?

▼ This view from the shores of Lake Michigan shows the many skyscrapers in Chicago's downtown area. The Sears Tower, to the left, is the tallest building in the United States.

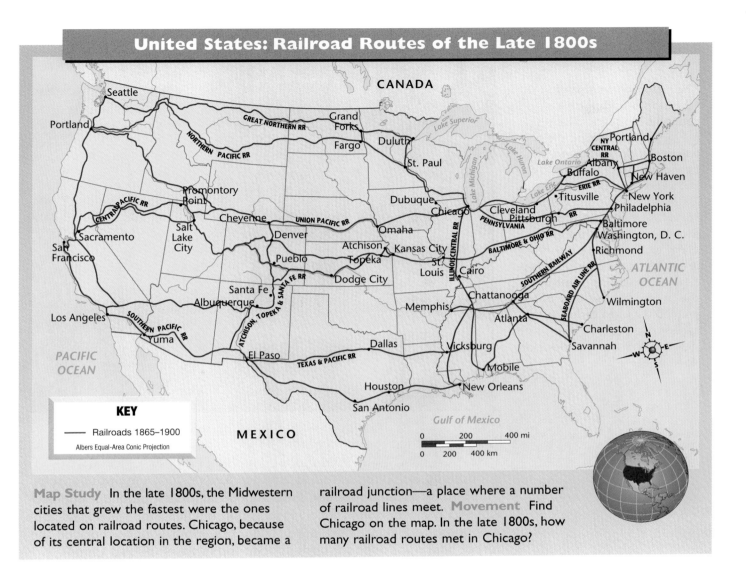

United States: Railroad Routes of the Late 1800s

KEY

—— Railroads 1865–1900

Albers Equal-Area Conic Projection

Map Study In the late 1800s, the Midwestern cities that grew the fastest were the ones located on railroad routes. Chicago, because of its central location in the region, became a railroad junction—a place where a number of railroad lines meet. **Movement** Find Chicago on the map. In the late 1800s, how many railroad routes met in Chicago?

Today, Chicago is the biggest city in the heartland. It is known for its ethnic diversity and lively culture. It is the hub of major transportation routes—highways, railroads, airlines, and shipping routes. Chicago is also the home of the first skyscraper—and many other architectural wonders. For a bird's-eye view of Chicago, go to the top of the Sears Tower, one of the tallest buildings in the world.

Other Cities The Midwest has other large cities. Two of them—Detroit and St. Louis—have played an important role in the country's history. Why do you think Detroit, Michigan, is called "the Motor City"? Here, you will find the headquarters of the American automobile industry. General Motors, Ford, and Chrysler have plants here.

Covered wagons, not cars, used to roll through St. Louis, Missouri. Located on the Mississippi River, this city was the starting point for pioneers heading west. Today, a huge stainless steel arch beside the river marks St. Louis as the "Gateway to the West." St. Louis is also a banking and commercial center.

LINKS ACROSS THE WORLD

Higher and Higher Until 1996, Chicago's Sears Tower, at 1,454 feet (443 m), was the world's tallest building. Now, the Petronas Twin Towers in Malaysia holds that title. It is 1,483 feet (452 m) high. But the world record may change again soon. When completed, the World Financial Center in Shanghai, China, will top out at 1,509 feet (460 m).

Suburban Minneapolis-St. Paul

The metropolitan area of Minneapolis-St. Paul covers about 4,620 square miles (11,965 sq km) around the point where the Mississippi and Minnesota rivers join. The area's population stands at about 2.7 million people and is growing steadily. The greatest population growth has taken place in Minneapolis-St. Paul's suburban areas, like the one pictured here. **Critical Thinking** Compare this photograph with the photograph of Chicago earlier in this section. How are the two scenes different? What similarities, if any, do you see?

Camille LeFevre moved to another Midwestern city, Minneapolis-St. Paul, Minnesota. These "Twin Cities" face each other on opposite sides of the Mississippi River. Publishing, medical, computer, and arts businesses are flourishing here. The city's suburbs have replaced the fertile land once used for farming. But the city has offered Camille the opportunity to build a career as a journalist. Camille's father still has his farm, and she visits him on the weekends. Perhaps Camille enjoys the best of both worlds.

SECTION 3 REVIEW

1. **Define** (a) mixed-crop farm, (b) recession, (c) corporate farm.

2. **Identify** (a) Chicago, (b) Detroit, (c) St. Louis, (d) Minneapolis-St. Paul.

3. Why did family farmers face hard times in the 1980s?

4. How are mixed-crop farming and corporate farming different?

Critical Thinking

5. **Identifying Central Issues** Think of how farming has changed with the development of corporate farms. List the advantages and disadvantages of corporate farming.

Activity

6. **Writing to Learn** Suppose you are a farmer and you have decided to sell your farm and move to a city. Write a letter to a friend explaining your decision.

The West

USING RESOURCES WISELY

Reach Into Your Background

Do you and your family take part in a recycling program, try to conserve water, or control the amount of electricity you use? In the western United States, people are trying to improve how they use resources.

Questions to Explore

1. What are the resources of the West?
2. How are people working to balance conservation with the need to use natural resources?

Key Terms
forty-niner
mass transit

Key Places
Sierra Nevada
Pacific Northwest
Portland
San Jose

An American President stood before Congress and made the following statement:

> "The conservation of our natural resources and their proper use constitute the fundamental problem which underlies almost every other problem of our national life. . . . But there must be . . . a realization . . . that to waste, to destroy our natural resources, to skin and exhaust the land instead of using it so as to increase its usefulness, will result in undermining . . . the very prosperity which we ought by right to hand down to [our children]."

Do you think this sounds like a modern plea for the environment? Actually, President Theodore Roosevelt made this statement nearly one hundred years ago. He understood that the vast resources of the West would not last without proper care.

▼ Congress declared Yosemite a national park in 1890. Yosemite Falls, which drops some 2,425 feet (740 m), are higher than any big-city skyscraper.

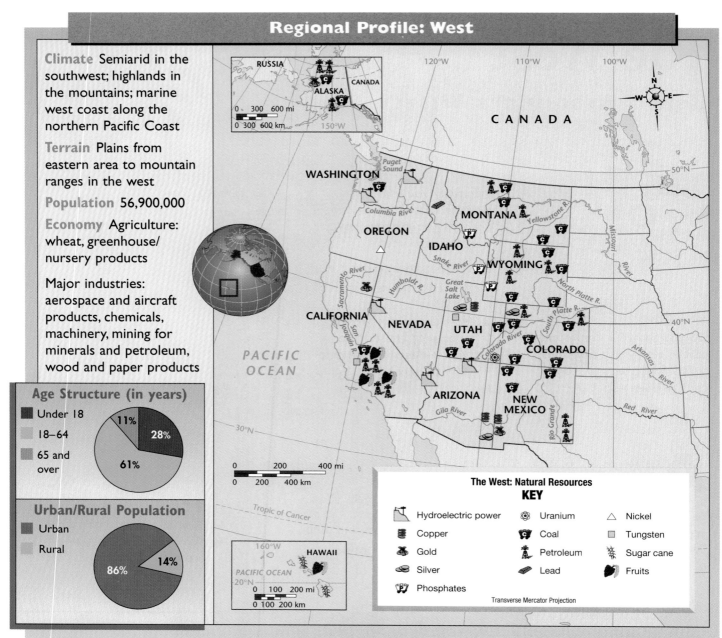

Climate Semiarid in the southwest; highlands in the mountains; marine west coast along the northern Pacific Coast

Terrain Plains from eastern area to mountain ranges in the west

Population 56,900,000

Economy Agriculture: wheat, greenhouse/ nursery products

Major industries: aerospace and aircraft products, chemicals, machinery, mining for minerals and petroleum, wood and paper products

Age Structure (in years)
- Under 18
- 18–64
- 65 and over

11%
28%
61%

Urban/Rural Population
- Urban
- Rural

86%
14%

The West: Natural Resources
KEY

- Hydroelectric power
- Copper
- Gold
- Silver
- Phosphates
- Uranium
- Coal
- Petroleum
- Lead
- Nickel
- Tungsten
- Sugar cane
- Fruits

Transverse Mercator Projection

Map and Chart Study This map shows the natural resources of the western states of the United States. **Place** What states have deposits of petroleum? What state's resources are mostly agricultural? **Movement** What states do you think are most likely to have been part of the Gold Rush in the late 1800s? **Critical Thinking** In the early 1800s, many people moved to the West to live in the region's wide open spaces. Look at the urban/rural population chart. Do you think that most people move to the West for the same reason today? Why or why not?

A Land of Precious Resources

An incredible wealth of natural resources has drawn people to the West for well over 400 years. The Spanish were well established on the West Coast even before the Pilgrims settled in New England in the 1620s. Then, after Lewis and Clark's exploration of the Louisiana Territory in the early 1800s, more people began to move westward.

Resources and Population   With the California Gold Rush in 1849, the population of the region exploded. The sleepy port of San Francisco boomed into a prosperous city. Hopeful miners arrived there, bought supplies, and headed off to the Sierra Nevada expecting to strike it rich.

A gold strike in Colorado led to the founding of the city of Denver. Further discoveries of valuable minerals drew more and more people to the region. New settlers here needed homes, and the place to find timber to build them was in the Pacific Northwest. After the Civil War, logging camps, sawmills, and paper mills sprang up in Washington, Oregon, and northern California.

At first, the resources of the West seemed unlimited. The use of these resources did create wealth and many jobs. However, it also created new challenges.

Managing Resources in the Sierras   Do you know the story of the goose that laid the golden egg? Its owner cut the goose open to see what was inside. For many years, people treated the Sierra Nevada in a similar way. The **forty-niners,** the first miners of the Gold Rush, washed small bits of gold from the streams. To get at larger deposits, big mining companies brought in water cannons that could blast away entire hillsides. They got their gold but left behind huge, ugly piles of rock.

After the Gold Rush, California's population soared. To meet the demand for new houses, loggers leveled many forests. Engineers built dams to send water through pipes to coastal cities. Next to the dams, they built hydroelectric (hy droh ee LEK trik) plants. Cities like San Francisco got water and power this way, but the dams flooded whole valleys of the Sierras.

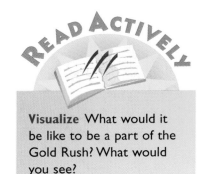

READ ACTIVELY

Visualize What would it be like to be a part of the Gold Rush? What would you see?

▼ The magnificent views at Grand Canyon National Park in Arizona attract crowds of tourists from all over the world.

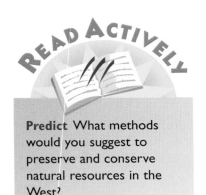

Predict What methods would you suggest to preserve and conserve natural resources in the West?

To save parts of the West as natural wilderness, Congress created several national parks and forests. Yet these, too, have developed problems. Yosemite (yoh SEM ut ee) National Park now gets so many visitors that it has traffic jams and air pollution in the summer.

Westerners are wrestling with new ways to manage the West's resources. For example, Yosemite now limits the number of campers in the park. Dam-building has stopped. Laws protect the habitats of certain animals. In addition, logging companies are limited in the amount of timber they can cut down.

The Urban West

Most Westerners today are not miners, farmers, or loggers. Rather, they work and live in cities. Their challenge is to figure out how to use natural resources wisely.

Portland, Oregon   "Your town or mine?" two land developers asked each other in 1845. The two developers were at the same site and predicted the development of a major port city. With such a great location near the junction of the Willamette and Columbia rivers, how could they lose? Francis W. Pettigrove of Portland, Maine, won the coin toss. He named the site after his hometown in the East.

Portland became a trade center for lumber, furs, grain, salmon, and wool. In the 1930s, new dams produced cheap electricity. Portland attracted many manufacturing industries. Over time, the factories polluted the Willamette River. Federal, state, and local governments—and industries—have worked to clean up this valuable resource.

A Black Bear in Its Natural Habitat

Many westerners are working to preserve the land areas where black bears and other wild animals live. Parts of the West have been made into national parks, forests, and wilderness areas. In addition, logging companies are working to preserve the environment by planting new trees to replace the ones that have been cut down.

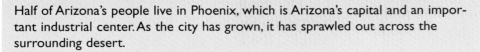

Phoenix, Arizona

Half of Arizona's people live in Phoenix, which is Arizona's capital and an important industrial center. As the city has grown, it has sprawled out across the surrounding desert.

San Jose, California   Urban sprawl is a problem in San Jose. The area around San Jose was known as "Valley of the Heart's Delight" for its beautiful orchards and farms. Now it is called "Silicon Valley," because it is the heart of the computer industry.

Instead of good soil and climate, San Jose's most valuable resource is its people. They come from all parts of the world. The greater population density has created crowded freeways and air pollution. To counter these problems, San Jose has built a light-rail **mass transit** system. Mass transit replaces individual cars with energy-saving buses or trains.

To Be a Leader Cesar Chavez and his family made a living as migrant farmworkers. Pay was low, and working conditions were hard. Chavez wanted to build a better future for migrant farmworkers. He helped to set up a farmworkers' union. Chavez's union organized national boycotts of farm products. As a result, farm owners agreed to improve pay and working conditions. Chavez had achieved his goal—fair treatment of migrant farmworkers.

SECTION 4 REVIEW

1. **Define**   (a) forty-niner, (b) mass transit.

2. **Identify**   (a) Sierra Nevada, (b) Pacific Northwest, (c) Portland, (d) San Jose.

3. (a) How have people used the resources of the West? (b) How are these resources being protected today?

4. What natural resources made Portland a good location for a city?

Critical Thinking

5. **Recognizing Cause and Effect**   How has rapid urban growth affected the natural resources of the West?

Activity

6. **Writing to Learn**   Do you think that there are better ways to use natural resources in your community? Write a letter to your representative in Congress expressing your ideas. To help you in this task, think about the efforts in the West to preserve and conserve resources.

SKILLS ACTIVITY

Understanding Circle Graphs

Chris walked across the playground with his new friend Kyung, who had just moved to Texas from Korea. Kyung looked up at the burning sun.

"Boy, it's really hot here. Does the whole United States get weather like this?"

"It depends," said Chris. "Let me think . . . in the Northwest it rains a lot, and I don't think it gets quite as hot as here. But Arizona and New Mexico do, for sure. In the Midwest, they have some really hot summers, but freezing cold winters. They have tornadoes, too. And then there's Alaska—their summers don't get too hot, even though the sun shines all night long. You know, it's hard to say. This country gets a lot of different weather."

▼ A typical sunny day in Myakka River State Park, Florida

Get Ready

Trying to describe the weather of the United States is no easy task. The United States has a great variety of weather. It can be hard to keep it all straight, but graphs can make it easier.

One common type of graph is a circle graph. Circle graphs show proportion, or the parts of a whole. The entire circle represents all, or 100 percent, of something. Half the circle represents 50 percent. Smaller slices represent smaller amounts, and larger slices represent larger amounts.

Try It Out

The best way to understand how circle graphs work is to try making one yourself. Working with a few other students, make a circle graph showing last week's weather. Follow the steps on the next page.

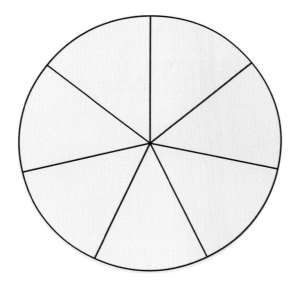

A. Record last week's weather. Write the days of the week in a column down the left-hand side of a sheet of paper. Working with your group, recall last week's weather. Which days had precipitation? Which days did not? Next to each day, note that day's weather activity as either *precipitation* or *no precipitation*. Now count the number of days with precipitation and with no precipitation and make a note of each on your paper.

B. Draw your circle graph. On another sheet of paper, copy the circle above. For your graph, the circle represents one week. Notice how the circle is divided into seven sections, one for each day of the week.

C. Fill in your circle graph. Using one color for each weather category, fill in your circle graph. You should color in one section of the graph for every day. For example, suppose there were three rainy days last week and you chose blue to represent precipitation. Color three sections blue. Be sure to keep the sections with the same color together.

D. Label your circle graph. Finally, label each color on your circle graph or create a key to show what each color stands for. Give your graph a title that tells what the graph is about.

E. Study your circle graph. Your graph lets you quickly see what proportion of last week had precipitation and what proportion did not. How would you describe last week's weather—as mostly wet or mostly dry?

Apply the Skill

A circle graph can show more than two categories of data. It can also be compared with other graphs showing the same kind of data, like the graphs on this page. Use the graphs to answer the questions below.

1 **Become familiar with the illustration.** Read the title. What is the subject of these two graphs? Read the graph key. What data do the graphs provide?

2 **Study the graphs.** Look at the graph for Los Angeles. How would you describe the weather in Los Angeles? Now study the graph for Boston. What percent of the year had no precipitation in this city?

3 **Use the graphs to make comparisons.** Which city has the most rain? What other comparisons can you make?

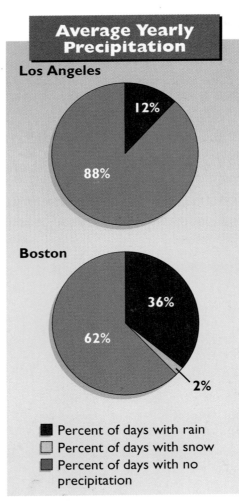

Average Yearly Precipitation

Los Angeles — 12%, 88%

Boston — 36%, 62%, 2%

■ Percent of days with rain
□ Percent of days with snow
■ Percent of days with no precipitation

Review and Activities

Reviewing Main Ideas

1. What are some of the large cities of the Northeast?
2. How does the Northeast serve as a gateway to the country?
3. How do people in the South make a living?
4. How does warm weather affect the economy of the South?
5. What major changes have occurred in the Midwest since the 1980s?
6. Describe the differences between family farms and corporate farms.
7. What are the main natural resources of the West?
8. How has life in the West changed since the days of the California Gold Rush?
9. How has the way people manage natural resources in the West changed since the 1800s?

Reviewing Key Terms

Use each key term below in a sentence that shows the meaning of the term.

1. commute
2. megalopolis
3. population density
4. petrochemical
5. industrialization
6. Sun Belt
7. mixed-crop farm
8. recession
9. corporate farm
10. forty-niner
11. mass transit

Critical Thinking

1. **Making Comparisons** Identify at least one major trend that two or more regions of the United States have in common.
2. **Drawing Conclusions** If the unwise use of resources continues in the West, what are some likely results?

Graphic Organizer

Copy the chart onto a separate sheet of paper. Then, using information from the chapter, fill in the empty boxes.

	Resources	Cities	Current Industries
Northeast			
South			
Midwest			
West			

Map Activity

United States

For each place listed below, write the letter from the map that shows its location.

1. Boston

2. New York City

3. Washington, D.C.

4. Atlanta

5. Chicago

6. Detroit

7. Portland

8. San Jose

Place Location

Writing Activity

Writing a Travel Guide

If you had friends who were visiting the United States for the first time, what information would you want to share with them? Which cities would you tell them to visit? Write a brief travel guide for your friends that takes them to all four regions of the United States. Do research to plan the trip. Suggest activities for each region. Provide background information to help your friends understand the history and culture of each region.

Internet Activity

Use a search engine to find *CityNet*. Take a virtual trip to cities in the Northeast, South, Midwest, and West. Make a chart to compare and contrast the cities. Work in small groups to write a television commercial to welcome tourists to one of the cities. Choose a group member to present the commercial to the class.

Skills Review

Turn to the Skills Activity.

Review how special graphs can give information. Then complete the following: (a) Explain what a circle graph shows. (b) Give two examples of kinds of information that could be shown in a circle graph.

How Am I Doing?

Answer these questions to help you check your progress.

1. Do I understand the history and economic development of the four regions of the United States?

2. Can I describe the major cities in the Northeast?

3. Can I identify the major resources and economic challenges in the South, the Midwest, and the West?

4. What information from this chapter can I use in my book project?

FROM

Childtimes

BY ELOISE GREENFIELD AND LESSIE JONES LITTLE,
WITH MATERIAL BY PATTIE RIDLEY JONES

BEFORE YOU READ

Reach Into Your Background

How much do people know about the lives of their grandparents? What about the lives of their parents as children? Suppose someone wanted to write a history of his or her family—how could they find information?

You can learn a lot from seeing how a single family lives through several generations. Every family history reflects the history of the country or region where that family lives. The following excerpts come from a book written by a mother and daughter, with help from the grandmother. They have written a *memoir,* or a true story of personal experience. This memoir tells the story of their family, and it also takes a peek into the history of the growth of their hometown, Parmele, North Carolina.

Questions to Explore

1. How does the town of Parmele change over three generations?
2. What do the memoirs of the three generations have in common?

Pattie Frances Ridley Jones
Born in Bertie County, North
Carolina, December 15, 1884

Parmele, North Carolina

Towns build up around work, you know. People go and live where they can find jobs. And that's how Parmele got started.

At first, it was just a junction, a place where two railroads crossed. Two Atlantic Coast Line railroads, one running between Rocky Mount and Plymouth, and one running between Kinston and Weldon. Didn't too many people live around there then, and those that did were pretty much spread out.

Well, around 1888, a Yankee named Mr. Parmele came down from New York and looked the place over, and he saw all those big trees and decided to start a lumber company. Everybody knew what that meant. There were going to be jobs! People came from everywhere to get work. I was right little at that time, too little to know what was going on, but everybody says it was something to see how fast that town grew. All those people moving in and houses going up. They named the town after the man who made the jobs, and they called it *Pomma-lee.*

The lumber company hired a whole lot of people. They hired workers to lay track for those little railroads they call tram roads that they were going to run back and forth between the town and the woods. They hired lumberjacks to chop the trees down and cut them up into logs and load them on the tram cars. They hired men to build the mill and put the machinery in, and millworkers to run the machines that would cut the logs into different sizes and dry them and make them nice and smooth.

Lessie Blanche Jones Little
Born in Parmele, North Carolina,
    October 1, 1906

Parmele

I used to hear Papa and Mama and their friends talking about the lumber mill that had been the center of life in Parmele before I was born, but there wasn't any mill when I was growing up. The only thing left of it was the sawdust from all the wood they had sawed there. The sawdust was about a foot thick on the land where the mill had been. I used to love to walk on it. It was spongy, and it made me feel like I was made of rubber. I'd take my shoes off and kind of bounce along on top of it. But that was all that was left of the mill.

My Parmele was a train town. The life of my town moved around the trains that came in and out all day long. About three hundred people lived in Parmele, most of them black. There were three black churches, a Baptist, a Methodist, and a Holiness, and one white church. Two black schools, one white. There wasn't even one doctor, and not many people would have had the money to pay one, if there had been. If somebody got down real bad sick, a member of the family would go by horse and buggy to a nearby town and bring the doctor back, or sometimes the doctor would ride on his own horse.

Most of the men and women in Parmele earned their living by farming. Some did other things like working at the tobacco factory in Robersonville, but most worked on the farms that were all around in the area, white

▼ These people were picking peppers in 1921 on a farm in Louisiana.

243

▲ Going to church in the South in the 1930s

READ ACTIVELY

Ask Questions What more would you like to know about farm life?

Pamlico Sound (PAM lih koh sound) a long body of water off the coast of North Carolina that separates the Hatteras Islands from the mainland

people's farms usually. When I was a little girl, they earned fifty cents a day, a farm day, sunup to sundown, plus meals. After they got home, they had all their own work to do, cooking and cleaning, laundry, chopping wood for the woodstove, and shopping.

***

Parmele had trains coming in and going out all day long. Passenger trains and freight trains. There was always so much going on at the station that I wouldn't know what to watch. People were changing trains and going in and out of the cafe and the restaurant. They came from big cities like New York and Chicago and Boston, and they were all wearing the latest styles. Things were being unloaded, like furniture and trunks and plows and cases of fruit and crates of clucking chickens, or a puppy, or the body of somebody who had died and was being brought back home. And every year around the last two weeks in May, a special

train would come through. It had two white flags flying on the locomotive, and it was carrying one hundred carloads of white potatoes that had been grown down near Pamlico Sound, where everybody said the soil was so rich they didn't even have to fertilize it.

The train station was a gathering place, too. A lot of people went there to relax after they had finished their work for the day. They'd come downtown to pick up their mail, or buy a newspaper, and then they'd just stand around laughing and talking to their friends. And on Sundays fellas and their girls would come all the way from other towns, just to spend the afternoon at the Parmele train station.

***

It was hard for Papa to find work. Not long after Sis Clara died, we moved to Mount Herman, a black section of Portsmouth, Virginia. Papa worked on the docks there, and even though he didn't make much money, the work was steady. But when we moved back to Parmele, it was hard for him to find any work at all.

***

Eloise Glynn Little Greenfield
Born in Parmele, North Carolina, May 17, 1929

Daddy Makes a Way

When I was three months old, Daddy left home to make a way for us. He went North, as thousands of black people had done, during slavery and since.

They went North looking for safety, for justice, for freedom, for work, looking for a good life. Often one member of a family would go ahead of the others to make a way—to find a job and a place to live. And that's what my father did.

In the spring of 1926, Daddy had graduated from high school, Parmele Training School. He had been offered a scholarship by Knoxville College in Tennessee, but he hadn't taken it. He and Mama had gotten married that fall, and now they had Wilbur and me to take care of. Mama had been teaching school since her graduation from Higgs, but she had decided to stop.

Nineteen twenty-nine was a bad time for Daddy to go away, but a worse time for him not to go. The Great Depression was about to begin, had already begun for many people. All over the United States, thousands of people were already jobless and homeless.

In Parmele, there were few permanent jobs. Some seasons of the year, Daddy could get farm work, harvesting potatoes and working in the tobacco fields. Every year, from August to around Thanksgiving, he worked ten hours a day for twenty-five cents an hour at a tobacco warehouse in a nearby town, packing tobacco in huge barrels and loading them on the train for shipping. And he and his father were house movers. Whenever somebody wanted a house moved from one place to another, Daddy and Pa would jack it up and attach it to a windlass, the machine that the horse would turn to move the house. But it was only once in a while that they were called on to do that.

So, one morning in August 1929, Mama went with Daddy to the train station and tried to hold back her tears as the Atlantic Coast Line train pulled out, taking him toward Washington, D.C. Then she went home, sat in the porch swing, and cried.

In Washington, friends helped Daddy find a room for himself and his family to live in, and took him job hunting. He found a job as a dishwasher in a restaurant, and in a few weeks, he had saved enough money for our train fare.

READ ACTIVELY

Visualize Picture the trains arriving at the station and the people and goods as they come off board.

Great Depression a period of time in the 1930s when businesses did not do well, causing many people to lose their jobs

EXPLORING YOUR READING

Look Back

1. How did the town of Parmele first begin to grow? What did adding a lumber company do that made more people come to the town?

Think It Over

2. Why were trains such an important part of Parmele?

Go Beyond

3. What do these memoirs tell you about the time period they cover?

Ideas for Writing: Memoir

4. Write a memoir of your own childhood from the point of view of yourself as an older person. What forces have most shaped your life?

CHAPTER 10

Exploring Canada

SECTION 1
Quebec
PRESERVING A CULTURE

SECTION 2
Saskatchewan
CANADA'S BREADBASKET

SECTION 3
British Columbia
TIES TO THE PACIFIC RIM

KEY

— National boundary

⊙ National capital

⊕ Provincial capital

• Other city

Lambert Azimuthal Equal-Area Projection

Canada is a nation of many cultures. People from all over the world have immigrated to Canada. This has given each region a distinct cultural identity. To get acquainted with some of these regions, do the following activities.

Study the map
Find the provinces of Quebec, Saskatchewan, and British Columbia on the map. Using information on the map, describe the relative location of each province.

Make historical connections
Which of the three provinces do you think was first settled by Europeans? Explain your answer.

Quebec

PRESERVING A CULTURE

Reach Into Your Background

In a democracy, citizens choose their leaders by voting. Sometimes they also vote on issues. The person or position on an issue that gets the most votes wins. Suppose that two of your classmates want to be class president. There is a vote—and each person gets half of the votes. What happens next? How can your class decide on the winner?

Questions to Explore

1. Why do French Canadians worry about preserving their culture?
2. What have French Canadians in Quebec done to preserve their culture?

Key Terms

Francophone
separatist
Quiet Revolution
referendum

Key People and Places

Jacques Cartier
Quebec City
Montreal

In 1977, a new law in the province of Quebec said that all street signs must be in French only. That pleased the majority of Quebeckers who speak French, but it upset other Quebeckers. In 1993, a change in the law allowed English on signs as well. But French is still the only language used in Quebec government, commerce, and education.

Canadian law states that the country has two official languages—English and French. French-speaking people live in every province. In Quebec, however, the first language of 83 percent of the people is French. The first language of 12 percent is English. The remaining 5 percent speak 35 different languages! Still, until the 1960s, government and business in Quebec were conducted in English, just as they were in the rest of Canada. It took a long political battle to change things in Quebec.

The French Influence in Quebec

Canada's history explains why Quebec is so French. In the 1530s, Jacques Cartier (zhahk kahr TYAY), a French explorer, sailed along the St. Lawrence River. In 1535, he landed near today's Quebec City. In his journal, Cartier wrote that he and his crew saw a land "as full of beautiful fields and

▼ In Quebec, bright red signs yell "STOP" in Canada's two official languages, French and English.

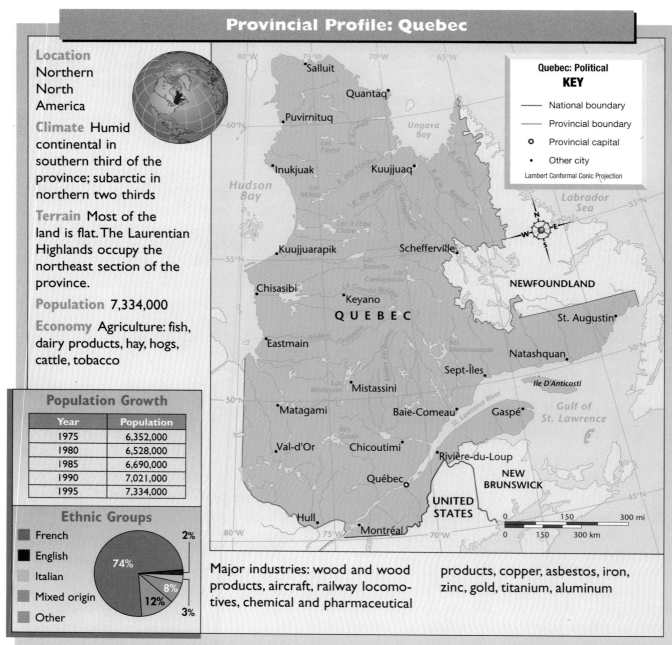

Location Northern North America

Climate Humid continental in southern third of the province; subarctic in northern two thirds

Terrain Most of the land is flat. The Laurentian Highlands occupy the northeast section of the province.

Population 7,334,000

Economy Agriculture: fish, dairy products, hay, hogs, cattle, tobacco

Population Growth

Year	Population
1975	6,352,000
1980	6,528,000
1985	6,690,000
1990	7,021,000
1995	7,334,000

Ethnic Groups

- French
- English
- Italian
- Mixed origin
- Other

74% 2% 8% 12% 3%

Quebec: Political KEY
- National boundary
- Provincial boundary
- ⊕ Provincial capital
- • Other city

Lambert Conformal Conic Projection

Major industries: wood and wood products, aircraft, railway locomotives, chemical and pharmaceutical products, copper, asbestos, iron, zinc, gold, titanium, aluminum

Map and Chart Study This map shows the borders and major cities of Quebec, Canada's largest province. **Location** Quebec shares a border with several Canadian provinces, including Newfoundland and New Brunswick. What country does Quebec share a border with? **Place** What features on the map show Quebec's French heritage? **Critical Thinking** Look at the charts on this page. What percentage of Quebeckers are French? About how much has Quebec's population grown since 1975?

meadows as any we have ever seen." The men became friends with the Stadacona (stad uh KOH nuh), the indigenous people of the area. Soon both groups were living in the area. Some places in Quebec and elsewhere in Canada have Stadacona names. Cartier and later explorers gave other places French names. *Montreal,* for instance, is French for "Mount Royal."

Cartier claimed the region we now know as Quebec for his nation and named it New France. But England also claimed the region. The two countries eventually fought over it. France lost, and in 1763 the territory went to the British. However, tens of thousands of French colonists lived in the region. Today, their descendants make up the majority of Quebec's population. They are **Francophones** (FRANG koh fohnz), or people who speak French as their first language.

Quebec—A Distinct Society Within Canada In the 1960s, many Francophones began to express concern about life in Quebec. They did not like using English at school and at work. They did not like the fact that new immigrants to Quebec learned English, not French. They felt that if this situation did not change, their language and culture might die. They also believed that they were contributing much to Canada but getting little back. Quebec is rich in natural resources, which are important to Canada's economy. For the most part, however, Francophones got only low-paying jobs. They faced prejudice because they were French speakers.

Soon some Francophone Quebeckers began to demand independence. They were called **separatists.** They wanted Quebec to separate, or break away, from Canada. To do this, they formed a political party called the *Parti Québécois* (PAHR tee keh beh KWAH). In a 1976 election, the party won control of the Quebec provincial legislature. This peaceful change in Quebec's government is called the **Quiet Revolution.**

READ ACTIVELY

Predict What problems developed when Britain took over French colonies in Canada?

◀ Quebec City's French heritage is shown in the French style of architecture. The Château Frontenac (sha TOH FRAHNT uh nak) Hotel, built in 1893, looks very much like the great country houses built by French nobles.

Just before the 1995 referendum, a Quebecker displays her opposition to separation. She has a "no" sign on her forehead and the maple leaf—the symbol of Canada—on her cheeks (left). Other Quebeckers, carrying signs calling for "independence" and "sovereignty," rallied to support the split from Canada (above). By the narrowest of margins, Quebeckers voted to remain part of Canada. **Critical Thinking** Why do you think that so many Quebeckers want their province to be an independent country?

READ ACTIVELY

Connect Suppose that California or New York state wanted to leave the United States and become a separate nation. What would be your response?

French became the official language, to be used in education, government, and commerce. Immigrants were required to learn French. Still, Quebec remained a province of Canada.

Not everyone in Quebec supported the idea of separation from Canada. In 1980, the provincial government held a referendum. In a **referendum,** voters cast ballots for or against an issue. This referendum asked voters whether Quebec should become a separate nation. A majority voted no.

The Canadian government knew that the separatists could force the nation to separate. For this reason, the government tried to meet their demands. Quebeckers wanted their province to be a "distinct society" within Canada. It would have its own special way of life. If this was guaranteed, they would stay part of Canada. There was only one way to do this—change Canada's constitution. In 1990 and 1992, the government held referendums about the issue. Quebeckers voted to change the constitution. Both times, Canadians in other provinces voted not to. The referendums failed.

In 1995, Quebec held another referendum. Again, Quebeckers voted to remain part of Canada. But the margin was very slim. The "no" vote was 50.6 percent; the "yes" vote was 49.4 percent. Canada's Prime Minister promised to try to change the constitution again, "so that Canada will move into the twenty-first century united." But Quebec's separatist leader warned, "The battle for a country is not over. And it will not be until we have one." The close vote on election day guaranteed that the issue will continue to be discussed.

Preserving Quebec's Culture

One of the ways in which Quebeckers celebrate their culture is through festivals. The *Fête des Neiges* (fet day NEZH), or winter festival, lasts 17 days. It even includes canoe races among the ice floes along the St. Lawrence River. A Quebec author notes that the city of Quebec

> "is liveliest in winter during the carnival . . . when the city is ruled by the carnival snowman and the newly elected carnival queen. Then a fairy ice palace is built on the hill facing the Quebec Parliament; people dance in the streets . . . visitors come from all over to admire the ice sculpture along the sidewalks of Sainte-Therese Street: a marvelous exhibition of dinosaur monsters . . . boats from the ice race, famous people, and all kinds of animals. . . . This fantasy world becomes really weird at night when all the sculptures are brilliantly lit by thousands of lamps."

LINKS ACROSS THE WORLD

A Copy of St. Peter's Basilica One sign of Quebec's religious heritage is Montreal's Cathedral-Basilica of Mary, Queen of the World. Built in 1870, this church was designed to look like Saint Peter's Basilica in Vatican City, in Rome, Italy. Montreal's church is one third as large as St. Peter's.

▼ During Quebec's Winter Carnival, artists compete to make the best sculptures of ice or packed snow.

A Summer Night in Quebec City

Quebeckers jam the sidewalk cafés in Upper Town, the old section of Quebec City. The capital of Quebec province, Quebec City is located on the site where the first permanent French settlement in Canada was set up. **Critical Thinking** Many French Canadians consider Quebec City to be an almost sacred place. Why do you think this is so?

This is only one festival in French-Canadian culture. Another honors Jean Baptiste (zhahn bah TEEST), the patron saint, or special guardian, of French Canadians. The festival is held June 24. All over the province, people celebrate with bonfires, firecrackers, and street dances.

French style and cooking are alive in Quebec—with Quebec variations. Sugar pie, for example, uses maple sugar from the province's forests. Quebec has French architecture—with Quebec variations. All in all, Quebeckers have a lively culture to preserve and protect.

SECTION 1 REVIEW

1. **Define** a) Francophone, (b) separatist, (c) Quiet Revolution, (d) referendum.

2. **Identify** (a) Jacques Cartier, (b) Quebec City, (c) Montreal.

3. What are some features of Quebec culture?

4. List several reasons for the Quiet Revolution.

5. What steps have Quebeckers and other Canadians taken to preserve French culture?

Critical Thinking

6. **Expressing Problems Clearly** Explain why many people in Quebec want to separate from Canada.

Activity

7. **Writing to Learn** List some features of Quebec culture that you would like to learn more about.

Saskatchewan

CANADA'S BREADBASKET

Reach Into Your Background

Think about something you heard that led you to believe that some experience was going to be wonderful. Were you ever disappointed when the real experience turned out to be less than what you had hoped for? What did you do? Did you try to maintain a good attitude?

Questions to Explore

1. Why did many immigrants from central and Eastern Europe come to Saskatchewan in the mid-1800s?

2. How do ethnic communities maintain their traditions in Saskatchewan?

Key Term
immunity

Key Places
Regina
Saskatoon

One August day in 1821, after a long, difficult journey, about 195 Swiss immigrants reached their new land. It was summertime. But it was chilly on the Hudson Bay in northern Canada. The Swiss watchmakers, mechanics, pastry cooks, and musicians wanted to become Canadian farmers in this region called "Rupert's Land." Later, the region became the Northwest Territory. The settlers had heard that these vast plains had good land and an excellent climate. Then they looked around. No shelter, food, or supplies were waiting for them. The settlers survived only because the native people of the region, the Saulteaux (sawl TOH), helped them.

The Rindisbacher (RIN dis baw kur) family was part of the group. All of them—father, mother, and seven children—later moved to the Red River region. Today it is part of Manitoba. One of the children, 15-year-old Peter, loved to draw. He sketched and painted pictures of life on the Canadian plains. He also drew the indigenous peoples, carefully adding details about their tools, clothing, and canoes.

Rindisbacher's pictures also tell us about the hard life of the settlers. During harsh winters they fought snow and ice. During summers they fought drought, floods, and swarms of grasshoppers.

▼ This photograph, taken in 1928, shows a group of young men on board the ship *Montcalm*. They are on their way to Canada to start a new life in the Prairie Provinces.

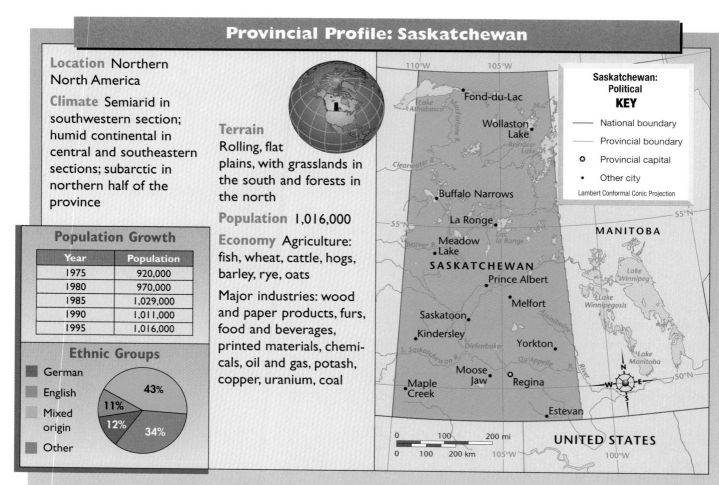

Provincial Profile: Saskatchewan

Location Northern North America

Climate Semiarid in southwestern section; humid continental in central and southeastern sections; subarctic in northern half of the province

Terrain Rolling, flat plains, with grasslands in the south and forests in the north

Population 1,016,000

Economy Agriculture: fish, wheat, cattle, hogs, barley, rye, oats

Major industries: wood and paper products, furs, food and beverages, printed materials, chemicals, oil and gas, potash, copper, uranium, coal

Population Growth

Year	Population
1975	920,000
1980	970,000
1985	1,029,000
1990	1,011,000
1995	1,016,000

Ethnic Groups

- German
- English
- Mixed origin
- Other

43%
11%
12%
34%

Saskatchewan: Political KEY
- National boundary
- Provincial boundary
- ✪ Provincial capital
- • Other city

Lambert Conformal Conic Projection

Map and Chart Study This map shows the borders and major cities of Saskatchewan. **Location** Where are most of Saskatchewan's major cities located? Why do you think these cities are located in this area?

Critical Thinking Look at the chart of Saskatchewan's ethnic groups. Is any one ethnic group much larger than the others? What conclusions can you draw about Saskatchewan's culture based on this chart?

There were few trees on the plains, so many people built their homes out of sod. They cut prairie sod into blocks and piled them up to make walls. "Soddies" were cheap, but if it rained, the roofs leaked! Most settlers had little experience in farming and had not expected such hardships.

Changing Ways of Life

Throughout the 1800s, European settlers continued to trickle into the Plains region. As they did, they changed the cultures of the indigenous peoples. In part, changes came from European trade goods, such as pots, needles, and guns. European diseases, such as measles, caused other changes. In Europe, people had suffered from measles for centuries. As a result, Europeans had **immunity,** or natural resistance. But measles had not existed in North America. Indigenous peoples had no immunity. In some groups, as many as 75 percent of the people died. European diseases killed millions of indigenous peoples in South America, too.

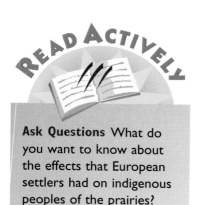

Ask Questions What do you want to know about the effects that European settlers had on indigenous peoples of the prairies?

A Way of Life Lost   In the late 1870s, the ways of life of many indigenous peoples in the Plains region of North America came to an end. For centuries, these people had built their lives around the buffalo. Then people of European descent began killing off the buffalo herds. In a few years, nearly all were gone. At the same time, the governments of Canada and the United States began to take over the indigenous peoples' land. Most agreed to give up their land and live on reserves. These were small areas of land set aside for the indigenous peoples. With a few exceptions, indigenous peoples in Canada did not go to war to protect their land as they did in the United States.

Free Land Draws Newcomers   The population of the indigenous peoples was shrinking. The European population, however, was increasing. Many early settlers, like the Rindisbacher family, moved away after a while. Other immigrants replaced them. The new people, too, were ready to farm the prairie. The Canadian government wanted even more people. Newcomers would help the economy grow. In the late 1800s and early 1900s, Canada advertised free land in European newspapers. The advertisements worked. Immigration increased.

Until then, most Canadians were indigenous peoples or settlers from France or Britain. That quickly changed. The newcomers were from many ethnic groups. The people in each group shared a history, religion, language, and customs. The Prairie Provinces saw an amazing variety of newcomers. Some were Ukrainians, Norwegians, or Finns.

Sanctuary Visitors to Saskatchewan's Grasslands National Park see some of North America's last untouched prairies. Ancient grasses called wheat grass, snowberry, and silver sage blow in the wind. The park is also home to 12 endangered and threatened species. They include certain kinds of hawks, burrowing owls, and short-horned lizards.

◄Settlers in the southwest of Saskatchewan made a living by ranching. Rodeos have become a popular form of entertainment in this area.

Others were Russians or Poles. The names of new settlements illustrated the changes. Swedes settled in New Stockholm. Icelanders founded Thingvalla. Danes founded New Denmark. Hungarians founded Esterhazy. And Germans founded Ebenezer. By the turn of the century, the Canadian prairies were a checkerboard of ethnic settlements. Each had its own language and customs.

All came looking for a better life. Life in Saskatchewan was not always as easy as the advertisements had claimed, however. One newspaper writer summed up the situation bluntly. He described the capital city of Regina as a village "in the midst of a vast plain of inferior soil . . . with about enough water in the miserable little creek . . . to wash a sheep." Nevertheless, the settlers stayed. Hope became an important part of Saskatchewan culture. When crops failed one year, people did not moan and complain. They just looked forward to the next year. This is how Saskatchewan earned the nickname "Next Year Country." The hard work of the people of Saskatchewan paid off. In 1923, the Saskatchewan Wheat Pool was started. Today, it is one of the world's largest grain cooperatives and is the leading company in the province.

READ ACTIVELY

Connect If you wanted to move to a new location, what kinds of things would attract you?

Maintaining Tradition on the Prairies

About one quarter of Canada's farmland is in Saskatchewan. Most European immigrants became wheat farmers. Two thirds of Saskatchewan's farmland is still devoted to wheat. For this reason, the province is sometimes called "Canada's Breadbasket."

Wheat Fields Near Saskatoon

This farmer is harvesting wheat near Saskatoon, Saskatchewan's largest city. Saskatchewan has more farmland than any other province in Canada. Saskatchewan is Canada's largest wheat producer. In fact, it is one of the largest wheat producers in the world. **Critical Thinking** What part of the United States is similar to this part of Canada?

Religious Diversity in Saskatchewan

The onion-shaped domes of St. Julien's Greek Orthodox Church pierce the blue sky of Alvena. This small town is located in central Saskatchewan about 150 miles (240 km) northwest of Regina. Saskatchewan's other Christian churches include Roman Catholic, Ukrainian Orthodox, and various Protestant denominations. **Critical Thinking** Why do you think that immigrant groups maintain the traditions and ways of life of the countries they came from?

Today, immigrants still come to the Canadian prairies. Most move to cities like Regina and Saskatoon. Each year, these cities celebrate ethnic festivals. Ukrainian, Icelandic, and German festivals include traditional dancing, art, and music. Every summer, indigenous peoples also host powwows. In some small towns, people still maintain the European languages and customs of their ancestors.

SECTION 2 REVIEW

1. **Define** immunity.

2. **Identify** (a) Regina, (b) Saskatoon.

3. What attracted thousands of European immigrants to the Canadian prairies?

4. How did the lives of indigenous peoples in Canada change after Europeans arrived?

5. How have European immigrants influenced the culture of Saskatchewan?

Critical Thinking

6. **Drawing Conclusions** Many immigrants came to the Canadian prairies in the 1800s. What advantages and disadvantages do you think this move had for them?

Activity

7. **Writing to Learn** Suppose that it is the year 1900. You want to encourage people to come and start farms in Saskatchewan. The government will give 160 acres of land to anyone willing to try. Make a poster advertising free land. You may show weather, soil, scenery, or settler communities. Describe conditions so many will want to come.

British Columbia

TIES TO THE PACIFIC RIM

BEFORE YOU READ

Reach Into Your Background

Think about the ways in which people use natural resources. How do we benefit from natural resources? What are some of the problems that using natural resources can cause?

Questions to Explore

1. Before the 1880s, what major events influenced British Columbia's culture?
2. Why does British Columbia have such a diverse population?
3. How does geography tie British Columbia to the Pacific Rim?

Key Terms
totem pole
boomtown

Key Places
Vancouver
Fraser River
Victoria
Cariboo Mountains
Pacific Rim

▼ Brightly painted totem poles are sometimes used to tell the history of a family or tribe.

A visitor starts her day at a tiny coffee shop. All around her, people are speaking Dutch, Japanese, Spanish, German, and English. After having breakfast, the visitor gets into her car. On the radio, she hears country music—sung in French. Driving downtown, she passes street signs in Chinese, Indian men wearing turbans, a Korean travel agency, and a Thai restaurant. Where in the world is she? It may seem like the United Nations. But it is Vancouver (van KOO vur), British Columbia—a truly international city.

Fishers, Hunters, Traders, Miners

The first people came to what is now British Columbia about 10,000 to 12,000 years ago. They belonged to several ethnic groups and spoke many different languages. Each group had its own customs and a complex society. The people along the coast caught fish, whales, and clams. They also carved giant **totem poles,** which were symbols for a group, a clan, or a family. Other groups lived and hunted game

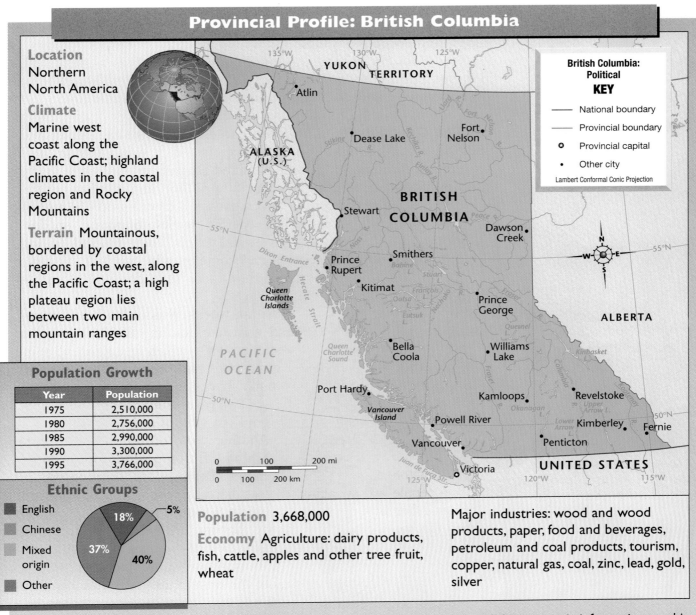

Provincial Profile: British Columbia

Location
Northern North America

Climate
Marine west coast along the Pacific Coast; highland climates in the coastal region and Rocky Mountains

Terrain Mountainous, bordered by coastal regions in the west, along the Pacific Coast; a high plateau region lies between two main mountain ranges

Population Growth

Year	Population
1975	2,510,000
1980	2,756,000
1985	2,990,000
1990	3,300,000
1995	3,766,000

Ethnic Groups

- English
- Chinese
- Mixed origin
- Other

5% 18% 37% 40%

British Columbia: Political
KEY
— National boundary
— Provincial boundary
⊙ Provincial capital
• Other city
Lambert Conformal Conic Projection

Population 3,668,000

Economy Agriculture: dairy products, fish, cattle, apples and other tree fruit, wheat

Major industries: wood and wood products, paper, food and beverages, petroleum and coal products, tourism, copper, natural gas, coal, zinc, lead, gold, silver

Map and Chart Study This map shows the borders and major cities of British Columbia. **Location** What U.S. state is separated from the rest of the United States by British Columbia? What other parts of Canada does British Columbia border? **Critical Thinking** Look at the charts and the economic information on this page. Is any one ethnic group much larger than the others? About how much has the population grown since 1975? How does British Columbia's growing population make a living?

in the dense inland forests. Some groups traded with each other and got along well. Others fought.

New Arrivals In the late 1500s, Spanish, British, and Russian explorers began to arrive in the area to trade. In 1778, James Cook, a British explorer, sailed to Vancouver Island, off the coast of British Columbia. A group of Nootka (NOOT kuh) people met the British and agreed to trade. These coastal people wanted iron tools, while the

Predict How did the discovery of gold affect life in British Columbia?

British wanted furs. When the British built a fur-trading post on the island, trade began to flourish.

Trade did not change the indigenous peoples' lives a great deal, however. Fur traders came and went. They did not settle. Then in 1858, everything changed. Someone discovered gold along Fraser River.

The Gold Rush　A few years earlier, the British had established Victoria, a trading village on Vancouver Island. It was a tidy town of traders and farmers. Its citizens attended church and cultivated lovely gardens. Then, one Sunday morning in April 1858, an American paddle-wheeler entered Victoria's harbor. It dropped off 450 men in red shirts. They carried packs, blankets, spades, pickaxes, knives, and pistols. These rugged-looking characters had come to mine gold. In a single morning, they more than doubled Victoria's population.

Within weeks, tens of thousands more had arrived. Victoria quickly became a "stumptown"—which meant that all of its great trees had been chopped down to build shacks and boats.

Two years later, miners also struck gold in the Cariboo Mountains. Another wave of miners came from China, Europe, and the United States. Because the Cariboo region was hard to reach, the government built a 400-mile (644-km) highway to it. Almost overnight, settlements called **boomtowns** sprang up along it. A boomtown's only purpose was to meet the miners' needs. When the gold rush was over, many boomtowns died out.

Changes for Indigenous Peoples

The indigenous peoples, said the governor of Victoria, were "naturally annoyed" that thousands were coming and taking gold from their land—even taking over the land itself. In 1888, the British government wanted to confine some indigenous peoples to a small reserve. The indigenous peoples protested. They had always lived on the land where the reserve was located. How, they asked, could the government now "give" it to them?

The indigenous peoples had little choice. In a few short years, they had gone from being the great majority to being the smallest minority of the population. They were pushed onto small reserves. Laws banned many of their customs, religions, and languages. Children were taken from their parents to be raised in European-run schools.

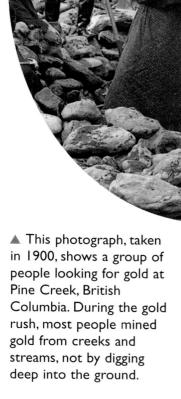

▲ This photograph, taken in 1900, shows a group of people looking for gold at Pine Creek, British Columbia. During the gold rush, most people mined gold from creeks and streams, not by digging deep into the ground.

Recently, the indigenous peoples of British Columbia have found new pride in their history and culture. They are demanding land and political rights, and their art is thriving.

The Canadian Pacific Railway In the spring of 1881, Canadians began work on an enormous project—building a railroad all the way from Montreal to Vancouver. The goal of the project was to unite Canada. Look at the map of British Columbia in the Provincial Profile and you may see what a major task this was. There were countless obstacles—soaring mountains, steep valleys, freezing weather, and glaciers. Workers built 600 bridges and blasted 27 tunnels through the mountains.

The railroad project brought more change. Immigrants from all over the world came to work on the railroad. Towns grew up along the railroad, and more newcomers moved in. All this activity attracted criminals, too. They caused so much trouble that the Mounted Police were brought in. In a few short years, British Columbia went from being a sparsely inhabited region to a settled one, complete with cities.

Trapping Shells Many native peoples of the Northwest used a shell called *dentalia* as money. The shells were difficult to gather. They lie on the ocean bottom, in beds 50 to 60 feet (15 to 18 m) deep. Native peoples would lower a broom-like device from a canoe. Stabbing the broom into the sand, they would trap a few shells at a time.

Hauling Freight

A huge freight train heads for Vancouver along the banks of the Thompson River, high in the mountains of British Columbia. **Critical Thinking** What difficulties do you think faced the workers who laid the railroad along the Thompson River?

Predict How has physical geography affected the culture of British Columbia?

British Columbia Today

The Canadian Pacific Railroad did unite all of Canada. However, the mountains have always been a big barrier between British Columbia and the rest of the country. Today, about two thirds of British Columbians live along the coast, west of the mountains. Many feel that their future lies with Pacific Rim countries—nations that border the Pacific Ocean—not with the rest of Canada.

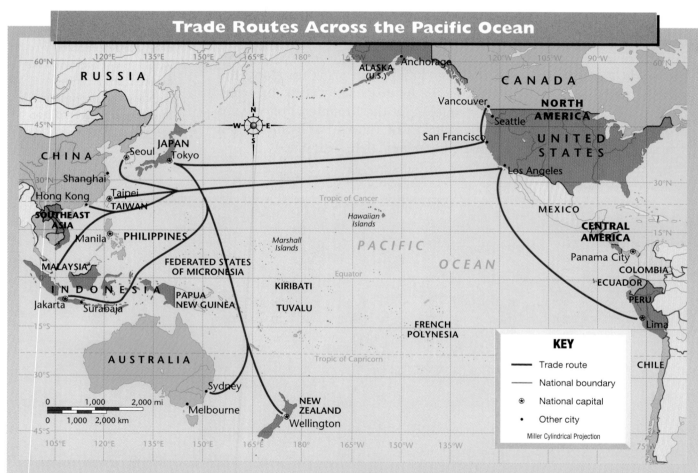

Trade Routes Across the Pacific Ocean

KEY
— Trade route
| National boundary
⊛ National capital
• Other city
Miller Cylindrical Projection

Map Study Traditionally, the United States and Europe have been Canada's most important trade partners. However, Canada is developing a thriving relationship with the countries that border the Pacific Ocean. In the mid-1970s, Japan replaced the United Kingdom as the second largest market for Canadian exports. Most of Canada's Pacific Rim trade passes through British Columbia's major port, Vancouver (right). **Movement** Name three Pacific countries, other than Japan, with which Canada might trade.

◀ The water in Vancouver's harbor never freezes. As a result, Vancouver is one of Canada's most important ports. Many people call Vancouver Canada's "Gateway to the Pacific" because almost all of Canada's trade with Asian countries is handled by this port.

Another link between British Columbia and the Pacific Rim is British Columbia's diverse people. About 11 percent have Asian ancestors. Trade is still another link between British Columbia and the Pacific Rim. Forty percent of the province's trade is with Asian countries. British Columbia wants good relationships with them. As a result, in British Columbian schools, students learn Asian languages. They learn Japanese, Cantonese Chinese, or Mandarin Chinese. Some even learn Punjabi (pun JAH bee), a language of India and Pakistan!

SECTION 3 REVIEW

1. **Define** (a) totem pole, (b) boomtown.

2. **Identify** (a) Vancouver, (b) Fraser River, (c) Victoria, (d) Cariboo Mountains, (d) Pacific Rim.

3. What brought Europeans to British Columbia between the late 1500s and the late 1800s?

4. Explain the effects of the gold rush on British Columbia.

5. What ties are there between the people of British Columbia and the Pacific Rim?

Critical Thinking

6. **Identifying Central Issues** What was the importance of the completion of the Canadian Pacific Railroad?

Activity

7. **Writing to Learn** What do you think it would be like to be a gold prospector in one of the gold rushes in Canada? Write a journal entry describing a gold prospector's typical workday.

Writing for a Purpose

Think about the last three or four conversations you have had.

You might have been talking with friends at school, a teacher, family members, a clerk in a store, or a friend. Chances are, the conversations were all very different. However, they probably also had something in common.

No matter what you talked about, or with whom you spoke, one of you probably *informed* the other. To inform someone simply means to give someone information. You might have informed a friend about how you were feeling, informed a store clerk about what you wanted to buy, or informed your mother that you had basketball practice after school.

People often write to inform, too. This entire book, for example, was written to inform you about the United States and Canada.

Get Ready

As a student and as an adult, you will often write to inform your readers. You may write reports to inform your teacher about a subject you have researched. You may write letters to inform friends about your life. You may fill in a job application to inform an employer about your work experience.

Try It Out

Writing to inform means writing to provide information. It involves five basic steps. As you read through the following steps, think about a one-page paper you could write to inform someone about something. Complete the activity at the end of each step.

A. Choose your topic. What will you write about? What do you want to tell your readers? Of course, there are millions of subjects. You can write about anything you want—a hobby, your last weekend, or a football game. Write down a few possibilities, then circle the one you like best.

Writing to Inform
about a process

Organize your writing around the steps in the process.

B. Choose your audience. You need to know to whom you are writing. You would write differently for a group of second-graders than you would for your parents. For this paper, your audience will be your teacher and your classmates.

C. Research your topic. In order to inform your audience, you have to first inform yourself. Read and take notes from books, magazines, newspapers, and other sources of information. Gather your information and know what you want to write before you begin the next step.

D. Plan your paper. This is how you will inform your audience. When you write to inform, you should organize your paper in the way that will make your topic easiest for your audience to understand. The box to the right tells you how to choose the best way.

Will you write about a process, an event, or a thing? How will you organize your paper? Write it down.

E. Write. Now you can start writing a one-page paper to inform. Make an outline before you start. Make sure it is organized in the same way that you will organize your final paper. Try to start your paper with an interesting opening and write clearly.

Apply the Skill

Now write a one-page paper to inform your teacher and classmates about a subject in this chapter of your textbook. Choose one of the following ideas, or choose your own subject.

- The immigration of Chinese Americans and other Americans to Canada from California (a process)
- The election to decide on Quebec's independence (an event)
- A wheat farm in Saskatchewan (a thing)

about a thing
Write about the object's purpose and its parts.

about an event
Organize your writing in chronological order, or order based on time.

Review and Activities

Reviewing Main Ideas

1. What is the largest cultural group in Quebec?
2. What is the main political aim of many French Canadians?
3. How has immigration shaped Saskatchewan's culture?
4. What is Saskatchewan's main contribution to Canada's economy?
5. Identify different groups of people who have shaped British Columbia's culture.
6. What part of the world has the strongest cultural ties with British Columbia today? Why?

Reviewing Key Terms

Use each key term below in a sentence that shows the meaning of the term.

1. Francophone
2. separatist
3. Quiet Revolution
4. referendum
5. immunity
6. totem pole
7. boomtown

Critical Thinking

1. **Recognizing Bias** The slogans "Masters in Our Own House" and "United From Sea to Sea" are from the dispute over Quebec. Determine which side of the issue each slogan supports.
2. **Recognizing Cause and Effect** Identify several different events in western Canada that led to the decline of the native peoples' cultures.

Graphic Organizer

Each of the provinces mentioned in this chapter has natural resources that attracted settlers. Copy this chart. Then fill in the blanks with resources found in each province.

Quebec		
Saskatchewan		
British Columbia		

Map Activity

Canada

For each place listed below, write the letter from the map that shows its location.

1. Quebec
2. Montreal
3. Saskatchewan
4. Regina
5. British Columbia
6. Rocky Mountains
7. Vancouver

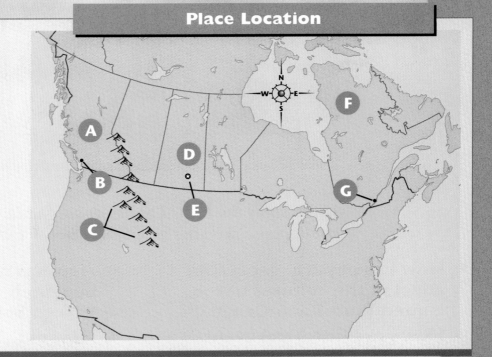

Place Location

Writing Activity

Writing a Paragraph

Make a list of the distinguishing characteristics of Quebec, Saskatchewan, and British Columbia. Then pick one province. Write a letter to a friend, trying to convince your friend to move to the province.

Internet Activity

Use a search engine to find **QuebecWeb.** Click **Regions,** then choose Quebec. Explore the various links to learn about the Quebecois heritage. What evidences of French culture did you find in Quebec? Use the information to make a time line of Quebecois heritage and history.

Skills Review

Turn to the Skills Activity.

Review the basic steps of writing to inform. Then complete the following: (a) Name some types of writing that inform. (b) Tell how you could organize informative writing about a process, an event, or an object.

How Am I Doing?

Answer these questions to help you check your progress.

1. Can I explain why French Canadians are worried about preserving their culture?
2. Can I visualize what life was like in Saskatchewan in the past?
3. Can I explain how the gold rush affected growth in British Columbia?
4. What information from this chapter can I use in my book project?

THE
UNITED STATES AND CANADA
PROJECT POSSIBILITIES

As you study the United States and Canada, you will be reading and thinking about these important questions.

- ☛ **How has physical geography affected the cultures of the United States and Canada?**

- ☛ **How have historical events affected the cultures of the United States and Canada?**

- ☛ **How has the variety of peoples in the United States and Canada benefited and challenged the two nations?**

- ☛ **How has modern technology benefited and challenged the United States and Canada?**

- ☛ **How did the United States and Canada become two of the wealthiest nations in the world?**

What do you know about the United States and Canada? It's time to show it.

GEO CLEO

Project Menu

The chapters in this book have some answers to these questions. Now you can find your own answers by doing projects on your own or with a group. Here are some ways to make your own discoveries about the United States and Canada.

Write a Children's Book Choose a topic from this book that interests you. Then write a short book about it for younger students. Take careful notes before you write, to be sure you get all the facts right. Write with simple language that younger children can understand. Include the main points of this topic in your book, along with a few interesting details. Illustrate your book with drawings and magazine photographs. Draw at least one map of the area you are writing about. Be sure to use the kind of map—physical, political, or other—that shows the right information for your topic. Finally, design a book cover, and bind your book. Share the book with younger students in your school.

From Questions to Careers

PARK RANGER

The national parks of the United States and Canada preserve and protect many of the great treasures of these two countries. Some parks preserve natural wonders, like deep forests and unusual geological formations. Other parks preserve important historic sites. Some simply give people a place to picnic, play, and camp outside.

Many people work for the park services in all kinds of jobs. Tour guides show visitors around historic sites, telling the story of each place. Scientists and park rangers often work together to keep wildernesses healthy and to protect the original land, water, plants, and animals. Writers create brochures for park visitors. On top of all that, the parks always hire people to work in gift shops, visitor offices, and snack bars, to help the thousands of people who visit the parks every year.

▼ This United States park ranger shows the famous cracked Liberty Bell to visitors in Philadelphia, Pennsylvania.

Set Up a Weather Station Set up a weather station to measure and record your local weather as you read this book. Measure the temperature each day at the same time. Also record the amount of precipitation and wind direction. Record all of your findings in a weather log.

Each day, compare your local weather with the weather in other parts of the country. You can get this information from television, radio, the newspaper, or the Internet. When you have finished your measurements and recordings, create graphs to display your local readings. In the end, compare your findings with the climate map in the Activity Atlas.

Make a Time Line of Local History Create a time line of the history of your community. What do you know about it? When was it founded? What famous people have lived there? What important events have shaped its history?

Find the answers to these and other questions about the history of your town, village, city, or county. Read about its history at the local public library. Write down the dates and descriptions of the most important events. Try to find between 10 and 20 events. On a sheet of paper, list the events in the order in which they happened. Then, make a time line large enough to hang on the wall of your classroom. Draw a picture of each event and place it next to its description on the time line. Add several major events of United States history.

Create a Diorama Make a diorama that represents a physical map of the United States and Canada, or of a smaller geographic region within the two countries. Use clay or dough to sculpt the major geographic forms, such as mountain ranges, valleys, rivers, and large bodies of water. Make your diorama with as much detail as possible, showing forests, farms, towns, and other landscapes. You can use materials such as rocks, twigs, and miniature buildings. Make a key that explains what each material represents. Display your finished diorama for the class.

LATIN AMERICA

The ancient peoples of Latin America built great civilizations from the riches of their land. Today, their descendants have mixed with newcomers from around the world to create a modern society with new traditions. Cities of steel and glass rise alongside ancient ruins. From villages in the rain forests, mountains, and countryside, people move to the thriving cities. Every day more families arrive, hoping to make a new life.

Guiding Questions

The readings and activities in this book will help you discover answers to these Guiding Questions.

- ☞ What are the main physical features of Latin America?
- ☞ What factors have affected cultures in Latin America?
- ☞ Why have many Latin Americans been moving to cities in recent years?
- ☞ What is the relationship of the nations of Latin America with the United States and the world?
- ☞ How has geography influenced the ways in which Latin Americans make a living?

Project Preview

You can also discover answers to the Guiding Questions by working on projects. Preview the following projects and choose one that you might want to do.

A Latin American Concert Research Latin American music and find some examples on tape to play for your class.

Visions of Latin America Create a diorama and write a short report to show how Latin America's geography affects the way people live.

Latin America in the News Collect articles on Latin America from magazines and newspapers for a bulletin board display.

Explorer's Dictionary Create an illustrated dictionary of important terms translated from Latin American languages.

The woman in the photo above left lives in Jamaica. In the photo above, the colorful clothing of people in Guatemala shows their famous skill with weaving. Students at a school in Lima, Peru, are shown in the photo at left.

EXPLORER'S JOURNAL

A journal can be your personal book of discovery. As you explore Latin America, you can use your journal to keep track of things you learn and do. You can also record your thoughts about your journey. For your first entry, write your thoughts on where in Latin America you would like to go and what you would want to see there.

Latin America

Learning about Latin America means being an explorer and a geographer. No explorer would start out without first checking some facts. Begin by exploring the maps of Latin America on the following pages.

Relative Location

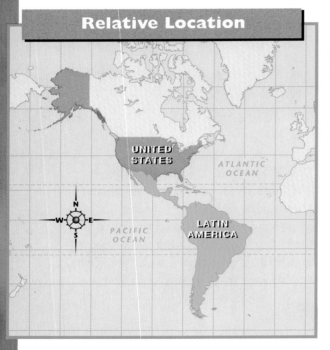

LOCATION

1. Explore Latin America's Location Notice where the United States and Latin America are located relative to the Equator. On the other side of the Equator, seasons come at the opposite time of year. For example, when it's summer here, it's winter there. Think about the season your birthday falls in. In what season would it fall if you lived in Argentina? What if you lived in Panama? How about in Bogotá, the capital city of Colombia? Or in Brasília, the capital of Brazil?

Relative Size

REGIONS

2. Estimate Latin America's Size How long is Latin America's west coast? To get an idea, curve a piece of string along the edge of the United States' west coast on the map above. Cut the string the same length as the coast. Now see how many string-lengths fit along the west coast of Latin America. Begin at the edge of the Pacific Ocean where Mexico borders California. Finish at the southern tip of South America. About how many times longer is Latin America's Pacific Coast than that of the United States?

LOCATION

3. Compare the Size of Countries The map below shows the countries that make up Latin America. Which two countries are the biggest in land area? Study the map to make your estimates. Check your answers in the World View section at the back of your textbook.

MOVEMENT

4. Investigate the Languages of Latin America The languages people speak give us clues about their history. Long ago, settlers from other countries took control of Latin America. Where were they from? Here are your clues: Portuguese is the official language of Brazil, and Spanish is spoken in most other Latin American countries.

Latin America: Political

KEY

—— National boundary

⊛ National capital

• Other city

Lambert Azimuthal Equal-Area Projection

5. Examine the Physical Features of Latin America Volcanoes created many of Latin America's dramatic features. Long ago, volcanoes erupting along the west coast of South America formed the Andes Mountains. Volcanoes that exploded under the Caribbean Sea became a chain of islands called the Lesser Antilles. Central America has volcanic mountains, too. Some are still active! Trace the Andes Mountains, the Lesser Antilles, and the mountains in Central America with your finger. Which of these areas has the highest altitude?

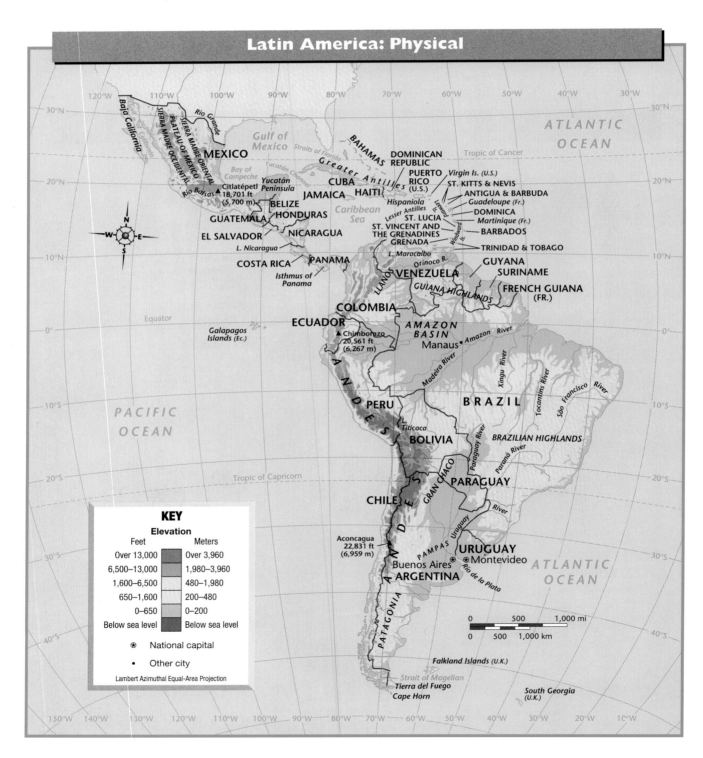

Latin America: Physical

KEY

Elevation

Feet	Meters
Over 13,000	Over 3,960
6,500–13,000	1,980–3,960
1,600–6,500	480–1,980
650–1,600	200–480
0–650	0–200
Below sea level	Below sea level

⊛ National capital

• Other city

Lambert Azimuthal Equal-Area Projection

6. **Guide Geo Leo** Geo Leo is exploring Latin America by boat, and he's taking you along to navigate. Read the passages below. To answer Geo Leo's questions, use the map below and the map on the opposite page.

A. We board our ship on the south side of the island of Hispaniola. A dense rain forest covers the island's mountain slopes. Which way to the Panama Canal?

B. We are sailing south past one of the Earth's driest deserts. It is in a long, skinny South American country that extends north and south along the continent's west coast. Steep mountains rise to the east. Where are we?

C. From the Falkland Islands, we travel north. For days we sail past desert. Finally, we see tropical rain forest along the coast. What two major cities will we come to next?

D. We continue sailing north, past grassland. We reach more rain forest and sail down a river through a low-lying area. Just ahead the Madeira River joins the one we are traveling on. Which way to the city of Manaus, our final destination?

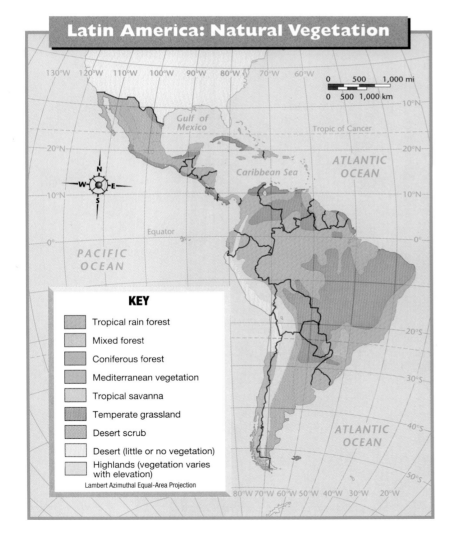

Latin America: Natural Vegetation

KEY
- Tropical rain forest
- Mixed forest
- Coniferous forest
- Mediterranean vegetation
- Tropical savanna
- Temperate grassland
- Desert scrub
- Desert (little or no vegetation)
- Highlands (vegetation varies with elevation)

Lambert Azimuthal Equal-Area Projection

GEO LEO

BONUS

List each body of water you and Geo Leo traveled over.

LOCATION

7. Investigate Latin America's Use of Hydroelectricity Hydroelectricity is electric power that is made by harnessing the power of water. One way to build a hydroelectric power plant is to build a dam across a river. The dam creates a large lake of water. To make electricity, the plant releases water from the lake into the river. As the water moves into the river, it turns a wheel. In some places, hydroelectric plants harness the power of ocean tides. Some of the largest hydroelectric plants are in Latin America. The world's largest is located on the border of Brazil and Paraguay. Look at the map below. What places in Latin America do you think would be good spots to build new hydroelectric power plants?

Latin America: Major Hydroelectric Plants

KEY

— National boundary

■ Hydroelectric Plants

Lambert Azimuthal Equal-Area Projection

Biggest Hydroelectric Dams

Name of Dam	Location
1. Itaipú	Brazil/Paraguay
2. Grand Coulee	United States
3. Guri (Raul Leoni)	Venezuela
4. Tucuruíi	Brazil
5. Sayano-Shushensk	Russia
6. Krasnoyarsk	Russia
7. Corpus-Posadas	Argentina/Paraguay
8. LaGrande 2	Canada
9. Churchill Falls	Canada
10. Bratsk	Russia

INTERACTION

8. Explore the Effects of a River Dam Unlike coal and petroleum, water power cannot be used up. It also does not cause air pollution. But building a dam does affect the environment of a river. It creates a large, artificial lake. It also reduces the amount of water that is in the river below the dam. What do you think are some advantages of building a dam across a river? What are some disadvantages?

◀▼ What percentage of its energy does Latin America get from hydroelectricity? How does this compare to energy use around the world?

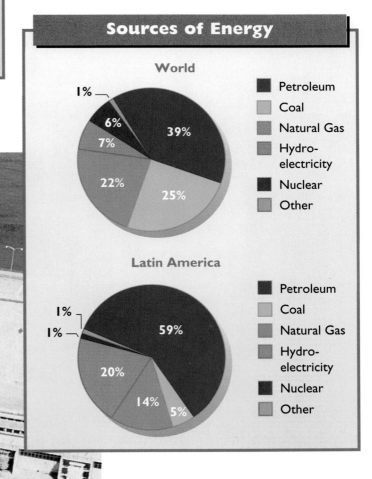

Sources of Energy

World

1% — 6% 7% 22% 25% 39%

Petroleum
Coal
Natural Gas
Hydro-electricity
Nuclear
Other

Latin America

1% — 1% — 59% 20% 14% 5%

Petroleum
Coal
Natural Gas
Hydro-electricity
Nuclear
Other

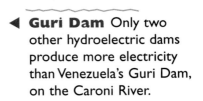

◀ **Guri Dam** Only two other hydroelectric dams produce more electricity than Venezuela's Guri Dam, on the Caroni River.

CHAPTER 11

LATIN AMERICA

Physical Geography

SECTION 1
Land and Water

SECTION 2
Climate and Vegetation

SECTION 3
Natural Resources

PICTURE ACTIVITIES

These rugged mountains are the Andes (AN deez). They run the length of South America. To help you get to know this part of Latin America, do the following.

Study the picture
What do you think it would be like to live in or near the Andes? Based on what you see in the photograph, where would be the best area to live?

Think about the climate
Have you ever climbed in the mountains? How did the temperature change as you climbed higher? Based on your experience, do you think the climate is the same at the top of the Andes as at the bottom? Where would it be colder? Where would it be warmer?

Land and Water

BEFORE YOU READ

Reach Into Your Background

No two places in the world are exactly the same. Think about the state in which you live. What features set it apart from other states? List some features that make your state special.

Questions to Explore

1. What are the main geographic regions of Latin America?

2. How do Latin America's geographic features affect the lives of the people?

Key Terms

plateau   pampas
isthmus   tributary
coral

Key Places

Mexico
Central America
Caribbean
South America

High in the Andes Mountains, planes take off and land at El Alto airport. *El Alto* (ehl AHL toh) is Spanish for "the high one." It is an accurate name, for El Alto is the highest airport in the world. El Alto is the airport for La Paz, Bolivia.

Shortly after leaving the plane, tourists may get mountain sickness. The "thin" air of the Andes contains less oxygen than most people are used to. Oxygen starvation makes visitors' hearts beat faster and leaves them short of breath. Later on in the day, they may get terrible headaches. It takes a few days for visitors' bodies to get used to the mountain air. But the people who live in the Andes do not have these problems. Their bodies are used to the mountain environment.

The Andes mountain range is one of Latin America's major landforms. In this section, you will learn about Latin America's other landforms and about the people who live there.

Where Is Latin America?

Latin America is located in the Western Hemisphere south of the United States. Look at the map in the Activity Atlas. You will see that Latin America includes all the nations from Mexico to the tip of South America. It also includes the islands that dot the Caribbean (ka ruh BEE un) Sea.

Geographic features divide Latin America into three smaller regions. They are (1) Mexico and Central America, (2) the Caribbean, and (3) South America. South America is so large that geographers classify it as a continent. Look at the physical map in the Activity Atlas. Can you identify the geographic features that separate these three areas?

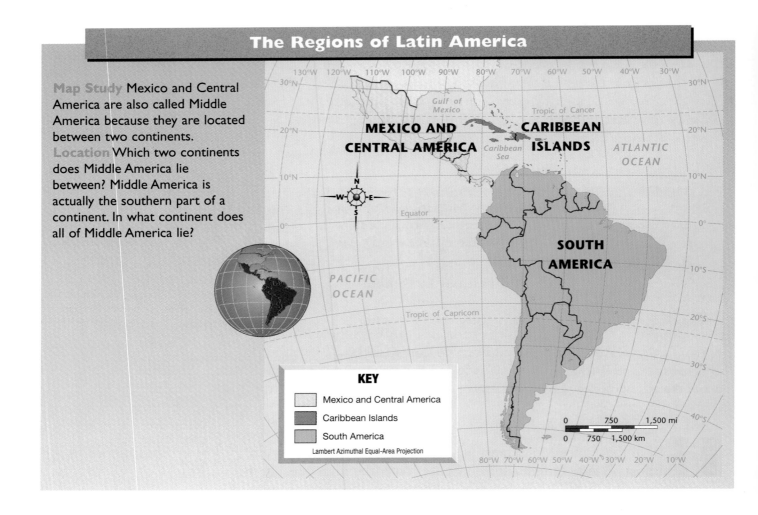

Map Study Mexico and Central America are also called Middle America because they are located between two continents. Location Which two continents does Middle America lie between? Middle America is actually the southern part of a continent. In what continent does all of Middle America lie?

KEY

☐ Mexico and Central America

■ Caribbean Islands

▨ South America

Lambert Azimuthal Equal-Area Projection

Perhaps you are wondering how Latin America got its name. About 500 years ago, Europeans sailed to Latin America. Most came from Spain and Portugal. European colonists brought their own languages and ways of life with them. Today, most Latin Americans speak Spanish, Portuguese, or French. These languages have their roots in the ancient language of Latin. As a result, the region is known as Latin America.

Landforms of Latin America

Imagine mountains that pierce the clouds and grassy plains that never seem to end. Picture wet rain forests and sunbaked deserts. This is Latin America, a region of variety and contrast.

Mexico and Central America Mexico and Central America stretch 2,500 miles (4,023 km) from the U.S. border to South America. It is a distance that is almost equal to the width of the mainland United States. Mountains dominate this region. These mountains are part of a long system of mountain ranges. This huge system extends from Canada through the United States all the way to the tip of South America.

READ ACTIVELY

Predict How do you think the physical features of Latin America might be like those of the United States?

Between the mountains in Mexico lies Mexico's Central Plateau. A **plateau** (pla TOH) is a large raised area of mostly level land. Mexico's Central Plateau makes up more than half of the country's area. Most of Mexico's people live here. However, the surrounding mountains make it hard for people to travel to and from the Central Plateau. Another major landform in Mexico is the narrow coastal plains.

Central America, located south of Mexico, is an isthmus. An **isthmus** is a narrow strip of land that has water on both sides and joins two larger bodies of land. Find Central America on the map in the Activity Atlas. What two large bodies of land does the isthmus of Central America connect? As in Mexico, narrow plains run along Central America's coasts. Between these coastal plains are rugged, steep mountains. More than a dozen of these mountains are active volcanoes. Volcanic ash has made the soil fertile. As a result, many people tend farms in the region.

The Caribbean Imagine islands made of skeletons. Imagine other islands that are the tops of underwater mountains. The Caribbean is made up of these two types of islands. The smaller islands are made up of the skeletons of tiny sea animals. Over hundreds of years, the skeletons meld together to form a rocklike substance called **coral.**

The larger islands of the Caribbean are the tops of huge underwater mountains. These include Cuba, Jamaica (juh MAY kuh), Hispaniola (his pun YOH luh), and Puerto Rico. Most people on the islands make a living farming.

The Tlaloques According to Aztec religion, a group of rain gods lived on the tops of mountains. They were called the Tlaloques. Tlaloc, the leader of the Tlaloques, was responsible for rain and lightning. The Aztecs were right, in a way—mountains affect rainfall. Clouds cool off and drop rain when they rise over the mountains.

Harvesting Alfalfa in Mexico

In Mexico, farming is an important way of making a living, even in the drier areas of the country. Raising crops requires fertile soil, a source of fresh water, and a long growing season. As in Central America, much of Mexico's fertile soil is the result of volcanic activity.

South America South America contains many types of landforms. Perhaps the most impressive landform is the Andes Mountains. The Andes run some 4,500 miles (7,250 km) along the western coast of South America. In some places, the Andes rise to heights of more than 20,000 feet (6,100 m). That's about the same height as twenty 100-story buildings stacked one on top of another. Except for the Himalaya Mountains in Asia, the Andes are the highest mountains in the world.

The Andes are steep and difficult to cross. But their rich soil has drawn farmers to the region. East of the Andes are rolling highlands. These highlands spread across parts of Brazil, Venezuela (ven uh ZWAY luh), Guyana (gy AN uh), and other South American countries. Farther south are the Pampas (PAHM puz), a large plains area that stretches through Argentina (ar jun TEE nuh) and Uruguay (YOOR uh gway). **Pampas** are flat grassland regions that are very similar to the Great Plains in the United States.

The Pampas and other plains areas, the eastern highlands, and the Andes frame the Amazon River Basin. The Amazon River Basin contains the largest tropical rain forest in the world. This dense forest covers more than a third of the continent.

The Rivers of Latin America

Latin America is famous for its rivers and lakes. They are some of the longest and largest bodies of water in the world. Latin America's waters are important to the people of the region. Rivers serve as natural

Herding Cattle on the Pampas

Grasslands known as the Pampas can also be found in Brazil. These grasslands are perfect for raising cattle. **Critical Thinking** How are these grasslands similar to the Great Plains in the United States?

highways in places where it is hard to build roads. The fish that swim the waters of Latin America provide food. Rushing water from large rivers provides electric power.

Amazon: The Ocean River
Latin America's Amazon (AM uh zahn) River is the second-longest river in the world. Only the Nile in Africa is longer. The Amazon flows 4,000 miles (6,437 km) from Peru across Brazil into the Atlantic Ocean.

How large is the Amazon? The Amazon River carries more water than any other river in the world. It contains about 20 percent of all the fresh river water on Earth. The Amazon River gathers power from the more than 1,000 tributaries (TRIB yoo tehr eez) that spill into it. **Tributaries** are the rivers and streams that flow into a larger river. With its tributaries, the Amazon drains an area of more than two million square miles. No wonder people call the Amazon the "Ocean River."

Other Rivers and Lakes Latin America has many other bodies of water besides the Amazon. The Paraná (pah rah NAH), Paraguay, and Uruguay rivers form the Río de la Plata system. The Río de la Plata separates Argentina and Uruguay. In Venezuela, people travel on the Orinoco River and Lake Maracaibo (mar uh KY boh). Lake Titicaca is the highest lake in the world on which ships can travel. It lies high in the Andes Mountains.

An Amazon Scene

The people who live near the Amazon River in Brazil rely on it for transportation, fish, and water. Families also wash their laundry right at the river bank.

READ ACTIVELY

Visualize How could a ship sail on a lake? What would the lake have to be like?

SECTION 1 REVIEW

1. **Define** (a) plateau, (b) isthmus, (c) coral, (d) pampas, (e) tributary.

2. **Identify** (a) Mexico, (b) Central America, (c) Caribbean, (d) South America.

3. Describe the main landforms of the three regions that make up Latin America.

4. Give one example of how the physical features of Latin America affect the people who live there.

Critical Thinking

5. **Making Comparisons** Explain two ways in which the three regions of Latin America are alike. Explain two differences.

Activity

6. **Writing to Learn** Suppose your family was planning to move to Latin America. If you had your choice, in which of the three regions of Latin America would you live? Explain why.

Climate and Vegetation

BEFORE YOU READ

Reach Into Your Background

Suppose the temperature outside is 90°F (32°C). Would you feel more comfortable lying on a sandy beach or sitting under a tree in the woods? In what type of climate would you want to vacation someday?

Questions to Explore

1. What kinds of climate and vegetation does Latin America have?

2. In what ways do climate and vegetation affect how Latin Americans live?

Key Terms

El Niño
elevation

Key Places

Andes
Atacama Desert
Patagonia
Amazonian rain forest

Every few years, a warm ocean current flows along the western coast of South America. This warm current drives away fish that thrive in the cold waters of the Pacific Ocean. The current brings other changes to Latin America, too. Instead of dry weather, heavy rains pour down and low-lying regions are flooded. In other places, drought plagues the land and the people.

Just what is this strange ocean current that brings disaster? It is **El Niño** (el NEEN yoh). Because it usually strikes near Christmas time, Latin Americans named the phenomena El Niño, Spanish for "the Christ child." El Niño is one of many factors that affect climate in Latin America.

Climate: Hot, Cold, and Mild

What's the climate like where you live? Is it hot? Cold? Rainy? If you lived in Latin America, the climate might be any of these. Climate in Latin America can vary greatly even within the same country.

In parts of the Andes, below-zero temperatures would set your teeth chattering. Travel down to the Amazon Basin, and you may be sweating in 80°F (27°C) heat. Don't forget your umbrella: This part of Latin America receives more than 80 inches (203 cm) of rain each year. If you prefer dry weather, visit the Atacama (ah tah KAH mah) Desert in Chile or the Sonoran Desert in Mexico. These are two of the driest places on Earth.

▼ Mexico's Sonoran Desert shows that even a hot, dry desert can be full of plant life.

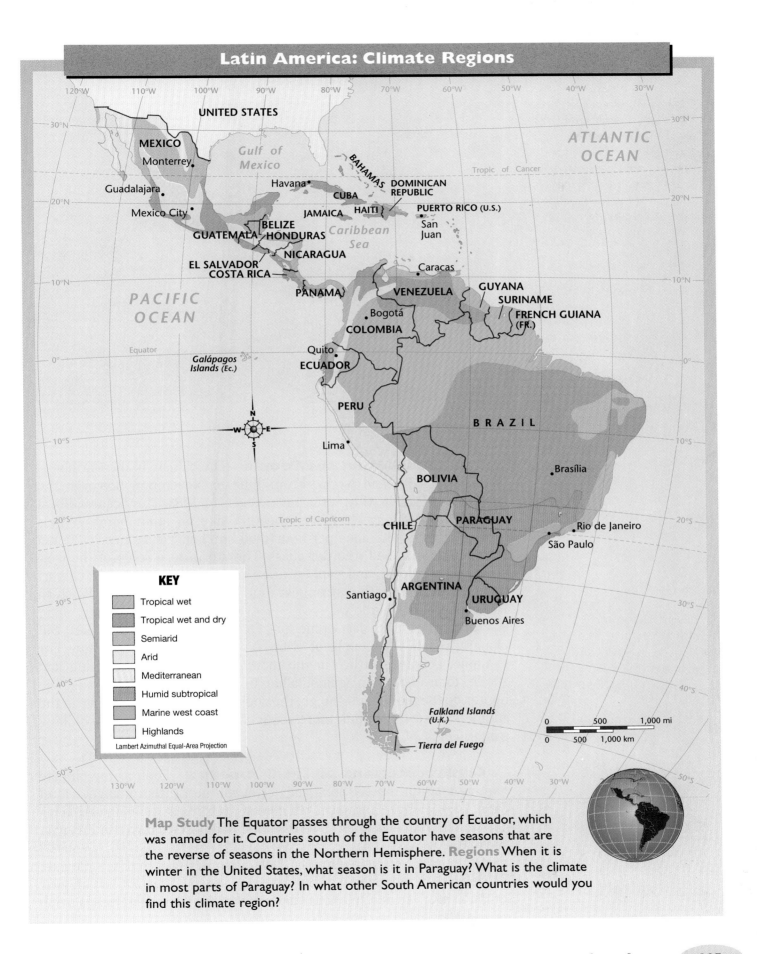

Latin America: Climate Regions

120°W   110°W   100°W   90°W   80°W   70°W   60°W   50°W   40°W   30°W

UNITED STATES

ATLANTIC OCEAN

30°N

MEXICO
Monterrey.

Gulf of Mexico

Tropic of Cancer

30°N

Guadalajara.

Havana.
BAHAMAS
DOMINICAN REPUBLIC

20°N

Mexico City.

CUBA
JAMAICA   **HAITI**
PUERTO RICO (U.S.)
San Juan

20°N

BELIZE
GUATEMALA **HONDURAS**

Caribbean Sea

EL SALVADOR
NICARAGUA

COSTA RICA

Caracas.

10°N

PACIFIC OCEAN

PANAMA

VENEZUELA
GUYANA
SURINAME
FRENCH GUIANA (FR.)

10°N

.Bogotá
COLOMBIA

Equator

Galápagos Islands (Ec.)

Quito.
ECUADOR

0°

0°

PERU

B R A Z I L

10°S

Lima.

10°S

.Brasília

BOLIVIA

Tropic of Capricorn

CHILE
PARAGUAY

.Rio de Janeiro

20°S

20°S

São Paulo.

ARGENTINA

Santiago.

URUGUAY

30°S

30°S

Buenos Aires

KEY

	Tropical wet
	Tropical wet and dry
	Semiarid
	Arid
	Mediterranean
	Humid subtropical
	Marine west coast
	Highlands

Lambert Azimuthal Equal-Area Projection

Falkland Islands (U.K.)

40°S

40°S

0   500   1,000 mi
0   500   1,000 km

Tierra del Fuego

50°S

50°S

130°W   120°W   110°W   100°W   90°W   80°W   70°W   60°W   50°W   40°W   30°W

Map Study The Equator passes through the country of Ecuador, which was named for it. Countries south of the Equator have seasons that are the reverse of seasons in the Northern Hemisphere. **Regions** When it is winter in the United States, what season is it in Paraguay? What is the climate in most parts of Paraguay? In what other South American countries would you find this climate region?

People in the Dominican Republic grow much of their own food, but they also grow sugar cane to export. **Regions** How does the climate in the Caribbean make the area good for farming? How is the climate in the Caribbean dangerous for farms?

The Climate and the People The climate in the Caribbean is usually sunny and warm. From June to November, however, the region is often hit with fierce hurricanes. In 1988, Hurricane Gilbert shattered the sunny Caribbean weather like an atom bomb. Winds howled at over 180 miles per hour (300 km/hr). Waves nearly 20 feet (6 m) high smashed into the coast. The storm tore roofs off houses, shattered windows, and yanked huge trees from the ground. Gilbert turned out to be the strongest hurricane to strike the Western Hemisphere this century.

Hurricanes are a part of life for people living in the Caribbean. But climate affects the people of Latin America in other ways, too. For example, people who live in the mountains need warm clothing and shelter to protect them against falling temperatures. That's because the higher up the mountains you go, the cooler it gets. Those who live in the sunny, warm tropics think more about cooling sea breezes than chilling winter winds.

Climate Regions of Latin America Look at the climate regions map on the previous page. You will notice that many parts of Latin America have a tropical wet climate. A tropical wet climate means hot, humid, rainy weather all year round. Rain forests thrive in this type of climate.

Other parts of Latin America have a tropical wet and dry climate. These areas are equally hot, but the rainy season does not last all year long. Parts of Mexico and Brazil and most of the Caribbean have a tropical wet and dry climate.

Much of Argentina, Uruguay, and Paraguay has a humid subtropical climate, similar to that of parts of the southern United States. People living in this climate usually have hot, wet summers and cool winters. Farmers in these areas can raise such crops as wheat and apples, which need a cold season to grow well. Farther south, the climate turns arid. Farmers raise sheep on the plains of this colder, drier area, called Patagonia (pat uh GOH nee uh).

What Factors Affect Climate? Have you ever hiked in the mountains? If you have, you probably noticed that as you climbed higher the temperature dropped. At some point during your hike, you may have stopped to put on a sweatshirt or jacket.

Elevation, the height of land above sea level, is a key factor in the climate of mountainous Latin America. Look at the diagram below. It shows how elevation affects climate. The higher the elevation, the colder the temperature. Suppose it is a warm 80°F (27°C) at sea level. At 3,000 feet (914 m), the temperature may be 72°F (25°C). Continue up to 6,000 feet (1,829 m), and the temperature may now be only about 65°F (13°C). Above 10,000 feet (3,048 m), the temperature may remain below freezing—too cold for people to live. Temperature also affects what crops people can grow in each region.

Other factors also affect Latin America's climate. Regions close to the Equator are generally warmer than those farther away. Look at the Latin America: Climate Regions map. Find the Equator. Which parts of Latin America are closest to the Equator? Which are farthest away?

READ ACTIVELY

Visualize Suppose that you were climbing a mountain. How would the vegetation you see change as you climb higher?

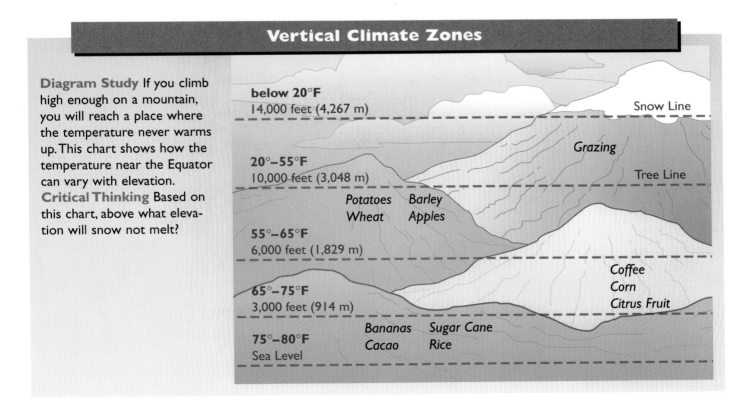

Vertical Climate Zones

Diagram Study If you climb high enough on a mountain, you will reach a place where the temperature never warms up. This chart shows how the temperature near the Equator can vary with elevation.
Critical Thinking Based on this chart, above what elevation will snow not melt?

below 20°F
14,000 feet (4,267 m)

Snow Line

Grazing

20°–55°F
10,000 feet (3,048 m)

Tree Line

Potatoes   Barley
Wheat   Apples

55°–65°F
6,000 feet (1,829 m)

Coffee
Corn
Citrus Fruit

65°–75°F
3,000 feet (914 m)

Bananas   Sugar Cane
Cacao   Rice

75°–80°F
Sea Level

Latin America: Vegetation Regions

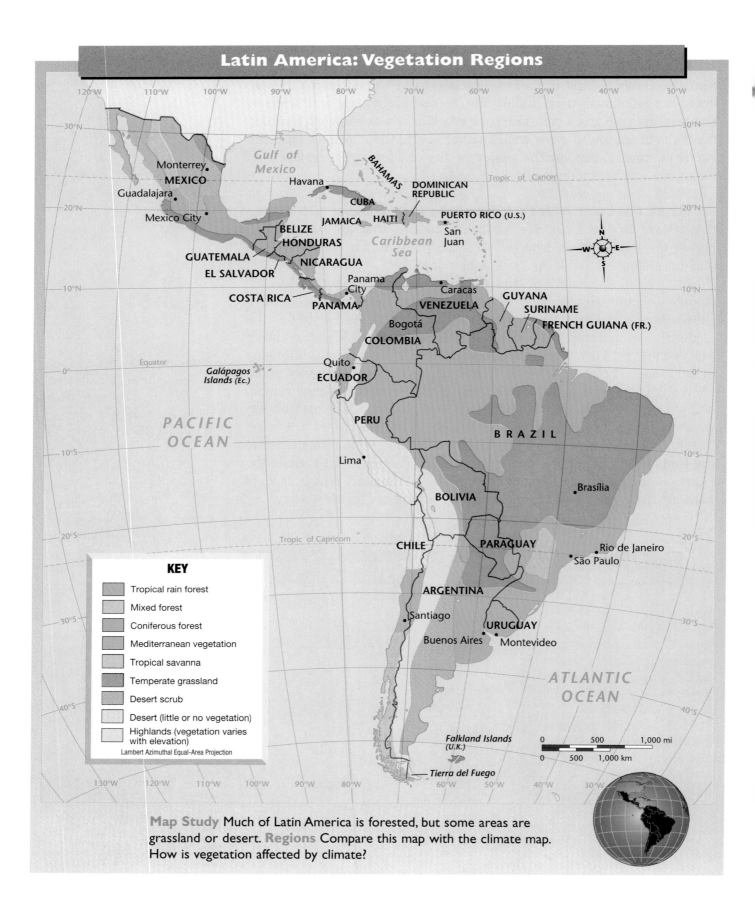

KEY

- Tropical rain forest
- Mixed forest
- Coniferous forest
- Mediterranean vegetation
- Tropical savanna
- Temperate grassland
- Desert scrub
- Desert (little or no vegetation)
- Highlands (vegetation varies with elevation)

Lambert Azimuthal Equal-Area Projection

Map Study Much of Latin America is forested, but some areas are grassland or desert. **Regions** Compare this map with the climate map. How is vegetation affected by climate?

Wind patterns affect the climate too. Winds move cold air from the North and South Poles toward the Equator. They also move warm air from the Equator toward the Poles. In the Caribbean, sea breezes blowing toward shore help to keep temperatures moderate. Winds also affect rainfall in the Caribbean. More rain falls on the sides of islands facing the wind than on sides facing away.

Ask Questions What would you like to know about living in the rain forest?

Natural Vegetation and Climate

Imagine a forest so dense and lush that almost no sunlight reaches the ground. Broad green leaves, tangled vines, and thousands of species of trees and plants surround you. The air is hot and heavy with moisture. Welcome to the Amazonian rain forest.

Now, suppose you have traveled to the coast of northern Chile. You're in the Atacama Desert. Winds carry no moisture to this barren land, and there is little sign of life. The Andes shield this parched region from rain. Parts of the desert have never felt a single raindrop.

Latin America's varied climate and physical features make such extremes possible. Look at the natural vegetation map on the previous page. How many different kinds of vegetation does the map show? Note which countries in Latin America have areas of tropical rain forest. Now, find these countries on the climate map. How do the tropical climate and heavy rainfall in these countries contribute to the vegetation that grows there?

Find Uruguay on the vegetation map and on the climate map. Uruguay's climate and vegetation have helped make sheep and cattle raising a key part of the country's economy.

Elevation also affects vegetation. For example, palm trees and fruit trees that grow well in the coastal plains of Mexico and Central America would not survive high in the Andes. To grow at higher elevations, plants must be able to withstand cooler temperatures, chill winds, and irregular rainfall.

▲Tree sloths live in the rain forest trees. They rarely descend from the trees.

SECTION 2 REVIEW

1. **Define** (a) El Niño, (b) elevation.

2. **Identify** (a) Andes, (b) Atacama Desert, (c) Patagonia, (d) Amazonian rain forest.

3. Describe two climates in Latin America. Then explain how climate affects the vegetation that grows in those regions.

4. How do Latin America's climate and vegetation affect how and where the people live?

Critical Thinking

5. **Drawing Conclusions** In what ways would the life of a family living on a Caribbean island be different from a family living high in the Andes?

Activity

6. **Writing to Learn** Latin America has been called a land of extremes. Do you agree or disagree? Write a paragraph or more telling why. Begin with the following sentences: "Many people have called Latin America a land of extremes. I believe that . . ." Support your opinion with examples.

Using Regional Maps to Show Climate

If you could follow the Earth's weather for many years, no two years would look exactly alike. Think how the weather in your own location varies. Some years are colder, warmer, wetter, or drier than others. The same is true for every place on the planet.

Still, you could notice patterns in the weather. For example, one place may tend to have hot, rainy summers and cold, dry winters. Another place might be hot and dry all year round. The typical weather patterns in a location are called its climate.

Traveling across the Earth, you would find that no two places have exactly the same climate. Even the next town might be a degree cooler than your own. Still, you would find some similarities. Places in a large area that have similar weather make up a climate region.

Get Ready

A region's climate affects how its inhabitants live. Learning to read a climate map can help you understand what life is like in different regions of the world.

Try It Out

Climates in Latin America fall into four general categories: *tropical, dry, mild,* and *highland.* Read about the climates described below. Use the map to answer each question.

A. Find a tropical climate zone. Tropical climates are hot year round. There are two types. Tropical wet zones have rain nearly every day. Tropical wet and dry zones have a wet season and a dry season. Where are tropical wet and

Latin America: Climates

UNITED STATES

Gulf of Mexico

C

MEXICO

Tropic of Cancer

CUBA HAITI DOMINICAN REPUBLIC

JAMAICA

BELIZE

B

HONDURAS   Caribbean Sea

PUERTO RICO (U.S.)

GUATEMALA

EL SALVADOR   NICARAGUA

COSTA RICA   VENEZUELA   SURINAME

PANAMA   H   GUYANA

COLOMBIA   FRENCH GUIANA (FR.)

Galapagos Is. (Ec.)   ECUADOR   A   Equator

PACIFIC OCEAN

BRAZIL

PERU

D   BOLIVIA

CHILE   PARAGUAY

Tropic of Capricorn

F

URUGUAY

E   ARGENTINA

ATLANTIC OCEAN

G

Falkland Is. (U.K.)

South Georgia (U.K.)

Tierra del Fuego

0   500   1,000 mi

0   500   1,000 km

120°W 110°W 100°W 90°W 80°W

30°N

20°N

10°N

0°

10°S

10°N

0°

20°S

30°S

40°S

80°W 70°W 60°W 50°W 40°W 30°W 20°W 10°W

KEY

- Tropical wet
- Tropical wet and dry
- Semiarid
- Arid
- Mediterranean
- Humid subtropical
- Marine west coast
- Highlands

Lambert Azimuthal Equal-Area Projection

dry zones usually located in relation to tropical wet zones?

B. Find a dry climate. Dry climates have little rain. There are two types. Arid zones may go years without rain. Semiarid zones receive enough rain for short grasses to grow. Where are semiarid zones usually located in relation to arid zones?

C. Find a mild climate. Mild climates are more comfortable than tropical or dry climates. There are three types. Marine climates are wet and have only moderate changes in temperature during the year. Humid subtropical areas are also wet but warmer than marine climates. Mediterranean climates are warm, too, but only rainy in the winter. Where are mild climate regions usually located in relation to large bodies of water?

D. Find a highland climate. Highland climates are found in mountainous regions. In a highland climate, temperatures vary. The higher you climb up a mountain, the colder it gets. Where is South America's highland climate located?

Apply the Skill

A region's climate can affect the kind of homes people build, the jobs they do, and the food they eat. Read the descriptions that follow. Then match each description with a letter on the map.

1. Few trees grow in Mexico's dry central region. Instead of building homes from wood, farmers often use sun-dried brick called adobe. Flat roofs are sometimes made of tile, straw, or sheet metal.

2. In the south of Mexico, more rain falls. The rain would eventually wash away an adobe home. So instead, some farmers build with wooden poles coated with a lime and clay mixture that keeps out the rain. Roofs are slanted so that rain water runs off.

3. Peru's west coast has one of the Earth's driest climates. To raise crops, farmers channel mountain streams to bring water to their fields.

4. Near the base of the Andes Mountains in Colombia, the weather is hot. High in the mountain peaks the climate is cold. In between, the mountain slopes have a mild climate perfect for growing coffee—one of Columbia's leading crops.

5. The Yanomamo are an Indian people living on the border between Brazil and Venezuela. A dense forest grows here. To clear land for crops, the Yanomamo must slash and burn trees. In addition to crops, they eat food found in the forest—anteaters, armadillos, and roasted caterpillars.

Natural Resources

Reach Into Your Background

Do you know what natural resources are? They are things found in nature that people can use to meet their needs. For example, trees are a natural resource. List two other natural resources. Describe how people use each one.

Questions to Explore

1. What are Latin America's important natural resources?

2. Why is it important for Latin American nations to have more than one source of income?

Key Terms
hydroelectricity
diversify

Key Places
Jamaica
Venezuela
Brazil
Colombia
Chile

Bolivia has always depended on mineral resources for wealth. At first, silver helped to bring money into Bolivia's treasury. Soon, however, another metal became even more important than silver. That metal was tin.

For many years, Bolivia enjoyed the good times that wealth from tin brought. Then, in the 1920s and 1930s, a world-wide economic crisis hit. Industries stopped buying tin, as well as other natural resources. Bolivia suffered as its main resource failed to bring money into the economy. This economic crisis hit all of Latin America hard. It brought home a problem many Latin American nations have: They rely too much on one resource.

▼ Latin America has about 12 percent of the world's petroleum.

Latin America's Resources

What do the following items have in common? Fish, petroleum, water, silver, and bananas. You have probably guessed that all these items are natural resources of Latin America. Latin America's resources are as varied as its physical features and climate.

Mexico and Central America: Riches of Land and Sea

Mexico is a treasure chest of minerals. The country has deposits of silver, gold, copper, coal, iron ore, and just about any other mineral you can name. How many of these mineral resources can you find on the map on the next page? Mexico also has huge amounts of oil and natural gas. In addition, trees cover nearly a quarter of Mexico's land. Wood from these trees is turned into lumber and paper products.

Central America's climate and rich soil are good for farming. The people grow coffee, cotton, sugar cane, and bananas. They also plant cacao trees. Cacao seeds are made into chocolate and cocoa.

Not all of Central America's resources are on land. People catch fish and shellfish in the region's waters. Central Americans use the power of rushing water to produce electricity. This type of power is called **hydro-electricity** (hy droh ee lek TRIS ih tee). Countries build huge dams to harness and control the energy that rushing water produces.

The Caribbean: Sugar, Coffee, and More Caribbean countries also have rich soil and a good climate for farming. Farmers grow sugar cane, coffee, bananas, cacao, citrus fruits, and other crops on the islands.

The Caribbean has other resources as well. For example, Jamaica is one of the world's main producers of bauxite—a mineral used to make aluminum. Cuba and the Dominican Republic have nickel deposits. Trinidad is rich in oil.

Drilling for Oil

Some of Mexico's petroleum reserves can only be reached through offshore drilling, or drilling into the ocean floor. **Interaction** What special precautions do you think that offshore drillers might have to take to avoid harming the environment?

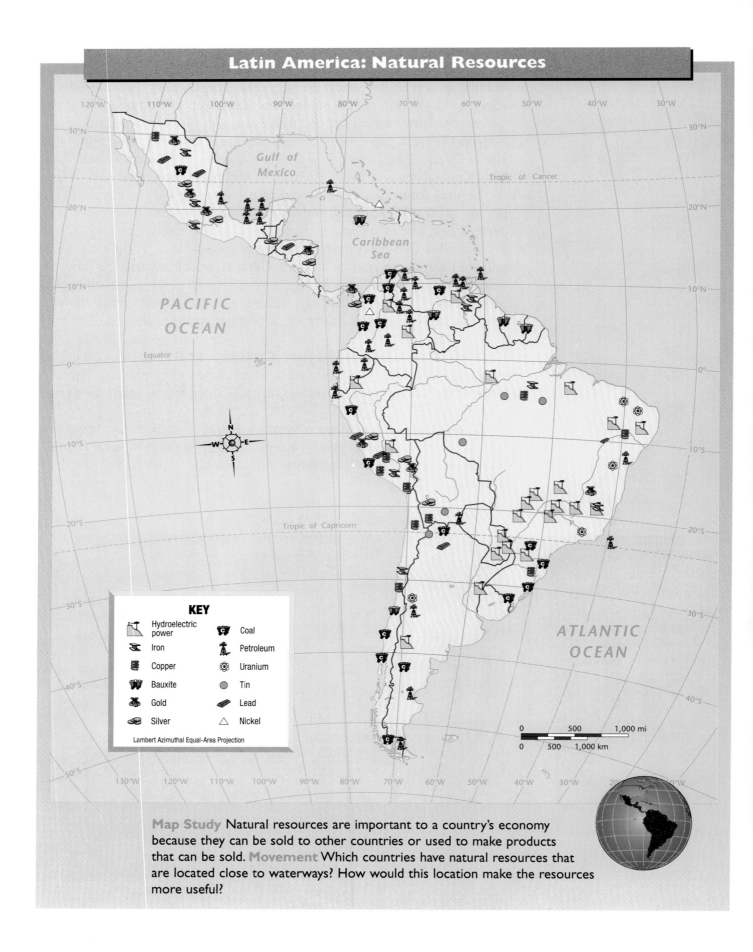

Latin America: Natural Resources

KEY

Hydroelectric power		Coal	
Iron		Petroleum	
Copper		Uranium	
Bauxite		Tin	
Gold		Lead	
Silver		Nickel	

Lambert Azimuthal Equal-Area Projection

0   500   1,000 mi

0   500   1,000 km

Map Study Natural resources are important to a country's economy because they can be sold to other countries or used to make products that can be sold. **Movement** Which countries have natural resources that are located close to waterways? How would this location make the resources more useful?

The hydroelectric power plant at Itaipú Dam is the largest in the world. It harnesses the energy of the Paraná River to provide electric power to Paraguay and Brazil. **Critical Thinking** What detail in this picture is a clue that the dam is used to produce electricity?

South America: A Wealth of Resources Like Mexico, South America is rich in minerals. It contains gold, copper, tin, bauxite, and iron ore. Businesses drill for oil in many South American countries. Much of South America's oil is found in Venezuela.

South America's plants and fish are natural resources, too. Forests cover about half the continent. Trees from these forests provide everything from wood for building to coconuts for eating. People harvest many rain forest plants to make medicines. Tuna, anchovies, and other fish are plentiful in the waters off the Pacific Coast.

Like other parts of Latin America, South America has rich soil. Farmers grow many different crops there. For example, coffee is a key crop in Brazil and Colombia. Wheat is important in Argentina. Many South American economies rely on the production of sugar cane, cotton, and rice.

Natural Resources and Latin America's Economy

Not every country shares in the wealth of Latin America's resources. Some Latin American countries have many resources, while others have few. Some countries do not have the money they need to develop all of their resources. Other countries rely too much on one resource or crop.

Sailors of the Seventh Century South Americans have been trading with the people of Mexico since at least A.D. 600. They sailed north from Ecuador, Colombia, and Peru on rafts. These adventurers traded not only goods, such as tweezers and bells, but also skills and ideas. For example, they taught people of Mexico how to make metal objects such as needles.

Cash Crop Farming

Many Latin American economies are based on agriculture. Half of Colombia's exports are coffee, and one third of Honduras' exports are bananas. **Critical Thinking** What problems do you think one-crop economies face?

Visualize How would the crops in a field look after a hurricane? How would they look after a drought?

Prices, Weather, and Other Factors   Depending on one resource or crop can lead to problems. For example, when world copper prices are high, the copper mining industry is very successful. But suppose copper prices drop sharply. Then copper exports are not worth as much. When this happens, the mining industry loses money. Mining workers may lose their jobs. Chile is the leading producer of copper in the world. When prices plunge, Chile's economy suffers.

Many people in Latin America make their living by farming. Some Latin American countries depend on one or two crops, such as coffee, bananas, or sugar. When the price of a crop goes down, exports of that crop bring less money into the country. As a result, workers' wages may drop, and some workers may lose their jobs.

Weather and disease also cause people and businesses to lose money. Hurricanes, droughts, and plant disease can damage crops. Weather sometimes hurts the fishing industry. The warm ocean current El Niño affects the fish that live in South America's coastal waters. Usually, the cold water of the Pacific supports a large number of small water plants on which the fish feed. When El Niño strikes, the warm water kills the plants and the fish die or move to other areas. Peru is among the countries affected by El Niño. Peruvian fishers have suffered great economic losses due to El Niño effects.

READ ACTIVELY

Depending on Oil   Oil is one of Latin America's most valuable resources. But it is risky to depend on oil. Oil prices increase and decrease. Sometimes they change suddenly. Mexico, like Venezuela, is a major oil producer. In the mid-1980s, oil companies produced more oil than the world needed. As a result, prices dropped. Mexico earned much less income than it had expected. The same thing happened to Trinidad.

There are other problems as well. In the 1960s, people discovered oil in Ecuador. Soon, oil became the country's main export. But in 1987, earthquakes destroyed Ecuador's major oil pipeline. The country's income was slashed.

Avoiding the Problems of a One-Resource Country

Latin American nations know the risks of depending on one resource or crop. They are trying to diversify their economies. To **diversify** is to add variety. When Latin American nations try to diversify their economies, it means that they are looking for other ways to make money. Many are building factories. Factories make products that can be sold to bring more money into the economy. Factories also provide jobs for people.

Venezuela has been trying to set up more factories and farms. Venezuela is also improving its bauxite and iron mines. Ecuador passed a law to encourage industry. Businesses there built factories to make cloth, electrical appliances, and other products.

Brazil has also been building up its industries. That way Brazil does not have to depend on agriculture. Brazil now exports machinery, steel, and chemicals. Brazil has also encouraged cotton farming. As a result, cotton weaving has become a successful industry.

El Salvador used to depend too heavily on its coffee crop. Now, cotton, sugar, corn, and other crops play an important role in the nation's economy. Trinidad has also encouraged its farmers to raise more kinds of crops. The government realizes that the country depends too much on oil and sugar.

SECTION 3 REVIEW

1. **Define**   (a) hydroelectricity, (b) diversify.

2. **Identify**   (a) Jamaica, (b) Venezuela, (c) Brazil, (d) Colombia, (e) Chile.

3. Describe the important natural resources of Latin America.

4. Why is it important for Latin American nations to diversify their economies?

Critical Thinking

5. **Recognizing Cause and Effect**   Suppose a disease destroyed Colombia's coffee crop. How would this loss affect coffee-plantation workers and their families? How would it affect Colombia's economy?

Activity

6. **Writing to Learn**   Imagine that you are the president of a Latin American country. Your nation depends on bananas for nearly all of its income. What arguments would you use to persuade people to diversify?

Review and Activities

Reviewing Main Ideas

1. List the three main regions of Latin America. Then choose two and describe their features.
2. In what ways do the physical features of Latin America affect the people and their way of life?
3. How does elevation affect climate?
4. (a) Give an example of how climate in one region of Latin America affects the vegetation that grows there.
   (b) How does this affect the way in which people live?
5. How are a country's natural resources tied to its economy?
6. What problems arise when a country depends too heavily on a single source of income? Support your answer with one or two examples.
7. How are the nations of Latin America trying to avoid the problems of relying on a single source of income?

Reviewing Key Terms

Match the definitions in Column I with the key terms in Column II

Column I

1. height of land above sea level
2. plains in Argentina and Uruguay
3. to add variety
4. river or stream that flows into a larger body of water
5. electricity generated by the power of moving water
6. large raised area of mostly level land
7. narrow strip of land that has water on both sides and joins two larger bodies of land

Column II

a. isthmus
b. pampas
c. plateau
d. tributary
e. elevation
f. diversify
g. hydro-electricity

Critical Thinking

1. **Identifying Central Issues** Explain the meaning of this statement, and give examples: "The weather in Latin America is a great friend to the people, but also a terrible enemy."
2. **Drawing Conclusions** "How a country uses its natural resources affects the well-being of its people." Do you agree or disagree with this statement? Explain your answer.

Graphic Organizer

Copy the chart to the right onto a separate sheet of paper. Then fill in the empty boxes to complete the chart. Use the maps in this chapter to help you.

	Physical Features	Climate	Vegetation	Natural Resources
Mexico and Central America				
The Caribbean				
South America				

Map Activity

For each place listed below, write the letter from the map that shows its location.

1. Colombia

2. Brazil

3. Jamaica

4. Mexico

5. Venezuela

Latin America: Place Location

Writing Activity

Writing a Letter
Imagine that you are a visitor to Latin America. You are touring the whole region: Mexico, Central America, the Caribbean, and South America. Write a letter home, describing your trip. Write about such items as these: impressive sights, the weather, interesting facts you've learned, places you liked or didn't like.

Internet Activity
Use a search engine to find **The Green Arrow Guide to Central America.** Click on **El Salvador.** Click on **An Introduction to El Salvador** and read about El Salvador's geography and climate. Use the information to make a physical map of El Salvador.

Skills Review

Turn to the Skill Activity.

Review the steps for reading a regional map. Then complete the following: (a) In your own words, describe two factors that vary from climate to climate. (b) What types of climates can be found in Latin America?

How Am I Doing?

Answer these questions to help you check your progress.

1. Can I identify and describe the main regions of Latin America?

2. Do I understand how Latin America's physical features, climate, and vegetation affect the people who live in the region?

3. Can I identify important natural resources of Latin America?

4. Can I explain why Latin American countries want to diversify their economies?

5. What information from this chapter can I use in my book project?

The Surveyor

BY ALMA FLOR ADA

BEFORE YOU READ

Reach Into Your Background

Do people in your family tell you stories about interesting or exciting events that have happened to them? What stories do you remember the best? What do you learn from these stories?

The stories that family members tell each other become part of the family history. Family stories are important because they teach people about their cultural heritage. Alma Flor Ada grew up in Cuba. The following story shows what Ada learned from one of the stories her father used to tell her.

Questions to Explore

1. What can you learn from this story about family life in Cuba?
2. What does this story tell you about how geography affects people's lives in Cuba?

surveyor (sir VAY ur) *n.:* a person who measures land and geographic features

My father, named Modesto after my grandfather, was a surveyor. Some of the happiest times of my childhood were spent on horseback, on trips where he would allow me to accompany him as he plotted the boundaries of small farms in the Cuban countryside. Sometimes we slept out under the stars, stringing our hammocks between the trees, and drank fresh water from springs. We always stopped for a warm greeting at the simple huts of the neighboring peasants, and my eyes would drink in the lush green forest crowned by the swaying leaves of the palm trees.

Since many surveying jobs called for dividing up land that a family had inherited from a deceased parent or relative, my father's greatest concern was that justice be achieved. It was not enough just to divide the land into equal portions. He also had to ensure that all parties would have access to roads, to water sources, to the most fertile soil. While I was able to join him in some trips, other surveying work involved large areas of land. On these jobs, my father was part of a team, and I would stay home, eagerly awaiting to hear the stories from his trip on his return.

◀ The equipment that surveyors use must be strong and lightweight.

Latin American families tend not to limit their family boundaries to those who are born or have married into it. Any good friend who spends time with the family and shares in its daily experiences is welcomed as a member. The following story from one of my father's surveying trips is not about a member of my blood family, but instead concerns a member of our extended family.

Félix Caballero, a man my father always liked to recruit whenever he needed a team, was rather different from the other surveyors. He was somewhat older, unmarried, and he kept his thoughts to himself. He came to visit our house daily. Once there, he would sit silently in one of the living room's four rocking chairs, listening to the lively conversations all around him. An occasional nod or a single word were his only contributions to those conversations. My mother and her sisters sometimes made fun of him behind his back. Even though they never said so, I had the impression that they questioned why my father held him in such high regard.

Then one day my father shared this story.

"We had been working on foot in mountainous country for most of the day. Night was approaching. We still had a long way to go to return to where we had left the horses, so we decided to cut across to the other side of the mountain, and soon found ourselves facing a deep gorge. The gorge was spanned by a railroad bridge, long and narrow, built for the sugarcane trains. There were no side rails or walkways, only a set of tracks resting on thick, heavy crossties suspended high in the air.

"We were all upset about having to climb down the steep gorge and up the other side, but

Predict Why do you think that Ada's father admires Félix so much?

recruit (ree KROOT) v.: to enlist or hire to join a group

gorge (gorj) n.: a narrow canyon with steep walls

span (span) v.: to extend across a space

▶ Walking across a railroad bridge is dangerous, because most are just wide enough for a train to pass.

dissuade (dis SWAYD) *v.*: to persuade not to do something

ominous (OM ih nus) *adj.*: threatening

the simpler solution, walking across the bridge, seemed too dangerous. What if a cane train should appear? There would be nowhere to go. So we all began the long descent . . . all except for Félix. He decided to risk walking across the railroad bridge. We all tried to dissuade him, but to no avail. Using an old method, he put one ear to the tracks to listen for vibrations. Since he heard none, he decided that no train was approaching. So he began to cross the long bridge, stepping from crosstie to crosstie between the rails, balancing his long red-and-white surveyor's poles on his shoulder.

"He was about halfway across the bridge when we heard the ominous sound of a steam engine. All eyes rose to Félix. Unquestionably he had heard it, too, because he had stopped in the middle of the bridge and was looking back.

"As the train drew closer, and thinking there was no other solution, we all shouted, 'Jump! Jump!', not even sure our voices would carry to where he stood, so high above us. Félix did look down at the rocky riverbed, which, as it was the dry season, held little water. We tried to encourage him with gestures and more shouts, but he had stopped looking down. We could not imagine what he was doing next, squatting down on the tracks, with the engine of the train already visible. And then, we understood. . . .

"Knowing that he could not manage to hold onto the thick wooden crossties, Félix laid his thin but resilient surveyor's poles across the ties, parallel to the rails. Then he let his body slip down between two of the ties, as he held onto the poles. And there he hung, below the bridge, suspended over the gorge but safely out of the train's path.

"The cane train was, as they frequently are, a very long train. To us, it seemed interminable. . . . One of the younger men said he counted two hundred and twenty cars. With the approaching darkness, and the smoke and shadows of the train, it was often difficult to see our friend. We had heard no human sounds, no screams, but could we have heard anything at all, with the racket of the train crossing overhead?

"When the last car began to curve around the mountain, we could just make out Félix's lonely figure still hanging beneath the bridge. We all watched in relief and amazement as he pulled himself up and at last finished walking, slowly and calmly, along the tracks to the other side of the gorge."

After I heard that story, I saw Félix Caballero in a whole new light. He still remained as quiet as ever, prompting a smile from my mother and her sisters as he sat silently in his rocking chair. But in my mind's eye, I saw him crossing that treacherous bridge, stopping to think calmly of what to do to save his life, emerging all covered with soot and smoke but triumphantly alive—a lonely man, hanging under a railroad bridge at dusk, suspended from his surveyor's poles over a rocky gorge.

If there was so much courage, such an ability to calmly confront danger in the quiet, aging man who sat rocking in our living room, what other wonders might lie hidden in every human soul?

resilient (rih ZIL yunt) *adj.*: able to withstand shock and bounce back from changes

treacherous (TRECH ur us) *adj.*: dangerous

READ ACTIVELY

Visualize Visualize the team of surveyors as they watch the train go by. How do you think they looked? How might they have acted?

EXPLORING YOUR READING

Look Back

1. How does this story change the way the author feels about Félix Caballero?

Think It Over

2. Why is surveying land important in Cuba?

3. Why do you think that the author's family accepts Félix Caballero as a member of their extended family?

4. What lesson does the author of this story hope to teach?

Go Beyond

5. What does this story tell you about the character traits that help a person to act in an emergency?

Ideas for Writing: A Short Story

6. Choose a story that has been told to you by a family member or friend. Or, choose a story that you have told others about an event that happened to you. Write the story. Include an introduction and conclusion that explain why the story is important to you.

LATIN AMERICA

Shaped by Its History

KEY

☐ Aztec Empire
A.D. 1200s–A.D. 1521

☐ Mayan Empire
A.D. 300–A.D. 900

☐ Incan Empire
A.D. 1400s–A.D. 1535

Lambert Azimuthal Equal-Area Projection

0   600   1,200 mi
0   600   1,200 km

This map shows the location of three civilizations in Latin America that existed before Europeans arrived in the region.

Study the map
(a) What are the names of the civilizations shown on the map?
(b) Which civilization is the oldest?

Consider the geography
Which civilization do you think was the most difficult to defend from invaders? Explain your answer.

Early Civilizations of Middle America

BEFORE YOU READ

Reach Into Your Background

What does the word *pyramid* bring to mind? Write down three things you know about pyramids. Then, compare what you know about pyramids with the pyramids you will read about in this section.

Questions to Explore

1. What were the chief characteristics and accomplishments of Mayan and Aztec civilizations?
2. How have Latin America's early civilizations affected present-day cultures in Latin America?

Key Terms
maize
hieroglyphics

Key Places
Copán
Tikal
Valley of Mexico
Tenochtitlán

Fans cheered as the players brought the ball down the court. Suddenly, the ball flew into the air and sailed through the hoop. Fans and players shouted and screamed. Although this may sound like a championship basketball game, it is actually a moment of a game played over 1,000 years ago. The game was called pok-a-tok.

Pok-a-tok was a game played by the ancient Mayas. Using only their leather-padded hips and elbows, players tried to hit a five-pound (1.9 kg), six-inch (15.2 cm) rubber ball through a stone hoop mounted 30 feet (9.1 m) above the ground.

Mayan Civilization

How do we know about this ancient game? Crumbling ruins of pok-a-tok courts and ancient clay statues of players have been found at sites in Central America and southern Mexico. In these areas, Mayan civilization thrived from about A.D. 300 to A.D. 900. By studying ruins, scientists have learned much about Mayan civilization.

▼ This pok-a-tok court is in Copán, Honduras. How is it similar to a basketball court?

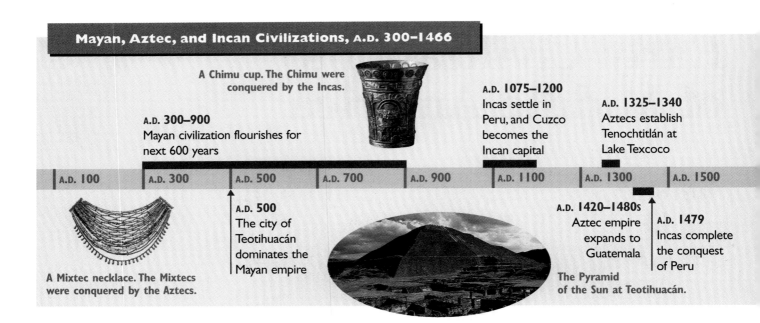

A Chimu cup. The Chimu were conquered by the Incas.

A.D. 1075–1200
Incas settle in Peru, and Cuzco becomes the Incan capital

A.D. 1325–1340
Aztecs establish Tenochtitlán at Lake Texcoco

A.D. 300–900
Mayan civilization flourishes for next 600 years

| A.D. 100 | A.D. 300 | A.D. 500 | A.D. 700 | A.D. 900 | A.D. 1100 | A.D. 1300 | A.D. 1500 |

A Mixtec necklace. The Mixtecs were conquered by the Aztecs.

A.D. 500
The city of Teotihuacán dominates the Mayan empire

A.D. 1420–1480s
Aztec empire expands to Guatemala

A.D. 1479
Incas complete the conquest of Peru

The Pyramid of the Sun at Teotihuacán.

The Mayas built great cities. One such city was Copán (ko PAHN) in the present-day country of Honduras. Another was Tikal (tee KAHL) in present-day Guatemala. Mayan cities were religious centers. A large pyramid-shaped temple stood in the center of the city. The Mayas worshipped their gods there. Farmers worked in fields surrounding the cities. Past the fields lay the dense tropical rain forest.

Mayan Farming and Science The Mayan farmers' most important crop was **maize,** or corn. Maize was the main food of the Mayas. They also grew beans, squash, peppers, avocados, and papayas. Mayan priests studied the stars and planets. They designed an accurate calendar, which they used to decide when to hold religious ceremonies. The Mayan calendar was more accurate than any used in Europe until the 1700s. The Mayas developed a system of writing using signs and symbols called **hieroglyphics** (hy ur oh GLIF iks). They also developed a number system that is similar to the present-day decimal system.

The Great Mystery of the Mayas About A.D. 900, the Mayas suddenly left their cities. No one knows why. Crop failures, war, disease, drought, or famine may have killed many Mayas. Or perhaps people rebelled against the control of the priests and nobles. The Mayas left their cities, but stayed in the region. Millions of Mayas still live in the countries of Mexico, Belize, Guatemala, Honduras, and El Salvador.

Aztec Civilization

Another ancient civilization of Middle America is that of the Aztecs. They arrived in the Valley of Mexico in the 1100s. The Valley of Mexico is in Central Mexico and includes the site of present-day Mexico City.

LINKS TO MATH

The Concept of Zero The Mayas created a numbering system that included the idea of zero. Zero is important in math because it is a symbol that shows that there is none of something. For example, to write the number 308, you need a symbol to show that there are no tens. Mathematicians consider the idea of zero to be one of the world's greatest inventions.

The Aztecs wandered about the valley looking for a permanent home until 1325. They finally settled on an island in Lake Texcoco. They changed the swampy lake into a magnificent city, which they called Tenochtitlán (tay nawch tee TLAHN). Tenochtitlán stood on the site of present-day Mexico City.

Tenochtitlán

Tenochtitlán, the Aztec capital, was built in the center of a lake. The Aztecs built floating islands by piling rich earth from the bottom of the lake onto rafts made of wood. After a while, the roots of plants and trees grew down to the lake bottom, anchoring the rafts. Some islands were the size of football fields. What do you think it would be like to live on a lake?

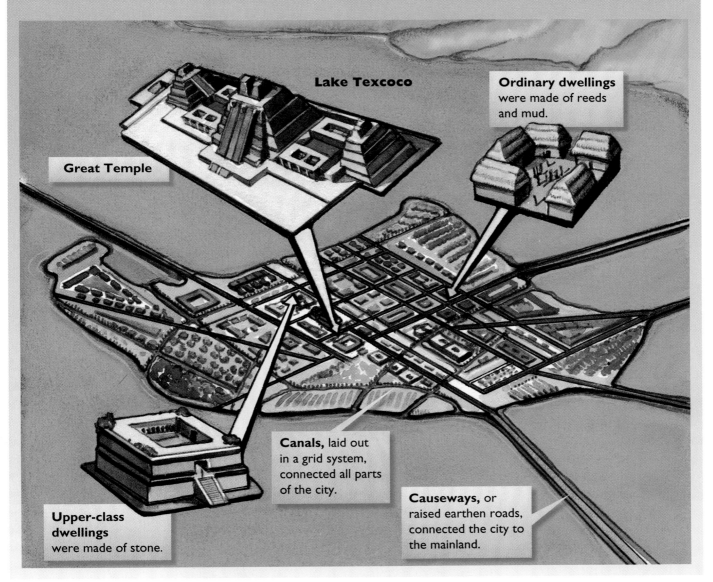

Lake Texcoco

Ordinary dwellings were made of reeds and mud.

Great Temple

Upper-class dwellings were made of stone.

Canals, laid out in a grid system, connected all parts of the city.

Causeways, or raised earthen roads, connected the city to the mainland.

Aztec Astronomy

The Aztecs observed the stars and planets carefully. They named them after their gods, like Quetzalcoatl, shown at right. The Aztecs used their knowledge of astronomy to make calendars like the one below.

The Aztecs Expand Their Empire   In the 1400s, Aztec warriors began conquering the other people in the region. They forced the people they conquered to pay tribute, or taxes. Tribute could be paid in food, cotton, gold, or slaves. The Aztecs grew rich from the tribute.

The Aztecs had an emperor who ruled over all Aztec lands. The rest of Aztec society had several classes. Nobles and priests helped the emperor. Warriors fought battles. Traders carried goods throughout the empire and beyond. Craftworkers created jewelry, garments, pottery, sculptures, and other goods. Most people, however, were farmers.

Other Aztec Accomplishments   Tenochtitlán was a center of trade and learning. Aztec doctors made more than 1,000 medicines from plants. They used the medicines to lower fevers, cure stomachaches, and heal wounds. Like the Mayas, Aztec astronomers predicted eclipses and the movements of planets. Aztec priests kept records using hieroglyphics similar to those used by the Mayas.

SECTION 1 REVIEW

1. **Define**   (a) maize, (b) hieroglyphics.

2. **Identify**   (a) Copán, (b) Tikal, (c) Valley of Mexico, (d) Tenochtitlán.

3. What were the main features of Mayan civilization?

4. How was Aztec society organized?

Critical Thinking

5. **Distinguishing Fact From Opinion**   Tell if the following statements are facts or opinions. Explain why. (a) Mayan calendars were very accurate. (b) Aztec civilization was more advanced than Mayan civilization.

Activity

6. **Writing to Learn**   What are some reasons for the decline of Mayan and Aztec civilizations? Does every society decline sooner or later?

The Incas

PEOPLE OF THE SUN

Reach Into Your Background

The United States has roads that run from state to state. These roads are called inter-state highways. Think about some ways that interstate highways are useful. Then, compare what you know about interstate highways with the roads you will read about in this section.

Questions to Explore

1. What was Incan civilization like?

2. How did the Incas interact with and change their environment to increase farmland and farm production?

Key Terms

aqueduct   quipu

Key People and Places

Pachacuti   Cuzco
Topa Inca

The runner sped along the mountain road. He lifted a horn made from a shell to his lips and blew. A second runner appeared and began running beside him. Without stopping, the first runner relayed to the second runner the message he carried. The second runner took off like the wind. He would not stop until he reached the next runner.

The Incas used runners to spread news from one place in their empire to another. Incan messengers carried news at a rate of 250 miles (402 km) a day. Without these runners, controlling the vast empire would have been very difficult.

The Rise of the Incas

This great and powerful empire had small beginnings. In about 1200, the Incas settled in Cuzco (KOOS koh), a village in the Andes that is now a city in the country of Peru. Most Incas were farmers. They grew maize and other crops. Through wars and conquest, the Incas won control of the entire Cuzco valley, one of many valleys that extend from the Andes to the Pacific Ocean.

In 1438, Pachacuti (PAHTCH an koo tee) became ruler of the Incas. The name Pachacuti means "he who shakes the earth." Pachacuti conquered the people who lived near the Pacific Ocean, from Lake Titicaca north to the city of Quito.

▼ The Incas shaped their stones so well that they did not need cement to hold a wall together.

Pachacuti demanded loyalty from the people he conquered. If they proved disloyal, he forced them off their land. He replaced them with people loyal to the Incas.

Pachacuti's son, Topa Inca, expanded the empire. In time, it stretched some 2,500 miles (4,023 km) from what is now Ecuador south along the Pacific coast through Peru, Bolivia, Chile, and Argentina. The 12 million people ruled by the Incas lived mostly in small villages.

Incan Accomplishments

The Incas were excellent farmers, builders, and managers. Their capital, Cuzco, was the center of government, trade, learning, and religion. In the 1500s, one of the first Spaniards to visit Cuzco described it as "large enough and handsome enough to compare to any Spanish city."

The emperor, and the nobles who helped him run the empire, lived in the city near the central plaza. They wore special headbands and earrings that showed their high rank. Most of the farmers and workers outside Cuzco lived in mud huts.

Roads and Aqueducts   The Incas built more than 19,000 miles (30,577 km) of roads. The roads went over some of the most mountainous land in the world. The road system helped the Incas to govern their vast empire. Not only did runners use the roads to deliver messages, but Incan armies and trade caravans also used the roads for speedy travel.

READ ACTIVELY

Connect How do your family and community depend on roads?

▼Pachacuti built many cities. The most famous one is the "lost city" of Machu Picchu. It lies high in the Andes Mountains, 54 miles (87 km) northwest of Cuzco. **Interaction** Look closely at the picture. How did the Incas adapt their city to the mountains?

The Incas used quipus to record information about births, deaths, trade, and taxes. **Critical Thinking** Think of some other ways to communicate information without using spoken or written words.

The Incas also built canals and aqueducts to carry water to dry areas. An **aqueduct** is a pipe or channel designed to carry water from a distant source. One stone aqueduct carried water from a mountain lake almost 500 miles (805 km) to its destination. The system of canals and aqueducts allowed the Incas to irrigate land that was otherwise too dry to grow crops.

Government and Records The Incas organized their government carefully. The emperor chose nobles to govern each province. Each noble conducted a census to count people so they could be taxed. Local officials collected some of each village's crops as a tax. The villagers also had to work on government building projects. However, the government took care of the poor, the sick, and the elderly.

The Incas did not have a written language. Incan government officials and traders recorded information on knotted strings called **quipus** (KEE poos). Every quipu had a main cord with several colored strings attached to it. Each color represented a different item, and knots of different sizes at certain intervals stood for numbers.

Religion Like the Mayas and the Aztecs, the Incas worshipped many gods. The sun god, Inti, was an important god of the Incas. They believed Inti was their parent. They referred to themselves as "children of the sun." Another important Incan god was Viracocha (vee ra KOCH ah), the creator of all the people of the Andes.

ACROSS TIME

Earthquake-proof Buildings Incan stone walls were so firmly constructed that even violent earthquakes could not knock them down. The walls swayed but did not crumble the way some modern buildings do. Engineers today are learning to make buildings that can resist an earthquake.

The Incas increased the amount of farmland in hilly areas by building terraces into the sides of steep slopes. The terraces helped keep soil from washing down the mountain. These terraces are at Pasaq, an ancient Incan fortress in Peru. Interaction Think of some other reasons why farming in the mountains might be hard.

Quechua Descendants of the Incas The Spanish conquered the Incan empire in the 1500s. However, descendants of the Incas still live in present-day Peru, Ecuador, Bolivia, Chile, and Colombia. They speak Quechua (KECH wah), the Incan language.

They use farming methods that are like those of the ancient Incas. The Incan culture also survives in the poncho and in other clothing styles, as well as in cloth woven into brightly colored complex patterns.

SECTION 2 REVIEW

1. **Define** (a) aqueduct, (b) quipu.
2. **Identify** (a) Pachacuti, (b) Topa Inca, (c) Cuzco.
3. Why was a good network of roads important to the Incan empire?

4. Describe a few features of the Incan religion.

Critical Thinking
5. **Drawing Conclusions** Look at the shape of the Incan empire on the map on the opening page of this chapter. In an attack, what features would make the empire difficult to defend? What features would help defend the empire?

Activity
6. **Writing to Learn** Make a list of some of the ways the Incas used land for farming. Do you think the Incas made good use of farmland? Why or why not?

European Conquest

SECTION 3

ernan Cortés was the Spanish soldier who conquered the Aztecs. He landed in Mexico in 1519 and soon met Malinche (mah LIHN chay). She was the daughter of a Mayan leader. Malinche, whom Cortés called Doña Marina, spoke several languages in addition to Mayan. She quickly learned Spanish. Malinche became Cortés's main translator. She also kept an eye on Aztec spies. Without Malinche, Cortés could not have conquered the Aztecs. Why did European explorers, like Cortés, want to conquer Native Americans? Why did some Native Americans, like Malinche, help the conquerers?

Europeans Arrive in the Americas

In the 1400s, Spain and Portugal searched for new trade routes to Asia. They knew that in Asia they would find expensive goods such as spices and silks. These goods could be traded for a profit.

Columbus Reaches America Christopher Columbus thought he could reach Asia by sailing west across the Atlantic Ocean. Columbus knew the world was round, as did most educated

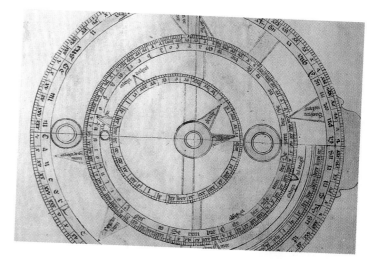

▼ Sailors in the 1400s guided their ships using only the stars, a compass, and an astrolabe. Below is a drawing of an astrolabe.

Map Study Columbus sailed to the Americas in 1492, 1493, 1498, and 1502. His 1502 voyage is shown here. Cortés sailed to the Americas in 1504 and conquered the Aztecs in 1519. Pizarro sailed in 1502 and conquered the Incas in 1533. **Movement** Once they reached the Caribbean, what factors do you think helped the Spanish to find the Aztec and Incan empires so quickly? **Regions** South America has two major language regions: Spanish and Portuguese. How did the Line of Demarcation create these regions?

Gulf of Mexico
YUCATÁN PEN.
Tenochtitlán
Tikal
Caribbean Sea
ATLANTIC OCEAN
PACIFIC OCEAN
Amazon R.
SOUTH AMERICA
BRAZIL
Cuzco
ANDES MOUNTAINS

KEY

→ Christopher Columbus 1502–1504

→ Hernan Cortés 1519–1521

→ Francisco Pizarro 1531

---- Line of Demarcation

Lambert Azimuthal Equal-Area Projection

0   600   1,200 mi
0 600 1,200 km

LINKS TO MATH

Navigating Without Modern Instruments Explorers like Columbus did not have radar, satellites, and computers to guide their ships. They used the stars as a reference. Sailors imagined a triangle with a straight line from the ship to the horizon, and a line from the horizon to a star. Measuring the angle between the line to the star and the horizon helped them figure out their location.

Europeans. But Columbus believed the distance around the world was shorter than it was. First Columbus asked Portugal to sponsor his voyage. Then he asked Spain. Queen Isabella of Spain finally agreed.

Columbus set sail in early August, 1492. Some 10 weeks later, on October 12, he spotted land. Columbus thought he had reached the East Indies in Asia, so he described the people there as Indians.

Dividing the World Spain and Portugal soon became fierce rivals. Each country tried to stop the other from claiming land in the Americas. In 1494, Spain and Portugal signed the **Treaty of Tordesillas** (tor day SEE yas). A **treaty** is an agreement in writing made between two or more countries. The treaty set an imaginary line from North Pole to South Pole at about 50° longitude, called the **Line of Demarcation.** It gave Spain the right to settle and trade west of the line. Portugal could do the same east of the line. The only part of South America that is east of the line is roughly the eastern half of present-day Brazil. Because of the Treaty of Tordesillas, the language and background of Brazil are Portuguese.

A Clash of Cultures

Spanish explorers heard stories of wealthy kingdoms in the Americas. They hoped to find gold and other treasures. Spanish rulers did not pay for the trips of the explorers. Instead, they gave the **conquistadors** (kon KEES ta dors), or conquerors, the right to hunt for treasure. The conquistadors could also settle in America. In exchange, conquistadors agreed to give Spain one fifth of any treasures they found. If a conquistador failed, he lost his own fortune. If he succeeded, both he and Spain gained fame, wealth, and glory.

Cortés Conquers the Aztecs   In 1519, Hernan Cortés sailed to the coast of Mexico in search of treasure. He brought a small army with him. The Aztec ruler Moctezuma (mahk the ZOOM uh) heard that a strange ship was offshore. He sent spies to find out about it. The spies reported back to Moctezuma:

> "We must tell you that we saw a house in the water, out of which came white men, with white hands and faces, and very long, bushy beards, and clothes of every color: white, yellow, red, green, blue, and purple, and on their heads they wore round hats."

The Aztecs demanded heavy tribute from the peoples who lived near them, so these groups disliked the Aztecs. Cortés made agreements with these groups. Then he headed for Tenochtitlán with 500 soldiers and 16 horses. Aztec spies told Moctezuma that the Spanish were coming. The Aztecs had never seen horses before. Moctezuma's spies described the Spanish as "supernatural creatures riding on hornless deer, armed in iron, fearless as gods." Moctezuma thought Cortés might be the god Quetzalcoatl (ket sahl koh AHTL). According to Aztec legend, Quetzalcoatl had promised to return to rule the Aztecs.

With a heavy heart, Moctezuma welcomed Cortés and his soldiers. Cortés tried to convince Moctezuma to surrender to Spain. After several months, Moctezuma agreed. But the peace did not last long. Spanish soldiers killed some Aztecs. Then the Aztecs began to fight against the Spanish. The battle was fierce and bloody. Moctezuma was killed, and Cortés and his army barely escaped.

With the help of the Aztecs' enemies, Cortés surrounded and attacked Tenochtitlán. In 1521, the Aztecs finally surrendered. By then, about 240,000 Aztecs had died and 30,000 of Cortés's allies had been killed. Tenochtitlán and the Aztec empire lay in ruins.

Pizarro Conquers the Incas   Francisco Pizarro (fran SIS koh pih ZAR oh), like Cortés, was a Spanish conquistador. He heard stories about the rich Incan kingdom. Pizarro planned to attack the Pacific coast of South America. In 1531, Pizarro set sail with a small force of 180 Spanish soldiers. Pizarro captured and killed the Incan

This historical painting shows Moctezuma welcoming Cortés to his court. **Critical Thinking** Based on this painting, what conclusions can you draw about Aztec wealth?

READ ACTIVELY

Connect How would you feel if you saw people riding on a large animal that you had never seen before?

Ask Questions Suppose that you were a doctor living in South America at the time of the Conquest. What questions would you ask to discover why so many Native Americans were dying of European diseases?

emperor. He also killed many other Incan leaders. By 1535, Pizarro had conquered most of the Incan empire, including the capital, Cuzco.

The conquistadors defeated the two most powerful empires in the Americas. It took them only 15 years. How did they do it? The Spanish had guns and cannons that the Native Americans had never seen. They also rode horses. At first, horses terrified Native Americans. The Europeans also carried diseases such as smallpox, measles, and chicken pox. These diseases wiped out entire villages. And, because of local rivalry, some Native Americans like Malinche helped the Spanish conquistadors.

Colonization

By the 1540s, Spain claimed land throughout much of the Americas. Spain's lands stretched from what today is Kansas all the way south to the tip of South America. Brazil was claimed by Portugal.

Spain Organizes Its Empire Spain divided its territory into provinces. Spain also set up a strong government. The two most important provinces were New Spain and Peru. The capital of New Spain was Mexico City. Lima became the capital city of Peru.

Lima's geographic layout was based on the Spanish social classes. The most powerful citizens lived in the center of Lima. They either came from Spain or had Spanish parents. **Mestizos,** people of mixed Spanish and Native American descent, lived on the outskirts of the city. Many

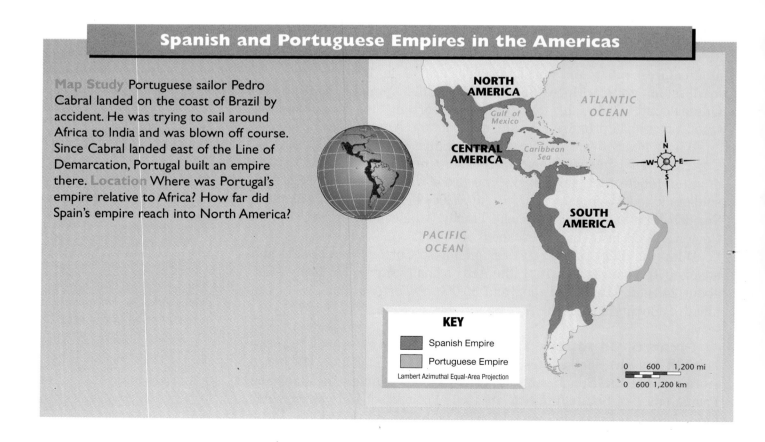

Spanish and Portuguese Empires in the Americas

Map Study Portuguese sailor Pedro Cabral landed on the coast of Brazil by accident. He was trying to sail around Africa to India and was blown off course. Since Cabral landed east of the Line of Demarcation, Portugal built an empire there. **Location** Where was Portugal's empire relative to Africa? How far did Spain's empire reach into North America?

NORTH AMERICA
Gulf of Mexico
ATLANTIC OCEAN
CENTRAL AMERICA
Caribbean Sea
SOUTH AMERICA
PACIFIC OCEAN

KEY
Spanish Empire
Portuguese Empire
Lambert Azimuthal Equal-Area Projection

0   600   1,200 mi
0   600   1,200 km

mestizos were poor. But some were middle class or quite wealthy. Native Americans were the least powerful class. Most Native Americans continued to live in the countryside. The Spanish forced them to work on haciendas. A **hacienda** (hah see EN duh) was a plantation owned by Spaniards or the Catholic Church.

The Effect of European Rule Spain gave its settlers **encomiendas** (en KOH mee en dus), which were rights to demand taxes or labor from Native Americans. Native Americans were allowed to stay on their own land, so the Spanish claimed that encomiendas protected Native Americans. In fact, encomiendas forced Native Americans to work for the settlers. At first, the Native Americans worked only on the haciendas. But when silver was discovered in Mexico and Peru, the Spanish forced Native Americans to also work in the mines. Some died from overwork and malnutrition. Many died from European diseases. In 1519, New Spain had a Native American population of 25 million. Only 3 million survived the first 50 years of Spanish rule. In 1532, 12 million Native Americans lived in Peru. Fifty years later, there were fewer than 2 million.

The Columbian Exchange

Western Hemisphere	Eastern Hemisphere
Pumpkin	Horse
Avocado	Cattle
Peanut	Sheep
Beans	Chicken
(lima, pole, navy, kidney)	Honeybee
Peppers (bell and chili)	Sugar cane
Pineapple	Wheat, barley, oats
Quinine	Onion
Wild rice	Lettuce
Corn	Peach and pear
Potato	Watermelon
Tomato	Citrus fruit
	Banana

Chart Study Goods, as well as people, crossed the Atlantic in the years after the conquest. . Do you think that the Eastern and Western hemispheres benefitted equally from the Columbian Exchange? Why or why not?

SECTION 3 REVIEW

1. Define (a) Treaty of Tordesillas, (b) treaty, (c) Line of Demarcation, (d) conquistador, (e) mestizo, (f) hacienda, (g) encomienda.

2. Identify (a) Hernan Cortés, (b) Malinche, (c) Christopher Columbus, (d) Moctezuma, (e) Francisco Pizarro.

3. What was the effect of the Treaty of Tordesillas on the European settlement of the Americas?

4. How did the Spanish conquest affect Native Americans?

Critical Thinking

5. Recognizing Bias The Treaty of Tordesillas affected the lives of millions of Native Americans. However, Native Americans were not asked about the treaty. What do you think this says about European attitudes toward Native Americans?

Activity

6. Writing to Learn Write two paragraphs: one by a Native American who has just seen a European for the first time and another by a European who has just seen a Native American for the first time.

Using a Time Line

The year is A.D. 2098. Biff Bucko, a star geography student, jumps into his shiny new time machine. He's off on a weekend trip to ancient Mayan civilization.

The centuries whiz by. As our hero approaches the year A.D. 1000, he slows to a stop. "When was Mayan culture at its height?" he wonders. Biff looks to the left and right. "Hmm . . . I think it's this way." Biff should have checked the time line in his glove compartment. If he had, he would have known that Mayan civilization declined after A.D. 900. Instead, he's landed in the 1400s where the Aztecs are busy conquering Middle America. "Oops," thinks Biff as a band of Aztec warriors descends upon him.

Studying the past makes you a kind of time traveler, too. Still, it's always best to know where you're going. Creating a time line can help.

Get Ready

A time line is like a map of the past. It keeps important dates in order so you don't get lost in time. Keep yours handy while you study for a test, research a report, or read for fun.

To make a time line you'll need:
- two sheets of paper
- thirteen paper clips

Try It Out

A. **Make a paper ruler.** Fold one sheet of paper in half the long way. Now fold it over again. You'll use this paper as a ruler to measure your time line.

B. **Mark the divisions of time periods.** Attach three paper clips along the top edge of your paper ruler. Slide one to the left corner, one to the right corner, and one to the exact center.

C. Look at dates for your time line. Your time line will cover a span of about 1,200 years. Label the left paper clip on your ruler with the year 300. Label the right paper clip 1500 and the middle one 900.

D. Figure out time intervals. Space your other paper clips evenly across the top of the ruler. The space between each will stand for 100 years. Label your clips with the years 400, 500, and so on.

E. Locate the dates on your time line. Turn your other paper so the long side is on top. Draw a straight line across it. Using your ruler, mark the 100-year intervals. Then mark where each of the four time line dates belongs on the line. (Estimate for the dates 1345 and 1438.) Label each mark with its date and event.

Dates for Your Time Line			
300	**900**	**1385**	**1438**
Mayan civilization rises	Mayas leave their cities	Aztecs found the city of Tenochtitlán	Pachacuti founds the Incan Empire

Apply the Skill

Now choose some other dates in Latin American history that you want to remember. Follow the steps below to create a time line.

1 **Design a time line ruler.** First look at the dates you've selected. What time span will your time line cover? For a long span, each paper clip could mark 100 years. For a shorter span, you could mark every 50 years, 10 years, or 1 year. Choose a measurement that makes sense.

2 **Find a date to start your ruler.** Take the earliest date you chose for your time line. Round it to a lower number. For example, if you are measuring every 50 years, round the date 1492 down to 1450.

3 **Find a date to end your ruler.** Take your last date. Round it up.

4 **Count the paper clips you'll need.** Say your ruler starts at 1450, ends at 1650, and marks every 50 years. Count: 1450, 1500, 1550, 1600, 1650. That's five clips.

5 **Put a clip at each end of the ruler.** Space the others evenly. Label each with its year. Now use the ruler to mark points on your time line. Label each point with its date and event.

Independence

On August 24, 1791, the night sky over Saint-Domingue (san duh MANG) glowed red and gold. The French Caribbean colony was on fire. The slaves were sick of being mistreated by their white masters. They finally had rebelled. Now they were burning every piece of white-owned property they could find. This Night of Fire was the beginning of the first great fight for freedom in Latin America. Toussaint L'Ouverture (too SAN loo vur TOOR), a former slave, led the people of Saint-Domingue in this fight for more than 10 years. Eventually they won. They founded the independent country of Haiti (HAY tee) in 1804.

The flame of liberty lit in Haiti soon spread across Latin America. By 1825, most of the region was independent. Latin Americans would no longer be ruled by Europe.

Independence in Mexico

Haiti's leaders drew encouragement from two famous revolutions. A **revolution** is a political movement in which the people overthrow the government and set up another. During the 1770s and early 1780s, the 13 British colonies in North America fought a war to free themselves from Britain's rule. In 1789, the ordinary people of France staged a violent uprising against their royal rulers. These actions inspired not only the people of Haiti, but also people across Latin America.

Criollos (kree OH yohz) paid particular attention to these events. A **criollo** had Spanish parents, but had been born in Latin America.

▼ Toussaint L'Ouverture was captured by the French, but his followers won Haiti's independence.

Criollos often were the wealthiest and best-educated people in the Spanish colonies. Few criollos had any political power, however. Only people born in Spain could hold government office. Many criollos attended school in Europe. There, they learned about the ideas that inspired revolution in France and the United States. The criollos especially liked the idea that people had the right to govern themselves.

The "Cry of Dolores"   Mexico began its struggle for self-government in 1810. Miguel Hidalgo (mee GEHL ee DAHL goh) led the way. He was a criollo priest in the town of Dolores. With other criollos in Dolores, he planned to begin a revolution.

In September 1810, the Spanish government discovered Hidalgo's plot. But before the authorities could arrest him, Hidalgo took action. He wildly rang the church bells. A huge crowd gathered. "Recover from the hated Spaniards the land stolen from your forefathers," he shouted. "Long live America, and death to the bad government!"

Hidalgo's call for revolution became known as the "Cry of Dolores." It attracted some 80,000 fighters in a matter of weeks. This army consisted mostly of mestizos and Native Americans. They were angry. They wanted revenge against anybody connected with the Spanish government. The rebels won some victories. Their luck, however, soon changed. By the beginning of 1811, they were in full retreat. Hidalgo tried to flee the country. However, government soldiers soon captured him. He was put on trial and convicted of treason. Hidalgo was executed by firing squad in July 1811.

Ask Questions What would you like to know about the attitudes of Mexican criollos toward the revolution?

The Cry of Dolores

Hidalgo made the "Cry of Dolores" on September 16. Mexico celebrates its independence every year on that day. **Critical Thinking** Why do you think that the painter of this mural included so many people in the background behind Hidalgo?

African Independence
Although Africa is closer to Europe than to Latin America, Europeans began to colonize Africa later. Europeans began claiming parts of Africa in the 1880s. Like the people of Latin America, many people in Africa later were inspired by the ideas of self-government and independence. African countries began to achieve independence in the 1950s and 1960s.

Independence Finally Comes The Spanish could execute the revolution's leaders, but they could not kill its spirit. Small rebel groups kept fighting. Then Agustín de Iturbide (ee toor BEE day) joined the rebels. He was a high-ranking officer in the Spanish army. Many people who had opposed the rebellion changed their minds. They had viewed Hidalgo as a dangerous hothead. But Iturbide was different. He was a criollo and an army officer. They could trust Iturbide to protect their interests. They decided to support the rebellion. In 1821, Iturbide declared Mexico independent.

South American Independence

Simón Bolívar (see MOHN boh LEE vahr) was not the first Latin American revolutionary leader. Almost certainly, however, he was the greatest. He was born in the country of Venezuela in 1783. His family was one of the richest and most important families in Latin America. Like most wealthy Latin Americans, he went to school in Spain. There, he met Prince Ferdinand, the heir to the Spanish throne. They decided to play a game similar to present-day badminton. Custom required that Bolívar show respect for the prince by losing. Instead, Bolívar played hard and tried to win. He even knocked the prince's hat off with his racquet! The angry prince demanded an apology. Bolívar refused. He claimed it was an accident. Furious, the prince insisted that they fight a duel. He soon calmed down, however.

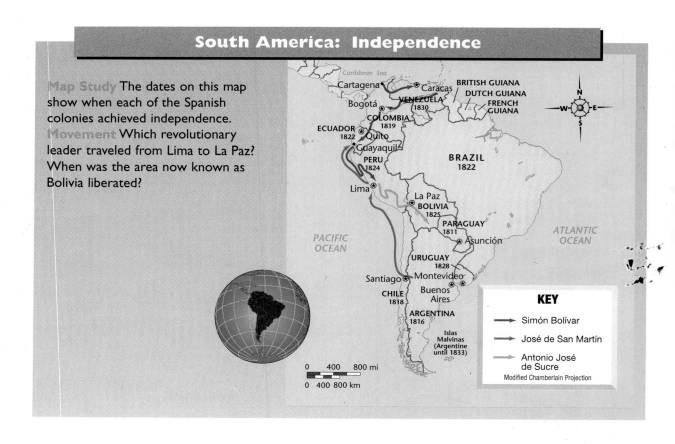

South America: Independence

Map Study The dates on this map show when each of the Spanish colonies achieved independence. **Movement** Which revolutionary leader traveled from Lima to La Paz? When was the area now known as Bolivia liberated?

Caribbean Sea

Cartagena
Bogotá
Caracas
VENEZUELA 1830
BRITISH GUIANA
DUTCH GUIANA
FRENCH GUIANA
COLOMBIA 1819
ECUADOR 1822
Quito
Guayaquil
PERU 1824
BRAZIL 1822
Lima
La Paz
BOLIVIA 1825
PARAGUAY 1811
Asunción
PACIFIC OCEAN
ATLANTIC OCEAN
URUGUAY 1828
Santiago
Montevideo
CHILE 1818
Buenos Aires
ARGENTINA 1816
Islas Malvinas (Argentine until 1833)

0   400   800 mi
0   400 800 km

KEY
→ Simón Bolívar
→ José de San Martín
→ Antonio José de Sucre
Modified Chamberlain Projection

Many years later, these two faced off again. This time, Bolívar knocked Spanish America from under Ferdinand's feet.

Bolívar and San Martín: The Liberators   Bolívar joined the fight for Venezuelan independence in 1804. Six years later he became its leader. Bolívar was completely certain that he would win. His confidence, courage, and daring inspired his soldiers. They enjoyed victory after victory. By 1822, Bolívar's troops had freed a large area from Spanish rule (the future countries of Colombia, Venezuela, Ecuador, and Panama). This newly liberated region formed Gran Colombia. Bolívar became its president. Even though his country was free, Bolívar did not give up the cause of independence. "The Liberator," as he was now known, turned south toward Peru.

José de San Martín (san mahr TEEN), an Argentine, had lived in Spain and served in the Spanish army. When Argentina began its fight for freedom, he quickly offered to help. San Martín took good care of his troops. He shared each hardship they had to suffer. They loved him for it. Many said they would follow San Martín anywhere—even over the snow-capped Andes Mountains. In 1817, his soldiers had to do just that. He led them through high passes in the Andes into Chile. This bold action took the Spanish completely by surprise. In a matter of months, Spain was defeated. San Martín declared Chile's independence. Then he turned his attention to Peru.

Again, San Martín took an unexpected action. This time, he attacked from the sea. The Spanish were not prepared for San Martín's tactics. Spanish defenses quickly collapsed. In July 1821, San Martín pushed inland and seized Lima, the capital of Peru.

▶ Nearly every town or city in South America has a central square with a statue of Bolívar or San Martín. These high school girls are visiting the statue of Bolívar in Meridá, Venezuela.

A year later, San Martín met with Bolívar to discuss the fight for independence. Historians do not know what happened in that meeting. But afterward, San Martín suddenly gave up his command. He left Bolívar to continue the fight alone. This Bolívar did. Eventually, he drove the remaining Spanish forces out of South America altogether. By 1825, only Cuba and Puerto Rico were still ruled by Spain.

Brazil Takes a Different Route to Freedom Portugal's colony, Brazil, became independent without fighting a war. In the early 1800s, French armies invaded Spain and Portugal. Portugal's royal family fled to Brazil for safety. The king returned to Portugal in 1821. However, he left his son, Dom Pedro, to rule the colony. Dom Pedro used more power than the king expected. He declared Brazil independent in 1822. Three years later, Portugal quietly admitted that Brazil was independent.

Challenges of Independence

After winning independence, Latin American leaders faced hard challenges. They had to decide how to govern their nations. Also, after years of fighting, Latin American nations were very poor.

Simón Bolívar dreamed of uniting South America as one country. Gran Colombia was the first step. Bolívar hoped it would become the "United States of South America." In trying to govern Gran Colombia, however, Bolívar found that his dream was impossible. Latin America was a huge area, divided by the Andes and dense rain forests. Also, the leaders of the countries in Gran Columbia wanted little to do with Bolívar. In poor health, he retired from politics.

Even though he did not last long in office, Bolívar set the standard for Latin American leaders. Most were **caudillos** (kow DEE yohs), military officers who ruled very strictly. Bolívar cared about the people he governed. Many other caudillos did not. These others just wanted to stay in power and get rich.

Ask Questions What questions would you ask Simón Bolívar about his dream of a "United States of South America"?

SECTION 4 REVIEW

1. **Define** (a) revolution, (b) criollo, (c) caudillo.
2. **Identify** (a) Miguel Hidalgo, (b) Agustín de Iturbide, (c) Simón Bolívar, (d) José de San Martín, (e) Dom Pedro.

3. What world events influenced the independence movement in Latin America?
4. How was Brazil's path to independence different from that of the rest of South America?

Critical Thinking
5. **Identifying Central Issues** What do you think Simón Bolívar had in mind when he wanted South America to become the "United States of South America"?

Activity
6. **Writing to Learn** Imagine you are a journalist with Bolívar's or San Martín's army. Describe the army's main actions.

Issues in Latin America Today

Reach Into Your Background

Most people like the feeling of being able to take care of themselves. What could you do now to prepare for your own independence?

Questions to Explore

1. How are Latin American nations trying to improve their economies?
2. What issues has the move to the cities created in Latin America?

Key Terms

invest
economy
campesino
rural
urban

Key Places

Brazil

Samuel Zemurray came from Russia to the United States in 1892. He worked for his aunt and uncle, who owned a store in Alabama. As part of his job, Zemurray sometimes traveled to the port city of Mobile. He noticed that fruit and vegetable traders there often threw away ripe bananas. They knew the bananas would spoil before reaching stores. Zemurray bought the ripe bananas and delivered them to stores overnight. The quick delivery meant that the fruit was still fit to be sold. Zemurray's business was so successful that he decided to expand. He did this by buying land in the country of Honduras, where bananas were grown. Zemurray soon became a leading banana grower.

▼ Many large-scale farming operations in Latin America are still foreign-owned.

Foreign Investment

In the 1900s, many companies like Zemurray's invested in Latin America. To **invest** means to spend money to earn more money. Some companies owned farms and grew crops such as sugar and bananas. Other foreign companies ran mines. By the mid-1900s, most businesses in Latin America were owned by or did work for foreign companies. As a result, foreign companies became powerful in Latin American economies. A country's **economy** is made up of the ways that goods and services are produced and made available to people. When money from the sale of goods and services comes into or goes out of a country, it affects the country's economy.

Predict What steps do you think Latin American countries took to balance their economies?

Foreign companies made huge profits from their businesses in Latin America. However, these companies did little to help Latin American countries build their economies. Many Latin Americans realized that it was important to improve their economies. They needed to build factories so that they could make their own manufactured goods. They also needed to grow many different kinds of crops and to develop a wide range of resources.

Some Latin American countries soon took steps to carry out these economic building plans. And they proved successful. During the 1960s and early 1970s, the economies of many Latin American countries grew. However, in the early 1980s, oil prices went up. Latin American countries needed oil to run their factories—and they had to pay higher and higher prices for it. At the same time, the prices of Latin American products fell. Latin American countries had to spend more money, but they were making less and less. To make up the difference, they borrowed money from wealthy countries such as the United States. By the 1980s, many Latin American countries had huge foreign debts.

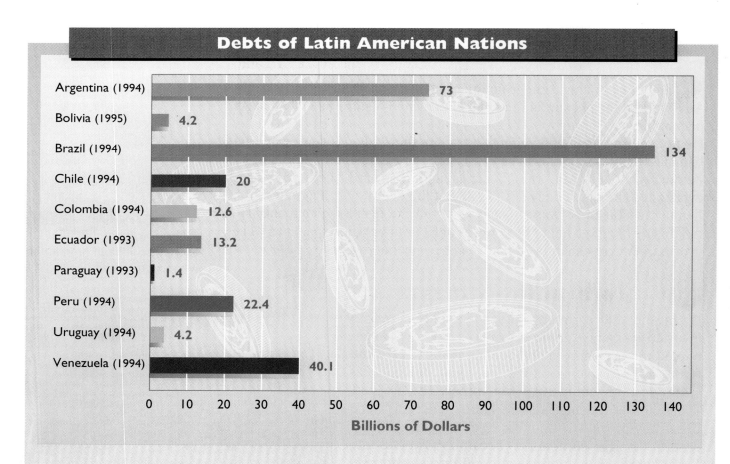

Debts of Latin American Nations

Country	Billions of Dollars
Argentina (1994)	73
Bolivia (1995)	4.2
Brazil (1994)	134
Chile (1994)	20
Colombia (1994)	12.6
Ecuador (1993)	13.2
Paraguay (1993)	1.4
Peru (1994)	22.4
Uruguay (1994)	4.2
Venezuela (1994)	40.1

Chart Study Argentina and Brazil are the two Latin American countries with the most industry. They also have the most foreign debt. **Critical Thinking** Why do you think that Argentina and Brazil have more debt than other countries?

Facing Economic Challenges

People in Latin American countries have expanded their economies by building more factories and growing different kinds of crops. And they have taken other steps to improve their economies.

Foreign companies still invest in Latin America. But most Latin American countries limit how investments can be made. They want to prevent foreign countries from having too much control over important parts of their economies. Some countries, for instance, have tried to stop foreign companies from acquiring too much land.

Latin American countries have tried to improve their economies by cooperating with one another. For a long time, most Latin American countries did not trade with one another. They did not need to because, for the most part, they all produced the same kinds of goods. Recently, however, some countries have developed new industries. The products these countries make can be traded to other countries in the region. This kind of trade has increased in the last few years. Latin American countries also have formed several organizations that encourage cooperation in the region.

LINKS ACROSS THE WORLD

African Economies Many African countries are also trying to improve their economies with less foreign investment. Africans are trying to earn more money by growing more types of cash crops. They are also working to build their own industries and mine their own resources without help from foreign companies.

Land Distribution

The issue of how land is used greatly affects the future of Latin America's economies. Land is one of Latin America's most important resources. Some people and companies own great amounts of land in

Building Televisions on an Assembly Line

In the last 50 years, Latin American countries have begun to produce many more products in factories like this one in Brazil. **Critical Thinking** What skills do you think these factory workers need?

In El Salvador, many farmers do not have modern farming equipment. They use traditional wooden plows and oxen. **Critical Thinking** What would it cost a farmer to own oxen? How would this cost compare to the cost of owning a tractor?

Latin America but most people in the region do not own any land. In Brazil, for example, 45 percent of the land is owned by only 1 percent of the population.

Dividing the Land Much of the farmland in Latin America is owned by a few wealthy families. This land is occupied by haciendas where crops are grown to sell abroad. In contrast, many poor farmers—known as **campesinos** (kahm peh SEE nohs)—own only small tracts of land. They often grow enough only to meet their own needs.

Starting in the 1930s, many Latin American countries tried to help the campesinos by dividing the land more equally. These programs have met with mixed success. In some cases, the land given to the campesinos was of poor quality. No matter how hard they tried, they could not make a living from it. In other cases, the campesinos struggled because they had neither the money to buy seeds and equipment nor the skills necessary for success. Many Latin American countries have begun to see that taking land from one person and giving it to another does not necessarily improve people's lives or the economy.

Using and Protecting the Land Dividing up the land has raised other issues. Brazil gave land to landless peasants by moving them to the Amazonian rain forest. The peasants burned down trees to clear the land for farming. After a few years, however, the soil in the rain forest became unfit for farming.

Many people around the world expressed worries about the clearing of the rain forest. Some believed that this would hurt the environment. Others said that it would change the way of life of the Native Americans who live there. Some people, however, have challenged this view. Economic progress, they say, will come only if Brazil uses all its resources. Brazilian leaders are looking for a balance. They want to find ways to help the economy and the campesinos without destroying the rain forest.

The Move to the City

Many campesinos have decided that making a living from the land is just too difficult. They have left the land and gone to the cities in search of different economic opportunities. This move has resulted in the rapid growth of the populations of large cities. Since the 1950s, many Latin American countries have had a population explosion. The population has increased dramatically in both the **rural,** or countryside, and the **urban,** or city, areas of Latin America. The population of urban areas, however, has gone up the most.

Many Latin Americans who move to the cities are looking for better jobs. They also want to improve the quality of their lives. They hope to find comfortable homes, better medical care, and good schools for their children. However, they do not always realize their hopes. As Latin American countries strive to build their economies, there will be greater opportunities for people to have a better life.

Farming in a Rain Forest

This pepper farmer has cleared land on an island in the Amazon River, in northern Brazil. **Critical Thinking** How does pepper farming contribute to Brazil's economy?

SECTION 5 REVIEW

1. **Define** (a) invest, (b) economy, (c) campesino, (d) rural, (e) urban.

2. **Identify** Brazil.

3. What steps have Latin American countries taken to improve their economies?

4. How have Latin American countries tried to change the landowning system in the region?

Critical Thinking

5. **Recognizing Cause and Effect** How has the increase in population contributed to the growth of cities in Latin America?

Activity

6. **Writing to Learn** You have read that many people oppose Brazil's plans to move poor farmers to the rain forest. Write a paper that explores both the pro and the con sides of the following statement: "A country has the right to use its resources as it sees fit."

Review and Activities

Reviewing Main Ideas

1. Why was an accurate calendar important to Mayan priests?
2. How did the Aztecs expand their empire?
3. How were the Incas able to change their environment in order to grow more food?
4. Give two examples of how the Mayan, Aztec, or Incan empires affect culture in Latin America today.

5. Why was Hernan Cortés able to persuade many Native Americans in the region to fight the Aztecs?
6. (a) Why did Spain gain control over most of Latin America?
   (b) How did Portugal come to control Brazil?

7. What role did the criollos play in the fight for Latin American independence?
8. How did José de San Martín surprise the Spanish in Chile and Peru?
9. How have many Latin American countries been trying to improve their economies in recent years?

Reviewing Key Terms

Use each key term below in a sentence that shows the meaning of the term.

1. maize
2. hieroglyphics
3. aqueduct
4. quipu
5. Line of Demarcation
6. conquistador
7. mestizo
8. hacienda
9. encomienda
10. criollo
11. caudillo
12. invest
13. economy
14. campesino
15. rural
16. urban

Critical Thinking

1. **Recognizing Cause and Effect** What were two causes of the fall of the Aztec and Incan empires? What were two effects on the Native American people of the region?
2. **Making Comparisons** Compare the way in which Mexico gained its independence with the way in which the countries of South America gained theirs.

Graphic Organizer

Copy this tree map onto a separate sheet of paper. Then use the empty boxes to outline Latin American history from Mayan civilization through the Spanish conquest.

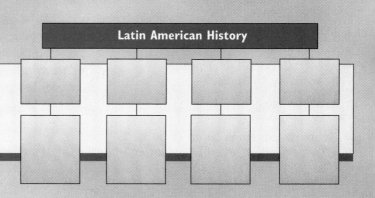

Latin American History

Map Activity

For each place listed below, write the letter from the map that shows its location.

1. Brazil

2. Guatemala

3. Mexico

4. Chile

5. Peru

6. Andes

7. Mexico City

Latin America: Place Location

Writing Activity

Writing a Story
The Mayas, Aztecs, and Incas had spoken histories. Information was passed from generation to generation in stories and songs. Suppose that you lived at the time of the Spanish conquest. Write a story or a song that tells about the conquest.

Internet Activity

Use a search engine to find the site **Rabbit in the Moon: Mayan Glyphs and Architecture.** Explore and learn about the ancient Mayan civilization. Then, click on **How to Write Your Name in Mayan Glyphs.** Write your name in Mayan hieroglyphics, or play Bul, the on-line Mayan Game of Chance.

Skills Review

Turn to the Skill Activity.

Review the steps for using a time line. Then: (a) Explain in your own words how using a time line can help you to understand history. (b) What kinds of events should you list on a time line?

How Am I Doing?

Answer these questions to help you check your progress.

1. Can I identify and describe characteristics of the Mayan, Aztec, and Incan civilizations?

2. Can I explain how European rule affected Native Americans?

3. Can I explain how Latin American countries achieved independence?

4. Can I explain how foreign investment has affected Latin America?

5. What information from this chapter can I use in my book project?

Cultures of Latin America

PICTURE ACTIVITIES

These people are attending a festival in Peru. Get to know more about the people of Latin America by completing the following.

Link culture and history
Look at the people in this scene. Based on what you know about the history of Latin America, what do you think is the ethnic background of the people in the picture.

Compare regions
The cultures of Latin America are a unique blend of Native American, African, and European influences. How do you think the variety of peoples found in Latin America compares with that in the United States?

The Cultures of Mexico and Central America

BEFORE YOU READ

Reach Into Your Background

What are your hopes and dreams for the future? Do you hope to work in a particular profession? Do you plan to go to college? Many Mexicans and Central Americans have the same kinds of dreams.

Questions to Explore

1. What is the ethnic heritage of the people of Mexico and Central America?
2. Why have many people in this region been moving from the country to the city?
3. What are the causes of Mexican and Central American immigration to the United States?

Key Terms
diversity
indigenous
injustice
maquiladora
emigrate
immigrant

Key Places
Mexico City

Elvia Alvarado (el VEE ah ahl vah RAH doh) walks the back roads of rural Honduras. She helps poor campesinos make a living. Honduran campesinos are like rural people in all of Central America. Many have little land of their own. It is hard for them to make enough money to support their families.

Alvarado is a mother and grandmother. She works for an organization of campesinos. She helps people get loans to buy seeds and farm machinery. Alvarado also helps them get more land. She works with community groups.

Alvarado's work is not easy. "The communities we work in are hard to get to," she says. "Sometimes I don't eat all day, and in the summertime the streams dry up and there's often no water to drink." Sometimes Alvarado does not get paid. "But I couldn't be happy if my belly was full while my neighbors didn't have a plate of beans and tortillas to put on the table," she says. "My struggle is for a better life for all Hondurans."

Cultural Heritage

Alvarado lives and works in Honduras, in Central America. It is one of seven nations in this area. Together they form a crooked, skinny isthmus. The isthmus links Mexico and South America.

One Region, Many Faces There is much **diversity,** or variety, among the people of Central America. Hondurans, like Alvarado, are mostly mestizo. They have both Spanish and indigenous ancestors. **Indigenous** (in DIJ uh nus) people are descendants of the people who first lived in a region. In Latin America, indigenous people are also called Native Americans or Indians. About half of Guatemala's people are mestizo. The other half are indigenous. Many Costa Ricans are direct descendants of Spaniards. And more than half the people of Belize are of African or mixed African and European descent.

These countries have many languages, too. Guatemala is home to more than 20 languages. Spanish is the language of government and business. But the indigenous people in Guatemala speak their own languages. So do indigenous people in Panama, El Salvador, and Nicaragua. Spanish is the main language in six of the seven countries. People in Belize speak English.

Mexico's Heritage Mexico blends Native American and Spanish influences. Spanish is the first language for most Mexicans, and Mexico is the largest Spanish-speaking country. Some Mexicans speak Native American languages. About 30 percent of the people of Mexico are indigenous, and some Mexicans are mestizos.

The Church Religion is important to the people of Mexico and Central America. In the 1500s and 1600s, Spanish missionaries converted many Native Americans to Christianity. The Roman Catholic Church has been important to this region ever since. Most of the people are Catholic. Native Americans have blended many elements of their religions with Christianity.

▶ The people of El Salvador are mostly mestizo, and their mixed heritage is reflected in their paintings. **Critical Thinking** What in this painting illustrates the Salvadorans' Spanish heritage?

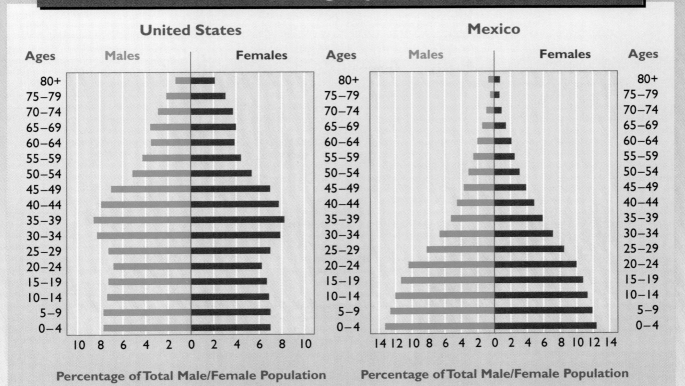

A Growing Population

United States

Ages	Males	Females	Ages

Mexico

Ages	Males	Females	Ages

Percentage of Total Male/Female Population   Percentage of Total Male/Female Population

Chart Study Unlike the United States, Mexico is a nation of young people.
Critical Thinking Think about what different skills and needs people have at different ages. What challenges do you think Mexico faces because so many of its people are very young?

Often, the Roman Catholic Church has fought injustice. **Injustice** is the unfair treatment of people. There are many examples of injustice. Injustice occurs when people have their property taken from them unfairly. It also occurs when people are imprisoned without first having a trial. Injustice often happens in countries that have undemocratic governments. Priests and bishops have called for all people to be treated fairly.

Following the Church's lead, many citizens have taken their own steps to end poverty and injustice. People have started their own health clinics, farms, and organizations. Like Elvia Alvarado and her campesino families, they hope that by working together they will be able to create a better way of life.

Looking for Work

The population of Mexico and Central America is growing rapidly. If it continues at the current rate, it will double in 20 to 30 years. Rapid population growth has made it hard for young people in rural areas to

CITIZEN HEROES

A Voice of Protest In the late 1600s, Mexican nun Sor Juana Inez de la Cruz was punished by her bishop for writing a letter defending women's right to learn. Sor Juana was a published poet, but the bishop took away her books and writing materials. However, Sor Juana's essay inspired later generations of women to stand up for their rights.

Many Mexican and Central American immigrants to the United States find jobs on farms, picking crops. The farm workers on the right are picking strawberries near Salinas, California. The worker below is harvesting broccoli in Texas' Rio Grande Valley.

READ ACTIVELY

Ask Questions What questions about maquiladoras would you like answered?

find jobs. Many have left their homes to look for work in the city. Today, most people in Mexico and Central America live in cities.

In Mexico, some people move to towns along the border with the United States. There, they can work in factories owned by American companies. These companies place their factories in Mexico because wages are lower there. Border factories are called **maquiladoras** (ma kee la DOR as).

Life in the City In many cities in the region, there are big contrasts between the lives of the wealthy and the lives of the poor. Wealthy people live in big houses on wide streets. They go to good schools and can afford to pay for medical care. Many of them have a lifestyle similar to that of wealthy people in the United States.

For the poor, however, life in the city can be hard. There is a shortage of housing. It is not easy to find work. Sometimes, the only job available is selling fruit or soda on street corners. It is hard to feed a family on the wages such work commands. Yet people are willing to live with hardships they find in the city. Cecilia Cruz can explain why. She moved with her husband and their two sons to Mexico City from the southern state of Oaxaca (wah HAH kah). They live in a two-room house made of cinder blocks. It is on the outermost boundary of the city. "We came here for the schools," says Cruz. "There are more choices here. The level of education is much higher." Most newcomers to the city would agree.

Moving to the United States   Most people in Mexico and Central America move somewhere else within their own country if they cannot find work. Some move to cities or border towns. In addition, however, thousands of people emigrate. To **emigrate** means to move out of one country into another. Most leave because they cannot find work at home. Also, rising prices have made living more expensive. Many people emigrate to the United States.

Fermin Carrillo (fair MEEN kah REE yoh) is one worker who did just that. He left his home town of Huaynamota, Mexico. There were no more jobs at home, and his parents needed food and medical care. Carrillo moved to a town in Oregon. Now he works in a fish processing plant. He sends most of the money he earns home to his parents. Carrillo hopes one day to become a U.S. citizen. Other immigrants are different. They want to return home after earning some money to help their families. An **immigrant** is a person who has moved into one country from another.

Many Mexicans and Central Americans, like Fermin Carrillo, have left the region in search of a better life. Many more have followed Elvia Alvarado's example. They have stayed and begun to build a better life for themselves at home.

READ ACTIVELY

Visualize What would a house made of cinder blocks look like? What problems might you notice if you went inside a cinder block house?

SECTION 1 REVIEW

1. **Define**   (a) diversity, (b) indigenous, (c) injustice, (d) maquiladora, (e) emigrate, (f) immigrant.
2. **Identify**   Mexico City.

3. (a) What is the main language and religion of the people of Mexico and Central America? (b) How do the languages and religions of the region reflect its history?
4. What is one reason that rural people in Mexico and Central America are moving to the cities?

Critical Thinking
5. **Recognizing Cause and Effect**   Explain several reasons for Mexican and Central American immigration to the United States.

Activity
6. **Writing to Learn**   Write a journal entry from the point of view of one of the people mentioned in this section. Write about that person's hopes and dreams. How are they like your own? How are they different?

The Cultures of the Caribbean

BEFORE YOU READ

Reach Into Your Background

Have you ever been on an island? Have you ever read a story about someone who lived on an island? What was the island like? What do you remember most about life there?

Questions to Explore

1. How did European, African, and Native American cultures blend to create unique Caribbean cultures?

2. What are the key characteristics of Caribbean cultures?

Key Terms
ethnic group
Carnival

Key Places
Jamaica
Cuba
Hispaniola
Trinidad and Tobago

Dorothy Samuels is a ten-year-old from Jamaica, a tropical island in the Caribbean Sea. She lives in a village near the ocean and goes to a village school. Dorothy is a good student. She hopes one day to go to college in Kingston, Jamaica's capital city. Jamaican laws require that women have as much opportunity to educate themselves as men do. Equality of women is important to Jamaican culture because many Jamaican women are independent farmers and business owners.

Dorothy's family are farmers. They plant yams and other vegetables and fruits. They also plant cocoa beans. Every Saturday, Dorothy's mother and grandmother take their fruits and vegetables to the market to sell. All the traders at the market are women.

▼ Many Jamaican women carry goods on their heads. This practice came to the Caribbean from Africa.

The People of the Caribbean

People in the Caribbean can make a living farming because most Caribbean islands have very fertile soil. These islands stretch over 2,000 miles (3,219 km) from Florida to the northeast coast of South America. As you might expect, a variety of peoples and cultures live within this large area.

The First People of the Caribbean The Caribbean islands are also called the West Indies because when Christopher Columbus arrived there, he thought he had reached the Indies in Asia.

The first people to live in the Caribbean were Native Americans, the Ciboney (SEE boh nay). The Ciboney lived on the islands for thousands of years. In about 300 B.C., they were joined by another indigenous group, the Arawaks (AR ah wahks), who came from South America. In about 1000, the Caribs (KA ribz), another South American group, arrived.

The Caribs gave the region its name. They lived there for more than 400 years before the first Europeans came to the area. Christopher Columbus and other Spaniards enslaved the Native Americans. Almost all of the Caribs, Arawaks, and other groups died of overwork and of diseases the Spanish brought with them. Today, just a few hundred Caribs still live on the island of Dominica.

Other Europeans followed the Spanish. They hoped to make money from the region's wealth of natural resources. Dutch, French, and English colonists began claiming territory in the 1600s. They built large sugar plantations and brought many enslaved Africans to work on them.

READ ACTIVELY

Predict What ethnic groups do you think live in the Caribbean today?

Caribbean Customs

	Jamaica	Puerto Rico	Dominican Republic
Greetings	A handshake; "Good morning/afternoon/evening"; use Mr., Mrs., Miss.	A handshake. Women kiss each other on the cheek.	Shake hands. Greet everyone when you enter a room. Ask about people's families.
Gestures	Show approval of an idea by touching fists. Suck air through your teeth to mean "Give me a break."	Wiggle your nose to mean, "What's going on?" Point with puckered lips.	Point with puckered lips. Clap hands to request your check in a restaurant.
Table Manners	Keep the fork in the left hand. If you buy food from a street cart, eat it on the spot.	Keep both hands above the table. Stay at the table after the meal to relax and chat.	Guests are served first and sometimes separately. They often are given more elaborate food than the hosts.
Clothing	Women wear colorful skirts and matching headdresses. Many people have tailors make their clothes. Jewelry is common.	Casual clothing is worn for everyday occasions. Parties and social events require formal clothing.	Dressing well is considered important. Clothing is always clean and well-pressed. Men have a traditional suit called a chacabana, which is a white shirt over dark trousers.

Chart Study When you visit another culture, knowing the local customs can help you understand what you see. **Critical Thinking** Name some customs that are unique to the United States.

Most of the Caribbean people today are descended from these Africans. Immigrants from China, India, and the Middle East also came to the area to work.

People in the Caribbean Today Since slavery was legally ended in the Caribbean, its population has grown to about 36 million. Nearly one third of these people live on the region's largest island, Cuba.

Because so many people came to the Caribbean as colonists, slaves, or immigrants, the area has great ethnic variety. An **ethnic group** is a group of people who share race, language, religion, or cultural traditions. The ethnic groups of the Caribbean are Native American, African, European, Asian, and Middle Eastern.

Depending on their island's history, the people of a Caribbean island may speak one of several European languages. Their language may also be a mixture of European and African languages. For example, two countries and two cultures exist on the island of Hispaniola. On the eastern half is one country, the Dominican Republic. Its population is Spanish-speaking and mostly mestizo. West of the Dominican Republic is the country of Haiti. Nearly all of Haiti's people are descended from Africans. They speak French and Creole, which is a blend of French and African languages.

Most West Indians are Christians, but there are also small groups of Hindus, Muslims, and Jews. Some people practice traditional African religions.

A Caribbean Family

Family life is very important to people in the Caribbean. This family, from Montserrat, British West Indies, is made up of parents and their children. Many people in the Caribbean live in family groups that also include grandparents, uncles, aunts, and cousins.

Haiti was one of the first places where the work of folk artists was recognized as real art. Large, colorful murals comment on religious and political themes. Bus drivers gain prestige by painting public buses, called taptaps.

Food, Music, Art, and Fun

Caribbean culture is known for its liveliness. People play music, dance, and tell stories. People also play many sports. Baseball, soccer, and track and field are popular. On some islands, people also play cricket, which is a British game similar to baseball. Dominoes is a popular game throughout the region.

Food Caribbean food is a mixture from all the cultures of the islands. Caribbean people can enjoy many types of seafood that are not found in U.S. waters. For instance, the people of Barbados love to eat flying fish and sea urchin eggs. Bammy—a bread made from the cassava plant—is still made the way the Arawaks made it. People also cook spicy curries from India, sausages from England, and Chinese dishes. Many tropical fruits grow on the islands. West Indians use the fruit to make many juices and other drinks that are not readily available in the United States.

Music Caribbean music is famous around the world. Calypso is a form of song that uses humor in its lyrics. You may have heard reggae (REG ay) music. It is from Jamaica. Steel drums are Caribbean musical instruments. They are made from recycled oil drums. A steel drum can be "tuned" so that different parts of it play different notes. Players strike the instruments with rubberized drumsticks. The rubber hitting the drum makes an almost liquid sound.

LINKS TO MUSIC

Soca—Calypso with Soul
In the 1970s, a new form of Caribbean music evolved. It blended calypso with two other styles—funk and ska. Funk is an earthy, blues music. Ska is similar to reggae. The first song to use this music was Lord Shorty's "Soul Calypso." The name of the new musical form comes from the title "Soul Calypso." It is called *soca*.

Many people in Caribbean countries dress in lavish, colorful costumes to celebrate before Lent. **Critical Thinking** What similar celebrations take place in the United States?

Carnival Many islanders observe the Roman Catholic tradition of Lent, which is the period of 40 days before Easter Sunday. People consider Lent to be a very solemn time, so just before Lent they throw a huge party. The party is called **Carnival.**

Different countries celebrate Carnival in different ways. The biggest Carnival takes place in Trinidad and Tobago. People spend all year making costumes and floats. Lent always starts on a Wednesday. At 5 A.M. the Monday before, people go into the streets in their costumes. Calypso bands play. Thousands of fans follow the bands through the streets, dancing and celebrating. At the stroke of midnight Tuesday, the party stops. Lent has begun.

SECTION 2 REVIEW

1. **Define** (a) ethnic group, (b) Carnival.

2. **Identify** (a) Jamaica, (b) Cuba, (c) Hispaniola, (d) Trinidad and Tobago.

3. Who were the first inhabitants of the Caribbean islands?

4. Which traditions does modern Caribbean culture blend?

Critical Thinking

5. **Making Comparisons** What common elements in their histories have shaped the cultures of the various Caribbean islands?

Activity

6. **Writing to Learn** Select one aspect of Caribbean culture (food, music, celebrations, and so on) and jot down what you have learned about it in this section. Then, write ways in which it is similar to and different from your own culture.

The Cultures of South America

Reach Into Your Background

Think about the books you read, the music you like to listen to, and the clothes you wear. These things are all part of your culture. How is your culture related to the history of your family and your region? How does the geography in your region affect your culture?

Questions to Explore
1. What major cultural groups live in South America?
2. How has geography created diversity in this region?

Key Terms
subsistence farming
import

Key Places
Andes
Chile
Argentina
Brazil

Between Peru and Bolivia is the deep lake called Lake Titicaca. It lies high in the Andes Mountains. This area is bitterly cold. There are few trees. Native Americans here make their living from totora reeds, a kind of thick, hollow grass that grows on the lakeshore. They use these reeds to make houses, mats, hats, ropes, sails, toys, roofs, and floors. They eat the reeds, feed them to livestock, and brew them into tea. Totora reeds can even be made into medicine. Long ago, some Native American groups built floating islands with tortora reeds. They used the islands to hide from the Incas. Today, some Native Americans live on floating islands.

The People of South America

Most South Americans today are descended from Native Americans, Africans, or Europeans. In this way, they are like the people of Mexico and Central America. South America's history is also like that of its neighbors to the north. It was colonized mainly by Spain. Most South Americans speak Spanish and are Catholic. Each nation has its own unique culture, however.

▼ The Native Americans who live on Lake Titicaca in Peru use tortora reeds to make boats.

Regions Within South America There are four cultural regions in South America. The first region includes Colombia, Venezuela, Guyana, Suriname, and French Guiana, which are in the northern part of South America. They each border the Caribbean Sea. The cultures of these countries are like those of the Caribbean islands.

To the south and west, the culture is very different. Peru, Ecuador, and Bolivia are Andean countries. Many Native Americans live high in the Andes. In Bolivia, there are more indigenous people than mestizos. The Quechua and Aymara (eye muh RAH) people each speak their own languages.

The third cultural region consists of Chile, Argentina, and Uruguay. The long, thin country of Chile has mountains, beaches, deserts, forests, and polar regions. Although its geography is diverse, its people are not. Most people in Chile are mestizos. The big cities of Argentina and Uruguay, however, are very diverse. Many different ethnic groups live there. Another culture exists on Argentina's Pampas, or plains. On the Pampas, gauchos (GOW chohz), or cowhands, herd cattle.

Brazil is South America's largest country. Brazil was a colony of Portugal. Its people speak Portuguese. However, Brazil is culturally diverse. Many Native Americans live in Brazil. So do people of African and European descent. Some Brazilians are of mixed descent. Many people have moved to Brazil from other countries. Brazil's largest city, São Paulo (sow PAW loh), is home to more Japanese than any other place in the world except Japan!

Connect How are the Pampas of Argentina like the plains of the United States?

Herding Llamas in Peru

Some of the indigenous people of the Andes raise llamas, a relative of the camel. Interaction How do you think the people of the Andes use llamas?

Yhaninc Puelles Enriquez age 12
Cuzco, Peru

The scene shown by this student artist is similar to the photograph on the previous page. **Critical Thinking** How are the scenes in the art and the photograph alike and different?

Art and Literature in South America South America has produced many famous artists, novelists, filmmakers, and poets. Chilean poets Pablo Neruda (PAH bloh nay ROO duh) and Gabriela Mistral (gah bree AY lah mees TRAHL) both were awarded the Nobel Prize for their work. Neruda wrote about everyday objects, including rain, tomatoes, and socks. Mistral wrote for and about children. Colombian Gabriel García Márquez (gah bree EL gar SEE uh MAR kays) and Chilean Isabel Allende (EES uh bel ah YEN day) both are famous for writing novels telling about several generations of life in one family. García Márquez was awarded the Nobel Prize.

Country and City Life

South America contains cities with millions of people, but it also has vast areas with hardly any people at all. Many people still live in the countryside. Others are leaving farms and moving to cities.

Farming in South America Outside of Chile, Argentina, and Uruguay, most rural people with land of their own do **subsistence farming.** That means they grow only enough food for their families to eat. They only have small plots of land. Farmers plant corn, beans, potatoes, and rice.

LINKS TO LANGUAGE ARTS

Gabriela Mistral Chilean poet Gabriela Mistral was awarded the Nobel Prize for Literature in 1945. But Mistral considered herself to be more a teacher than a writer. Mistral taught school in rural Chile in the early 1900s, but she was frustrated by the low quality of the textbooks that were available. In response, Mistral began to write poetry and prose for children.

Very large farms grow crops to export to other countries. The main export crops of South America are coffee, sugar, cocoa, and bananas. Export farming uses so much land for cash crops that South America has to import food to eat. To **import** means to buy from another country.

EXPLORING TECHNOLOGY

Brasília

Brasília is a planned city. Some people think it looks like a bow and arrow. Others think it looks like a jet plane. Government offices and shopping areas are located in the middle of the city, where the two "wings" meet. The wings contain superblocks, or residential neighborhoods. Each includes 10 to 16 apartment buildings, a school, and shops. What would you like about living in a completely new city? What would you dislike?

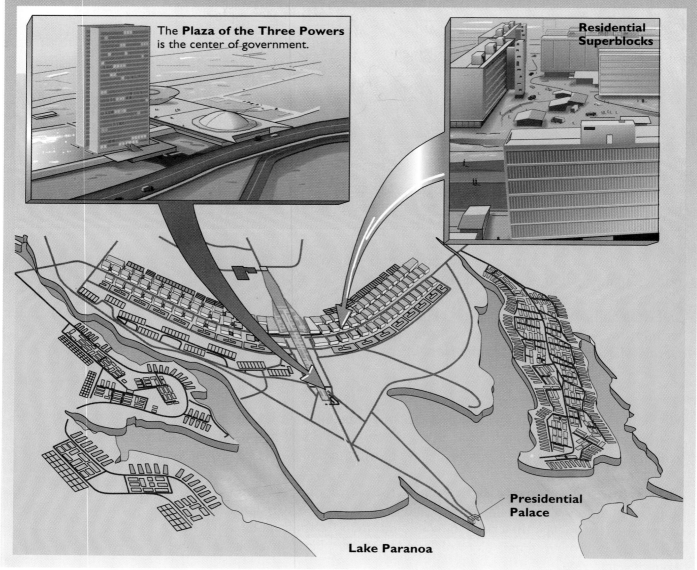

The **Plaza of the Three Powers** is the center of government.

Residential Superblocks

Presidential Palace

Lake Paranoa

The population of South America is booming. Latin America is the fastest-growing region in the world. Like Mexicans and Central Americans, South Americans cannot find enough jobs in rural areas. Every day, thousands of rural South Americans move to the cities looking for work.

South America's Cities   The cities of South America illustrate the region's mix of cultures. Many major cities—Lima, Peru, and Buenos Aires, Argentina, for example—were built by Spanish colonists more than 400 years ago. Some of the buildings in these older cities follow Native American designs. In contrast, modern office blocks and apartment buildings of concrete, steel, and glass tower above the downtown areas. One or two cities were built quite recently. Brasília, the Brazilian capital, was constructed in the 1950s. It was a completely planned city, designed to draw people to the country's interior.

By contrast, one of the unplanned things about many South American cities is the slums. They are called *favelas* (fuh VEH luz) in Brazil and *barrios* (BAR ee ohs) in Venezuela. More and more people have migrated into the cities in recent years. Usually they have ended up in poor neighborhoods. City governments try to provide electricity and running water to everyone. But people move into cities so quickly that it is hard for city governments to keep up.

The Role of Women   In some ways, women do not yet play a role equal to that of men in South America. Women in South America are more likely than men to be poor. They also do not attend school for as many years as men do.

More and more women in South America today are fighting to make a living for themselves and their children. They are demanding equal rights. Women are struggling for the rights to go to school, to get into different types of jobs, to have good health care, and to have a voice in government. Some women are getting bank loans to start small businesses. These businesses are sometimes based on traditional skills such as sewing, weaving, or preparing food.

Working Together From 1976 to 1983, Argentina had a military government. The government took thousands of people prisoner. Many were never seen again. The mothers and grandmothers of the "disappeared" marched in protest every day for six years in Buenos Aires. Their actions forced the government to explain what happened to the missing people.

SECTION 3 REVIEW

1. **Define**   (a) subsistence farming, (b) import.
2. **Identify**   (a) Andes, (b) Chile, (c) Argentina, (d) Brazil.
3. What pressures does rapid population growth place on the countries of South America?
4. Name two ways in which the geography of South America has shaped how people live.

Critical Thinking
5. **Recognizing Cause and Effect**   What is one cause of rapid population growth in the cities? What is one effect?

Activity
6. **Writing to Learn**   Choose one region of South America you'd like to visit, and write a paragraph explaining why.

SKILLS ACTIVITY

Distinguishing Facts From Opinions

Kate was nervous, but excited. This was her first trip out of the United States. For two weeks, she had seen more fantastic things in Mexico than she could have dreamed of: beautiful countryside, ancient ruins . . . the list was endless. Now, she was about to start a new adventure.

Today, she would travel from Mexico City to Paplanta, a small town near the coast to the east. A fellow traveler had discouraged her. "The train trip is very long," she had said.

The train trip is very long and boring!

The train ride to Paplanta is three hours long.

"And boring. There's nothing to look at out the windows. The town is not interesting, either. You should skip that trip altogether."

"Hmmm," Kate thought as she pulled out her guidebook and train schedule. The guidebook said that the ruins of an old Spanish mission were located at Paplanta. The El Tajin ruins were also there. On Sundays, the town hosted an open-air market. The train schedule said it was only a three-hour train ride away, through mountainous country. "A long trip? Nothing to look at? Ha!" More determined than ever, Kate headed to the train station.

Get Ready

Kate decided to go to Paplanta because she relied on facts instead of opinions. Facts are statements that can be proved true. Opinions are beliefs. That the train ride was three hours long is a fact. The traveler's statement that the train ride "is very long" is an opinion. Distinguishing facts from opinions, as Kate found out, is a valuable skill.

Distinguishing facts from opinions is something you will need to do almost every day of your life. You will do it as you watch television, read books and magazines, and—like Kate—as you reach your own decisions.

How can you distinguish, or tell the difference between, facts and opinions? It's as simple as A-B-C:

A. Facts can be proved true.

B. Opinions cannot be proved true.

C. Opinions are often indicated by words and phrases like "I think," "I believe," "should," and "ought to," and by adjectives like "beautiful" or "ugly."

Ladinos make up about 50 percent of the population of Guatemala.

Guatemala is the most beautiful country in Latin America.

F

O

Try It Out

Learn to distinguish facts from opinions by playing a simple game. All you need are some note cards, a couple of pens, and a partner.

A. Deal the cards. Deal ten note cards to your partner and ten to yourself. Each of you should then write one fact or one opinion about Latin America on each of your note cards. You can get the facts from your textbook. The opinions should be your own beliefs. On the back of each note card, write an F if you wrote a fact and an O if you wrote an opinion. Don't let your partner see these!

B. Shuffle the cards. Shuffle your cards, and give them to your partner. Challenge him or her to identify each sentence as a fact or an opinion. Award one point for each correct answer. Give a bonus point if your partner can explain how the statement could be proved true if it is a fact or how your partner knew it was an opinion. Total your partner's score, and write it down.

C. Switch cards. Now try your hand at your partner's note cards. Compare scores. Which of you won? The winner should help the loser learn more about distinguishing fact from opinion.

Apply the Skill

Now distinguish facts from opinions in a real case.

1 Read for understanding. Read the paragraph in the box below once or twice, until you are sure you understand its meaning.

2 Read for facts and opinions. Now reread *one sentence at a time.* For each sentence, apply the A-B-C method of distinguishing facts from opinions. Ask yourself: A) Is this a fact that *can* be proved true? B) Is this an opinion that *cannot* be proved true? C) Are there words in the sentence that identify it as an opinion? Which sentences are facts and which are opinions? How could you prove the facts true? How do you know the other sentences express opinions?

> Urbanization takes place when people move from rural areas to urban areas. I believe that urbanization in Mexico is a bad thing. First, the cities are already too crowded. There are thousands of homeless people in urban areas. Lots of people can't find jobs. Second, the city streets were not designed for so many cars. Traffic jams are a huge headache. Finally, the water and electric systems do not have the capacity to serve more people. I think the time has come for the government to try to stop urbanization.

CHAPTER

13

Review and Activities

Reviewing Main Ideas

1. **(a)** What are maquiladoras?
   (b) Why are they important to the economy of Mexico?
2. To which country are some Mexicans and Central Americans emigrating to find jobs?
3. **(a)** Who were the first people on the Caribbean islands?
   (b) What happened to those people?
4. What are some of the musical styles that began in the Caribbean?
5. How do some of the people of the Andes make a living?
6. **(a)** How is the country of Chile geographically diverse?
   (b) How is Brazil culturally diverse?

Reviewing Key Terms

Decide whether each statement is true or false. If it is true, write "true." If it is false, change the underlined term to make the statement true.

1. Border factories are called <u>mestizos.</u>
2. <u>Indigenous</u> people are descendants of a region's first inhabitants.
3. To <u>emigrate</u> is to move from one's home country to another country.
4. Many Mexicans become <u>pampas</u> in the United States because they cannot find jobs in their home countries.
5. Ethnic <u>diversity</u> refers to people with a variety of cultures, customs, religions, or languages.
6. <u>Imports</u> occur when a government does not respect people's human rights.
7. To <u>immigrate</u> means to buy from another country.

Critical Thinking

1. **Making Comparisons** Consider these three regions: Mexico and Central America; the Caribbean; South America. What do the cultures of these regions have in common? How are they different?
2. **Recognizing Cause and Effect** What is the main reason that many Latin Americans move from one region or one country to another?

Graphic Organizer

Copy the chart to the right onto a separate sheet of paper. Then fill in the empty boxes to complete the chart.

	Mexico and Central America	The Caribbean	South America
Languages			
Religions			
Ethnic Background			
Special Features			

Map Activity

For each place listed below, write the letter from the map that shows its location.

1. Andes
2. Argentina
3. Brazil
4. Honduras
5. Jamaica
6. Mexico City
7. Trinidad and Tobago

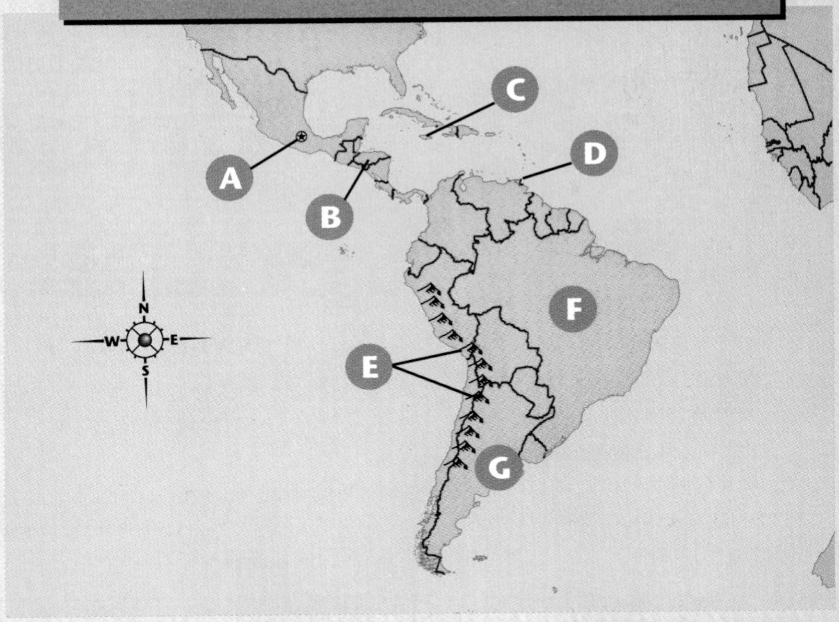

Writing Activity

Writing a Magazine Article
In this chapter, you've taken a guided tour of the cultures of Latin America. Write an article for a travel magazine describing the "high points" of your tour. As you write, consider how historical events and geography influenced the region's culture.

Internet Activity

Use a search engine to find the site **amigo! Mexican Art & Culture.** Explore several links to learn about various aspects of Mexican culture. Make a travel brochure highlighting some of your favorite findings, create a portfolio of Mexican culture, or give a class presentation on the aspect that interested you the most.

Skills Review

Turn to the Skill Activity. Review the steps for distinguishing facts from opinions. Then, write a brief paragraph about the cultures of Latin America that includes both facts and opinions.

How Am I Doing?

Answer these questions to help you check your progress.

1. Can I explain how the cultures in a region reflect its history?

2. Can I explain how most people make a living in the countryside?

3. Can I identify the reasons why many people in Latin America are moving from rural to urban areas?

4. What information from this chapter can I use in my book project?

CHAPTER 14

Exploring Mexico and Central America

SECTION I
Mexico
ONE FAMILY'S MOVE
TO THE CITY

SECTION 2
Guatemala
DESCENDANTS OF AN
ANCIENT PEOPLE

SECTION 3
Panama
WHERE TWO
OCEANS MEET

MAP ACTIVITIES

Look at the map above. Notice that the shape of Mexico and Central America is like a funnel, wide at the top and narrowing to a point. To learn more about this region, complete the following activities.

Study the map
How many countries are there in Central America? What bodies of water do they border?

Consider the geography
Mexico is a large country, while the countries of Central America are small. How do you think geography helped divide Central America into small countries?

Mexico

ONE FAMILY'S MOVE TO THE CITY

Reach Into Your Background

Have you ever moved from one house to another or from one city to another? Did you have to change schools? Think about what the move was like and make a few notes about how you felt at the time.

Questions to Explore

1. Why have many Mexicans been moving from the countryside to the city?

2. What challenges do Mexicans from the country face when they build new lives in the city?

Key Terms

squatter
plaza
migrant farmworker

Key Places

Mexico City

Ramiro Avila (rah MEE roh ah VEE lah) is one of seven children. He grew up in the state of Guanajuato (gwah nuh HWAH toh), in central Mexico. In his small village, Ramiro knew everyone and everyone knew him.

Ramiro's family were campesinos who owned no land. Even as a young child, Ramiro had to work to help support the family. He and his father had jobs as farm laborers. They worked on someone else's farm. They made less than a dollar a day.

The Move to Mexico City

Ramiro's village is located in the southern part of the Mexican Plateau. This area has Mexico's best farmland. It also is home to more than half of the country's people. Not surprisingly, it is the location of Mexico's largest city—Mexico City. Find Mexico City on the map on the previous page.

When Ramiro was 13, his parents decided to move the family to Mexico City. They hoped to find better work. The city was far away and their lives would be completely different. But moving offered them a chance to make a decent living.

Mexico's Population

Chart Study What pattern of population movement does this chart show?

	Total Population	Urban (%)	Rural (%)
1995	93,986,000	71.	29.
2000	102,912,000	77.7	22.3
2010	120,115,000	81.6	18.4

*Projected population

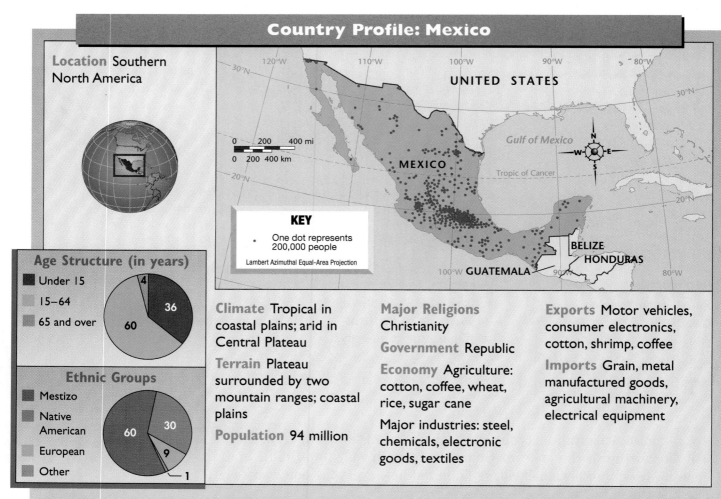

Location Southern North America

Age Structure (in years)
- Under 15
- 15–64
- 65 and over

4
36
60

Ethnic Groups
- Mestizo
- Native American
- European
- Other

60
30
9
1

KEY
One dot represents 200,000 people

Lambert Azimuthal Equal-Area Projection

Climate Tropical in coastal plains; arid in Central Plateau

Terrain Plateau surrounded by two mountain ranges; coastal plains

Population 94 million

Major Religions Christianity

Government Republic

Economy Agriculture: cotton, coffee, wheat, rice, sugar cane

Major industries: steel, chemicals, electronic goods, textiles

Exports Motor vehicles, consumer electronics, cotton, shrimp, coffee

Imports Grain, metal manufactured goods, agricultural machinery, electrical equipment

Map Study The map above shows Mexico's population distribution. Some parts of Mexico are sparsely populated, while others are very crowded.

Location Where do most of Mexico's people live? Why do you think that they live in that area and not elsewhere?

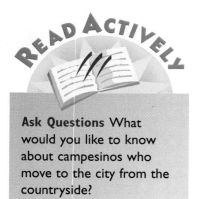

READ ACTIVELY

Ask Questions What would you like to know about campesinos who move to the city from the countryside?

Housing in the City Like thousands of other campesino families coming to the city, Ramiro's family did not have much money. When they arrived in Mexico City, they could not afford a house. They went to live in Colonia Zapata, which is one of many neighborhoods where poor people become **squatters.** That means they settle on someone else's land without permission. Many small houses of squatters cling to the sides of a steep hill in the Colonia. The older houses near the bottom of the hill are built of concrete. However, most people cannot afford to make sturdy houses when they first arrive. Therefore, many of the newer houses higher up the hill are constructed of scrap metal.

Ramiro's family made a rough, one-room house of rock. Ramiro felt that his new house was ugly. He and his family hoped that soon they would be able to buy land from the government. Then they could build a real house with a garden and a patio.

Work and School   Ramiro went to school in Mexico City, but he also worked as a cook in a tiny restaurant. He started work at 7 A.M. and worked until 2 P.M., preparing scrambled eggs and sausage. For these seven hours of work he earned about $3. His mother and some of his brothers and sisters worked, too. Ramiro went to a school that held night classes, attending classes until 9:30 at night.

Ramiro's father could not get a job in Mexico City. He decided to go to Texas in the United States. He found work as a farm laborer there. He sent money home every month. The move to Mexico City brought a lot of responsibilities for Ramiro. It became his job to look after his younger brothers and sisters while his father was gone. Ramiro's life was very different from how it had been in his village.

Life in Rural Mexico

Before Ramiro's family moved, they lived in a village where life has changed little over the years. Every village has a church and a market. At the center of most villages is a public square called a **plaza.** Farm families grow their own food. If they have extra food, they sell it at the market. Rural people buy nearly everything they need—clothing, food, toys, housewares—at the market rather than in stores.

Markets of Rural Mexico

This photograph shows a market in Oaxaca, Mexico. People in rural Mexico buy many of their groceries and housewares from markets like these. **Critical Thinking** What details in this photograph show similarities between rural markets and urban supermarkets? What details show differences?

Farm Work Most farm families in Mexico and Central America are poor. Many campesinos work their own small farms. They often plow the land and harvest their crops by hand because they cannot afford expensive equipment. **Migrant farmworkers** do not own land. Like Ramiro and his father, they work on large farms owned by rich landowners. Migrants travel from one area to another, picking the crops that are in season.

Lack of Jobs Mexico's population has risen dramatically over the last 20 years. The country's population is growing at a rate of more than two percent each year—one of the highest rates in the world. There is not enough farm work for so many people. A large family cannot support itself on a small farm. And there are not enough jobs for all the migrant workers. Many people move to the cities because they cannot find work in the countryside.

About 70 percent of Mexico's people now live in cities and large towns. Many of them live in Mexico City. If you count the people in all the outlying areas, Mexico City has over 23 million people. Only Tokyo, Japan, has more people than Mexico City.

Mexico City: A Megacity

Mexico City is huge. Its population sprawls over a large area. It is a megacity, an urban center where many of Mexico's people live. Unlike most big cities, Mexico City does not have many skyscrapers and major streets. Two- and three-story buildings still form its downtown. Only a

Predict What problems might occur as more people move into a city?

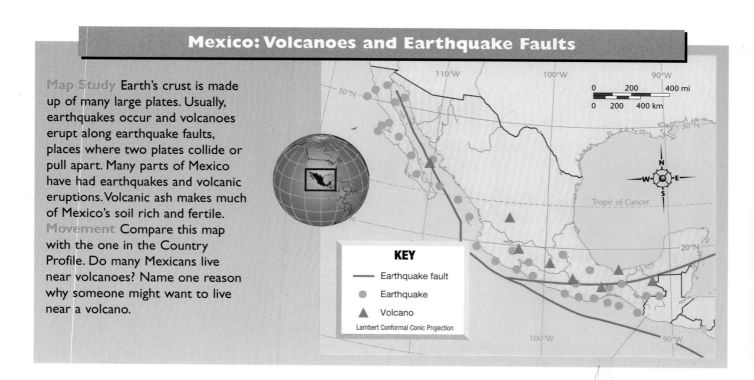

Mexico: Volcanoes and Earthquake Faults

Map Study Earth's crust is made up of many large plates. Usually, earthquakes occur and volcanoes erupt along earthquake faults, places where two plates collide or pull apart. Many parts of Mexico have had earthquakes and volcanic eruptions. Volcanic ash makes much of Mexico's soil rich and fertile. Movement Compare this map with the one in the Country Profile. Do many Mexicans live near volcanoes? Name one reason why someone might want to live near a volcano.

KEY
— Earthquake fault
● Earthquake
▲ Volcano
Lambert Conformal Conic Projection

Lake Zumpango

Lake Texcoco (dry)

KEY

City limits, 1945

City limits, 1995

Lambert Azimuthal Equal-Area Projection

0   5   10 mi

0   5   10 km

Map Study Mexico City covers more than twice the land that it did in 1945. **Interaction** How do you think the challenges of living in a city might be different from the challenges of living in a rural area?

few streets are wide enough for the city's traffic. The subway, the underground railroad system, carries thousands of people each day.

Small neighborhoods of very wealthy people are tucked away from the rest. But most of Mexico City's residents are not wealthy. They live in all areas of the city. The poorest, like Ramiro and his family, live on the outskirts. Some must travel several hours a day to get to their jobs and back.

Pollution and Geography   Because the cities have grown so large, Mexico's capital and other large cities in the region are facing problems of pollution and traffic jams. Four million cars and trucks jam Mexico City's narrow streets. They compete with taxis, trolleys, and buses. Mexico City's location traps pollution close to the city. The city spreads across a bowl-shaped valley. The mountains surrounding the valley stop winds from carrying away factory smoke, automobile exhaust fumes, and other pollution. The pollution creates smog. It hangs over the city like a black cloud.

Making a Living   Large cities offer many ways to make a living. Factories and offices employ millions of people. Thousands more sell goods from stalls in the street. Ramiro's sister, Carmela, is a street vendor. She sells juice at a stand in the bus station near their neighborhood.

LINKS

ACROSS TIME

Tenochtitlán—A Clean City Tenochtitlán, the Aztec capital, did not have a pollution problem. In fact, the first Europeans to visit Tenochtitlán were amazed at how clean the city was. At least 1,000 workers cleaned and swept the city's streets. Clean water was piped in from springs. At the time, European cities did not have fresh, clean water.

Even on a sunny day, buildings a few blocks away appear dim and blurry in Mexico City because of smog. **Interaction** Why do you think Mexico City has so much smog? How do you think the smog affects the way people in Mexico City live?

Every morning, she gets up at 5:30 to make juice from oranges and carrots. People on their way to work buy her juice for their long trip into the city.

Mexico City is not the only city that is growing. All of Mexico's major cities are becoming more crowded. City life is not easy for most Mexicans. Hard work and hope are what keep people going.

SECTION 1 REVIEW

1. **Define** (a) squatter, (b) plaza, (c) migrant farmworker.

2. **Identify** Mexico City.

3. What is the main reason that rural people from all over Mexico have been moving to the cities?

4. What difficulties do rural people face when they move to Mexico City?

Critical Thinking

5. **Expressing Problems Clearly** How do the lives of rural Mexicans improve when they move to the city? How do their lives continue to be difficult?

Activity

6. **Writing to Learn** Write an entry in your journal comparing and contrasting Ramiro's life with your own. How are your lives different? What similarities do you notice?

Guatemala

DESCENDANTS OF AN ANCIENT PEOPLE

BEFORE YOU READ

Reach Into Your Background

Each year the Nobel Peace Prize is awarded to someone who has worked for peace in the world. What qualities do you think a person should have in order to receive such a prize?

Questions to Explore

1. How are the indigenous people of Guatemala a unique culture?
2. What are the main issues that indigenous people face?
3. How did Rigoberta Menchú become a leader of her people?

Key Terms

ladino
ethnic group
strike

Key People and Places

Rigoberta Menchú
Guatemala

"Where I live is practically a paradise, the country is so beautiful. There are no big roads and no cars. Only people can reach it." These are the words of a Guatemalan woman named Rigoberta Menchú (ree goh BEHR tah men CHOO). Menchú is a Mayan woman. She was born in 1959. She speaks a language called Quiché (kee CHAY). In 1984, Menchú wrote a book about her life in Guatemala.

The mountains where Menchú was born are beautiful. But Menchú's family was very poor. They farmed their land, but the soil was not good. "Where we live in the mountains," Menchú wrote, "you can barely grow maize and beans. The land isn't fertile enough for anything else."

▼ Most Mayas who live in the highlands of Guatemala have only small plots of land to farm.

The Struggle for Land

Menchú's mountain home is in the country of Guatemala. This southern neighbor of Mexico is "first" in Central America in many categories. For example, it has the largest population among Central American countries. To learn more about Guatemala, study the Country Profile on the next page.

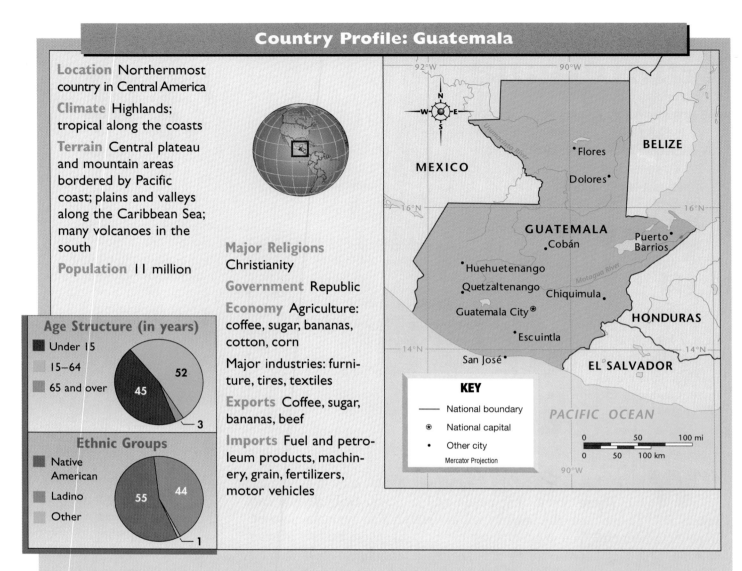

Country Profile: Guatemala

Location Northernmost country in Central America

Climate Highlands; tropical along the coasts

Terrain Central plateau and mountain areas bordered by Pacific coast; plains and valleys along the Caribbean Sea; many volcanoes in the south

Population 11 million

Major Religions Christianity

Government Republic

Economy Agriculture: coffee, sugar, bananas, cotton, corn

Major industries: furniture, tires, textiles

Exports Coffee, sugar, bananas, beef

Imports Fuel and petroleum products, machinery, grain, fertilizers, motor vehicles

Age Structure (in years)
- Under 15
- 15–64
- 65 and over

52
45
3

Ethnic Groups
- Native American
- Ladino
- Other

55
44
1

Map Study This map shows the country of Guatemala. **Location** What four countries border Guatemala? **Chart Study** The chart on the bottom left shows the percentages of ethnic groups in Guatemala. Most Mayas live in rural communities, speak a Mayan language, and follow Mayan customs. Ladinos speak Spanish, have adopted Spanish customs, and often live in towns or cities. **Critical Thinking** Which ethnic group do you think has been more involved in Guatemala's government? Why?

Menchú's parents lived in the mountains because it was the only land available to Native Americans. Most land in Guatemala belongs to a few rich families. The rich landowners of Guatemala are **ladinos** (luh DEE nohs), mestizos who are descended from Native Americans and Spaniards. Native Americans who follow European ways are also considered to be ladinos.

Menchú's parents worked hard to make their land produce crops. "You had to pay a fee so that you could clear the land," she wrote. "Of course, it's not very easy to make things grow on land that's just been cleared. You don't get a good yield for at least eight or nine years."

Losing a Home During most of Menchú's childhood, there was a civil war going on in Guatemala. The Mayas were caught in the middle. Indigenous people do not always think of themselves as citizens of the country in which they live. A Mayan woman is more likely to think of herself as a Maya than as a Guatemalan.

Also, most Native Americans in Guatemala cannot read or write. Most Mayas have not filed any papers with the government showing that they own land. The Mayas often have no way to prove that their land belongs to them. The people of Menchú's village worked hard for many years, and soon the land began to produce crops. But then the civil war and landowners caught up with Menchú's village.

Menchú wrote that when she was twelve years old, the landowners came with soldiers. They disagreed with the village's claim to the land. Now that it was cleared and producing crops, they wanted it. They forced Menchú's family and their neighbors to leave.

"First they went into our houses without permission and got all the people out," Menchú remembered. Then, the soldiers were ordered to throw away each family's belongings. The soldiers took all the corn the people had stored. The villagers had nowhere to go but out into the rain.

ACROSS THE WORLD

The Sami The Sami, or Lapps, live in the far north of Norway, Sweden, Finland, and Russia. The governments of these countries consider the Sami their citizens. Most Sami, however, look upon themselves as part of a separate nation. In recent years, the Sami have won some degree of self-government. The Sami of Norway, for example, have their own elected assembly.

A Guatemalan Market

Mayas in rural Guatemala do much of their shopping at open-air markets like this one. Movement What types of goods are being traded or sold at this market?

Mayan communities each have their own hand-woven style of clothing. **Critical Thinking** What skills do you think are needed to weave cloth into a certain pattern?

CITIZEN HEROES

Overcoming Obstacles
Justina Tzoc travels through rural Guatemala, teaching Quiché Maya women about their rights and teaching them to read. Her work is dangerous, because she sometimes travels through areas that are torn by civil war. But Tzoc is determined to help every woman she can reach.

A 500-Year-Old Struggle   Menchú's story is a common one. The indigenous people of Guatemala have fought against injustice for 500 years. They started when the Spanish first arrived.

The Spanish conquered Native Americans by force. Many were killed. Others died of hunger or the hardships of slavery. Still others died from European diseases. In many Latin American countries, there are few indigenous people left.

But in Guatemala, Native Americans are the majority of the population. They form 23 ethnic groups. An **ethnic group** is a group of people who share language, religion, and cultural traditions. The indigenous groups of Guatemala are related to each other. However, each group is different. Each has its own language and customs. Rigoberta Menchú comes from the largest group, the Quiché Maya.

Rigoberta Menchú Takes a Stand

Rigoberta Menchú began working with campesinos all over the country. She learned several other indigenous languages. She also learned Spanish. She wanted to be able to work with ladinos who supported Native American land rights. Menchú became part of a nationwide political movement, which is a large group of people who work together to defend their rights or to change the leaders in power. This political movement was to defend campesino rights. Menchú helped villages plan ways to protect themselves. She taught people how to read. She also taught people about the history of their land. Menchú helped the movement organize meetings, protests, and **strikes,** or work stoppages. She was determined to defend Native American land rights.

Menchú's mother, father, and brother were killed fighting against the landowners. But Menchú continued to fight for the rights of her people. Her life, too, was in danger. For her own safety, Menchú had to leave the country. She went to live in Mexico.

Rigoberta Menchú

Rigoberta Menchú never went to school. Instead, she worked on farms and as a maid. Later, she taught herself to speak and read several languages. She knew that command of these languages would help her get her message to all Guatemalans.

Peace in Guatemala In 1992, Rigoberta Menchú was awarded the Nobel Peace Prize. She was the first indigenous person in the world ever to win the prize. Since 1992, Menchú has continued to work for justice in Guatemala. Her efforts have brought important changes. Recently, Guatemala's government appointed 21 Mayan priests to advise officials about Mayan culture. New Mayan organizations are being formed every day. In addition, Mayan languages are being used in books, newspapers, and radio programs. Government officials and Mayan leaders hope these changes will bring peace to Guatemala.

READ ACTIVELY

Ask Questions What questions would you like to ask Rigoberta Menchú about her activities?

SECTION 2 REVIEW

1. **Define** (a) ladino, (b) ethnic group, (c) strike.
2. **Identify** (a) Rigoberta Menchú, (b) Guatemala.
3. How does Rigoberta Menchú describe the land where she was born?

4. How do most indigenous people in Guatemala make a living? What difficulties do they face?

Critical Thinking

5. **Identifying Cause and Effect** Explain the main reason that Guatemala's indigenous people and other farmers have formed a political movement.

Activity

6. **Writing to Learn** Write a short essay explaining what you would have done if you were in Rigoberta Menchú's position. Then, explain what you would do if you were the president of Guatemala.

Previewing a Reading Selection

Sean asked his mom if he could go for a bike ride before it got dark. His mom said, "Sure, if you finish your homework first." Sean didn't have much homework. "If I can finish it in an hour," Sean thought to himself, "I'll have a whole hour for a killer mountain bike adventure."

He settled down to study. His assignment was to answer ten questions about the Panama Canal using two books he had checked out from the school library. He read the first question: "What are three obstacles workers faced when building the Panama Canal?" He picked up the first book and began reading on page 1. Five pages and 10 minutes later he didn't have his answer. He tried the other book. Ten pages and 20 minutes later he still hadn't found what he was looking for. "Half an hour gone and not one question answered!" he thought, disgustedly. "No bike ride tonight!"

Sean missed out on his bike ride because he forgot to apply an important skill: previewing. Previewing means looking over a book or chapter before you read it or try to find information in it. Previewing is a valuable study skill that will help you read more efficiently.

Get Ready

How do you preview? You might be surprised to learn that this is one skill you already know! If you've ever seen a preview for a movie, you've "previewed" that movie. You have a gen-

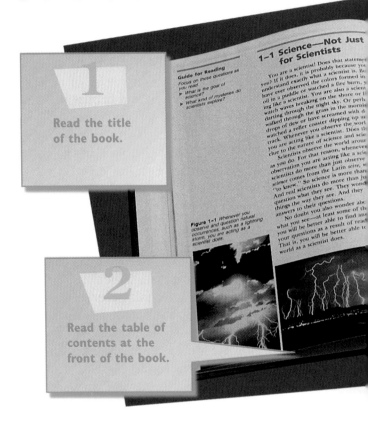

1. Read the title of the book.

2. Read the table of contents at the front of the book.

eral idea what the movie is about. If you've ever looked over a menu, you've "previewed" your meal. You have a general idea of what the food will be like.

Of course, previewing a reading selection is a little different from previewing a movie or meal. Previewing means looking over something you are about to read in a general way to become familiar with it. The idea is to get a "sense" of the material. To get a sense of what a book is about, you can use five things: the title, the table of contents, the illustrations, the index, and sample paragraphs. To do this with a chapter, you can use titles, subtitles, illustrations, and captions.

3
Study the illustrations throughout the book. They include pictures, charts, diagrams, and maps.

4
Thumb through the book, reading short passages.

5
Scan the index at the back of the book.

Group Member 1: "The title indicates the main subject of the book. Many books have a subtitle that gives even more information. What does the title of our book tell us?"

Group Member 2: "The table of contents is like a menu at a restaurant. It tells us what general topics are available in the book. What does the table of contents tell us?"

Group Member 3: "The illustrations in a book provide clues to the subjects discussed in the book. What do the illustrations tell us about the book?"

Group Member 4: "The index lists the specific topics in a book and the pages where they are discussed. What does the index tell us about the content of our book?"

Group Member 5: "By thumbing through a book and reading a few paragraphs here and there, you can get an idea of how a book is written. You can see if there are special headings in the book. What does a little reading tell us about our book?"

When you've completed this process, use the secretary's notes to find specific information in the book. If you are going to read the whole book, this process can help you get the most out of your reading.

Apply the Skill

Now that you know how to preview, practice by previewing Chapter 4. What do the titles and subtitles tell you about the chapter? How about the illustrations and captions? Take notes as you preview the chapter. Then, use your notes to write a short description of the chapter. Finally, as you read through the chapter, see how it matches your description.

Try It Out

You can practice previewing a book in a fun and easy way by playing a "What Does It Tell Us?" game with a group of six students. Choose your group members, and choose a book. Then sit down and preview it together. Your group will follow the script to the right. After each person reads his or her part to the group, the other group members should work together to answer the question. Group Member 6 is the group secretary, who writes the answers down.

Panama

WHERE TWO OCEANS MEET

Reach Into Your Background

Have you ever agreed to a deal or given away something and then wondered if you made the best choice? Think about how you felt. Write down some ways you might try to undo the deal.

Questions to Explore

1. What geographic and political factors made Panama a good site for a canal?
2. How was the Panama Canal built?
3. How did Panama gain control of the Panama Canal?

Key Term
lock

Key Places
Panama Canal
Canal Zone

The Panama Canal is the shortcut of the Western Hemisphere. It's the only way to get from the Pacific Ocean to the Atlantic by ship without going all the way around South America. That's a savings of 7,800 miles (12,553 km).

But be prepared to wait. Traffic jams can leave you bobbing in the ocean for up to 20 hours. Then the trip through the 40-mile (64.4-km) canal takes another eight hours. That's about walking speed. Then there is the toll: as much as $34,000.

Going Through the Canal

Cruising through the Pacific Ocean, a tanker approaches the city of Balboa, in the country of Panama. It is heading for the Panama Canal. The ship is loaded with petroleum. Other ships sailing toward the canal carry lumber, metal ores, and other cargo. Ships pass through the Panama Canal 24 hours a day, 365 days a year. The canal is crowded. The tanker must get in line.

The tanker enters the canal at sea level. But parts of the canal go through mountains and are not at sea level. The tanker will need to be raised and lowered several times as it travels toward the Atlantic Ocean.

Miraflores Lock The ship sails north to Miraflores (mee ruh FLOR uhs) Lock. A **lock** is a section of waterway in which ships are raised or lowered by adjusting the water level. The tanker passes through a set of gates into a lock chamber. The water in the chamber is still at sea level. Then, more water comes pouring into the chamber

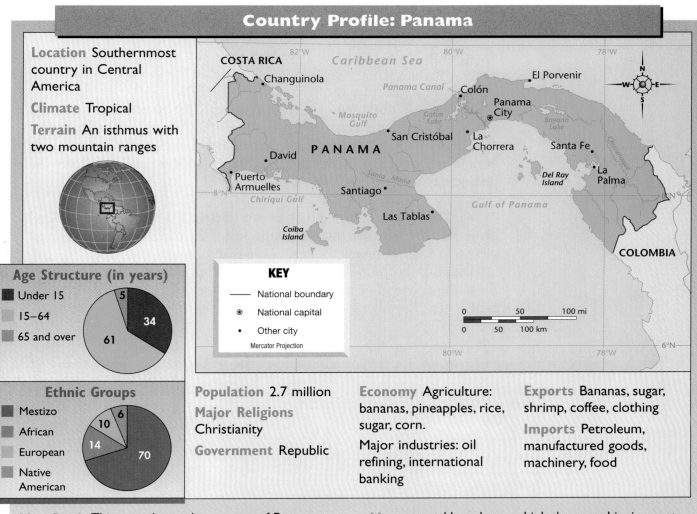

Country Profile: Panama

Location Southernmost country in Central America

Climate Tropical

Terrain An isthmus with two mountain ranges

Age Structure (in years)

- Under 15
- 15–64
- 65 and over

5
34
61

Ethnic Groups

- Mestizo
- African
- European
- Native American

6
10
14
70

Population 2.7 million

Major Religions Christianity

Government Republic

Economy Agriculture: bananas, pineapples, rice, sugar, corn.

Major industries: oil refining, international banking

Exports Bananas, sugar, shrimp, coffee, clothing

Imports Petroleum, manufactured goods, machinery, food

KEY

— National boundary

⊛ National capital

• Other city

Mercator Projection

0   50   100 mi
0   50   100 km

Map Study This map shows the country of Panama and the location of the Panama Canal. Find the Panama Canal on the map.

Movement How do you think the new shipping route created by the canal affected the economy of the city of Colón? Explain your answer.

---

through valves. The tanker rises like a toy boat in a bathtub filling with water. When the water rises high enough, the ship passes through a second set of gates and enters a small lake. It proceeds to the next lock, and the water level is raised again.

Galliard Cut During the voyage, the tanker will pass through two more sets of locks. It will zigzag through the eight-mile (13-km) Galliard (GAL yurd) Cut. The Galliard Cut was blasted through the hard rock of Panama's mountains. The tanker will sail through a huge artificial lake and past an island that is home to a wild game preserve. Finally, eight hours after entering the canal, the tanker exits at Limón (lih MOHN) Bay in the city of Colón (kuh LOHN). It has traveled only 40 miles (64 km), but it is now in the Atlantic Ocean.

The Idea for a Canal Takes Hold

Look at the map on this page and trace the route the canal follows across Panama. This waterway has dominated life in Panama for much of the twentieth century.

Sailors had dreamed of a canal through Central America since the 1500s. A canal could shorten the trip from the Atlantic to the Pacific by thousands of miles. It would cut the cost of shipping goods by thousands of dollars for each ship. But not until the 1900s did engineers have the technology to make such a canal.

A Struggle Over Rights to Build The first real attempt came in 1881. At that time, Panama was part of Colombia. Colombia gave a French company the rights to build a canal.

Digging through Panama posed several problems for the builders. First, they struggled with mud slides as they dug. Second, a mountain range, the Cordillera de San Blas (kord ul YEHR uh day san blas),

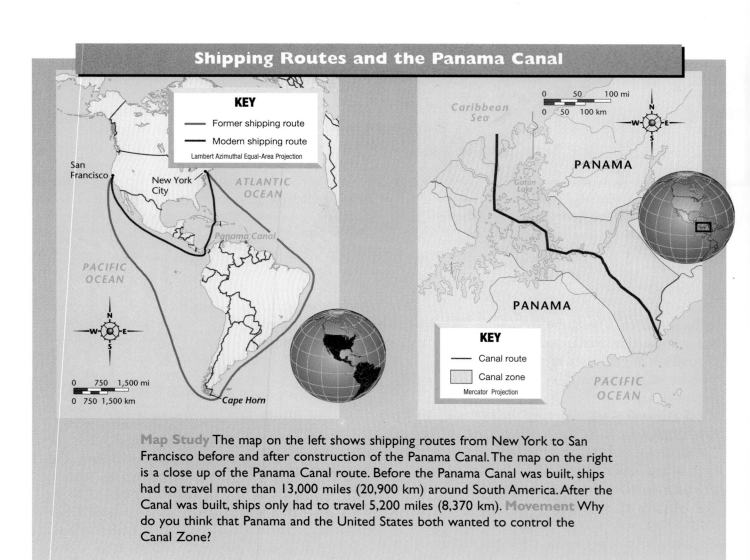

Shipping Routes and the Panama Canal

KEY
—— Former shipping route
—— Modern shipping route
Lambert Azimuthal Equal-Area Projection

San Francisco
New York City
ATLANTIC OCEAN
PACIFIC OCEAN
Panama Canal
Cape Horn

0   750   1,500 mi
0   750   1,500 km

Caribbean Sea
0   50   100 mi
0   50   100 km
PANAMA
Gatún Lake
PANAMA
PACIFIC OCEAN

KEY
—— Canal route
☐ Canal zone
Mercator Projection

Map Study The map on the left shows shipping routes from New York to San Francisco before and after construction of the Panama Canal. The map on the right is a close up of the Panama Canal route. Before the Panama Canal was built, ships had to travel more than 13,000 miles (20,900 km) around South America. After the Canal was built, ships only had to travel 5,200 miles (8,370 km). **Movement** Why do you think that Panama and the United States both wanted to control the Canal Zone?

Panama's Tropical Rain Forest

Panama's Barro Colorado rain forest is inside the Canal Zone. **Critical Thinking** This photograph shows a trail through the rain forest. Where is it? Based on this photograph, think of some difficulties that might have faced the Panama Canal workers.

blocked the way. Disease was also a problem. Much of Panama is covered with dense tropical forest. Tropical diseases such as malaria and yellow fever killed many workers. After several years of digging and blasting, the French company went bankrupt. Work on the canal stopped.

In 1902, the United States government bought what was left of the French company. Then, the United States began talks with Colombia about getting the rights to continue building a canal.

Colombia refused to grant the United States rights to build the canal. The businesspeople of Panama were disappointed. They knew that a canal would bring business to Panama. They wanted the canal to be built as soon as possible. Also, many Panamanians wanted to be free of Colombia's rule. They saw the canal as a chance to win independence.

In November 1903, the United States helped Panama revolt against Colombia. Two weeks after Panama declared its independence, the United States received the rights needed to build the canal.

LINKS ACROSS THE WORLD

Not Made in Panama You would assume the "Panama hat," a hand-woven straw hat, is made in Panama. However, you would be wrong—the hats were originally made in Ecuador. They were named for Panama because it was a shipping center for hats in the 1800s. Ecuadorans still make the Panama hat. But today, many hats are made even farther from Panama—in Asia.

Like Digging Through Sand

The cut through Panama's soft earth hills was the hardest part of the canal to build. Earth still slides into the canal there today. *Movement* Based on the picture on the left, how were workers and supplies moved to and from the canal?

Predict How do you think workers overcame problems to build the Panama Canal?

Building the Canal The builders of the canal faced numerous problems. They had to scoop out and remove mountains of earth and rock. The hills were made of soft earth. Whenever the diggers carved out a hole, more earth would slide into its place. The project called for a dam to be built to form a lake. There were locks to design and build.

While the work was difficult and slow, by far the biggest problem facing the project was disease. Some 25,000 workers had died of malaria and yellow fever while the French worked on the canal. Scientists did not know what caused these diseases, so they could do little to prevent them.

In the early 1900s, doctors discovered that malaria and yellow fever were both carried by mosquitoes. The mosquitoes bred in swamps and also in people's drinking water. In 1904, the Panama Canal Company hired a doctor and a large crew to deal with the mosquito problem. It took one year, 1,000 tons (907 metric tons) of timber, 200 tons (181 metric tons) of wire mesh, and 4,500 workers to do the job. Workers burned sulfur in every house to kill mosquitoes. They covered every water vessel with mesh so mosquitoes could not get in. They filled in swampy breeding grounds with dirt. Without this effort, the Panama Canal probably could not have been built.

Modern medicine and machinery were important to the project. So was good planning. Still, it took eight years and the sweat of 45,000 workers, mostly Caribbean islanders, to make the waterway. The Panama Canal remains one of the greatest engineering feats of modern times.

Control of the Canal

When the United States gained rights to build a canal, it signed a treaty with Panama. The treaty gave the United States the right to build the Panama Canal, and to control it forever.

The Canal Zone The United States also controlled an area called the Canal Zone. The Canal Zone included the land on either side of the canal, the ports, the port cities, and the railroad. The treaty allowed the United States to run the Zone according to its laws, and gave the United States the right to invade Panama to protect the canal.

Many Panamanians felt this was too high a price to pay for the privilege of having the canal in their country. The canal gave the United States a great deal of power in Panama. The United States built 14 military bases in the Canal Zone and stationed thousands of soldiers there.

For years, Panama talked with the United States about regaining control of the canal. In the 1960s and 1970s, many Panamanians grew angry. They rioted to protest U.S. control.

A Change of Ownership In 1978, after years of talks, U.S. President Jimmy Carter signed two new treaties with Panama's government. The Panama Canal Neutrality Treaty and the Panama Canal Treaty gave Panama more control over the canal. In 1999, the Panama Canal will belong to Panama for the first time.

Ask Questions What would you like to know about life near the Canal Zone?

SECTION 3 REVIEW

1. **Define** lock.

2. **Identify** (a) Panama Canal, (b) Canal Zone.

3. How did a canal come to be built in Panama?

4. What difficulties did the builders of the canal face?

5. How did the United States gain control of rights to build the canal?

6. Two sets of treaties have determined the control of the Panama Canal, the original treaty of 1903 and two in 1978. Describe the terms of these treaties.

Critical Thinking

7. **Identifying Central Issues** It has been very important to Panamanians to regain control of the canal. Explain why, in both political and economic terms.

Activity

8. **Writing to Learn** Imagine that you are a newspaper editor in 1900. Decide whether you think Panama or Nicaragua is a better choice for the location of the canal, and write a short editorial defending your position.

CHAPTER 14 Review and Activities

Reviewing Main Ideas

1. Describe the movement of Mexicans from one area to another—rural to rural, rural to urban. Why do many people make these moves?
2. What problems has Mexico City experienced as a result of its rapid population growth?
3. How are the indigenous cultures of Guatemala distinct from the ladino culture?
4. What are the main challenges that indigenous Guatemalans face?
5. How did the United States gain the rights to build a canal in Panama?
6. (a) Why was the canal important to the United States and Panama?
   (b) How is control of the canal currently changing?

Reviewing Key Terms

Match the definitions in Column I with the key terms in Column II.

Column I

1. a landless person who travels from one area to another working other people's land
2. a section of a waterway in which ships are raised or lowered by adjusting the water level
3. a person who settles on someone else's land without permission
4. a work stoppage
5. a public square
6. people who share race, language, religion, and cultural traditions

Column II

a. squatter
b. plaza
c. migrant farmworker
d. ethnic group
e. strike
f. lock

Critical Thinking

1. **Identifying Central Issues** What are the main demands that Rigoberta Menchú and others like her have made of the government and landowners? How has the government responded?
2. **Drawing Conclusions** Over the years, the United States has exercised a great deal of economic and political influence in Central America. How does the Panama Canal demonstrate U.S. influence in the region? What do you think the changes taking place over the control of the canal say about U.S. influence in the region today?

Graphic Organizer

Copy the tree map onto a piece of paper. In the first set of boxes, note the three kinds of population movement. In the second set, note details about these movements.

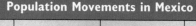
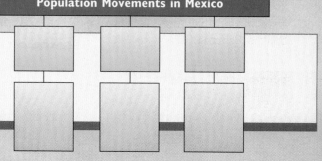

Population Movements in Mexico

Map Activity

For each place listed below, write the letter from the map that shows its location.

1. Guatemala
2. Colón, Panama
3. Panama
4. Mexico City

Mexico and Central America: Place Location

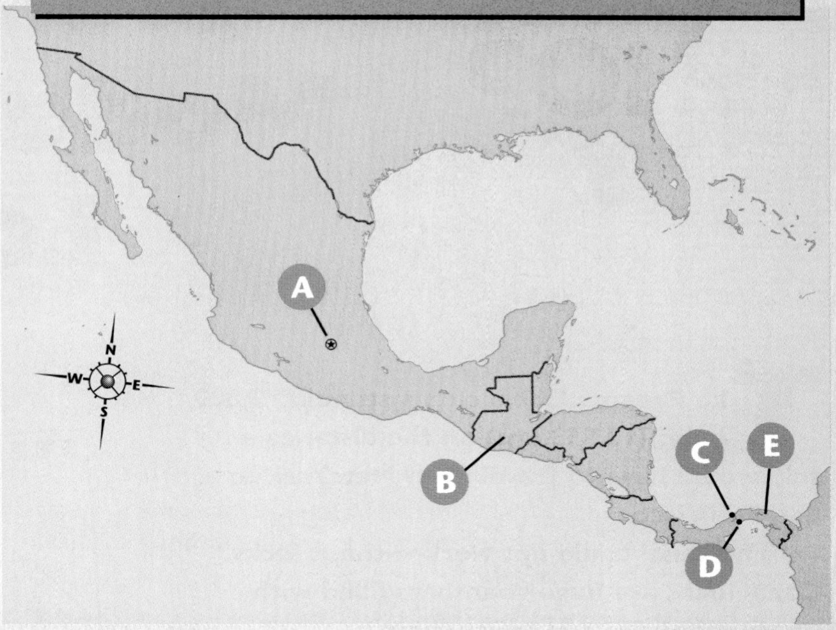

Writing Activity

Writing News Stories
Imagine you are a writer for a radio news program. Write brief news stories on population movements in Mexico, the work of Rigoberta Menchú, and the history of the Panama Canal. Be sure that each of your stories can be read in two to three minutes.

Internet Activity

Use a search engine to find the site **Ancient Guatemala.** Read **Our Mayan Legacy**. Then, click on **Guatemalan Home Page.** Click on the links **Modern Guatemala and Our People.** Make a chart comparing the architecture, language, people, and culture of ancient and modern Guatemala.

Skills Review

Turn to the Skill Activity.

Review the steps for previewing. Then use these steps to preview Chapter 5. Based on your preview, write a brief paragraph describing what you expect to read in the chapter.

How Am I Doing?

Answer these questions to help you check your progress.

1. Can I explain why a Mexican family might decide to leave the countryside for the city?
2. Do I understand the major challenges that face the indigenous peoples of Guatemala?
3. Can I describe the building of the Panama Canal and its impact on the Panamanian people?
4. What information from this chapter can I use in my book project?

Making a Model Canal Lock

The Panama Canal cuts a stunning 7,800 miles (12,553 km) off the distance a ship would have to travel from New York to San Francisco.

The canal could not work without locks. Canal locks are huge chambers filled with water that raise and lower ships.

The Panama Canal needs locks because the sea level at the Atlantic and the Pacific entrances to the canal is not the same. Also, the path of the canal is not level—it goes up one slope to the continental divide and down the other.

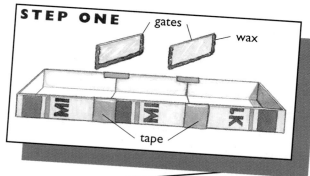

STEP ONE — gates — wax — tape

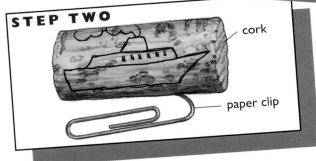

STEP TWO — cork — paper clip

Purpose

The best way to understand how canal locks work is to build a model of one. As you complete this activity, you will understand how a real ship travels through a real canal.

Materials

- two half-gallon cardboard juice or milk cartons
- modelling wax
- scissors
- duct tape
- a ballpoint pen
- a cork
- a paper clip
- a pitcher of water

Procedure

STEP ONE

Construct a model canal and lock.
Follow the illustrations. Cut the cartons in half lengthwise. Line up three of the four halves lengthwise and connect them on the outside with duct tape. Then carefully cut out the walls of cardboard that separate the boxes and divide your canal. Line three edges of each cut-out wall with modelling wax. Then replace the walls. Use

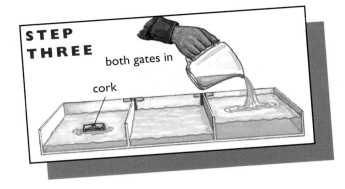

STEP THREE

both gates in

cork

STEP FOUR

first gate is out

cork

both gates in

cork

second gate is out

cork

both gates in

cork

enough wax to make a watertight seal. These are the gates in the canal lock.

STEP TWO

Use the pen, cork, and paper clip to make a model ship. Look at the picture for an example. Stick the paper clip into the bottom of the ship to make it float upright.

STEP THREE

Fill your canal with water. Fill one end and the middle of the carton with water about one inch deep. Fill the other end with water almost to the top. Float your boat in the end of the canal with the lower water level.

STEP FOUR

Operate the canal lock to raise your ship to the higher water level. Remove the gate that separates your ship from the middle chamber. Sail your ship into the middle chamber and close the gate behind it by carefully replacing it. To raise your ship to the next level, slowly pour water into the middle chamber until the water level matches the level in the last chamber. Remove the second gate, sail your ship into the last chamber, and replace the gate. You have successfully navigated a canal!

Observations

1 How did you raise your ship from one level to a higher level?

2 Why does the canal lock need gates to work?

ANALYSIS AND CONCLUSION

1. How do you think the water level is raised in a real lock?

2. Repeat the activity in reverse. How will you lower your ship?

CHAPTER 15

Exploring the Caribbean

SECTION 1
Cuba
CLINGING TO COMMUNISM

SECTION 2
Haiti
THE ROAD TO DEMOCRACY

SECTION 3
Puerto Rico
CULTURAL IDENTITY OF A PEOPLE

MAP ACTIVITIES

The islands of the Caribbean stretch about 1,500 miles (2,414 km) across blue-green waters. Each island has its own traditions and cultures. To learn more about the Caribbean, complete the following activities.

Understanding geography
How do you think the sea may have affected the economies of the Caribbean islands?

Study the map
Before the Europeans arrived in the region, how do you think the sea may have served as both a highway and a barrier to contact with other people?

Cuba

CLINGING TO COMMUNISM

BEFORE YOU READ

Reach Into Your Background

Suppose that you had to move tomorrow and you could pack exactly one suitcase. You could never come back for the things you left behind. What would you pack?

Questions to Explore

1. What is life in Cuba like today?
2. What ties do Cuban Americans have to Cuba?

Key Terms

dictator
communist
exile
illiterate

Key People and Places

Fidel Castro
Fulgencio Batista
Miami

Twelve-year-old Venesa Alonso (vuh NEH suh uh LAHN zoh) lives in Miami, Florida. Her home is just a few miles away from the ocean. Venesa hardly ever goes to the beach, however. The blue waves and roaring surf remind her of her trip from Cuba to the United States. The memory still gives her nightmares.

Venesa and her family left Cuba in the summer of 1994. They built a rickety raft and carried it to the ocean. They were among the 35,000 Cubans who took to the sea that summer. They sailed on anything that would float—rubber tires, old boats, and home-made rafts. One hope kept them going. It was the thought of making it to the United States. They planned to apply to enter the United States as immigrants.

Venesa's family and thousands of others left Cuba for two main reasons. The first reason was that Cuba's economy was in bad shape. People often did not have enough food to eat. Clothing, medicine, and other basic necessities were hard to get. A desire for freedom was the second reason why many people left. Cuba's leader, Fidel Castro (fee DEL KAS troh), does not allow Cubans to speak out against government policies they disagree with.

▼ Cubans trying to reach the United States in 1995 took to the sea in boats like this one.

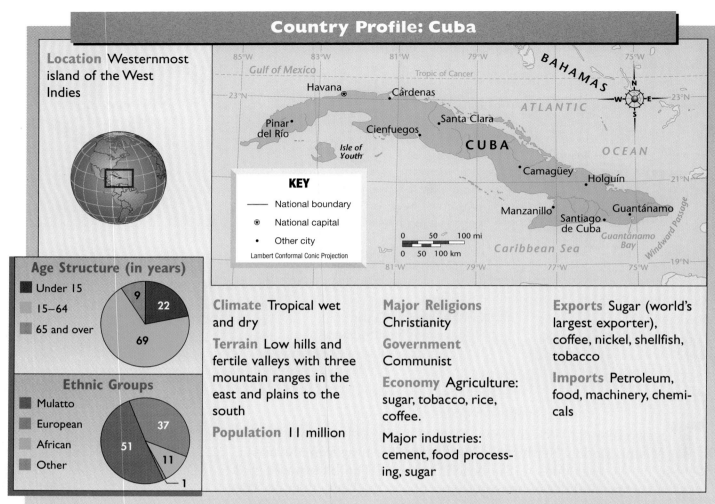

Location Westernmost island of the West Indies

Age Structure (in years)
- Under 15
- 15–64
- 65 and over

9, 22, 69

Ethnic Groups
- Mulatto
- European
- African
- Other

37, 51, 11, 1

Climate Tropical wet and dry

Terrain Low hills and fertile valleys with three mountain ranges in the east and plains to the south

Population 11 million

Major Religions Christianity

Government Communist

Economy Agriculture: sugar, tobacco, rice, coffee.

Major industries: cement, food processing, sugar

Exports Sugar (world's largest exporter), coffee, nickel, shellfish, tobacco

Imports Petroleum, food, machinery, chemicals

Map Study Hundreds of thousands of Cubans have left Cuba in recent years. Many Cubans traveled on small boats and on rafts made of plywood and inner tubes. They were trying to cross 90 miles (145 km) of ocean to reach Florida. **Location** What is the capital of Cuba? Where are Cuba's capital and most of its major cities located?

Cuba's History

Cuba is a small country. It is about the size of the state of Pennsylvania. Cuba's farmland is fertile, and Cuba is the third largest sugar producer in the world. Look at the political map in the Activity Atlas in the front of your book. Cuba is located between the two entrances to the Gulf of Mexico. It also has excellent harbors. This makes it a good place to trade with the United States and other parts of the Caribbean. But Cuba's relationship with the United States and many of its neighbors has not been friendly since the 1960s.

Cuban Independence Cuba's government and economy were not always like they are now. Cuba was a Spanish colony. In 1898, the United States defeated Spain in the Spanish-American War, and Cuba won its independence. In the years that followed, Cuba became the richest country in the Caribbean. Sugar planters made money

A Fiery Speechmaker

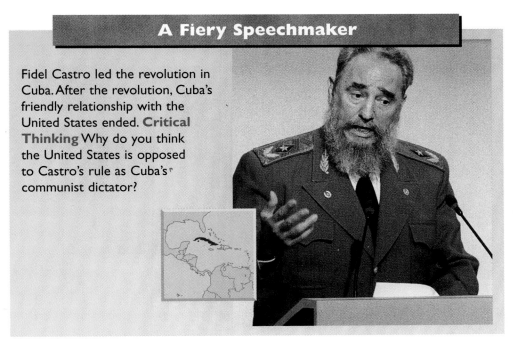

Fidel Castro led the revolution in Cuba. After the revolution, Cuba's friendly relationship with the United States ended. **Critical Thinking** Why do you think the United States is opposed to Castro's rule as Cuba's communist dictator?

READ ACTIVELY

Ask Questions If you could interview Fidel Castro, what questions would you ask him?

selling to people in the United States. Hotels were built, and tourists came to Cuba to enjoy its beautiful beaches and great climate. Many Cubans became businesspeople, teachers, doctors, and lawyers.

Not all Cubans shared the country's wealth, however. Most farm and factory workers earned low wages. Cuba also had many harsh leaders who ruled as dictators. A **dictator** is a ruler who has complete power. In the 1950s, Fulgencio Batista (fool HEN see yoh bah TEE stah) was Cuba's leader. During his rule, some people formed rebel groups to remove Batista and change the country.

Communism in Cuba   A young lawyer named Fidel Castro led one of these small rebel groups. He tried three times to overthrow the government during the 1950s. By his third attempt, he had gained many supporters. Finally, Batista gave up and left the country in 1959.

When Batista left, Fidel Castro took control of Cuba. He still holds power today. Castro's government is **communist.** In a communist country, the government owns all large businesses and most of the country's land. Under Castro, the Cuban government took over private businesses and land. Further, Castro said that newspapers and books could print only information supporting his government. Anyone who disagreed with government policy was put in jail. Huge numbers of Cubans fled the island. Many settled in Miami, Florida.

Cuba became a communist country in the early 1960s. At the same time, it became friendly with the Soviet Union. The Soviet Union was then the most powerful communist nation in the world. It sent money and supplies to Cuba. The United States and the Soviet Union, however, were not friendly. As a result, Cuba's relationship with the United States became tense. Relations grew worse when the United States openly welcomed the people who fled from Cuba.

CITIZEN HEROES

To Be a Leader When José Martí grew up in Cuba in the 1800s, it was still a colony of Spain. At age 16, he started a newspaper dedicated to Cuban independence. Martí later became famous for his poems and essays. In 1895, he led the revolution that eventually liberated Cuba. By the time independence was achieved, however, Martí had died in a battle with the Spanish.

There is a large Cuban American community in Miami, Florida. These men are playing dominoes in a Miami park. Behind them is a mural showing the presidents of many countries in the Western Hemisphere.

Cubans Leaving Cuba

Lydia Martin left Cuba in 1970. She was only six years old. Her mother had grown tired of the limits on freedom and lack of opportunity in communist Cuba. She wanted to take Lydia to the United States with her. Lydia's father begged her to stay.

"For years [my mother] had been anxious to leave Cuba . . . to take me to a place where I could learn about freedom. Her exit papers had finally arrived, but my father wouldn't let me go. . . . There was no talking sense into a man who feared losing his little girl forever. . . . While my mother was away at the church, I called him.

"I'm leaving with my mother," I told him with all the bravery a six-year-old could muster. . . .

"Have you stopped to think you may never see me again?" my father asked. . . . "

Cuban Exiles   Many Cuban exiles tell stories like Lydia's. An **exile** is a person who leaves his or her homeland for another country because of political problems. From the 1960s onwards, large numbers of people left Cuba. Many families were torn apart.

Dreams of Returning to Cuba Some Cubans never got over the loss of their home. In the 1970s, relations between the United States and Cuba grew worse. Even if she wanted to, Lydia Martin could not write to her father. The government might punish him if he got a letter from the United States. Still, Lydia hoped to reunite with him one day. Lydia's mother now spoke of Cuba with longing. She said that in Cuba, the sky was bluer, the sand whiter, and the palm trees greener.

In 1991, the government of the Soviet Union collapsed and could no longer help Cuba. Food, medicine, tools, and other necessities became more scarce. Lydia began worrying about her father and her other relatives. In 1995, she flew back to the island for the first time. Visitors from the United States are not always welcome in Cuba, especially if they once fled the island. Lydia was nervous.

Cuba: Today and Tomorrow

When Lydia stood on the beach in Cuba, she thought of her mother. Her mother had been right. The sky did seem bluer here, the sand whiter, and the palm trees greener.

Lydia had heard about the food shortages in Cuba, but she had not known how bad they were. Her father's new family sometimes had little more than rice to eat. When Lydia unpacked the shoes, soap, powdered milk, and underwear she had brought, her father and his new family took them with joy. They cooked her a delicious meal of lobster and rice on her first night. They had been saving money for it for months.

LINKS ACROSS THE WORLD

Livan Hernandez At 21 years old, Livan Hernandez was close to becoming a star pitcher in the Cuban Baseball League. He left Cuba for a chance to make millions of dollars pitching for a major league team in the United States. If that decision sounds easy, consider that Hernandez left behind everyone who is dear to him in Cuba. Hernandez hopes his family can one day enjoy the same freedom he has found.

◀ After Lydia Martin (left) departed from Cuba, she did not see or talk to her father (right) again for 25 years.

A Cuban High School

At many of Cuba's rural schools, students spend four hours in the classroom and four hours doing manual labor. **Critical Thinking** How is this school similar to yours? How is it different?

One thing that Cubans do not need to save money for is education. In the 1960s and 1970s, Castro overhauled Cuba's schools. At the time, many Cubans were **illiterate,** or unable to read and write. Castro sent students and teachers into the countryside to teach. Soon, more Cubans could read and write than ever before. Today, about 95 percent of Cubans can read and write.

Schools in Cuba may have helped many Cubans to learn how to read. However, they teach only communist ideas. But because Cuba is close to the United States, Cubans can tune in to American radio stations. Cuban teenagers listen to popular American dance music. They wear jeans from the United States whenever they can get them. Castro has allowed some businesses to be privately owned. The tourist industry is growing.

No one knows what Cuba's future will bring. Many think the time is near when those who left Cuba will be able to return home to visit or live there in freedom.

SECTION 1 REVIEW

1. **Define** (a) dictator, (b) communist, (c) exile, (d) illiterate.

2. **Identify** (a) Fidel Castro, (b) Fulgencio Batista, (c) Miami.

3. How did the collapse of the Soviet Union affect Cuba's economy?

4. What problems did communism bring to Cuba?

Critical Thinking

5. **Drawing Conclusions** Do you think that Cubans born in the United States feel as strongly about Cuba as their Cuban-born parents do? Why or why not?

Activity

6. **Writing to Learn** Work with a partner. One of you will write a letter to a relative in Cuba from the point of view of a Cuban exile in the United States. The other will write a response from the point of view of a Cuban who has never left Cuba.

Haiti

THE ROAD TO DEMOCRACY

Reach Into Your Background

Is there something in your life that you have had to try many times to achieve? What strate-

gies did you use to try to get what you wanted? Did they work? Why or why not?

Questions to Explore

1. How did Haiti's struggle for democracy affect people's lives?
2. How does the history of Haiti affect the culture of its people?

Key Terms

Creole
dialect

Key People and Places

Jean-Bertrand Aristide
Toussaint L'Ouverture
François Duvalier
Jean-Claude Duvalier
Port-au-Prince

▼ After his exile, Haitian President Jean-Bertrand Aristide returned to Haiti amid cheers of support.

The plane dipped toward Port-au-Prince (port oh PRINS), the capital of Haiti. It flew over a spreading slum. The slum was a neighborhood of crumbling cardboard huts with tin roofs. In the streets, people were jammed into a solid mass. All heads turned up toward the sky.

As if in one voice, a cheer of joy rose from the crowd. In the plane, Haiti's president, Jean-Bertrand Aristide (zhan behr TRAHND uh ris TEED), was returning to his country after a three-year exile. He had been elected by the people, but Haiti's military had forced him to leave. Then, a group of generals had taken over the country. The United States and other nations had pressured the military to give power back to Aristide. Many hoped that Aristide's return would also bring back democracy.

Haiti's Struggle for Democracy

Aristide was the first president to be elected democratically in many years. This does not mean that most Haitians did not want democracy. Their country was born out of a desperate struggle for freedom. Haiti is the only nation in the Americas formed from a successful revolt of enslaved Africans.

Country Profile: Haiti

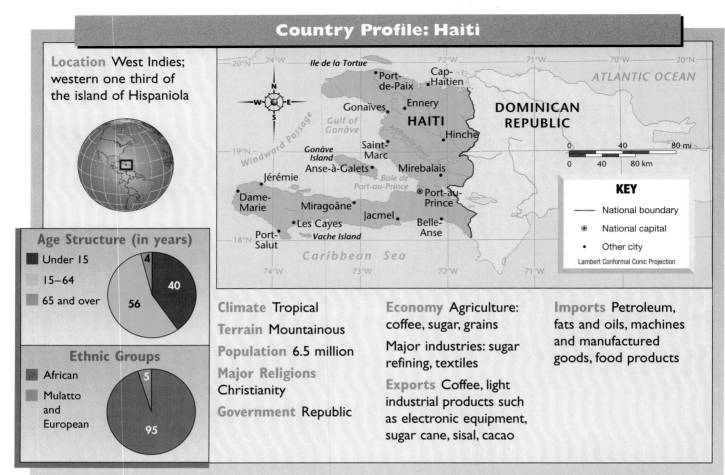

Location West Indies; western one third of the island of Hispaniola

Age Structure (in years)
- Under 15
- 15–64
- 65 and over

4 / 40 / 56

Ethnic Groups
- African
- Mulatto and European

5 / 95

Climate Tropical

Terrain Mountainous

Population 6.5 million

Major Religions Christianity

Government Republic

Economy Agriculture: coffee, sugar, grains

Major industries: sugar refining, textiles

Exports Coffee, light industrial products such as electronic equipment, sugar cane, sisal, cacao

Imports Petroleum, fats and oils, machines and manufactured goods, food products

Map and Chart Study This map shows the country of Haiti. Haiti is on the island of Hispaniola. **Region** What other country is on the island? Find the city of Cap-Haïtien. This is near the spot where Columbus landed in 1492. **Location** On what side of the island is Cap-Haïtien? In 1492, the Arawaks lived on Hispaniola. Look at the chart of ethnic groups. Do the Arawaks, a Native American group, still live in Haiti? What group makes up the largest part of the population?

The Birth of Haiti As you can see on the Country Profile above, Haiti lies on the western third of the island of Hispaniola. Haiti was once a colony of France. Europeans brought enslaved Africans to Haiti to work on sugar cane and coffee plantations. In the 1790s, slave revolts began. A Haitian leader named Toussaint L'Ouverture helped banish slavery from Haiti in 1801. He also offered Haitians a new way of life, based on the idea that all people could live as equals.

Troubled Years In the years that followed, Toussaint L'Ouverture's goal of freedom and equality was never fully realized. Most of Haiti's presidents became dictators once they got into power. One of the worst was François Duvalier (frahn SWAH doo VAHL yay), who took power in 1957. Because Duvalier had been a country doctor, Haitians called him "Papa Doc."

Papa Doc died in 1971. He was followed by his son, Jean-Claude Duvalier (zhan KLAHD doo VAHL yay), or "Baby Doc." Both Papa Doc and Baby Doc were cruel leaders. They stole government funds and used violence to keep power. During their rule, Haiti became the poorest country in the Western Hemisphere.

In 1986, rebels forced Baby Doc to leave the country. Many Haitians thought a period of freedom and prosperity was about to begin. But this was not to be. Haiti was ruled by one military leader after another. And most Haitians still made a living trying to farm small plots of land.

READ ACTIVELY

Connect How do most people in the United States make a living?

Life on a Farm When farmer Pierre Joseph stands at the top of his land, he can see the calm waters of the Caribbean. When he looks down, he sees the dry, cracked earth of his one acre.

About two thirds of the people in Haiti make their living by farming. The land has been overused. Most trees have been cut. Rains wash the topsoil into the sea. Joseph is thin because he rarely gets enough to eat. "The land just doesn't yield enough," he says. He points to the few rows of corn and beans that he can grow on his one acre.

Farmers like Pierre Joseph can barely make a living, but many feel they are rich in other ways. Haitian culture blends African, French, and West Indian tradition. The blend of traditions gives Haiti a Creole culture. **Creole** is a word referring to people of mixed ancestry.

Creole also refers to the dialect spoken in Haiti. A **dialect** is the different version of a language that is spoken in a particular region. The Creole dialect is based on both French and African languages.

Papa Doc and Baby Doc

François (left) and Jean-Claude Duvalier (right) often used violence to rule Haiti. The country also became much poorer during their rule. By the time Baby Doc was forced from power, the average Haitian earned only about $300 a year.

Predict Why do you think that Haitians were so glad to see Jean-Bertrand Aristide?

Life in the City   Haiti's capital, Port-au-Prince, is a blend not only of cultures, but also of rich and poor. The wealthy live in spacious wooden houses on the hills overlooking the city. There is a small middle class of doctors, lawyers, teachers, and owners of small businesses, that also live fairly well. Many poor people from the country live in tiny homes of crumbling concrete.

Hopes for the Future

In December 1990, Jean-Bertrand Aristide was elected president. Haitians held high hopes for the future. Aristide was a Catholic priest who had long defended the rights of the poor. He took office in February 1991.

A Military Takeover   Aristide served as president for seven months. Then Haiti's military forced him to leave the country. The military also attacked his supporters. "We have been in hiding since police shot up our house in October," an Aristide supporter told reporters in 1991. "We got away because people warned us they were coming."

The year after the election, thousands of Aristide supporters fled the capital. They feared for their lives. They squeezed into trucks by the dozen and went to hide in the hills. Others tore their homes apart to make rafts. Then they took to the sea. Many headed for the United States. Some were sent back.

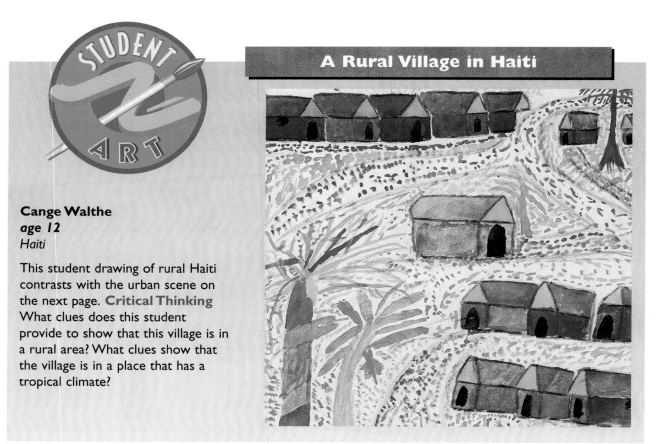

A Rural Village in Haiti

Cange Walthe
age 12
Haiti

This student drawing of rural Haiti contrasts with the urban scene on the next page. **Critical Thinking** What clues does this student provide to show that this village is in a rural area? What clues show that the village is in a place that has a tropical climate?

Dancing in the Streets

Haiti's people danced in the streets of Port-au-Prince when they heard that Aristide was returning to the country. They hoped that peace would return to Haiti along with Aristide.

Hundreds of children also left Haiti on rafts. Fifteen-year-old Fresenel Pierre (frehz uh NEL pea EHR) was one. He had an older brother waiting for him in Miami, where there is a large Haitian community. The children Fresenel sailed with were the children of Aristide supporters. Many were coming to the United States with no one to take them in.

Returning to Roots   In 1995, Aristide came back to Haiti. Since his return, a new spirit seems to be everywhere in Haiti. It has led to a movement to return to Haiti's Creole roots. For many Haitians, the idea of Creole has become an idea of equality. It suggests that people of different races and cultures must all work together to give Haiti its special identity.

SECTION 2 REVIEW

1. **Define**   (a) Creole, (b) dialect.

2. **Identify**   (a) Jean-Bertrand Aristide, (b) Toussaint L'Ouverture, (c) François Duvalier, (d) Jean-Claude Duvalier, (e) Port-au-Prince.

3. How did Haiti win its independence?

4. What obstacles to making a living do farmers like Pierre Joseph face?

Critical Thinking

5. **Making Comparisons** Give an example of how Haitian culture blends African and European traditions.

Activity

6. **Writing to Learn**   Write a diary entry from the point of view of Pierre Joseph about how economic and political conditions in Haiti affect his life.

Locating Information

Marisol felt like a sailor lost at sea.

She was surrounded by an ocean of information. Shelves overflowing with books towered above her. Beyond the bookshelves, more shelves loomed, filled with magazines. Past the magazines were computer terminals. Enough information to fill millions of pages could be accessed through them. Although she was in her community library, Marisol felt just as lost as if she were adrift in a lifeboat.

Marisol had gone to the library to find information about Toussaint L'Ouverture. Marisol had read in her textbook how L'Ouverture had led the Haitian people to freedom more than 200 years ago. Marisol's assignment was to write a one-page biography, or life story, about L'Ouverture. One question loomed in her mind: Where should she begin?

Get Ready

Locating information is an essential skill. Throughout your school career, you will need to locate information to complete homework assignments and class projects. As an adult, you will need to locate information to help you decide many things such as where to live, what job to do, and how to do it.

The first rule about locating information is *Don't panic!* Marisol felt lost in the library. But libraries and other sources of information are carefully designed to make your search for information as easy as possible. Just like a sailor at sea, it's a matter of choosing your destination, planning your route, and finally sailing to the one little island where the information you need is located.

Try It Out

Locating the information you need can be an exciting adventure. When you locate the information you've been searching for, you will feel the satisfaction and excitement of an explorer who finds the right island. Work with a partner to plan a voyage out into the Sea of Information:

A. Choose your destination. Your destination is the information you need. You and your partner should pick one now, and write it down. It might look like this: *"Destination: Information about how many Cubans live in the United States."*

B. Determine the best way to get there. Just as there are many ways to travel, there are many ways to locate information. Five important routes to information are listed in the box to the right. Discuss each source of information with your partner. Choose the source most likely to have the information you seek.

C. Prepare for your journey. You're about to depart, so pack your bags! You'll need a notebook and a pencil to jot down information. You might need a few coins for the copy machine.

D. Use signposts. Just as signposts can help you find your way on a real journey, different "signposts" can help you on your journey to find information. Read about these "signposts" in the box.

Five Important Routes To Information

Libraries Most of the world's information is stored in libraries. *Signposts:* the card catalog and librarians.

Books There are books about nearly every subject. *Signposts:* book titles and tables of contents.

Periodicals Magazines and newspapers can provide up-to-date information on a huge range of topics. *Signposts:* magazine indexes and newspaper indexes found in libraries.

The Internet The Internet is a worldwide network of computers containing information. *Signposts:* special electronic search indexes on the Internet.

People By interviewing experts, you can learn what they know about their specialties. *Signposts:* the telephone directory to locate appropriate people to interview.

Apply the Skill

Now that you've made an information-seeking journey with a partner, it's time to do it alone. Choose one of the following destinations:

- Destination: Information that identifies the chief agricultural product grown in Cuba.

- Destination: Information that identifies the President of Haiti.

- Destination: Information that identifies three historic sites you could visit in Puerto Rico.

Once you have reached your destination by locating the information, draw a map to show how you found it.

Puerto Rico

CULTURAL IDENTITY OF A PEOPLE

Reach Into Your Background

Do you ever feel that you have "two selves"? One that acts a certain way with some people? And another that comes out when you are with other people? Are both of them the real you?

Questions to Explore

1. What factors influenced Puerto Rican culture?

2. What is Puerto Rico's relationship with the United States?

Key Terms

citizen
commonwealth
constitution

Key Places

San Juan
Condado

▼ Esmeralda Santiago moved from Puerto Rico to New York City when she was 13 years old.

Puerto Rican Esmeralda Santiago (ez mur EL duh sant ee AHG oh) can never forget the first time she saw the movie *West Side Story.* She was living in New York. It was 1961 and she was 13 years old. The movie was about Puerto Ricans living in New York, but most of the actors who played them were English-speaking whites. To her, they just didn't seem like Puerto Rican people.

Seeing the movie was a turning point in Esmeralda's life. She knew the movie was not about her. But she did not know what the film should have been like. Realizing this made her feel confused.

66**I** had no sense of Puerto Rican culture or what it was to me. Where did I come from? Who is this person who calls herself a Puerto Rican and what does that mean? . . . [W]hen I think Puerto Rican, there's this big void, this empty space where my history should be.99

Puerto Rican and American

Even though Esmeralda felt confused about who she was, she remembered her early days in Puerto Rico vividly. When Esmeralda's mother brought her to New York City, everything changed.

Country Profile: Puerto Rico

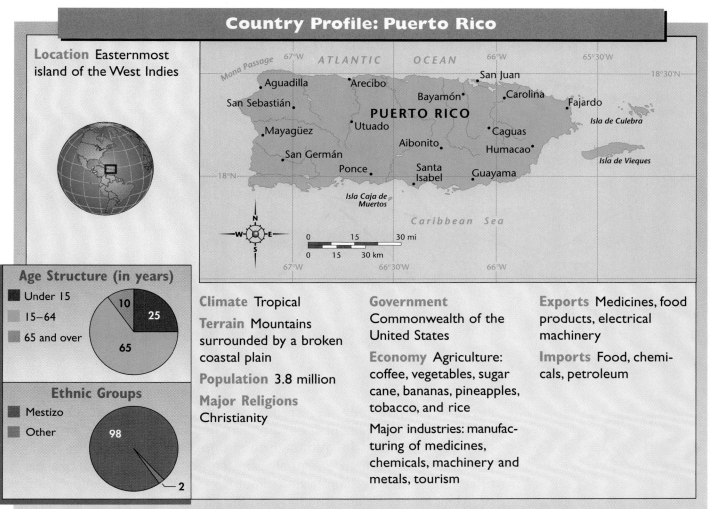

Location Easternmost island of the West Indies

Age Structure (in years)
- Under 15
- 15–64
- 65 and over

10
25
65

Ethnic Groups
- Mestizo
- Other

98
2

Climate Tropical

Terrain Mountains surrounded by a broken coastal plain

Population 3.8 million

Major Religions Christianity

Government Commonwealth of the United States

Economy Agriculture: coffee, vegetables, sugar cane, bananas, pineapples, tobacco, and rice

Major industries: manufacturing of medicines, chemicals, machinery and metals, tourism

Exports Medicines, food products, electrical machinery

Imports Food, chemicals, petroleum

Map and Chart Study This map shows Puerto Rico. **Location** Read the description of Puerto Rico's terrain. Where are Puerto Rico's mountains located? How do you know? **Movement** How do you think most exports are shipped out of Puerto Rico? **Critical Thinking** Look at the chart that shows age structure. Would you say that Puerto Rico's population is old, young, or evenly balanced? Why?

It was not that Esmeralda was completely separated from her people. Puerto Ricans are U.S. citizens. **Citizens** are individuals with certain rights and responsibilities under a particular government. However, Puerto Ricans cannot vote in U. S. presidential elections. They do not pay U.S. taxes. And they have only a non-voting representative in the U.S. Congress. Puerto Rico is a commonwealth of the United States. A **commonwealth** is a place that has its own government but also has strong ties to another country. Esmeralda had the right to return to Puerto Rico whenever she chose.

Esmeralda found life on the mainland strange and confusing. One problem was that to succeed in school, she had to improve her English. Esmeralda was also confused by her new group of friends. She found that Puerto Ricans living on the mainland were different from her friends on the island of Puerto Rico. Instead of the salsa and merengue

Chart Study Many Puerto Ricans have moved to the mainland United States. **Critical Thinking** Which region of the mainland has the most Puerto Ricans? What do you think draws Puerto Ricans to a particular area?

Population	
Total	2,728,000
Northeast	1,872,000
Midwest	258,000
South	406,000
West	192,000

Distribution by Region

- 9.4%
- 7.0%
- 14.9%
- 68.6%

- Northeast
- Midwest
- South
- West

READ ACTIVELY

Connect What kind of music do you listen to? Does the music you listen to reflect your feelings about your life and your community? Why or why not?

music she loved, they preferred rock music. Most of the time they spoke neither pure Spanish nor English, but a mixture of the two that they called "Spanglish." Although they were Puerto Rican, Esmeralda felt different from them. Eventually, she learned their ways. She became more like them and thought less about her old life on the island.

Most Puerto Ricans who move to the mainland keep connections to Puerto Rico. As people travel back and forth between the mainland and Puerto Rico, they bring customs and products with them. If you visited Puerto Rico, you would see many influences from the U.S. mainland. You would also see that in Puerto Rico, there is a strong cultural connection to the Caribbean. Most people are a mix of Spanish and African ancestry. Some Puerto Ricans like to look even further back into their history by calling themselves "Boricuas" (bohr ee KOO uhs). The name comes from the Boriqueno (bohr ee KAY noh), an indigenous farming people who lived on the island before the Spanish arrived.

More Than the Four Walls

The land of Puerto Rico is a memory no Puerto Rican forgets. Some, like Esmeralda Santiago, never go back to it. But others return, longing for the familiar ways they left behind. Julia de Jesus Chaparro (HOO lee a day HAY soos sha PAHR ro) moved back to a small mountain village in Puerto Rico after more than 14 years in Boston. She is fond of saying that where she lives now there are "more than the four walls of the city." To prove what she means, she takes visitors to her back porch. Outside it, one can see a row of steep mountains. Peeking between them is the bright blue of the Caribbean Sea. The mountain slopes steeply down from her back porch, but she has managed to clear some land. Her garden of mangoes, coconuts, grapefruit, and lemons thrives in the sun. Behind a nearby tree, a hen and six chickens are pecking in the dirt.

On other parts of the island, farmers ride horses through fields of tall sugar cane. Higher in the hills, Puerto Rican cowhands, called *jíbaros* (HEE bahr ohs), hunt, fish, and raise chickens, pigs, and cattle. To the southwest, where the land gets lower, fishing villages dot the coast.

Puerto Rico is an island of cities as well as countryside. Puerto Rican cities show influences of Spanish, Caribbean, and U.S. mainland cultures. About 70 percent of Puerto Ricans live in cities. Many city people work in factories. Others work in the hotels and restaurants that draw many tourists. Puerto Rico's capital, San Juan (san HWAHN), has a large waterfront area known as the Condado (kohn DAH do). It is packed with luxury hotels. Not far away, modern skyscrapers pierce the brilliant sky. In the old section of San Juan, Spanish-style buildings are everywhere. A 450-year-old Catholic church built by the Spanish has been carefully restored. Not far from it sit ancient houses graced with iron balconies in lacy Spanish style.

READ ACTIVELY

Visualize What might you see if you looked out the back door of an apartment in the city? What might you see if you looked out the back door of a house in the countryside?

A Commonwealth in Question

In 1951, Puerto Ricans voted to adopt their own constitution. A **constitution** is a statement of a country's basic laws and values. This gave Puerto Rico its own group of lawmakers. But it was still connected

New York City's Spanish Harlem

Puerto Ricans are the largest ethnic group in New York City's Lower East Side, and they make up about 12 percent of the city's total population.

to the United States. Puerto Rico is bound by many United States laws. Puerto Ricans have many questions about this. Is it good for Puerto Rico? Should Puerto Rico become independent? Or should it become a state of the United States?

What Direction to Take? Puerto Ricans have many disagreements over the answers to these questions. Many feel that having "one foot" in Puerto Rico and "one foot" in the United States can lead to problems. Others point out how the relationship with the United States has helped Puerto Rico. U.S. businesses on the island have raised the standard of living. Each year, the U.S. government sends millions of dollars to the island to help people in need.

Some people still feel that Puerto Rico has a disadvantage because people there cannot vote in U.S. elections. They say Puerto Rico should try to become a state. But if it does, it will become the poorest state in the union. Puerto Ricans earn more money than people in other Caribbean countries. However, they earn less than people on the U.S. mainland. Also, if Puerto Rico becomes a state, Puerto Ricans will have

READ ACTIVELY

Connect Would people in your area want to become part of another state? Why or why not?

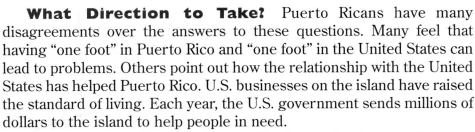

San Juan: Old and New

San Juan, Puerto Rico's oldest city, is famous for historic forts and the wrought iron balconies of its oldest neighborhoods. But San Juan is also a vacation spot for tourists, with modern hotels lining its sandy beaches.

▶ These women are celebrating Puerto Rico's Spanish heritage. Puerto Ricans celebrate many holidays with traditional music and dancing.

to pay U.S. taxes. This could lower the earnings of many who have little to spare. For these reasons, in 1993, Puerto Ricans voted not to become the 51st state of the United States.

The Question of Independence   Some people who voted against statehood have even bigger dreams for the country. They want Puerto Rico to become a separate nation. If not, they fear that Puerto Ricans will become confused about their identity, just as Esmeralda Santiago became confused about hers. They stress Puerto Rico's connection to other Caribbean nations. They want to make sure that Puerto Ricans always identify with the Spanish language and Spanish culture. But for now, Puerto Rico will keep its links to the mainland. Many Puerto Ricans hope that their relationship with the United States will lead to a profitable and peaceful future.

SECTION 3 REVIEW

1. **Define** (a) citizen, (b) commonwealth, (c) constitution.

2. **Identify** (a) San Juan, (b) Condado.

3. What is the political connection between Puerto Rico and the United States?

4. Compare life in the mainland United States with life in Puerto Rico.

Critical Thinking

5. **Identifying Central Issues** What are the three options Puerto Ricans consider in terms of their relationship with the United States? What are the benefits and drawbacks of each?

Activity

6. **Writing to Learn** Try to put yourself in Esmeralda Santiago's place. Write a paragraph telling what it was like to move to New York from Puerto Rico.

Review and Activities

Reviewing Main Ideas

1. What happened to Cuba when the communist regime in the Soviet Union fell?
2. What changes did Lydia Martin notice when she visited Cuba in 1995?
3. How is Haiti's history unique?
4. What were two results of Jean-Bertrand Aristide's forced exile from Haiti?
5. How do the cultures of Spain and the United States influence Puerto Rico? Give one example of how each has influenced Puerto Rico.
6. How have frequent trips to the U.S. mainland affected some Puerto Rican families?

Reviewing Key Terms

Use each key term below in a sentence that shows the meaning of the term.

1. communist
2. dictator
3. exile
4. illiterate
5. Creole
6. dialect
7. commonwealth
8. citizen
9. constitution

Critical Thinking

1. **Making Comparisons** Both Cubans and Puerto Ricans have settled in the United States. How has the experience been similar for both? How has it been different?
2. **Drawing Conclusions** How do you think Toussaint L'Ouverture's fight for independence inspires Haitians to fight for democracy?

Graphic Organizer

Copy the chart to the right onto a piece of paper, then fill in the empty boxes to complete the chart.

	Cuba	Haiti	Puerto Rico
Form of government			
United States Influence			

Map Activity

For each place listed below, write the letter from the map that shows its location.

1. Port-au-Prince

2. San Juan

3. Havana

4. Miami

5. Gulf of Mexico

6. Guantánamo Bay

7. Dominican Republic

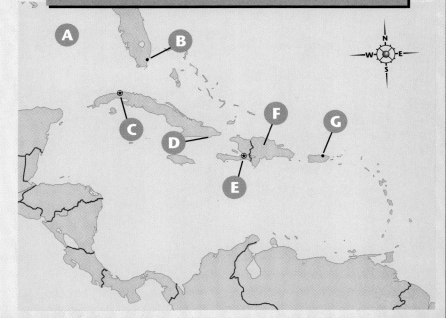

The Caribbean: Place Location

Writing Activity

Writing a Poem
Write a poem describing the culture in your region. Does your region have a blend of cultures, like Haiti?

Why or why not? How does the culture in your region affect the way you feel about yourself?

Internet Activity
Use a search engine to find the site **Nueva Vista: Latino/Puerto Rican Home Page.** Click on **Viewpoint.** Then, click on **The 51st State: the State of Confusion** and read one person's view on Puerto Rico's status as a U.S. commonwealth. Use this information to debate the issue with your classmates.

Skills Review

Turn to the Skill Activity.
Review the steps for locating information. Then write a one page biography of Fidel Castro. Make a list of four routes you could take to find information.

How Am I Doing?

Answer these questions to help you check your progress.

1. Do I understand why many Cubans have emigrated to the United States?

2. Can I explain how Haiti's people have struggled for democracy?

3. Do I understand Puerto Rico's relationship with the United States?

4. Can I describe what factors have affected culture in the Caribbean islands?

5. What information from this chapter can I use in my book project?

Exploring South America

MAP ACTIVITIES

South America is more than two times as large as the mainland United States. Because it is so large, its geography and cultures are diverse. To learn more about South America, complete the following activities.

Understanding geography
Much of South America is located south of the Equator. If you were to start at the Equator and travel south, how do you think the climate would change? Why?

Study the map
How do you think the Andes Mountains may have affected political boundaries in South America?

Brazil

RESOURCES OF THE RAIN FOREST

SECTION 1

BEFORE YOU READ

Reach Into Your Background
In this section, you will learn about the rain forests in Brazil.

List three things you already know or can guess about the rain forests.

Questions to Explore
1. Why are the rain forests in Brazil a global issue?
2. How does what happens to the rain forests affect Brazil's economy?

Key Terms
canopy
photosynthesis

Key People and Places
Rio de Janeiro
Salvador
Yanomamo
Brasília

D eep in the rain forest in Brazil, the light barely penetrates. At the top of the trees, the leaves form a dense mass called a **canopy.** Sun and rain beat down upon the canopy. But on the ground, the air feels almost chilly. The only sounds are the calls of birds, monkeys, and insects.

Brazil and Its Rain Forests

Brazil, the largest country in South America, is nearly as large as the United States. It is also one of the richest countries in the world in land and resources. Until recently, its immense rain forests remained undisturbed. Only the few Native American groups that had lived in them for centuries ever explored them.

Brazil's Geography Brazil's rain forests take up about one half of the country. Look at the map in the Country Profile. In the southeast, the forests give way to a large plateau divided by mountain ranges and river valleys. The plateau reaches Brazil's long coast. Many harbors lie along the coast. Large cities, such as Rio de Janeiro (ree oh day zhuh NER oh), grew up around harbors. Most of Brazil's people live near the coast, far from the rain forests.

▼ The canopy of Brazil's rain forest parts only where rivers slice through it.

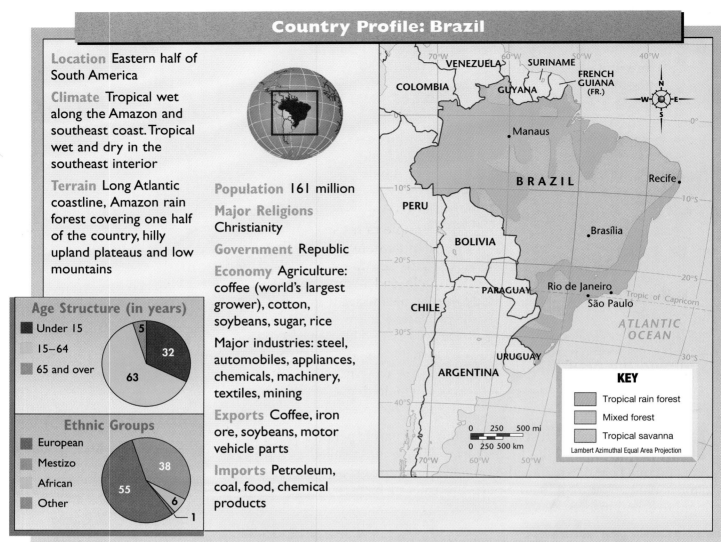

Location Eastern half of South America

Climate Tropical wet along the Amazon and southeast coast. Tropical wet and dry in the southeast interior

Terrain Long Atlantic coastline, Amazon rain forest covering one half of the country, hilly upland plateaus and low mountains

Population 161 million

Major Religions Christianity

Government Republic

Economy Agriculture: coffee (world's largest grower), cotton, soybeans, sugar, rice

Major industries: steel, automobiles, appliances, chemicals, machinery, textiles, mining

Exports Coffee, iron ore, soybeans, motor vehicle parts

Imports Petroleum, coal, food, chemical products

Age Structure (in years)

- Under 15
- 15–64
- 65 and over

5
32
63

Ethnic Groups

- European
- Mestizo
- African
- Other

38
55
6
1

KEY

- Tropical rain forest
- Mixed forest
- Tropical savanna

Lambert Azimuthal Equal Area Projection

0   250   500 mi
0   250 500 km

Map Study This map shows the vegetation regions of Brazil. Brazil contains over 1 million square miles (2,589,900 sq km) of rain forest. Northern Brazil contains part of the largest rain forest in the world, the Amazonian rain forest. Alaska could fit inside Brazil's Amazonian rain forest twice. Texas could fit inside it five times. **Location** What four Brazilian cities are located in the rain forest?

The People of Brazil

The Native Americans living in the rain forest were some of the first people to live in Brazil. Today, most Brazilians are a mix of Native American, African, and European heritages.

Many parts of African culture still flourish in Brazil. The most African of Brazilian cities, Salvador, lies on the coastal plains. Visitors are surprised by how much Salvador is like a town in Africa. Most of the people who live here descend from the millions of Africans brought to Brazil as slaves.

Working on Farms and in Factories   Many Africans in Brazil were forced to work the coffee plantations. Brazil used their labor to become the world's largest coffee grower. When the slaves were freed in the late 1800s, they became paid but cheap labor.

Coffee prices dropped in the first few years of the 1900s. Brazilians realized that they could not depend on one or two crops to survive. In the 1930s, the government discouraged coffee production and tried to diversify the economy by building more factories. Today, Brazil produces many goods, including iron and steel, cars, and electrical equipment. Since 1960, about 30 million people have left farms and plantations to get jobs in these new industries. They moved into the cities.

A Brazilian City   Brazilian cities are home to the rich and the very poor. Rio de Janeiro is a good example of these contrasts. It lies on the coast, surrounded by huge mountains that dip to the sea. If you climbed to the top of one, you could see the whole city. To the south, you would see expensive hotels and shops for tourists. In the downtown area, you would see old palaces and government buildings.

But to the north, you would see clusters of small houses where factory workers live. Below this neighborhood is an even poorer one, crowded with homes that have no electricity or running water. About a quarter of Rio's 12 million people live in these neighborhoods known as *favelas* (fuh VEH lus). However, most of Rio's people live in well-built houses with electricity and running water.

READ ACTIVELY

Connect How is the history of Africans in Brazil like the history of Africans brought to the United States?

Brazil's African Heritage

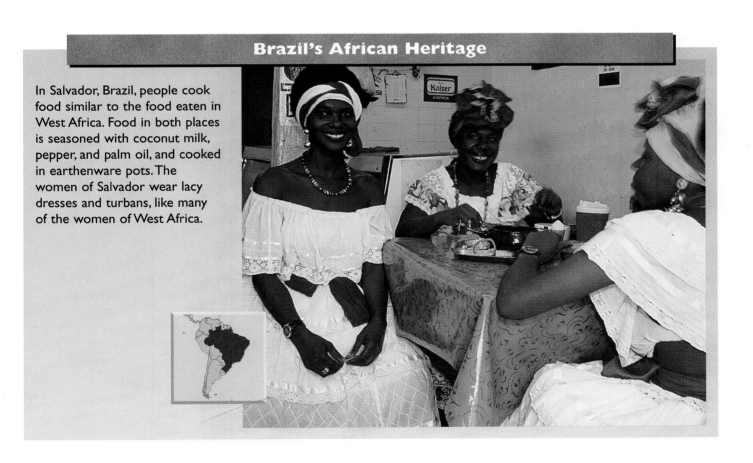

In Salvador, Brazil, people cook food similar to the food eaten in West Africa. Food in both places is seasoned with coconut milk, pepper, and palm oil, and cooked in earthenware pots. The women of Salvador wear lacy dresses and turbans, like many of the women of West Africa.

Using the Rain Forest's Resources

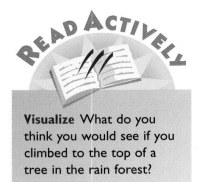

Visualize What do you think you would see if you climbed to the top of a tree in the rain forest?

On a sunny January in 1994, two boys who lived in the rain forest scrambled up the trees. The boys were Yanomamos. The Yanomamo are a Native American group that lives in the rain forests. The boys pointed to a plane soaring close to the treetops. The plane dipped down and landed on a dirt strip. "Foreign visitors!" the boys called excitedly.

Brazil's New Capital: Brasília The visitors were from Brasília (bruh ZIL yuh), the capital city of Brazil. Brasília is closer to the rain forest than the coastal cities are. On the vast interior plain where Brasília now stands, there used to be nothing but a savanna called the Cerrado (suh RAH doh). The Cerrado was a region 10 times larger than the state of Kansas. The government thought that moving the capital there would attract some people from the coastal areas.

The government wanted to develop Brazil's interior region using the resources of the rain forest. The rain forests are important to Brazil's economy because people cut timber, mine for gold, and farm there. Now, the government hoped to develop industry using the resources of the rain forest.

Worldwide Impact of the Rain Forest The rain forest where the Yanomamo live is very important to life all around the Earth. Scientists estimate that rain forests produce about one third of the world's oxygen. Green plants and trees produce their own food using

▼São Paulo is the largest city in Brazil. It contains more than 20,000 factories, which provide jobs for 600,000 workers.

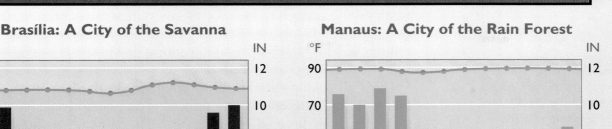

Two Cities, Two Climates

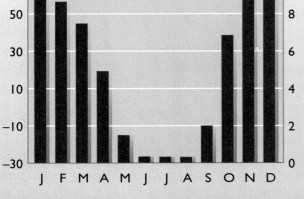

Brasília: A City of the Savanna

°F / IN

Months: J F M A M J J A S O N D

Manaus: A City of the Rain Forest

°F / IN

Months: J F M A M J J A S O N D

Curved lines show temperatures in Fahrenheit degrees. **Bars** show rainfall in inches.

Chart Study A climate graph shows rainfall and temperature in the same space. The bars show rainfall, while the curved lines show temperature. **Critical Thinking** How are the seasons in Brasília and Manaus different from each other?

water, carbon dioxide, and sunlight. This process is called **photosynthesis** (foht oh SIN thuh sis). In the process of photosynthesis, oxygen is given off. All people and animals need oxygen to breathe.

The rain forest also holds about one fifth of the world's fresh water. Many scientists think that when people come to the rain forest, they may upset the delicate balance of nature.

Protecting the Rain Forest Brazil's government is taking care to use the rain forest's resources without upsetting this balance. The government has started using satellites to keep an eye on the rain forest. That way, the government can respond fast to protect the rain forest from the following dangers.

First, if too much timber is cut down, there will not be enough trees to absorb the carbon dioxide in the atmosphere. The carbon dioxide layer may trap heat near the Earth, changing the world's climate. When part of the forest is destroyed, the animals and plants that live there may not survive. When plant life is destroyed, less oxygen is produced.

CITIZEN HEROES

A Voice of Protest Friar Hector Turrini moved from Italy to Brazil more than 45 years ago. At that time, there were so few roads that Turrini had to learn to fly a plane to get around his parish. He dedicated himself to protecting the Native Americans and rubber tappers who depend on the rain forest. Now Turrini is working to protect the rain forest.

Second, there is the problem of smuggling. Each year, Brazil loses about 12 million animals to smugglers. Many of these animals are endangered. Smugglers look for monkeys, parrots, and other animals. One parrot can be sold for $10,000. One woolly monkey can be sold for as much as $50,000. It is illegal to capture or kill these animals, but the smugglers often get away with it.

Third, development can cause pollution. In the late 1980s, the discovery of gold attracted many miners to the rain forest. Mining gold involves mixing the gold with mercury. The mercury polluted streams in the forest. It made people in several Yanomamo villages sick.

The gold mining in the rain forest attracted the attention of the world. The government of Brazil passed strict laws about mining in the rain forest. Sometimes the government insisted that the miners leave. At times, military police had to be called in to make sure they did.

Giving Land to the Poor   One of the main reasons that people come to the rain forest is the lack of land to farm. This may seem strange when one considers Brazil's large size. However, most of Brazil's land is owned by a few people who may choose not to farm their land. About one third of Brazil's farmland is unused. This represents about 300 million acres (122 million hectares) of crop and ranch land.

In 1995, Brazil's president gave some of this unused land to poor farmers. The goal is to resettle more than 3,600 poor families who want a new place to live and who want to return to farming. The process is a slow one. However, life for some resettled Brazilians is improving.

People are starting small farms just north of Rio de Janeiro. The farms help people make a living for themselves. On a balmy July day in 1995, farmer Joe Brum showed a reporter his farm. Brum had received the 17-acre plot from the government. Now his tin-roofed house was shaded by the coconut and banana trees he had planted. He had a couple of pigs and had earned enough money to buy a satellite dish and a television.

Brum's eyes gleamed as he pointed to the rows of vegetables. "What I have here," he explained to the reporter, "I made myself."

SECTION 1 REVIEW

1. Define (a) canopy, (b) photosynthesis.

2. Identify (a) Rio de Janeiro, (b) Salvador, (c) Yanomamo, (d) Brasília.

3. Why are Brazil's rain forests important to the whole world?

4. In what ways does Brazil depend on its rain forest?

Critical Thinking

5. Expressing Problems Clearly Some people want Brazil to stop using rain forests completely. Is this reasonable? What do you think it would do to Brazil's economy?

Activity

6. Writing a Journal Entry Use what you know about the rain forest to write a journal entry about a visit to it.

Peru

LIFE IN THE ALTIPLANO

Reach Into Your Background

Did you choose your clothing according to the weather report this morning? The decision you make is affected by climate. Think of other ways that climate affects your life.

Questions to Explore

1. How has geography affected the lifestyle of Native Americans of the altiplano?

2. How do people on the altiplano survive?

Key Terms

altiplano
sierra
montaña
tundra

Key People and Places

Lake Titicaca
Aymara
Quechua
Cuzco

When people on Tribuna, an island in Lake Titicaca, play soccer, they must be careful. That's because the island is made of straw. The ground is uneven, and when they walk on it they can feel the water shifting below. "It seems crazy to play soccer on water," says Luis Colo, who lives on Tribuna. "We don't jump on each other after a goal, or we'd probably fall through the field."

Tribuna is one of about 70 islands made by the Aymara (eye muh RAH). The Aymara have adapted to the geography of Lake Titicaca. The Aymara make their islands out of tortora reeds. They join the floating roots of tortora reeds together and then lay cut reeds on top. This process creates an island that is firm enough to support small communities of people with huts and livestock. When the Aymara need more land, they build another island.

▲ When the wind comes up, the Aymara must anchor their islands to keep them from being swept away.

Peru's Three Geographic Regions

The Aymara live on Lake Titicaca. Find Lake Titicaca on the map in the Country Profile. Lake Titicaca lies high in Peru's altiplano (al tih PLAH noh), a high plateau region in the Andes. The altiplano is about 12,000 feet (3,658 m) above sea level. It lies in the southern part of Peru near the Bolivian border.

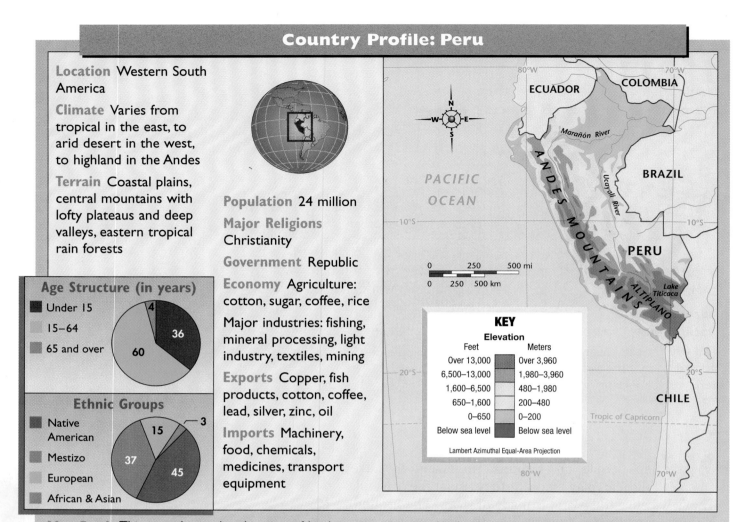

Country Profile: Peru

Location Western South America

Climate Varies from tropical in the east, to arid desert in the west, to highland in the Andes

Terrain Coastal plains, central mountains with lofty plateaus and deep valleys, eastern tropical rain forests

Population 24 million

Major Religions Christianity

Government Republic

Economy Agriculture: cotton, sugar, coffee, rice

Major industries: fishing, mineral processing, light industry, textiles, mining

Exports Copper, fish products, cotton, coffee, lead, silver, zinc, oil

Imports Machinery, food, chemicals, medicines, transport equipment

Age Structure (in years)

- Under 15
- 15–64
- 65 and over

4, 36, 60

Ethnic Groups

- Native American
- Mestizo
- European
- African & Asian

3, 15, 37, 45

KEY
Elevation

Feet		Meters
Over 13,000		Over 3,960
6,500–13,000		1,980–3,960
1,600–6,500		480–1,980
650–1,600		200–480
0–650		0–200
Below sea level		Below sea level

Lambert Azimuthal Equal-Area Projection

Map Study This map shows the elevation of land in Peru. The higher you climb in the mountains, the colder the climate gets. In the Andes Mountains, trees will not grow above 10,000 feet (3,048 m) because it is too cold. But east of the Andes, the elevation is lower. Much of the eastern lowlands is covered with a dense tropical rain forest. **Location** How high in the mountains is Lake Titicaca? What direction do the rivers on this map flow? How can you tell?

Peru's mountains divide the country into three geographic regions. The altiplano and Peru's highest mountains are in the **sierra,** the mountains that run from northwest to southeast Peru. The mountains are so high that the temperature can drop as low as 20°F (–7°C). People who live in this region must sleep under many blankets. They sometimes wear sweaters to bed.

Their life is far different from the lives of those who live on the coastal plain, which is Peru's second geographical region. This dry region is warmed by the sun and cooled by sea breezes. Several cities, including Trujillo (troo HEE yoh), Chimbote (chim BOH tay), and Lima (LEE muh), dot the coast.

The third region is called the **montaña.** The montaña is made of large stretches of tropical forests on the lower slopes of mountains in northeast Peru. Here the weather is warm and humid all year round.

Peru's People

Native Americans make up almost half of Peru's population. Most Native Americans living in Peru are Quechua. About 15 percent of Peruvians are of European descent. Another 37 percent are mestizo. The remaining Peruvians are of African and Asian descent.

Peru's Cities   The altiplano contains cities and isolated towns. City life is very different from village life. Most city dwellers have electricity. The streets are paved, and there are telephones. But in Peru's cities, the old mixes with the new.

One Peruvian city, Cuzco, is the site of the ancient Incan capital. Parts of the old Incan wall that once surrounded the city are still standing. Today's modern houses are made of adobe, with red tile roofs. But their foundations are the remains of Incan stonework. There are buildings from the time of the Spanish colonists as well.

Spanish conquistador Francisco Pizarro founded Peru's largest city and capital, Lima, in 1535. Lima lies on the coastal plain. Like Cuzco, Lima is a mix of old and new. Historic Spanish cathedrals and government buildings from the 1600s and 1700s stand next to modern skyscrapers.

LINKS ACROSS TIME

Bridging Canyons The Incas invented the technology for building suspension bridges. First, they built stone towers on each side of a canyon. They suspended cables woven from plants from the stone towers. Then, they laid wooden slats across the cables to make a bridge. They used smaller cables for railings. People still use Incan bridges today. Modern suspension bridges have steel cables and are reinforced with iron beams.

◀ Lima is the busiest and most modern of Peru's cities. What details in the photo are modern? What details are more traditional?

Life in Rural Areas   In the isolated towns of the altiplano, life is very different from life in the city. There are no telephones to ring. Few buses drive through the villages. Most people are Quechua or Aymara.

A Day in a Quechua Village   Modesto Mamani (moh DES toh muh MAN ee) is a 13-year-old Quechua boy. He wakes before dawn to the freezing mountain air. He eats breakfast as soon as the sun comes up. Breakfast is always the same: a couple of rolls, coffee with sugar, and whole wheat kernels that can be eaten like popcorn. The only other meal may be lunch. It is usually potato and barley soup with chunos—freeze-dried potato skins.

For much of the day, Modesto works in the field with his father and brothers. On other days, he looks after the sheep or goes with his mother to the market. Despite all of these chores, Modesto finds time to play soccer on the tundra in back of his house. A **tundra** is an area where no trees grow because the soil is always cold.

Predict How do you think the Quechuas of the altiplano make a living?

Modesto Mamani at School and at Work

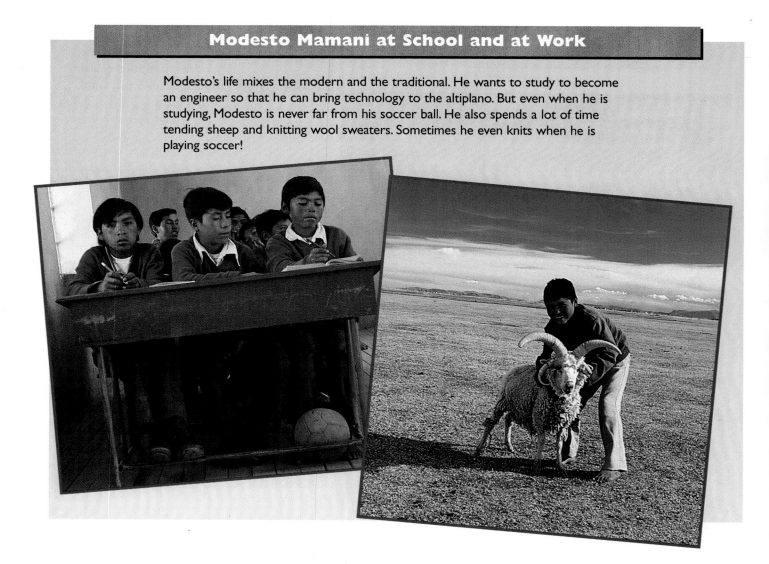

Modesto's life mixes the modern and the traditional. He wants to study to become an engineer so that he can bring technology to the altiplano. But even when he is studying, Modesto is never far from his soccer ball. He also spends a lot of time tending sheep and knitting wool sweaters. Sometimes he even knits when he is playing soccer!

The Straw People Modesto's village is not far from the Aymara islands on Lake Titicaca. The people there live on one of the 70 tortora reed islands that float on the lake. The islanders use tortora reeds for many other purposes besides building islands. They weave it to make boats. They use it as fuel for cooking. They eat the soft inside of the reeds. Most important, though, they use the reeds to repair the islands. Tortora reeds last only a few months before they start to rot. A person who slipped through them could die in the lake's icy waters.

On the straw islands, women wake at dawn to get water from the lake for cooking and washing. They spend the rest of the day washing clothes, untangling fishing nets, and making new homes out of reeds. Once or twice a week they go to market to trade fish for rice, potatoes, and sugar. Meanwhile, the men fish and help to repair the straw islands.

A Modern Future Quechuas and other Native Americans living on the altiplano follow traditions that are hundreds of years old. Their communities, however, are slowly changing. Thousands of Native Americans have left for jobs in the city. Life is changing even for those who stay in the village. The future holds a promising mix of old and new ways.

Quechua Market Day

On market days, Quechua from several communities gather together to buy and sell goods. What kinds of goods are being sold at this market?

SECTION 2 REVIEW

1. **Define** (a) altiplano, (b) sierra, (c) moñtana, (d) tundra.

2. **Identify** (a) Lake Titicaca, (b) Aymara, (c) Quechua, (d) Cuzco.

3. How is the daily life of the Quechua affected by the high altitude of the altiplano?

4. Describe people's lives on the straw islands of Lake Titicaca.

Critical Thinking

5. **Recognizing Bias** Do you think the Quechua see their way of life as outsiders see it? Explain.

Activity

6. **Writing to Learn** Compare life in a Peruvian city with life in a rural Quechua or Aymara community.

Using Isolines to Show Elevation

limb straight up, hike over the side, or walk all the way around? That was the question Melissa and José faced.

They stared up at the huge hill in front of them. According to the map, the campsite they were hiking to was exactly on the opposite side of the hill. What was the best route to take?

Melissa spread the map out on a fallen log. "Look," she said, pointing at the map. "This hill is steep on this side, but we can climb it." She traced the route on the map. "But look what we'd run into on the other side!"

"A cliff!" José responded. "We'd never be able to get down. It's way too steep. I guess we'll have to walk around the hill."

"Not so fast. If we head to our left, we can climb up a gentle slope and work our way past the cliff down the hill on the other side. It's kind of steep, but at least we'll be going downhill!"

Get Ready

How could Melissa tell from the map how steep different parts of the hill were? The answer is that the map showed isolines. The word *isolines* comes from the Greek word *iso,* which means "equal," and our word *lines.* Isolines link together equal parts of a map. On the map Melissa and José used, every part of the hill that was the same elevation was linked by an isoline. By studying the pattern of the isolines, Melissa could figure out the best route to take.

Isolines that show elevation are also called contour lines, because their pattern shows the contour, or shape, of the land.

You can make your own contour map. To do this, you will need:

- an irregularly shaped rock, about the size of a cantaloupe
- a pan of water big enough and deep enough to submerge the rock
- a crayon or waterproof marker
- a sheet of blank paper and a pencil

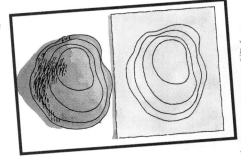

Try It Out

A. Fill the pan with water deep enough to cover the rock.

B. Holding the top of the rock, dip the bottom of it evenly about one inch into the water. Don't drop it! Remove the rock. Use the crayon or marker to trace the waterline all the way around the rock.

C. Dip the rock again, about one inch deeper. The waterline will now be about one inch higher up on the rock. Trace the new waterline with the crayon or marker, all the way around the rock.

D. Continue this process, dipping the rock about one inch deeper each time. Do this until you can go no farther.

E. Now, put the rock on the floor, and look at it from above. Can you see how each crayon or marker line connects the parts of the rock that are the same height? These are isolines. Using a pencil, copy the pattern you see looking down on the rock onto to your piece of paper. Next, label each of your isolines from the outside in. The outside line should be marked "1 inch," the next line "2 inches," and so on.

You have just drawn a map of the top of the rock using isolines.

Apply the Skill

The map on this page shows isolines of a region around the city of Lima, Peru. Use the map to visualize the shape of the land.

① **Remember that isolines connect places of equal elevation.** Just like the isolines you made on the rock, the isolines on this map connect places of equal elevation. The lines are numbered to show their elevation. What is the lowest elevation shown on the map? What is the highest elevation?

② **Use the isolines to get useful information from the map.** Remember that where the land is steep, isolines are close together. Where the land is flatter, isolines are farther apart. As you head east from Lima, does the elevation increase or decrease? Now sketch a side view of the map. What is the highest point? What is the lowest? How can you tell?

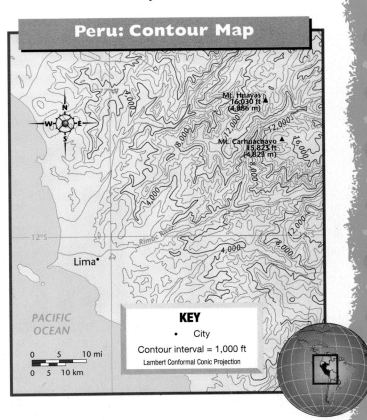

Peru: Contour Map

Mt. Huayas
16,030 ft
(4,886 m)

Mt. Carhuacbayo
15,823 ft
(4,823 m)

Rímac River

Lima

12°S

77°W

PACIFIC OCEAN

0   5   10 mi
0   5   10 km

KEY
• City
Contour interval = 1,000 ft
Lambert Conformal Conic Projection

Chile

A GROWING ECONOMY BASED ON AGRICULTURE

BEFORE YOU READ

Reach Into Your Background

Do you like eating fresh fruit in summer? What if you could have fresh, juicy strawberries and peaches in the middle of winter? Think of ways to make this possible.

Questions to Explore

1. How does Chile's location affect the crops it grows?
2. How does producing more crops help Chile?

Key Terms
pesticide

Key Places
Santiago
Andes
Atacama Desert

▼ Maracas are normally used to play music.

It was a fairly quiet day at the airport of Santiago (san tee AH goh), the capital of Chile. Two passengers from Venezuela stepped off a plane. They had their carry-on luggage and a couple of maracas. A maraca is a musical instrument that sounds like a rattle. It is made from a hollow gourd filled with dried-out seeds or pebbles.

There is nothing very surprising about seeing maracas in South America. They are used in many orchestras and bands to play Latin music. So why was the customs officer staring at them suspiciously? Before the travelers had time to pass through customs, the officer grabbed the maracas and X-rayed them. Then he broke them open. Just as he thought, they did not contain dried-up seeds or pebbles. They were full of new seeds that were good for planting.

Life in Chile

Chile may be the only country in the world that inspects maracas brought into its borders. In recent years, Chile's agriculture has been booming. Chile makes millions of dollars a year by exporting peaches, grapes, cherries, and other

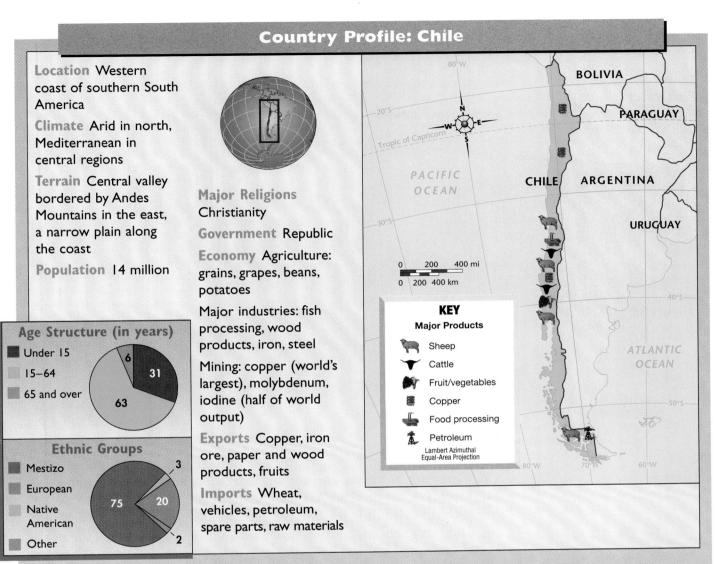

Country Profile: Chile

Location Western coast of southern South America

Climate Arid in north, Mediterranean in central regions

Terrain Central valley bordered by Andes Mountains in the east, a narrow plain along the coast

Population 14 million

Major Religions Christianity

Government Republic

Economy Agriculture: grains, grapes, beans, potatoes

Major industries: fish processing, wood products, iron, steel

Mining: copper (world's largest), molybdenum, iodine (half of world output)

Exports Copper, iron ore, paper and wood products, fruits

Imports Wheat, vehicles, petroleum, spare parts, raw materials

Age Structure (in years)
- Under 15
- 15–64
- 65 and over

6
31
63

Ethnic Groups
- Mestizo
- European
- Native American
- Other

3
75
20
2

KEY
Major Products
- Sheep
- Cattle
- Fruit/vegetables
- Copper
- Food processing
- Petroleum

Lambert Azimuthal Equal-Area Projection

Map Study This map shows the major products of each region in Chile. Most of Chile's people live in its central valley. Read the description of the climate and terrain in central Chile. **Place** How do the climate and terrain of central Chile make it a good region for farming? **Movement** The Andes Mountains run down the whole length of Chile. What do you think would be the easiest way to ship Chile's products out of the country?

fruits and vegetables. Their country is protected by the Andes mountains, so some of the insect pests and animal diseases that plague other countries never reach Chile. That is why the government is so concerned about what enters now. Protecting Chile's crops is very important. No plant or animal matter from foreign places is allowed because it might bring disease to the crops.

The Geography of Chile Look at the physical map of Latin America in the Activity Atlas at the front of your book. Find the Andes Mountains. They run down the whole length of this long country like a giant spine. Chile is narrow. On average, it is about 100 miles (161 km) wide. If Chile were flat, it would take less than two hours to drive

The Atacama Desert looks barren and empty compared to Cerro Santa Lucia, a park in Santiago. But they are both in Chile. **Critical Thinking** What factors do you think make it possible for one country to have such different climates?

LINKS TO LANGUAGE ARTS

What Makes a Poem? What do you think is a proper topic for a poem? Chilean poet Pablo Neruda was willing to write a poem about anything. He wrote many poems about everyday subjects, like dusty wheels, sweat, and his socks. He even wrote a poem about a person wearing out a pair of shoes. He called it "You Flame Foot!"

across it. However, because of the mountains, it takes much longer. Chile may not be very wide, but it is extremely long. It runs 2,650 miles (4,265 km) down the Pacific Coast. Chile reaches all the way to the tip of South America. It is the longest, narrowest country in the world.

Chile contains an amazing variety of lands and climates. In the north is the Atacama Desert, one of the driest regions in the world. The long central valley near the coast has rolling hills, high grasses, and dense forests. This is the region where most of the people live.

The People of Chile Chile's early Spanish settlers married Native Americans already living there. Today, mestizos make up about 75 percent of the population. Only 3 percent of Chileans are Native Americans.

The lifestyles of Chileans vary from region to region. In the far south, sheep herders in heavy wool sweaters brave the strong winds. Farther north in the central valley, farmers grow wheat, potatoes, sugar beets, corn, tomatoes, and many fruits. In the cities, people in business suits hurry in and out of tall skyscrapers. Few people live in the Atacama Desert of the far north. Not many plants or animals can survive here either. But the desert is rich in copper, so the region is dotted with mines. Chile exports more copper than any country in the world.

A Chilean City A visit to Santiago is unforgettable. Old Spanish buildings stand near gleaming skyscrapers. The city is in the valley of the central plain, so the altitude is low enough to produce mild weather.

The sea makes the air humid. Palm trees grow in the public parks. The snowcapped Andes lie to the east.

The beautiful sights of Santiago are sometimes blocked by a thick layer of smog. Pollution has become so bad that it makes many small children and old people sick. The signs of pollution are everywhere. On a bad day, people wear surgical masks in order to breathe, or they press scarves to their faces. Few mothers bring their babies out on a day like this. If they do, the babies may have to be rushed to the hospital to receive oxygen.

The Problems of Industry How did pollution get to be so bad in Santiago? One cause is the city's location. It is surrounded by the Andes on three sides. The mountains trap the exhaust from vehicles and smoke from factories in the valley. This is especially true during the winter, when there is not much wind.

Another reason for the increase in pollution is the economy. Before the 1980s, Chile's economy depended mostly on its copper exports. Part of the copper industry was owned by the government. The profits went into projects that were supposed to help everyone in the country.

READ ACTIVELY

Connect What cities in the United States have problems with pollution? Which of these cities, like Santiago, are surrounded by mountains?

▼ German architecture can be found in many parts of southern Chile. German immigrants arrived here more than 100 years ago.

In northern Chile, the soil is not very good for farming. Many people here fish for a living. Chile's fishing industry is one of the largest in the world. **Critical Thinking** What difference do you see between people who fish for a living and those who fish for fun?

LINKS ACROSS THE WORLD

Falling Copper Prices Other countries besides Chile suffered when copper prices dropped in the 1980s. Zaire, in Central Africa, paid all its trade bills in 1980, mostly from the money it earned selling copper. By 1990, however, Zaire was heavily in debt because of the fall in copper prices.

In the early 1980s, world copper prices began to drop. The government tried to solve the problem by encouraging industry. The government relaxed the laws that protected the environment from pollution. Government leaders thought that if the laws were too strict, some private industries would not survive. Encouraging private industry did save Chile's economy. It was easier to mine and process copper. Tons of steel, cement, glass, and electronic equipment were made and sold.

The standard of living rose. But so did pollution levels. Also, more people moved to the cities to get jobs in the new industries. More than 80 percent of Chile's people now live in cities.

During the 1990s, Chile's government took action to reduce the problems of pollution in the city. On days when the wind does not blow, industries are shut down. And only a limited number of cars may enter the city. Further, the government may also require new cars to have special exhaust systems that do not produce much pollution. No one knows how well these solutions will work. But most Chileans are hoping for a cleaner and healthier future.

Chile's Agricultural Revolution

The drop in copper prices in the early 1980s made it clear that Chile could not depend on copper to survive. Chile decided that one way to improve the economy was to sell more crops.

Pest-Free Produce   Chile's fruits and vegetables are free of many common plant pests. As a result, these products are welcome in many other countries. To supply the demands of these countries, about 15 percent of Chile's people farm. Chilean workers are also employed at packing plants for fruits and vegetables. Modern farming methods help grow even more crops.

By the late 1980s, agriculture was especially important for Chile. It had become a billion dollar industry, providing jobs for about 900,000 Chileans. Chile shipped wheat, potatoes, sugar beets, corn, grapes, melons, apples, peaches, apricots, cherries, and other fruits and vegetables around the world.

The United States, Japan, and Europe are an especially good market for Chilean produce from October through May. These months are winter in the Northern Hemisphere, but summer in the Southern Hemisphere. This means that Chile can provide fruits and vegetables to the United States, for example, during the months when American farmers cannot.

Although the Andes mountains protect Chile from many common plant pests and diseases, Chile has some pests of its own. To prevent them from destroying the fruits and vegetables, Chilean farmers use different kinds of pesticides. A **pesticide** (PES tuh syd) is a chemical used to kill insects and stop diseases that can hurt crops. Pesticides have helped farmers to increase crop production. But some people think that the pesticides may have caused certain kinds of illness in young children. As a result, Chilean scientists and farmers are trying to find ways to control pests without using chemicals. They want to make sure that Chilean fruits and vegetables are the tastiest and healthiest that people can buy.

SECTION 3 REVIEW

1. **Define**   pesticide.

2. **Identify**   (a) Santiago, (b) Andes, (c) Atacama Desert.

3. What aspect of Chile's location gives it an advantage in agriculture?

4. How has the growth of agriculture helped Chileans?

Critical Thinking

5. **Expressing Problems Clearly**   Industries can cause pollution, but when industries close down, people lose their jobs. If you were the mayor of an industrial city with a pollution problem, what would you do?

Activity

6. **Writing to Learn**   Like many places around the world, Chile is a popular tourist destination. Think about the reasons why a tourist might like to visit Chile. Describe the country's most interesting features. Present these paragraphs in the form of a tourist brochure.

Venezuela

OIL POWERS THE ECONOMY

Reach Into Your Background

There are some things in life that people can control and others that they cannot. Think of at least one thing in your life that you can control. Think of another thing that is beyond your control.

Questions to Explore

1. How was Venezuela affected by the oil boom?
2. How is Venezuela trying to change its economy for the future?

Key Terms

boom
privatization

Key Places

Caracas
Lake Maracaibo

Welcome to Caracas (kuh RAHK us), population about 3.3 million. The view from a high-rise apartment can be breathtaking. At night, thousands of lights dot the surrounding hills. Below, on the street, fashionable-looking people walk by on their way to dinner or a movie.

Outside, the air is balmy. You won't find much pollution in the air, either. The city is in a valley that runs from east to west. Winds blow through it. They sweep the exhaust of the many cars out of the city.

Why not visit one of the cafes? Or if you're lucky, you might find a party for teenagers going on right in the street. They may be listening to American-style rap music. But the words will be in Spanish. If you have the time, take the Caracas subway. It cost the government millions to build, more than any other subway in the world. You can get almost anywhere in the city on it, and the fare is only about 25 cents.

▼ Many of Venezuela's largest petroleum deposits lie beneath the floor of Lake Maracaibo.

A Land Made Wealthy by Oil

Venezuela's government could pay for the subways because of money it made from the sale of oil. Venezuela has vast supplies of oil. The Country Profile map shows where Venezuela's oil is located. Venezuela's oil has earned millions of dollars on the world market. People migrated from the countryside to work for the oil companies.

Country Profile: Venezuela

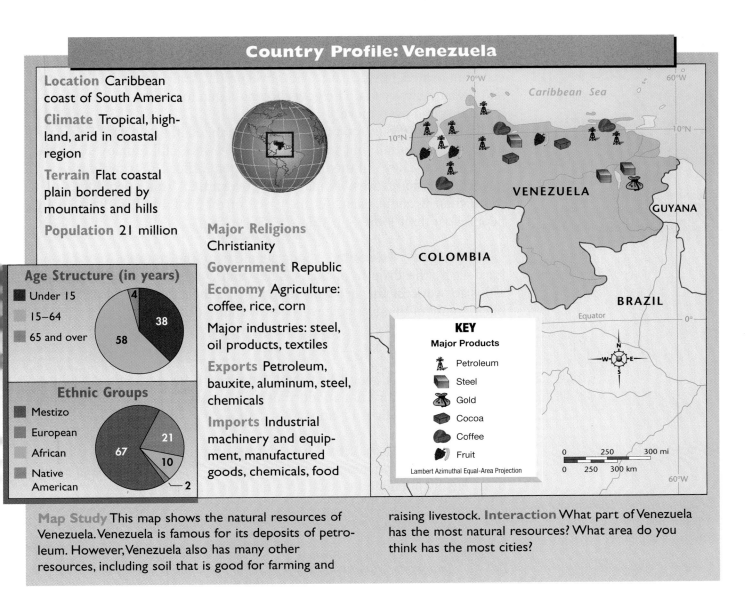

Location Caribbean coast of South America

Climate Tropical, highland, arid in coastal region

Terrain Flat coastal plain bordered by mountains and hills

Population 21 million

Major Religions Christianity

Government Republic

Economy Agriculture: coffee, rice, corn

Major industries: steel, oil products, textiles

Exports Petroleum, bauxite, aluminum, steel, chemicals

Imports Industrial machinery and equipment, manufactured goods, chemicals, food

Age Structure (in years)

- Under 15
- 15–64
- 65 and over

4
38
58

Ethnic Groups

- Mestizo
- European
- African
- Native American

67
21
10
2

KEY
Major Products

- Petroleum
- Steel
- Gold
- Cocoa
- Coffee
- Fruit

Lambert Azimuthal Equal-Area Projection

Map Study This map shows the natural resources of Venezuela. Venezuela is famous for its deposits of petroleum. However, Venezuela also has many other resources, including soil that is good for farming and raising livestock. **Interaction** What part of Venezuela has the most natural resources? What area do you think has the most cities?

They helped maintain the giant oil rigs in Lake Maracaibo. They also worked in oil refineries.

Both the government and individuals own oil companies in Venezuela. They have grown rich mining, processing, and selling oil. By the early 1980s, Venezuela was the richest country in Latin America. Much of the money has gone to Caracas, where most Venezuelans live.

Ups and Downs of Oil Prices Venezuela's oil was discovered about 75 years ago. Since then, Venezuela has pumped about 67 billion barrels of oil. There seemed to be no end to the money that could be made in the oil industry. Except for the Persian Gulf region, Venezuela has the biggest oil reserves in the world.

During the 1970s, the price of oil went up. An oil boom began. A **boom** is a period of increased prosperity during which more of a product is produced and sold. The standard of living of many Venezuelans went up, too. That is when the government started spending huge sums

READ ACTIVELY

Predict Do you think that one resource, such as oil, can support a country forever? Why or why not?

of money. Many people were hired to run government agencies and government-owned businesses. The government built expensive subways and high-quality roads. The government began to borrow money so that it could spend even more.

In the mid-1980s, too much oil was produced in the world. The price of oil started to fall, but millions of people were still employed by the government. They ran the many government offices. Or they worked in government industries. Finally, the government was spending much more than it could earn. As the price of oil continued to drop, many people lost their jobs.

The New Poverty   Poor people from the country were hit the hardest by the drop in oil sales. They had come to Caracas and other cities to work in the growing industries. When the oil industries cut back, many of these people were left without jobs.

Venezuelan Culture

During the oil boom, Venezuela changed from a traditional culture based on agriculture to a modern urban country. Now about 80 percent of the population lives in cities.

A Venezuelan Life   Juan Varderi (hwahn var DEHR ee) is about 28 years old. He is a good example of the new Venezuelan. Juan grew up in a densely populated coastal area north of Caracas.

▼ Caracas is the largest city in Venezuela. It is also the country's capital.

U.S. Petroleum Imports From Venezuela, 1984–1996

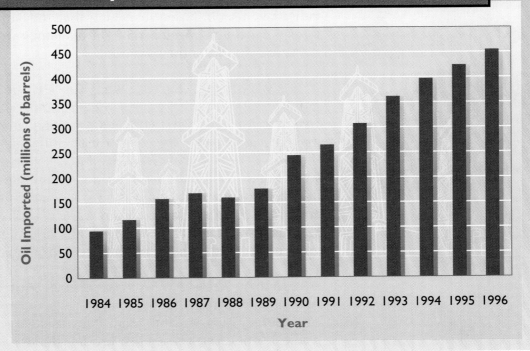

Chart Study The United States has several major petroleum deposits, but still uses more petroleum than it produces. The United States imports petroleum from Canada, Mexico, Nigeria, Saudi Arabia, and Venezuela. **Critical Thinking** When did the United States import the least amount of petroleum from Venezuela? When did it import the most?

Oil Imported (millions of barrels)

500
450
400
350
300
250
200
150
100
50
0

1984 1985 1986 1987 1988 1989 1990 1991 1992 1993 1994 1995 1996

Year

Juan's grandfather raised sheep on a ranch east of Lake Maracaibo. He made a fairly good living selling wool and meat to people in Caracas. He fully expected that his son, Juan's father, would work with him, so he never encouraged him to go to school. But in the 1970s, Juan's father was lured by the oil industry, which was beginning to boom.

Varderi's father left the ranch at age 16. He went to work on an oil rig that was owned by the government. By the time Juan was born, the family was living in Caracas in a small apartment. They had a radio but no telephone. Juan Varderi grew up playing baseball on the streets of Caracas. Baseball is very popular in Venezuela.

By the early 1980s, Juan's father was making more money. The family bought a television. Televisions had become popular. Varderi remembers those years as the most exciting time of his life.

❝There were American programs you could watch on television, dubbed into Spanish. My friends and I paid attention to the clothes that the Americans wore. We tried to dress like them. We thought their music was the coolest in the world. We used to watch rock videos and try to learn the words of songs. In the early 1980s, we thought we could live just like rich Americans seemed to live. We didn't understand it was only taking place on TV. We didn't know what was going to happen to us in just a few years.❞

LINKS ACROSS THE WORLD

Germany in Venezuela In 1843, the Venezuelan government recruited almost 400 Germans to live in the mountains west of Caracas. For over 100 years their colony, Colonia Tovar, was isolated. The people spoke German, ate German food, and married only Germans. The town is still so different from the rest of the country that it deserves its nickname, "Germany in Venezuela."

Ask Questions If you had a chance to meet Juan Varderi, what questions would you ask? What questions do you think that Juan would ask you?

A few years later, when Juan Varderi turned 15, oil prices fell. His father lost his job. Three years after that, the family was in danger of losing its apartment. Varderi thought his family would have to move. But his father found another solution.

Government Businesses Go Public The solution Juan's father found lay in a new government policy of privatization. **Privatization** (pry vuh tih ZAY shun) occurs when the government sells its industries to individuals or private companies. In the late 1980s and the 1990s, the government decided to sell some of its businesses to private corporations. It hoped that the corporations would make big profits. The profits would help workers. When the government turned over an oil refinery to a private company, Varderi's father applied for a job there. He was hired. The salary was less than he had earned working for the government, but it was enough to keep his family in their apartment.

Finding Other Ways to Make Money Venezuela started new industries in an attempt to make its economy less dependent on oil. The country is producing goods such as steel, gold, cocoa, coffee, and tropical fruits. Varderi's oldest brother, Julio, received money from the government to start a small fruit orchard. This year he made enough money to support his family and help pay for a ticket for Juan to visit New York City. It was a trip Juan had always dreamed of.

Planting Corn in Venezuela

The Piaroa, one of Venezuela's Native American groups, farm on land they have cleared in Amazonas Territory. **Critical Thinking** What details from this photograph provide clues that these men are planting?

CONTRA LA GUERRA

Many Venezuelans like to wear fashions from the United States, especially jeans. They also like to meet each other in plazas, or public squares. In fact, addresses in Caracas are given by plazas and corners, not streets.

A Changed Venezuela   Whatever Venezuela's economic fortune is, one thing is certain. The oil boom brought Venezuela into the modern world. When televisions, cellular phones, and other conveniences came into Venezuelan homes, life changed permanently. Juan Varderi dreams of having these things again in the future. And he is willing to work as hard as necessary to get them.

SECTION 4 REVIEW

1. **Define** (a) boom, (b) privatization.

2. **Identify** (a) Caracas, (b) Lake Maracaibo.

3. (a) What happened to many Venezuelans during the oil boom? (b) What happened to them after?

4. Explain how Venezuela is trying to improve its economy.

Critical Thinking

5. **Drawing Conclusions** (a) Why did the drop in oil prices affect Venezuela so much? (b) What do you think Venezuela should do to avoid economic problems in the future?

Activity

6. **Writing Activity** Juan Varderi learned about United States culture from television programs. Describe America as shown on television.

Review and Activities

Reviewing Main Ideas

1. Why are the rain forests so important for the environment?
2. In what ways does the Brazilian economy depend upon the rain forest?
3. (a) What challenges does life on the altiplano present?
   (b) How do the people who live there overcome these challenges?
4. Why are many Quechua and Aymara moving to the cities of Peru?
5. Why does Chile have such strict customs laws?
6. (a) How does geography contribute to Chile's pollution problem?
   (b) How does it contribute to its agricultural boom?
7. What type of lifestyle changes did many Venezuelans make during the oil boom of the 1970s?
8. Why is it important for Venezuela to develop new ways to boost its economy?

Reviewing Key Terms

Use each key term below in a sentence that shows the meaning of the term.

1. canopy
2. photosynthesis
3. altiplano
4. sierra
5. montaña
6. tundra
7. pesticide
8. boom
9. privatization

Critical Thinking

1. **Making Comparisons** In what ways have Chile's and Venezuela's economic histories been similar? How have they differed?
2. **Recognizing Cause and Effect** How do you think the coming of modern conveniences like electricity will change life for the Quechua?

Graphic Organizer

Copy the chart onto a piece of paper. Then fill in the empty boxes to complete the chart.

	Brazil	Peru	Chile	Venezuela
Important exports				
Major cities				

Map Activity

For each place listed below, write the letter from the map that shows its location.

1. Amazon River
2. Rio de Janeiro
3. Brasília
4. Cuzco
5. Lake Titicaca
6. Santiago
7. Andes
8. Caracas
9. Orinoco River

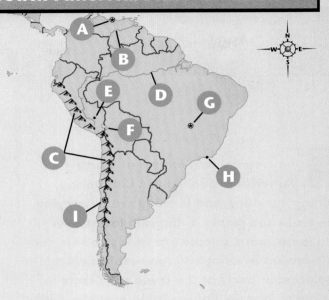

South America: Place Location

Writing Activity

Writing a Test
Write your own test about the economies of Chile and Venezuela. You may include multiple choice, true/false, fill in the blank, and essay questions on your test. Ask questions about how natural resources are important in each country's economy. Ask about benefits and problems that have affected each economy. Write an answer key to go with your test. Then trade tests with a partner. Take each other's tests. How did you do?

Internet Activity
Use a search engine to find the site **Rainforest Action Network.** Click on **Kid's Corner.** Here you can learn about life in the rain forest, issues of concern, and action that you can take. After exploring, click the BACK button on your browser. Click on **Rainforest Information.** Then click on **Take a Rainforest Quiz** to take a fun, on-line quiz.

Skills Review

Turn to the Skill Activity.

Review the steps for making a contour map. Then answer the following: (a) What are isolines? (b) Explain in your own words how you can use isolines to get useful information from a map.

How Am I Doing?

Answer these questions to help you check your progress.

1. Can I explain how changes in Brazil's rain forests affect the rest of the world?
2. Do I understand how geography has affected the lifestyles of Native Americans in Peru?
3. Can I explain why agriculture is important to Chile's economy?
4. Do I understand how the oil boom affected Venezuela's economy?
5. What information from this chapter can I use in my book project?

Rain Forest Resources

The tropical rain forests of South America are in danger. Lumbering, mining, ranching, and farming are destroying the trees and plants of the rain forests. As you know, some people are trying to save the rain forests by using the renewable, or replaceable, parts of the trees and plants in products for sale. For example, cashews and brazil nuts from rain forest trees can be harvested without harming the trees themselves. Oils from rain forest plants and nuts can be used in lotions and shampoos. If people can make money from a rain forest without cutting or burning it, people will have reasons to preserve the forests.

Purpose

In this activity, you will invent a new rain forest product. As you work on this activity, you will discover how rain forest products can be used without destroying rain forest resources.

Invent a Product

Think of a product that can be made with a renewable rain forest resource. Rain forest nuts are used in candy, ice cream, and cookies. Natural rubber from rubber trees is used to make bath toys. Use encyclopedias and other references to find out about the fruits of the assai tree, the oil of the babacu tree, and the resin of the copaiba tree. Think of something from the rain forest that many people need. Once you decide on your product, give it a name that people will remember.

Design a Package

When you have a product in mind, decide how it should look in a store. Should it come in a bag, a box, a can, or a bottle? Design the package, including art work and a product description.

Set a Price

Do some research to find out what products like yours cost. Visit or call a store. Then decide on the price for your product that is in the range of similar products. Put the price on your package.

Figure Your Costs

Now figure out how much money is needed to make your product. Assume that your costs are half of the selling price. For example, if your selling price is $6.50, then your manufacturing cost is $3.25. Divide your total manufacturing cost into the categories listed below.

- 50 percent for labor
- 25 percent for materials
- 10 percent for transportation
- 10 percent for advertising
- 5 percent for taxes

Then make a circle graph showing the percentage and dollar amount for each type of expense.

Make a Poster

Make a poster showing the layers of rain forest life: herb layer, shrub layer, understory, canopy, and emergent layer. Use encyclopedias and reference books such as *Usborne Science and Experiments: Ecology* (Usborne Publishing, 1988). Show the different kinds of creatures that live at each level and explain how they survive.

Links to Other Subjects

Designing a package
for a new product .... **Art**

Making a circle graph .... **Math**

Doing research on the
layers of the rain forest .... **Science**

Writing a script .... **Language Arts**

Writing a song .... **Music**

Create a Commercial

You can make a commercial to advertise your rain forest product. Use the poster you made as a prop for your commercial. Write a short script that explains why it is important to protect rain forests and how your product helps in that effort. Write and perform an original jingle or music for the commercial. You can produce your commercial on computer or shoot it with a video camera. Or, you can perform your commercial for the rest of the class. Remember that your commercial should make people want to buy your product.

ANALYSIS AND CONCLUSION

Write a summary that describes the process you used to create your product. Be sure to answer the following questions in your summary.

1. What did you learn about using rain forest resources?

2. How can rain forest resources be used without destroying them?

3. Do you think it is possible for people to protect rain forests by using their renewable resources?

Question Book

BY PABLO NERUDA

Reach Into Your Background

Do you pay close attention to the world around you? Describe a plant, a building, or a person that you saw on your way to school today. Remember as many details as you can. If you saw a tree, try to remember the shape of its leaves and whether its roots were visible above the ground. If you saw a person, try to remember what the person was wearing and how old the person seemed to be.

Many of Pablo Neruda's poems help readers pay more attention to the world around them. Neruda, who lived in Chile, often wrote about subjects that people take for granted. The following poem is from a book of Neruda's poetry called *Question Book*.

Questions to Explore

1. How does this poem help you look more closely at the changes of the seasons?
2. Because Chile is in the Southern Hemisphere, its seasons are the reverse of the seasons in the United States. Does knowing this change your understanding of the poem? Why or why not?

Ask Questions If you were going to write a poem of questions, what questions would you ask?

LXXII

Si todos los ríos son dulces
de dónde saca sal el mar?

Cómo saben las estaciones
que deben cambiar de camisa?

Por qué tan lentas en invierno
y tan palpitantes después?

Y cómo saben las raíces
que deben subir a la luz?

Y luego saludar al aire
con tantas flores y colores?

Siempre es la misma
    primavera
la que repite su papel?

LXXII

If all rivers are sweet
where does the sea get its salt?

How do the seasons discover
it's time to change shirts?

Why are winters so slow
and the aftermaths, volatile?

How do the roots know
they must climb toward the light?

And then greet the air
with such colors and flowers?

Is it always the same spring,
repeating the same role?

◄▲ These photos show
winter and summer in
Chile's Patagonian Andes.
How can you tell which
season is which?

READ ACTIVELY

Visualize What does a
root look like as it pushes
away from a seed and up
toward the sky?

EXPLORING YOUR READING

Look Back

1. What do all the questions
in this poem have in
common?

Think It Over

2. Seasons don't wear shirts.
What does Neruda mean
when he refers to the seasons changing their shirts?

3. How is spring like an actor
playing a role in a play?

4. Based on this poem, does
Neruda seem to think
that nature is friendly or
unfriendly? Explain your
answer.

Go Beyond

5. How can paying attention
to details around you help
you appreciate nature?

Ideas for Writing: Answer Poem

6. The questions that Neruda
asks all have scientific
explanations. Find out
the scientific answer to
Neruda's questions. Then,
write an answer poem in
response to Neruda's.

LATIN AMERICA
PROJECT POSSIBILITIES

As you study Latin America, you will be reading and thinking about these important questions.

☞ **What are the main physical features of Latin America?**

☞ **What factors have affected cultures in Latin America?**

☞ **Why have many Latin Americans been moving to cities in recent years?**

☞ **What is the relationship of the nations of Latin America with the United States and the world?**

☞ **How has geography influenced the ways in which Latin Americans make a living?**

Doing a project shows what you know! Are you doing this project? Muy bueno!

GEO LEO

Project Menu

The chapters in this book have some answers to these questions. Now it's time for you to find your own answers by doing projects on your own or with a group. Here are some ways to make your own discoveries about Latin America.

A Latin American Concert As you study Latin America, find out about the music of each region. Find out what kinds of instruments people play and what the instruments are made of. Then try to find examples of each kind of music. You might find some in public libraries, which usually have a music collection. Play the music for your class. You might explain how history and geography had an effect on the development of each kind of music. For example, in the Andes, people make a kind of rattle out of llamas' hooves. Talk about the roles of different types of music. For example, merengue is dance music, and reggae often serves as political protest.

From Questions to Careers

INTERPRETER

When people who speak different languages need to talk to each other, they often need an interpreter. An interpreter is someone who speaks both languages and can translate for both people as they talk.

In the United States, most interpreters work for the government. They translate during meetings between U.S. officials and visitors from other countries. Interpreters are especial-ly important when there is an emergency. For example, when a major earthquake struck San Francisco in 1989, interpreters helped Spanish speakers get medical attention and talk to telephone operators.

Interpreters also work for companies doing business in other countries. Large corporations often have a whole team of interpreters.

Many interpreters have a degree in their second language and additional training in interpreting. However, some bilingual people are able to become interpreters for small companies or agencies without training.

Visions of Latin America

Create a diorama showing the effect of geography on the way people live in Latin America. Your diorama can be realistic or it can show a symbol. Work in groups of three or four.

After you finish your diorama, write a short report to explain how the subject of your diorama affects the people of Latin America today. Display the whole set of dioramas with the reports. Invite other students to look at them. You might also display them at parents' night.

Latin America in the News

As you read about Latin America, keep a bulletin board display called *Latin America in the News*. Look in magazines and newspapers for articles that describe life in Latin America. For example, when you study Mexico, you can collect articles about Mexican culture, politics, or economics.

When you have finished your study of Latin America, choose the articles that you want to keep. Make a scrapbook to contain the articles. Display the scrapbook in the school library or resource center.

Explorer's Dictionary

Many languages are spoken in Latin America. As you work on this book, create a dictionary of important terms. Use a foreign-language dictionary to translate your terms into Spanish or another Latin American language.

Illustrate your dictionary with drawings or pictures cut out from magazines or travel brochures. Bind the pages together with yarn or staples. Display your dictionary so other students can use it.

Reference

TABLE OF CONTENTS

MAP AND Handbook GLOBE

This Map and Globe Handbook is designed to help you develop some of the skills you need to be a world explorer. These can help you whether you explore from the top of an elephant in India or from a computer at school.

You can use the information in this handbook to improve your map and globe skills. But the best way to sharpen your skills is to practice. The more you practice, the better you'll get.

GEO CLEO and GEO LEO

Table of Contents

Five Themes of Geography

Studying the geography of the entire world can be a huge task. You can make that task easier by using the five themes of geography: location, place, human-environment interaction, movement, and regions. The themes are tools you can use to organize information and to answer the where, why, and how of geography.

1 Location answers the question, "Where is it?" You can think of the location of a continent or a country as its address. You might give an absolute location such as "22 South Lake Street" or "40°N and 80°W." You might also use a relative address, telling where one place is by referring to another place. "Between school and the mall" and "eight miles east of Pleasant City" are examples of relative locations.

2 Place identifies the natural and human features that make one place different from every other place. You can identify a specific place by its landforms, climate, plants, animals, people, or cultures. You might even think of place as a geographic signature. Use the signature to help you understand the natural and human features that make one place different from every other place.

1. Location
Chicago, Illinois, occupies one location on the Earth. No other place has exactly the same absolute location.

2. Place
Ancient cultures in Egypt built distinctive pyramids. Use the theme of place to help you remember features that exist only in Egypt.

3 Human-Environment Interaction focuses on the relationship between people and the environment. As people live in an area, they often begin to make changes to it, usually to make their lives easier. For example, they might build a dam to control flooding during rainy seasons. Also, the environment can affect how people live, work, dress, travel, and communicate.

4 Movement answers the question "How do people, goods, and ideas move from place to place?" Remember that, often, what happens in one place can affect what happens in another. Use the theme of movement to help you trace the spread of goods, people, and ideas from one location to the next.

5 Region is the last geographic theme. A region is a group of places that share common features. Geographers divide the world into many types of regions. For example, countries, states, and cities are political regions. The people in these places live under the same type of government. Other features can be used to define regions. Places that have the same climate belong to a particular climate region. Places that share the same culture belong to a cultural region. The same place can be found in more than one region. The state of Hawaii is in the political region of the United States. Because it has a tropical climate, Hawaii is also part of a tropical climate region.

PRACTICE YOUR WORLD EXPLORER SKILLS

1. What is the absolute location of your school? What is one way to describe its relative location?

2. What might be a "geographic signature" of the town or city you live in?

3. Give an example of human-environment interaction where you live.

4. Name at least one thing that comes into your town or city and one that goes out. How is each moved? Where does it come from? Where does it go?

5. What are several regions you think your town or city belongs in?

3. Human-Environment Interaction
Peruvians have changed steep mountain slopes into terraces suitable for farming. Think how this environment looked before people made changes.

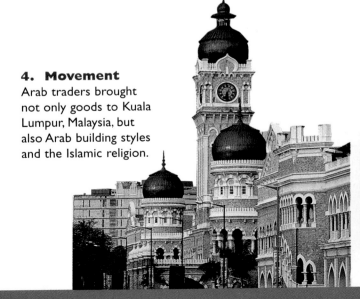

4. Movement
Arab traders brought not only goods to Kuala Lumpur, Malaysia, but also Arab building styles and the Islamic religion.

5. Regions
Wheat farming is an important activity in Kansas. This means that Kansas is part of a farming region.

Understanding Movements of the Earth

Planet Earth is part of our solar system. The Earth revolves around the sun in a nearly circular path called an orbit. A revolution, or one complete orbit around the sun, takes 365 1/4 days, or a year. As the Earth revolves around the sun, it is also spinning around in space. This movement is called a rotation. The Earth rotates on its axis—an invisible line through the center of the Earth from the North Pole to the South Pole. The Earth makes one full rotation about every 24 hours. As the Earth rotates, it is daytime on the side facing the sun. It is night on the side away from the sun.

The Earth's axis is tilted at an angle. Because of this tilt, sunlight strikes different parts of the Earth at certain points in the year, creating different seasons.

Earth's Revolution and the Seasons

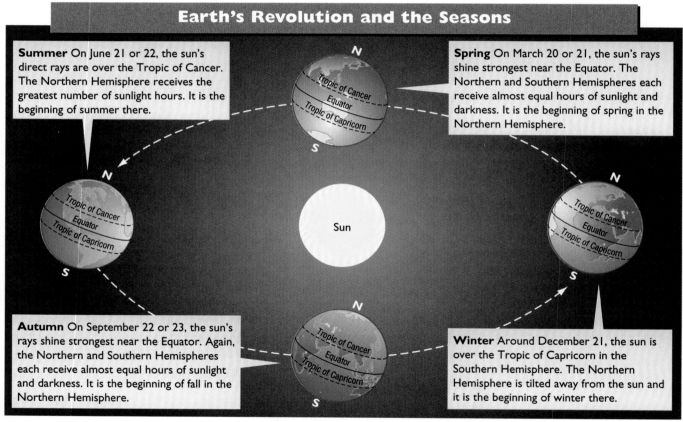

Summer On June 21 or 22, the sun's direct rays are over the Tropic of Cancer. The Northern Hemisphere receives the greatest number of sunlight hours. It is the beginning of summer there.

Spring On March 20 or 21, the sun's rays shine strongest near the Equator. The Northern and Southern Hemispheres each receive almost equal hours of sunlight and darkness. It is the beginning of spring in the Northern Hemisphere.

Autumn On September 22 or 23, the sun's rays shine strongest near the Equator. Again, the Northern and Southern Hemispheres each receive almost equal hours of sunlight and darkness. It is the beginning of fall in the Northern Hemisphere.

Winter Around December 21, the sun is over the Tropic of Capricorn in the Southern Hemisphere. The Northern Hemisphere is tilted away from the sun and it is the beginning of winter there.

▲ **Location** This diagram shows how the Earth's tilt and orbit around the sun combine to create the seasons. Remember, in the Southern Hemisphere the seasons are reversed.

PRACTICE YOUR WORLD EXPLORER SKILLS

1 What causes the seasons in the Northern Hemisphere to be the opposite of those in the Southern Hemisphere?

2 During which two months of the year do the Northern and Southern Hemispheres have about equal hours of daylight and darkness?

Maps and Globes Represent the Earth

Globes

A globe is a scale model of the Earth. It shows the actual shapes, sizes, and locations of all the Earth's landmasses and bodies of water. Features on the surface of the Earth are drawn to scale on a globe. This means a smaller unit of measure on the globe stands for a larger unit of measure on the Earth.

Because a globe is made in the true shape of the Earth, it offers these advantages for studying the Earth.

- The shape of all land and water bodies are accurate.
- Compass directions from one point to any other point are correct.
- The distance from one location to another is always accurately represented.

However, a globe presents some disadvantages for studying the Earth. Because a globe shows the entire Earth, it cannot show small areas in great detail. Also, a globe is not easily folded and carried from one place to another. For these reasons, geographers often use maps to learn about the Earth.

Maps

A map is a drawing or representation, on a flat surface, of a region. A map can show details too small to be seen on a globe. Floor plans, mall directories, and road maps are among the maps we use most often.

While maps solve some of the problems posed by globes, they have some disadvantages of their own. Maps flatten the real round world. Mapmakers cut, stretch, push, and pull some parts of the Earth to get it all flat on paper. As a result, some locations may be distorted. That is, their size, shape, and relative location may not be accurate. For example, on most maps of the entire world, the size and shape of the Antarctic and Arctic regions are not accurate.

PRACTICE YOUR WORLD EXPLORER SKILLS

1. What is the main difference between a globe and a map?

2. What is one advantage of using a globe instead of a map?

Global Gores

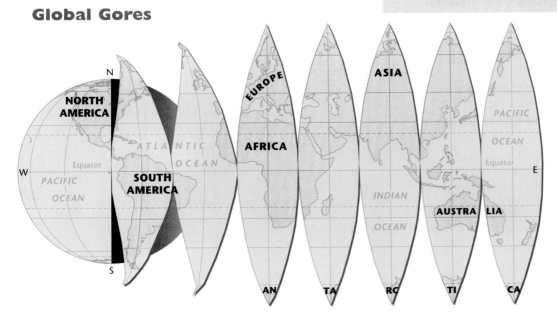

◀ **Location**
When mapmakers flatten the surface of the Earth, curves become straight lines. As a result, size, shape, and distance are distorted.

Locating Places on a Map or a Globe

The Hemispheres

Another name for a round ball like a globe is a sphere. The Equator, an imaginary line halfway between the North and South Poles, divides the globe into two hemispheres. (The prefix *hemi* means "half.") Land and water south of the Equator are in the Southern Hemisphere. Land and water north of the Equator are in the Northern Hemisphere.

Mapmakers sometimes divide the globe along an imaginary line that runs from North Pole to South Pole. This line, called the Prime Meridian, divides the globe into the Eastern and Western Hemispheres.

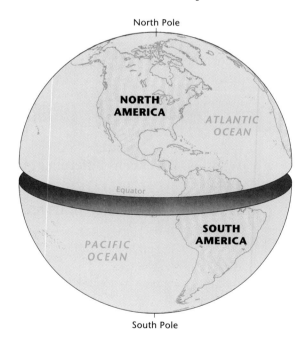

Southern Hemisphere

▲ The Equator divides the Northern Hemisphere from the Southern Hemisphere.

Western Hemisphere   **Eastern Hemisphere**

▲ The Prime Meridian divides the Eastern Hemisphere from the Western Hemisphere.

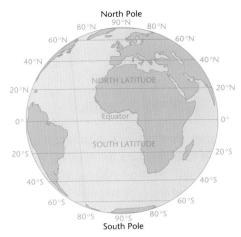

Parallels of Latitude

The Equator, at 0° latitude, is the starting place for measuring latitude or distances north and south. Most globes do not show every parallel of latitude. They may show every 10, 20, or even 30 degrees.

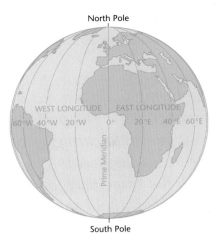

Meridians of Longitude

The Prime Meridian, at 0° longitude, runs from pole to pole through Greenwich, England. It is the starting place for measuring longitude or distances east and west. Each meridian of longitude meets its opposite longitude at the North and South Poles.

The Global Grid

Two sets of lines cover most globes. One set of lines runs parallel to the Equator. These lines, including the Equator, are called *parallels of latitude*. They are measured in degrees (°). One degree of latitude represents a distance of about 70 miles (112 km). The Equator has a location of 0°. The other parallels of latitude tell the direction and distance from the Equator to another location.

The second set of lines runs north and south. These lines are called *meridians of longitude*. Meridians show the degrees of longitude east or west of the Prime Meridian, which is located at 0°. A meridian of longitude tells the direction and distance from the Prime Meridian to another location. Unlike parallels, meridians are not the same distance apart everywhere on the globe.

Together the pattern of parallels of latitude and meridians of longitude is called the global grid. Using the lines of latitude and longitude, you can locate any place on Earth. For example, the location of 30° north latitude and 90° west longitude is usually written as 30°N, 90°W. Only one place on Earth has these coordinates—the city of New Orleans, in the state of Louisiana.

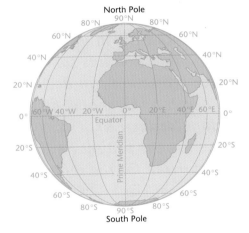

The Global Grid

By using lines of latitude and longitude, you can give the absolute location of any place on the Earth.

1. Which continents lie completely in the Northern Hemisphere? The Western Hemisphere?

2. Is there land or water at 20°S latitude and the Prime Meridian? At the Equator and 60°W longitude?

Map Projections

magine trying to flatten out a complete orange peel. The peel would split. The shape would change. You would have to cut the peel to get it to lie flat. In much the same way, maps cannot show the correct size and shape of every landmass or body of water on the Earth's curved surface. Maps shrink some places and stretch others. This shrinking and stretching is called distortion—*a change made to a shape.*

To make up for this disadvantage, mapmakers use different map projections. Each map projection is a way of showing the round Earth on flat paper. Each type of projection has some distortion. No one projection can accurately show the correct area, shape, distance, and direction for the Earth's surface. Mapmakers use the projection that has the least distortion for the information they are studying.

Same-Shape Maps

Some map projections can accurately show the shapes of landmasses. However, these projections often greatly distort the size of landmasses as well as the distance between them.

One of the most common same-shape maps is a Mercator projection, named for the mapmaker who invented it. The Mercator projection accurately shows shape and direction, but it distorts distance and size. In this projection, the northern and southern areas of the globe appear stretched more than areas near the Equator. Because the projection shows true directions, ships' navigators use it to chart a straight line course between two ports.

Mercator Projection

Equal-Area Maps

Some map projections can show the correct size of landmasses. Maps that use these projections are called equal-area maps. In order to show the correct size of landmasses, these maps usually distort shapes. The distortion is usually greater at the edges of the map and less at the center.

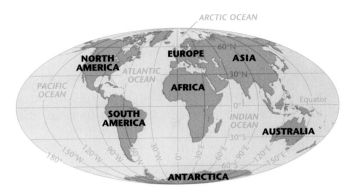

Equal-Area Projection

Robinson Maps

Many of the maps in this book use the Robinson projection. This is a compromise between the Mercator and equal-area projections. It gives a useful overall picture of the world. The Robinson projection keeps the size and shape relationships of most continents and oceans but does distort size of the polar regions.

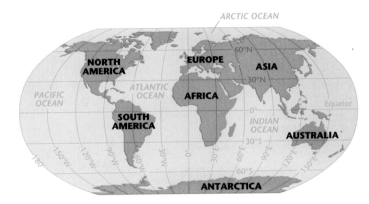

Robinson Projection

Azimuthal Maps

Another kind of projection shows true compass direction. Maps that use this projection are called azimuthal maps. Such maps are easy to recognize—they are usually circular. Azimuthal maps are often used to show the areas of the North and South Poles. However, azimuthal maps distort scale, area, and shape.

WORLD EXPLORER

1 What feature is distorted on an equal-area map?

2 Would you use a Mercator projection to find the exact distance between two locations? Tell why or why not.

3 Which would be a better choice for studying the Antarctic—an azimuthal projection or a Robinson projection? Explain.

Azimuthal Projection

Parts of a Map

Mapmakers provide several clues to help you understand the information on a map. As an explorer, it is your job to read and interpret these clues.

Compass
Many maps show north at the top of the map. One way to show direction on a map is to use an arrow that points north. There may be an N shown with the arrow. Many maps give more information about direction by displaying a compass showing the directions, north, east, south, and west. The letters N, E, S, and W are placed to indicate these directions.

Title
The title of a map is the most basic clue. It signals what kinds of information you are likely to find on the map. A map titled *West Africa: Population Density* will be most useful for locating information about where people live in West Africa.

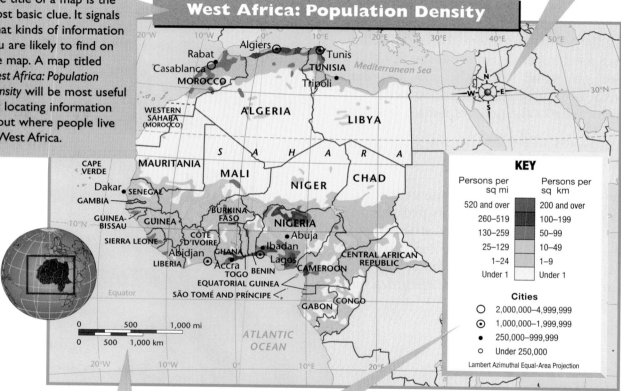

West Africa: Population Density

KEY

Persons per sq mi	Persons per sq km
520 and over	200 and over
260–519	100–199
130–259	50–99
25–129	10–49
1–24	1–9
Under 1	Under 1

Cities
- ⃝ 2,000,000–4,999,999
- ⊙ 1,000,000–1,999,999
- • 250,000–999,999
- ○ Under 250,000

Lambert Azimuthal Equal-Area Projection

Scale
A map scale helps you find the actual distances between points shown on the map. You can measure the distance between any two points on the map, compare them to the scale, and find out the actual distance between the points. Most map scales show distances in both miles and kilometers.

Key
Often a map has a key, or legend, that shows the symbols used on the map and what each one means. On some maps, color is used as a symbol. On those maps, the key also tells the meaning of each color.

PRACTICE YOUR WORLD EXPLORER SKILLS

1. What part of a map tells you what the map is about?

2. Where on the map should you look to find out the meaning of this symbol? •

3. What part of the map can you use to find the distance between two cities?

Comparing Maps of Different Scale

ere are three maps drawn to three different scales. The first map shows Moscow's location in the northeastern portion of Russia. This map shows the greatest area—a large section of northern Europe. It has the smallest scale (1 inch = about 900 miles) and shows the fewest details. This map can tell you what direction to travel to reach Moscow from Finland.

Find the red box on Map 1. It shows the whole area covered by Map 2. Study Map 2. It gives a closer look at the city of Moscow. It shows the features around the city, the city's boundary, and the general shape of the city. This map can help you find your way from the airport to the center of town.

Now find the red box on Map 2. This box shows the area shown on Map 3. This map moves you closer into the city. Like the zoom on a computer or camera, Map 3 shows the smallest area but has the greatest detail. This map has the largest scale (1 inch = about 0.8 miles). This is the map to use to explore downtown Moscow.

Map 1

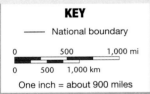

KEY

—— National boundary

0   500   1,000 mi
0   500   1,000 km

One inch = about 900 miles

Map 2

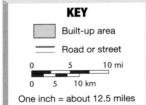

KEY

☐ Built-up area

—— Road or street

0   5   10 mi
0   5   10 km

One inch = about 12.5 miles

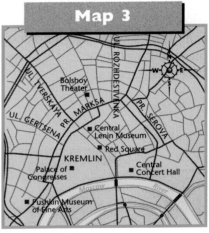

Map 3

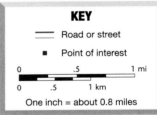

KEY

—— Road or street

■ Point of interest

0   .5   1 mi
0   .5   1 km

One inch = about 0.8 miles

PRACTICE YOUR **WORLD EXPLORER** SKILLS

1. Which map would be best for finding the location of Red Square? Why?

2. Which map best shows Moscow's location relative to Poland? Explain.

3. Which map best shows the area immediately surrounding the city?

Political Maps

Mapmakers create maps to show all kinds of information. The kind of information presented affects the way a map looks. One type of map is called a political map. Its main purpose is to show continents, countries, and divisions within countries such as states or provinces. Usually different colors are used to show different countries or divisions within a country. The colors do not have any special meaning. They are used only to make the map easier to read.

Political maps also show where people have built towns and cities. Symbols can help you tell capital cities from other cities and towns. Even though political maps do not give information that shows what the land looks like, they often include some physical features such as oceans, lakes, and rivers.

Political maps usually have many labels. They give country names, and the names of capital and major cities. Bodies of water such as lakes, rivers, oceans, seas, gulfs, and bays are also labeled.

PRACTICE YOUR WORLD EXPLORER SKILLS

1. What symbol shows the continental boundary?

2. What symbol is used to indicate a capital city? A major city?

3. What kinds of landforms are shown on this map?

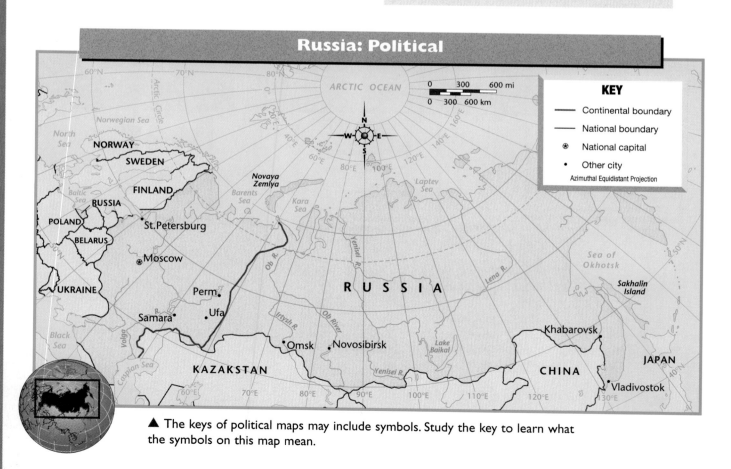

Russia: Political

KEY
— Continental boundary
— National boundary
⊛ National capital
• Other city
Azimuthal Equidistant Projection

▲ The keys of political maps may include symbols. Study the key to learn what the symbols on this map mean.

Physical Maps

Like political maps, physical maps show country labels and labels for capital cities. However, physical maps also show what the land of a region looks like by showing the major physical features such as plains, hills, plateaus, or mountains. Labels give the names of features such as mountain peaks, mountains, plateaus, and river basins.

In order to tell one landform from another, physical maps often show elevation and relief.

Elevation is the height of the land above sea level. Physical maps in this book use color to show elevation. Browns and oranges show higher lands while blues and greens show lands that are at or below sea level.

Relief shows how quickly the land rises or falls. Hills, mountains, and plateaus are shown on relief maps using shades of gray. Level or nearly level land is shown without shading. Darkly shaded areas indicate steeper lands.

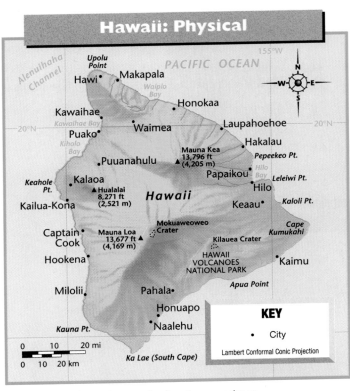

▲ On a physical map, shading is sometimes used to show relief. Use the shading to locate the moutains in Hawaii.

1 How is relief shown on the map to the left?

2 How can you use relief to decide which areas will be the most difficult to climb?

3 What information is given with the name of a mountain peak?

▼ Mauna Kea, an extinct volcano, is the highest peak in the state of Hawaii. Find Mauna Kea on the map.

Special Purpose Maps

As you explore the world, you will encounter many different kinds of special purpose maps. For example, a road map is a special purpose map. The title of each special purpose map tells the purpose and content of the map. Usually a special purpose map highlights only one kind of information. Examples of special purpose maps include land use, population distribution, recreation, transportation, natural resources, or weather.

The key on a special purpose map is very important. Even though a special purpose map shows only one kind of information, it may present many different pieces of data. This data can be shown in symbols, colors, or arrows. In this way, the key acts like a dictionary for the map.

Reading a special purpose map is a skill in itself. Look at the map below. First, try to get an overall sense of what it shows. Then, study the map to identify its main ideas. For example, one main idea of this map is that much of the petroleum production in the region takes place around the Persian Gulf.

PRACTICE YOUR WORLD EXPLORER SKILLS

1. What part of a special purpose map tells what information is contained on the map?

2. What part of a special purpose map acts like a dictionary for the map?

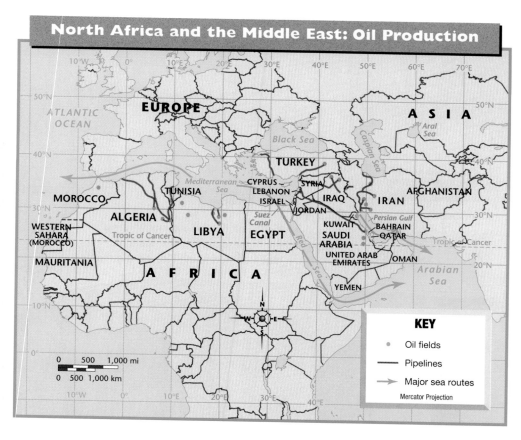

North Africa and the Middle East: Oil Production

KEY
- Oil fields
- Pipelines
- Major sea routes

Mercator Projection

◀ The title on a special purpose map indicates what information can be found on the map. The symbols used on the map are explained in the map's key.

Landforms, Climate Regions, and Natural Vegetation Regions

Maps that show landforms, climate, and vegetation regions are special purpose maps. Unlike the boundary lines on a political map, the boundary lines on these maps do not separate the land into exact divisions. A tropical wet climate gradually changes to a tropical wet and dry climate. A tundra gradually changes to an ice cap. Even though the boundaries between regions may not be exact, the information on these maps can help you understand the region and the lives of people in it.

Landforms

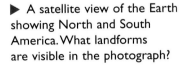

Understanding how people use the land requires an understanding of the shape of the land itself. The four most important landforms are mountains, hills, plateaus, and plains. Human activity in every region in the world is influenced by these landforms.

- **Mountains** are high and steep. Most are wide at the bottom and rise to a narrow peak or ridge. Most geographers classify a mountain as land that rises at least 2,000 feet (610 m) above sea level. A series of mountains is called a mountain range.

- **Hills** rise above surrounding land and have rounded tops. Hills are lower and usually less steep than mountains. The elevation of surrounding land determines whether a landform is called a mountain or a hill.

- A **plateau** is a large, mostly flat area of land that rises above the surrounding land. At least one side of a plateau has a steep slope.

- **Plains** are large areas of flat or gently rolling land. Plains have few changes in elevation. Many plains areas are located along coasts. Others are located in the interior regions of some continents.

▶ A satellite view of the Earth showing North and South America. What landforms are visible in the photograph?

Climate Regions

Another important influence in the ways people live their lives is the climate of their region. Climate is the weather of a given location over a long period of time. Use the descriptions in the table below to help you visualize the climate regions shown on maps.

Climate	Temperatures	Precipitation
Tropical		
Tropical wet	Hot all year round	Heavy all year round
Tropical wet and dry	Hot all year round	Heavy when sun is overhead, dry other times
Dry		
Semiarid	Hot summers, mild to cold winters	Light
Arid	Hot days, cold nights	Very light
Mild		
Mediterranean	Hot summers, cool winters	Dry summers, wet winters
Humid subtropical	Hot summers, cool winters	Year round, heavier in summer than in winter
Marine west coast	Warm summers, cool winters	Year round, heavier in winter than in summer
Continental		
Humid continental	Hot summers, cold winters	Year round, heavier in summer than in winter
Subarctic	Cool summers, cold winters	Light
Polar		
Tundra	Cool summers, very cold winters	Light
Ice Cap	Cold all year round	Light
Highlands	Varies, depending on altitude and direction of prevailing winds	Varies, depending on altitude and direction of prevailing winds

Natural Vegetation Regions

Natural vegetation is the plant life that grows wild without the help of humans. A world vegetation map tells what the vegetation in a place would be if people had not cut down forests or cleared grasslands. The table below provides descriptions of natural vegetation regions shown on maps. Comparing climate and vegetation regions can help you see the close relationship between climate and vegetation.

Vegetation	Description
Tropical rain forest	Tall, close-growing trees forming a canopy over smaller trees, dense growth in general
Deciduous forest	Trees and plants that regularly lose their leaves after each growing season
Mixed forest	Both leaf-losing and cone-bearing trees, no type of tree dominant
Coniferous forest	Cone-bearing trees, evergreen trees and plants
Mediterranean vegetation	Evergreen shrubs and small plants
Tropical savanna	Tall grasses with occasional trees and shrubs
Temperate grassland	Tall grasses with occasional stands of trees
Desert scrub	Low shrubs and bushes, hardy plants
Desert	Little or no vegetation
Tundra	Low shrubs, mosses, lichens; no trees
Ice Cap	No vegetation
Highlands	Varies, depending on altitude and direction of prevailing winds

PRACTICE YOUR WORLD EXPLORER SKILLS

1. How are mountains and hills similar? How are they different?

2. What is the difference between a plateau and a plain?

Atlas

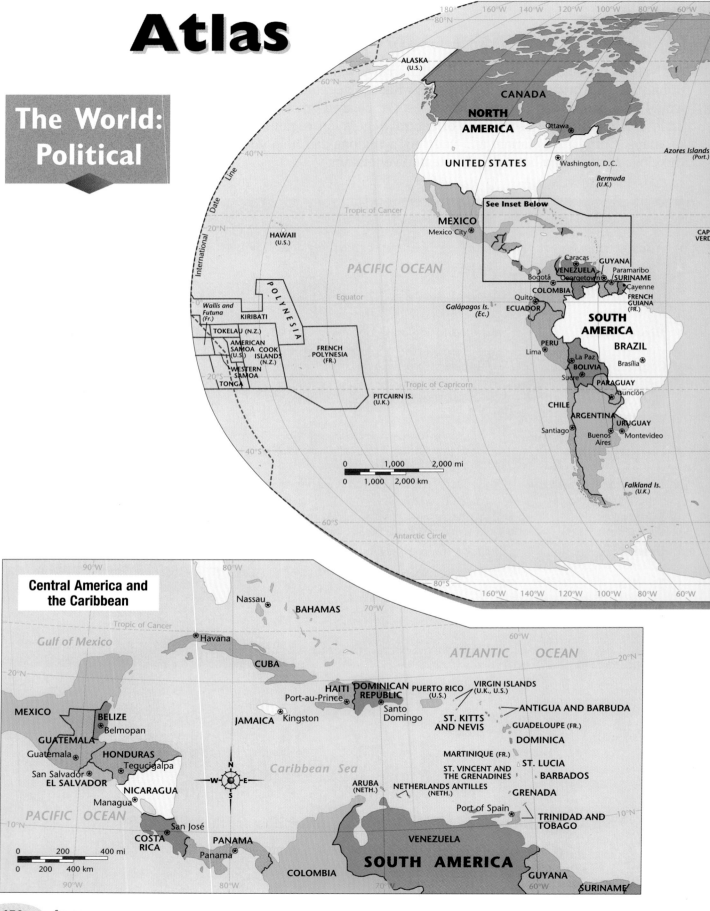

180° 160°W 140°W 120°W 100°W 80°W 60°W
80°N

ALASKA (U.S.)

60°N

CANADA

NORTH AMERICA

Ottawa ⊛

40°N

UNITED STATES

Washington, D.C. ⊛

Azores Islands (Port.)

Bermuda (U.K.)

Tropic of Cancer

See Inset Below

CAPE VERDE

20°N

HAWAII (U.S.)

MEXICO

Mexico City ⊛

PACIFIC OCEAN

Caracas ⊛ GUYANA

VENEZUELA Paramaribo ⊛

Bogotá ⊛ Georgetown ⊛ SURINAME

Equator

Galápagos Is. (Ec.)

COLOMBIA Cayenne ⊛

Quito ⊛ FRENCH GUIANA (FR.)

ECUADOR

SOUTH AMERICA

Wallis and Futuna (Fr.)

KIRIBATI

POLYNESIA

TOKELAU (N.Z.)

AMERICAN SAMOA (U.S) COOK ISLANDS (N.Z.)

FRENCH POLYNESIA (FR.)

PERU **BRAZIL**

Lima ⊛

La Paz ⊛ Brasília ⊛

20°S

WESTERN SAMOA

BOLIVIA

Sucre ⊛

PARAGUAY

TONGA

Tropic of Capricorn

Asunción ⊛

PITCAIRN IS. (U.K.)

CHILE ARGENTINA URUGUAY

40°S

Santiago ⊛ Buenos Aires ⊛ Montevideo ⊛

0   1,000   2,000 mi

0   1,000   2,000 km

Falkland Is. (U.K.)

60°S

Antarctic Circle

80°S

160°W 140°W 120°W 100°W 80°W 60°W

International Date Line

Central America and the Caribbean

90°W 80°W

Nassau ⊛

BAHAMAS 70°W

Tropic of Cancer

Gulf of Mexico

Havana ⊛

ATLANTIC OCEAN

60°W 20°N

20°N

CUBA

HAITI DOMINICAN PUERTO RICO VIRGIN ISLANDS (U.K., U.S.)

Port-au-Prince ⊛ REPUBLIC (U.S.)

MEXICO BELIZE

⊛ Belmopan

Santo ANTIGUA AND BARBUDA

JAMAICA Kingston ⊛ Domingo

ST. KITTS GUADELOUPE (FR.)

GUATEMALA AND NEVIS

Guatemala ⊛ DOMINICA

HONDURAS

San Salvador ⊛ Tegucigalpa ⊛ MARTINIQUE (FR.) ST. LUCIA

EL SALVADOR Caribbean Sea ST. VINCENT AND

NICARAGUA THE GRENADINES BARBADOS

Managua ⊛ ARUBA (NETH.) NETHERLANDS ANTILLES GRENADA

PACIFIC OCEAN (NETH.)

10°N Port of Spain ⊛ TRINIDAD AND

San José ⊛ TOBAGO 10°N

COSTA PANAMA VENEZUELA

0 200 400 mi RICA

0 200 400 km Panama ⊛ GUYANA

SOUTH AMERICA

COLOMBIA SURINAME

90°W 80°W 70°W 60°W

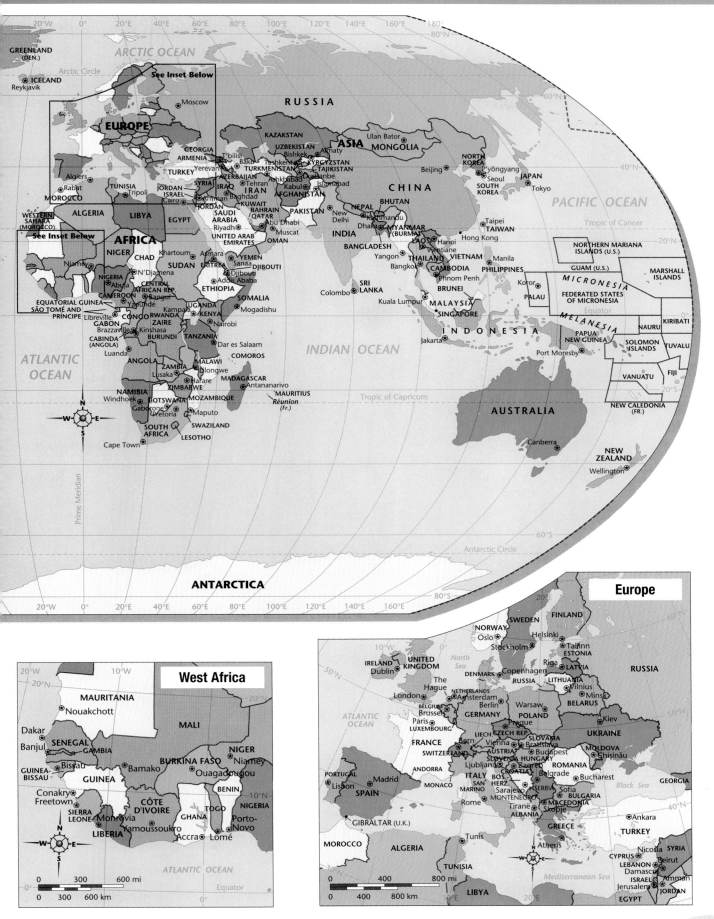

ARCTIC OCEAN

GREENLAND
(DEN.)

ICELAND
Reykjavik

See Inset Below

EUROPE

Moscow

RUSSIA

ASIA

KAZAKSTAN

MONGOLIA
Ulan Bator

UZBEKISTAN
GEORGIA
ARMENIA
TURKEY
Algiers
Rabat
MOROCCO

T'bilisi
Yerevan
Baku
AZERBAIJAN
SYRIA
JORDAN
ISRAEL
Cairo

TUNISIA
Tripoli

TURKMENISTAN
Ashkhabad
Tehran
Baghdad
IRAQ
IRAN

KYRGYZSTAN
TAJIKISTAN
Dushanbe
Kabul
AFGHANISTAN
Islamabad

Bishkek
Almaty
Tashkent

NORTH
KOREA
P'yŏngyang
Seoul
SOUTH
KOREA

Beijing

CHINA

JAPAN
Tokyo

PACIFIC OCEAN

WESTERN
SAHARA
(MOROCCO)

ALGERIA

LIBYA

EGYPT

JORDAN
KUWAIT
BAHRAIN
QATAR
Riyadh
SAUDI
ARABIA
Abu Dhabi
UNITED ARAB
EMIRATES
Muscat
OMAN

PAKISTAN

NEPAL
Kathmandu
New
Delhi
Dhaka
BHUTAN

INDIA

MYANMAR
(BURMA)
Yangon

LAOS
Vientiane
THAILAND
Bangkok
CAMBODIA
Phnom Penh

Hanoi
VIETNAM

Taipei
TAIWAN
Hong Kong

Tropic of Cancer

NORTHERN MARIANA
ISLANDS (U.S.)

GUAM (U.S.)

MARSHALL
ISLANDS

See Inset Below

AFRICA

NIGER
CHAD

Khartoum
SUDAN

Asmara
ERITREA
Sanaa
YEMEN
Addis Ababa
DJIBOUTI
Djibouti

BANGLADESH

Colombo
SRI
LANKA

Kuala Lumpur
MALAYSIA

Manila

PHILIPPINES

BRUNEI

SINGAPORE

MICRONESIA
Koror
PALAU
FEDERATED STATES
OF MICRONESIA

Equator

KIRIBATI

NAURU

Niamey
NIGERIA
Abuja
N'Djamena
CENTRAL
AFRICAN REP.
Bangui
Yaoundé
CAMEROON
EQUATORIAL GUINEA
SÃO TOMÉ AND
PRÍNCIPE
Libreville
GABON
CONGO
Brazzaville
Kinshasa
ZAIRE

ETHIOPIA

SOMALIA
Mogadishu

UGANDA
Kampala
RWANDA
Nairobi
KENYA
BURUNDI
TANZANIA
Dar es Salaam

Luanda

COMOROS

INDIAN OCEAN

Jakarta
INDONESIA

MELANESIA
PAPUA
NEW GUINEA
Port Moresby

SOLOMON
ISLANDS

TUVALU

ATLANTIC
OCEAN

ANGOLA
CABINDA
(ANGOLA)

ZAMBIA
Lusaka
MALAWI
Lilongwe

MADAGASCAR
Antananarivo

NAMIBIA
Windhoek
ZIMBABWE
BOTSWANA
Gaborone
Pretoria
SOUTH
AFRICA
Cape Town

Harare
MOZAMBIQUE
Maputo
SWAZILAND
LESOTHO

MAURITIUS
Réunion
(Fr.)

Tropic of Capricorn

AUSTRALIA

Canberra

VANUATU

NEW CALEDONIA
(Fr.)

FIJI

NEW
ZEALAND
Wellington

N W E S

ANTARCTIC Circle

ANTARCTICA

SWEDEN
FINLAND
NORWAY
Oslo
Stockholm
Helsinki
IRELAND
Dublin
UNITED
KINGDOM
North
Sea
Tallinn
ESTONIA
Riga
LATVIA
RUSSIA
LITHUANIA
Vilnius
Minsk
BELARUS

DENMARK
Copenhagen
RUSSIA

The
Hague
London
NETHERLANDS
BELGIUM
Amsterdam
Brussels
Berlin
GERMANY
Warsaw
POLAND
Prague
Kiev
UKRAINE

ATLANTIC
OCEAN

Paris
LUXEMBOURG
FRANCE
SWITZERLAND
Bern
LIECH.
Vienna
AUSTRIA
SLOVENIA
CZECH REP.
SLOVAKIA
Bratislava
Budapest
HUNGARY
Zagreb
CROATIA
Ljubljana
MOLDOVA
Chişinău
ROMANIA
Bucharest

GEORGIA

PORTUGAL
Lisbon
SPAIN
Madrid
ANDORRA
MONACO
ITALY
SAN
MARINO
Rome
BOS.
HERZ.
Sarajevo
SERBIA
MONTENEGRO
Tiranë
ALBANIA
MACEDONIA
Skopje
Sofia
BULGARIA
Belgrade
Black Sea

GIBRALTAR (U.K.)

MOROCCO

ALGERIA

TUNISIA

Tunis

GREECE
Athens

LIBYA

EGYPT

Mediterranean Sea

Ankara
TURKEY
CYPRUS
Nicosia
SYRIA
LEBANON
Beirut
Damascus
ISRAEL
Jerusalem
JORDAN
Amman

N W E S

MAURITANIA
Nouakchott

MALI

Dakar
SENEGAL
Banjul
GAMBIA
GUINEA-
BISSAU
Bissau
GUINEA
Conakry
Freetown
SIERRA
LEONE
LIBERIA
Monrovia

BURKINA FASO
Bamako
Ouagadougou
NIGER
Niamey

BENIN

CÔTE
D'IVOIRE
Yamoussoukro
GHANA
Accra
TOGO
Lomé
NIGERIA
Porto-
Novo

ATLANTIC OCEAN

Equator

0   300   600 mi
0   300   600 km

0   400   800 mi
0   400   800 km

N W E S

The World: Physical

KEY

Elevation

Feet		Meters
Over 13,000		Over 3,960
6,500–13,000		1,980–3,960
1,600–6,500		480–1,980
650–1,600		200–480
0–650		0–200
Below sea level		Below sea level

Ice cap

Ice shelf

Robinson Projection

ARCTIC OCEAN
GREENLAND (DEN.)
Beaufort Sea
Yukon R.
Mackenzie R.
Bering Sea
Aleutian Islands
ROCKY MOUNTAINS
GREAT PLAINS
CANADIAN SHIELD
Hudson Bay
NORTH AMERICA
Great Lakes
St. Lawrence R.
Missouri R.
Mississippi R.
APPALACHIAN MTS.
ATLANTIC OCEAN
Colorado R.
Rio Grande
SIERRA MADRE ORIENTAL
SIERRA MADRE OCCIDENTAL
Gulf of Mexico
West Indies
Hawaiian Islands
Tropic of Cancer
Caribbean Sea
PACIFIC OCEAN
Orinoco R.
GUIANA HIGHLANDS
AMAZON BASIN
Amazon R.
Equator
SOUTH AMERICA
ANDES
BRAZILIAN HIGHLANDS
Tropic of Capricorn
PAMPAS
Rio de la Plata
PATAGONIA
Cape Horn
Drake Passage
Antarctic Circle
ANTARCTIC PENINSULA
POLYNESIA

South Pole

ATLANTIC OCEAN
INDIAN OCEAN
QUEEN MAUD LAND
Permanent Ice Pack
Weddell Sea
COATS LAND
ENDERBY LAND
Antarctic Peninsula
Amery Ice Shelf
Ronne Ice Shelf
TRANSANTARCTIC MTS.
ANTARCTICA
South Pole
0   800 mi
QUEEN MAUD MTS.
0   800 km
Ross Ice Shelf
WILKES LAND
Roosevelt I.
Permanent Ice Pack
Ross Sea
VICTORIA LAND
South Magnetic Pole
Prime Meridian
International Date Line
PACIFIC OCEAN

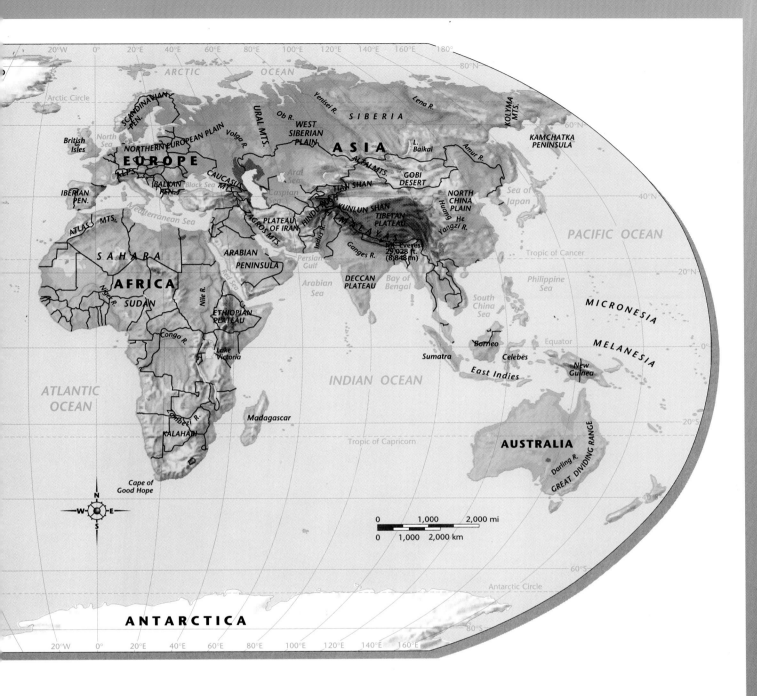

20°W   0°   20°E   40°E   60°E   80°E   100°E   120°E   140°E   160°E   180°

ARCTIC   OCEAN   80°N

Arctic Circle

SCANDINAVIAN PEN.   SIBERIA   Lena R.   KOLYMA MTS.   60°N

British Isles   North Sea   NORTHERN EUROPEAN PLAIN   Volga R.   Ob R.   WEST SIBERIAN PLAIN   Yenisei R.   ASIA   L. Baikal   Amur R.   KAMCHATKA PENINSULA

EUROPE   ALPS   Black Sea   CAUCASUS MTS.   Aral Sea   Caspian   ALTAI MTS.   TIAN SHAN   GOBI DESERT   NORTH CHINA PLAIN   Sea of Japan   40°N

IBERIAN PEN.   BALKAN PEN.   ZAGROS MTS.   PLATEAU OF IRAN   HINDU KUSH   KUNLUN SHAN   TIBETAN PLATEAU   Huang He   Yangzi R.   PACIFIC OCEAN

ATLAS MTS.   Mediterranean Sea   HIMALAYAS   Mt. Everest 29,028 ft. (8,848 m)   Tropic of Cancer

SAHARA   ARABIAN PENINSULA   Indus R.   Ganges R.   Persian Gulf   DECCAN PLATEAU   Bay of Bengal   Philippine Sea   20°N   MICRONESIA

AFRICA   Niger R.   SUDAN   Red Sea   Nile R.   Arabian Sea   South China Sea   MELANESIA

ETHIOPIAN PLATEAU   Borneo   Equator   0°

Congo R.   Sumatra   Celebes   New Guinea

Lake Victoria   INDIAN OCEAN   East Indies

ATLANTIC OCEAN   Zambezi R.   Madagascar   20°S

KALAHARI   Tropic of Capricorn   AUSTRALIA   Darling R.   GREAT DIVIDING RANGE

Cape of Good Hope   N W E S

0   1,000   2,000 mi
0   1,000   2,000 km

60°S

Antarctic Circle

ANTARCTICA   80°S

20°W   0°   20°E   40°E   60°E   80°E   100°E   120°E   140°E   160°E

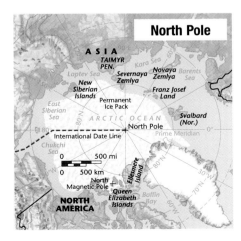

North Pole

ASIA   TAIMYR PEN.   Kara Sea   Barents Sea

Laptev Sea   Severnaya Zemlya   Novaya Zemlya

New Siberian Islands   Franz Josef Land

East Siberian Sea   Permanent Ice Pack   Svalbard (Nor.)

ARCTIC OCEAN   80   North Pole   Prime Meridian

International Date Line

Chukchi Sea   0   500 mi

0   500 km   North Magnetic Pole   Ellesmere Island

NORTH AMERICA   Queen Elizabeth Islands   Baffin Bay

United States: Political

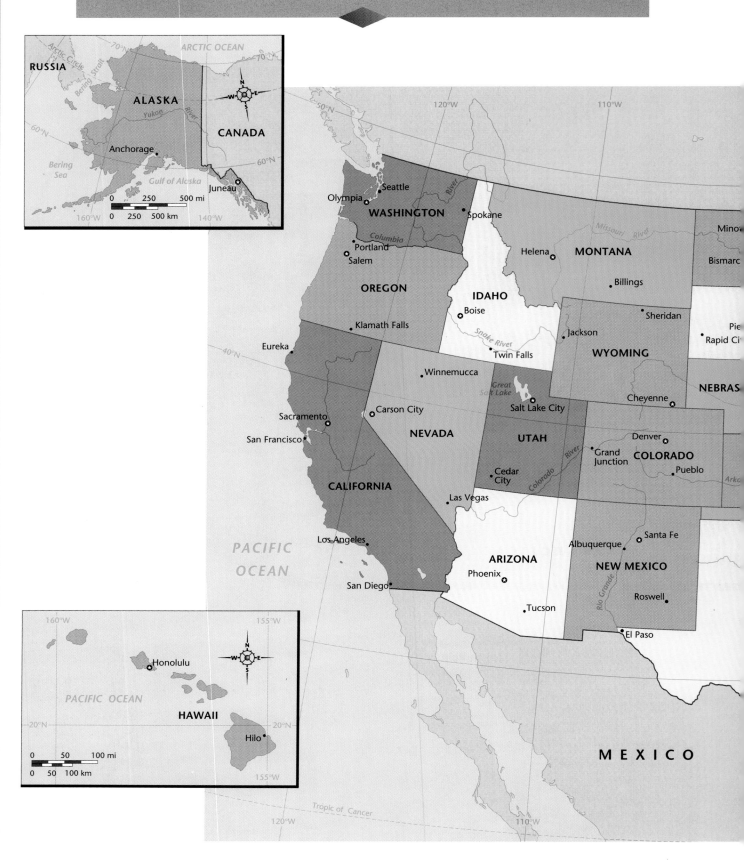

ARCTIC OCEAN

RUSSIA

ALASKA

CANADA

Arctic Circle

Bering Strait

Yukon River

70°N

70°N

60°N

60°N

Anchorage

Bering Sea

Gulf of Alaska

Juneau

0   250   500 mi
0   250   500 km

160°W   140°W

50°N   120°W   110°W

WASHINGTON

Seattle
Olympia
Spokane

Columbia

Portland
Salem

OREGON

Klamath Falls

Eureka

40°N

Carson City

Sacramento

San Francisco

NEVADA

Winnemucca

CALIFORNIA

Los Angeles

PACIFIC
OCEAN

San Diego

Cedar City

Las Vegas

IDAHO

Boise

Snake River

Twin Falls

Helena

MONTANA

Billings

Sheridan

Jackson

WYOMING

Great Salt Lake

Salt Lake City

UTAH

Grand Junction

Colorado River

ARIZONA

Phoenix

Tucson

Cheyenne

Denver

COLORADO

Pueblo

Albuquerque

Santa Fe

NEW MEXICO

Roswell

Rio Grande

El Paso

Missouri River

Mino

Bismarc

Pie

Rapid Ci

NEBRAS

Arka

MEXICO

160°W   155°W

Honolulu

PACIFIC OCEAN

20°N

20°N

HAWAII

Hilo

0   50   100 mi
0   50   100 km

155°W

Tropic of Cancer

120°W   110°W

CANADA

NORTH DAKOTA

MINNESOTA

Duluth

Lake Superior

Sault Ste. Marie

MICHIGAN

Lake Huron

MAINE

Presque Isle

Augusta

Portland

Montpelier

VERMONT

NEW HAMPSHIRE

Concord

Boston

SOUTH DAKOTA

MINNESOTA

Minneapolis   St. Paul

WISCONSIN

Lake Michigan

Milwaukee

Madison

Lansing

Detroit

Lake Ontario

NEW YORK

Albany

Buffalo

Lake Erie

Cleveland

MASSACHUSETTS

Hartford

New Haven

Providence

RHODE ISLAND

CONNECTICUT

Missouri

IOWA

Des Moines

Chicago

Cedar Rapids

ILLINOIS

Springfield

INDIANA

Indianapolis

OHIO

Columbus

Cincinnati

PENNSYLVANIA

Harrisburg

Pittsburgh

New York City

Trenton

Philadelphia

NEW JERSEY

Baltimore

Dover

DELAWARE

Washington, D.C.

Annapolis

MARYLAND

Omaha

Lincoln

KANSAS

Topeka

Kansas City

Jefferson City

MISSOURI

Wichita

St. Louis

Louisville

Frankfort

KENTUCKY

WEST VIRGINIA

Charleston

Richmond

VIRGINIA

Norfolk

Raleigh

NORTH CAROLINA

Charlotte

ATLANTIC OCEAN

OKLAHOMA

Tulsa

Oklahoma City

ARKANSAS

Little Rock

Pine Bluff

Memphis

Nashville

TENNESSEE

Columbia

SOUTH CAROLINA

Charleston

Red River

Dallas

Shreveport

MISSISSIPPI

Birmingham

Jackson

ALABAMA

Montgomery

Hattiesburg

Columbus

Atlanta

GEORGIA

Savannah

TEXAS

Austin

San Antonio

Baton Rouge

LOUISIANA

Houston

New Orleans

Tallahassee

Jacksonville

FLORIDA

Tampa

Lake Okeechobee

Miami

Rio Grande

Gulf of Mexico

0   150   300 mi
0   150   300 km

N
W   E
S

KEY

—— National boundary
—— State boundary
⊛ National capital
⊙ State capital
• Other city

Transverse Mercator Projection

Mississippi River

Ohio River

Tennessee River

North and South America: Political

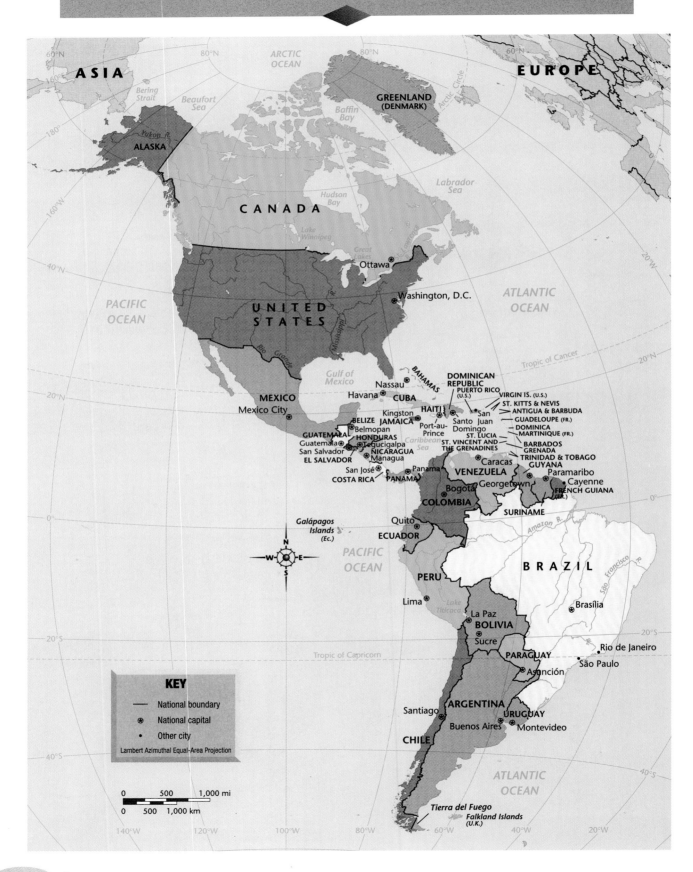

ASIA

ARCTIC OCEAN

EUROPE

Bering Strait

Beaufort Sea

GREENLAND (DENMARK)

Baffin Bay

Arctic Circle

Yukon R.

ALASKA

Labrador Sea

Hudson Bay

C A N A D A

Lake Winnipeg

Great Lakes

St. Lawrence R.

Ottawa

PACIFIC OCEAN

U N I T E D S T A T E S

Washington, D.C.

ATLANTIC OCEAN

Rio Grande

Mississippi R.

Tropic of Cancer

Gulf of Mexico

Nassau

BAHAMAS

DOMINICAN REPUBLIC

PUERTO RICO (U.S.)

VIRGIN IS. (U.S.)

MEXICO

Havana

CUBA

ST. KITTS & NEVIS

ANTIGUA & BARBUDA

Mexico City

Kingston

HAITI

San Juan

Santo Domingo

GUADELOUPE (FR.)

BELIZE

JAMAICA

Port-au-Prince

DOMINICA

MARTINIQUE (FR.)

Belmopan

ST. LUCIA

GUATEMALA

HONDURAS

Caribbean Sea

ST. VINCENT AND THE GRENADINES

BARBADOS

Guatemala

Tegucigalpa

GRENADA

San Salvador

NICARAGUA

TRINIDAD & TOBAGO

EL SALVADOR

Managua

Caracas

GUYANA

San José

Panama

VENEZUELA

Paramaribo

COSTA RICA

PANAMA

Georgetown

Cayenne

Bogotá

FRENCH GUIANA (FR.)

COLOMBIA

SURINAME

Amazon R.

Quito

ECUADOR

Galápagos Islands (Ec.)

PACIFIC OCEAN

B R A Z I L

São Francisco R.

PERU

Lima

Lake Titicaca

Brasília

La Paz

Rio de Janeiro

BOLIVIA

Sucre

Tropic of Capricorn

PARAGUAY

São Paulo

Asunción

KEY

— National boundary
⊛ National capital
• Other city

Lambert Azimuthal Equal-Area Projection

ARGENTINA

Santiago

URUGUAY

Buenos Aires

Montevideo

CHILE

| 0 | 500 | 1,000 mi |
| 0 | 500 | 1,000 km |

ATLANTIC OCEAN

Tierra del Fuego

Falkland Islands (U.K.)

60°N   80°N   80°N   60°N   20°W

160°W

180°

40°N

160°W

40°N

20°N

0°

20°S

40°S

140°W   120°W   100°W   80°W   60°W   40°W   20°W

20°N

0°

20°S

40°S

North and South America: Physical

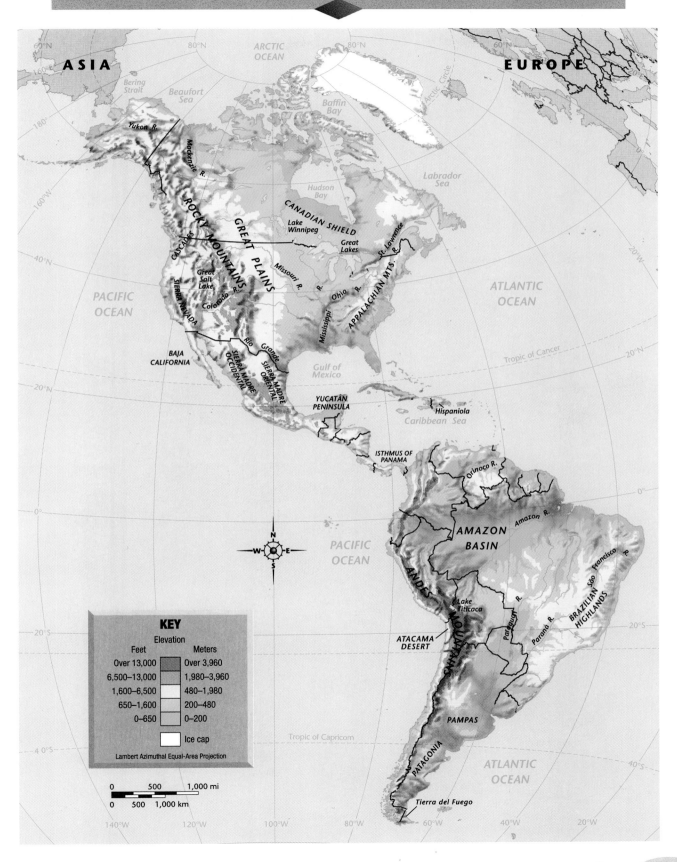

ASIA

ARCTIC OCEAN

EUROPE

Bering Strait

Beaufort Sea

Baffin Bay

Labrador Sea

Yukon R.

Mackenzie R.

ROCKY MOUNTAINS

GREAT PLAINS

CANADIAN SHIELD

Lake Winnipeg

Great Lakes

St. Lawrence R.

CASCADES

Great Salt Lake

Missouri R.

Ohio R.

APPALACHIAN MTS.

PACIFIC OCEAN

SIERRA NEVADA

Colorado R.

Mississippi R.

ATLANTIC OCEAN

BAJA CALIFORNIA

Rio Grande

SIERRA MADRE OCCIDENTAL

SIERRA MADRE ORIENTAL

Gulf of Mexico

Tropic of Cancer

YUCATÁN PENINSULA

Hispaniola

Caribbean Sea

ISTHMUS OF PANAMA

Orinoco R.

AMAZON BASIN

Amazon R.

PACIFIC OCEAN

ANDES

São Francisco R.

ALTIPLANO

Lake Titicaca

Paraguay R.

BRAZILIAN HIGHLANDS

Paraná R.

ATACAMA DESERT

PAMPAS

Tropic of Capricorn

PATAGONIA

ATLANTIC OCEAN

Tierra del Fuego

KEY

Elevation

Feet	Meters
Over 13,000	Over 3,960
6,500–13,000	1,980–3,960
1,600–6,500	480–1,980
650–1,600	200–480
0–650	0–200
Ice cap	

Lambert Azimuthal Equal-Area Projection

0   500   1,000 mi

0   500   1,000 km

Europe: Political

KEY

— National boundary
⊛ National capital
• Other city

Lambert Azimuthal Equal-Area Projection

ARCTIC OCEAN

Arctic Circle

ICELAND
Reykjavik

ATLANTIC
OCEAN

Faeroe Is.
(Den.)

Shetland Is.
(U.K.)

NORWAY
Lillehammer
Oslo

SWEDEN
Göteborg
Stockholm

FINLAND
Turku
Helsinki
St. Petersburg

RUSSIA
Moscow

ESTONIA
Tallinn

LATVIA
Riga

LITHUANIA
Vilnius

BELARUS
Minsk

North
Sea

Baltic
Sea

DENMARK
Copenhagen

IRELAND
Dublin

UNITED
KINGDOM
Manchester
London

Amsterdam
The Hague
NETHERLANDS

Brussels
BELGIUM

English Channel

LUXEMBOURG
Luxembourg

Paris

FRANCE

Bay
of
Biscay

PORTUGAL
Lisbon

SPAIN
Madrid

ANDORRA

Barcelona

Marseille

Corsica

Balearic Is.

Strait of
Gibraltar

GIBRALTAR
(U.K.)

AFRICA

Berlin

GERMANY
Cologne
Bonn
Frankfurt

Munich

LIECHTENSTEIN
Bern
SWITZERLAND

Milan

MONACO

SAN MARINO

ITALY
Rome

VATICAN
CITY

Naples

Sardinia

Mediterranean

Sea

MALTA

Sicily

Gdańsk

RUSSIA

POLAND
Warsaw
Łódź

Katowice
Kraków

CZECH
REPUBLIC
Prague
Brno

SLOVAKIA
Bratislava

Vienna

AUSTRIA

Budapest

HUNGARY

Danube R.

SLOVENIA
Ljubljana
Zagreb

CROATIA

BOSNIA &
HERZEGOVINA
Sarajevo

MONTENEGRO
Podgorica

SERBIA
Belgrade

Adriatic

Sea

ALBANIA
Tiranë

Skopje
MACEDONIA

GREECE
Athens

UKRAINE
Kiev

MOLDOVA
Chișinău

Cluj
ROMANIA
Bucharest

Black
Sea

BULGARIA
Sophia

Tyrrhenian
Sea

Ionian
Sea

Aegean
Sea

Crete

| 0 | 250 | 500 mi |
| 0 | 250 | 500 km |

Europe: Physical

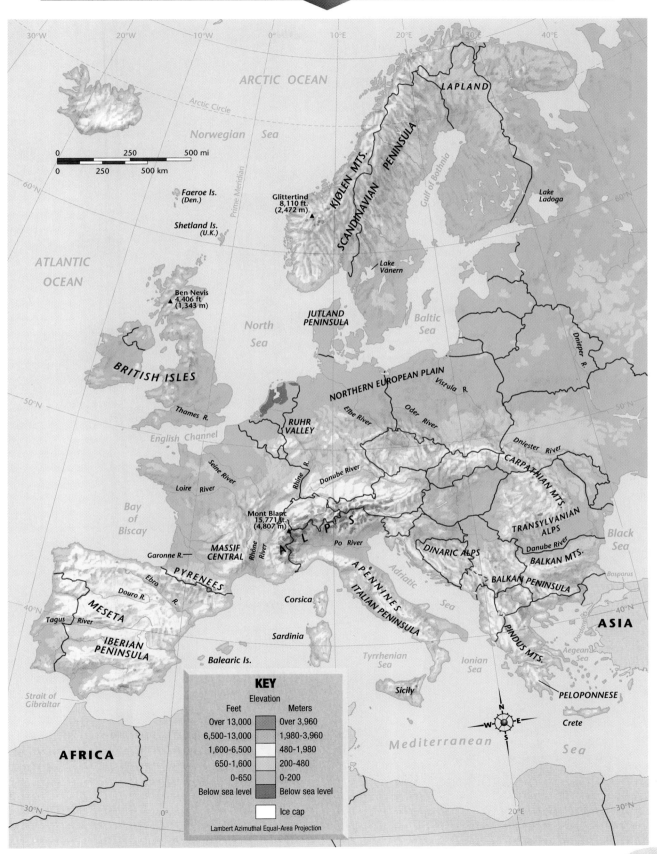

ARCTIC OCEAN

Norwegian Sea

LAPLAND

Faeroe Is.
(Den.)

Shetland Is.
(U.K.)

Arctic Circle

Prime Meridian

KJØLEN MTS.

SCANDINAVIAN PENINSULA

Glittertind
8,110 ft.
(2,472 m)

Gulf of Bothnia

Lake Ladoga

ATLANTIC OCEAN

Ben Nevis
4,406 ft
(1,343 m)

Lake Vänern

North Sea

JUTLAND PENINSULA

Baltic Sea

Dnieper R.

BRITISH ISLES

English Channel

Thames R.

Seine River

Loire River

RUHR VALLEY

NORTHERN EUROPEAN PLAIN

Elbe River

Oder River

Vistula R.

Dniester River

CARPATHIAN MTS.

Bay of Biscay

Mont Blanc
15,771 ft.
(4,807 m)

Garonne R.

MASSIF CENTRAL

PYRENEES

Rhône River

Rhine R.

Danube River

A L P S

Po River

TRANSYLVANIAN ALPS

Danube River

DINARIC ALPS

BALKAN MTS.

BALKAN PENINSULA

Black Sea

Bosporus

ASIA

MESETA

Douro R.

Ebro R.

Corsica

APENNINES

ITALIAN PENINSULA

Adriatic Sea

PINDUS MTS.

Dardanelles

40°N

Tagus River

IBERIAN PENINSULA

Sardinia

Tyrrhenian Sea

Ionian Sea

Aegean Sea

Strait of Gibraltar

Balearic Is.

Sicily

PELOPONNESE

Crete

AFRICA

Mediterranean Sea

KEY

Elevation

Feet	Meters
Over 13,000	Over 3,960
6,500–13,000	1,980–3,960
1,600–6,500	480–1,980
650–1,600	200–480
0–650	0–200
Below sea level	Below sea level
	Ice cap

Lambert Azimuthal Equal-Area Projection

0   250   500 mi
0   250   500 km

Africa: Political

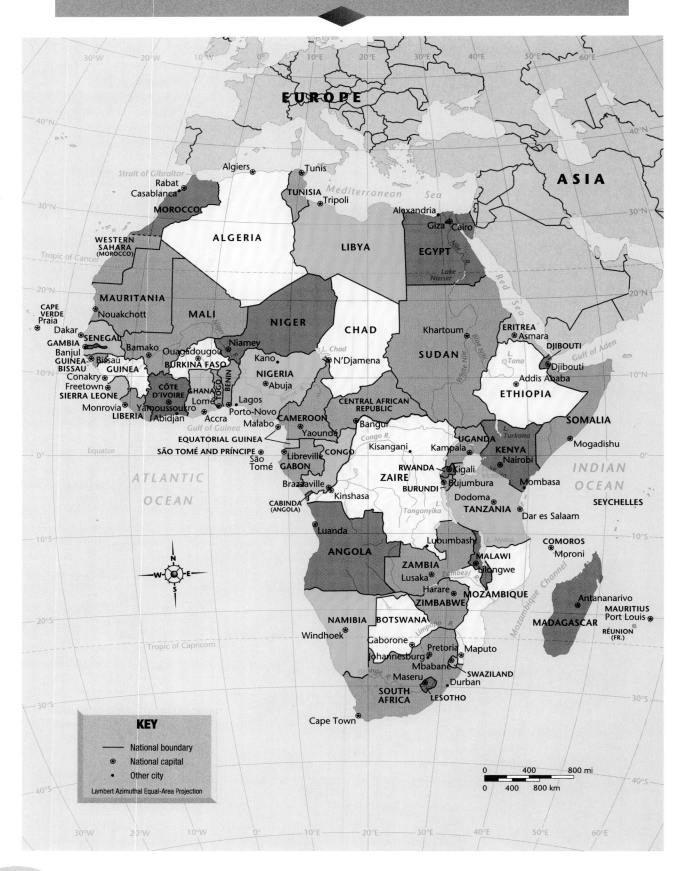

EUROPE

ASIA

Strait of Gibraltar

Algiers ⊛   Tunis ⊛

Rabat ⊛
Casablanca •
MOROCCO
TUNISIA
⊛ Tripoli
Mediterranean Sea

Alexandria •
Giza • ⊛ Cairo

WESTERN SAHARA (MOROCCO)
Tropic of Cancer

ALGERIA

LIBYA

EGYPT
Nile R.
Lake Nasser

MAURITANIA

⊛ Nouakchott
MALI

NIGER

CHAD

Khartoum ⊛
ERITREA
Asmara ⊛
DJIBOUTI
Gulf of Aden

CAPE VERDE
Praia ⊛
• Dakar
SENEGAL
GAMBIA
Banjul ⊛
Bamako ⊛
Ouagadougou ⊛
Niamey ⊛
Kano •
⊛ N'Djamena
SUDAN
L. Tana
⊛ Djibouti
Red Sea

GUINEA-BISSAU ⊛ Bissau
Conakry ⊛
GUINEA
BURKINA FASO
NIGERIA
⊛ Abuja
L. Chad
Niger R.
Blue Nile
White Nile
Addis Ababa ⊛
ETHIOPIA

Freetown ⊛
SIERRA LEONE
CÔTE D'IVOIRE
GHANA
TOGO
BENIN
• Lagos
Benue R.

Monrovia ⊛
Yamoussoukro ⊛
Lomé ⊛
Porto-Novo ⊛
CENTRAL AFRICAN REPUBLIC
L. Turkana
SOMALIA

LIBERIA
Abidjan •
Accra ⊛
Malabo ⊛
CAMEROON
Bangui ⊛
⊛ Mogadishu

Gulf of Guinea
EQUATORIAL GUINEA
Yaoundé ⊛
Congo R.
UGANDA
Kampala ⊛
KENYA

SÃO TOMÉ AND PRÍNCIPE
São Tomé •
Libreville ⊛
CONGO
Kisangani •
Nairobi ⊛
INDIAN OCEAN

Equator
GABON
ZAIRE
RWANDA
Kigali ⊛
L. Victoria
• Mombasa

ATLANTIC OCEAN
Brazzaville ⊛
Kinshasa ⊛
BURUNDI
Bujumbura ⊛
Dodoma ⊛
SEYCHELLES

CABINDA (ANGOLA)
L. Tanganyika
TANZANIA
Dar es Salaam •

Luanda ⊛
Lubumbashi •
L. Nyasa
COMOROS
Moroni •

ANGOLA
ZAMBIA
Lusaka ⊛
MALAWI
Lilongwe ⊛
Zambezi R.

Harare ⊛
MOZAMBIQUE
Antananarivo •
MAURITIUS
Port Louis ⊛

NAMIBIA
BOTSWANA
ZIMBABWE
MADAGASCAR
RÉUNION (FR.)

Tropic of Capricorn
Windhoek ⊛
Gaborone ⊛
Pretoria ⊛
Maputo ⊛
Limpopo R.
Mozambique Channel

Johannesburg •
Mbabane ⊛
SWAZILAND
Maseru ⊛
• Durban
Orange R.

SOUTH AFRICA
LESOTHO

Cape Town ⊛

KEY
— National boundary
⊛ National capital
• Other city

Lambert Azimuthal Equal-Area Projection

0 400 800 mi
0 400 800 km

Africa: Physical

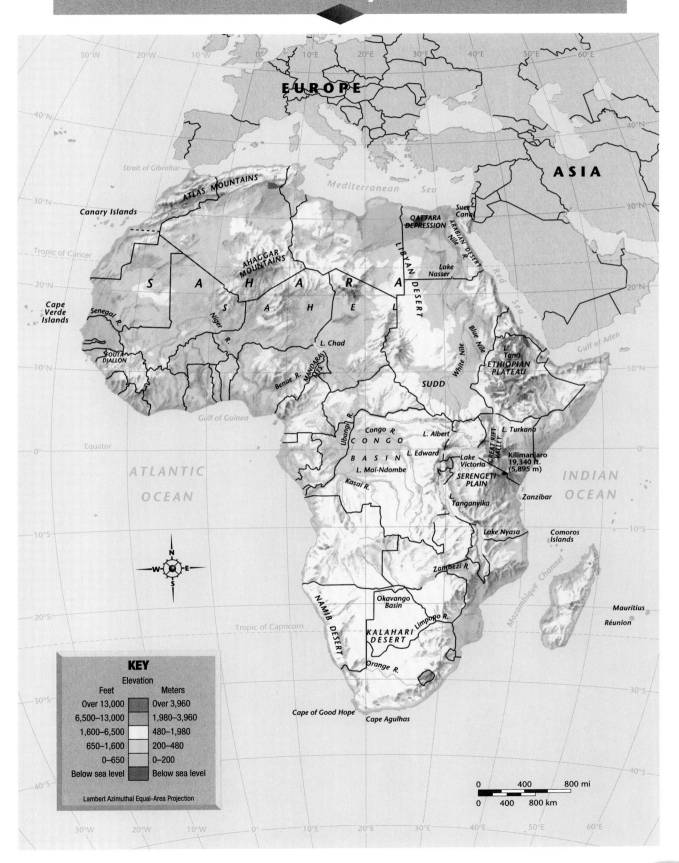

EUROPE

ASIA

Strait of Gibraltar

Mediterranean Sea

ATLAS MOUNTAINS

Canary Islands

QATTARA DEPRESSION

Suez Canal

Tropic of Cancer

AHAGGAR MOUNTAINS

ARABIAN DESERT

Lake Nasser

S A H A R A

Cape Verde Islands

Senegal R.

Niger R.

S A H E L

LIBYAN DESERT

Red Sea

Gulf of Aden

FOUTA DJALLON

L. Chad

MANDARA MTS.

White Nile

Blue Nile

L. Tana

ETHIOPIAN PLATEAU

Benue R.

Gulf of Guinea

SUDD

Ubangi R.

Congo R.

C O N G O

L. Albert

L. Turkana

GREAT RIFT VALLEY

Kilimanjaro 19,340 ft. (5,895 m)

ATLANTIC OCEAN

Equator

B A S I N

L. Edward

Lake Victoria

SERENGETI PLAIN

L. Mai-Ndombe

Zanzibar

INDIAN OCEAN

Kasai R.

L. Tanganyika

Lake Nyasa

Comoros Islands

Zambezi R.

Mozambique Channel

Mauritius

Réunion

NAMIB DESERT

Okavango Basin

Tropic of Capricorn

KALAHARI DESERT

Limpopo R.

Orange R.

Cape of Good Hope

Cape Agulhas

KEY

Elevation

Feet	Meters
Over 13,000	Over 3,960
6,500–13,000	1,980–3,960
1,600–6,500	480–1,980
650–1,600	200–480
0–650	0–200
Below sea level	Below sea level

Lambert Azimuthal Equal-Area Projection

0   400   800 mi

0   400   800 km

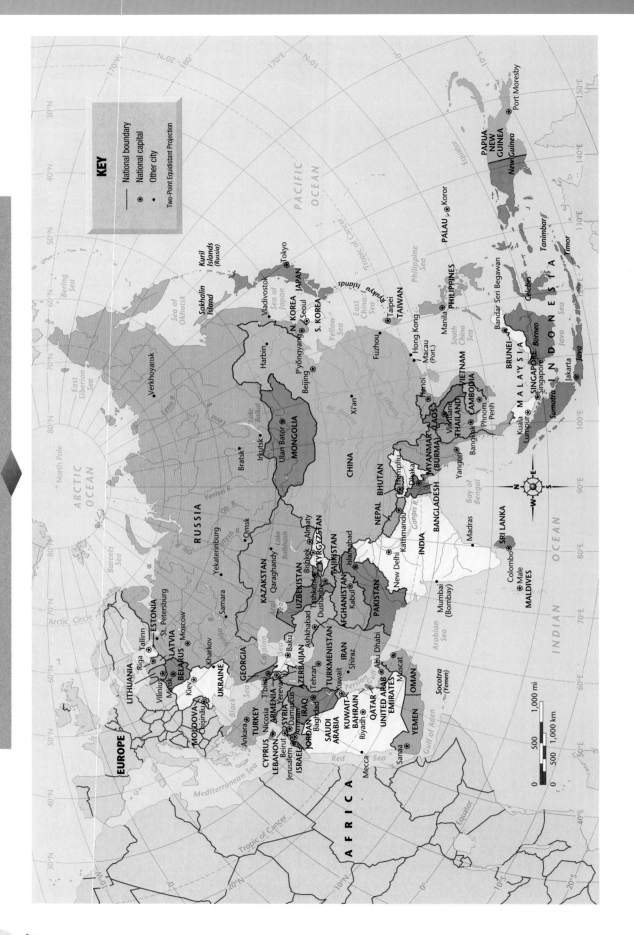

Asia: Political

KEY
— National boundary
⊛ National capital
• Other city
Two-Point Equidistant Projection

EUROPE

AFRICA

ARCTIC OCEAN
+North Pole

PACIFIC OCEAN

INDIAN OCEAN

Bering Sea
East Siberian Sea
Barents Sea
Sea of Okhotsk
Sea of Japan
Yellow Sea
East China Sea
Philippine Sea
South China Sea
Java Sea
Celebes Sea
Bay of Bengal
Arabian Sea
Gulf of Aden
Red Sea
Persian Gulf
Caspian Sea
Aral Sea
Black Sea
Mediterranean Sea

RUSSIA
Verkhoyansk
Vladivostok
Harbin
Irkutsk
Bratsk
Yekaterinburg
Omsk
Samara
Moscow
St. Petersburg
Kharkov

Sakhalin Island
Kuril Islands (Russia)
Tokyo ⊛ JAPAN
N. KOREA ⊛ Pyŏngyang
Seoul ⊛ S. KOREA
Beijing ⊛
Ulan Bator ⊛ MONGOLIA
CHINA
Xi'an •
Fuzhou •
Hong Kong •
Macau (Port.)
TAIWAN Taipei ⊛
Manila ⊛ PHILIPPINES
Koror ⊛ PALAU
PAPUA NEW GUINEA ⊛ Port Moresby
New Guinea
Tanimbars
Timor
Java
Jakarta
Sumatra
INDONESIA
Borneo
Celebes
BRUNEI ⊛ Bandar Seri Begawan
MALAYSIA
Kuala Lumpur ⊛
SINGAPORE ⊛ Singapore
VIETNAM
LAOS ⊛ Vientiane
Hanoi ⊛
CAMBODIA ⊛ Phnom Penh
THAILAND ⊛ Bangkok
MYANMAR (BURMA)
Yangon •
Ryukyu Islands

KAZAKHSTAN
Qaraghandy •
Almaty •
Qaraghandy
UZBEKISTAN
Tashkent ⊛ Bishkek ⊛ KYRGYZSTAN
Dushanbe ⊛ TAJIKISTAN
Ashkhabad ⊛
TURKMENISTAN
AFGHANISTAN
Kabul ⊛
PAKISTAN
Islamabad ⊛
Baku ⊛
AZERBAIJAN
Tehran ⊛
IRAN
Shiraz •
Abu Dhabi ⊛
UNITED ARAB EMIRATES
OMAN ⊛ Muscat
Socotra (Yemen)
YEMEN ⊛ Sanaa
QATAR
BAHRAIN
Kuwait ⊛ KUWAIT
SAUDI ARABIA ⊛ Riyadh
Mecca •
IRAQ ⊛ Baghdad
JORDAN ⊛ Amman
ISRAEL ⊛ Jerusalem
SYRIA ⊛ Damascus
LEBANON ⊛ Beirut
CYPRUS ⊛ Nicosia
TURKEY ⊛ Ankara
GEORGIA ⊛ Tbilisi
ARMENIA ⊛ Yerevan
MOLDOVA ⊛ Chişinău
UKRAINE ⊛ Kiev
BELARUS ⊛ Minsk
LITHUANIA ⊛ Vilnius
LATVIA ⊛ Riga
ESTONIA ⊛ Tallinn

NEPAL ⊛ Kathmandu
BHUTAN ⊛ Thimphu
BANGLADESH ⊛ Dhaka
INDIA
New Delhi ⊛
Mumbai (Bombay) •
Madras •
SRI LANKA ⊛ Colombo
MALDIVES ⊛ Male

Lena R.
Ob R.
Yenisei R.
Irtysh R.
Volga R.
Lake Baikal
Lake Balkhash
Ganges R.
Huang He
Chang Jiang
Indus R.

Arctic Circle
Tropic of Cancer
Equator
Tropic of Cancer

1,000 mi
0   500   1,000 km
0   500

162   ATLAS

Asia: Physical

KEY

Elevation

Feet	Meters	
Over 13,000	Over 3,960	
6,500–13,000	1,980–3,960	
1,600–6,500	480–1,980	
650–1,600	200–480	
0–650	0–200	
Below sea level	Below sea level	

Two-Point Equidistant Projection

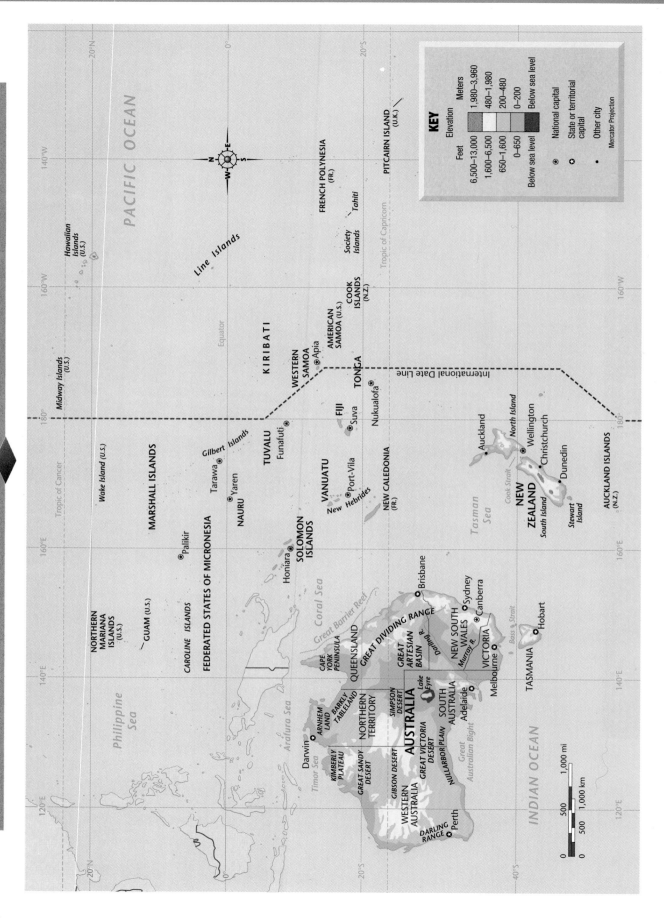

KEY

Elevation

Feet	Meters
6,500–13,000	1,980–3,960
1,600–6,500	480–1,980
650–1,600	200–480
0–650	0–200
Below sea level	Below sea level

⊛ National capital

✪ State or territorial capital

• Other city

Mercator Projection

PACIFIC OCEAN

Hawaiian Islands (U.S.)

Line Islands

FRENCH POLYNESIA (FR.)

Tahiti

Society Islands

PITCAIRN ISLAND (U.K.)

Tropic of Capricorn

Midway Islands (U.S.)

Equator

KIRIBATI

WESTERN SAMOA
⊛ Apia

AMERICAN SAMOA (U.S.)

COOK ISLANDS (N.Z.)

TONGA

International Date Line

Wake Island (U.S.)

MARSHALL ISLANDS

Gilbert Islands

Tarawa ⊛

Yaren

⊛ NAURU

TUVALU
Funafuti

FIJI
✪ Suva

Nukualofa

VANUATU
⊛ Port-Vila

New Hebrides

NEW CALEDONIA (FR.)

Auckland •

North Island

Wellington ⊛
Christchurch •
Dunedin •

Cook Strait

NEW ZEALAND
South Island

Stewart Island

AUCKLAND ISLANDS (N.Z.)

Tasman Sea

Tropic of Cancer

NORTHERN MARIANA ISLANDS (U.S.)

GUAM (U.S.)

CAROLINE ISLANDS

FEDERATED STATES OF MICRONESIA

Palikir ⊛

SOLOMON ISLANDS
Honiara ⊛

Coral Sea

Great Barrier Reef

Brisbane ✪

Sydney •
Canberra ⊛

GREAT DIVIDING RANGE

CAPE YORK PENINSULA

QUEENSLAND

GREAT ARTESIAN BASIN

NEW SOUTH WALES

Darling R.

VICTORIA
Melbourne ✪

Bass Strait

TASMANIA
Hobart ✪

Philippine Sea

Arafura Sea

Timor Sea

Darwin •

ARNHEM LAND

BARKLY TABLELAND

NORTHERN TERRITORY

SIMPSON DESERT

Lake Eyre

SOUTH AUSTRALIA

Adelaide ✪

AUSTRALIA

GREAT VICTORIA DESERT

NULLARBOR PLAIN

Great Australian Bight

Murray R.

KIMBERLY PLATEAU

GREAT SANDY DESERT

GIBSON DESERT

WESTERN AUSTRALIA

DARLING RANGE
Perth •

INDIAN OCEAN

1,000 mi

500   1,000 km

0   500

0

The Arctic

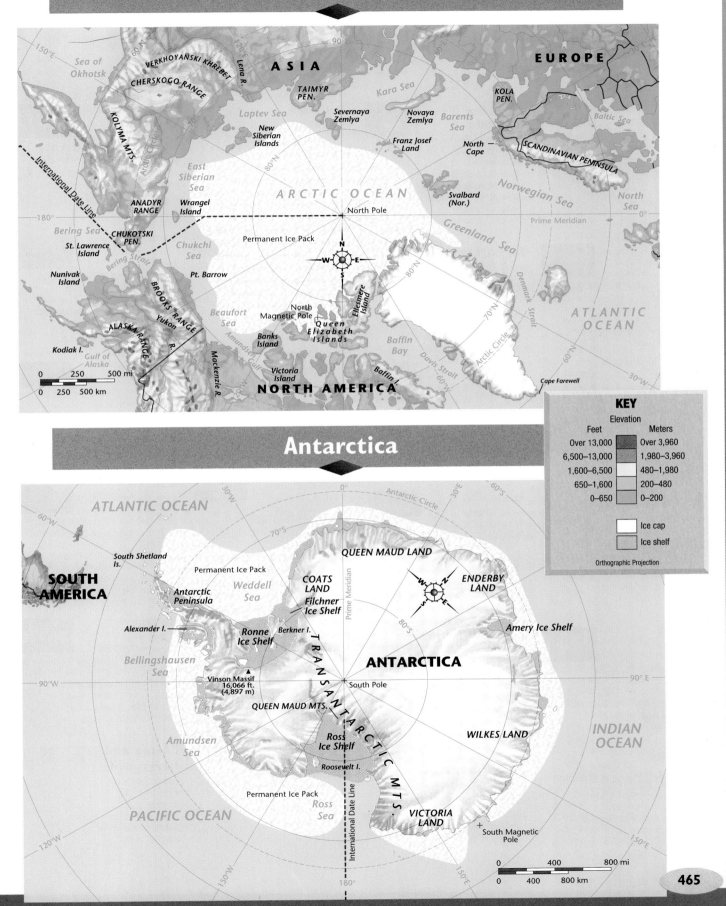

150°E

Sea of Okhotsk

VERKHOYANSKI KHREBET

CHERSKOGO RANGE

Lena R.

ASIA

TAIMYR PEN.

EUROPE

KOLA PEN.

Kara Sea

Severnaya Zemlya

Novaya Zemlya

Barents Sea

Baltic Sea

SCANDINAVIAN PENINSULA

KOLYMA MTS.

Laptev Sea

New Siberian Islands

Franz Josef Land

North Cape

Arctic Circle

International Date Line

East Siberian Sea

ARCTIC OCEAN

Svalbard (Nor.)

Norwegian Sea

North Sea

ANADYR RANGE

Wrangel Island

North Pole

Greenland Sea

Prime Meridian

0°

Bering Sea

CHUKOTSKI PEN.

Chukchi Sea

Permanent Ice Pack

N
W   E
S

80°N

Denmark Strait

ATLANTIC OCEAN

St. Lawrence Island

Bering Strait

Nunivak Island

Pt. Barrow

North Magnetic Pole

Ellesmere Island

70°N

Kodiak I.

BROOKS RANGE

Yukon R.

Beaufort Sea

Queen Elizabeth Islands

Baffin Bay

Arctic Circle

60°N

ALASKA RANGE

Banks Island

Davis Strait

Gulf of Alaska

Amundsen Gulf

Mackenzie R.

Victoria Island

Baffin I.

60°N

Cape Farewell

30°W

0   250   500 mi
0   250   500 km

Baffin I.

NORTH AMERICA

Antarctica

KEY

Elevation

Feet	Meters
Over 13,000	Over 3,960
6,500–13,000	1,980–3,960
1,600–6,500	480–1,980
650–1,600	200–480
0–650	0–200

Ice cap

Ice shelf

Orthographic Projection

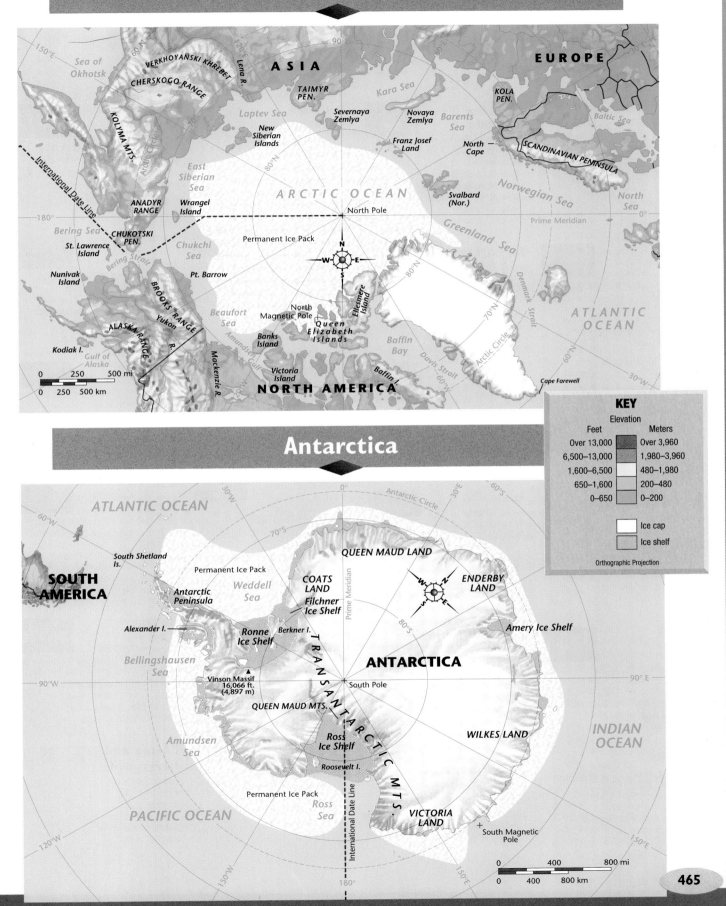

60°W

ATLANTIC OCEAN

Antarctic Circle

0°

30°E

60°S

30°W

70°S

QUEEN MAUD LAND

60°E

South Shetland Is.

Permanent Ice Pack

COATS LAND

ENDERBY LAND

SOUTH AMERICA

Antarctic Peninsula

Weddell Sea

Filchner Ice Shelf

Prime Meridian

Alexander I.

Ronne Ice Shelf

Berkner I.

N
W   E
S

80°S

Amery Ice Shelf

Bellingshausen Sea

Vinson Massif 16,066 ft. (4,897 m)

TRANSANTARCTIC MTS.

ANTARCTICA

90°E

South Pole

QUEEN MAUD MTS.

WILKES LAND

INDIAN OCEAN

Amundsen Sea

Ross Ice Shelf

Roosevelt I.

90°W

Permanent Ice Pack

Ross Sea

International Date Line

VICTORIA LAND

120°W

PACIFIC OCEAN

South Magnetic Pole

150°E

150°W

180°

0   400   800 mi
0   400   800 km

World View

Afghanistan
CAPITAL: Kabul
POPULATION: 21,251,821
MAJOR LANGUAGES: Pashtu, Afghan Persian, Turkic, and 30 various languages
AREA: 250,010 sq mi; 647,500 sq km
LEADING EXPORTS: fruits and nuts, handwoven carpets, and wool
CONTINENT: Asia

Albania
CAPITAL: Tiranë
POPULATION: 3,413,904
MAJOR LANGUAGES: Albanian, Tosk dialect, and Greek
AREA: 11,101 sq mi; 28,750 sq km
LEADING EXPORTS: asphalt, metals and metallic ores, and electricity
CONTINENT: Europe

Algeria
CAPITAL: Algiers
POPULATION: 28,539,321
MAJOR LANGUAGES: Arabic (official), French, and Berber dialects
AREA: 919,626 sq mi; 2,381,740 sq km
LEADING EXPORTS: petroleum and natural gas
CONTINENT: Africa

Andorra
CAPITAL: Andorra La Vella
POPULATION: 65,780
MAJOR LANGUAGES: Catalan (official), French, and Castilian
AREA: 174 sq mi; 450 sq km
LEADING EXPORTS: electricity, tobacco products, and furniture
CONTINENT: Europe

Angola
CAPITAL: Luanda
POPULATION: 10,069,501
MAJOR LANGUAGES: Portuguese (official), Bantu, and various languages
AREA: 481,370 sq mi; 1,246,700 sq km
LEADING EXPORTS: oil, diamonds, and refined petroleum products
CONTINENT: Africa

Anguilla
CAPITAL: The Valley
POPULATION: 7,099
MAJOR LANGUAGE: English (official)
AREA: 35 sq mi; 91 sq km
LEADING EXPORTS: lobster and salt
LOCATION: Caribbean Sea

Antigua and Barbuda
CAPITAL: Saint John's
POPULATION: 65,176
MAJOR LANGUAGES: English (official) and various dialects
AREA: 170 sq mi; 440 sq km
LEADING EXPORTS: petroleum products and manufactures
LOCATION: Caribbean Sea

Argentina
CAPITAL: Buenos Aires
POPULATION: 34,292,742
MAJOR LANGUAGES: Spanish (official), English, Italian, German, and French
AREA: 1,068,339 sq mi; 2,766,890 sq km
LEADING EXPORTS: meat, wheat, corn, oilseed, and manufactures
CONTINENT: South America

Armenia
CAPITAL: Yerevan
POPULATION: 3,557,284
MAJOR LANGUAGES: Armenian and Russian
AREA: 11,506 sq mi; 29,800 sq km
LEADING EXPORTS: gold and jewelry, and aluminum
CONTINENT: Asia

Australia
CAPITAL: Canberra
POPULATION: 18,322,231
MAJOR LANGUAGES: English and various languages
AREA: 2,968,010 sq mi; 7,686,850 sq km
LEADING EXPORTS: coal, gold, meat, wool, and alumina
CONTINENT: Australia

Austria
CAPITAL: Vienna
POPULATION: 7,986,664
MAJOR LANGUAGE: German
AREA: 32,376 sq mi; 83,850 sq km
LEADING EXPORTS: machinery and equipment, and iron and steel
CONTINENT: Europe

Azerbaijan
CAPITAL: Baku
POPULATION: 7,789,886
MAJOR LANGUAGES: Azeri, Russian, Armenian, and various languages
AREA: 33,438 sq mi; 86,600 sq km
LEADING EXPORTS: oil and gas, chemicals, and oil field equipment
CONTINENT: Asia

Bahamas
CAPITAL: Nassau
POPULATION: 256,616
MAJOR LANGUAGES: English and Creole
AREA: 5,382 sq mi; 13,940 sq km
LEADING EXPORTS: pharmaceuticals, cement, rum, and crawfish
LOCATION: Caribbean Sea

Bahrain
CAPITAL: Manama
POPULATION: 575,925
MAJOR LANGUAGES: Arabic, English, Farsi, and Urdu
AREA: 239 sq mi; 620 sq km
LEADING EXPORTS: petroleum and petroleum products
CONTINENT: Asia

Bangladesh
CAPITAL: Dhaka
POPULATION: 128,094,948
MAJOR LANGUAGES: Bangla and English
AREA: 55,600 sq mi; 144,000 sq km
LEADING EXPORTS: garments, jute and jute goods, and leather
CONTINENT: Asia

Barbados
CAPITAL: Bridgetown
POPULATION: 256,395
MAJOR LANGUAGE: English
AREA: 166 sq mi; 430 sq km
LEADING EXPORTS: sugar and molasses, and rum
LOCATION: Caribbean Sea

Belarus
CAPITAL: Minsk
POPULATION: 10,437,418
MAJOR LANGUAGES: Byelorussian and Russian
AREA: 79,926 sq mi; 207,600 sq km
LEADING EXPORTS: machinery and transportation equipment
CONTINENT: Europe

Belgium
CAPITAL: Brussels
POPULATION: 10,081,880
MAJOR LANGUAGES: Dutch, French, and German
AREA: 11,780 sq mi; 30,510 sq km
LEADING EXPORTS: iron and steel, and transportation equipment
CONTINENT: Europe

Belize
CAPITAL: Belmopan
POPULATION: 214,061
MAJOR LANGUAGES: English (official), Spanish, Maya, and Garifuna
AREA: 8,865 sq mi; 22,960 sq km
LEADING EXPORTS: sugar, citrus fruits, bananas, and clothing
CONTINENT: North America

Benin
CAPITAL: Porto-Novo
POPULATION: 5,522,677
MAJOR LANGUAGES: Fon, Yoruba, and at least 6 various languages
AREA: 43,484 sq mi; 112,620 sq km
LEADING EXPORTS: cotton, crude oil, palm products, and cocoa
CONTINENT: Africa

Bermuda
CAPITAL: Hamilton
POPULATION: 61,629
MAJOR LANGUAGE: English
AREA: 19.3 sq mi; 50 sq km
LEADING EXPORTS: semitropical produce and light manufactures
LOCATION: Atlantic Ocean

Bhutan
CAPITAL: Thimphu
POPULATION: 1,780,638
MAJOR LANGUAGES: Dzongkha (official), Tibetan dialects, and Nepalese dialects
AREA: 18,147 sq mi; 47,000 sq km
LEADING EXPORTS: cardamon, gypsum, timber, and handicrafts
CONTINENT: Asia

Bolivia
CAPITAL: La Paz
POPULATION: 7,896,254
MAJOR LANGUAGES: Spanish, Quechua, and Aymara
AREA: 424,179 sq mi; 1,098,580 sq km
LEADING EXPORTS: metals, natural gas, soybeans, jewelry, and wood
CONTINENT: South America

Bosnia and Herzegovina

CAPITAL: Sarajevo
POPULATION: 3,201,823
MAJOR LANGUAGE: Serbo-Croatian
AREA: 19,782 sq mi; 51,233 sq km
LEADING EXPORTS: none
CONTINENT: Europe

Botswana

CAPITAL: Gaborone
POPULATION: 1,392,414
MAJOR LANGUAGES: English and Setswana
AREA: 231,812 sq mi; 600,370 sq km
LEADING EXPORTS: diamonds, copper and nickel, and meat
CONTINENT: Africa

Brazil

CAPITAL: Brasília
POPULATION: 160,737,489
MAJOR LANGUAGES: Portuguese, Spanish, English, and French
AREA: 3,286,600 sq mi; 8,511,965 sq km
LEADING EXPORTS: iron ore, soybean, bran, and orange juice
CONTINENT: South America

British Virgin Islands

CAPITAL: Road Town
POPULATION: 13,027
MAJOR LANGUAGE: English
AREA: 58 sq mi; 150 sq km
LEADING EXPORTS: rum, fresh fish, gravel, sand, and fruits
LOCATION: Caribbean Sea

Brunei

CAPITAL: Bandar Seri Begawan
POPULATION: 292,266
MAJOR LANGUAGES: Malay, English, and Chinese
AREA: 2,228 sq mi; 5,770 sq km
LEADING EXPORTS: crude oil and liquefied natural gas
LOCATION: South China Sea

Bulgaria

CAPITAL: Sofia
POPULATION: 8,775,198
MAJOR LANGUAGE: Bulgarian
AREA: 42,824 sq mi; 110,910 sq km
LEADING EXPORTS: machinery and agricultural products
CONTINENT: Europe

Burkina Faso

CAPITAL: Ouagadougou
POPULATION: 10,422,828
MAJOR LANGUAGES: French (official) and Sudanic languages
AREA: 105,873 sq mi; 274,200 sq km
LEADING EXPORTS: cotton, gold, and animal products
CONTINENT: Africa

Burundi

CAPITAL: Bujumbura
POPULATION: 6,262,429
MAJOR LANGUAGES: Kirundi, French, and Swahili
AREA: 10,746 sq mi; 27,830 sq km
LEADING EXPORTS: coffee, tea, cotton, and hides and skins
CONTINENT: Africa

Cambodia

CAPITAL: Phnom Penh
POPULATION: 10,561,373
MAJOR LANGUAGES: Khmer and French
AREA: 69,902 sq mi; 181,040 sq km
LEADING EXPORTS: timber, rubber, soybeans, and sesame
CONTINENT: Asia

Cameroon

CAPITAL: Yaounde
POPULATION: 13,521,000
MAJOR LANGUAGES: 24 various languages, English, and French
AREA: 183,574 sq mi; 475,440 sq km
LEADING EXPORTS: petroleum products and lumber
CONTINENT: Africa

Canada

CAPITAL: Ottawa
POPULATION: 28,434,545
MAJOR LANGUAGES: English and French
AREA: 3,851,940 sq mi; 9,976,140 sq km
LEADING EXPORTS: newsprint, wood pulp, timber, and crude petroleum
CONTINENT: North America

Cape Verde

CAPITAL: Praia
POPULATION: 435,983
MAJOR LANGUAGES: Portuguese and Crioulo
AREA: 1,556 sq mi; 4,030 sq km
LEADING EXPORTS: fish, bananas, and hides and skins
CONTINENT: Africa

Cayman Islands

CAPITAL: George Town
POPULATION: 33,192
MAJOR LANGUAGE: English
AREA: 100 sq mi; 260 sq km
LEADING EXPORTS: turtle products and manufactured goods
LOCATION: Caribbean Sea

Central African Republic

CAPITAL: Bangui
POPULATION: 3,209,759
MAJOR LANGUAGES: French, Sangho, Arabic, Hunsa, and Swahili
AREA: 240,542 sq mi; 622,980 sq km
LEADING EXPORTS: diamonds, timber, cotton, coffee, and tobacco
CONTINENT: Africa

Chad

CAPITAL: N'Djamena
POPULATION: 5,586,505
MAJOR LANGUAGES: French, Arabic, Sara, Songo, and over 100 various languages and dialects
AREA: 495,772 sq mi; 1,284,000 sq km
LEADING EXPORTS: cotton, cattle, textiles, and fish
CONTINENT: Africa

Chile

CAPITAL: Santiago
POPULATION: 14,161,216
MAJOR LANGUAGE: Spanish
AREA: 292,269 sq mi; 756,950 sq km
LEADING EXPORTS: copper and other metals and minerals
CONTINENT: South America

China

CAPITAL: Beijing
POPULATION: 1,203,097,268
MAJOR LANGUAGES: Mandarin, Putonghua, Yue, Wu, Minbei, Minnan, Xiang, and Gan and Hakka dialects
AREA: 3,705,533 sq mi; 9,596,960 sq km
LEADING EXPORTS: textiles, garments, footwear, and toys
CONTINENT: Asia

Colombia

CAPITAL: Bogota
POPULATION: 36,200,251
MAJOR LANGUAGE: Spanish
AREA: 439,751 sq mi; 1,138,910 sq km
LEADING EXPORTS: petroleum, coffee, coal, and bananas
CONTINENT: South America

Comoros

CAPITAL: Moroni
POPULATION: 549,338
MAJOR LANGUAGES: Arabic, French, and Comoran
AREA: 838 sq mi; 2,170 sq km
LEADING EXPORTS: vanilla, ylang-ylang, cloves, and perfume oil
LOCATION: Indian Ocean

Congo

CAPITAL: Brazzaville
POPULATION: 2,504,996
MAJOR LANGUAGES: French, Lingala, Kikongo, and other languages
AREA: 132,051 sq mi; 342,000 sq km
LEADING EXPORTS: crude oil, lumber, plywood, sugar, and cocoa
CONTINENT: Africa

Cook Islands

CAPITAL: Avarua
POPULATION: 19,343
MAJOR LANGUAGES: English and Maori
AREA: 95 sq mi; 240 sq km
LEADING EXPORTS: copra, fresh and canned fruit, and clothing
LOCATION: Pacific Ocean

Costa Rica

CAPITAL: San José
POPULATION: 3,419,114
MAJOR LANGUAGES: Spanish and English
AREA: 19,730 sq mi; 51,100 sq km
LEADING EXPORTS: coffee, bananas, textiles, and sugar
CONTINENT: North America

Côte d'Ivoire

CAPITAL: Yamoussoukro
POPULATION: 14,791,257
MAJOR LANGUAGES: French, Dioula, and 59 other dialects
AREA: 124,507 sq mi; 322,460 sq km
LEADING EXPORTS: cocoa, coffee, tropical woods, and petroleum
CONTINENT: Africa

Croatia

CAPITAL: Zagreb
POPULATION: 4,665,821
MAJOR LANGUAGE: Serbo-Croatian
AREA: 21,830 sq mi; 56,538 sq km
LEADING EXPORTS: machinery and transportation equipment
CONTINENT: Europe

Cuba

CAPITAL: Havana
POPULATION: 10,937,635
MAJOR LANGUAGE: Spanish
AREA: 42,805 sq mi; 110,860 sq km
LEADING EXPORTS: sugar, nickel, shellfish, and tobacco
LOCATION: Caribbean Sea

Cyprus

CAPITAL: Nicosia
POPULATION: 736,636
MAJOR LANGUAGES: Greek, Turkish, and English
AREA: 3,572 sq mi; 9,250 sq km
LEADING EXPORTS: citrus, potatoes, grapes, wines, and cement
LOCATION: Mediterranean Sea

Czech Republic

CAPITAL: Prague
POPULATION: 10,432,774
MAJOR LANGUAGES: Czech and Slovak
AREA: 30,388 sq mi; 78,703 sq km
LEADING EXPORTS: manufactured goods
CONTINENT: Europe

Denmark

CAPITAL: Copenhagen
POPULATION: 5,199,437
MAJOR LANGUAGES: Danish, Faroese, Greenlandic, and German
AREA: 16,630 sq mi; 43,070 sq km
LEADING EXPORTS: meat and meat products, and dairy products
CONTINENT: Europe

Djibouti

CAPITAL: Djibouti
POPULATION: 421,320
MAJOR LANGUAGES: French, Arabic, Somali, and Afar
AREA: 8,495 sq mi; 22,000 sq km
LEADING EXPORTS: hides and skins, and coffee (in transit)
CONTINENT: Africa

Dominica

CAPITAL: Roseau
POPULATION: 82,608
MAJOR LANGUAGES: English and French patois
AREA: 290 sq mi; 750 sq km
LEADING EXPORTS: bananas, soap, bay oil, and vegetables
LOCATION: Caribbean Sea

Dominican Republic

CAPITAL: Santo Domingo
POPULATION: 7,511,263
MAJOR LANGUAGE: Spanish
AREA: 18,815 sq mi; 48,730 sq km
LEADING EXPORTS: ferronickel, sugar, gold, coffee, and cocoa
LOCATION: Caribbean Sea

Ecuador

CAPITAL: Quito
POPULATION: 10,890,950
MAJOR LANGUAGES: Spanish, Quechua, and various languages
AREA: 109,487 sq mi; 283,560 sq km
LEADING EXPORTS: petroleum, bananas, shrimp, and cocoa
CONTINENT: South America

Egypt

CAPITAL: Cairo
POPULATION: 62,359,623
MAJOR LANGUAGES: Arabic, English, and French
AREA: 386,675 sq mi; 1,001,450 sq km
LEADING EXPORTS: crude oil and petroleum products
CONTINENT: Africa

El Salvador

CAPITAL: San Salvador
POPULATION: 5,870,481
MAJOR LANGUAGES: Spanish and Nahua
AREA: 8,124 sq mi; 21,040 sq km
LEADING EXPORTS: coffee, sugar cane, and shrimp
CONTINENT: North America

Equatorial Guinea

CAPITAL: Malabo
POPULATION: 420,293
MAJOR LANGUAGES: Spanish, Pidgin English, Fang, Bubi, and Ibo
AREA: 10,831 sq mi; 28,050 sq km
LEADING EXPORTS: coffee, timber, and cocoa beans
CONTINENT: Africa

Eritrea

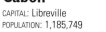

CAPITAL: Asmara
POPULATION: 3,578,709
MAJOR LANGUAGES: Tigre, Kunama, Cushitic dialects, Nora Bana, and Arabic
AREA: 46,844 sq mi; 121,320 sq km
LEADING EXPORTS: salt, hides, cement, and gum arabic
CONTINENT: Africa

Estonia

CAPITAL: Tallinn
POPULATION: 1,625,399
MAJOR LANGUAGES: Estonian, Latvian, Lithuanian, and Russian
AREA: 17,414 sq mi; 45,100 sq km
LEADING EXPORTS: textiles, food products, vehicles, and metals
CONTINENT: Europe

Ethiopia

CAPITAL: Addis Ababa
POPULATION: 55,979,018
MAJOR LANGUAGES:
Amharic, Tigrinya, Orominga, Guaraginga, Somali, Arabic, English, and various languages
AREA: 435,201 sq mi; 1,127,127 sq km
LEADING EXPORTS: coffee, leather products, and gold
CONTINENT: Africa

Fiji

CAPITAL: Suva
POPULATION: 772,891
MAJOR LANGUAGES: English, Fijian, and Hindustani
AREA: 7,054 sq mi; 18,270 sq km
LEADING EXPORTS: sugar, clothing, gold, processed fish, and lumber
LOCATION: Pacific Ocean

Finland

CAPITAL: Helsinki
POPULATION: 5,085,206
MAJOR LANGUAGES: Finnish, Swedish, Lapp, and Russian
AREA: 130,132 sq mi; 337,030 sq km
LEADING EXPORTS: paper and pulp, machinery, and chemicals
CONTINENT: Europe

France

CAPITAL: Paris
POPULATION: 58,109,160
MAJOR LANGUAGES: French and regional dialects and languages
AREA: 211,217 sq mi; 547,030 sq km
LEADING EXPORTS: machinery and transportation equipment
CONTINENT: Europe

Gabon

CAPITAL: Libreville
POPULATION: 1,185,749
MAJOR LANGUAGES: French, Fang, Myene, Bateke, Bapounou/Eschira, and Bandjabi
AREA: 103,351 sq mi; 267,670 sq km
LEADING EXPORTS: crude oil, timber, manganese, and uranium
CONTINENT: Africa

The Gambia

CAPITAL: Banjul
POPULATION: 989,273
MAJOR LANGUAGES: English, Mandinka, Wolof, Fula, and various languages
AREA: 4,363 sq mi; 11,300 sq km
LEADING EXPORTS: peanuts and peanut products, and fish
CONTINENT: Africa

Georgia

CAPITAL: T'bilisi
POPULATION: 5,725,972
MAJOR LANGUAGES: Armenian, Azeri, Georgian, Russian, and various languages
AREA: 26,912 sq mi; 69,700 sq km
LEADING EXPORTS: citrus fruits, tea, and wine
CONTINENT: Asia

Germany

CAPITAL: Berlin
POPULATION: 81,337,541
MAJOR LANGUAGE: German
AREA: 137,808 sq mi; 356,910 sq km
LEADING EXPORTS: machines and machine tools, and chemicals
CONTINENT: Europe

Ghana

CAPITAL: Accra
POPULATION: 17,763,138
MAJOR LANGUAGES: English, Akan, Moshi-Dagomba, Ewe, Ga, and various languages
AREA: 92,104 sq mi; 238,540 sq km
LEADING EXPORTS: cocoa, gold, timber, tuna, and bauxite
CONTINENT: Africa

Greece

CAPITAL: Athens
POPULATION: 10,647,511
MAJOR LANGUAGES: Greek, English, and French
AREA: 50,944 sq mi; 131,940 sq km
LEADING EXPORTS: manufactured goods, foodstuffs, and fuels
CONTINENT: Europe

Grenada

CAPITAL: Saint George's
POPULATION: 94,486
MAJOR LANGUAGES: English and French patois
AREA: 131 sq mi; 340 sq km
LEADING EXPORTS: bananas, cocoa, nutmeg, and fruits and vegetables
LOCATION: Caribbean Sea

Guatemala

CAPITAL: Guatemala
POPULATION: 10,998,602
MAJOR LANGUAGES: Spanish, Quiche, Cakchiquel, Kekchi, and various languages and dialects
AREA: 42,044 sq mi; 108,890 sq km
LEADING EXPORTS: coffee, sugar, bananas, cardamom, and beef
CONTINENT: North America

Guinea

CAPITAL: Conakry
POPULATION: 6,549,336
MAJOR LANGUAGES: French and various languages
AREA: 94,930 sq mi; 245,860 sq km
LEADING EXPORTS: bauxite, alumina, diamonds, gold, and coffee
CONTINENT: Africa

Guinea Bissau

CAPITAL: Bissau
POPULATION: 1,124,537
MAJOR LANGUAGES: Portuguese, Criolo, and various languages
AREA: 13,946 sq mi; 36,210 sq km
LEADING EXPORTS: cashews, fish, peanuts, and palm kernels
CONTINENT: Africa

Guyana

CAPITAL: Georgetown
POPULATION: 723,774
MAJOR LANGUAGES: English and various dialects
AREA: 83,003 sq mi; 214,970 sq km
LEADING EXPORTS: sugar, bauxite/alumina, rice, and shrimp
CONTINENT: South America

Haiti

CAPITAL: Port-au-Prince
POPULATION: 6,539,983
MAJOR LANGUAGES: French and Creole
AREA: 8,784 sq mi; 22,750 sq km
LEADING EXPORTS: light manufactures and coffee
LOCATION: Caribbean Sea

Holy See (Vatican City)

CAPITAL: Vatican City
POPULATION: 830
MAJOR LANGUAGES: Italian, Latin, and various languages
AREA: 17 sq mi; 44 sq km
LEADING EXPORTS: none
CONTINENT: Europe

Honduras

CAPITAL: Tegucigalpa
POPULATION: 5,549,743
MAJOR LANGUAGES: Spanish and various dialects
AREA: 43,280 sq mi; 112,090 sq km
LEADING EXPORTS: bananas, coffee, shrimp, lobsters, and minerals
CONTINENT: North America

Hungary

CAPITAL: Budapest
POPULATION: 10,318,838
MAJOR LANGUAGES: Hungarian and various languages
AREA: 35,920 sq mi; 93,030 sq km
LEADING EXPORTS: raw materials and semi-finished goods
CONTINENT: Europe

Iceland

CAPITAL: Reykjavik
POPULATION: 265,998
MAJOR LANGUAGE: Icelandic
AREA: 39,770 sq mi; 103,000 sq km
LEADING EXPORTS: fish and fish products, and animal products
LOCATION: Atlantic Ocean

India

CAPITAL: New Delhi
POPULATION: 936,545,814
MAJOR LANGUAGES: English, Hindi, Bengali, Telugu, Marathi, Tamil, Urdu, Gujarati, Malayam, Kannada, Oriya, Punjabi, Assamese, Kashmiri, Sindhi, Sanskrit, and Hindustani (all official)
AREA: 1,269,389 sq mi; 3,287,590 sq km
LEADING EXPORTS: clothing, and gems and jewelry
CONTINENT: Asia

Indonesia

CAPITAL: Jakarta
POPULATION: 203,583,886
MAJOR LANGUAGES: Bahasa Indonesia, English, Dutch, Javanese, and various dialects
AREA: 741,052 sq mi; 1,919,251 sq km
LEADING EXPORTS: manufactures, fuels, and foodstuffs
CONTINENT: Asia

Iran

CAPITAL: Tehran
POPULATION: 64,625,455
MAJOR LANGUAGES: Farsi (official) and Turkic languages
AREA: 634,562 sq mi; 1,643,452 sq km
LEADING EXPORTS: petroleum, carpets, fruit, nuts, and hides
CONTINENT: Asia

Iraq

CAPITAL: Baghdad
POPULATION: 20,643,769
MAJOR LANGUAGES: Arabic, Kurdish, Assyrian, and Armenian
AREA: 168,760 sq mi; 437,072 sq km
LEADING EXPORTS: crude oil and refined products, and fertilizers
CONTINENT: Asia

Ireland

CAPITAL: Dublin
POPULATION: 3,550,448
MAJOR LANGUAGES: Irish Gaelic and English
AREA: 27,136 sq mi; 70,280 sq km
LEADING EXPORTS: chemicals and data processing equipment
CONTINENT: Europe

Israel

CAPITAL: Jerusalem
POPULATION: 7,566,447
MAJOR LANGUAGES: Hebrew, Arabic, and English
AREA: 10,421 sq mi; 26,990 sq km
LEADING EXPORTS: machinery and equipment, and cut diamonds
CONTINENT: Asia

Italy

CAPITAL: Rome
POPULATION: 58,261,971
MAJOR LANGUAGES: Italian, German, French, and Slovene
AREA: 116,310 sq mi; 301,230 sq km
LEADING EXPORTS: metals, and textiles and clothing
CONTINENT: Europe

Jamaica

CAPITAL: Kingston
POPULATION: 2,574,291
MAJOR LANGUAGES: English and Creole
AREA: 4,243 sq mi; 10,990 sq km
LEADING EXPORTS: alumina, bauxite, sugar, bananas, and rum
LOCATION: Caribbean Sea

Japan

CAPITAL: Tokyo
POPULATION: 125,506,492
MAJOR LANGUAGE: Japanese
AREA: 145,888 sq mi; 377,835 sq km
LEADING EXPORTS: machinery, motor vehicles, and electronics
CONTINENT: Asia

Jordan

CAPITAL: Amman
POPULATION: 4,100,709
MAJOR LANGUAGES: Arabic and English
AREA: 34,447 sq mi; 89,213 sq km
LEADING EXPORTS: phosphates, fertilizers, and potash
CONTINENT: Asia

Kazakhstan

CAPITAL: Almaty
POPULATION: 17,376,615
MAJOR LANGUAGES: Kazakh and Russian
AREA: 1,049,191 sq mi; 2,717,300 sq km
LEADING EXPORTS: oil, and ferrous and nonferrous metals
CONTINENT: Asia

Kenya

CAPITAL: Nairobi
POPULATION: 28,817,227
MAJOR LANGUAGES: English, Swahili, and various languages
AREA: 224,970 sq mi; 582,650 sq km
LEADING EXPORTS: tea, coffee, and petroleum products
CONTINENT: Africa

Kiribati

CAPITAL: Tarawa
POPULATION: 79,386
MAJOR LANGUAGES: English and Gilbertese
AREA: 277 sq mi; 717 sq km
LEADING EXPORTS: copra, seaweed, and fish
LOCATION: Pacific Ocean

Korea, North

CAPITAL: P'yongyang
POPULATION: 23,486,550
MAJOR LANGUAGE: Korean
AREA: 46,542 sq mi; 120,540 sq km
LEADING EXPORTS: minerals and metallurgical products
CONTINENT: Asia

Korea, South

CAPITAL: Seoul
POPULATION: 45,553,882
MAJOR LANGUAGES: Korean and English
AREA: 38,025 sq mi; 98,480 sq km
LEADING EXPORTS: electronic and electrical equipment
CONTINENT: Asia

Kuwait

CAPITAL: Kuwait
POPULATION: 1,817,397
MAJOR LANGUAGES: Arabic and English
AREA: 6,881 sq mi; 17,820 sq km
LEADING EXPORT: oil
CONTINENT: Asia

Kyrgyzstan

CAPITAL: Bishkek
POPULATION: 4,769,877
MAJOR LANGUAGES: Kyrgyz and Russian
AREA: 76,644 sq mi; 198,500 sq km
LEADING EXPORTS: wool, chemicals, cotton, metals, and shoes
CONTINENT: Asia

Laos

CAPITAL: Vientiane
POPULATION: 4,837,237
MAJOR LANGUAGES: Lao, French, English, and various languages
AREA: 91,432 sq mi; 236,800 sq km
LEADING EXPORTS: electricity, wood products, coffee, and tin
CONTINENT: Asia

Latvia

CAPITAL: Riga
POPULATION: 2,762,899
MAJOR LANGUAGES: Lettish, Lithuanian, Russian, and various languages
AREA: 24,750 sq mi; 64,100 sq km
LEADING EXPORTS: oil products, timber, and ferrous metals
CONTINENT: Europe

Lebanon

CAPITAL: Beirut
POPULATION: 3,695,921
MAJOR LANGUAGES: Arabic, French, Armenian, and English
AREA: 4,016 sq mi; 10,400 sq km
LEADING EXPORTS: agricultural products, chemicals, and textiles
CONTINENT: Asia

Lesotho

CAPITAL: Maseru
POPULATION: 1,992,960
MAJOR LANGUAGES: Sesotho, English, Zulu, and Xhosa
AREA: 11,719 sq mi; 30,350 sq km
LEADING EXPORTS: wool, mohair, wheat, cattle, and peas
CONTINENT: Africa

Liberia

CAPITAL: Monrovia
POPULATION: 3,073,245
MAJOR LANGUAGES: English and Niger-Congo
AREA: 43,002 sq mi; 111,370 sq km
LEADING EXPORTS: iron ore, rubber, timber, and coffee
CONTINENT: Africa

Libya

CAPITAL: Tripoli
POPULATION: 5,248,401
MAJOR LANGUAGES: Arabic, Italian, and English
AREA: 679,385 sq mi; 1,759,540 sq km
LEADING EXPORTS: crude oil and refined petroleum products
CONTINENT: Africa

Liechtenstein

CAPITAL: Vaduz
POPULATION: 30,654
MAJOR LANGUAGES: German and Alemannic
AREA: 62 sq mi; 160 sq km
LEADING EXPORTS: small specialty machinery and dental products
CONTINENT: Europe

Lithuania

CAPITAL: Vilnius
POPULATION: 3,876,396
MAJOR LANGUAGES: Lithuanian, Polish, and Russian
AREA: 25,175 sq mi; 65,200 sq km
LEADING EXPORTS: electronics, petroleum products, and food
CONTINENT: Europe

Luxembourg

CAPITAL: Luxembourg
POPULATION: 404,660
MAJOR LANGUAGES: Luxembourgisch, German, French, and English
AREA: 998 sq mi; 2,586 sq km
LEADING EXPORTS: finished steel products and chemicals
CONTINENT: Europe

Macedonia

CAPITAL: Skopje
POPULATION: 2,159,503
MAJOR LANGUAGES: Macedonian, Albanian, Turkish, Serb, Gypsy, and various languages
AREA: 9,781 sq mi; 25,333 sq km
LEADING EXPORTS: manufactured goods and machinery
CONTINENT: Europe

Madagascar

CAPITAL: Antananarivo
POPULATION: 13,862,325
MAJOR LANGUAGES: French and Malagasy
AREA: 226,665 sq mi; 587,040 sq km
LEADING EXPORTS: coffee, vanilla, cloves, shellfish, and sugar
CONTINENT: Africa

Malawi

CAPITAL: Lilongwe
POPULATION: 9,808,384
MAJOR LANGUAGES: English, Chichewa, and various languages
AREA: 45,747 sq mi; 118,480 sq km
LEADING EXPORTS: tobacco, tea, sugar, coffee, and peanuts
CONTINENT: Africa

Malaysia

CAPITAL: Kuala Lumpur
POPULATION: 19,723,587
MAJOR LANGUAGES: Malay, English, Mandarin, Tamil, Chinese dialects, and various languages and dialects
AREA: 127,322 sq mi; 329,750 sq km
LEADING EXPORTS: electronic equipment
CONTINENT: Asia

Maldives

CAPITAL: Male
POPULATION: 261,310
MAJOR LANGUAGES: Divehi dialect and English
AREA: 116 sq mi; 300 sq km
LEADING EXPORTS: fish and clothing
CONTINENT: Asia

Mali

CAPITAL: Bamako
POPULATION: 9,375,132
MAJOR LANGUAGES: French, Bambara, and various languages
AREA: 478,783 sq mi; 1,240,000 sq km
LEADING EXPORTS: cotton, livestock, and gold
CONTINENT: Africa

Malta

CAPITAL: Valletta
POPULATION: 369,609
MAJOR LANGUAGES: Maltese and English
AREA: 124 sq mi; 320 sq km
LEADING EXPORTS: machinery and transportation equipment
LOCATION: Mediterranean Sea

Marshall Islands

CAPITAL: Majuro
POPULATION: 56,157
MAJOR LANGUAGES: English, Marshallese dialects, and Japanese
AREA: 70 sq mi; 181.3 sq km
LEADING EXPORTS: coconut oil, fish, live animals, and trichus shells
LOCATION: Pacific Ocean

Mauritania

CAPITAL: Nouakchott
POPULATION: 2,263,202
MAJOR LANGUAGES: Hasaniya Arabic, Wolof, Pular, and Soninke
AREA: 397,969 sq mi; 1,030,700 sq km
LEADING EXPORTS: iron ore, and fish and fish products
CONTINENT: Africa

Mauritius

CAPITAL: Port Louis
POPULATION: 1,127,068
MAJOR LANGUAGES: English (official), Creole, French, Hindi, Urdu, Hakka, and Bojpoori
AREA: 718 sq mi; 1,860 sq km
LEADING EXPORTS: textiles, sugar, and light manufactures
LOCATION: Indian Ocean

Mayotte

CAPITAL: Mamoutzou
POPULATION: 97,088
MAJOR LANGUAGES: Mahorian and French
AREA: 145 sq mi; 375 sq km
LEADING EXPORTS: ylang-ylang and vanilla
CONTINENT: Africa

Mexico

CAPITAL: Mexico City
POPULATION: 93,985,848
MAJOR LANGUAGES: Spanish and Mayan dialects
AREA: 761,632 sq mi; 1,972,550 sq km
LEADING EXPORTS: crude oil, oil products, coffee, and silver
CONTINENT: North America

Micronesia

CAPITAL: Federated states of Kolonia (on the Island of Pohnpei)
*a new capital is being built about 10 km southwest in the Palikir Valley
POPULATION: 122,950
MAJOR LANGUAGES: English, Turkese, Pohnpeian, Yapese, and Kosrean
AREA: 271 sq mi; 702 sq km
LEADING EXPORTS: fish, copra, bananas, and black pepper
LOCATION: Pacific Ocean

Moldova

CAPITAL: Chisinau
POPULATION: 4,489,657
MAJOR LANGUAGES: Moldovan (official), Russian, and Gagauz dialect
AREA: 13,012 sq mi; 33,700 sq km
LEADING EXPORTS: foodstuffs, wine, and tobacco
CONTINENT: Europe

Monaco

CAPITAL: Monaco
POPULATION: 31,515
MAJOR LANGUAGES: French (official), English, Italian, and Monegasque
AREA: .73 sq mi; 1.9 sq km
LEADING EXPORTS: exports through France
CONTINENT: Europe

Mongolia

CAPITAL: Ulaanbaatar
POPULATION: 2,493,615
MAJOR LANGUAGES: Khalkha Mongol, Turkic, Russian, and Chinese
AREA: 604,270 sq mi; 1,565,000 sq km
LEADING EXPORTS: copper, livestock, animal products, and cashmere
CONTINENT: Asia

Morocco

CAPITAL: Rabat
POPULATION: 29,168,848
MAJOR LANGUAGES: Arabic (official), Berber dialects, and French
AREA: 172,420 sq mi; 446,550 sq km
LEADING EXPORTS: food and beverages
CONTINENT: Africa

Mozambique

CAPITAL: Maputo
POPULATION: 18,115,250
MAJOR LANGUAGES: Portuguese and various dialects
AREA: 309,506 sq mi; 801,590 sq km
LEADING EXPORTS: shrimp, cashews, cotton, sugar, copra, and citrus
CONTINENT: Africa

Myanmar (Burma)

CAPITAL: Rangoon
POPULATION: 45,103,809
MAJOR LANGUAGE: Burmese
AREA: 261,979 sq mi; 678,500 sq km
LEADING EXPORTS: pulses and beans, teak, rice, and hardwood
CONTINENT: Asia

Namibia

CAPITAL: Windhoek
POPULATION: 1,651,545
MAJOR LANGUAGES: English (official), Afrikaans, German, Oshivambo, Herero, Nama, and various languages
AREA: 318,707 sq mi; 825,418 sq km
LEADING EXPORTS: diamonds, copper, gold, zinc, and lead
CONTINENT: Africa

Nauru

CAPITAL: Government offices in Yaren District
POPULATION: 10,149
MAJOR LANGUAGES: Nauruan and English
AREA: 8 sq mi; 21 sq km
LEADING EXPORTS: phosphates
LOCATION: Pacific Ocean

Nepal

CAPITAL: Kathmandu
POPULATION: 21,560,869
MAJOR LANGUAGES: Nepali (official) and 20 various languages divided into numerous dialects
AREA: 54,365 sq mi; 140,800 sq km
LEADING EXPORTS: carpets, clothing, and leather goods
CONTINENT: Asia

Netherlands

CAPITAL: Amsterdam
POPULATION: 15,452,903
MAJOR LANGUAGE: Dutch
AREA: 14,414 sq mi; 37,330 sq km
LEADING EXPORTS: metal products and chemicals
CONTINENT: Europe

New Caledonia

CAPITAL: Noumea
POPULATION: 184,552
MAJOR LANGUAGES: French and 28 Melanesian-Polynesian dialects
AREA: 7,359 sq mi; 19,060 sq km
LEADING EXPORTS: nickel metal and nickel ore
LOCATION: Pacific Ocean

New Zealand

CAPITAL: Wellington
POPULATION: 3,407,277
MAJOR LANGUAGES: English and Maori
AREA: 103,741 sq mi; 268,680 sq km
LEADING EXPORTS: wool, lamb, mutton, beef, fish, and cheese
LOCATION: Pacific Ocean

Nicaragua

CAPITAL: Managua
POPULATION: 4,206,353
MAJOR LANGUAGES: Spanish (official), English, and various languages
AREA: 50,000 sq mi; 129,494 sq km
LEADING EXPORTS: meat, coffee, cotton, sugar, seafood, and gold
CONTINENT: North America

Niger

CAPITAL: Niamey
POPULATION: 9,280,208
MAJOR LANGUAGES: French (official), Hausa, and Djerma
AREA: 489,208 sq mi; 1,267,000 sq km
LEADING EXPORTS: uranium ore and livestock products
CONTINENT: Africa

Nigeria

CAPITAL: Abuja
POPULATION: 101,232,251
MAJOR LANGUAGES: English (official), Hausa, Yoruba, Ibo, and Fulani
AREA: 356,682 sq mi; 923,770 sq km
LEADING EXPORTS: oil, cocoa, and rubber
CONTINENT: Africa

Niue

CAPITAL: (Free association with New Zealand)
POPULATION: 1,837
MAJOR LANGUAGES: Polynesian and English
AREA: 100 sq mi; 260 sq km
LEADING EXPORTS: canned coconut cream, copra, and honey
LOCATION: Pacific Ocean

Norway

CAPITAL: Oslo
POPULATION: 4,330,951
MAJOR LANGUAGES: Norwegian (official), Lapp, and Finnish
AREA: 125,186 sq mi; 324,220 sq km
LEADING EXPORTS: petroleum and petroleum products
CONTINENT: Europe

Oman

CAPITAL: Muscat
POPULATION: 2,125,089
MAJOR LANGUAGES: Arabic (official), English, Baluchi, Urdu, and Indian dialects
AREA: 82,034 sq mi; 212,460 sq km
LEADING EXPORTS: petroleum, re-exports, and fish
CONTINENT: Asia

Pakistan

CAPITAL: Islamabad
POPULATION: 131,541,920
MAJOR LANGUAGES: Urdu (official), English (official), Punjabi, Sindhi, Pashtu, Urdu, Balochi, and other languages
AREA: 310,414 sq mi; 803,940 sq km
LEADING EXPORTS: cotton, textiles, clothing, rice, and leather
CONTINENT: Asia

Palau

CAPITAL: Koror
POPULATION: 16,661
MAJOR LANGUAGES: English (official), Sonsorolese, Angaur, Japanese, Tobi, and Palauan
AREA: 177 sq mi; 458 sq km
LEADING EXPORTS: trochus, tuna, copra, and handicrafts
LOCATION: Pacific Ocean

Panama

CAPITAL: Panama
POPULATION: 2,680,903
MAJOR LANGUAGES: Spanish (official) and English
AREA: 30,194 sq mi; 78,200 sq km
LEADING EXPORTS: bananas, shrimp, sugar, clothing, and coffee
CONTINENT: North America

Papua New Guinea

CAPITAL: Port Moresby
POPULATION: 4,294,750
MAJOR LANGUAGES: English, pidgin English, and Motu
AREA: 178,266 sq mi; 461,690 sq km
LEADING EXPORTS: gold, copper ore, oil, logs, and palm oil
LOCATION: Pacific Ocean

Paraguay

CAPITAL: Asuncion
POPULATION: 5,358,198
MAJOR LANGUAGES: Spanish (official) and Guarani
AREA: 157,052 sq mi; 406,750 sq km
LEADING EXPORTS: cotton, soybeans, timber, and vegetable oils
CONTINENT: South America

Peru

CAPITAL: Lima
POPULATION: 24,087,372
MAJOR LANGUAGES: Spanish (official), Quechua (official), and Aymara
AREA: 496,243 sq mi; 1,285,220 sq km
LEADING EXPORTS: copper, zinc, and fish meal
CONTINENT: South America

Philippines

CAPITAL: Manila
POPULATION: 73,265,584
MAJOR LANGUAGES: Pilipino and English (official)
AREA: 115,834 sq mi; 300,000 sq km
LEADING EXPORTS: electronics, textiles, and coconut products
CONTINENT: Asia

Poland

CAPITAL: Warsaw
POPULATION: 38,792,442
MAJOR LANGUAGE: Polish
AREA: 120,731 sq mi; 312,680 sq km
LEADING EXPORTS: intermediate goods
CONTINENT: Europe

Portugal

CAPITAL: Lisbon
POPULATION: 10,562,388
MAJOR LANGUAGE: Portuguese
AREA: 35,553 sq mi; 92,080 sq km
LEADING EXPORTS: clothing and footwear, and machinery
CONTINENT: Europe

Qatar

CAPITAL: Doha
POPULATION: 533,916
MAJOR LANGUAGES: Arabic (official) and English
AREA: 4,247 sq mi; 11,000 sq km
LEADING EXPORTS: petroleum products, steel, and fertilizers
CONTINENT: Asia

Romania

CAPITAL: Bucharest
POPULATION: 23,198,330
MAJOR LANGUAGES: Romanian, Hungarian, and German
AREA: 91,702 sq mi; 237,500 sq km
LEADING EXPORTS: metals and metal products, and mineral products
CONTINENT: Europe

Russia

CAPITAL: Moscow
POPULATION: 149,909,089
MAJOR LANGUAGES: Russian and various languages
AREA: 6,952,996 sq mi; 17,075,200 sq km
LEADING EXPORTS: petroleum and petroleum products
CONTINENT: Europe and Asia

Rwanda

CAPITAL: Kigali
POPULATION: 8,605,307
MAJOR LANGUAGES: Kinyarwanda (official), French (official), and Kiswahili
AREA: 10,170 sq mi; 26,340 sq km
LEADING EXPORTS: coffee, tea, cassiterite, and wolframite
CONTINENT: Africa

Saint Kitts and Nevis

CAPITAL: Basseterre
POPULATION: 40,992
MAJOR LANGUAGE: English
AREA: 104 sq mi; 269 sq km
LEADING EXPORTS: machinery, food, and electronics
LOCATION: Caribbean Sea

Saint Lucia

CAPITAL: Castries
POPULATION: 156,050
MAJOR LANGUAGES: English and French patois
AREA: 239 sq mi; 620 sq km
LEADING EXPORTS: bananas, clothing, cocoa, and vegetables
LOCATION: Caribbean Sea

Saint Vincent and the Grenadines

CAPITAL: Kingstown
POPULATION: 117,344
MAJOR LANGUAGES: English and French patois
AREA: 131 sq mi; 340 sq km
LEADING EXPORTS: bananas, and eddoes and dasheen (taro)
LOCATION: Caribbean Sea

San Marino

CAPITAL: San Marino
POPULATION: 24,313
MAJOR LANGUAGE: Italian
AREA: 23 sq mi; 60 sq km
LEADING EXPORTS: building stone, lime, wood, and chestnuts
CONTINENT: Europe

Sao Tome and Principe

CAPITAL: Sao Tome
POPULATION: 140,423
MAJOR LANGUAGE: Portuguese (official)
AREA: 371 sq mi; 960 sq km
LEADING EXPORTS: cocoa, copra, coffee, and palm oil
CONTINENT: Africa

Saudi Arabia

CAPITAL: Riyadh
POPULATION: 18,729,576
MAJOR LANGUAGE: Arabic
AREA: 757,011 sq mi; 1,960,582 sq km
LEADING EXPORTS: petroleum and petroleum products
CONTINENT: Asia

Senegal

CAPITAL: Dakar
POPULATION: 9,007,080
MAJOR LANGUAGES: French (official), Wolof, Pulaar, Diola, and Mandingo
AREA: 75,752 sq mi; 196,190 sq km
LEADING EXPORTS: fish, ground nuts, and petroleum products
CONTINENT: Africa

Serbia and Montenegro

CAPITAL: Belgrade
POPULATION: 11,101,833
MAJOR LANGUAGES: Serbo-Croatian and Albanian
AREA: 39,436 sq mi; 102,350 sq km
LEADING EXPORTS: none
CONTINENT: Europe

Seychelles

CAPITAL: Victoria
POPULATION: 72,709
MAJOR LANGUAGES: English (official), French (official), and Creole
AREA: 176 sq mi; 455 sq km
LEADING EXPORTS: fish, cinnamon bark, and copra
CONTINENT: Africa

Sierra Leone

CAPITAL: Freetown
POPULATION: 4,753,120
MAJOR LANGUAGES: English (official), Mende, Temne, and Krio
AREA: 27,700 sq mi; 71,740 sq km
LEADING EXPORTS: rutile, bauxite, diamonds, coffee, and cocoa
CONTINENT: Africa

Singapore

CAPITAL: Singapore
POPULATION: 2,890,468
MAJOR LANGUAGES: Chinese, Malay, Tamil, and English
AREA: 244 sq mi; 633 sq km
LEADING EXPORTS: computer equipment
CONTINENT: Asia

Slovakia

CAPITAL: Bratislava
POPULATION: 5,432,383
MAJOR LANGUAGES: Slovak and Hungarian
AREA: 18,860 sq mi; 48,845 sq km
LEADING EXPORTS: machinery and transportation equipment
CONTINENT: Europe

Slovenia

CAPITAL: Ljubljana
POPULATION: 2,051,522
MAJOR LANGUAGES: Slovenian, Serbo-Croatian, and various languages
AREA: 7,837 sq mi; 20,296 sq km
LEADING EXPORTS: machinery and transportation equipment
CONTINENT: Europe

Solomon Islands

CAPITAL: Honiara
POPULATION: 399,206
MAJOR LANGUAGES: Melanesian pidgin and English
AREA: 10,985 sq mi; 28,450 sq km
LEADING EXPORTS: fish, timber, palm oil, cocoa, and copra
LOCATION: Pacific Ocean

Somalia

CAPITAL: Mogadishu
POPULATION: 7,347,554
MAJOR LANGUAGES: Somali (official), Arabic, Italian, and English
AREA: 246,210 sq mi; 637,660 sq km
LEADING EXPORTS: bananas, live animals, fish, and hides
CONTINENT: Africa

South Africa

CAPITAL: Pretoria (administrative), Cape Town (legislative), Bloemfontein (judicial)
POPULATION: 45,095,459
MAJOR LANGUAGES: Afrikaans, English, Ndebele, Pedi, Sotho, Swazi, Tsonga, Tswana, Venda, Xhosa, and Zulu (all official)
AREA: 471,027 sq mi; 1,219,912 sq km
LEADING EXPORTS: gold, other minerals and metals, and food
CONTINENT: Africa

Spain

CAPITAL: Madrid
POPULATION: 39,404,348
MAJOR LANGUAGES: Spanish, Catalan, Galician, and Basque
AREA: 194,892 sq mi; 504,750 sq km
LEADING EXPORTS: cars and trucks, and semifinished goods
CONTINENT: Europe

Sri Lanka

CAPITAL: Colombo
POPULATION: 18,342,660
MAJOR LANGUAGES: Sinhala (official) and Tamil
AREA: 25,333 sq mi; 65,610 sq km
LEADING EXPORTS: garments and textiles, teas, and diamonds
CONTINENT: Asia

Sudan

CAPITAL: Khartoum
POPULATION: 30,120,420
MAJOR LANGUAGES: Arabic (official), Nubian, Ta Bedawie, Nilotic, Nilo-Hamitic, and Sudanic dialects
AREA: 967,532 sq mi; 2,505,810 sq km
LEADING EXPORTS: gum arabic, livestock/meat, and cotton
CONTINENT: Africa

Suriname

CAPITAL: Paramaribo
POPULATION: 429,544
MAJOR LANGUAGES: Dutch (official), English, Sranang, Tongo, Hindustani, and Japanese
AREA: 63,041 sq mi; 163,270 sq km
LEADING EXPORTS: alumina, aluminum, and shrimp and fish
CONTINENT: South America

Swaziland

CAPITAL: Mbabane
POPULATION: 966,977
MAJOR LANGUAGES: English (official) and SiSwati (official)
AREA: 6,641 sq mi; 17,360 sq km
LEADING EXPORTS: sugar, edible concentrates, and wood pulp
CONTINENT: Africa

Sweden

CAPITAL: Stockholm
POPULATION: 8,821,759
MAJOR LANGUAGES: Swedish, Lapp, and Finnish
AREA: 173,738 sq mi; 449,964 sq km
LEADING EXPORTS: machinery, motor vehicles, and paper products
CONTINENT: Europe

Switzerland

CAPITAL: Bern
POPULATION: 7,084,984
MAJOR LANGUAGES: German, French, Italian, Romansch, and various languages
AREA: 15,943 sq mi; 41,290 sq km
LEADING EXPORTS: machinery and equipment
CONTINENT: Europe

Syria

CAPITAL: Damascus
POPULATION: 15,451,917
MAJOR LANGUAGES: Arabic (official), Kurdish, Armenian, Aramaic, Circassian, and French
AREA: 71,501 sq mi; 185,180 sq km
LEADING EXPORTS: petroleum, textiles, cotton, and fruits
CONTINENT: Asia

Taiwan

CAPITAL: Taipei
POPULATION: 21,500,583
MAJOR LANGUAGES: Mandarin Chinese (official), Taiwanese, and Hakka dialects
AREA: 13,892 sq mi; 35,980 sq km
LEADING EXPORTS: electrical machinery and electronics
CONTINENT: Asia

Tajikistan

CAPITAL: Dushanbe
POPULATION: 6,155,474
MAJOR LANGUAGES: Tajik (official) and Russian
AREA: 55,253 sq mi; 143,100 sq km
LEADING EXPORTS: cotton, aluminum, fruits, and vegetable oil
CONTINENT: Asia

Tanzania

CAPITAL: Dar Es Salaam
POPULATION: 28,701,077
MAJOR LANGUAGES: Swahili, English, and various languages
AREA: 364,914 sq mi; 945,090 sq km
LEADING EXPORTS: coffee, cotton, tobacco, tea, and cashew nuts
CONTINENT: Africa

Thailand

CAPITAL: Bangkok
POPULATION: 60,271,300
MAJOR LANGUAGES: Thai and English
AREA: 198,463 sq mi; 511,770 sq km
LEADING EXPORTS: machinery and manufactures
CONTINENT: Asia

Togo

CAPITAL: Lome
POPULATION: 4,410,370
MAJOR LANGUAGES: French, Ewe and Mina, Dagomba, and Kabye
AREA: 21,927 sq mi; 56,790 sq km
LEADING EXPORTS: phosphates, cotton, cocoa, and coffee
CONTINENT: Africa

Tonga

CAPITAL: Nukualofa
POPULATION: 105,600
MAJOR LANGUAGES: Tongan and English
AREA: 289 sq mi; 748 sq km
LEADING EXPORTS: squash, vanilla, fish, root crops, and coconut oil
LOCATION: Pacific Ocean

Trinidad and Tobago

CAPITAL: Port-of-Spain
POPULATION: 1,271,159
MAJOR LANGUAGES: English, Hindu, French, and Spanish
AREA: 1,981 sq mi; 5,130 sq km
LEADING EXPORTS: petroleum and petroleum products
LOCATION: Caribbean Sea

Tunisia

CAPITAL: Tunis
POPULATION: 8,879,845
MAJOR LANGUAGES: Arabic and French
AREA: 63,172 sq mi; 163,610 sq km
LEADING EXPORTS: hydrocarbons and agricultural products
CONTINENT: Africa

Turkey

CAPITAL: Ankara
POPULATION: 63,405,526
MAJOR LANGUAGES: Turkish, Kurdish, and Arabic
AREA: 301,394 sq mi; 780,580 sq km
LEADING EXPORTS: manufactured products, and foodstuffs
CONTINENT: Europe and Asia

Turkmenistan

CAPITAL: Ashgabat
POPULATION: 4,075,316
MAJOR LANGUAGES: Turkmen, Russian, Uzbek, and various languages
AREA: 188,463 sq mi; 488,100 sq km
LEADING EXPORTS: natural gas, cotton, and petroleum products
CONTINENT: Asia

Tuvalu

CAPITAL: Fongafale, on Funafuti atoll
POPULATION: 9,991
MAJOR LANGUAGES: Tuvaluan and English
AREA: 10 sq mi; 26 sq km
LEADING EXPORT: copra
LOCATION: Pacific Ocean

Uganda

CAPITAL: Kampala
POPULATION: 19,573,262
MAJOR LANGUAGES: English, Luganda, Swahili, Bantu languages, and Nilotic languages
AREA: 91,139 sq mi; 236,040 sq km
LEADING EXPORTS: coffee, cotton, and tea
CONTINENT: Africa

Ukraine

CAPITAL: Kiev
POPULATION: 51,867,828
MAJOR LANGUAGES: Ukranian, Russian, Romanian, Polish, and Hungarian
AREA: 233,098 sq mi; 603,700 sq km
LEADING EXPORTS: coal, electric power, and metals
CONTINENT: Europe

United Arab Emirates

CAPITAL: Abu Dhabi
POPULATION: 2,924,594
MAJOR LANGUAGES: Arabic, Persian, English, Hindi, and Urdu
AREA: 29,183 sq mi; 75,581 sq km
LEADING EXPORTS: crude oil, natural gas, re-exports, and dried fish
CONTINENT: Asia

United Kingdom

CAPITAL: London
POPULATION: 58,295,119
MAJOR LANGUAGES: English, Welsh, and Scottish Gaelic
AREA: 94,529 sq mi; 244,820 sq km
LEADING EXPORTS: manufactured goods, machinery, and fuels
CONTINENT: Europe

United States

CAPITAL: Washington, D.C.
POPULATION: 263,814,032
MAJOR LANGUAGES: English and Spanish
AREA: 3,618,908 sq mi; 9,372,610 sq km
LEADING EXPORTS: capital goods and automobiles
CONTINENT: North America

Uruguay

CAPITAL: Montevideo
POPULATION: 3,222,716
MAJOR LANGUAGES: Spanish and Brazilero
AREA: 68,041 sq mi; 176,220 sq km
LEADING EXPORTS: wool and textile manufactures
CONTINENT: South America

Uzbekistan

CAPITAL: Tashkent
POPULATION: 23,089,261
MAJOR LANGUAGES: Uzbek, Russian, Tajik, various languages
AREA: 172,748 sq mi; 447,400 sq km
LEADING EXPORTS: cotton, gold, natural gas, and minerals
CONTINENT: Asia

Vanuatu

CAPITAL: Port-Vila
POPULATION: 173,648
MAJOR LANGUAGES: English, French, pidgin, and Bislama
AREA: 5,699 sq mi; 14,760 sq km
LEADING EXPORTS: copra, beef, cocoa, timber, and coffee
LOCATION: Pacific Ocean

Venezuela

CAPITAL: Caracas
POPULATION: 21,004,773
MAJOR LANGUAGES: Spanish and various languages
AREA: 352,156 sq mi; 912,050 sq km
LEADING EXPORTS: petroleum, bauxite and aluminum, and steel
CONTINENT: South America

Vietnam

CAPITAL: Hanoi
POPULATION: 74,393,324
MAJOR LANGUAGES: Vietnamese, French, Chinese, English, Khmer, and various languages
AREA: 127,248 sq mi; 329,560 sq km
LEADING EXPORTS: petroleum, rice, and agricultural products
CONTINENT: Asia

Western Samoa

CAPITAL: Apia
POPULATION: 209,360
MAJOR LANGUAGES: Samoan and English
AREA: 1,104 sq mi; 2,860 sq km
LEADING EXPORTS: coconut oil and cream, taro, copra, and cocoa
LOCATION: Pacific Ocean

Yemen

CAPITAL: Sanaa
POPULATION: 14,728,474
MAJOR LANGUAGE: Arabic
AREA: 203,857 sq mi; 527,970 sq km
LEADING EXPORTS: crude oil, cotton, coffee, hides, and vegetables
CONTINENT: Asia

Zaire (Democratic Republic of Congo)

CAPITAL: Kinshasa
POPULATION: 44,060,636
MAJOR LANGUAGES: French, Lingala, Swahili, Kingwana, Kikongo, and Tshiluba
AREA: 905,599 sq mi; 2,345,410 sq km
LEADING EXPORTS: copper, coffee, diamonds, cobalt, and crude oil
CONTINENT: Africa

Zambia

CAPITAL: Lusaka
POPULATION: 9,445,723
MAJOR LANGUAGES: English (official) and about 70 various languages
AREA: 290,594 sq mi; 752,610 sq km
LEADING EXPORTS: copper, zinc, cobalt, lead, and tobacco
CONTINENT: Africa

Zimbabwe

CAPITAL: Harare
POPULATION: 11,139,961
MAJOR LANGUAGES: English, Shona, and Sindebele
area: 150,809 sq mi; 390,580 sq km
LEADING EXPORTS: agricultural products and manufactures
CONTINENT: Africa

Glossary of Geographic Terms

basin
a depression in the surface of the land; some basins are filled with water

bay
a part of a sea or lake that extends into the land

butte
a small raised area of land with steep sides

▲ butte

canyon
a deep, narrow valley with steep sides; often has a stream flowing through it

cataract
a large waterfall; any strong flood or rush of water

delta
a triangular-shaped plain at the mouth of a river, formed when sediment is deposited by flowing water

flood plain
a broad plain on either side of a river, formed when sediment settles on the riverbanks

glacier
a huge, slow-moving mass of snow and ice

hill
an area that rises above surrounding land and has a rounded top; lower and usually less steep than a mountain

island
an area of land completely surrounded by water

isthmus
a narrow strip of land that connects two larger areas of land

mesa
a high, flat-topped landform with cliff-like sides; larger than a butte

mountain
an area that rises steeply at least 2,000 feet (300 m) above surrounding land; usually wide at the bottom and rising to a narrow peak or ridge

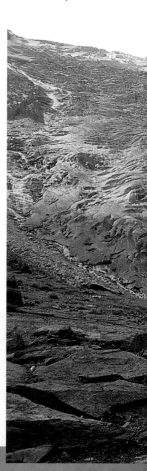

▶ glacier

◀ cataract

◀ delta

mountain pass
a gap between mountains

peninsula
an area of land almost completely surrounded by water and connected to the mainland by an isthmus

plain
a large area of flat or gently rolling land

plateau
a large, flat area that rises above the surrounding land; at least one side has a steep slope

river mouth
the point where a river enters a lake or sea

strait
a narrow stretch of water that connects two larger bodies of water

tributary
a river or stream that flows into a larger river

volcano
an opening in the Earth's surface through which molten rock, ashes, and gasses from the Earth's interior escape

▶ volcano

Gazetteer

A

Africa world's second-largest continent, surrounded by the Mediterranean Sea, the Atlantic Ocean, and the Red Sea, p. 57

Amazon Rain Forest a large tropical rain forest occupying the drainage basin of the Amazon River in northern South America and covering an area of 2,700,000 square miles, p. 289

Andes Mountains a mountain system extending along the western coast of South America, p. 278

Antarctic Circle (66°S) line of latitude around the Earth near the South Pole, p. 29

Antarctica the continent located at the South Pole; almost completely covered by an ice sheet, p. 47

Appalachian Mountains a mountain system in eastern North America, p. 139

Arctic Circle (66°N) line of latitude around the Earth near the North Pole, p. 29

Arctic region located at the North Pole, p. 59

Argentina (35°S, 67°W) a country in South America, p. 282

Asia the world's largest continent, surrounded by the Arctic Ocean, the Pacific Ocean, the Indian Ocean, and Europe, p. 57

Atacama Desert a desert in Chile, South America; the driest place on the Earth, p. 28

Atlanta (33°N, 84°W) the capital of the state of Georgia, p. 221

Australia an island continent in the Southern Hemisphere; a country including the continent and Tasmania, p. 57

B

Bolivia (17°S, 64°W) a country in South America, p. 273

Boston (42°N, 71°W) the capital of the state of Massachusetts, p. 215

Brasília (15°S, 47°W) the capital city of Brazil, p. 346

Brazil the largest country in South America, p. 282

C

California Current a southward-flowing oceanic current along the West Coast of North America; flows between 48°N and 23°N, p. 40

Canal Zone a 10-mile strip of land along the Panama Canal, stretching from the Atlantic Ocean to the Pacific Ocean, p. 371

Caracas (10°N, 66°W) the capital city of Venezuela, p. 418

Caribbean Sea part of the southern Atlantic Ocean, pp. 41, 279

Cariboo Mountains a mountain range in eastern British Columbia, Canada; a place where miners struck gold in the 1800s, p. 260

Central America the part of Latin America between Mexico and South America; includes the seven republics of Guatemala, Honduras, El Salvador, Nicaragua, Costa Rica, Panama, and Belize, p. 279

Chicago (41°N, 87°W) a major city in the state of Illinois, on Lake Michigan, p. 230

Chile a country on the west coast of South America, p. 284

China a country occupying most of the mainland of East Asia, p. 90

Colombia a country in northwest South America, p. 295

Condado a waterfront area of San Juan, Puerto Rico, p. 393

Copán (14°N, 89°W) a ruined ancient Mayan city in western Honduras, p. 306

Cuba (22°N, 79°W) an island country, the largest of the Caribbean islands, pp. 65, 281

Cuyahoga River a river in northeastern Ohio, p. 185

Cuzco (13°S, 71°W) a city in Peru; capital of the Incan empire, p. 309

D

Death Valley the hottest, driest region of North America, located in southeastern California, p. 139

Detroit (42°N, 83°W) an industrial city in the state of Michigan, p. 231

E

Egypt a country in North Africa, p. 85

Europe the world's second-smallest continent; a peninsula of the Eurasian landmass bounded by the Arctic Ocean, the Atlantic Ocean, the Mediterranean Sea, and Asia, p. 57

F

Fraser River a major river of western North America, along the border between British Columbia and Alberta, p. 260

G

Galapagos Islands group of islands located in the eastern Pacific Ocean; part of Ecuador, p. 40

Germany a country in Europe, p. 83

Grand Coulee Dam (47°N, 119°W) a dam on the Columbia River in the state of Washington, p. 151

Great Britain popular name of the United Kingdom, a country in western Europe; the largest island of the United Kingdom, including England, Scotland, and Wales, p. 83

Great Lakes a group of five large lakes in central North America: Lakes Superior, Michigan, Huron, Erie, and Ontario, p. 141

Great Plains a dry area of short grasses located in North America, stretching from the Rio Grande at the U.S.-Mexico border in the south to the Mackenzie River Delta in the north, and from the Canadian Shield in the east to the Rocky Mountains in the west; also called "The Great American Desert," p. 46

Greenland a large, self-governing island in the northern Atlantic Ocean, part of Denmark, p.14

Guatemala (15°N, 91°W) a country in Central America, p. 306

Gulf Stream a warm ocean current in the North Atlantic, flowing northeastward off the North American coast, p. 40

H

Haiti (19°N, 72°W) a country in the Caribbean Sea, on the island of Hispaniola, p. 320

Hispaniola (17°N, 73°W) an island in the Caribbean Sea, divided between Haiti in the west and the Dominican Republic in the east, p. 281

I

Imperial Valley a valley in the Colorado Desert, extending from southeastern California to Mexico, p. 150

India a large country occupying most of the Indian subcontinent in South Asia, p. 37

Indian Ocean the world's third-largest ocean, lying between Africa, Asia, and Australia, p. 9

Indonesia a country in Southeast Asia consisting of many islands, including Sumatra, Java, Sulawesi (Celebes), Bali, and the western half of New Guinea, p. 68

Israel (32°N, 34°E) a country in Southwest Asia, p. 91

Italy (43°N, 11°E) a boot-shaped country in southern Europe, including the islands of Sicily and Sardinia, p. 89

J

Jakarta (6°S, 106°E) the capital and largest city of the Republic of Indonesia, p. 68

Jamaica (17°N, 78°W) an island country in the Caribbean Sea, p. 281

Jamestown the first permanent British settlement in North America, located in present-day Virginia; now a site of historic preservation, p. 164

Japan (36°N, 133°E) an island country in the Pacific Ocean off the east coast of Asia, consisting of four main islands—Honshu, Hokkaido, Kyushu, and Shikoku—and many smaller islands, p. 55

L

Lake Erie the fourth largest of the five Great Lakes; forms part of the boundary between Canada and the United States, p. 185

Lake Maracaibo (9°N, 72°W) a lake in northwestern Venezuela, p. 283

Lake Titicaca the world's largest lake, in the Andes Mountains in South America, p. 283

M

Mexico (23°N, 104°W) a country in North America, pp. 41, 279

Mexico City (19°N, 99°W) the capital of and largest city in Mexico; one of the largest urban areas in the world, p. 306

Miami (25°N, 80°W) a city in southeastern Florida, p. 377

Minneapolis-St. Paul (44°N, 93°W) two cities in Minnesota; also called the Twin Cities, p. 232

Mississippi River a large river in the central United States flowing south from Minnesota to the Gulf of Mexico, p. 142

Montreal (45°N, 73°W) the largest city in the province of Quebec, Canada, p. 248

Mount Everest (28°N, 86°E) highest point on the Earth, located on the Great Himalaya Range in Asia, p. 47

Myanmar (Burma) (21°N, 95°E) a country in Southeast Asia, p. 9

N

Nepal (28°N, 83°E) a country in south Asia, p. 47

New York City (40°N, 73°W) a large city and port at the mouth of the Hudson River in the state of New York, p. 215

Niagara Falls (43°N, 79°W) a waterfall on the Niagara River between Ontario, Canada, and New York state; one of North America's most famous spectacles, p. 188

Nile Valley the fertile land located on both sides of the Nile River in Africa; site of one of the earliest civilizations, p. 59

North America the world's third-largest continent, consisting of Canada, the United States, Mexico, and many islands, p. 57

North Pole (90°N) northernmost end of the Earth's axis, located in the Arctic Ocean, p. 39

Nunavut a section of land in the Northwest Territories of Canada, granted by the government as Inuit "homeland," p. 206

O

Ontario (50°N, 88°W) the second-largest province in Canada, p. 180

P

Pacific Northwest the region in the northwestern United States that includes Oregon, Washington, and part of Idaho, p. 235

Pacific Rim the countries bordering on the Pacific Ocean, p. 262

Panama (9°N, 80°W) southern-most country of Central America, p. 323

Panama Canal an important shipping canal across the Isthmus of Panama, linking the Caribbean Sea (and the Atlantic Ocean) to the Pacific Ocean, p. 366

Pangaea (pan jee uh) according to scientific theory, a single landmass that broke apart to form today's separate continents; thought to have existed about 180 million years ago, p. 33

Paraguay (24°S, 57°W) a country in central South America, p. 273

Patagonia a desert in southern Argentina; the largest desert in the Americas, p. 287

Pennsylvania Colony a colony in America founded in 1680 by William Penn, who purchased land from the Native Americans, p. 164

Peru (10°S, 75°W) a country in northwest South America, p. 283

Peru Current a cold-water current of the southeast Pacific Ocean; flows between 40°S and 4°S, p. 40

Philadelphia (40°N, 75°W) a city and port in Pennsylvania, located on the Delaware River, p. 215

Port-au-Prince (18°N, 72°W) the capital city and chief port of Haiti, p. 383

Portland (45°N, 122°W) the largest city in the state of Oregon, p. 236

Puerto Rico (18°N, 66°W) an island commonwealth of the United States in the Caribbean Sea, p. 281

Q

Quebec (51°N, 70°W) a province in southeastern Canada, p. 179

Quebec City (46°N, 71°W) the capital city of the province of Quebec, Canada, p. 247

R

Regina (50°N, 104°W) the capital of the province of Saskatchewan, Canada, p. 257

Ring of Fire a circle of volcanic mountains that surrounds the Pacific Ocean, including those on the islands of Japan and Indonesia, in the Cascades of North America, and in the Andes of South America, p. 31

Rio de Janeiro (22°S, 43°W) a major city in Brazil, p. 399

Rocky Mountains the major mountain range in western North America, extending south from Alberta, Canada, through the western United States to Mexico, p. 138

S

Salvador (12°S, 38°W) the capital city and major port of Bahia state, in northeastern Brazil, p. 400

San Francisco (37°N, 122°W) a seaport city in California, p. 40

San Jose (37°N, 121°W) a city in western California, p. 237

San Juan (18°N, 66°W) the capital and largest city in Puerto Rico, p. 393

Santiago (33°S, 70°W) the capital city of Chile, p. 412

São Paulo (23°S, 46°W) the largest city in Brazil, p. 342

Saskatoon (52°N, 106°W) a city in the province of Saskatchewan, Canada, p. 257

Sierra Nevada Mountains a mountain range in California in the western United States, p. 235

South America the world's fourth-largest continent, bounded by the Caribbean Sea, the Atlantic Ocean, and the Pacific Ocean, and linked to North America by the Isthmus of Panama, pp. 40, 279

South Pole (90°S) southernmost end of the Earth's axis located in Antarctica, p. 39

St. Lawrence Lowlands a major agricultural region in the prairie provinces of Canada, p. 152

St. Lawrence River a river in eastern North America; the third-longest river in Canada, p. 140

St. Lawrence Seaway a navigable seaway from the Atlantic Ocean to the western end of the Great Lakes, maintained jointly by the United States and Canada, p. 188

St. Louis (38°N, 90°W) the largest city in Missouri, on the Mississippi River, pp. 40, 231

T

Tenochtitlán name of the ancient Aztec metropolis covering more than five square miles near modern Mexico City; originally located on two small islands in Lake Texcoco, it gradually expanded; one of two Aztec capitals, its name means "stone rising in the water," p. 307

Tikal (17°N, 89°W) site of the largest Mayan city, in the northern part of Guatemala, p. 306

Trinidad and Tobago (11°N, 61°W) republic of the West Indies, on the two islands called Trinidad and Tobago, p. 273

Tropic of Cancer (23.5°N) the northern boundary of the tropics, or the band of the Earth that receives the most direct light and heat energy from the sun, p. 29

Tropic of Capricorn (23.5°S) the southern boundary of the tropics, or the band of the Earth that receives the most direct light and heat energy from the sun, p. 29

V

Valley of Mexico the area in Mexico where Lake Texcoco, Tenochtitlán, and modern Mexico City are located, p. 306

Vancouver (49°N, 123°W) a city in southwestern British Columbia, Canada, p. 144

Venezuela (8°N, 65°W) a country in South America, p. 282

Victoria (48°N, 123°W) the capital of British Columbia, Canada, p. 260

Vietnam (18°N, 107°E) a country located in Southeast Asia, p. 66

W

Washington, D.C. (38°N, 77°W) the capital city of the United States, located between Maryland and Virginia on the Potomac River, pp. 215, 226

West Indies the islands of the Caribbean, p. 273

Winnipeg (49°N, 97°W) the capital city of Manitoba, Canada, p. 144

Y

Yukon (63°N, 135°W) a territory in northwestern Canada, p. 181

Glossary

A

abolitionist a person who believed that enslaving people was wrong and who wanted to end the practice, p. 170

acculturation the process of accepting, borrowing, and exchanging ideas and traits among cultures, p. 95

acid rain rain whose high level of chemicals can pollute or damage the environment; usually caused by pollutants from the burning of fossil fuels, pp. 118, 186

agribusiness a large company that runs huge farms to produce, process, and distribute agricultural products, p. 150

agriculture farming; includes growing crops and raising livestock, p. 80

alliance formal agreement to do business together, sometimes formed between governments, p. 166

alluvial deposited by water, relating to the fertile topsoil left by rivers after a flood, p. 150

altiplano [al tih plah noh] a high plateau region; a region of high plateaus in the Andes, p. 405

amid in the middle of; within, p. 201

aqueduct a pipe or channel used to carry water from a distant source to dry areas, p. 311

atmosphere the multilayered band of gases that surrounds the Earth, p. 35

axis an imaginary line around which a planet turns; the Earth turns around its axis, which runs between its North and South poles, p. 28

B

bilingual speaking two languages; having two official languages, p. 183

birthrate the number of live births each year per 1,000 people, p. 61

bison buffalo; a large animal something like an ox, p. 161

boom a period of increased prosperity; period of economic activity when more of a product is produced and sold, p. 419

boomtown a settlement that sprang up quickly, often to serve the needs of miners, p. 260

boycott a refusal to buy or use goods and services, p. 165

C

campesino [kahm pe see noh] a poor Latin American farmer, p. 328

canopy a dense mass of leaves forming the top layer of a forest, pp. 44, 399

capitalism an economic system in which people and privately owned companies own both basic and nonbasic businesses and industries, p. 89

cardinal direction one of the four compass points: north, south, east, and west, p. 19

Carnival an annual celebration in Latin America with music, dances, and parades, p. 342

caudillo [kow dee yoh] a military officer who rules strictly, p. 324

citizen an individual with certain rights and responsibilities under a particular government, p. 391

civil rights movement the efforts of a large group of people who worked together in the United States beginning in the 1960s to end the segregation of African Americans and to support equal rights for all minorities, p. 176

Civil War the war between the northern and southern states in the United States, which began in 1861 and ended in 1865, p. 170

clear-cutting a type of logging in which all the trees in an area are cut down, p. 187

climate the weather patterns that an area typically experiences over a long period of time, p. 38

Cold War a period of great tension between the United States and the former Soviet Union, which lasted for more than 40 years after World War II, p. 176

commercial farming farming that is done by companies; commercial farms are large and use modern technology; also, the raising of crops and livestock for sale in outside markets, p. 114

commonwealth a self-governing political unit with strong ties to a particular country, p. 391

communism a system of government in which the government controls the means of industrial production, determining what goods are to be made, how much workers will be paid, and how much items will cost, pp. 90, 176

communist having an economic system in which the government owns all large businesses and most of a country's land, p. 379

commute to travel regularly to and from a place, particularly to and from a job, p. 215

compass rose a map feature that usually shows the four cardinal directions, p. 19

complex complicated; not simple, p. 258

conquistador [kon kees ta dor] sixteenth-century conquerors working for the Spanish government who were in charge of gaining land and wealth in the Americas, p. 314

conservation preserving and protecting from loss, p. 233

constitution a set of laws that defines a country's basic values and limits a government's power, pp. 91, 393

consumer a person who buys goods and services, p. 88

Continental Divide the boundary that separates rivers flowing toward opposite sides of a continent; in North America, the Rocky Mountains, p. 142

continental United States the geographical area that includes all states of the United States except Alaska and Hawaii, p. 57

cooperative an organization managed by a group of people working together for a shared purpose, p. 256

coral a rock-like substance formed from the skeletons of tiny sea animals, p. 281

corporate farm a large farm run by a corporation; may consist of many smaller farms once owned by families, p. 229

counter to act in defense, p. 237

Creole a person, often of European and African descent, born in the Caribbean or other parts of the Americas, whose culture has strong French and African influence; a dialect spoken by Creoles, p. 385

criollo [kree oh yoh] a person born of Spanish parents but born outside of Spain; criollos were often among the best-educated and wealthiest people in the Spanish colonies, p. 320

crucial extremely important, p. 180

cultural diffusion the movement of customs and ideas from one culture to another, p. 95

cultural diversity a wide variety of cultures, p. 197

cultural exchange a process in which different cultures share ideas and ways of doing things, p. 198

cultural landscape a landscape that has been changed by human beings and that reflects their culture, p. 79

cultural trait a behavioral characteristic of a people, such as a language, skill, or custom, passed from one generation to another, p. 78

culture the way of life of people who share similar customs and beliefs, p. 78

D

death rate the number of deaths each year per 1,000 people, p. 61

debate argument; disagreement expressed in words, p. 169

deforestation the process of clearing land of forests or trees, usually to make room for farms and homes, p. 118

degree a unit of measure used to determine absolute location; on globes and maps, latitude and longitude are measured in degrees, p. 11

demographer a scientist who studies human populations, including their size; growth; density; distribution; and rates of births, marriages, and deaths, p. 55

dense thick and crowded, p. 259

descendant child, grandchild, great-grandchild (and so on) of an ancestor, p. 249

developed nation a modern industrial society with a well-developed economy, p. 113

developing nation a country with relatively low industrial production, often lacking modern technology, p. 113

dialect a version of a language that is spoken in a particular region, p. 385

dictator a person who has absolute power to rule a country, pp. 92, 175, 379

direct democracy a system of government in which the people participate directly in decision making, p. 91

distinct clearly different; separate, p. 163

distortion a misrepresentation of the true shape; each map projection used by a cartographer produces some distortion, p. 15

diverse varied, p. 163

diversify to add variety; to expand, p. 297

diversity variety, p. 334

dominion a self-governing area subject to Great Britain; for example, Canada prior to 1939, p. 181

drought a long period of weather with no rain, p. 253

dwindle to become fewer in number, p. 228

E

economy a system for producing, distributing, consuming, and owning goods, services, and wealth, pp. 88, 136, 325

ecosystem a community of living things and their environment; the elements of an ecosystem interact with one another, p. 117

El Niño [el neen yoh] a warm ocean current that flows along the western coast of South America; this current influences global weather patterns, p. 294

elevation height of land above sea level, p. 297

emigrate move out of one country into another, p. 337

encomienda [en koh mee en duh] a right that was granted by the Spanish government to its settlers in the Americas to demand taxes or labor from Native Americans, p. 317

enslave to force someone to become a slave, p. 163

Equator an imaginary line that circles the globe at its widest point (halfway between the North and South poles), dividing the Earth into two halves called hemispheres; used as a reference point from which north and south latitudes are measured, p. 11

erosion a process by which water, wind, or ice wears away landforms and carries the material to another place, p. 35

ethics the standards or code of moral behavior that distinguishes between right and wrong for a particular person, religion, group, profession, and so on, p. 85

ethnic group a group of people who share a language, a religion, a history, and cultural traditions, pp. 199, 340, 362

exile a person who leaves or is forced to leave his or her homeland for another country because of political reasons, p. 340

expanse a wide open space or area, p. 150

extended family a family unit that may include parents, children, grandparents, aunts, uncles, cousins, and other relatives, p. 84

F

fertile able to produce many crops, p. 139

foreign aid economic and military aid to another country, p. 116

forty-niner one of the first miners of the California Gold Rush of 1849, p. 235

fossil fuel a nonrenewable resource formed over millions of years from animal and plant remains; includes coal, petroleum, and natural gas, pp. 108, 186

Francophone a person who speaks French as his or her first language, p. 249

free trade trade with no tariffs, or taxes, on imported goods, p. 189

freshwater consisting of water that has no salt in it, p. 141

fugitive a runaway; someone who runs from danger, p. 169

fundamental basic; being the foundation on which something is built, p. 233

G

gangplank a movable bridge or walkway people cross to get on or off a ship, p. 220

geographic diversity a variety of landforms, climates, and vegetation, p. 198

geography the study of the Earth's surface and the processes that shape it, the connections between places, and the relationship between people and their environment, p. 10

glacier a large mass of ice that moves slowly over the land, formed over a long period of time from tightly compressed snow, p. 140

global warming a slow increase in the Earth's temperature due to the increasing amount of carbon dioxide in the atmosphere; if there is too much carbon dioxide in the atmosphere, more heat than normal is trapped in the Earth's atmosphere, and temperatures around the world increase, p. 120

globe a round model of the Earth that shows the continents and oceans in their true shapes, p. 15

goods products that are made to be sold; cars, baskets, computers, and paper are all examples of goods, p. 88

government the system that establishes and enforces the laws and institutions of a society; some governments are controlled by a few people, and others are controlled by many, or are representative p. 90

Green Revolution changes in agriculture since the 1950s that have greatly increased the world's food supply; the Green Revolution comes with a price tag, however, since reliance on costly technologies and dangerous pesticides can be both financially and environmentally damaging to nations, p. 61

gunnysack a bag or sack made of burlap or other coarse materials, p. 227

H

habitat the area in which a plant or an animal naturally grows or lives, pp. 118, 236

hacienda [hah see en duh] plantation owned by the Spanish settlers or the Catholic Church in Spanish America, p. 317

haze foglike air, often caused by pollution, p. 186

hieroglyphics [hy ur oh glif iks] a system of writing using signs and symbols, used by the Maya and other cultures, p. 316

high latitudes the region between the Arctic Circle and the North Pole and the Antarctic Circle and the South Pole, p. 29

hill a landform that rises above the surrounding land and that has a rounded top; a hill is lower and usually less steep than a mountain, p. 32

Homestead Act a law passed in 1862 giving 160 acres (65 hectares) of land on the Midwestern plains to any adult willing to live on the land and farm it for five years, p. 173

hydroelectricity electric power produced by moving water, usually generated by releasing water from a dam across a river, pp. 151, 293

I

illiterate unable to read or write, p. 382

immigrant a person who has moved to a new country for the purpose of settling there, pp. 64, 168, 337

immunity a natural resistance to disease, p. 254

import to bring products into one country from another in order to sell them, p. 346

indentured servant a person who, in exchange for benefits received, must work for a period of years to gain freedom, p. 163

indigenous [in dij uh nus] describes people who are descendants of the people who first lived in a region, pp. 163, 334

Industrial Revolution the change from making goods by hand to making them by machine; the Industrial Revolution began in England in the 1700s and later spread to the United States and Europe, p. 168

industrialization the process of building new industries in an area previously dominated by farming; the development of large industries, p. 224

injustice lack of fairness, p. 335

interdependent dependent upon each other, p. 188

invest to spend money to earn more money, p. 325

isthmus narrow strip of land that has water on both sides and joins two larger bodies of land, p. 281

K

key the section of a map that explains the symbols for the map features; also called a legend, p. 19

L

labor force the supply of workers, p. 173

lacrosse ballgame played by two teams with long rackets, p. 207

ladino [luh dee noh] in Guatemala, a mestizo, p. 360

land bridge a bridge formed by a narrow strip of land connecting one landmass to another, p. 161

landform an area of the Earth's surface with a definite shape; mountains and hills are examples of landforms, p. 32

landmass a large area of land, p. 138

latitude lines the series of imaginary lines, also called parallels, that circle the Earth parallel to the Equator; used to measure a distance north or south of the Equator in degrees, p. 11

life expectancy the number of years that a person may be expected, on average, to live, p. 61

Line of Demarcation an imaginary line from the North Pole to the South Pole (at about 50° longitude) set forth in the 1494 Treaty of Tordesillas; Spain had the right to settle and trade west of the line and Portugal had the right to settle and trade east of the line, p. 314

lock an enclosed section of a canal in which ships are raised or lowered by adjusting the water level, pp. 141, 366

longitude lines the series of imaginary lines, also called meridians, that run north and south from one pole to the other; used to measure a distance east or west of the Prime Meridian in degrees, p. 11

Louisiana Purchase the sale of land in 1803 by France to the United States; all the land between the Mississippi River and the eastern slope of the Rocky Mountains, p. 166

low latitudes the region between the Tropic of Cancer and the Tropic of Capricorn, p. 29

lowlands lands that are lower than the surrounding land, p. 139

M

maize both the plant and the kernel of corn, p. 306

mammoth a huge animal something like an elephant, now extinct, p. 161

Manifest Destiny a belief that the United States had a right to own and rule all the land from the Atlantic Ocean to the Pacific Ocean, p. 168

manufacturing the process of turning raw materials into a finished product, p. 112

maquiladora [ma kee la dor a] a U.S.-owned factory in Mexico that is located close to the U.S.-Mexico border, p. 336

mass transit a system of subways, buses, and commuter trains used to transport large numbers of people, p. 237

megalopolis a number of cities and suburbs that blend into one very large urban area, p. 215

meridian an imaginary line that circles the globe from north to south and runs through both the North and South poles; the lines of longitude on maps or globes are meridians, p. 11

mestizo a person of mixed Spanish and Native American ancestry, p. 316

middle latitudes the region between the Tropic of Cancer and the Arctic Circle and the Tropic of Capricorn and the Antarctic Circle, p. 30

migrant farmworker a laborer who travels from one area to another, picking crops that are in season, p. 356

migration movement of people from one country or region to another in order to make a new home, pp. 64, 161

missionary a person who tries to convert others to his or her religion, p. 163

mixed-crop farm a farm that grows several different kinds of crops, p. 228

monarchy a system of authoritarian government headed by a monarch—usually a king or queen—who inherits the throne by birth, p. 91

montaña in northeast Peru, large stretches of tropical forests on the lower slopes of mountains, p. 406

mountain a landform that usually rises more than 2,000 ft (610 m) above sea level and is wide at the bottom and narrow at the peak, p. 32

N

NAFTA North American Free Trade Agreement, signed in 1994 by Canada, the United States, and Mexico to establish mutual free trade, p. 189

navigate to plot or direct the course of a ship or aircraft, p. 141

nomadic moving from one place to another frequently in search of food or pastureland, p. 206

nonrenewable resource a resource that cannot be replaced once it is used; nonrenewable resources include fossil fuels such as coal and oil, and minerals such as iron, copper, and gold, p. 107

nuclear family a family unit that includes a mother, a father, and their children, p. 83

O

obstacle something that is in the way, p. 261

orbit the path followed by an object in space as it moves around another, such as that of the Earth as it moves around the sun, p. 28

ore rock that contains valuable metal or minerals, p. 153

ozone layer the layer of gas in the upper part of the atmosphere that blocks out most of the sun's harmful ultraviolet rays, p. 119

P

pampas [pahm puhs] flat grassland regions in the southern part of South America; a region similar to the Great Plains in the United States, p. 282

parallel in geography, any of the imaginary lines that circle the Earth parallel to the Equator; a latitude line, p. 11

pastime recreation; activity that makes time pass pleasantly, p. 201

permafrost permanently frozen layer of ground below the top layer of soil, p. 147

pesticide [pes tuh syd] a chemical used to kill insects and diseases that can attack crops, p. 417

petrochemical a substance, such as plastic, paint, or asphalt, that is made from petroleum, p. 223

photosynthesis [foht oh sin thuh sis] the process by which green plants and trees produce their own food using water, carbon dioxide, and sunlight; oxygen is released as a result of photosynthesis, p. 403

plain a large area of flat or gently rolling land, pp. 13, 32

plantation a large estate, usually in a warm climate, on which crops are grown by workers living there; plantations usually raise a single crop for export, and were common in the Southern United States before the Civil War pp. 115, 164

plate in geography, a huge section of the Earth's crust, p. 33

plate tectonics the theory that the Earth's crust is made of huge, slowly moving slabs of rock called plates, p. 33

plateau [pla toh] a large, mostly flat area that rises above the surrounding land; at least one side has a steep slope, pp. 32, 281

plaza public square at the center of a village, town, or city, p. 355

population density the average number of people per square mile or square kilometer living in a given area, pp. 58, 216

population distribution how a population is spread over an area, p. 55

population the people living in a particular region; especially the total number of people in an area, p. 55

prairie a region of flat or rolling land covered with tall grasses, p. 147

precipitation all the forms of water, such as rain, sleet, hail, and snow, that fall to the ground from the atmosphere, p. 38

prejudice unfair judgment against someone based on hatred of his or her race, religion, or culture, p. 249

Prime Meridian an imaginary line of longitude, or meridian, that runs from the North Pole to the South Pole through Greenwich, England; it is designated 0° longitude and is used as a reference point from which east and west lines of longitude are measured, p. 11

privatization [pry vuh tih zay shun] a policy of a government to sell its industries to individuals or private companies, p. 422

producer a person who makes products that are used by other people, p. 88

projection a representation of the Earth's rounded surface on a flat piece of paper; a map p. 16

prosperity continued success or good fortune, especially concerning wealth, p. 167

province a political division of land in Canada, similar to a state in the United States, p. 147

"push-pull" theory a theory of migration that says people migrate because certain things in their lives "push" them to leave a place, and certain things in a new place "pull" them to go there, p. 65

Q

Quiet Revolution a peaceful change in the government of the Province of Quebec, Canada, in which the Parti Québécois won control of the legislature and made French the official language, p. 249

quipu [kee poo] knotted strings used by Incan government officials and traders for record keeping, p. 311

R

rain shadow an area on the side of a mountain away from the wind that receives little rainfall, p. 145

raw material a resource or material that is still in its natural state, before being processed or manufactured into a useful product, p. 106

recession a downturn in business activity and economic prosperity, not as severe as a depression, p. 229

Reconstruction United States plan for rebuilding the nation after the Civil War, p. 171

recyclable resource a resource that cycles through natural processes in the environment; water, nitrogen, and carbon are recyclable resources, p. 107

recycle to reuse materials to make new products, p. 121

referendum a ballot or vote in which voters decide for or against a particular issue, p. 250

renewable resource a natural resource that the environment continues to supply or replace as it is used; trees and water are renewable resources, p. 107

represent to speak for someone else and guard their interests, p. 165

representative democracy a system of government in which the people elect representatives to run the affairs of the country, p. 91

reserve land set aside for a specific purpose, as by the Canadian government for indigenous peoples, p. 205

revolution a political movement in which people overthrow the existing government and set up another, p. 320

revolution one complete orbit of the Earth around the sun; the Earth completes one revolution every 365 1/4 days, or one year, p. 28

Revolutionary War the war in which the American colonies won their independence from Britain, fought from 1775 to 1781, p. 165

rotation the spinning motion of the Earth, like a top on its axis; the Earth takes about 24 hours to rotate one time, p. 28

rural area an area with low population density, such as a village or the countryside, pp. 68, 224, 329

S

scale the size of an area on a map as compared with the area's actual size, p. 15

segregate to set apart and force to use separate schools, housing, parks, and so on because of race or religion, p. 171

separatist in Canada, someone who wants the province of Quebec to break away from the rest of the country, p. 249

services work done or duties performed for other people, such as the work of a doctor or of a television repair person, p. 88

settlement house a community center for poor immigrants to the United States, for example, Jane Addams's Hull House in Chicago, p. 173

shield a lowland area of exposed bedrock, p. 140

sierra a group of mountains, such as the one that runs from northwest to southeast Peru, p. 406

slum a usually crowded area of a city, often with poverty and poor housing, p. 172

social structure the ways in which people within a culture are organized into smaller groups; each smaller group has its own particular tasks, p. 82

socialism an economic system in which the government owns most basic industries, such as transportation, communications, and banking; nonbasic industries are privately owned, p. 89

sod top layer of soil containing grass plants and their roots, p. 254

sparsely thinly; in a scattered, uncrowded way, p. 261

squatter a person who settles on someone else's land without permission, p. 354

strike work stoppage; a refusal to continue to work until certain demands of workers are met, p. 363

subsistence farming farming that provides only enough food and animals for the survival of a family or a village, p. 115, 345

subway commuter train that travels underground, p. 215

Sun Belt the broad area of the United States that stretches from the southern Atlantic Coast to the coast of California; known for its warm weather, p. 97

T

tariff a fee charged on imported goods, p. 189

technology tools and the skills that people need to use them; the practical use of scientific skills, especially in industry, p. 79

temperature the degree of hotness or coldness of something, such as water or air, usually measured with a thermometer, p. 38

tenement an apartment house that is poorly built and crowded, p. 172

totem pole a tall, carved wooden pole containing tribe, clan, or family symbols, found among Native Americans of the Pacific Northwest, p. 258

treaty an agreement in writing made between two or more countries, p. 344

Treaty of Tordesillas [tor day see yas] the 1494 treaty setting up the Line of Demarcation, giving Spain the right to settle and trade west of the line and Portugal the same rights east of the line, p. 314

tributary a river or stream that flows into a larger river, pp. 142, 283

tropics the area on the Earth between the 23.5°N and 23.5°S lines of latitude, where the climate is almost always hot, p. 145

tundra a cold region with little vegetation except for low grasses; in mountains, the area above the tree line; an area covered with snow for more than half the year; a vast, treeless plain where the subsoil is frozen even in summer, pp. 46, 147, 408

U

unique having no equal; the only one of its kind, p. 139

urban having to do with cities, p. 329

urban area an area with a high population density; a city or town, p. 68

urbanization the growth of city populations caused by the movement of people to cities, p. 68

V

vast huge; enormous in size, p. 138

vegetation the plants in an area, p. 43

vertical climate the overall weather patterns of a region as influenced by elevation; the higher the elevation, the colder the climate, p. 47

W

weather the condition of the bottom layer of the Earth's atmosphere in one place over a short period of time, p. 37

weathering the breaking down of rocks by wind, rain, or ice, p. 35

Index

birthrate, 62; during the Agricultural Revolution, 81
bison, 161
Black River Falls, Wisconsin, 227
blizzard, 42
blue jeans: cultural impact of, 93, 95
bluegrass, 201
Bolívar, Simón, 322–324
Bolivia, *m 285, m 288,* 310, 312, 343, 344, *m 398;* altiplano of, 405; economy of, 292; natural resources of, 292
boll weevil, 222
Bond, Rebecca, 182
boom, 419
boomtowns. *See* Gold Rush: Canadian
border: Canadian and U.S., *p 184,* 185
Boricuas (Boriqueno), 392
Boston, Massachusetts, 217
bottomlands, 102
Botts, Lee, 121
boycott: American, of British goods, 37; by Mexican-American farm-workers, 237
Brazil, 282, 283, *m 285, m 288,* 295, *p 295,* 314, 324, 344, *p 346,* 347, *m 398,* 399–404; ancestry of, 400; Cerrado of, 402; climate of, *m 285,* 286; coffee plantations in, 401; coffee production in, 295, 401; Country Profile of, 400; diversification in, 297, 401; economy of, 297, 401, 402; enslavement of Africans in, 344, 400–401; factories in, 401; farming in, 401, 404; geography of, 399; government in, 402, 403–404; industry in, 297, 402; land in, 328, 399, 404; language of, 314, 344; Native Americans in, 344, 399, 400, 402; natural vegetation of, *m 288;* people of, 399, 400; rain forests of, 328–329, 399–404; resources of, 399; urbanization in, 401; Yanomamo in, 402
Bressette, Thomas M., 205–206
British Columbia, 140; 246, *m 246;* Canadian Pacific Railway and, 261; Provincial Profile of, *m 259,* 259; timber industry and, 153
British North American Act, 181
broadcast, 95
Broadway. *See* New York City: art in

Brooklyn Bridge, *p 218*
Buddhism, *m 86*
Buenos Aires, Argentina, 347
buffalo: European slaughter of, in Canada, 255
bullet train, 55, *p 55*
Burgess Shale, 140
Burma. *See* Myanmar
burrowing owls, 255

C

cacti, 43, *p 43*
Cairo, Egypt: overcrowding in, *p 69*
Cajuns, 179
California Current, 40
California, 139; Lake Casitas, *p 97;* land area of, 59; population of, 59; San Francisco, *p 8,* 40
Cambridge, Massachusetts, 217
campesino, 328, 329
Canada, 113; British control of, 179–180; independence of, 182; and laws to reduce acid rain, 119; Ontario, 37; political system of, 90, 91; population of, 58; Quebec, 90; representative democracy of, 91
"Canada's breadbasket." *See* Saskatchewan
Canadian Mounted Police, 261
Canadian Pacific Railway, *p 181,* 262
Canadian Shield, 140, 153, 157
cancer research: "Marathon of Hope" and, 207
canopy, 399; rain forest, 44
Cape Canaveral, Florida, 225
capitalism, 89, *c 89*
Caracas, Venezuela, 418; subway in, 418
carbon dioxide, 119
cardinal directions, 19
Caribbean (region), 279, *m 280,* 281, 293, 338–342, 344, 376–395, *m 376;* Carnival in, 342; climate of, 286, *p 286;* culture in, 338–342, *c 339;* Europeans in, 339; farming in, 293, 338; food and music in, 341; landforms of, 279, 281; languages of, 340; migration from other countries to, 340; name origination, 339; natural resources of, 293, *m 294;* people of, 338–340; and Puerto Rico, 392; religion in the, 340, 342

Caribbean Sea, 18, 41, 163
Cariboo Mountains, 260
Caribs, 339
Carlotta, California, 149
Carnival, 342
Carrying the Fire, 9
Cartier, Jacques, 247–249
Cascade Mountains, 139
Castro, Fidel, 377, 379, 382; and Cuba's education system, 382
Cathedral-Basilica of Mary, Queen of the World, 251
Catholicism: in the Caribbean, 342; in Mexico and Central America, 335; Roman Catholic Church, 334-335; in South America, 343
Catskill Mountains, *p 75*
cattle: and the Great Plains, 147
caudillo, 324
Census Bureau, 73
Central America, *m 280,* 288, 305, 333, 352, *m 352,* 359–371; Aztecs, 306–308; Central Plains, 139, 140; culture in, 333–335; employment in, 336, 337; farming in, 281, 293, 356; hydroelectricity in, 293; landforms of, 279, 280–281; languages of, 334; location of, 280–281; Mayan civilization in, 305–306; and Mexico, 279, 280–281, 293, 305, 306, 333–335, 336, 337, 352, *m 352,* 356; natural resources of, 293, *m 294;* natural vegetation of, 291; population of, 336; religion in, 334–335; urbanization in, 336–337 Cerrado, 402
Central Powers, 174
centralized economy, *c 89*
CFCs. *See* chlorofluorocarbons (CFCs)
Chamberland, Paul, 204
Charleston, South Carolina, *g 49,* 226
Chavez, Cesar, 237
Chemainus, British Columbia, *p 205*
Cherokee nation: Supreme Court case and, *m 167. See also* Native Americans; Sequoyah
Chesapeake Bay, 224
Cheyenne, *m 198. See also* Native Americans
Chicago, Illinois, 230–231, *p 230;* child labor, 173, 177, *p 103*

Acknowledgments

Program Development, Design, Illustration, and Production
Proof Positive/Farrowlyne Associates, Inc.

Cover Design
Martucci Studio

Maps
GeoSystems Global Corp.

Text
9, Excerpt from *Carrying the Fire* by Michael Collins. Copyright © 1974 by Michael Collins. Reprinted by permission from Farrar, Straus & Giroux, Inc. 27, Excerpt from *North American Indian Mythology* by Cottie Burland, rev. by Marion Wood. Copyright © 1965 by Cottie Burland, Copyright © renewed 1985 by the Estate of Cottie Burland. Reproduced by permission of Reed Books. 31, Excerpt from "The Kobe Earthquake: A Chance to Serve," by Megumi Fujiwara, JAMA, January 3, 1996, volume 275, p. 79. Copyright © 1996, American Medical Association. Reprinted with permission of the American Medical Association. 74, From *My Side of the Mountain* by Jean Craighead George. Copyright © 1959 by Jean Craighead George, renewed 1987 by Jean Craighead George. Used by permission of Dutton Children's Books, a division of Penguin Books USA Inc. 102, "Rough Country" copyright © 1991 by Dana Gioia. Reprinted from *The Gods of Winter* with the permission of Graywolf Press, Saint Paul, Minnesota. 163, From *The Crown of Columbus* by Louise Erdrich and Michael Dorris. Copyright © 1991 by Michael Dorris and Louise Erdrich. Reprinted by permission of HarperCollins Publishers, Inc. 172, From *How the Other Half Lives* by Jacob A. Riis. Copyright © 1971 by Dover Publications, Inc. Reprinted by permission. 197, 200 From *New Kids on the Block: Oral Histories of Immigrant Teens* by Janet Bode. Copyright © 1989 by Janet Bode. Published by Franklin Watts. 203, From *The Land and People of Canada* by Andrew H. Malcolm. Text copyrighted © 1992 by Andrew H. Malcolm. Reprinted with permission of HarperCollins Publishers, Inc. 206, From "Chippewas Push Claims for Land in Canada," by Clyde H. Farnsworth, *New York Times,* August 27, 1995. Copyright © 1995 by The New York Times Co. Reprinted by permission. 212, From *The Book of Americans* by Rosemary and Stephen Vincent Benét. Copyright © 1933 by Rosemary and Stephen Vincent Benét. Copyright © renewed 1961 by Rosemary Carr Benét. Reprinted by permission of Brandt & Brandt Literary Agents, Inc. 213, "The chief of the world," "Glooscap's wigwam," from *Whirlwind Is a Ghost Dancing* by Natalia Belting. Copyright © 1974 by Natalia Belting. Used by permission of Dutton Children's Books, a division of Penguin Books USA Inc. 223, *From Fannie Lou Hamer: From Sharecropping to Politics* by David Rubel. Copyright © 1990 by Silver Burdett Press, Simon & Schuster Elementary. Used by permission. 233, From *History of the United States* by Thomas V. DiBacco, Lorna C. Mason, and Christian G. Appy. Copyright © 1991 by Houghton Mifflin Company. Reprinted by permission. 242, From *Childtimes: A Three-Generation Memoir* by Eloise Greenfield and Lessie Jones Little. Copyright © 1979 by Eloise Greenfield and Lessie Jones Little. Reprinted by permission of HarperCollins Publishers, Inc. 251, From *Quebec, I Love You* by Miyuki Tanobe. Copyright © 1976 by Miyuki Tanobe, published by Tundra Books. Reprinted by permission. 300, "Where the Flame Trees Bloom," by Alma Flor Ada. Text © 1994 Alma Flor Ada. Reprinted with the permission of Atheneum Books for Young Readers, an imprint of Simon & Schuster Children's Publishing Division. 380, Excerpt from "Finding My Father," by Lydia Martin, *The Miami Herald,* June 18, 1995. Reprinted with permission of *The Miami Herald.* 428, Poem LXXII (Question Book) by Pablo Neruda. Spanish original reprinted from *Libros de las Preguntas,* by Pablo Neruda. © Pablo Neruda and Fundación Pablo Neruda, 1974. English translation from *Late and Posthumous Poems* 1968-1974, by Pablo Neruda, translated by Ben Belitt. © 1988 by Ben Belitt. Used by permission of Grove/Atlantic, Inc.

Photo Research
Feldman & Associates, Inc.

Photos
1 T, © Karen Kasmauski/Woodfin Camp & Associates, 1 BL, © SuperStock International, 1 BR, © Paul Chesley/Tony Stone Images, 2 T, © Ken Graham/Tony Stone Images, 2 B, Peter Carmichael/Tony Stone Images, 3 T, © Alan Abromowitz/Tony Stone Images, 3 B, Robert Frerck/Odyssey Productions, 4, © Mark Thayer, Boston, 8, © Baron Wolman/Tony Stone Images, 9, © Kevin Kelley/Tony Stone Images, 12, The Rift Valley—Lake Naivasha, by Edwin Rioba, age 16, Kenya. Courtesy of the International Children's Art Museum, 14, © British Museum, 15 T, M, BL, BR, © Custom Medical Stock Photo, 20, 21, © David Young-Wolff/PhotoEdit, 24 L, © Mike McQueen/Tony Stone Images, 24 R, © Stephen Studd/Tony Stone Images, 26, © ESA/TSADD/Tom Stack & Associates, 27, © Photri, 37, © David Falconer/Tony Stone Images, 43, © Rod Planck/Tom Stack & Associates, 46 TR, © John Beatty/Tony Stone Images, 46 BL, © Jonathan Nourok/PhotoEdit, 49, © Grant Taylor/Tony Stone Images, 53, © David Young-Wolff/PhotoEdit, 54, © Robert Fox/Impact Visuals, 55, © Paul Chesley/Tony Stone Images, 56, © Tony Stone Images, 58 TL, © Connie Coleman/Tony Stone Images, 58 TR, © Bill Pogue/Tony Stone Images, 58 B, SuperStock International, 61, © Jason Laure'/Laure' Communications, 64, © Chris Brown/SABA Press Photos, 66, © Ted Streshinsky/Corbis, 67, © Mariella Furrer/SABA Press Photos, 69, © Donna DeCesare/Impact Visuals, 70, © Earth Imaging/Tony Stone Images, 74, © Carr Clifton/Carr Clifton Photography, 76, © Lawrence Migdale/Tony Stone Images, 77, © Paul Conklin/PhotoEdit, 78,